Human Resource

management

Seventh Edition

HUMAN RESOURCE MANAGEMENT

DAVID A. DECENZO   TOWSON UNIVERSITY

STEPHEN P. ROBBINS   SAN DIEGO STATE UNIVERSITY

 JOHN WILEY & SONS, INC.

EDITOR . . . . JEFF MARSHALL

MARKETING MANAGER . . . . CHARITY ROBEY

SENIOR PRODUCTION EDITOR . . . . KELLY TAVARES

PHOTO EDITOR . . . . SARA WIGHT

SENIOR ILLUSTRATION EDITOR . . . . SANDRA RIGBY

COVER DESIGNER . . . . CAROL GROBE

TEXT DESIGNER . . . . JILL YUTKOWITZ

ART DIRECTOR . . . . DAWN L. STANLEY

COVER ART . . . . ©GARY KAEMMER/THE IMAGE BANK

This book was set in Sabon by TechBooks and printed and bound by Von Hoffman Press. This book is printed on acid-free paper. ⊗

Library of Congress Cataloging-in-Publication Data

DeCenzo, David A.
  Human resource management / David A. DeCenzo, Stephen P. Robbins.—7th ed.
    p. cm.
  Includes bibliographical references and index.
  ISBN 0-471-39785-7 (pbk. : alk. paper)
    1. Personnel management. I. Robbins, Stephen P., 1943– II. Title.

HF5549.D396 2001
658.3–dc21   2001045365

Printed in the United States of America

10 9 8 7 6 5 4 3 2 1

PREFACE

Welcome to the seventh edition of our Human Resource Management text, and thank you for taking the time to read this preface to better understand this book. We want to use this section to address three important aspects about the book. These are: (1) what this book is about, (2) what important in-text learning aids exist, and (3) who, besides the authors named on the cover, were instrumental in the book's development.

About-the-Book

When we revised the book for the fifth edition, we made some major changes. We downsized the book, eliminated material that at the time we felt was courageous, added a heavy dose of pedagogy to make the book more "student-friendly." We also brought the book to market in paperback. We took some risks, bucking the "market" to some extent, and kept our fingers crossed that we had made the correct decisions. For the sixth edition, we continued this trend, moving material around in response to users, adding elements that appeared to help facilitate learning, and cut the number of chapters again.

We are happy to report that thanks to you and countless others, the sixth edition continued the tradition of a successful book. The market accepted our changes, students appreciated the effort to provide them good learning tools, and almost everyone was appreciative of the book continually offered in paperback. We knew for the seventh edition that we'd have to continue with this tradition, offer our readers more, and once again produce a market-leading product.

We started this process by going back to our users—and even sought advice from those who hadn't chosen us as their HRM text. What we got was plenty of advice—and a lot of very good suggestions. Some of these suggestions even reflected a concern to "undo" something we had done in the sixth edition—ordering of chapters. We again looked hard at our research, and made the changes that clearly will make this edition of HRM even better than the last. For this information, and to those who provided it, we are grateful. So what did we do?

We began with a set of goals—to once again produce a text that addressed the most critical issues in human resource management (HRM). We also continued with our tradition of achieving a delicate balance between basic HRM functions, and the new world of HRM. Moreover, in a dynamic field like HRM, a completely updated research base is a must. You want to know, after all, the current state of the field. We have undertaken an extensive literature review to include hundreds of current citations from business periodicals and academic journals in this text. This became a more challenging task as

THIS BOOK HAS BEEN DEVELOPED BASED UPON THE HUMAN RESOURCES BODY OF KNOWLEDGE AS DEFINED BY THE HUMAN RESOURCE CERTIFICATION INSTITUTE (HRCI), AN AFFILIATE OF THE SOCIETY FOR HUMAN RESOURCE MANAGEMENT.

we entered the new millennium. For example, with citations now reflecting 2000 and 2001 dates of publications, those 1980s and early 1990s citations that existed cannot be "hidden." They stuck out like a sore thumb. So we sought the latest information available to make this book as current as publishing a book allows. That's not to say that you won't find a citation two decades old. When that citation is the leading citation for some research, or when a particular court case ruling was published, we used the original source and its original date of publication. But other than that, you'll see a "currentness of endnotes" that should give you a clear indication of the currentness of this seventh edition.

Of course, relevant HR topics that are making news today also are covered in the text. This includes, for example, such topics as technology and its effect on HRM, the use of the Internet in recruiting, and recent updates to legal and societal issues like sexual harassment and diversity. Yet, one of the major elements of this new edition is the addition of more pedagogy.

I recently completed a short course in HR Management, preparatory to taking the SHRM certification exam. [Your] text was used in the course. I found it to be a comprehensive review of the broad subject matter included in HR Management. I passed the certification exam and believe the course and text contributed to my success.

Nina Paula Marchioni, PHR
  Nuclear Fuel Services, Inc.

Learning Aids

Our experience has led us to conclude that a text becomes highly readable when the writing is straightforward and conversational, the topics flow logically, and the authors make extensive use of examples to illustrate concepts. These factors guided us in developing this text as a highly effective learning tool. Previous text users have regularly commented on how clearly our books present ideas. We think this one, too, is written in a clear, lively, concise, and conversational style. Furthermore, our classroom experience tells us that students remember and understand concepts and practices most clearly when they are illustrated through examples. So we've used a wealth of examples to clarify ideas.

Each chapter of this book is organized to provide clarity and continuity. Each begins with Learning Outcomes, which identify specifically what the reader should gain after reading the chapter. Within the chapters themselves, we address and highlight the some current concepts with features such as Workplace Issues, Diversity and EEO, Technology and HRM, and Ethical Decisions in HRM. These features can be used also as class discussion or for writing assignments. We've also included margin notes in each chapter which are highlighted in the text and defined in the Glossary of the book.

New to this edition is our HRM Workshop. It's not enough to know about Human Resource Management. Today's students—especially those entering the HRM field—want the skills to succeed at their organizations. So we emphasized the skill component in this edition. You'll see this in the HRM workshop sections at the end of each chapter. These workshops are designed to help students build analytical, diagnostic, team-building, investigative, Internet search, and writing skills. We address these skill areas in several ways. For example, we include experiential exercises to develop team building skills; a case to case to build diagnostic, analytical, and decision making skills; and suggested topical writing assignments to enhance writing skills—some of which require Internet search exercises to develop skills at doing research on the Internet.

Have you had students tell you that they read the assignments and thought they understood the material, but still didn't do well on the exam? Well, we have both had this experience and know that many students have, too. In fact, much

tive on this point. So we've continued the concept of Testing Your Understanding questions that relate to each chapter. However, rather than place them in the back of each chapter, we've moved this learning tool to our Website-www.wiley.com/college/decenzo. These questions are designed to assist readers in determining if they understood the chapter material. In most cases, questions link directly to the learning outcomes. Each question is answered for readers. These questions have been specifically written to challenge your critical thinking, and generally require some application from the chapter's content.

This book is supported by a comprehensive learning package that helps instructors create a motivating environment and provides students with additional instruments for understanding and reviewing major concepts.

Supplemental Material

Instructor's Resource Guide: This includes, for each chapter, a chapter overview, a description of additional features within the chapter, a chapter outline, additional lecture and activity suggestions, answers to class exercises, answers to case applications, additional review and discussion questions, and one additional case.

Test Bank: Contains approximately 80 questions per chapter. The general breakdown being 50 multiple-choice, 10 true/false, 10 matching, and 10 completion questions.

Computerized Test Bank: A Test Bank powered by a program called Microtest which allows instructors to customize their quizzes and exams for each chapter of the text.

Video Package: Contains a selection of news segments from "Nightly Business Report," the longest running, most watched daily business, financial, and economic news program on television. The segments within this package relate to various topics throughout the text.

Website with PowerPoint Presentations: Includes electronic files for all of the instructor resources along with lecture outline PowerPoint Presentations for each chapter and an interactive feature for students called *"How would you handle this?"*. This feature, which is new to the 7th edition of this text, provides students with on-line HR Experiences that challenge the effectiveness of their management skills.

Acknowledgments

Getting a finished book into a reader's hands requires the work of many people. The authors do their part by efficiently developing an outline, thoroughly researching topics, and accurately keyboarding sentences into their computers. We would like to recognize just a few of the people who contributed to this text.

First of all are our reviewers. Authors cannot survive without good feedback from its reviewers. Ours were outstanding, and we appreciate the feedback they gave us. We do recognize that the book before you is better because of the insight they provided. We'd like to recognize reviewers from this edition as well as reviewers of previous editions: Dr. Kristin Backhause of Suny New Paltz; Dr. Ellen D. Durnin, Chair of the Management Dept. Western Connecticut State University; Prof. Michael Bedell, California State University, Bakersfield; Dr. Judith Weisinger, Northeastern University; Prof. Janice M. Feldbauer, Austin Community College; Dr. Mary Connerly, Virginia Tech; Dr. K. Shannon Davis, North Carolina State University; Dr. Lucy N. McClurg, Robinson College of Business, Georgia State University; Dr. Kenneth M. York, Oakland University.

A book doesn't simply appear automatically on bookstore shelves. It gets there through the combined efforts of many people. For us, this is the outstanding publishing team at John Wiley & Sons, consisting of Jeff Marshall, our editor; Charity Robey, Marketing Manager; Kelly Tavares, Senior Production Editor; Dawn Stanley, Senior Designer; Sandra Rigby, Illustrations Editor; and Sara Wight, Photo Editor.

Last, we want to acknowledge a few people individually. For Dave, I wish again to thank my wife and children who continue to give me the best support anyone could want. To my wife of 19 years, where did the time go? But the years get better as they go on. To Mark, Meredith, Gabriella, and Natalie, what more can a proud father say about his kids. You clearly bring joy to my life in all that you do.

For Steve, I wish to acknowledge my wife, Laura, without whose patience and support this "writing business" would be a chore.

Dave DeCenzo   Steve Robbins

$\mathcal{A}$BOUT THE AUTHORS

David A. DeCenzo received his Ph.D. from West Virginia University. He is the Director of Partnership Development and Professor of Management at Towson University. His major teaching and research interests focus on the general areas of human resource management, management, and organizational behavior. He has published articles in such journals as Harvard Business Review, Business Horizons, Risk Management, Hospital topics, and Performance and Instruction.

Dr. DeCenzo has spent his recent years writing textbooks. His books include Human Resource Management, 7th edition (2002) with Stephen Robbins; Fundamentals of Management, 3rd edition (2001) with Stephen Robbins; Human Relations (2002) with Beth Silhanek, Essentials of Labor Relations (1992) with Molly Bowers; and Employee Benefits (1990) with Stephen Holoviak, all published by Prentice Hall. These books are used widely at colleges and universities in the U.S., as well as schools throughout the world.

Dr. DeCenzo also has industry experience as a corporate trainer, and has served as a consultant to a number of companies, including G&K Services, Inc., Fairpoint Communications, Moen, Inc., HealthCare Strategies, Inc., AlliedSignal Technical Services Corportation, Citicorp, Teledyne/Landis Machine Company, Blue Cross & Blue Shield of Maryland, the Tnemec Company, the James River Corporation, Packaging Division, and the Managerial and Professional Society of Baltimore.

In Dr. DeCenzo's other life, he participates in raising his four children (Mark, Meredith, Gabriella, and Natalie) with his wife, Terri. He isn't setting any world record times, but does plenty of "running" around.

Stephen P. Robbins received his Ph.D. from the University of Arizona. He previously worked for the Shell Oil Company and Reynolds Metals Company. Since completing his graduate studies, Dr. Robbins has taught at the University of Nebraska at Omaha, Concordia University in Montreal, the University of Baltimore, Southern Illinois University at Edwardsville, and San Diego State University. Dr. Robbins' research interests have focused on conflict, power, and politics in organizations, as well as the development of effective interpersonal skills. His articles on these and other topics have appeared in such journals as Business Horizons, the California Management Review, Business and Economic Perspectives, International Management, Management Review, Canadian Personnel and Industrial Relations, and the Journal of Management Education.

In recent years, Dr. Robbins has been spending most of his professional time writing textbooks. These include Management 7th edition (2002) with Mary Coulter, Organizational Behavior, 9th edition (2001); Supervision Today! 3rd edition, (2000) with David DeCenzo; Managing Today! (2000); Essentials of Organizational Behavior, 6th edition (2000); Training in InterPersonal Skills,

ganizational Behavior, 6th edition (2000); Training in InterPersonal Skills, 2nd edition, (1996) with Philip Hunsaker; and Organization Theory, 3rd edition (1990), all published by Prentice Hall. These books are used at more than a thousand U.S. colleges and universities, as well as hundreds of schools throughout Canada, Latin America, Australia, New Zealand, Asia, Scandinavia, and Europe.

In Dr. Robbins' "other life," he participates in masters' track competition. Since turning 50 he has set numerous indoor and outdoor world sprint records. He's also won gold medals in World Veteran Games in 100m, 200m, and 400m. Robbins has been named the outstanding age-40-and-over male track and field athlete by the Masters Track and Field Committee of USA Track & Field, the national governing body for athletes in the United States.

All authors of a textbook generally include a preface that describes why they wrote the book and what's unique about it, and then thank a lot of people for the role they played in getting the book completed. Well, we're no different. We just did that, too. But it has become crystal-clear to us that two things are common about a book's preface. First, it's usually written for the professor, especially one who's considering selecting the book. Second, students usually don't read the preface. That's unfortunate because it often includes information that students would find useful.

As authors, we do listen to our customers. And many of ours have told us that they'd enjoy some input from us. So, we've written this memo. Our purpose is to provide you with our ideas about the book, how it was put together, and more importantly, how you can use it to better understand the field of HRM— and do better in this class!

This book was written to provide you with the foundations of HRM. Whether you intend to work in HRM or not, most of these elements will affect you at some point in your career. How? Take, for example, the performance appraisal. Although you might not currently be in a position to evaluate another individual's work performance, if you are working, you're more than likely to have your performance appraised. For that matter, each time you take an exam in a class, your performance is being evaluated. Consequently, it's important for you to have an understanding of how it should work, and the potential problems that may exist.

We began Part I of this book with an emphasis on providing you with an overview of the ever-changing world of work and the effect it is having on HRM. With that as a foundation, we then proceed to introduce you to HRM, its approach, and its cast of characters. Part 2, we turn our attention to the laws that affect HRM activities. Much of how HRM operates is guided by legislation and court decisions that prohibit practices that adversely affect certain groups of people. Without a good understanding of these laws, an organization's performance can suffer, and the organization can be vulnerable to costly lawsuits. Part 2 ends with a discussion of several areas focusing on employee rights.

Parts 3 through 5 provide coverage of the fundamental activities that exist in HRM. Part 3 explores the staffing function, with discussions on employment recruiting, and selection. Part 4 addresses means for socializing, training, and developing employees. Part 5 looks at how organizations encourage high performance by evaluating, paying, and rewarding its employees. Then, in Part 6, we look at ways for management to keep their high-performing employees through effective HR communications.

Much of the discussion in Part 2 through 5 reflects typical activities in an organization that is not unionized. When a union is present, however, many of these practices might need modification to comply with another set of laws. As such, we reserved the final chapter for dealing with labor-management relations.

While we are confident that completing the 15 chapters contained in the book will provide the fundamentals of HRM, a text has to offer more. It should not only cover topics (we hope, in an interesting and lively way), it should also assist in the learning process. It should be written in such a way that you can understand it, it keeps your attention, and it provides you an opportunity for feedback. We think we've met each of these goals. Of course, only you can be the judge of our claim. But let's look at how we arrived at our conclusion.

To be understandable and lively means that we need to communicate with you. We make every attempt in this text to have it sound as if we were in front of your class speaking with you. Writing style is important to us. We use examples whenever possible—real companies, so you can see that what we talk about is happening in the "real world." In the past, people using our books have indicated that our writing style does help hold their attention. But the communication connection, albeit critical, is only half of the equation. The ultimate tests for you are: Does the book help you do well on exams? Does it help prepare you for a job?

We start every chapter with learning outcomes. We view these as the critical learning points. They present a logic flow from which the material will be presented. If you can explain what is proposed in each learning objective, you'll be on the right track to understanding the material. But memory sometimes fools us. We read the material, think we understand it, see how the summaries directly tie the learning outcomes together, then take the exam and receive a grade that is not reflective of "what we knew we knew." We have given a lot of thought to that issue, and think we've come up with something that will help—putting a feedback test on the Website that supports our book! Let's explain.

The typical textbook ends each chapter with a set of review questions. Sometimes, your tests look much like these types of questions. But exams also have a tendency to emphasize multiple-choice exams. So we've included sample test questions on our Website to help you prepare for exams in this class. These questions are actual questions that we've used to test our students' understanding of the material. If you can correctly answer these questions, then you're one step closer to enhancing your understanding of HRM. Recognize, of course, that these are only a learning aid. They help you to learn but don't replace careful reading or intensive studying. And don't assume that getting a question right means you fully understand the concept covered. Why? Because any set of multiple-choice questions can only test a limited range of information. So don't let correct answers lull you into a sense of false security. If you miss a question or don't fully understand why you got the correct response, go back to the material in the chapter and reread the material.

Learning, however, goes beyond just passing a test. It also means preparing yourself to perform successfully in tomorrow's organizations. You'll find that organizations today require their employees to work more closely together than at any time in the past. Call it teams, horizontal organizational structures, matrix management, or the like, the fact remains that your success will depend on how well you work closely with others. To help model this group concept for you, we have included class exercises in this text. Each of these team experiential learning efforts is designed to highlight a particular topic in the text and give you an opportunity to work in groups to solve the issue at hand.

One last thing before we close: What can you take out of this course and use in the future? Many business leaders have complained about how business schools train their graduates. Although business schools have made many positive accomplishments, one critical component appears lacking—practical skills. The skills you need to succeed in today's business environment are increasing. You must be able to communicate (both verbally and in a written format), think creatively, make good and timely decisions, plan effectively, and deal with people. In HRM, we have an opportunity to build our skills bank. As you go through this text, you'll find a dozen or more practical skills that you can use on your job. We hope you give them special attention, practice them often, and add them to your repertoire. We've also included suggestions for writing assignments—2–3 page reports that cover an important aspect of the Chapter's material. Look at these as a learning tool, not as an assignment that you have to do. We think you find working on these will help prepare you for dealing with the kinds of "writing" requests you get are on the job.

Finally, if you'd like to tell us how we might improve the next edition of this book, we encourage you to write Dave DeCenzo at the College of Business and Economics, Towson University, Towson, Maryland 21252-0001; or e-mail him at ddecenzo@towson.edu. To those of you who have done so in the previous editions, we appreciate you taking the time to write us. Thanks for helping us out.

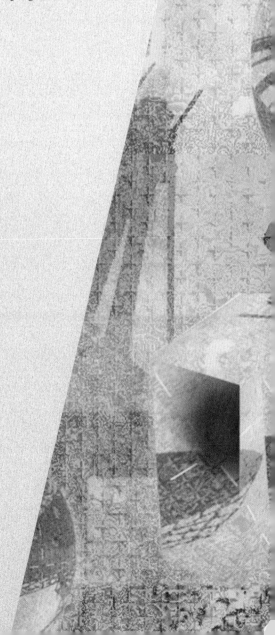

BRIEF TABLE OF CONTENTS

CONTENTS

PART 3: STAFFING THE ORGANIZATION   124

*C*HAPTER 5:
EMPLOYMENT PLANNING AND JOB ANALYSIS   124

PART 6: MAINTAINING EFFECTIVE RELATIONSHIPS   390

CHAPTER 14:
EFFECTIVE HRM COMMUNICATIONS   390

CHAPTER 15:
LABOR RELATIONS AND COLLECTIVE BARGAINING   412

This book is dedicated to Stephen E. Marshall and Andrew D. Freeman, who through their tremendous efforts on our behalf helped us deal with one of the most difficult issues a parent could encounter. Thanks for all you did for us.

1

HRM in a Dynamic Environment

What do Spectech Systems, InterDent, and Chesapeake Auto Wholesalers Association have in common? Is it that they're successful medium-sized businesses that are growing every year? Is it the fact that each has demonstrated a particular niche on which to capitalize and meet customer needs? While both of these may be true, the main thing each of these organizations has in common is that none of them employ their own employees. Instead, they have a co-employment relationship with Selective HR, a Bradenton, Florida-based professional employee organization.[1]

A professional employer organization (PEO) is a firm that "provides integrated human resource administration and risk management services" to other organizations. That is, a PEO recruits, trains, pays employees, offers employee benefits, and handles all the necessary compliance and government reporting requirements.[2] PEOs like Selective HR (formerly Modern Employers, Inc.) provide an avenue for companies to outsource all their human resources activities. The employees, while they are technically PEO employees, permanently work for client organizations. Modern Employers, Inc. was founded in 1984 by two insurance agents, Rick Ratner and Ed Bongart. It was acquired by Selective Insurance Group, Inc. in 1999 and renamed Selective HR. Under the direction of Bob Clancy, president and CEO, Selective HR recognizes that human resource services—especially employee benefits and government compliance programs—are major headaches for the small and mid-sized business owners. That's because these owners often want to do the things they enjoy most—selling the services of their business. But they need employees, and with each employee comes a variety of responsibilities. For example, once an organization employees 15 individuals, they are required to follow a wide variety of government regulations relating to hiring, firing, and promoting employees. Completing the requisite payroll documentation as well as employee safety forms is generally more involved than most entrepreneurs envision. Furthermore, attracting skilled employees in smaller businesses is often more difficult because they typically cannot afford the full array of employee benefits that many of today's workers seek. For Selective HR, this challenge created an opportunity for them to provide a valuable service to businesses.

Valuable services in what way? PEOs frequently target employers with fewer than 500 employees. In many cases, it's these organizations that need a fully functioning human resource department but can't justify the costs. For a percentage of their total payroll costs, PEOs handle all the human resource activities for a client organization. For example, they issue paychecks, deposit payroll taxes, handle unemployment and workers' compensation claims, provide employee benefits, screen applicants, and develop employee handbooks. They will also assist in handling layoffs and terminations if necessary. But freeing these business owners from endless paperwork and government regulations is only one piece of the puzzle. By hiring the employees and leasing them to client organizations, PEOs are able to provide employee benefits at a much lower cost than if small business owners had to buy them separately. For the client organizations, this means that they can offer the benefits "their" employees desire at a fraction of the cost. This includes comprehensive health insurance plans, retirement programs, credit union membership, and life insurance. This aspect alone has helped reduce turnover in many of the PEOs' client organizations.

Has a PEO like Selective HR "built a better mousetrap"? It looks like it! Selective HR is one of the top 20 PEOs in the United States. With branch offices in Marietta, Georgia, Charlotte, North Carolina, Branchville, New Jersey, and Baltimore, Maryland, Selective HR provides HR support to more than 500 client organizations in 17 eastern, midwestern, and southern states—and currently "leases" more than 14,000 employees.

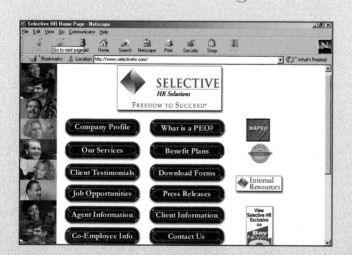

Introduction

There's no doubt that the world of work as we know it is rapidly changing. Even as little as fifteen years ago, the times were calmer than they are today. But that doesn't mean that we didn't experience change back then. On the contrary, we were then, as we are today, in a state of flux. It's just that today the changes appear to be happening more rapidly.

As part of an organization then, HRM must be prepared to deal with the effects of the changing world of work. For them, this means understanding the implications of globalization, technology changes, work-force diversity, changing skill requirements, continuous improvement initiatives, the contingent work force, decentralized work sites, and employee involvement. Let's look at how these changes are affecting HRM goals and practices.

Welcome to the Global Village

Back in 1973, with the first oil embargo, U.S. businesses began to realize the important effects that international forces had on profit and loss statements. The world was changing rapidly, with other countries making significant inroads into traditional U.S. markets. Unfortunately, U.S. businesses did not adapt to this changing environment as quickly or adeptly as they should have. The result was that U.S. businesses lost out in world markets and have had to fight much harder to get in. Only by the late 1980s did U.S. businesses begin to get the message. But when they did, they aggressively began to improve production standards, focusing more on quality (we'll look further at this issue later in this chapter) and preparing employees for the global village.[3] It is on this latter point that human resources will have the biggest effect.

What Is the Global Village?

Global Village The production and marketing of goods and services worldwide.

The **global village** is a term that reflects the state of businesses in our world. Business today doesn't have "national" boundaries—it reaches around the world. The rise of multinational and transnational corporations[4] places new requirements on human resource managers. For instance, human resources must ensure that the appropriate mix of employees in terms of knowledge, skills, and cultural adaptability is available to handle global assignments.

In order for human resources to meet this goal, they must train individuals to meet the challenges of the global village. First of all, there must be the means for these workers to gain a working knowledge of the language of the country in which they will work. The importance of understanding the language cannot be overstated. There have been too many examples of embarrassing situations and lost business because executives or lower-level managers were unprepared. Product names or marketing strategies have translated poorly in some foreign countries. Embarrassing situations have even happened to several former presidents of the United States! Accordingly, before any organization sends any employee overseas, human resources should ensure that the employee can handle the language.[5]

Language requirements are also going to extend into communication programs for employees, such as memos and employee handbooks being written in multiple languages. When we go abroad, for instance, searching for people with specific skills, we may be bringing into an organization someone who speaks very little English. Accordingly, we will be required to assist these individuals in learning English as a foreign language—or go even further! That is, while our foreign-born employees may learn English as a second language, it is advantageous for HRM to assure that any communication provided be understood. To achieve that outcome, companies have moved toward multilingual communications. That is, anything transmitted to employees should appear in more than one language to help the message get through. While there are no hard-and-fast rules in sending such messages, it appears safe to say that such a message should be transmitted in the languages that employees speak to ensure adequate coverage.

All HRM communications must be sent in multiple languages to assure that all employees can understand the message.

In addition to the language, human resources must also ensure that workers going overseas understand the host country's culture. All countries have different values, morals, customs, and laws. Accordingly, people going to another country must have exposure to those cultural issues before they can be expected to commence working. It is also equally important for human resource managers to understand how the host society will react to one of these mobile employees. For example, although U.S. laws guard against employers discriminating against individuals on the basis of such factors as race, religion, or sex, similar laws may not exist in other countries. Consequently, cultural considerations are critical to the success of any global business. Although it is not our intent here to provide the scope of cultural issues needed to enable an employee to go to any country, we do want to recognize that some similarities do exist (see Exhibit 1-1). Research findings allow us to group countries according to such cultural variables as status differentiation, societal uncertainty, and assertiveness.[6] These variables indicate a country's means of dealing with its people and how the people see themselves. For example, in an individualistic society like the United States, people are primarily concerned with their own family. On the contrary, in a collective society (the opposite of individualistic) like that in Japan, people care for all individuals who are part of their group. Thus, a strongly individualistic U.S. manager may not work well if sent to a Pacific Rim country where collectivism dominates. Accordingly, flexibility and adaptability are key components for managers going abroad. It will be critical, then, for those in human resources to have an understanding "of the working conditions and social systems globally so that they can counsel management on decisions and issues crossing national frontiers."[7]

HRM must also develop mechanisms that will help multicultural individuals work together. As background, language, custom, or age differences become more prevalent, there are indications that employee conflict will increase. HRM must make every effort to acclimate different groups to each other, finding ways

EXHIBIT 1-1
Cultural Similarities

COUNTRIES THAT VALUE INDIVIDUALISM AND ACQUIRING THINGS	COUNTRIES THAT VALUE COLLECTIVISM, RELATIONSHIPS, AND CONCERN FOR OTHERS
United States	Japan
Great Britain	Colombia
Australia	Pakistan
Canada	Singapore
Netherlands	Venezuela
New Zealand	Philippines

to build teams and thus reduce conflict. For instance, at Corning Inc., efforts have been made to assist these issues with respect to African-American and female employees. The purpose of this process is to "identify gender and race issues, find remedial actions, guide program development, and measure results."[8] Such action, however, is not geared to U.S. citizens only;[9] workers from different countries bring with them their own biases toward individuals from other countries, and that also can be problematic. For example, while initiatives have been underway to bring about peace in the Middle East, the dichotomy between Israel and its surrounding Arab neighbors continues. Accordingly, requiring workers from these two areas to work together could create an uneasiness that must be addressed.

How Does One Understand a Cultural Environment?

Understanding cultural environments is critical to the success of an organization's operations, but training employees in these is not the only means of achieving the desired outcomes. Companies like Amadeus Global Travel Distribution, Levi Strauss, Mars, and Hewlett-Packard are dealing with this issue by hiring nationals in foreign countries in which they operate.[10] What that has meant to these corporations is a ready supply of qualified workers who are well versed in their home country's language and customs. This recruiting has other benefits, too. Because these individuals come from differing backgrounds and are mixed together, there is a spillover training effect: that is, while working closely with one another, individuals informally learn the differences that exist between them and their two cultures. The Mars Company, for example, builds on this informal development by providing formalized training that focuses on the "major differences that lead to problems."[11] But not all employees come from the home country. In Caracas, Venezuela, for example, more than 50,000 Americans are working in the telecom construction industry. Helping them adjust to the Venezuelan culture is critical to their success.

Companies like Levi Strauss recognize that when searching for areas where work can be performed effectively in the global village, extra efforts sometimes must be made. In Bangladesh, Levi helps fund education programs for members of companies who contract out work for them.

HRM also will be required to train management to be more flexible in its practices. Because today's workers come in all different colors, nationalities, and so on, managers will be required to change their ways. This will necessitate managers being trained to recognize differences in workers and to appreciate—even celebrate—those differences. The various requirements of workers because of different cultural backgrounds, customs, work schedules, and the like must all be taken into account.[12] In addition, extensive training to recognize these differences and "change the way [managers] think about people different from themselves"[13] has positive outcomes. Companies like Honeywell, Wang Laboratories, Xerox, and Avon have already begun to formalize this process.[14]

*T*ECHNOLOGY

It's easy to forget that just 25 years ago, no one had a fax machine, a cellular phone, or a laptop computer. Terms we now use in our everyday vocabulary, like *e-mail, Internet,* and *Palm Top,* were known to maybe, at best, a few hundred people. Computers often took up expansive space, quite unlike the 1-pound notebook computer today. Moreover, if you were to talk about networks 25 years ago, people would have assumed you were talking about ABC, CBS, or NBC—the major television networks.

technology corner

HRM CHANGING TIMES

A FEW AS 10 YEARS AGO, finding information about any subject, let alone HRM, was a tedious task. The legwork, the time spent looking things up, and the cost were high. Today, however, all that has changed. With the advent of the Internet, finding information is just a "click" away. For example, the following web addresses are just a sampling of the wealth of information available to you that may be helpful in this class and in your personal pursuits.

http://www.knowledgepoint.com	Provides a human resources library
http://www.JobMark.com	A site for recruiting information and job searching
http://www.shrm.org	A premier site containing information about all aspects of human resources, as well as the certification process for HR professionals
http://www.hrfree.com	General HR information
http://hrstrategy.com	Strategic human resource management information
http://www.workforce.com	Provides information on work-force issues
http://www.eeoc.gov	The Equal Employment Opportunity Commission's web sites with case law and legal matters concerning all aspects of equal employment opportunities
Http://www.ahrd.com	Provides recent HRM research
http://www.nlrb.gov	The National Labor Relations Board's web site providing information regarding labor and management relationships
http://www.osha.gov	The Occupational Safety and Health Administration's web site providing information on health and safety issues in today's organizations
http://www.erbi.org	Provides information on employee benefit matters
http://bcsolutionsmag.com	Provides information on employee compensation matters
http://www.diversityhotwire.com	Focuses on diversity issues in organizations
http://www.trainngsupersite.com	Provides information on training and development, and career issues
http://www.chrt.com.au	Provides information on technology in HR
http://www.wfpma.com	Focuses on global/international HRM issues

The silicon chip and other advances in technology have permanently altered the economies of the world, the way people work, and the way we manage an organization's human resources. When we talk about **technology,** we are referring to any equipment, tools, or operating methods that are designed to make work more efficient (see Technology Corner). Technological advances reflect integrating any technology into any process for changing inputs into outputs. For example, digital electronics, optical data storage, more powerful and portable computers, and the ability for computers to communicate with each other are changing the way information is created, stored, used, and shared. One individual who has studied these changes and predicted some of their implications is futurist Alvin Toffler.

Toffler has written extensively about social change.[15] Classifying each period of social history, Toffler has argued that modern civilization has evolved over three "waves." With each wave came a new way of doing things. Some groups of people gained from the new way; others lost.

The first wave was driven by *agriculture*. Until the late nineteenth century, all economies were agrarian. For instance, in the 1890s, approximately 90 percent of people were employed in agriculture-related jobs. These individuals were typically their own boss and were responsible for performing a variety of tasks. Their success—or failure—was contingent on how well they produced. Since the 1890s, the proportion of the population engaged in farming has consistently dropped. Now less than 5 percent of the global work force is needed to provide our food; in the United States, it's under 3 percent.

The second wave was *industrialization*. From the late 1800s until the 1960s, most developed countries moved from agrarian societies to ones based on machines. In doing so, work left the fields and moved into formal organizations. The industrial wave forever changed the lives of skilled craftsmen. No longer did they grow something or produce a product in its entirety. Instead, workers were hired into tightly structured and formal workplaces. Mass production, specialized jobs, and authority relationships became the mode of operation. It gave rise to a new group of workers—the blue-collar industrial worker—individuals who were paid for performing routine work that relied almost exclusively on physical stamina. By the 1950s, industrial workers had become the largest single group in every developed country. They made products such as steel, automobiles, rubber, and industrial equipment. Ironically, "no class in history has ever risen faster than the blue-collar worker. And no class in history has ever fallen faster."[16] Today, blue-collar industrial workers account for less than 30 percent of the U.S. work force and will be less than half that in just a few short years.[17] The shift since World War II has been away from manufacturing work and toward service jobs. Manufacturing jobs today are highest, as a proportion of the total civilian work force, in Japan at 24.3 percent. In the United States, manufacturing jobs make up about 18 percent of the civilian work force. In contrast, services make up 59 percent of jobs in Italy (the lowest percentage of any industrialized country) and more than 80 percent in the United States and Canada.[18]

By the start of the 1970s a new age was gaining momentum, one based on *information*. Technological advancements were eliminating many low-skilled, blue-collar jobs. Moreover, the information wave was transforming society from a manufacturing focus to one of service. People were increasingly moving from jobs on the production floor to clerical, technical, and professional jobs. Job growth in the past 25 years has been in low-skilled service work (such as fast-food employees, clerks, and home health aides) and knowledge work. This latter group includes professionals such as registered nurses, accountants, teachers, lawyers, and engineers. It also includes technologists—people who work with their hands and with theoretical knowledge—commonly referred to as information technologists.[19] Computer programmers, software designers, and systems analysts are examples of jobs in this category. Knowledge workers as a group currently make up about a third of the U.S. work force.[20]

What Is a Knowledge Worker?

Knowledge Workers Individuals whose jobs are designed around the acquisition and application of information.

Knowledge workers are at the cutting edge of this third wave. Their jobs are designed around the acquisition and application of information. Organizations need people who can fill these jobs—the demand for them is great. And because the supply of information technologists is low, those in the field are paid a premium for their services.[21] Meanwhile, the number of blue-collar workers has shrunk dramatically. Unfortunately, some of the blue-collar workers don't have the education and flexibility necessary to exploit the new job opportunities in the information revolution. They don't have the specific skills to move easily into high-paying technologists' jobs. This situation contrasts with the shift from the first wave to the second. The transition from the farm to factory floor required little additional skill—often just a strong back and a willingness to learn, follow directions, and work hard.

In What Ways Does Technology Affect HRM Practices?

Technology has had a positive effect on the internal operations of organizations. But it has also changed the way human resource managers work. They work in, and provide support in what have become integrative communication centers. By linking computers, telephones, fax machines, copiers, printers, and the like, information can be disseminated more quickly. With that information, human resource plans can be better facilitated, decisions can be made faster, jobs may be more clearly defined, and communications with both the external community and employees can be enhanced. How? Let's look at some specific examples.

Recruiting Getting information out to individuals is one of the most critical aspects of recruiting. Word of mouth, newspaper advertisements, college visits, and the like, are being supplemented or replaced altogether by job postings on the Internet. Posting jobs on company web sites, or through specific job search web sites like hotjobs.com, headhunter.net, or monster.com, are giving human resource managers the opportunity to reach a larger pool of potential job applicants. It also can serve as a means of determining if an applicant possesses some of the basic technology skills. Rather than ask for a paper copy of a resume, some of these organizations are requiring the submission of an electronic resume—one that can be scanned very quickly for "relevance" to the job in question.

Employee Selection Hiring good people is particularly challenging in technology-based organizations because they require a unique brand of technical and professional people. They have to be smart and able to survive in the demanding cultures of today's dynamic organizations. In addition, many of these "qualified"

individuals are in short supply and are able to go wherever they like. Once applicants have been identified, HRM must carefully screen final candidates to ensure they fit well into the organization's culture. The realities of organizational life today may focus on an informal, team-spirited workplace, one in which intense pressure to complete projects quickly and on time is critical, and a 24/7 (24 hours a day, 7 days a week) work mentality dominates. Selection tools used by HRM need to "select out" people that aren't team players and can't handle ambiguity and stress.

Training and Development Technology is also dramatically changing how human resource managers orient, train, and develop employees—including their career management. The Internet has provided HRM opportunities to deliver specific information to employees on demand—whenever the employee has the time to concentrate on the material. These training media are also making it possible to "send" employees to training without having to physically transport them from one location to another.

Ethics and Employee Rights Electronic surveillance of employees by employers is an issue that pits an organization's desire for control against an employee's right to privacy. The development of increasingly sophisticated surveillance software only adds to the ethical dilemma of how far an organization should go in monitoring the behavior of employees who do their work on computers.[22] For instance, the web activity of every one of Xerox's 92,000 employees—in countries around the world—is routinely monitored by the company. In October 1999, Xerox fired 40 of its employees because they were caught in the act of surfing to forbidden web sites. The company's monitoring software recorded the unauthorized visits to shopping and pornography sites, and every minute they had spent at those sites.[23] Is Xerox unique? No. A recent survey by the American Management Association found that more than 50 percent of employers monitored their employees' phone calls, computer files, or e-mail messages.[24]

Motivating Knowledge Workers Are there unique challenges to motivating knowledge workers in organizations? The answer appears to be "yes." Knowledge workers appear to be more susceptible to distractions that can undermine their work effort and reduce their productivity. And with access to the Internet, some of these workers play online games, trade stocks, shop, and search for another job. The average U.S. employee with Net access is spending 90 minutes each day visiting sites unrelated to his or her job. Recent estimates indicate that 30 to 40 percent of lost worker productivity is due solely to cyberloafing; and this cyberloafing is costing U.S. employers alone $54 billion a year.[25] Ironically, it's these same workers who often have skills which make them very marketable, and many realize their employers' dependence on these skills. As a result human resource managers are facing an unusual dilemma.

Paying Employees Market Value It's becoming more difficult today for organizations to find and keep technical and professional employees. So many have implemented an extensive list of attractive incentives and benefits rarely seen by nonmanagerial employees in typical organizations: for instance, signing bonuses, stock options, cars, free health-club memberships, full-time onsite concierges, and cell phone bill subsidies. These incentives may benefit their recipients but there are downsides. One is the effect these rewards have on others who don't get them. The other is the increasing problem created by stock options. Specifically, while they look very good when a firm is growing and the stock market looks favorably on the company's future, stock options can demotivate employees when conditions turn negative.

Communications The rules of communication are being rewritten. Because these rules are designed around comprehensive, integrated information networks, communication is no longer constrained. Employees today are able to communicate with any individual directly without going through channels. Employees can communicate instantly anytime, with anyone, anywhere. At the Ford Motor Company, for instance, all of its 400,000 employees were given a home computer and Internet access for $5 a month.[26] This will allow Ford management to keep in close touch with its employees, and allow employees to easily communicate with each other and readily access company information and services.

These open communication systems break down historical organizational communication pattern flows. They also redefine how activities such as meetings, negotiations, supervision, and water-cooler talk are conducted. For instance, virtual meetings allow people in geographically dispersed locations to meet regularly. Moreover, it's now easier for employees in Charlotte and Singapore to covertly share company gossip than for those offline employees who work two cubicles apart. And employees in a number of industries even have web sites that are becoming electronic grapevines.[27]

A Legal Concern   Organizations that use technology—especially the Internet and electronic mail—must address the potential for harassment, bias, discrimination, and offensive sexual behavior from Internet and e-mail abuses.[28] There is increasing evidence that many employees fail to use the same constraints in electronic communications that they use in traditional work settings. As one individual noted, human resource managers "all know that they can't hang up a Penthouse calendar in the workplace. They all know that they can't make a racist or sexist joke in the workplace."[29] But those same people may think it's acceptable to send racist and sexist jokes via e-mail or download pornography at work. HRM must have a policy that defines inappropriate electronic communications, reserves the right to monitor employee Internet and e-mail usage, and specifies disciplinary actions for violations.

Work-Life Balance   An increasing number of employees are putting in 12-hour days, plus working 6 and 7 days a week. Many of today's dynamic organizations appear to be at the forefront of the trend toward workaholic cultures. These organizations are increasingly expecting people to work 60 to 70 hours a week. Add in the ability of technology to blur the lines separating work and home plus the dramatic increase in two-career couples, and you have the ingredients for a potential crisis. People are increasingly finding that work is squeezing out personal lives.[30] And many are questioning this lifestyle. Balancing work life and personal life is likely to become one of the most important upcoming issues for HRM.[31] Recent articles in business periodicals—with titles like "How Much Is Enough?" "9-to-5 Isn't Working Anymore," and "A Living or a Life?"—attest to this crisis.[32] And a recent survey of more than 2,000 college students and recent graduates further confirms the relevance of this issue.[33] When asked what they value most in their career decision, 42 percent chose balancing work and personal life, while only 26 and 23 percent selected compensation and advancement potential, respectively.

$\mathcal{W}$ORK-FORCE DIVERSITY

Nearly six decades ago, human resource management (or personnel as it was referred to back then) was considerably simpler because our work force was strikingly homogeneous. In the 1950s, for example, the U.S. work force consisted primarily of white males employed in manufacturing, who had wives who stayed at home, tending to the family's two-plus children. Inasmuch as these workers were alike, personnel's job was certainly easier. Recruiting for these workers was done locally, if in fact, new employees weren't related to a current worker. Because those workers all shared the same interests and needs, personnel's responsibility was to get them in the door, sign them up, tell them about the standardized benefit program, and plan the company's annual Christmas party. Then, when the time came, it was personnel's responsibility to purchase the traditional gold watch, have it engraved, and present it to the employee in a gala event in honor of the employee's retirement. But times have changed.

Until very recently, organizations took a "melting-pot" approach to differences in organizations. It was assumed that people who were different would somehow automatically want to assimilate. But today's HRM managers have found that employees do not set aside their cultural values and lifestyle preferences when they come to work. The challenge for them, therefore, is to make their organizations more accommodating to diverse groups of people by addressing different lifestyles, family needs, and work styles. The melting-pot assumption is being replaced by the recognition and celebration of differences.[34] Interestingly, those who do celebrate the differences are finding that their organization's profits are higher.[35]

What Does the Work Force Look Like?

Much of the change that has occurred in the work force is attributed to the passage of federal legislation in the 1960s prohibiting employment discrimination.[36] Based on such laws (we'll look at discrimination legislation in Chapter 3), avenues began to open up for minority and female applicants. These two groups have since become the fastest-growing segment in the work force, and accommodating their needs has become a vital responsibility for human resource managers. Furthermore, during this time, birthrates in the United States began to decline. The Baby Boom generation had already reached its apex in terms of employment opportunities, which meant that as hiring continued, there were fewer Baby Boomers left to choose.[37] And as globalization became more pronounced, Hispanic, Asian, and other immigrants came to the United States and sought employment.[38]

Projecting into the future is often an educated guess at best. Trying to predict the exact composition of our **work-force diversity** is no exception, even though we do know it will be made up of "males, females, whites, blacks, Hispanics, Asians, Native Americans, the disabled, homosexuals, straights, and the elderly."[39] Nonetheless, we do have some excellent predictors available to us, the results of which give us a good indication of what is to come. The landmark investigation into work-force composition was conducted by the Hudson Institute and the Department of Labor.[40] Their findings, originally published in 1987, illuminated the changes we could expect over the next two decades. Although there is some debate over the original findings of the Hudson Report, including the Hudson Institute's own sequel to the study, and how rapidly the work-force composition change will occur,[41] three groups in particular are projected to supply significant increases of workers to U.S. firms. These are minorities, women, and immigrants (see Exhibit 1-2).[42]

One final group that has a significant impact on the work force is the aging Baby Boom population. Commonly referred to as the "graying of the work force," our work force is increasingly witnessing those individuals who desire to work past "retirement" age.[43] Brought about by necessity (a need to have a greater income to sustain current living standards), or desire (to remain active), more individuals over the age of 55 are expected in the work force, with more than 80 percent of the Baby Boom generation indicating that they expect to work past age 65. Couple this with the fact that Congress passed the Senior Citizen's Freedom to Work Act, which eliminated the benefits penalty for those individuals on Social Security who earn more than $17,000 per year. Moreover, near-full employment levels at the beginning of the millennium has created a labor shortage—some of which is being overcome by enticing those who have previously retired to return to the workplace. In short, we can expect our work force to continue to get older, with 70- and 80-year-old workers no longer uncommon.

Work-Force Diversity The varied personal characteristics that make the work force heterogeneous.

EXHIBIT 1-2
Work-Force Diversity

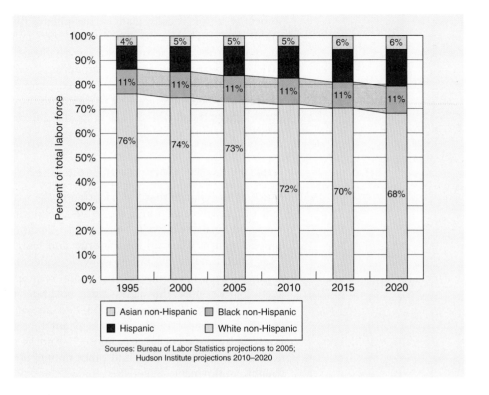

Sources: Bureau of Labor Statistics projections to 2005;
Hudson Institute projections 2010–2020

How Does Diversity Affect HRM?

As organizations become more diverse—with **diversity** in terms of gender, race, age, sexual orientation, and ethnicity—management has been adapting its human resource practices to reflect those changes (see Workplace Issues). Many organizations today, like BankAmerica, have work-force diversity programs. They tend to "hire, promote and retain minorities,[44] as well as focus on training employees. Some, like Motorola, actually conduct cultural audits to ensure that diversity is pervasive in the organization.[45] Furthermore, other organizations—both large and small—are modifying their benefit programs to make them more "family-friendly."[46]

To better meet the needs of the diverse work force, some organizations, such as Bell Atlantic, Deloitte & Touche, Ford, Pfizer, and Target, are also offering family-friendly benefits.[47] **Family-friendly benefits** include a wide range of work and family programs such as on-site day care, child and elder care, flexible work hours, job sharing, telecommuting, temporary part-time employment, unpaid leaves of absences, personal concierge services, relocation programs, adoption benefits, and parental leave.[48] With more women working and more two-career couples, family-friendly benefits are seen as a means of helping employees better balance their work and family lives.[49] And studies indicate that helping employees resolve work and family conflicts boosts morale, increases productivity, reduces absenteeism, and makes it easier for employers to recruit and retain skilled workers.[50] For example, a study at Johnson & Johnson found that absenteeism among employees who used flexible work hours and family-leave policies was on average 50 percent less than those who did not take advantage of these family-friendly benefits.[51] We'll come back to family-friendly benefits in Chapter 12.

Family-Friendly Benefits   Flexible benefits that are supportive of caring for one's family.

workplace issues

DIVERSITY AWARENESS

THE WORK FORCE IS CHANGING, AND ANYONE not sensitive to diversity issues needs to stop and check his or her attitude at the door. Today, people of color, white women, and immigrants account for nearly 85 percent of our labor force. In 1980, blacks made up 10 percent of the total work force; by the year 2000 that number had increased to 12 percent. Over the next 20 years, U.S. population is expected to grow by 42 million, and African Americans will account for 22 percent of that growth.

People are a company's no. 1 asset—not the computers, not the real estate—the people. To waste people is to waste assets, and that is not only bad business, it is the kind of thinking that today, in our competitive marketplace, will put a business out of business. Management must realize that legal requirements are simply not enough to meet the needs of our changing work force, to improve our workplace culture and environment, or to fully utilize the skills of all employees, thereby increasing a company's competitiveness. To fully maximize the contributions of African Americans and other people of color, we must commit to voluntarily focus on opportunities to foster mutual respect and understanding.[52] This can be done by valuing our differences, which enrich our workplace. And it should be done not only because it's the law, or because it's morally and ethically the right thing to do, or because it makes good business sense, but also because when we open our minds and hearts we feel better about ourselves. And decency is a hard thing to put a price tag on.

What can companies and organizations do to facilitate diversity? Here are a few suggestions:[53]

- Enlist leadership from all levels to accomplish diversity goals.
- Identify goals, barriers, obstacles, and solutions and develop a plan to meet the goals and overcome the obstacles.
  - Develop awareness through training, books, videos, and articles. Use outside speakers and consultants, as well as internal resources, to determine how to motivate and maximize the skills of a diverse work force.
  - Establish internally sanctioned employee support systems, networks, or groups.
  - Challenge each employee to question his or her beliefs, assumptions, traditions, and how they impact their relationships and decisions.
  - Modify existing policies or create diversity policies, and communicate them to all current and future hires.
- Hold managers accountable and reward them for developing, mentoring, or providing awareness training.
- Build in accountability through surveys and audits to measure progress as diligently as you would increasing production quotas or maintaining zero loss-time accidents. Then communicate the results and repeat the process. Continuous improvement applies to diversity as well as production.

CHANGING SKILLS REQUIREMENTS

In any discussion of the changing world of work, the issues of skill requirements must be addressed. As recently as the end of the nineteenth century, the United States was primarily an agrarian economy. Our great-great-grandparents worked the land with sheer brawn, growing food for themselves and those in the community. As the Industrial Revolution continued to introduce machine power, assembly lines, and mass production, workers left the farm, moved to cities, and went to work in factories. For a generation or two, these workers led the United States in becoming the world's leading industrialized nation, producing quality goods in our smokestack industries. But many of these manufacturing jobs have disappeared—replaced by more efficient machines or sent overseas to be done by lower-cost labor. Today, the U.S. economy is essentially driven by service, not manufacturing. The vast majority of employees in the United States are now employed in service-related jobs.

What does all this imply about our workers? Segments of our work force are deficient in skills necessary to perform the jobs required in the twenty-first century. The United States as a whole lags behind Singapore, Denmark, Germany, Japan, and Norway in terms of a skilled work force.[54] Some new entrants to the work force simply are not adequately prepared. High-school graduates sometimes lack the necessary reading, writing, and mathematics skills needed to perform today's high-tech jobs.[55] Others in the work force are computer illiterate. Just think of what these deficiencies imply. Imagine tomorrow's aerospace engineers who cannot properly read a blueprint or explain how wing icing affects lift on an airplane. Or tomorrow's traffic engineer who cannot properly adjust the light sequencing at a busy intersection. Just how bad has it gotten? It is estimated that about 36 percent of all job applicants who are tested for basic reading and math skills fail to pass the tests.[56]

Skill deficiencies translate into significant losses for the organization in terms of poor-quality work and lower productivity, increases in employee accidents, and customer complaints.[57] These losses run into the billions of dollars.[58] This is a major problem that must be addressed, but it is one that cannot be tackled by companies alone. To attack and to begin to correct functional illiteracy will require the resources of companies and government agencies.[59] Human resources will become the hub for providing remedial education. For example, in an effort to acquire potentially productive employees, Aetna Life offers a basic course in clerical and mathematical skills to inner-city residents. Such an attempt was made because the company was experiencing a drastic reduction in clerical applications. Since the program's inception, Aetna reports that all individuals who have entered this remedial course have moved on to become productive workers for the company.[60] But such programs do not come cheap. A significant portion of the current $80 billion spent annually on employee job training must be targeted to assisting the functionally illiterate. Ford Motor Company spends more than $200 million in remedial education.[61]

CONTINUOUS IMPROVEMENT PROGRAMS

Total Quality Management   A continuous process improvement.

There continues to be a quality revolution taking place in both the private and the public sectors.[62] The generic terms that have evolved to describe this revolution are **total quality management** or **continuous improvement**. The revolution was inspired by a small group of quality experts—individuals like Joseph Juran and the late W. Edwards Deming.[63] Today, many of these individuals' original beliefs have been expanded into a philosophy of organizational life that is driven by customer needs and expectations.[64] Importantly, however, total quality management expands the term *customer* beyond the traditional definition to

Skill deficiencies translate into significant losses for the organization.

include everyone involved with the organization, either internally or externally—encompassing employees and suppliers as well as the people who buy the organization's products or services.[65] The objective is to create an organization committed to continuous improvement, or as the Japanese call it, *kaizen.*[66]

Although continuous improvement plans have been criticized by some for overpromising and underperforming, their overall record is impressive.[67] Varian Associates, Inc., a maker of scientific equipment, used total quality management in its semiconductor unit to cut the time it took to put out new designs by 14 days. Another Varian unit, which makes vacuum systems for computer clean rooms, boosted on-time delivery from 42 percent to 92 percent through continuous improvement methods. Globe Metallurgical, Inc., a small Ohio metal producer, credits total quality management for having helped it become 50 percent more productive. And the significant improvements made over the past decade in the quality of cars produced by GM, Ford, and DaimlerChrysler can be directly traced to the implementation of total quality methods.

What Is Work Process Engineering?

Although continuous improvement methods are positive starts in many of our organizations, they generally focus on incremental change. Such action—a constant and permanent search to make things better—is intuitively appealing. Many organizations, however, operate in an environment of rapid and dynamic change. As the elements around them change so quickly, a continuous improvement process may keep them behind the times.

The problem with a focus on continuous improvements is that it may provide a false sense of security. It may make organizational members feel as if they are actively doing something positive, which is somewhat true. Unfortunately, ongoing incremental change may prevent a company from facing up to the possibility that what the organization may really need is radical or quantum change, referred to as **work process engineering.**[68] Continuous change may also make employees feel as if they are taking progressive action while, at the same time, avoiding having to implement quantum changes that will threaten certain aspects of organizational life. The incremental approach of continuous improvement, then, may be today's version of rearranging the deck chairs on the *Titanic*.[69] It is imperative in today's business environment that all organizational members consider the challenge that work process engineering may have for their organizational processes. Why? Because work process engineering can lead to "major gains in cost, service, or time,"[70] as well as assist an organization in preparing to meet the challenges technology changes foster.[71]

Work Process Engineering Radical, quantum change in an organization.

Work process engineering requires all organizational members to rethink what work should be done.

How Can HRM Support Improvement Programs?

Human resource management plays an important role in the implementation of continuous improvement programs. Whenever an organization embarks on any improvement effort, it is introducing change into the organization. As such, organization development efforts dominate.

Specifically, HRM must prepare individuals for the change. This requires clear and extensive communications of why the change will occur, what is to be expected, and the effects it will have on employees. Improvement efforts may result in changes in work patterns, changes in operations, and even changes in reporting relationships. HRM must avail itself to help the affected employees overcome barriers that may result in resistance to the change. That is, the fear dimension that is often associated with change must be overcome.

Looking for better ways of working often results in new ways of doing things. Consequently, HRM must be prepared to train employees in these new processes and help them to attain new skills levels that may be associated with the "new, improved" operations.[72]

How Does HRM Assist in Work Process Engineering?

If we accept the premise that work process engineering will change how we do business, it stands to reason that our employees will be directly affected. As such, generating the gains that work process engineering offers will not occur unless we address the people issues.

First of all, work process engineering may have left employees, at least the survivors, confused and angry. Although a preferred method of "change" would have been to involve employees throughout the process, we need to recognize that work process engineering may have left some of our employees frustrated and unsure of what to expect.[73] Long-time work relationships may have been severed—and stress levels may be magnified. Accordingly, HRM must have mechanisms in place for employees to get appropriate answers and direction for what to expect—as well as assistance in dealing with the conflicts that may permeate the organization.

Although the emotional aspect is difficult to resolve, for work process engineering to generate its benefits, HRM needs to train its employee population. Whether it's a new process, a technology enhancement, working in teams, or having more decision-making authority, our employees are going to need new skills. Consequently, HRM must be in a position to offer the skills training that is necessary in the "new" organization. Even the best process will fail if employees do not have the requisite skills to perform as the process task dictates.

Furthermore, as many components of the organization have been redefined, so too will many of the HRM activities that affect employees. For example, if redesigned work practices have resulted in changes in employee compensation packages (e.g., bonus/incentive pay), such changes need to be communicated to employees. Likewise, performance standards and how employees will be evaluated must also be understood.

THE CONTINGENT WORK FORCE

Years ago, employment patterns in our organizations were relatively predictable. In good times, when work was plentiful, large numbers of employees were hired. Then as the economy went into a recession and fewer goods were being purchased, companies simply laid off their "surplus" employee population. When the economic picture improved, a new cycle started. This process has changed, however, for most organizations.

Organizations today often do not have the luxury of hiring lots of individuals when times are good and severing them from organizational service when downtimes occur. Simply the costs of frequently hiring employees, coupled with increases in unemployment insurance rates (based, in part, on how frequently an employer lays off employees), and the costs associated with separating employees (like severance pay) have required employers to rethink their work population.

Core Employees An organization's full-time employee population.

In a number of organizations, this dynamic situation has led organizations to employ two types of workers. The first group are the core employees. **Core employees** are workers who hold full-time jobs in organizations. These employees usually provide some essential job tasks—like the chief software designer of a high-tech software development company—that require commitment and permanence in the organization. Employees who hold key core positions enjoy the full slate of employee benefits that typically were provided to full-time employees. Beyond these essential employees are many individuals who "sell" their services to an organization. We collectively call these individuals the contingent work

Contingent Workers The part-time, temporary, and contract workers used by organizations to fill peak staffing needs, or perform work unable to be done by core employees.

force. **Contingent workers** include individuals who are typically hired for shorter periods of time. They perform specific tasks that often require special job skills, and are employed when an organization is experiencing significant deviations in its work flow. Then, when the special need for them is fulfilled, these workers are let go—but not let go in the traditional layoff sense. Contingent workers have no "full-time" rights in the organization. Consequently, when their project is completed, so, too, may be their affiliation with the organization. Similarly, because of their status, these workers often do not receive any of the employee benefits that are provided to core workers. About 5 percent of the work force in 2000 was comprised of contingent workers, and that number is expected to climb in the years ahead. So who makes up the contingency pool? Contingent workers are any individuals who work part-time, as temporaries, or as contract workers (see Exhibit 1-3). And they may hold such diverse jobs as secretaries, accountants, nurses, assembly line workers, lawyers, dentists, computer programmers, engineers, marketing representatives, and human resource professionals. Even some senior management positions are filled with contingent workers.[74]

Are Contingent Workers Throw-Away Workers?

Does the fact that an organization uses contingent workers imply that management views employees less positively? Undoubtedly, since the early 1990s, we

EXHIBIT 1-3
The Contingent Work Force

Part-time Employees:	Part-time employees are those employees who work fewer than forty hours a week. Generally, part-timers are afforded few, if any, emloyee benefits. Part-time employees are generally a good source of employees for organizations to staff their peak hours. For example, the bank staff that expects its heaviest clientele between 10 A.M and 2 P.M. may bring in part-time tellers for those four hours. Part-time employees may also be a function of job sharing, where two employees split one full-time job.
Temporary Employees:	Temporary employees, like part-timers, are generally employed during peak production periods. Temporary workers also act as fill-ins when some employees are off of work for an extended period of time. For example, a secretarial position may be filled using a "temp" while the secretary is off work during his twelve-week unpaid leave of absence for the birth of his daughter. Temporary workers create a fixed cost to an employer for labor "used" during a specified period.
Contract Workers:	Contract workers, subcontractors, and consultants (who may be referred to as freelance individuals) are hired by organizations to work on specific projects. These workers, typically very skilled, perform certain duties for an organization. Often their fee is set in the contract and is paid when the organization receives particular deliverables. Organizations use contract workers because their labor cost is then fixed, and they don't incur any of the costs associated with a full-time employee population. Additionally, some contract arrangements may exist because the contractor can provide virtually the same good or service in a more efficient manner.

have witnessed significant changes in how organizations are staffed. As the changing world of work affects our businesses, reality has indicated that today's organizations simply cannot be efficient if they have surplus employees. The strategic nature of both business and HRM requires that they both be prepared for "just-in-time" employees. What that means is that organizations must find the proper blend of having a ready supply of skilled workers available when the need arises—not delayed in any manner that might create a serious shortage that would cause deadlines to be missed—and not having a surplus pool of workers waiting for something to arise. In order to meet this dual goal, however, organizations must remain flexible in their staffing levels.[75] Contingent workers conveniently fill that void. But at what cost?

Are workers freely becoming contingent workers out of their desire to fulfill personal work, family, lifestyle, or financial needs? Or have individuals been forced into this employment "limbo" as a result of downsizing and the like? The answer to both questions is unequivocally "yes."[76] There are those individuals who prefer the contingent work relationship. This offers workers some of the greatest flexibility in work scheduling—and that's something that workers, especially women, have been requesting from Corporate America.[77] With the increasing diversity of the work force, contingent work arrangements permit one to blend family and career goals.[78] Using this logic, we find that contingent positions are, in fact, beneficial to employees (see Ethical Issues in HRM).

But we cannot overlook the other side of this issue. Many organizations are using contingent work concepts to save money. Employing contingent workers saves an organization about 40 percent in labor costs, because no benefits are provided. Furthermore, hiring contingent workers protects an organization's core

---

THE CONTINGENT WORK FORCE

HIRING CONTINGENT WORKERS CAN BE A BLESSING for both organizations and individuals. Contingent workers provide employers with a rich set of diverse skills on an as-needed basis. In addition, hiring precisely when the specific work is to begin is very cost-effective. Moreover, individuals who desire to work less than full time are also given the opportunity to keep their skills sharp. Simultaneously, being contingent workers permits them to balance their commitment to personal matters and their careers.

Many of the blessings for individuals, however, revolve around a central theme: that an individual chooses to be a contingent worker. Unfortunately, that is not always the case. Jobs in the United States have shifted in terms of requisite skills and locations, and that trend is expected to continue. Consequently, the involuntary contingent work force will be expected to grow in the years ahead.

Being part of the contingent work force—even if not by choice—might not be so bad if employees received benefits typically offered to full-time core employees. Although hourly rates sometimes are higher for the contingent workers, these individuals have to pay themselves for the benefits that organizations typically provide to their full-time permanent employees. For instance, as a contract worker, you are required to pay all of your Social Security premiums. For core and some part-time employees, the employee and the employer share in this "tax." So some of that "extra" hourly rate of the contingent worker is taken away as an expense. Added to Social Security are such things as paying for one's health insurance. Buying health insurance through an organization that receives group rates is generally cheaper than having to buy the insurance yourself. This is yet another added expense to the contingent worker. So too is having to pay for one's office supplies and equipment. As for time off with pay benefits, forget about it. Vacation, holidays, sick leave? It's simple. Take all you want. But remember, when you don't work, you don't get paid!

Do you believe organizations that hire contingent workers who would rather have permanent employment are exploiting them? Should organizations be legally required to provide some basic level of benefits—such as health insurance, vacation, sick leave, and retirement—to contingent workers? What's your opinion?

employees from work fluctuations.[79] For instance, Blue Cross and Blue Shield of Rhode Island was able to trim its work force by more than 40 percent over a five-year period without having to lay off one full-timer. To achieve this, some employees are, in fact, being forced into contingent employee roles. A Bank of America employee with more than 14 years of experience was given a choice: reduce work time to 19 hours a week and receive no benefits, or be severed from the bank permanently.[80] This employee, given financial responsibilities, took what was minimally available from the bank and looked elsewhere for another part-time job. Unfortunately, individuals in this situation may work 40 hours or more each week, for several organizations, and not have the luxury of the benefits package had those 40 hours been spent in one organization.

The debate over the use of contingent workers will surely continue. There will always be those who want to be full-time employees in certain organizations, but simply cannot find that opportunity. However, the increasing trend to be lean-and-mean, the increasing competitive nature of business, and the more diverse work force will result in the creation of more temporary jobs.

What Are the HRM Implications of Contingent Workers?

When an organization makes its strategic decision to employ a sizable portion of its work force from the contingency ranks, several HRM issues come to the forefront. These include being able to have these "virtual" employees available when needed, providing scheduling options that meet their needs, and making decisions about whether benefits will be offered to the contingent work force.[81] No organization can make the transition to a contingent work force without sufficient planning. As such, when these strategic decisions are being made, HRM must be an active partner in the discussions. After all, it is HRM's responsibility to locate and bring into the organization these temporary workers. Just as employment has played an integral role in recruiting full-time employees, so too will it play a major part in securing needed just-in-time talent.

As temporary workers are brought in, HRM will also have the responsibility of quickly adapting them to the organization. Although orientation for full-time employees is more detailed, the contingent work force, nonetheless, needs to be made aware of the organization's personality. Along this line, too, some training may be required. Even a network analyst brought in to work on a specific intranet problem will need to be brought up to speed rather quickly on the uniqueness of the organization's system.

HRM will also have to give some thought to how it will effectively attract quality temporaries. As this becomes the status quo in business, there will be significant competition for the "good" talent. Accordingly, HRM will need to re-examine its compensation philosophy. If temporaries are employed solely as a cost-cutting measure, the pay and benefits offered to contingent workers might be different from those offered to other workers who are used part-time as a result of restructuring and work process engineering. HRM, then, will need to begin understanding specifically what these employees want. Is it the flexibility in scheduling, the autonomy these jobs offer, or the control over one's career destiny that such a situation affords individuals that attracts them? Or is it just bad luck, and they are forced into this situation? Understanding the reasons will surely affect the motivation of these workers.[82] For example, Half-Price Books, a Dallas, Texas, book retailer, offers health insurance coverage, retirement, vacation, and sick and holiday pay to its part-time employees. It provides these benefits because it needs an ample supply of contingent workers and wants to reduce the turnover that often occurs in their industry. By recognizing that many of its workers prefer to work part-time, yet need basic employee benefits, Half-Price Books attracts a higher quality of temporary worker.[83]

Finally, HRM must be prepared to deal with the potential conflict that may arise between core and contingent workers. The core employees may become envious of the higher pay rates and flexibility in scheduling that the contingent workers receive. In the total compensation package, which includes benefits, core employees might earn substantially more money, but these employees may not immediately include the "in-kind" pay (their benefits) in the rate of pay received. For example, paying a training consultant $3,800 for a two-day presentation skills training program might cause some conflict with core HRM trainers, although the HRM trainer may not have the time or resources to develop such a program. If the consultant offers 20 of these two-day programs over the year, earning $76,000 in consulting fees, a $50,000-a-year company trainer might take offense. Consequently, HRM must ensure that its communication programs anticipate some of these potential conflicts and address them before they become detrimental to the organization—or worse, provide an incentive for core employees to leave!

Decentralized Work Sites

Perkin-Elmer Company, the Norwalk, Connecticut, manufacturer of scientific and laboratory equipment, recently found itself facing a dilemma.[84] It had closed about 35 of its sales offices in the United States and made the decision that several hundred of its sales staff employees would work out of their homes. One employee, Wayne Wolinger, took offense! It wasn't that Wolinger objected to working out of his home. He clearly saw the benefit of being closer to his customers. What he did challenge, however, was the fact that Perkin-Elmer wouldn't compensate him for the costs he would incur by having his office at home. Although the company was setting up the office—furnishings, supplies, and equipment—Wolinger knew his monthly electric bill, insurance premiums, and the like would increase. Simply put, Wolinger wanted to be reimbursed for added expenses. Furthermore, because the company was saving money on warehousing by requiring employees to have spare parts frequently needed by customers at their homes, Wolinger wanted to be compensated for the "lost" space in his house. But company policy was clear—employees were not going to be paid any additional money for working out of their home. As a result of an inability to reach a satisfactory compromise, Wayne Wolinger was fired.

What happened to Wayne Wolinger may be an extreme case, but one that may come to light as more companies move to having workers do their jobs at home. This decentralized work site arrangement has advantages and disadvantages, and is creating new issues for HRM.

Where Do You Work?

Where one works can almost be smugly answered—wherever one's computer is! If you go back 175 years in U.S. history, it was not uncommon for workers to be performing their "craft" out of their homes. In fact, most workers performed some tasks, produced a finished product, and took it to a market to sell. But the Industrial Revolution changed all that. Large manufacturing companies drew workers away from rural areas and into the cities. Along with this movement came the traditional job—one that required employees to show up at the company's facility and spend their eight-to-twelve-hour work day there.

New management practices—like work process engineering—are changing all of that again. Jobs as our parents and grandparents knew them are disappearing. And when you factor in technological changes that have occurred in the past decade, even where we do our jobs may change. Computers, modems, fax machines, and even the telephone are making decentralized work sites attractive. Why? Several reasons have been cited.[85] **Telecommuting** capabilities that exist today have made it possible for employees to be located anywhere on the globe.[86] With this potential, employers no longer have to consider locating a business near its work force. For example, if Progressive Auto Insurance in Nebraska finds that it is having problems attracting qualified local applicants for its claims-processing jobs, and a pool of qualified workers is available in Berlin, Maryland, Progressive doesn't need to establish a facility in Maryland. Rather, by providing these employees with computer equipment and appropriate ancillaries, the work can be done hundreds of miles away and then be transmitted to the home office.

Telecommuting also offers an opportunity for a business in a high-labor-cost area to have its work done in an area where lower wages prevail. Take the publisher in New York City who finds manuscript editing costs have skyrocketed. By having that work done by a qualified editor in Little Rock, Arkansas, the publisher could reduce labor costs. Likewise, not having to provide office space in the city to this editor, given the cost per square foot of real estate in the area, adds to the cost savings. Today, nearly 8 percent of the workforce telecommutes, and this trend is expected to grow.[87]

Telecommuting Employees who do their work at home on a computer that is then linked to their office.

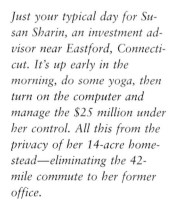

Just your typical day for Susan Sharin, an investment advisor near Eastford, Connecticut. It's up early in the morning, do some yoga, then turn on the computer and manage the $25 million under her control. All this from the privacy of her 14-acre homestead—eliminating the 42-mile commute to her former office.

Decentralized work sites also offer opportunities that meet the needs of the diversified work force. Those who have family responsibilities, like child or elder care, or those who have disabilities may prefer to work in their homes, rather than travel to the organization's facility. Telecommuting, then, provides the flexibility in work scheduling that many members of the diversified work force desire. Finally, there's some incentive from government agencies for companies to consider these alternative work arrangements. For example, the federal government, in its effort to address environmental concerns in the United States, may make state highway funds contingent on the state's ability to reduce traffic congestion in heavily populated areas. One means of achieving that goal is for businesses to receive some incentive, like a tax break, for implementing decentralized work sites. In a similar fashion, state departments of labor may also provide an incentive to businesses to relocate their work activities from more affluent communities to economically depressed areas.[88]

This trend is expected to continue. Currently, about 15 percent of the work force works at home, and that number is expected to rise sharply in the future.[89] And this trend isn't solely found in processing or sales-type jobs. Instead, telecommuting is affording doctors, lawyers, accountants, service workers, and managers the opportunities to conduct their business directly out of their homes.[90] Of course, as this occurs, it is creating some issues that HRM must deal with.

What Are the HRM Challenges of Decentralized Work Sites?

Generally, individuals get excited about the opportunities and freedom of working out of their homes. Although there are instances such as that of Wayne Wolinger that must be resolved, many home workers see this work arrangement as a major benefit. For HRM, however, decentralized work sites present a challenge.

Much of that challenge revolves around training managers in how to establish and ensure appropriate work quality and on-time completion. Traditional "face-time" is removed in decentralized work sites, and managers' need to "control" the work will have to change. Instead, there will have to be more employee involvement, allowing workers the discretion to make those decisions that affect them. For instance, although a due date is established for the work assigned to employees, managers must recognize that home workers will work at their own pace. That may mean that instead of an individual focusing work efforts over an eight-hour period, the individual may work two hours here, three hours at another time, and another three late at night. The emphasis, then, will be on the final product, not on the means by which it is accomplished. Work at home may also require HRM to rethink its compensation policy. Will it pay workers by the hour, on a salary basis, or by the job performed? More than likely, because certain jobs, like claims processing, can be easily quantified and standards set, pay plans will be in the form of pay for actual work done.

Beyond these issues, HRM must also anticipate potential legal problems that may arise from telecommuting.[91] For example, what if the employee works more than 40 hours during the work week? Will that employee be entitled to overtime pay? The answer is yes! As such, decentralized work-site activities will have to be monitored by HRM to ensure that employees are not abusing overtime privileges, and that those workers who rightfully should be paid overtime are compensated.

Because employees in decentralized work sites are full-time employees of an organization, as opposed to contingent workers, it may appear that it is the organization's responsibility to ensure the health and safety of the decentralized work site. Equipment provided by the company, for example, that leads to an employee injury or illness was thought to be the responsibility of the organization. Realization is that HRM cannot constantly monitor workers in their homes, and it is nearly impossible to ensure that these workers understand the proper techniques for using the equipment. In addition, government safety regulators have backed away from requiring employers to ensure the safety of decentralized work sites.

$\mathcal{E}$MPLOYEE INVOLVEMENT

Whenever significant changes occur in an organization, subsequent changes in the way work gets done must also occur. With respect to work process engineering and continuous improvements, many companies today are requiring their employees to do more, faster, and better, with less. Involving employees means different things to different organizations and people. But by and large, for today's workers to be successful, there are a number of employee involvement concepts that appear to be accepted.[92] These are delegation, participative management, work teams, goal setting, and employer training—the empowering of employees! Let's elaborate on these a bit.

How Can Organizations Involve Employees?

To be successful when facing multiple tasks, often on multiple projects, more employees at all levels will need to delegate some of their activities and responsibilities to other organizational members. This means that employees are going to have to be given certain amounts of authority to make decisions that directly affect their work. Even though **delegation** was once perceived as something that managers did with lower levels of management, delegation will be required at all levels of the organization—in essence, peer delegation, or using influence without authority!

Delegation A management activity in which activities are assigned to individuals at lower levels in the organization.

In addition to being required to take on more responsibilities, employees will be expected to make decisions without the benefit of the tried-and-true decisions of the past. And because all these employees are part of the process today, there is more of a need for them to contribute to the decision-making process. In most organizations, the days of autocratic management are over. To facilitate customer demands and fulfill corporate expectations, today's employees need to be more involved. Group decision making enables these employees to have more input into the processes, and greater access to needed information.[93] Such actions are also consistent with work environments that require increased creativity and innovation.

Another phenomenon of involving employees will be an emphasis on work teams.[94] The bureaucratic structure of yesterday—where clear lines of authority existed and the chain of command was paramount—is not appropriate for many of today's companies. Workers from different specializations in an organization are increasingly required to work together to successfully complete complex projects. As such, traditional work areas have given way to more of

GUIDELINES FOR ACTING ETHICALLY

ABOUT THE SKILL: MAKING ETHICAL choices can often be difficult for human resource managers. Obeying the law is mandatory, but acting ethically goes beyond mere compliance with the law. It means acting responsibly in those "gray" areas where right and wrong are not defined. What can you do to enhance your abilities in acting ethically? We offer some guidelines.

1. *Know your organization's policy on ethics.* Company policies on ethics, if they exist, describe what the organization perceives as ethical behavior and what it expects you to do. This policy will help you to clarify what is permissible and the discretion you will have. This becomes your code of ethics to follow!

2. *Understand the ethics policy.* Just having the policy in your hand does not guarantee that it will achieve what it is intended to do. You need to fully understand it. Behaving ethically is rarely a cut-and-dried process. But the policy can act as a guiding light, providing a basis from which you will do things in the organization. Even if a policy does not exist, there are still several steps you can take before you deal with the difficult situation.

3. *Think before you act.* Ask yourself, "Why am I going to do what I'm about to do? What led up to the problem? What is my true intention in taking this action? Is my reason valid? Or are there ulterior motives behind it — such as demonstrating organizational loyalty? Will my action injure someone? Would I disclose to my boss or my family what I'm going to do?" Remember, it's your behavior and your actions. You need to make sure that you are not doing something that will jeopardize your role as a manager, your organization, or your reputation.

4. *Ask yourself what-if questions.* If you are thinking about why you are going to do something, you should also be asking yourself what-if questions. For example, the following questions may help you shape your actions. "What if I make the wrong decision: what will happen to me? to my job?" "What if my actions were described, in detail, on the local TV news show or in the newspaper: would it bother or embarrass me or those around me?" "What if I get caught doing something unethical: am I prepared to deal with the consequences?"

5. *Seek opinions from others.* If it is something major that you must do, and about which you are uncertain, ask for advice from other managers. Maybe they have been in a similar situation and can give you the benefit of their experience. Or maybe they can just listen and act as a sounding board for you.

6. *Do what you truly believe is right.* You have a conscience, and you are responsible for your behavior. Whatever you do, if you truly believe it was the right action to take, then what others say, or what the "Monday morning quarterbacks" say is immaterial. You need to be true to your own internal ethical standards. Ask yourself: "Can I live with what I've done?"

a team effort, building and capitalizing on the various skills and backgrounds that each member brings to the team. Consider, for example, what kind of group it takes to put together a symphony. One musician could not possibly handle the various instruments—especially playing them all at one time. Accordingly, to blend the music of the orchestra, symphonies have string sections, brass instruments, percussion, and the like. At times, however, a musician may cross over these boundaries, like the trombonist who also plays the piano. The basis of these work teams, then, is driven by the tasks at hand. Involving employees allows them an opportunity to focus on the job goals. By giving them more freedom, employees are in a better position to develop the means to achieve the desired ends.

What Are the Employee Involvement Implications for HRM?

We have addressed some components of employee involvement; for an organization, however, addressing them is not enough. What is needed is demonstrated leadership, as well as supportive management. Additionally, employees need to be trained, and that's where human resource management can make a valuable contribution. Employees expected to delegate, to have decisions participatively handled, to work in teams, or to set goals cannot do so unless they know and understand what it is they are to do. Empowering employees requires extensive training in all aspects of the job. Workers may need to understand new job design processes. They may need training in interpersonal skills to make participative management and work teams function properly. We can anticipate much more involvement from HRM in all parts of the organization.

But make no mistake about it. Employee involvement comes at a price. First of all, better control over one's work activities, coupled with better "tools," has been shown to improve productivity.[95] We are doing more with less, but are doing it smarter and more productively. Additionally, there is evidence that as employees see the commitment the organization and HRM have made to them, their own commitment and loyalty to the organization will increase.[96]

HRM WORKSHOP

*S*UMMARY

(This summary relates to the Learning Outcomes identified on p. 2.)
After having read this chapter, you should be able to:

1. **Discuss how the global village affects human resource management practices.** Globalization is creating a situation where human resource management must begin to search for mobile and skilled employees capable of successfully performing their job duties in a foreign land. This means that these employees must understand the host country's language, culture, and customs.

2. **Describe how technology is changing HRM.** Technology is having a major impact on HRM. It's giving all employees instant access to information and changing the skill requirements of employees. As a result of technological changes, HRM has had to address or change its practices when it deals with such activities as recruiting and selecting employees, motivating and paying individuals, training and developing employees, and legal and ethical matters.

3. **Identify the significant changes that have occurred in the composition of the work force.** The work-force composition has changed considerably over the past 35 years. Once characterized as having a dominant number of white males, the work force of the new millennium is

comprised of a mixture of women, minorities, immigrants, and white males.

4. **Explain the implications for human resource management of the changing work-force composition.** The most significant implications for human resource management regarding the changing work-force composition are language and skill deficiencies of available workers, changing management practices to accommodate a diverse work group, dealing with conflict among employees, and providing family-friendly benefits.

5. **Describe how changing skill requirements affect human resource management.** Changing skill requirements necessitate that human resource management provide extensive training. This training can be in the form of remedial help for those who have skill deficiencies, or specialized training dealing with technology changes.

6. **Explain why organizational members focus on quality and continuous improvements.** Organizational members focus on quality and continuous improvements for several reasons; today's educated consumers demand it and quality improvements have become strategic initiatives in the organization. HRM is instrumental in quality initiatives by preparing employees to deal with the change and training them in new techniques.

7. **Describe how work process engineering differs from continuous improvements and its implications for HRM.** Continuous incremental improvements focus on enhancing the quality of a current work process. Work process engineering focuses on major or radical change in the organization.

8. **Identify who makes up the contingent work force and its HRM implications.** The contingent work force includes those part-time, temporary, consultants, and contract workers who provide services to organizations on an as-needed basis. The HRM implications of a contingent work force include attracting and retaining skilled contingent workers, adjusting to their special needs, and managing any conflict that may arise between core and contingent workers.

9. **Explain why work sites may be decentralized and what their implications are for HRM.** Organizations use decentralized work sites because telecommuting arrangements enable organizations to find qualified employees without having to relocate business facilities. Decentralized work sites also provide cost savings to the organization, as well as fulfilling some special needs of a diversified work force. For HRM, decentralized work sites will require training for managers in managing and controlling work, and establishing pay systems to reflect this work arrangement. HRM will also have to monitor the hours home workers spend on the job, as well as ensuring the health and safety of workers in the home office.

10. **Define employee involvement and list its critical components.** Employee involvement can be best defined as giving each worker more control over his or her job. To do this requires delegation, participative management, work teams, goal setting, and employee training. If handled properly, involving employees should lead to developing more productive employees who are more loyal and committed to the organization.

DEMONSTRATING COMPREHENSION: *Questions for Review and Discussion*

1. How has the global village contributed to the need for diversity awareness in our organizations?

2. Which groups will comprise the greatest influx into the U.S. work force over the next 10 years? What will be the HRM effect of these groups?

3. "Work force diversity is nothing new. We need only look back to the early 1900s when thousands of immigrants came to the United States, understand how we handled them, and then implement similar practices again." Do you agree or disagree with the statement? Explain.

4. How does workplace illiteracy affect an organization? What can HRM do to deal with the illiteracy issue?

5. "Our public school systems have created a significant problem for Corporate America. Many recent graduates cannot read, write, or do the simplest math calculations. What is needed is a restructuring of our high school curriculum to demand higher levels of rigor that will result in better prepared employees." Build an argument for and against this statement.

6. What is a knowledge worker? What HRM changes can be expected to deal with knowledge workers with respect to recruiting, selection, motivation, and work-life issues?

7. What is the purpose of a continuous improvement program? What role does HRM play in assisting continuing improvements?

8. What are the necessary ingredients for a successful empowerment program?

9. "Family-friendly benefits are crucial to attracting and retaining quality workers today. Without them, work-life stressors will only become worse." Do you agree or disagree with this statement? Defend your position.

10. What are the advantages and disadvantages of decentralized work sites? What effect do these have on employers? On employees?

Case Application: *TEAM FUN!*

Kenny and Norton founded TEAM FUN!, a sporting goods and equipment store and manufacturer, ten years ago. They now have 125 employees and 3 suburban branches. Overlooking their LAGOON, where employees try out new water gear (kayaks, swim fins, wet suits, racing suits, goggles), Norton says to Kenny, "Maybe we are getting too old for this. I got the prototype for the new soccer gear, and it's labeled funny." Kenny frowns. Norton continues, "Some funny language. Maybe two. Looks like Spanish. 'Agua' is water, right?"

Kenny slugs Norton's shoulder, "Si!"

Norton: "Maybe French or German for the other. Why would SideKick do that? We've been doing business for 10 years."

Kenny scratches his head: "I dunno. Lots of things going on around here that I don't understand. Charley asked me if we could make a corner of the lunch room into a baby sitting place. Said we'd be family-friendly. We've always been that, right?" They head outside to the GREEN, their golf supply area, and past a few people who smile and nod. Kenny comments, "I don't even know everyone who works here anymore. Edna in personnel asked me about an insurance file claim on Jane Edwards. I don't even know who Jane is or why we have eye insurance. Edna talked about 'human resources issues.'"

Norton offers, "Last week I played racquetball with Keith." Kenny frowns and Norton goes on, "Sure, you know Keith. He runs that football recleater operation in Springfield. He was bragging about their strategic new Human Resources Manager."

Kenny picks up the new TEAM TigerPutter at the sign, TRY THIS OUT. "This golf club is a strategic advantage. What is a strategic human resource?"

Questions:
1. Is TEAM FUN! impacted by globalization?
2. What other major workforce issues are evident?
3. Does TEAM FUN! need a human resources professional? Explain your answer to Kenny and Norton.

Working with a Team: *Understanding Diversity Issues*

Work-force diversity has become a major issue for managers. Although there are often similarities among individuals, obvious differences do exist. A means of identifying some of those differences is to get to know individuals from the diverse groups. For this exercise, you will need to contact people from a different country. If you don't know any, the office of your college that is responsible for coordinating international students can give you a list of names. Interview at least three people to get responses to such questions as:
1. What country do you come from?
2. What is your first language?
3. Describe your country's culture in terms of, for example, form of government, emphasis on individual versus group, role of women in the work force, benefits provided to employees, and how employees are treated.
4. What were the greatest difficulties in adapting to your new culture?
5. What advice would you give me if I had an HRM position in your country?

In groups of three to five class members, discuss your findings. Are there similarities in what each of you found? If so, what are they? Are there differences? Describe them. What implications for managing in the global village has this exercise generated for you and your group?

Enhancing Your Writing Skills

1. Visit a human resource management department—either on elect a dot-com organization. Research information on this organization in terms of human resource activities. For instance, if the organization has a "job posting" web site, visit it and critique its usefulness to you.
2. Provide a two- to three-page write up on a technology-based organization (e.g., Amazon.com; Dell, Varsitybooks.com) and the effect technology is having on the human resource aspects of the business. Emphasize the way the business has had to change its HRM practices to accommodate the technology changes, and the benefits that have accrued or are anticipated.
3. Family-friendly benefits have a tendency to be perceived as benefits that are primarily offered to female employees. But fathers have rights, too. Research what organizations are doing to provide male employees with family-friendly benefits. In presenting your results, include a discussion on the benefits and the costs accruing to organizations from offering these benefits.

ENDNOTES

1. Vignette based on Selective HR profile, <http://www. se-lectivehr.com/profile.htm> (September 30, 2000), pp. 1–3. See also K. A. Goeldner, "Professional Employee Organizations—Opportunities and Considerations," *CPCU Journal* (Spring 1999), pp. 17–21; M. Cody, "Serving Small Firms Pays Off Big for HR Tech," *Columbia Flyer* (December 3, 1998), p. 26; J. J. Occhiogrosso, "Professional Employers for Small Companies," *Management Accounting* (December 1998), pp. 38–42; K. Fleming, "Columbia Entrepreneurs Honored," *Business Monthly* (August 1998), p. 17; "Largest Private Sector Employers in the Baltimore Area," *Baltimore Business Journal* (August 28, 1998), p. 22; and "HR Tech's Leaders of the Pack, *Proemp Journal* (May 1998), pp. 76–79.

2. "Outsourcing HR," *Industry Week* (May 15, 2000), p. 71.

3. William H. Wagel, "On the Horizon: HR in the 1990s," *Personnel* (January 1990), p. 6.

4. A multinational corporation is an organization that has significant operations in two or more countries. A transnational corporation is one that maintains significant operations in two or more countries simultaneously, and gives each the decision-making authority to operate in the local country.

5. Because of the global nature of work, it is important for students to be bilingual. In terms of gaining employment, those who speak more than one language will have an advantage in the job market.

6. For a more comprehensive coverage of the cultural dimension, see Geert Hofstede, *Cultural Consequences: International Differences in Work-Related Values* (Beverly Hills, CA: Sage Publications, 1980).

7. Wagel, p. 17.

8. Stephanie Overman, "Managing the Diverse Work Force," *HRMagazine* (April 1991), p. 31.

9. Bruce W. Nolan, "Racism," *Time* (August 12, 1991), pp. 36–38.

10. *HRMagazine* (January 1991), pp. 40–41.

11. Ibid., p. 40.

12. William H. Wagel, *Personnel* (January 1990), p. 12.

13. "Riding the Tide of Change," *Wyatt Communicator* (Winter 1991), p. 11.

14. Ibid.

15. See, for example, A. Toffler, *The Third Wave* (New York: Bantam Books, 1981).

16. P. F. Drucker, "The Age of Social Transformation," *Atlantic Monthly* (November 1994), p. 56.

17. A. Fox, "Leaders Offer Insights on the Workforce of the 21st Century," *HRNews* (May 1999), p. 3.

18. See, for example, G. Epstein, "Economic Beat: The Economy Runs on Service Jobs (Not That There's Anything Wrong with That)," *Barron's* (March 8, 1999), p. 40.

19. P. F. Drucker, "The Age of Social Transformation," p. 56.

20. Ibid.

21. M.A. Verespej, "Name That Salary," *Industry Week* (February 15, 1999), p. 33; and D. North, "Revenge of the Nerds," *Canadian Business* (December 1996), p. 39.

22. See, for instance, M. J. McCarthy, "You Assumed 'Erase' Wiped Out That Rant Against the Boss? Nope," *Wall Street Journal* (March 7, 2000), p. A1; and S. Boehle, "They're Watching You: Workplace Privacy is Going . . . Going . . . ," *Training* (August 2000), pp. 50–60.

23. L. Guernscy, "The Web: New Ticket to a Pink Slip," *New York Times* (December 16, 1999), p. D1+.

24. American Management Association Survey of 2,133 corporations (January 2000).

25. Cited in M. Conlin, "Workers, Surf at Your Own Risk," *Business Week* (June 12, 2000), p. 105.

26. "Ford Motor Company's CEO Jac Nasser on Transformational Change, E-Business, and Environmental Responsibility," *Academy of Management Executive* (August 2000), pp. 46–51; and "Ford Employees to Receive Home Computers, Internet Access," www.uaw. com (February 3, 2000).

27. A. Cohen, "Click Here for a Hot Rumor About Your Boss," *Time* (September 11, 2000), p. 48.

28. M. A. Verespej, "Inappropriate Internet Surfing," *Industry Week* (February 7, 2000), pp. 59–64.

29. Ibid., p. 59.

30. Alan Goldstein, "The Average Workday Used to Be 9 to 5. Now with Technology and the Internet's Reach, It's Almost 24/7. So Where Does the Workday End and the Personal Life Begin? All Work, No Play," *Dallas Morning News* (September 20, 2000), p. 1H.

31. See, for instance, P. Cappelli, J. Constantine, and C. Chadwick, "It Pays to Value Family: Work and Family Tradeoffs Reconsidered," *Industrial Relations* (April 2000), pp. 175–198; and R. D. Winsor and E. A. Ensher, "Choices Made in Balancing Work and Family," *Journal of Management Inquiry* (June 2000), pp. 218–231.

32. C. Fishman, "How Much Is Enough?" *Fast Company* (July–August 1999), pp. 108–116; M. Conlin, "9 To 5 Isn't Working Anymore," *Business Week* (September 20, 1999), pp. 94–98; and A. Field, "A Living or a Life?" *Fast Company* (January–February 2000), pp. 256–267.

33. "Students Place High Value on Work/Life Issues," *HR Magazine* (March 2000), p. 30.

34. I. Taylor, "Winning at Diversity," *Working Woman* (March 1999), p. 36; L. Urresta and J. Hickman, "The Diversity Elite," *Fortune* (August 3, 1998).

35. Sherry Kuczynski, "If Diversity, Then Higher Profits," *HRMagazine* (December 1999), pp. 66–74. See also Orlando C. Richard, "Racial Diversity, Business Strategy, and Firm Performance: A Resource Based View," *Academy of Management Journal* (April 2000), pp. 164–177.

36. Donna Fenn, "Diversity: More Than Just Affirmative Action," *Inc.* (July 1995), p. 93.

37. The Baby-Boom generation refers to those individuals born between 1946 and 1964.

38. Jonathan A. Degal, "Diversify for Dollars," *HRMagazine* (April 1997), pp. 134–140.

39. Sharon Nelton, "Winning with Diversity," *Nation's Business* (September 12, 1992), p. 18.

40. The Hudson Institute, *Workforce 2000: Work and Workers for the 21st Century* (Indianapolis, IN: Hudson Institute, 1987).

41. Ann Crittenden, "Where Workforce 2000 Went Wrong," p. 18.

42. Richard W. Judy and Carol D'Amico, *Workforce 2020: Work and Workers in the 21st Century* (Indianapolis, IN: Hudson Institute, 1997), p. 109; Betty Holcomb, "No, We're Not Going Home Again," *Working Mother* (November 1994), p. 28. See also James Aley, "Men Ditch the Labor Market," *Fortune* (August 22, 1994), p. 24.

43. Neal Thompson, "American Work Force Is Seeing More Gray," *Baltimore Sun* (October 8, 2000), pp. A1; A13.

44. See Geoffrey Colvin, "The 50 Best Companies for Asians, Blacks, and Hispanics," *Fortune* (July 19, 1999), pp. 53–78.

45. R. LaGow, "Motorola Official Downplays Formal Cultural Audits," *HRNews* (December 1998), p. 3.

46. See, for instance, "Friends of the Family: 100 Best Companies for Working Mothers — 15th Annual Survey," *Working Mother* (October 2000), pp. 60–148; R. S. Johnson, "The 50 Best Companies for Asians, Blacks, and Hispanics," pp. 94–110; M. Evanstock, "Women and Children First," *Working Woman* (February 1999), pp. 28–29; J. K. Ford and S. Fisher, "The Role of Training in a Changing Workplace: New Perspectives and Approaches," and S. A. Lobel and E. E. Kossek, "Human Resource Strategies to Support Diversity in Work and Personal Lifestyles: Beyond the "Family-Friendly" Organization," both in E. E. Kossek and S. A. Lobel (eds.), *Managing Diversity* (Cambridge, MA: Blackwell Publishers, 1996), pp. 164–193 and 221–244, respectively.

47. See, for example, S. Branch, "The 100 Best Companies to Work for in America," *Fortune* (January 11, 1999), pp. 118–144.

48. J. Lynn, "Fathers Figure," *Entrepreneur* (March 1999), p. 33; and M. N. Martinez, "An Inside Look at Making the Grade," *HRMagazine* (March 1998).

49. F. J. Milliken, L. L. Martins, and H. Morgan, "Explaining Organizational Responsiveness to Work-Family Issues: The Role of Human Resource Executives as Issue Interpreters," *Academy of Management Journal* (October 1998), pp. 580–591; and R. W. Judy and C. D'Amico, *Workforce 2020* (Indianapolis, IN: Hudson Institute, 1997), p. 109.

50. A. Fisher, "The 100 Best Companies to Work for in America," *Fortune* (January 12, 1998), pp. 69–70; and L. Grant, "Happy Workers, High Returns," *Fortune* (January 12, 1998), p. 81.

51. M Galen, "Work & Family," *Business Week* (June 28, 1993), p. 82.

52. See, for example, Robert J. Grossman, "Race in the Workplace," *HRMagazine* (March 2000), pp. 41–45.

53. See also Society of Human Resource Management, "What Are Some Strategies for Recruiting and Retaining a Diverse Workforce?" *Workplace Diversity Initiative* (September 29, 2000), pp. 1–3.

54. Jane A. Sasseen, Robert Neff, Shekar Hattangadi, and Silvia Sansoni, "The Winds of Change Blow Everywhere," *Business Week* (October 17, 1994), p. 93.

55. Commerce Clearing House, "Employers to Bear Burden of Adult Literacy," *Human Resources Management: Ideas and Trends* (November 10, 1993), p. 182.

56. Commerce Clearing House, "AMA Surveys: Drug Testing, Basic Skills, and AIDS Policy Benchmarks," *Human Resources Management: Ideas and Trends* (June 8, 1994), p. 97.

57. "Employee Literacy," *Inc.* (August 1992), p. 81.

58. Ibid.

59. See, for example, Samuel Fromartz, "Tomorrow's Workforce," *Inc. Tech 2000* (September 2000), pp. 88–92.

60. *Fortune* (April 23, 1990), p. 176.

61. Ibid.; see also Louis S. Richman, "The New Work Force Builds Itself," *Fortune* (June 27, 1994), pp. 68–69.

62. See, for example, B. Krone, "Total Quality Management: An American Odyssey," *Bureaucrat* (Fall 1990), pp. 35–38; A. Gabor, *The Man Who Discovered Quality* (New York: Random House 1990); J. Clemmer, "How Total Is Your Quality Management?" *Canadian Business Review* (Spring 1991), pp. 38–41; and M. Sashkin and K. J. Kiser, *Total Quality Management* (Seabrook, MD: Ducochon Press, 1991).

63. For an excellent review of the theory of development and the implications of Deming's TQM, see J. W. Dean Jr. and D. E. Bowen, "Management Theory and Total Quality: Improving Research and Practice through Theory Development," *Academy of Management Review* (July 1994), pp. 392–418; and J. C. Anderson, M. Rungtusanatham, and R. G. Schroeder, "A Theory of Quality Management Underlying the Deming Management Method," *Academy of Management Review* (July 1994), pp. 472–509. See also T. A. Stewart, "A Conversation with Joseph Juran," *Fortune* (January 11, 1999), pp. 168–170.

64. A. C. Hyde, "Rescuing Quality Management from TQM," *Bureaucrat* (Winter 1990–91), p. 16.

65. M. Hendricks, "Step by Step," *Entrepreneur* (March 1996), p. 70.

66. J. H. Sheridan, "Kaizen Blitz," *Industry Week* (September 1997), pp. 18–28.

67. See A. R. Korukonda, J. G. Watson, and T. M. Rajkumar, "Beyond Teams and Empowerment: A Counterpoint to Two Common Precepts in TQM," *SAM Advanced Management Journal* (Winter 1999), pp. 29–36; T. Y. Choi and O. C. Behling, "Top Managers and TQM Success: One More Look After All These Years," *Academy of Management Executive* February 1997), pp. 37–46.

68. T. A. Stewart, "Reengineering: The Hot New Managing Tool," *Fortune* (August 23, 1993), pp. 41–48.

69. A. B. Shani and Y. Mitki, "Reengineering, Total Quality Management, and Sociotechnical Systems Approaches to Organizational Change: Towards an Eclectic Approach?" *Journal of Quality Management* (1996), pp. 133–134; and M. Hammer and S. A. Stanton, *The Reengineering Revolution* (New York: Harper Business, 1995).

70. Hammer and Stanton, *The Reengineering Revolution*, p. 42.

71. S. Hamm and M. Stepanek, "From Reengineering to E-Engineering," *Business Week* (March 22, 1999), pp. EB-13–EB-18.

72. Edward E. Lawler III, "Total Quality Management and Employee Involvement: Are They Compatible?" *Academy of Management Executive*, Vol. 8, No. 1 (1994), pp. 68–76; and Richard Blackman and Benson Rosen, "Total Quality and Human Resources Management: Lessons Learned from Baldrige Award–Winning Companies," *Academy of Management Executive*, Vol. 7, No. 3 (1993), pp. 49–66.

73. Julie Connelly, "Have We Become Mad Dogs in the Office?" *Fortune* (November 28, 1994), p. 197.

74. Beth Rogers, "Temporary Help Industry Evolving as It

Grows," *HRNews* (January 1995), p. 4.

75. See, for instance, Audrey Freedman, "Human Resources Forecast 1995: Contingent Workers," *HRMagazine Supplement* (1994), pp. 13–14.

76. Maggie Mahar, "Part-time: By Choice or By Chance," *Working Woman* (October 1993), p. 20.

77. Ann Crittenden, "Temporary," p. 32.

78. Jaclyn Fierman, "The Contingent Work Force," p. 33.

79. Keith H. Hammonds, Kevin Kelly, and Karen Thurston, "The New World of Work," *Business Week* (October 17, 1994), p. 85.

80. Ann Crittenden, "Temporary," p. 33.

81. Ani Hadjian, "Hiring Temps Full-Time May Get the IRS On Your Tail," *Fortune* (January 24, 1994), p. 34.

82. See, for example, Leon Rubis, "Benefits Boost Appeal of Temporary Work," *HRMagazine* (January 1995), pp. 54–58; and Anne Murphy, "Do-It-Yourself Job Creation," *Inc.* (January 1994), pp. 36–50.

83. Michael P. Cronin, "The Benefits of Part-Time Work," *Inc.* (December 1994), p. 127.

84. Based on Sue Shellenbarger, "Refusing In-Home Work Costs Him His Job," *Wall Street Journal* (April 8, 1994), p. B–1.

85. See, for example, Wayne F. Casio, "Managing a Virtual Workplace," *Academy of Management Executive,* Vol. 14, No. 3 (March 2000), pp. 81–89.

86. Robert Barker, "Work a'la Modem," *Business Week* (October 4, 1999), pp. 170–174.

87. Ibid, p. 176.

88. Ibid.

89. Thomas Roberts, "Who Are the High-Tech Home Workers?," *Inc. Technology* (1994), p. 31.

90. Ibid.

91. Commerce Clearing House, "Work at Home Increasingly Appealing to Employers, But Legal Pitfalls Abound," *Human Resources Management: Ideas and Trends* (February 16, 1994), pp. 25–26.

92. For a comprehensive overview of empowering employees, see Jay A. Conger and Rabindra N. Kanungo, "The Empowerment Process: Integrating Theory and Practice," *Academy of Management Review,* Vol. 13, No. 3 (July 1988), pp. 471–482.

93. See, for example, Jeffrey Pfeffer, "Producing Sustainable Competitive Advantage Through the Effective Management of People," *Academy of Management Executive,* Vol. 9, No. 1 (1995), pp. 55–72.

94. Keith H. Hammond, Kevin Kelly, and Karen Thurston, "The New World of Work," *Business Week* (October 17, 1994), p. 81.

95. See, for example, Jon L. Pierce, Stephen A. Rubenfeld, and Susan Morgan, "Employee Ownership: A Conceptual Model of Process and Effects," *Academy of Management Review,* Vol. 16, No. 1 (January 1991), pp. 121–144.

96. Ibid., pp. 136–137; and Brian O'Reilly, "The New Deal: What Companies and Employees Owe One Another," *Fortune* (June 13, 1994), p. 44.

2

FUNDAMENTALS OF HRM

LEARNING OUTCOMES

AFTER READING THIS CHAPTER, YOU WILL BE ABLE TO:

1. Define management and identify its primary functions.
2. Describe the importance of human resource management.
3. Explain what is meant by the term *human resource management*.
4. Identify the primary environmental influences affecting human resource management.
5. Characterize how management practices affect human resource management.
6. Discuss the effect of labor unions on human resource management.
7. Outline the components and the goals of the staffing, training, and development functions.
8. List the components and goals of the motivation and maintenance functions of human resource management.
9. Outline the major activities in the employment, training and development, compensation and benefits, and employee relations departments of human resource management.
10. Explain how human resource management practices differ in small businesses and in an international setting.

"Good morning staff," said Robin Alexander, vice president of HRM. "As you know, it's time once again for us to take a look at where we've been, and what issues need addressing as we continue to support this organization's strategic directions. Even though we meet weekly to discuss day-to-day activities, I feel it's necessary for us to have these planning sessions to reassess how we are helping this organization achieve its goals. So, now that you have settled in, let me start by giving you my 'state-of-HRM' recap.[1]

"We have been providing a first-class service to our clients. Over the past couple of years, we have worked hard to put in place many of the programs that have truly aided this company and supported its strategic direction. For example, we now have our family-friendly benefits program fully functioning. In its first year alone, we were able to cut recruiting costs by more than 23 percent. We've done this in part through our intranet access to our HR systems. We were also one of the first in the area to implement a detailed policy on employee monitoring—keeping informed on employee activities. But a policy alone wouldn't suffice. We effectively enlightened each employee of this organization about the policy and what is unacceptable behavior. We have helped design online interactive training programs that support senior management's continuous improvement program. And let me remind you of these findings just released by our president. Through these efforts, productivity has improved more than 20 percent in the past twelve months. Much of this productivity increase has been attributable to our changing emphasis from specialized jobs to ones that have a more employee-involved, team approach. We'll need to continue to assist organizational members, and ourselves, in how to effectively work as teams. Although I could go on about our accomplishments, we cannot take the position that we've succeeded. On the contrary, there are new challenges ahead. Let me address some of the more important issues facing us over the next few years.

"Organizations continue to rapidly evolve. Change is no longer something that occurs in a controlled fashion. Rather, it is constantly before us, creating chaos as we deal with the uncertainty brought about by a dynamic world. As such, we all learn how to become more flexible in dealing with the changes that will arise. We must assist others in taking active roles in managing the change, as opposed to sitting back and helping them react to it. This means that we've got to retrain ourselves and others in terms of effective managerial skills and competencies such as project management, team building, and technology skills.

"Closely aligned with these new job requirements will be our continued effort toward enhancing the skill levels of our workers. Today's jobs are more complex and require significant interaction with sophisticated technology. We must keep in mind that competition for employees is global. We must ensure that we have the right people for those jobs, which, in most cases, will require us to continuously train and upgrade our employees' skills. We must be at the forefront of developing knowledge workers by using a variety of methods.

"But keep in mind this will not be an easy task; all employees are not alike—either in skill level or in their backgrounds. Thus, we need to pay more attention to the diversity that exists in the work force. What do I mean by attention to diversity? By and large, I think that it means recognizing and respecting differences in people. We have employees from all walks of life. Accordingly, we need to be more sensitive to each person's background and their needs. In doing so, we can capitalize on their strengths they bring to us. Consequently, we must advocate more acceptance of one another in the organization as we work toward achieving our common goals by valuing differences as well as similarities.

"Let's also continue to remember the legislation that we face. Each day we make decisions that may be reviewed or questioned by people external to our organization. We must ensure that our HRM practices do not adversely affect any one group. We must give all employees an equal chance to realize their potential and fulfill their career dreams. When that happens, the organization can only benefit. But we can do this only by continuing to have in place effective HRM practices. Finally, let's remember that we must help our employees as well as ourselves to balance work and life issues, enabling a quality of life that helps each individual achieve his or her goals.

"Thank you for your wonderful years of service to HR and this organization."

*I*NTRODUCTION

When you reflect for a moment on Robin's comments, it is important to note that achieving organizational goals cannot be done without human resources. What is Microsoft without its employees? A lot of buildings, expensive equipment, and some impressive bank balances. Similarly, if you removed the employees from such varied organizations as the St. Louis Rams football team, Cisco, Southwest Airlines, or Cedars-Sinai Hospital, what would you have left? Not much. It's people—not buildings, the equipment, or brand names—that really make a company.

This point is one that many of us take for granted. When you think about the millions of organizations that provide us with goods and services, any one or more of which will probably employ you during your lifetime, how often do you explicitly consider that these organizations depend on people to make them operate? Only under unusual circumstances, such as when you get put on hold for an extended period of time on a company's toll-free customer-service line or when a major corporation is sued for a discriminatory HRM practice, do you recognize the important role that employees play in making organizations work. But how did these people come to be employees in their organizations? How were they selected? Why do they come to work on a regular basis? How do they know what to do on their jobs? How does management know if the employees are performing adequately? And if they are not, what can be done about it? Will today's employees be adequately prepared for the technologically advanced work the organization will require of them in the years ahead? What happens in an organization if a union is present?

It's people, not buildings . . . that make a company successful.

These are some of the many questions whose answers lie in the subject of the foundations of human resource management. It's our intention to discuss these elements as a set of activities that need to be accomplished by someone—whether or not they are actual members of an organization, or providing a service (like a PEO) for an organization. Regardless of who is doing them, certain actions must take place—actions that serve as the fundamentals of HRM. Yet the field of HRM is not one that exists in isolation. Rather, it's part of the larger field of management. So, before we attempt to understand how an organization should manage its human resources, let's briefly review the essentials of management.

What Are the Management Essentials?

Management is the process of efficiently achieving the objectives of the organization with and through people. To achieve its objective, management typically requires the coordination of several vital components that we call functions. The primary functions of management that are required are **planning**[2] (e.g., establishing goals), **organizing** (i.e., determining what activities need to be completed to accomplish those goals), **leading** (i.e., ensuring that the right people are on the job with appropriate skills, and motivating them to levels of high productivity), and **controlling** (i.e., monitoring activities to ensure that goals are met). When these four functions operate in a coordinated fashion, we can say that the organization is heading in the correct direction toward achieving its objectives. Common to any effort to achieve objectives are three elements: goals, limited resources, and people.

In any discussion of management, one must recognize the importance of setting goals. Goals are necessary because activities undertaken in an organization

Management The process of efficiently getting activities completed with and through other people.

Planning A management function focusing on setting organizational goals and objectives.

Organizing A management function that deals with what jobs are to be done, by whom, where decisions are to be made, and the grouping of employees.

Leading A management function concerned with directing the work of others.

Controlling A management function concerned with monitoring activities.

must be directed toward some end. For instance, your goal in taking this class is to build a foundation of understanding HRM, and obviously, to pass the class. There is considerable truth in the observation, "If you don't know where you are going, any road will take you there." The established goals may not be explicit, but where there are no goals, there is no need for managers.

Limited resources are a fact of organizational life. Economic resources, by definition, are scarce; therefore, the manager is responsible for their allocation. This requires not only that managers be effective in achieving the established goals, but that they be efficient in doing so. Managers, then, are concerned with the attainment of goals, which makes them effective, and with the best allocation of scarce resources, which makes them efficient.

The need for two or more people is the third and last requisite for management. It is with and through people that managers perform their work. Daniel Defoe's legendary Robinson Crusoe could not become a manager until Friday's arrival.

In summary, managers are those who work with and through other people, allocating resources, in the effort to achieve goals. They perform their tasks through four critical activities—planning, organizing, leading, and controlling.

Why Is HRM Important to an Organization?

Prior to the mid-1960s,[3] personnel departments in organizations were often perceived as the "health and happiness" crews.[4] Their primary job activities involved planning company picnics, scheduling vacations, enrolling workers for health-care coverage, and planning retirement parties. That has certainly changed during the past three decades.

Federal and state laws have placed many new requirements concerning hiring and employment practices on employers. Jobs have also changed. They have become more technical and require employees with greater skills. Furthermore, job boundaries are becoming blurred. In the past, a worker performed a job in a specific department, working on particular job tasks with others who did similar jobs. Today's workers are just as likely, however, to find themselves working on project teams with various people from across the organization. Others may do the majority of their work at home—and rarely see any of their coworkers. And, of course, global competition has increased the importance of organizations improving the productivity of their work force, and looking globally for the best-qualified workers. This has resulted in the need for HRM specialists trained in psychology, sociology, organization and work design, and law.[5]

Federal legislation requires organizations to hire the best-qualified candidate without regard to race, religion, color, sex, disability, or national origin—and someone has to ensure that this is done. Employees need to be trained to function effectively within the organization—and again, someone has to oversee this. Furthermore, once hired and trained, the organization has to provide for the continuing personal development of each employee. Practices are needed to ensure that these employees maintain their productive affiliation with the organization. The work environment must be structured to induce workers to stay with the organization, while simultaneously attracting new applicants. Of course, the "someones" we refer to, those responsible for carrying out these activities, are human resource professionals.

Today, professionals in the human resources area are important elements in the success of any organization. Their jobs require a new level of sophistication.

Many organizations are restructuring their work forces, rearranging them into teams. At Saturn, teams have been popular for years. From the start, Saturn management recognized the need to have employees involved in decisions that affect them. Accordingly, when individuals apply for jobs at Saturn, they are informed that they will be assigned to a team, and being a fully functioning team member is a prerequisite for successful job performance.

Not surprisingly, their status in some organizations has also been elevated. Even the name has changed. Although the terms *personnel* and *human resource management* are frequently used interchangeably, it is important to note that the two connote quite different aspects.[6] Once a single individual heading the personnel function, today the human resource department head may be a vice president sitting on executive boards and participating in the development of the overall organizational strategy.[7]

The Strategic Nature   Many companies today recognize the importance of people in meeting their goals. HRM must therefore balance two primary responsibilities—that of "being a strategic business partner and representative of employees."[8] Clearly HRM has a significant role in today's organization. HRM must be forward thinking. They must not simply react to what "management" states. Rather they must take the lead in assisting management with the "people" component of the organization. Moreover, employees of an organization can assist it in gaining and maintaining a competitive advantage. Attracting and keeping such employees requires HRM to have policies and practices that such employees desire. Being a strategic partner also involves supporting the business strategy. This means working with line management in analyzing organizational designs, the culture, and performance systems—and recommending and implementing changes where necessary.[9]

HRM must be a strategic partner and the employees' representative simultaneously.

HRM Certification   Many colleges and universities are also helping to prepare HRM professionals by offering concentrations and majors in the discipline. Additionally, there exists an accreditation process for HRM professionals. The Society for Human Resource Management offers opportunities for individuals to distinguish themselves in the field by achieving a level of proficiency that has been predetermined by the Human Resource Certification Institute as necessary for successful handling of Human Resource Management affairs (see Learning an HRM Skill at the end of this chapter).

Human resource management is the part of the organization that is concerned with the "people" dimension. HRM can be viewed in one of two ways. First, HRM is a staff, or support, function in the organization. Its role is to provide assistance in HRM matters to line employees, or those directly involved in producing the organization's goods and services. Second, HRM is a function of every manager's job. Whether or not one works in a formal HRM department, the fact remains that to effectively manage employees requires all managers to handle the activities we'll describe in this book. That's important to keep in mind!

Every organization is comprised of people. Acquiring their services, developing their skills, motivating them to high levels of performance, and ensuring that they continue to maintain their commitment to the organization are essential to achieving organizational objectives. This is true regardless of the type of organization—government, business, education, health, recreation, or social action. Getting and keeping good people is critical to the success of every organization.

To look at HRM more specifically, we propose that it is an approach consisting of four basic functions: (1) staffing, (2) training and development, (3) motivation, and (4) maintenance. In less academic terms, we might say that HRM is made up of four activities: (1) getting people, (2) preparing them, (3) stimulating them, and (4) keeping them.

When one attempts to piece together an approach for human resource management, many variations and themes may exist.[10] However, when we begin to focus on HRM activities as being subsets of the four functions, a clearer picture arises (see Exhibit 2-1). Let's take a closer look at each component.

EXHIBIT 2-1
Human Resource Management: Primary Activities

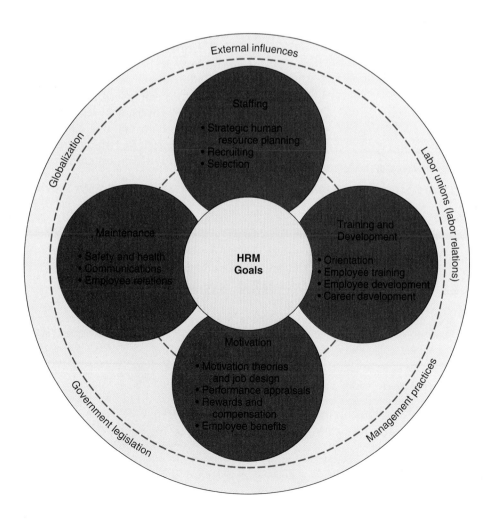

How Do External Influences Affect HRM?

The four HRM activities don't exist in isolation. Rather, they are highly affected by what is occurring outside the organization. It is important to recognize these environmental influences because any activity undertaken in each of the HRM processes is directly, or indirectly, affected by these external elements. For example, when a company downsizes (sometimes referred to as rightsizing) its work force, does it lay off workers by seniority? If so, are an inordinate number of minority employees affected?

Although any attempt to identify specific influences may prove insufficient, we can categorize them into four general areas—the dynamic environment, governmental legislation, labor unions, and current management practice.

The Dynamic Environment of HRM   It has been stated that the only thing that remains constant during our lifetimes is change (and paying taxes!). We must, therefore, prepare ourselves for events that have a significant effect on our lives. HRM is no different. Many events help shape our field. Some of the more obvious ones include globalization, technology, work-force diversity, changing skill requirements, continuous improvement, work process engineering, decentralized work sites, and employee involvement. If these sound familiar to you, congratulations, you are reading carefully. They were, in fact, the topics presented in Chapter 1.

Governmental Legislation   Many employees today wishing to take several weeks of unpaid leave to be with their newborn children, and to return to their previous job without any loss of seniority, have an easier time making the request. Although some employers may see such an application as negatively affecting the work flow, government legislation has given employees the right to take this leave. Laws supporting this and other employer actions are important to the HRM process. Listed in Exhibit 2-2 are a number of laws that have had a tremendous effect on HRM in organizations. We'll explore this critical area in depth in Chapter 3.

technology corner

HRM Basics

SOME OF THE MORE ROUTINE APPLICATIONS in HRM can be computerized in hope that it will assist HRM members in becoming more efficient in their daily duties. Here are two applications that can be purchased off the shelf and used immediately.

Personnel Ready Works: A software package that provides more than 150 personnel-related forms that can be used in HR functions. These include forms such as job-offer letters, applicant ratings, attitude surveys, exit interviews, and regulatory reporting forms.

Agreement Builder: This ready-to-use software package provides more than 100 easy-to-understand employment agreements that can minimize misunderstandings in employment relationships. Forms address a variety of areas of HRM, including nondisclosures, termination and separation, and independent contractor agreements.

Forms for either software program can be used as is, or they can be customized to meet the specific needs of an organization. Personnel Ready Works and Agreement Builders are sold by HR Press (http://www.hrpress-software.com) and sell for $129 each.

EXHIBIT 2-2
*Relevant Laws Affecting
HRM Practices*

YEAR ENACTED	LEGISLATION	FOCUS OF LEGISLATION
1866	Civil Rights Act	prohibits discrimination based on race
1931	Davis–Bacon Act	paying prevailing wage rates
1935	Wagner Act	legitimized unions
1938	Fair Labor Standards Act	requires premium pay rates for overtime
1947	Taft–Hartley Act	balanced union power
1959	Landrum–Griffin Act	requires financial disclosure for unions
1963	Equal Pay Act	requires equal pay for equal jobs
1964	Civil Rights Act	prohibits discrimination
1967	Age Discrimination in Employment Act	adds age to protected group status
1970	Occupational Safety and Health Act	protects workers from workplace hazards
1974	Privacy Act	permits employees to review personnel files
1974	Employee Retirement Income and Security Act	protects employee retirement funds
1976	Health Maintenance Organization Act	requires alternative health insurance coverage
1978	Mandatory Retirement Act	raises mandatory retirement age from 65 to 70; uncapped in 1986
1986	Immigration Reform and Control Act	requires verification of citizenship or legal status in the United States
1986	Consolidated Omnibus Budget Reconciliation Act	provides for benefit continuation when laid off
1988	Employment Polygraph Protection Act	prohibits use of polygraphs in most HRM practices
1989	Plant Closing Bill	requires employers to give advance notice to affected employees
1990	Americans with Disabilities Act	prohibits discrimination against those with disabilities
1991	Civil Rights Act	overturns several Supreme Court cases concerning discrimination
1993	Family and Medical Leave Act	permits employees to take unpaid leave for family matters

Labor Unions   Labor unions were founded and exist today to assist workers in dealing with the management of an organization. As the certified third-party representative, the union acts on behalf of its members to secure wages, hours, and other terms and conditions of employment. Another critical aspect of unions is that they promote and foster what is called a *grievance procedure,* or a specified process for the resolving of differences between workers and management. In many instances, this process alone constrains management from making unilateral decisions. For instance, a current HRM issue is the debate over employers' ability to terminate employees whenever they want. When a union is present and HRM practices are spelled out in a negotiated agreement, employers cannot fire for unjustified reasons. Because of the complexities involved in operating under the realm of unionization and the special laws that pertain to it, we will defer that discussion until Chapter 15, when we will explore the unique world of labor relations and collective bargaining.

Management Thought
Early theories of management that promoted today's HRM operations.

Management Thought   The last area of external influence is current **management thought.** Since the inception of the first personnel departments, management practices have played a major role in promoting today's HRM operations. Much of the emphasis has come from some of the early, and highly regarded, management theorists. Four individuals specifically are regarded as the forerunners of HRM support: Frederick Taylor, Hugo Munsterberg, Mary Parker Follet, and Elton Mayo.

Frederick Taylor, who is often regarded as the father of **scientific management,** developed a set of principles to enhance worker productivity. By systematically studying each job and detailing methods to attain higher productivity levels, Taylor's work was the first sense of today's human resource practices that we see. For instance, Taylor advocated that workers needed appropriate job training and should be screened according to their ability to do the job (a forerunner of skill-based hiring). Hugo Munsterberg and his associates made suggestions to improve methods of employment testing, training, performance evaluations, and job efficiency. Mary Parker Follet, a social philosopher, advocated people-oriented organizations. Her writings focused on groups as opposed to the individuals in the organization. Thus, Follet's theory was one of the forerunners of today's teamwork concept and group cohesiveness. But probably the biggest advancement in HRM came from the works of Elton Mayo and his famous Hawthorne studies.

Scientific Management
A set of principles designed to enhance worker productivity.

Hawthorne Studies   A series of studies that provided new insights into group behavior.

The **Hawthorne studies,** so named because they were conducted at the Hawthorne Plant of Western Electric just outside of Chicago, ran for nearly a decade beginning in the late 1920s. They gave rise to what today is called the human relations movement. The researchers found that informal work groups had a significant effect on worker performance. Group standards and sentiments were more important determinants of a worker's output than the wage incentive plan. Results of the Hawthorne studies justified many of the paternalistic programs that human resource managers have instituted in their organizations. We can point to the advent of employee benefit offerings, safe and healthy working conditions, and the concern by every manager for human relations as directly stemming from the work of Mayo and his associates at Hawthorne.[11]

In today's organizations, we can see the influence of management practice affecting HRM in a variety of ways. Motivation techniques that have been cited in management literature, as well as W. Edwards Deming's influence on continuous improvement programs to enhance productivity, have made their way into HRM activities. Writers like Tom Peters and Peter Drucker emphasize letting employees have a say in things that affect their work, teams, and work process engineering. Implementing these will ultimately require the assistance of HRM professionals.

Now that you have a brief picture of the external influences affecting this field, let's turn our attention to the functions and activities within HRM.

What Activities Occur in the Staffing Function?

Staffing Function   Activities in HRM concerned with sourcing and hiring qualified employees.

Although recruiting is frequently perceived as the initial step in the **staffing function,** there are a number of prerequisites. Specifically, before the first job candidate is sought, the HR specialist must embark on employment planning. This area alone has probably fostered the most change in human resource departments during the past 20 years. We can no longer hire individuals haphazardly. We must have a well-defined reason for needing individuals who possess specific skills, knowledge, and abilities that are directly likened to specific jobs required in the organization.[12] No longer does the HR manager exist in total darkness, or for that matter, in a reactive mode. Not until the mission and strategy of the

The Hawthorne studies showed that informal work groups had a significant effect on employee productivity.

organization have been fully developed can human resource managers begin to determine the human resource needs.[13]

Specifically, when a company plans strategically, it determines its goals and objectives for a given period of time. These goals and objectives often result in structural changes being made in the organization; that is, these changes foster changes in job requirements, reporting relationships, how individuals are grouped, and the like. As such, these new or revised structures bring with them a host of pivotal jobs. It is these jobs that HRM must be prepared to fill.[14]

As these jobs are analyzed, specific skills, knowledge, and abilities are identified that the job applicant must possess to be successful on the job. This aspect cannot be understated, for herein lies much of the responsibility and success of HRM.[15] Through the job analysis process, HRM identifies the essential qualifications for a particular job. Not only is this sound business acumen, for these jobs are critically linked to the strategic direction of the company, but it is also well within the stated guidelines of major employment legislation. Additionally, almost all activities involved in HRM revolve around an accurate description of the job. One cannot recruit without knowledge of the critical skills required, nor can one appropriately set performance standards and pay rates, or invoke disciplinary procedures fairly without this understanding. Once these critical competencies have been identified, the recruiting process begins.[16] Armed with information from employment planning, we can begin to focus on our prospective candidates. When involved in recruiting, HR specialists should be attempting to achieve two goals. These goals are to obtain an adequate pool of applicants, thereby giving human resources and line managers more choices, while simultaneously providing enough information about the job such that those who are unqualified will not apply. Recruiting, then, becomes an activity designed to locate potentially good applicants, conditioned by the recruiting effort's constraints, the job market, and the need to reach members of underrepresented groups like minorities and women.

Once applications have come in, it is time to begin the selection phase. Selection, too, has a dual focus. It attempts to thin out the large set of applications that arrived during the recruiting phase and to select an applicant who will be successful on the job. To achieve this goal, many companies use a variety of steps to assess the applicants. The candidate who successfully completes all steps is typically offered the job, but that is only half of the equation. HRM must also ensure that the good prospects accept the job offer, if made. Accordingly, HRM must communicate a variety of information to the applicant, such as the organization culture, what is expected of employees, and any other information that is pertinent to the candidate's decision-making process.

Once the selection process is completed, the staffing function has come to an end.[17] The goals, then, of the staffing function are to locate competent employees and get them into the organization. When this goal has been reached, it is time for HRM to begin focusing its attention on the employee's training and development.

What Are the Goals of the Training and Development Function?

Whenever HRM embarks on the hiring process, it attempts to search and secure a candidate whom we labeled as the "best" possible candidate. And while HRM professionals pride themselves on being able to determine those who are qualified versus those who are not, the fact remains that few, if any, new employees

RESPONDING TO LAYOFF SURVIVORS

ONE OF THE SIGNIFICANT MANAGEMENT TRENDS during the 1990s was organizational downsizing. Because downsizing typically involved shrinking the organization's work force, it was an issue in human resource management that needed to be addressed.

Many organizations had done a fairly good job of helping layoff victims by offering a variety of job-help services, psychological counseling, support groups, severance pay, extended health insurance benefits, and detailed communications. Although some affected individuals reacted very negatively to being laid off (the worst cases involve returning to the separating organization and committing some form of violence), the assistance offered revealed that the organization did care about its former employees. Unfortunately, very little has been done for those who have been left behind and have the task of keeping the organization going or even of revitalizing it.

It may surprise you to learn that both victims and survivors experience feelings of frustration, anxiety, and loss.[18] But layoff victims get to start over with a clean slate and a clear conscience. Survivors don't. As one author suggested, "The terms could be reversed: Those who leave become survivors, and those who stay become victims."[19] A new syndrome seems to be popping up in more and more organizations: **layoff-survivor sickness.** It is a set of attitudes, perceptions, and behaviors of employees who remain after involuntary employee reductions.[20] Symptoms include job insecurity, perceptions of unfairness, guilt, depression, stress from increased workloads, fear of change, loss of loyalty and commitment, reduced effort, and an unwillingness to do anything beyond the required minimum.

To address this survivor syndrome, managers may want to provide opportunities for employees to talk to counselors about their guilt, anger, and anxiety. Group discussions can also provide an opportunity for the "survivors" to vent their feelings. Some organizations have used downsizing efforts as the spark to implement increased employee participation programs such as empowerment and self-managed work teams. In short, to keep morale and productivity high, every attempt should be made to ensure that those individuals who are still working in the organization know that they are a valuable and much-needed resource.

Layoff-survivor Sickness   A set of attitudes, perceptions, and behaviors of employees who remain after involuntary employee reductions.

can truly come into an organization and immediately become fully functioning, 100 percent performers. First, employees need to adapt to their new surroundings. Socialization is a means of bringing about this adaptation. While it may begin informally in the late stages of the hiring process, the thrust of socialization continues for many months after the individual begins working. During this time, the focus is to orient the new employee to the rules, regulations, and goals of the organization, department, and work unit. Then, as the employee becomes more comfortable with his or her surroundings, more intense training can occur.

Reflection over the past few decades tells us that, depending on the job, employees often take a number of months to adjust to their new organizations and positions. Does that imply that HRM has not hired properly, or the staffing function goals were not met? On the contrary, it indicates that intricacies and peculiarities involved in each organization's positions result in jobs being tailored to adequately meet organizational needs. Accordingly, HRM plays an important role in shaping this reformulation of new employees so that within a short period of time they, too, will be fully productive. To accomplish this, HRM typically embarks on four areas in the training and development phase: employee training, employee development, organization development, and career development. It is important to note that employee and career development are more employee centered, whereas employee training is designed to promote competency in the new job. Organization development, on the other hand, focuses on systemwide changes.[21] While each area has a unique focus, all four are critical to the success of the training and development phase. We have summarized these four in Exhibit 2-3.

Exhibit 2-3
*Training and Development
Activities*

Employee Training:	Employee training is designed to assist employees in acquiring better skills for their current job. The focus of employee training is on current job-skill requirements.
Employee Development:	Employee development is designed to help the organization ensure that it has the necessary talent internally for meeting future human resource needs. The focus of employee development is on a future position within the organization for which the employee requires additional competencies.
Career Development:	Career development programs are designed to assist employees in advancing their work lives. The focus of career development is to provide the necessary information and assessment in helping employees realize their career goals. However, career development is the responsibility of the individual, not the organization.
Organization Development:	Organization development deals with facilitating systemwide changes in the organization. The focus of organization development is to change the attitudes and values of employees according to new organizational strategic directions.

Training and Development Function Activities in HRM concerned with assisting employees to develop up-to-date skills, knowledge, and abilities.

At the conclusion of the **training and development function**, HRM attempts to reach the goal of having competent, adapted employees who possess the up-to-date skills, knowledge, and abilities needed to perform their current jobs more successfully. If that is attained, HRM turns its attention to finding ways to motivate these individuals to exert high energy levels.

What Is the Motivation Function?

Motivation Function Activities in HRM concerned with helping employees exert high energy levels.

The **motivation function** is one of the most important, yet probably the least understood, aspects of the HRM process. Why? Because human behavior is so complex. Trying to figure out what motivates various employees has long been a concern of behavioral scientists. However, research has given us some important insights into employee motivation.

First of all, one must begin to think of motivation as a multifaceted process—one that has individual, managerial, and organizational implications. Motivation is not just what the employee exhibits, but a collection of environmental issues surrounding the job. It has been proposed that one's performance in an organization is a function of two factors: ability and willingness to do the job.[22] Thus, from a performance perspective, employees need to have the appropriate skills and abilities to adequately do the job. This should have been accomplished in the first two phases of HRM, by correctly defining the requirements of the job, matching applicants to those requirements, and training the new employee in how to do the job. But there is also another concern, which is the job design itself. If jobs are poorly designed, inadequately laid out, or improperly described, employees will perform below their capabilities. Consequently, HRM must look at the job. Has the latest technology been provided in order to permit maximum efficiency? Is the office setting appropriate (properly lit and adequately ventilated, for example) for the job? Are the necessary tools readily available for employee use? For example, imagine an employee who spends considerable time each day developing product designs. This employee, however, does not have ready access to a computer-aided design (CAD) software program or a powerful enough computer system to run it. Compared to another employee who does have access to such technology, the first individual is going to be less productive. While not trying to belittle the problem with such an example, the point should be clear. Office automation and industrial engineering techniques must be incorporated into the job design. Without such planning, the best intentions of organizational members to motivate employees may be lost or significantly reduced.

Additionally, many organizations today are recognizing that motivating employees also requires a level of respect between management and the workers. This respect can be seen as involving employees in decisions that affect them, listening to employees, and implementing their suggestions where appropriate.

The next step in the motivation process is to understand the implications of motivational theories. Some motivational theories are well known by most practicing managers, but recent motivation research has given us new and more valid theories for understanding what motivates people at work. We've summarized the highlights of the more popular theories in Exhibit 2-4. Performance standards for each employee must also be set. While no easy task, managers must be sure that the performance evaluation system is designed to provide feedback to employees regarding their past performance, while simultaneously addressing any performance weaknesses the employee may have. A link should be established between employee compensation and performance: the compensation and benefit activity in the organization should be adapted to, and coordinated with, a pay-for-performance plan.[23]

Throughout the activities required in the motivation function, the efforts all focus on one primary goal: to have those competent and adapted employees, with up-to-date skills, knowledge, and abilities, exerting high energy levels. Once that is achieved, it is time to turn the HRM focus to the maintenance function.

How Important Is the Maintenance Function?

Maintenance Function Activities in HRM concerned with maintaining employees' commitment and loyalty to the organization.

The last phase of the HRM process is called the **maintenance function.** As the name implies, the objective of this phase is to put into place activities that will help retain productive employees.[24] When one considers how job loyalty of employees has declined in the last decade, it's not difficult to see the importance of maintaining employee commitment.[25] To do so requires some basic common sense and some creativity. HRM must work to ensure that the working environment is safe and healthy; caring for employees' well-being has a major effect on their commitment. HRM must also realize that any problem an employee faces in his or her personal life will ultimately be brought into the workplace. Employee assistance programs, such as programs that help individuals deal with stressful life situations, are needed. Such programs provide many benefits to the organization while simultaneously helping the affected employee.[26]

Communications Programs HRM programs designed to provide information to employees.

In addition to protecting employees' welfare, it is necessary for HRM to operate appropriate **communications programs** in the organization. Included in such programs is the ability for employees to know what is occurring around them and to vent frustrations. Employee relations programs should be designed to ensure that employees are kept well informed—through e-mail, bulletin boards, town hall meetings, or teleconferencing—and to foster an environment where employee voices are heard. If time and effort are expended in this phase, HRM

Exhibit 2-4
Key Elements of Classic Motivation Theories

Theory	Individual	Summary
Hierarchy of Needs	Abraham Maslow	Five needs rank in a hierarchical order from lowest to highest: physiological, safety, belonging, esteem, and self-actualization. An individual moves up the hierarchy and, when a need is substantially realized, moves up to the next need.
Theory X— Theory Y	Douglas McGregor	Proposes two alternative sets of assumptions that managers hold about human beings' motivations—one, basically negative, labeled Theory X; and the other, basically positive, labeled Theory Y. McGregor argues that Theory Y assumptions are more valid than Theory X and that the employee motivation would be maximized by giving workers greater job involvement and autonomy.
Motivation— Hygiene	Frederick Herzberg	Argues that intrinsic job factors motivate, whereas extrinsic factors only placate employees.
Achievement, Affiliation, and Power Motives	David McClelland	Proposes that there are three major needs in workplace situations: achievement, affiliation, and power. A high need to achieve has been positively related to higher work performance when jobs provide responsibility, feedback, and moderate challenge.
Equity Theory	J. Stacey Adams	An individual compares his or her input/outcome ratio to relevant others. If there is a perceived inequity, the individual will augment his or her behavior, or choose another comparison referent.
Expectancy Theory	Victor Vroom	Proposes that motivation is a function of valence (value) of the effort-performance and the performance–reward relationships.

may be able to achieve its ultimate goal of having competent employees, who have adapted to the organization's culture, with up-to-date skills, knowledge, and abilities, who exert high energy levels, and who are now willing to maintain their commitment and loyalty to the company. This process is difficult to implement and maintain, but the rewards should be such that the effort placed in such endeavors is warranted.

How Are HRM Functions Translated into Practice?

The areas of HRM can take on a number of characteristics. Describing the various permutations and combinations goes well beyond the scope of this book.[27] Realize, too, that more than half of all HR departments also offer some type of administrative service to the organization. These might include operating the company's credit union, making childcare arrangements, providing security, or

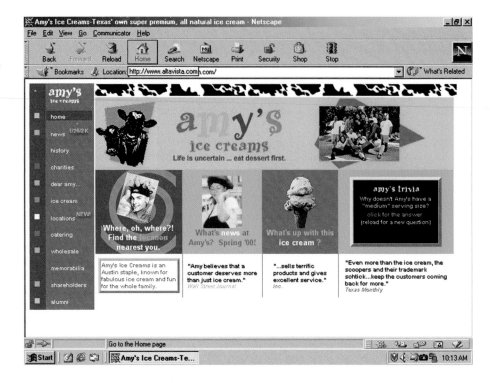

operating in-house medical or food services.[28] Yet, in spite of the different configurations, in a typical nonunion HRM department, we generally find four distinct areas: (1) employment, (2) training and development, (3) compensation/benefits, and (4) employee relations. Usually reporting to a vice president of human resources, managers in these four areas have specific responsibilities. Exhibit 2-5 is a simplified organizational representation of HRM areas, with some typical job titles and a sampling of what these job incumbents earn.[29]

Employment   The main thrust of the employment function is to promote the activities of the staffing function. Working in conjunction with position control specialists (either in compensation, in benefits, or in a comptroller's office), the employment department embarks on the process of recruiting new employees.[30] This means correctly advertising the job to ensure that the appropriate knowledge and abilities are being sought. After sorting through resumes or applications, the employment specialist usually conducts the first weeding-out of candidates who applied but do not meet the job's requirements. The remaining applications are then typically forwarded to the line area for its review. After reviewing the resumes, the line manager may then instruct the employment specialist to interview the selected candidates. In many cases, this initial interview is another step in the hiring process. Understanding what the line manager desires in an employee, the employment specialist begins to further filter down the list of prospective candidates. During this phase, candidates who appear to "fit" the line area's need typically are scheduled to meet with the line manager for another interview.

It is important to note that the employment specialist's role is not to make the hiring decision, but to coordinate the effort with line management. Once the line area has selected its candidate, the employment specialist usually makes the job offer and handles the routine paperwork associated with hiring an employee.

Training and Development   The training and development section of an organization is often responsible for helping employees to maximize their potential. Their focus is to enhance the personal qualities of the employees such that the improvements made will lead to greater organizational productivity.[31] More importantly, the training and development members are often better known as the organization's internal change agents. The role of these change agents, or organizational development specialists, is to help the members of the organization cope with change. Changes that occur in an organization come in many forms. It can be a cultural change where the philosophy, values, and ways of operating are changed by top management. For instance, changing from a production focus of producing whatever the company wants and selling it to the public, to a marketing focus whereby what is produced and sold is contingent on consumer demand, requires a new organizational orientation. A change may also occur in the organization's structure, which can result in layoffs, new job assignments, team involvement, and the like, and again requires new orientations by the organizational members. We may also see changes in procedures or policies where employees must be informed and taught to deal with such occurrences. For instance, a growing concern of companies has been to implement policies to stop sexual harassment from occurring in the organization. Not only must employees understand what constitutes sexual harassment, but they must also become more sensitive to issues surrounding a diverse work force. Training and education often leads this charge as the best form of prevention.

Training and development may also include career development activities and employee counseling to help people make better choices about their careers and to achieve their desired goals.

EXHIBIT 2-5
Sample HRM Organizational Chart, Sample Activities, and Selected Salaries

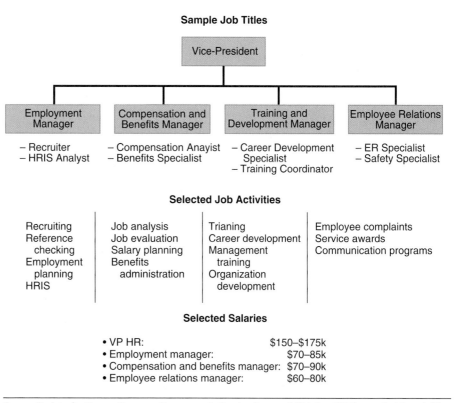

Sample Job Titles

Vice-President

| Employment Manager | Compensation and Benefits Manager | Training and Development Manager | Employee Relations Manager |

– Recruiter
– HRIS Analyst

– Compensation Anayist
– Benefits Specialist

– Career Development Specialist
– Training Coordinator

– ER Specialist
– Safety Specialist

Selected Job Activities

Recruiting	Job analysis	Trianing	Employee complaints
Reference checking	Job evaluation	Career development	Service awards
Employment planning	Salary planning	Management training	Communication programs
HRIS	Benefits administration	Organization development	

Selected Salaries

- VP HR: $150–$175k
- Employment manager: $70–85k
- Compensation and benefits manager: $70–90k
- Employee relations manager: $60–80k

Source: Society for Human Resource Management, *Spectra Personnel* (October 2000), pp. 1–16; and *HR Basics 2000* (October 2000), pp. 1–2.

Compensation and Benefits   Work in a compensation and benefits area[32] is often described as dealing with the most objective areas of a subjective field. As the name implies, compensation and benefits is concerned with paying employees and administering their benefits package. These tasks are by no means easy ones. First of all, job salaries are not paid on a whim; rather, dollar values assigned to positions come from elaborate investigations and analyses. These investigations run the gamut of simple, logical job rankings (i.e., the position of president of a company should be paid more than the position of a maintenance engineer) to extensive analyses. Once these analyses are finished, job ratings are statistically compared to determine the relative worth of the job to the company. External factors, such as market conditions, limited supply of potential workers, and the like, may affect the overall range of job worth. Additionally, analysis is conducted to ensure that there is internal equity in the compensation system. This means that as job rates are set, they are determined on such dimensions as skill, job responsibility, effort, and accountability—not by personal characteristics that may be suspect under employment law.

On the benefits side of the equation, much change has occurred over the past decade. As benefit offerings to employees have become significantly more costly, the benefits administrator (who may also have the title of risk manager) has the responsibility of piecing together a benefits package that meets the needs of the employees while simultaneously being cost-effective to the organization. As such, much effort is expended searching for lower-cost products, like health or workers compensation insurance, while concurrently maintaining or improving quality. Additionally, various new products are often reviewed, such as flexible benefits programs and utilization reviews, to help in benefit cost containment. But benefits should not be viewed solely from a cost-containment perspective. Benefits are of a strategic nature in that they are helpful in attracting and retaining high-quality employees.[33]

The benefits administrator also serves as the resource information officer to employees regarding their benefits. This information may be provided through a variety of methods, including a company's intranet. Activities such as helping employees prepare for their retirement, looking for various payout options, keeping abreast of recent tax law changes, or helping executives with their perquisites, are conducted.[34] This gives this individual a great deal of responsibility, but also high visibility in the organization.

Employee Relations   The final phase in our scheme of HRM operations is the **employee relations function**. Employee relations (ER) has a number of major responsibilities. Before we go further, however, we must differentiate between employee relations and labor relations. While the two are structurally similar, labor relations involves dealing with labor unions. As such, because other laws apply, some of the techniques in employee relations may not be applicable. For instance, in a unionized setting, a specific grievance procedure might be detailed in the labor-management contract, and might involve the union, management, and the alleged wronged employee. In a nonunion environment, a similar procedure might exist or the grievance might be handled one-on-one. While these may be subtle differences, the fact remains that labor relations requires a different set of competencies and understanding.

In the nonunion setting, however, we see employee relations specialists performing many tasks. As mentioned earlier, one of their key responsibilities is to ensure that open communications permeates the organization.[35] This is done

Employee Relations Function   Activities in HRM concerned with effective communications among organizational members.

by fostering an environment where employees talk directly to supervisors and settle any differences that may arise. If needed, employee relations representatives intervene to assist in achieving a fair and equitable solution. ER specialists are also intermediaries in helping employees understand the rules. Their primary goal is to ensure that policies and procedures are enforced properly, and to permit a wronged employee a forum to obtain relief. As part of this role, too, comes the disciplinary process. These representatives are in place to ensure that appropriate disciplinary sanctions are used consistently throughout the organization.

In addition to the communications role, the employee relations department is responsible for additional assignments. Typically in such a department, recruiting, employment, and turnover statistics are collected, tabulated, and written up in the company's affirmative action plan documentation. This material is updated frequently and made available to employees on request. Part of their responsibility is to ensure safe and healthy work sites. This may range from casual work inspections to operating nursing stations and coordinating employee-assistance programs. However involved, the premise is the same—to focus on those aspects that help make an employee committed and loyal to the organization through fair and equitable treatment, and by listening to employees.

Lastly, there is the festive side of employee relations. This department is typically responsible for company outings, company athletic teams, and recreational and recognition programs. Whatever they do under this domain, the goal remains having programs that benefit the workers and their families and make them feel part of a community.

ethical issues in HRM

PURPOSEFULLY DISTORTING INFORMATION

THE IDEA OF WITHHOLDING INFORMATION IS an issue for all HRM managers. Read the following two scenarios and think about ethical dilemmas that those in HRM might face when relating to the intentional distortion of information.

Scenario 1:   At the President's monthly executive staff meeting, you were informed of the past quarter's revenue figures. Moreover, you also were informed that the organization is going to more than double its quarterly expected "numbers" and the value of your company's stock will likely surge. Your organization has a bonus plan where profits are shared with employees. But this profit sharing is based solely on management's discretion and does not follow any systematic formula. If word gets out that profits are outstanding, employees might expect larger bonuses. The executive committee wants to share about half of the windfall with employees and reinvest most of the rest into capital equipment and save some for less favorable times. Your staff and several employees from a cross section of departments are meeting with you tomorrow to begin the process of making profit-sharing decisions for the year. What do you tell them?

Scenario 2:   An employee asks you about a rumor she's heard that your

HR may be outsourced to a company in Atlanta. You know the rumor to be true, but you'd rather not let the information out just yet. You're fearful that it could hurt departmental morale and lead to premature resignations. What do you say to your employee?

These two scenarios illustrate dilemmas that HRM managers may face relating to evading the truth, distorting facts, or lying to others. And here's something else that makes the situation even more problematic: it might not always be in a manager's best interest or that of his or her unit to provide full and complete information. Keeping communications fuzzy can cut down on questions, permit faster decision making, minimize objections, reduce opposition, make it easier to deny one's earlier statements, preserve the freedom to change one's mind, permit one to say "no" diplomatically, help to avoid confrontation and anxiety, and provide other benefits that work to the advantage of the individual.

Is it unethical to purposely distort communications to get a favorable outcome? What about "little white lies" that really don't hurt anybody? Are these ethical? What guidelines could you suggest for those in HRM who want guidance in deciding whether distorting information is ethical or unethical?

CONCLUSION

Although we have presented four generic areas of HRM, we would be remiss not to recognize the changing nature of HRM in today's organizations. As organizations change structures (to reflect global competition and the like), there has been a movement away from centralization of functional areas toward more self-contained units. In companies where strategic business units or market-driven units dominate,[36] an HRM professional may be assigned to these units to handle all the HRM operations. While a headquarters HRM staff remains to coordinate the activities, the HRM representative is expected to perform all the HR functions. Accordingly, the movement toward generalist positions in HRM appears to be on the rise.[37]

Another trend is also closely aligned with the generalist-versus-specialist discussion. That trend is called **shared services.** In large organizations like Allied Signal and du Pont, companies that are geographically dispersed are finding it more cost effective to share their HRM services among the divisions.[38] For example, at Ford, shared HRM services enabled the company to cut its work force from 14,000 to approximately 3000 employees, supporting more than 300,000 Ford employees worldwide. And at General Electric, shared services enabled the company to reduce its HR staff by 75 percent, and provide more cost-effective, high-quality HR services.[39]

Under shared services, each location is staffed by a few generalists who handle routine local matters like recruiting, policy implementation, grievances, employee training, and the like. Specialized services, like organization development and compensation and benefits, are handled by a staff located at a centralized location, frequently called the **HR Services Center.**[40] Each location, then, shares these services offered by the centralized unit, and uses only what is necessary for the division. As such, each location gets specialized care on an as-needed basis without the cost of having full-time staff.

There's one last area to be addressed about the changing nature of HRM. In some organizations, top management has made a decision to outsource some of the work HRM professionals once handled.[41] For example, private staffing agencies may perform the recruiting and selection activities, with several consulting firms providing training programs, and yet another financial organization handling the majority of a company's benefits administration. It is our contention that when much of HRM is outsourced, managers and employees still need to understand what the basic HRM issues and activities are. So whether what we will describe in this book is done by you or another company employee, or by someone external to your organization, you need some familiarity with these fundamental HRM practices.

Shared Services Sharing HRM activities among geographically dispersed divisions.

HR Shared Services Centeralized HRM activities focusing on activities such as organization development, and compensation and benefits.

HRM IN A SMALL ENTERPRISE

The discussion about the four departments of HRM refers to situations where there are sufficient resources available for functional expertise to exist. However, such is not always the case. Take, for instance, the small business operation. In these organizations, the owner-manager often is responsible for and may perform these activities. In other situations, small-business human resource departments are staffed with one individual and possibly a full-time secretary. Accordingly, such individuals are forced, by design, to be HRM generalists. Irrespective of the unit's size, the same activities are required in small businesses, but on a smaller scale. These small-business HRM managers must be able to properly perform the four functions of HRM and achieve the same goals that a larger department achieves. The main difference is that they are doing the work themselves without benefit of a specialized staff. There may be a tendency to use outside consultants to assist in or perform all HRM activities. For instance, benefit administration may be beyond the capability of the small businessperson. In that case, benefit administration may need to be contracted out. HRM in a small business requires that individuals keep current in the field and legal issues. For example, the Family and Medical Leave Act of 1993 is applicable to those organizations that have 50 or more employees. Accordingly, the small business may be exempt from many laws affecting employment practices. Being aware of this information can save the small business time and money. Before we begin to pity this small-business HRM manager, let's look at the potential benefits from such an arrangement. Often, these individuals feel that they are less constrained in their jobs. That is, the bureaucratic hierarchy that typically accompanies larger organizations is often absent in the small business. Furthermore, some small-business HRM managers use this arrangement to their advantage. For instance, in recruiting efforts, a selling point to attract a good applicant might be the aspect of freedom from a rigid structure that the small-business opportunity offers, as well as the opportunity to share in the success of the business. A good number of dot-com startup companies in the late 1990s used this to their advantage in recruiting seasoned executives from much larger, traditional organizations.

A good number of dot-com startup companies used their small-business opportunities to their advantage in recruiting seasoned executives from much larger organizations.

$\mathcal{H}$RM IN A GLOBAL VILLAGE

As a business grows from a regional to a national, to an international one, the human resource management function must take on a new and broader perspective.[42] As a national company expands overseas, first with a sales operation, then to production facilities and fully expanded operations or to international joint ventures, the human resource function must adapt to a changing and far more complex environment.[43]

Where is one of the world's leading steel mills located. Pennsylvania, Ohio? How about in Mexico. Like many other industries, steel production has truly become a global business. Here these workers at the Lazaro Cardenas steel mill manufacture steel products that will be used in autos, appliances, and construction sectors around the world.

HRM Skills

WHAT SKILLS AND COMPETENCIES ARE necessary for successful performance in HRM? Although it is extremely difficult to pinpoint exactly what competencies will serve you best when dealing with the uncertainties of human behavior, we can turn to the certifying body in HRM for answers. Specifically, the Human Resources Certification Institute (HRCI) suggests that certified HR practitioners must have exposure and an understanding in six specific areas of the field. These include Management Practices, Selection and Placement, Training and Development, Compensation and Benefits, Employee and Labor Relations, and Health, Safety, and Security. Let's briefly look at each one, and relate these specifically to the part of this book where they are addressed.

MANAGEMENT PRACTICES:

As a subset of management, HRM practitioners are required to have a general understanding of the field of management, its history and theories (especially those relating to the behavioral component), and the trends and their implications that exist today. They must also understand the financial aspects of the business, its technology, and the capabilities of organizational members. Specific reference to this text: Chapters 1, 2, and 11.

GENERAL EMPLOYMENT PRACTICES:

One must understand the broad areas of HRM, its environment, and its practices. This includes an understanding of the legal framework and of workplace issues. Specific reference to this text: Chapters 1, 2, 3, and 4.

STAFFING:

HRM practitioners require an understanding of why and how jobs are filled and the various methods of recruiting candidates. Emphasis in this area is on making good decisions within the legal parameters about job candidates that use valid and reliable measures. Specific reference to this text: Chapters 6 and 7.

HUMAN RESOURCE DEVELOPMENT:

For employees to be successful in an organization, they must be trained and developed in the latest technologies and skills relevant to their current and future jobs. This means an understanding of adult learning methodologies, relating training efforts to organizational goals, and evaluating the effort. Specific reference to this text: Chapters 8 and 9.

COMPENSATION AND BENEFITS:

One of the chief reasons people work is to fulfill needs. Intrinsic or extrinsic aside, one major need is compensation and benefits. Yet, these offerings are probably the most expensive ones with respect to the employment relationship. As such, the HRM practitioner must understand the intricacies involved in establishing a cost-effective compensation and benefits package. Specific reference to this text: Chapters 10, 11, and 12.

EMPLOYEE AND LABOR RELATIONS:

Working with employees requires an understanding of what makes employees function. Satisfying monetary needs alone will not have a lasting impact. Employees need to be kept informed and have an avenue in which to raise suggestions or complaints. When the case involves unionized workers, the HRM/labor relations practitioner must understand the various laws that affect the labor-management work relationship. Specific reference to this text: Chapters 1 and 15.

HEALTH, SAFETY, AND SECURITY:

A basic need of individuals is the safety one must feel at the workplace. This means freedom from physical and emotional harm. Mechanisms must be in place to provide a safe work environment for employees. Programs must permit employees to seek assistance for those things affecting their work and personal lives. Specific reference to this text: Chapters 1, 13, and 14.

All the basic functions of domestic HRM are more complex when the organization's employees are located around the world, and additional human resource management activities are often necessary that would be considered invasions of employee privacy in domestic operations. This is necessary partially because of the increased vulnerability and risk of terrorism sometimes experienced by American executives abroad.

When a corporation sends its American employees overseas, that corporation takes on responsibilities that add to the basic HRM functions. For example, the staffing and training and development functions take on greater emphasis.[44] Not only are organizations concerned about selecting the best employee for the job, they must also be aware of the entire family's needs. Why? Many individuals who take international assignments fail because their spouses or family just can't adjust to the new environment. Furthermore, the relocation and orientation process before departure may take months of foreign language training and should involve not just the employee, but the employee's entire family. Details such as work visas, travel, safety, household moving arrangements, taxes, and family issues such as the children's schooling, medical care, and housing, all must be provided for.[45] Administrative services for the expatriate employees also must be available once they are placed in their overseas posts. All these additional functions make international human resource management a very costly undertaking.

HRM WORKSHOP

SUMMARY

(This summary relates to the Learning Outcomes identified on p. 34.)

After having read this chapter, you should be able to:

1. **Define management and identify its primary functions.** Management is the process of efficiently achieving the strategic objectives of the organization with and through people. The four main functions of management are planning, organizing, leading, and controlling. Three factors common to the definition of organizations are goals, limited resources, and people.

2. **Describe the importance of human resource management.** Human resource management is responsible for the people dimension of the organization. It is responsible for getting competent people, training them, getting them to perform at high effort levels, and providing mechanisms to ensure that these employees maintain their productive affiliation with the organization.

3. **Explain what is meant by the term *human resource management*.** Human resource management is comprised of the staffing, development, motivation, and maintenance functions. Each of these functions, however, is affected by external influences.

4. **Identify the primary environmental influences affecting human resource management.** Environmental influences are those factors that affect the functions of HRM. They include the dynamic environment of HRM, government legislation, labor unions, and management thought.

5. **Characterize how management practices affect human resource management.** Management practices affect HRM in a number of ways. As new ideas or practices develop in the field, they typically have HRM implications. Accordingly, once these practices are implemented, they typically require support from HRM to operate successfully.

6. **Discuss the effect of labor unions on human resource management.** Labor unions affect HRM practices in a variety of ways. If a union exists, HRM takes on a different focus—one of labor relations as opposed to employee relations. Additionally, what occurs in the unionized sector frequently affects the activities in organizations where unions are not present.

7. **Outline the components and the goals of the staffing, training, and development functions.** The components of the staffing function include strategic human resource planning, recruiting, and selection. The goal of the staffing function is to locate and secure competent employees. The training and development function includes orientation, employee training, employee development, organization development, and career development. The goal of the development function is to take competent workers, adapt them to the organization, and help them to obtain up-to-date skills, knowledge, and abilities for their job responsibilities.

8. **List the components and goals of the motivation and maintenance functions of human resource management.**

The components of the motivation function include motivation theories, appropriate job design, reward and incentive systems, compensation, and benefits. The goal of the motivation function is to take competent, adapted employees, with up-to-date skills, knowledge, and abilities, and provide them with an environment that encourages them to exert high energy levels. The components of the maintenance function include safety and health issues, and employee communications. The goal of the maintenance function is to help competent, adapted employees, with up-to-date skills, knowledge, and abilities, who are exerting high energy levels, to maintain their commitment and loyalty to the organization.

9. **Outline the major activities in the employment, training and development, compensation and benefits, and em-**

ployee relations departments of human resource management.** The departments of employment, training and development, compensation and benefits, and employee relations support the components of the staffing, training and development, motivation, and maintenance functions, respectively.

10. **Explain how human resource management practices differ in small businesses and in an international setting.** In large HRM operations, individuals perform functions according to their specialization. Such may not be the case with small-business HRM practitioners. Instead, they may be the only individuals in the operation, and thus, must operate as HRM generalists. In an international setting, HRM functions become more complex and typically require additional activities associated with staffing and training and development.

DEMONSTRATING COMPREHENSION: *Questions for Review and Discussion*

1. Contrast management, personnel, and human resource management.
2. Explain the purpose of HRM in an organization.
3. What activities are involved in the staffing function of HRM?
4. What are the goals of the training and development function of HRM?
5. Describe the primary goals of the motivation function of HRM.
6. "Motivation is the primary responsibility of line managers. HRM's role in motivating organizational employees is limited to providing programs that equip line managers with means of motivating their employees." Do you agree or disagree with the statement? Explain your position.
7. In what ways can HRM meet its goals of the maintenance function?
8. You have been offered two positions in HRM. One is a generalist position in a smaller business, and one is a recruiting position in a large corporation. Which one of the two jobs do you believe will give you more opportunities to be involved in a variety of HRM activities? Defend your answer.
9. What role does HRM play in the strategic direction of an organization?
10. "Globalization had led us to the realization that workers are interchangeable between countries so long as language issues are resolved." Do you agree or disagree with this statement? Explain your position.

CASE APPLICATION: *TEAM FUN!*

Kenny and Norton own TEAM FUN!, a medium sized company that manufacturers and sells sporting goods and equipment. They are watching a CROSSKATES video about cross country roller skates in the LOUNGE. Norton says, "I don't know. This stuff looks dangerous! What do you think? Remember that bungee jumping thing we tried?"

Kenny responds, "Edna was out a long time with that knee problem. She sure is a good sport. Keith said we were lucky not to get sued for that. Do you think employees could sue us if they are hurt on product test assignments?"

Norton: "Let's ask Tony, that guy you hired for—what did you call him—Director of Human Resources?"

Norton smiles broadly, "Yep. He sure seems to be busy. He's pulled together all that paperwork for insurance and retirement that Edna used to handle and named her Compensation and Benefits Manager."

Kenny: "He wants to send Joe and Eric to a supervisor's school for work scheduling, job team assignments, and project management. He started those picnics by the LAGOON for people to talk about work conditions and issues."

Norton asks, "I guess we should let him hire a fulltime secretary. I thought Edna could do that, but Tony said she has a full plate. Did you tell him to do that employee bulletin board he tacked into the website?"

Kenny shook his head no.

Norton wonders: "Me neither. Wonder why he did that? Guess we better talk to him."

Questions:
1. Which of the functional HR processes can be identified in Tony's area?
2. Identify the environmental influences that are important to TEAM FUN!.

3. How are the functional areas of HR lined up with the overall HR process?
4. Which motivation theorists has Tony applied to TEAM FUN!?

5. Does Tony need to do anything else to set up a strategic HR function?

WORKING WITH A TEAM: *Making a Layoff Decision*

Every human resource manager, at some point in his or her career, is likely to be faced with the difficult task of managing laying off employees. Assume that you are the human resource director of a 720 technology company. You have been notified by top management that you must permanently reduce your staff by two individuals. Below are some data about your five employees.

Jasmine Carver: African-American female, age 36. Jasmine has been employed with your company for five years, all in the HRM. Her evaluations over the past three years have been outstanding, above average, and outstanding. Jasmine has an MBA from a top-25 business school. She has been on short-term disability the past few weeks because of the birth of her second child and is expected to return to work in twenty weeks.

George Reynolds: White male, age 49. George has been with you for four months and has eleven years of experience in the company in systems management. He has a degree in computer science and master's degrees in accounting information systems. He's also a CPA. George's evaluations over the past three years in the systems department have been average, but he did save the company $150,000 on a suggestion he made regarding using electronic time sheets.

Rickie Hernandez: Hispanic male, age 31. Rickie has been with the company almost four years. His evaluations over the past three years in your department have been outstanding. He is committed to getting the job done and devoting whatever it takes. He has also shown initiative by taking job assignments that no one else wanted. And he has been instrumental in getting your benefits adminis-

tration intranet on line and rolled out to the employees.

Connie Nelson: White female, age 35. Connie has been with your company seven years. Four years ago, Connie was in an automobile accident while traveling on business to a customer's location. As a result of the accident, she was disabled and is wheelchair-bound. Rumors have it that she is about to receive several million dollars from the insurance company of the driver that hit her. Her performance the last two years has been above average. She has a bachelor's degree in human resource management and a master's degree in human development. Connie specializes in training, career, and organization development activities.

Chuck Jones: African-American male, age 43. Chuck just completed his joint MBA and law program, and recently passed the Bar exam. He has been with your department the past four years. His evaluations have been good to above-average. Five years ago, Chuck won a lawsuit against your company for discriminating against him in a promotion to a supervisory position. Rumors have it that now, with his new degree, Chuck is actively pursuing another job outside the company.

Given these five brief descriptions, make a recommendation to your boss in which two employees will be laid off. Discuss any other options that you feel can be used to meet the requirement of downsizing by two employees—yet not resorting to layoffs. Discuss what you will do to (1) assist the two individuals who have been let go and (2) assist the remaining three employees. Then, in a group of three to five students, seek consensus on the questions posed above. Be prepared to defend your actions.

ENHANCING YOUR WRITING SKILLS

1. Visit a human resource management department—either on or off campus. During your meeting, ask an HRM representative for insight on what he or she does on the job. Focus specifically on what the person's job title is, his or her key job responsibilities, and why the individual got into HRM. Once your appointment is completed, provide a three- to five-page summary of the interview, highlighting how the information can be useful for you in better understanding HRM practices.

2. Discuss how the Hawthorne studies have influenced HRM. Find three examples of HRM applications that can be linked to these studies. What benefits have these applications provided to the organization?

3. Go to the Society of Human Resource Management's web sites <http://www.shrm.org>. Research the process one must follow to prepare for the Human Resource Certification Exam and what certification means.

www.wiley.com/college/decenzo

ℰNDNOTES

1. Concepts for this opening vignette are based in part on John McMorrow, "Future Trends in Human Resources," *HR Focus* (September 1999), pp. 7–9; and Lynn Miller, "What's New," *HRMagazine* (May 1999), pp. 140–143.

2. For a comprehensive overview of management, see Stephen P. Robbins and David A. DeCenzo, *Fundamentals of Management,* 3rd ed. (Upper Saddle River, NJ: Prentice Hall, 2001), Ch. 1. It is also worth noting that changes in the world of work reveal that these work functions may no longer be just the purview of managers, but instead, be part of every worker's job responsibility.

3. While no specific date is identified regarding the "birth" of personnel departments, the generally accepted inception of personnel was in the early 1900s in the BF Goodrich Company.

4. They were seen as performing relatively unimportant activities. In fact, the personnel department was often seen as an "employee graveyard"—a place to send employees who were past their prime and couldn't do much damage. See also Vitor M. Marciano, "The Origins of Development of Human Resource Management," *Published in Best Papers Proceedings, Academy of Management,* Dorothy Perrin Moore, Ed. (August 6–9, 1995), Vancouver, British Columbia, Canada, pp. 223–227.

5. Rebecca B. Edwards, "Legal Skills Important Part of HR Professional's Tool Kit," *HR News* (May 1996), p. 26; and Vitor M. Marciano, "The Origins and Development of Human Resource Management," *Published in Best Papers Proceedings, Academy of Management,* Dorothy Perrin More, Ed. (August 6–9, 1995), Vancouver, British Columbia, Canada, pp. 223–227.

6. Jeffrey Pfeffer, "Producing Sustainable Competitive Advantage Through the Effective Management of People," *Academy of Management Executive,* Vol. 9, No. 1 (1995), p. 55.

7. Mitchell Lee Marks, "Let's Make a Deal," *HRMagazine* (April 1997), 125–131; Alan Bush, "The Business of HR Is Business," *HRMagazine* (May 1996), p. 112; and Timothy J. Galpin and Patrick Murray, "Connect Human Resource Strategy to the Business Plan," *HRMagazine* (March 1997), pp. 99–104.

8. Mike Verespej, "How to Manage Adversity," *Industry Week* (January 1998), p. 24; Russell W. Coff, "Human Assets and Management Dilemmas: Coping with Hazards on the Road to Resource-Based Theory," *Academy of Management Review,* Vol. 22, No. 2 (Summer 1997), pp. 374–402; Martha I. Finney, "The Catbert Dilemma: The Human Side of Tough Decisions," *HRMagazine* (February 1997), pp. 70–76; and "HR Must Balance Demands of Dual Roles, Ellig Says," *HR News* (July 1996), p. 9.

9. Robert W. Thompson, "Survey Targets Relationship Between HR, Line Managers," *HR News* (July 1998), p. 5; James W. Down, Walter Mardis, Thomas R. Connolly, and Sarah Johnson, "A Strategic Model Emerges," *HR Focus* (June 1997), pp. 22–23; R. Wayne Anderson, "The Future of Human Resources: Forging Ahead or Falling Behind," *Human Resource Management* (Spring 1997), pp. 17–22; Michael Beer, "The Transformation of the Human Resource Function: Resolving the Tension Between a Traditional Administrative and a New Strategic Role," *Human Resource Management* (Spring 1997), pp. 49–56; John E. Delery and D. Harold Doty, "Models of Theorizing in Strategic Human Resource Management: Tests of Universalistic, Contingency, and Configurational Performance Prediction," *Academy of Management Journal* (August 1996), pp. 802–823; Mark A. Huselid, Susan E. Jackson, and Randall S. Schuler, "Technical and Strategic Human Resource Management Effectiveness as Determinants of Firm Performance," *Academy of Management Journal* (February 1997), pp. 171–188; and Richard Niehaus and Paul M. Swiercz, "Summary of the 1997 HRPS Research Symposium 'Positioning the Human Function for the 21st Century,'" *HR: Human Resource Planning* (Fall 1997), pp. 42–54.

10. See, for instance, Nancy Wong Bryan, "HR by the Numbers," *Workforce* (June 2000), pp. 94–104.

11. Although there has been much criticism of the Hawthorne studies regarding the conclusions they drew, this has in no way diminished the significance of opinions they represent in the development of the field of HRM.

12. Scott Hayes, "Basic Skills Training 101," *Workforce* (April 1999), pp. 76–78.

13. Arnold Packer, "Getting to Know the Employee of the Future," *Training and Development* (August 2000), pp. 39–43.

14. "Strategic HR—Aligning Human Resources with Corporate Goals," *Management Services* (August 2000), p. 5; Jennifer Laabs, "Strategic HR Won't Come Easily," *Workforce* (January 2000), pp. 52–56; and Richard M. Hodgetts, Fred Luthans, and John W. Slocum, Jr., "Strategy and HRM Initiatives for the '00 Environment: Redefining Roles and Boundaries, Linking Competencies and Resources," *Organizational Dynamics* (Autumn 1999), pp. 7–21.

15. Bill Leonard, "Investment in HR Reaps Benefits," *HRMagazine* (June 2000), p. 22.

16. See also, Timothy R. Athey and Michael S. Orth, "Emerging Competency Methods of the Future," *Human Resource Magazine* (Fall 1999), pp. 215–225.

17. Of course we recognize that staffing, as with other HRM activities, is continuous, and all functions occur simultaneously. However, for the sake of explanation, we present each function as a linear process.

18. See, for instance, D. M. Noer, *Healing the Wounds* (San Francisco: Jossey-Bass, 1993).

19. S. P. Robbins, "Layoff-Survivor Sickness: A Missing Topic in Organizational Behavior," *Journal of Management Accounting* (February 1999).

20. Ibid.

21. Pamela A. McLagan, "As the HRD World Churns," *Training and Development* (December 1999), p. 20.

22. See, for example, Richard Henderson, *Compensation Management in a Knowledge-Based World,* 8th ed. (Upper Saddle River, NJ: Prentice-Hall, 2000).

23. "Money Still Talks When It Comes to Retention," *Workforce* (September 2000), p. 30.

24. Christopher Gaggiano, "How're You Gonna Keep 'Em Down on the Firm?" *Inc.* (January 1998), pp. 71–82.

25. See, for instance, Edward L. Powers, "Employee Loyalty in the New Millennium," *SAM Advanced Management Journal* (Summer 2000), pp. 4–8.

26. Linda Micco, "Work-Life Policies Enhance Bottom Line," *HR News* (January 1997), p. 2.

27. For a review of the different types of HRM models, see Terrence R. Bishop and Albert S. King, "The Effects of Varying Human Resource Management Models on Perceptions of Human Resource Department Integration in Organizational Management," *Business Journal* (Fall–Spring 1997), pp. 79–85.

28. Carla Johnson, ". . . and Other Duties as Assigned," *HR Magazine* (February 2000), pp. 66–72.

29. Information based on Society for Human Resource Management, "HR Basics 2000" (October 2000).

30. As we will show in Chapter 5, during a period of downsizing, employment may also be the department handling the layoffs.

31. See, for example, John T. Delaney and Mark A. Huselid, "The Impact of Human Resource Management Practices on Perceptions of Organizational Performance," *Academy of Management Journal,* Vol. 39, No. 4 (August 1996), pp. 949–969; Mark A. Youndt, Scott A. Snell, James W. Dean, Jr., and David P. Lepak, "Human Resource Management, Manufacturing Strategy, and Firm Performance," *Academy of Management Journal,* Vol. 39, No. 4 (August 1996), pp. 836–866; Mark A. Huselid, Susan E. Jackson, and Randall S. Schuler, "Technical and Strategic Human Resource Management Effectiveness as Determinants of Firm Performance," *Academy of Management Journal,* Vol. 40, No. 1 (February 1997), pp. 171–188.

32. It should be noted that compensation and benefits may be, in fact, two separate departments. However, for reading flow, we will consider the department as a combined, singular unit.

33. See, for example, Karen S. Whelan-Berry and Judith R. Gordon, "Strengthening Human Resource Strategies: Insights from the Experiences of Mid-Career Professional Women," *Human Resource Planning* (January 2000), pp. 27–37; and "Flexible Benefits: Beyond the New Regulations," *Employee Benefit Plan Review* (June 2000), pp. 43–45.

34. Perquisites, or perks, are special offerings accorded to senior managers in an attempt to attract and retain the best managers possible.

35. See also Jonathan A. Segal, "Cybertraps for HR," *HRMagazine* (June 2000), pp. 217–231.

36. A strategic business unit, or market-driven unit, refers to a situation whereby these units operate as independent entities in an organization with their own set of strategies and mission.

37. Patricia Wamser, "How Does Your Pay Stack Up," *HRMagazine* (November 1995), pp. 41–43.

38. Bill Leonard, "Organizations Benefit from Sharing HR Services," *HRMagazine* (February 2000), p. 32; and Samuel Greengard, "Fair Share," *Industry Week* (March 15, 1999), pp. 42–46.

39. Bob Cecil, "Shared Services: Moving Beyond Success," *Strategic Finance* (April 2000), pp. 64–68.

40. Michael George and Gary Lowe, "Eight Steps to a Superior HR Service Center," *Call Center Solutions* (September 1999), pp. 106–113.

41. Donna Fenn, "Managing: Do You Need an HR Director," *Inc.* (February 1996), p. 97; and John Mariotti, "Outsourcing Shouldn't Be a Dirty Word," *Industry Week* (September 16, 1996), p. 17.

42. Manpower Argus, "More Than 100 Million Children Are in Global Workforce," *Employment Trends* (October 1996), p. 4.

43. Sarah Cuthill, "Cross-Cultural Training: A Critical Step in Ensuring the Success of International Assignments," *Human Resource Management* (Summer Fall 2000), pp. 239–250.

44. Society of Human Resource Management, "Selection Criteria, Procedures and Success Indicators for Managers in International Assignments," *SHRM Information Center* (April 1999), pp. 1–7; and "International Transfers: Making Relocation Offers Employees Can't Refuse," *SHRM Information Center* (April 2000), pp. 1–6.

45. See, for instance, Maria Antonia del Rio, "Expatriate Tax: Understanding the Spanish System," *Benefits and Compensation* (July–August 2000), pp. 27–30.

46. Certification Institute, *Certification Information Handbook* (Alexandria, VA: Society for Human Resource Management, 2000).

3

EQUAL EMPLOYMENT OPPORTUNITY

LEARNING OUTCOMES

AFTER READING THIS CHAPTER, YOU WILL BE ABLE TO:

1. Identify the groups protected under the Civil Rights Act of 1964, Title VII.
2. Discuss the importance of the Equal Employment Opportunities Act of 1972.
3. Describe affirmative action plans.
4. Define what is meant by the terms *adverse impact, adverse treatment,* and *protected group members.*
5. Identify the important components of the Americans with Disabilities Act of 1990.
6. Explain the coverage of the Family and Medical Leave Act of 1993.
7. Discuss how a business can protect itself from discrimination charges.
8. Specify the HRM importance of the *Griggs v. Duke Power* case.
9. Define what constitutes sexual harassment in today's organizations.
10. Discuss what is meant by the term *glass ceiling.*

magine you're looking for a job in your local area. You've come from a proud heritage of United Auto Workers and are about to be the fourth generation in your family to go to work in an automotive plant. You're excited about the opportunity, the potential for a career, and the resurgence of American automobile manufactures. And you firmly believe in "Quality is Job 1"—the slogan that served as the vision propelling the quality revolution at the Ford Motor Company. Plus, given the past press that Ford is an employer committed to diversity only adds to your excitement. And so, when the job is offered, you excitedly accept. But before long, your excitement turns to aggravation, as the work environment you're working in has become anything but positive.[1]

At the center of the controversy at Ford were two of its Chicago area plants. A few years ago, about 30 women employees at the parts stamping plant complained to company management and the Equal Employment Opportunity Commission that their work environment was hostile. They were subjected to crude language being spoken on the plant floor, being called sexually explicit names, groped and grabbed unwantedly, and even massaged by male co-workers and supervisors at times. Investigating the matter, the Equal Employment Opportunity Commission found that some of the complaints were valid, and Ford agreed to pay a $2 million settlement to those involved, and make some organizational changes to eliminate this from happening again. But more changes apparently were needed.

Even though company officials have terminated 10 male employees and disciplined 29 others for inappropriate actions, and have implemented a policy in which a supervisor who tolerates a hostile environment will be denied salary increases and promotions, the harassment apparently didn't stop. In addition to continuing harassment at the parts plant, a second Chicago-area plant—the one that produced the Taurus and Sable models—found itself at the center of controversy. Complaints from more than 850 employees poured in. Complaints centered on the behaviors previously witnessed, plus being subjected to sexually explicit graffiti and pornographic materials. Moreover, some male members even used the company facility for parties involving strippers and prostitutes. Not only have pictures of these events been circulated to female employees in the plants, the Chicago police were once called to the plant late at night to break up one of these events.

Recognizing that problems may exist, Ford management attempted to take the high road in solving the matter. They agreed with the Equal Employment Opportunity Commission to a $17.5 million settlement in late 1999. Of this settlement money, $7.5 million was to be awarded to the 850 women employees subjected to harassment; and the remaining $10.5 million was to be spent on training all employees, and specifically supervisors, about sexual harassment. Furthermore, the company agreed to triple the number of female supervisors working in the plants.

Did Ford act responsibly knowing that harassment was evident in these two plants? That's a question a judge will have to answer. Even with the Equal Employment Opportunity settlement in place, a district court judge granted all females who worked at the two plants any time after December 2, 1993 the right to file a class action suit against the company. The judge's rationale focused on the facts that the agreement reached didn't involve the affected employees, some women who were part of the settlement were experiencing retaliation, and enforcing the agreement may be lacking. Accordingly, even though Ford attempted to correct the situation, it may face a bigger liability in the near future.

Introduction

What do Domino's, Astra Pharmaceuticals, Mitsubishi, Morgan Stanley, and State Farm Insurance have in common? Each has been singled out for practices that allegedly discriminated against minorities or women. In the last chapter, we briefly introduced the concept of government legislation as it affects employment practices. In this chapter, we will explore this critical influence to provide an understanding of the legislation. Why? Because it is a fact of doing business. Almost every U.S. organization, both public and private, must abide by the guidelines established in the 1964 Civil Rights Act, its subsequent amendment (1972), and other federal laws governing employment practices. The importance of such legislation cannot be overstated, as these laws permeate all HRM functions in the organization.

Keep in mind that although our discussion will be limited to federal employment legislation, there may also be state or municipal laws that go beyond what the federal government requires. For example, in eleven states, sexual orientation is considered a "protected class."[2] While it is impossible to cover all of these laws, HRM managers must know and understand what additional requirements they face. Interestingly, 14 countries around the globe have national laws that protect gays, lesbians, and bisexuals from employment discrimination.[3]

Laws Affecting Discriminatory Practices

Civil Rights Acts of 1991 Employment discrimination law that nullified selected Supreme Court decisions, reinstated burden of proof by the employer, and allowed for punitive and compensatory damage through jury trials.

The beginning of equal employment opportunity is usually attributed to the passage of the 1964 Civil Rights Act. Even though the focus of the activities we will explore in this chapter is rooted in this 1964 act, equal employment's beginning actually goes back more than one hundred years. For instance, Section 1981 of Title 42 of the U.S. Code, referred to as the **Civil Rights Act of 1866,** coupled with the Fourteenth Amendment to the Constitution (1868), prohibited discrimination on the basis of race, sex, and national origin. Although these earlier actions have been overshadowed by the 1964 act, they've gained prominence in years past as being the laws that white male workers could use to support claims of reverse discrimination. In such cases, white males used the Civil Rights Act of 1866 and the Fourteenth Amendment to support their argument that minorities were given special treatment in employment decisions that placed them at a disadvantage. Under the Civil Rights Act of 1866 employees could sue for racial discrimination.[4] As a result of this act, individuals could also seek punitive and compensatory damages under Section 1981, in addition to the awarding of back pay.[5] However, in 1989, a Supreme Court ruling limited Section 1981 use in discrimination suits in that the law does not cover racial discrimination after a person has been hired.[6] We'll look more at reverse discrimination in our discussion of relevant Supreme Court decisions.

Although earlier attempts were rudimentary in promoting fair employment practices among workers, it was not until the 1960s that earnest emphasis was placed on achieving such a goal. Let's turn our attention, then, to the landmark piece of employment legislation, the Civil Rights Act of 1964.

The Civil Rights Act of 1964

No single piece of legislation in the 1960s had a greater effect on reducing employment discrimination than the Civil Rights Act of 1964. It was divided into a number of parts called *titles*—each dealing with a particular facet of discrimination. On college campuses, you may have heard about Title IX issues—usually in the context of what a university spends on both men and women's sports programs. For HRM purposes, however, **Title VII** is especially relevant.

Title VII The most prominent piece of legislation regarding HRM, it states that it is illegal to discriminate against individuals based on race, religion, color, sex, or national origin.

Title VII prohibits discrimination in hiring, compensation, and terms, conditions, or privileges of employment based on race, religion, color, sex, or national origin. Title VII also prohibits retaliation against an individual who files a charge of discrimination, participates in an investigation, or opposes any unlawful practice. Most organizations, both public and private, are bound by the law. The law, however, specifies compliance based on the number of employees in the organization. Essentially, as originally passed in 1964, any organization with 25 or more (amended to 15 or more in 1972) employees is covered.[7] This

Title VII prohibits discrimination in hiring, compensation, and terms and conditions of employment.

minimum number of employees serves as a means of protecting, or removing from the law, small, family-owned businesses.[8] The organizations initially covered by the EEO regulations, however, found compliance confusing.

Organizations were faced with relatively new requirements, but detailed guidelines for compliance were lacking. Days of purposefully excluding certain individuals significantly decreased, yet practices like testing applicants appeared to create the same effect.[9] In an attempt to clarify this procedure, several cases were challenged in the Supreme Court. The outcomes of these cases indicated that any action that had the effect of keeping certain groups of people out of particular jobs was illegal, unless the company could show why a practice was required. The implication of these decisions, for example, was that a company could not hire a maintenance employee using an aptitude test and a high-school diploma requirement unless those criteria could be shown to be directly relevant to the job. In one of these cases, *Griggs v. Duke Power Company* (1971), the company was unable to show job relatedness. Griggs, an applicant for a maintenance job, demonstrated that the power company's tests and degree requirements were unrelated to performance on the job in question. The decision in the *Griggs* case, though, did not mean that specific selection criteria couldn't be used. For instance, in the case of *Washington v. Davis* (1967),[10] the Supreme Court held that the use of aptitude tests was permissible. In this case, Davis was an applicant for a position as a metropolitan Washington, D.C., police officer. The police force required all applicants to pass a comprehensive aptitude test. The Supreme Court held that the test measured necessary competencies required to be successful as a police officer.

Griggs v. Duke Power Landmark Supreme Court decision stating that tests must fairly measure the knowledge or skills required for a job.

Even though we began to gain a better understanding of what Congress meant in the writing of Title VII, something was clearly lacking—enforcement mechanisms. By 1972, after realizing that the Civil Rights Act was left much to interpretation, Congress passed an amendment to the act called the **Equal Employment Opportunity Act** (EEOA). This act was designed to provide a series of amendments to Title VII.[11] Probably the greatest consequence of the EEOA was the granting of enforcement powers to the Equal Employment Opportunity Commission (EEOC). The EEOC was granted authority to effectively prohibit all forms of employment discrimination based on race, religion, color, sex, or national origin. The EEOC was given the power to file civil suits (individuals may also file a suit themselves if the EEOC declines to sue) against organizations if it was unable to secure an acceptable resolution of discrimination charges within 120 days. In addition, the EEOA also expanded Title VII coverage to include employees of state and local governments, employees of educational institutions, and employers or labor organizations—as we mentioned earlier, those with 15 or more employees or members.

Equal Employment Opportunity Commission The arm of the federal government empowered to handle discrimination in employment cases.

Affirmative Action   A practice in organizations that goes beyond discontinuance of discriminatory practices, including actively seeking, hiring, and promoting minority group members and women.

Title VII, as it exists today, stipulates that organizations must do more than just discontinue discriminatory practices. Enterprises are expected to actively recruit and give preference to minority group members in employment decisions. This action is commonly referred to as **affirmative action.**

Affirmative Action Plans   Affirmative action programs are programs instituted by an organization to correct past injustices in an employment processes. There were four primary reasons for these plans:

- Affirmative action programs were built on the premise that white males made up the majority of workers in our companies.
- U.S. companies were still growing and could accommodate more workers.
- As a matter of public policy and decency, minorities should be hired to correct past prejudice that has kept them out.
- "Legal and social coercion [were] necessary to bring about the change."[12]

What do these reasons imply about affirmative action programs? Affirmative action means that an organization must take certain steps to show that it is not discriminating. For example, the organization must conduct an analysis of the demographics of its current work force. Similarly, the organization must analyze the composition of the community from which it recruits. If the work force resembles the community for all jobs classifications, then the organization may be demonstrating that its affirmative action program is working. If, however, there are differences, affirmative action also implies that the organization will establish goals and timetables for correcting the imbalance, and have specific plans for how to go about recruiting and retaining protected group members.[13]

In coordinating an EEO program, a few issues arise. First of all, the company must know what the job requires in terms of skills, knowledge, and abilities. Candidates are then evaluated on how well they meet the essential elements of the job. If candidates meet these criteria, then they are essentially qualified, meaning that they should be successful performers of the job. Nowhere under EEO does the federal government require an organization to hire unqualified workers. They do require organizations to actively search for qualified minorities by recruiting from places like predominantly African-American or women's colleges, but they do not force hiring of these individuals under this process. However, as a result of affirmative action programs, an organization should be able to show significant improvements in hiring and promoting women and minorities, or justify why external factors prohibited them from achieving their affirmative action goals.[14]

Over the past few years, there has been a backlash against affirmative actions programs.[15] Much of the criticism has focused on the realization that affirmative action bases employment decisions on group membership rather than individual performance.[16] This tugs at the heart of fair employment, whereby certain groups of individuals (e.g., race, sex, age) are given preferential treatment.[17] As the argument goes, if it was wrong 50 years ago to give white males preference for employment, why is it right today to give other individuals preference simply because they possess certain traits?[18] Although there has been some movement in a few states to eliminate affirmative action plans, and the issue has been debated in the Congress of the United States, at this point in time, affirmative action plans still exist. And it appears that they will be around for some time.[19]

Irrespective of the controversy surrounding affirmative action plans, throughout much of this discussion we have addressed practices that are designed to assure equal employment opportunity for all individuals. But how do we know if equal employment programs are not operating properly? The answer to that question may lie in the concept of **adverse (disparate) impact.**

Adverse Impact   Adverse impact can be described as any employment consequence that is discriminatory toward employees who are members of a protected group. Protected status categories include race, color, religion, national origin, citizenship status, sex, age 40 and above, pregnancy-related medical conditions, disability, and Vietnam-era veteran military status.

For an example of an adverse impact, we can look at the prior height and weight requirements police departments around the country had years ago. The height requirement was frequently 5' 10" or greater. As such, many women who wished to become police officers were unable to. Why? Because the average height of females is shorter than that of males. Accordingly, using this height requirement had the effect of significantly reducing the job opportunities for this group of people. The concept of adverse impact, then, results from a seemingly neutral, even unintentional consequence of an employment practice.[20]

There is another issue that differs from adverse impact but follows a similar logic. This is called **adverse (disparate) treatment.** Adverse treatment occurs when a member of a protected group receives less favorable outcomes in an employment decision than a nonprotected group member. For example, if a protected group member is evaluated as performing poorly more often, or receives fewer organizational rewards, adverse treatment may have occurred.

The Civil Rights Act of 1964 led the way to change how HRM would function. As the years progressed, other amendments and legislation were passed that extended equal employment opportunity practices to diverse groups. Let's take a look at the more critical of these laws summarized in Exhibit 3-1.

Other Laws Affecting Discrimination Practices

In addition to the Civil Rights Act of 1964, there are a number of other laws and presidential orders that equally affect HRM practices. Specifically, we'll address the Age Discrimination in Employment Act of 1967 (amended in 1978 and 1986), the Pregnancy Discrimination Act of 1978, the Americans with Disabilities Act of 1990, the Family and Medical Leave Act of 1993, and three Executive Orders: 11246, 11375, and 11478.

Age Discrimination in Employment Act of 1967   The **Age Discrimination in Employment Act (ADEA)** of 1967 prohibited the widespread practice of requiring workers to retire at the age of 65.[21] It gave protected-group status to individuals between the ages of 40 and 65. Since 1967, this act has been amended twice—once in 1978, which raised the mandatory retirement age to 70, and again in 1986, where the upper age limit was removed altogether.[22] As a result, anyone over age 39 is covered by the ADEA. Organizations with 20 or more employees, state and local governments, employment agencies, and labor organizations are covered by the ADEA.[23]

Of course, there are and have been exceptions to this law. Employees holding certain types of jobs, such as college professors, didn't come under full protection until 1994. Furthermore, other employees—like commercial pilots—may be required to leave their current positions because of strict requirements of the job. For instance, pilots may not captain a commercial airplane upon reaching the age of 60.[24] Why age 60? That age is a benchmark after which the Federal Aviation Agency believes that medical research can show that the necessary skills

---

Adverse (Disparate) Impact   A consequence of an employment practice that results in a greater rejection rate for a minority group than it does for the majority group in the occupation.

Adverse (Disparate) Treatment   An employment situation where protected group members receive different treatment than other employees in matters like performance evaluations, promotions, etc.

Age Discrimination in Employment Act   Passed in 1967 and amended in 1978 and 1986, this act prohibits arbitrary age discrimination, particularly among those over age 40.

EXHIBIT 3-1
Summary of Laws Affecting
Discrimination

Civil Rights Act of 1964	Title VII prohibits employment discrimination in hiring, compensation, and terms, conditions, or privileges of employment based on race, religion, color, sex, or national origin.
Executive Order (E.O.) 11246	Prohibits discrimination on the basis of race, religion, color, and national origin, by federal agencies as well as those working under federal contracts.
Executive Order 11375	Added sex-based discrimination to E.O. 11246.
Age Discrimination in Employment Act of 1967	Protects employees 40–65 years of age from discrimination. Later amended to age 70 (1978), then amended (1986) to eliminate the upper age limit altogether.
Executive Order 11478	Amends part of E.O. 11246, states practices in the federal government must be based on merit; also prohibits discrimination based on political affiliation, marital status, or physical handicap.
Equal Employment Opportunity Act of 1972	Granted the enforcement powers for the EEOC.
Vocational Rehabilitation Act of 1973	Prohibits employers who have federal contracts greater than $2,500 from discrimination against individuals with handicaps, racial minorities, and women.
Vietnam Veterans Readjustment Act of 1974	Provided for equal employment opportunities for Vietnam War veterans. Administered and enforced by the Office of Federal Contract Compliance Programs.
Age Discrimination in Employment Act of 1978	Increased mandatory retirement age from 65 to 70. Later amended (1986) to eliminate upper age limit.
Pregnancy Discrimination Act of 1978	Affords EEO protection to pregnant workers and requires pregnancy to be treated like any other disability.
Americans with Disabilities Act of 1990	Prohibits discrimination against an essentially qualified individual, and requires enterprises to reasonably accommodate individuals.
Civil Rights Act of 1991	Nullified selected Supreme Court decisions. Reinstates burden of proof by employer. Allows for punitive and compensatory damages through jury trials.
Family and Medical Leave Act of 1993	Permits employees in organizations of 50 or more workers to take up to 12 weeks of unpaid leave for family or medical reasons each year.

to handle an emergency may be lacking or may significantly decline.[25] Thus, using age 60 as the determining factor, airlines are permitted to remove a pilot at that age for public safety reasons. But that does not mean that they must leave the organization. Should a 60-year-old pilot decide to be a flight engineer or even an airport ticket agent, and if an opening exists, the individual may apply for the job. Failure to allow their retiring pilots to do so is in violation of ADEA.

In applying this act to the workplace, a four-pronged test is typically used to determine if age discrimination has occurred. This test involves proving that one is "a member of a protected group, that adverse employment action was taken, the individual was replaced by a [younger] worker, and the individual was qualified for the job."[26] For example, assume that in an organization's attempt to cut salary costs, it lays off senior employees. Yet, instead of leaving the jobs unfilled, the organization hires recent college graduates who are paid significantly less. This action may be risky and may lead to a charge of discrimination. Should the organization be found guilty of age discrimination, punitive damages up to double the compensatory amount may be awarded by the courts.

Pregnancy Discrimination Act Law prohibiting discrimination based on pregnancy.

The Pregnancy Discrimination Act of 1978 The **Pregnancy Discrimination Act of 1978** (and supplemented by various state laws) prohibits discrimination based on pregnancy. Under the law, companies may not terminate a female employee for being pregnant, refuse to make a positive employment decision based on one's pregnancy, or deny insurance coverage to the individual. The law also requires organizations to offer the employee a reasonable period of time off from work. Although no specific time frames are given, the pregnancy leave is typically six to ten weeks. At the end of this leave, the worker is entitled to return to work. If the exact job she left is unavailable, a similar one must be provided.

It is interesting to note that this law is highly contingent on other benefits the company offers.[27] Should the organization not offer health or disability-related (like sick leave) benefits to its employees, it is exempt from this law. However, any type of health or disability insurance offered, no matter how much or how little, requires compliance. For instance, if a company offers a benefit covering 40 percent of the costs associated with any short-term disability, then it must include pregnancy in that coverage.

Americans with Disabilities Act of 1990 Extends EEO coverage to include most forms of disability, requires employers to make reasonable accommodations, and eliminates post-job-offer medical exams.

The Americans with Disabilities Act of 1990 The **Americans with Disabilities Act of 1990** (ADA) extends employment protection to most forms of disability status, including those afflicted with AIDS.[28] It's important, however, to recognize that ADA doesn't protect all forms of disability. For example, some

Years ago, people like Lawrence Scadden would have had difficulty finding a job in many organizations. Blind since age 5, Scadden is the Director of the National Science Foundation's (NSF) program for people with disabilities–a group that funds math and science education programs for students with disabilities. To perform his job effectively and to accommodate his disability, NSF has provided Scadden with a braille typewriter, as well as a sophisticated speech system that interacts with his computer enabling it to talk. The "tools" to accommodate Scadden cost the NSF just over $1,500. More than reasonable given his productivity.

psychiatric disabilities (like pyromania and kleptomania) may disqualify an individual from employment. And while some mental illness advocates have raised concerns, the EEOC and some courts have held that the employer is not held accountable in these special cases.[29] In addition to the extended coverage, companies are further required to make **reasonable accommodations** to provide a qualified individual access to the job.[30] A company may also be required to provide necessary technology to enable an individual to do his or her job. For example, suppose a worker is legally blind. If special "reading" equipment is available and could assist this individual in doing the job, then the company must provide it if that accommodation does not present an undue hardship.[31]

The ADA extends its coverage to private companies and all public service organizations. Compliance with ADA was phased in over four years, with full compliance for companies with 15 or more employees effective July 26, 1994. As a final note on this act, it's important to mention that contagious diseases, including HIV+ and AIDS, are considered conditions of being disabled.[32] In advancing the decision in the 1987 Supreme Court case of *Arline v. Nassau County*, the ADA views contagious diseases as any other medical disability. With respect to AIDS, there are exceptions that can be implemented, but most of these are rare. In restaurants, for example, the individual may simply be assigned other duties, rather than terminated. Under this law, you must treat the AIDS worker in the same way that you would treat a worker suffering from cancer, and all job actions must be based on job requirements.

Reasonable Accommodations Providing the necessary technology to enable an affected individual to do his or her job.

The Americans with Disabilities Act extends employment protection to most forms of disability.

The Family and Medical Leave Act of 1993   The Family and Medical Leave Act of 1993 (FMLA) provides employees in organizations[33] employing 50 or more workers the opportunity to take up to 12 weeks of unpaid leave[34] each year for family matters (like childbirth or adoption, or for their own illness or to care for a sick family member). These employees are guaranteed their current job, or one equal to it, upon their return.[35] Furthermore, during this period of unpaid leave, employees retain their employer-offered health insurance coverage (see Exhibit 3-2). Currently, about 66 percent of all U.S. workers are covered under FMLA.[36] The Act, while providing a benefit to employees, has, however, created some hardships for organizations. The hardships for these organizations stem from compliance with the law as well as the administrative complexity in processing FMLA matters.[37]

Since its passage, the FMLA has taken on more substance. For example, the Department of Labor has issued guidelines regarding what constitutes a serious health condition.[38] For example, in one case, an employee sued her employer for failing to provide her with FMLA protection to care for her child who was suffering with an ear infection and had to miss school for four days.[39] The court's ruling in this case was that an ear infection was not a serious illness. Moreover, for those employers covered under the FMLA, the Department of Labor implemented certain communication requirements for employers. These requirements went into effect on April 6, 1995 (see Exhibit 3-3).

Family and Medical Leave Act Federal legislation that provides employees up to twelve weeks of unpaid leave each year to care for family members, or for their own medical reasons.

Relevant Executive Orders   In 1965, President Lyndon Johnson issued Executive Order 11246. This executive order prohibited discrimination on the basis of race, religion, color, or national origin by federal agencies as well as by contractors and subcontractors who worked under federal contracts. This was

Executive Order 11246 Executive order which prohibited discrimination on the basis of race, religion, color, or national origin by federal agencies as well as by contractors and subcontractors who worked under federal contracts.

EXHIBIT 3-2
Family and Medical Act

Your Rights
Under The
Family and Medical Leave Act of 1993

FMLA requires covered employers to provide up to 12 weeks of unpaid, job-protected leave to "eligible" employees for certain family and medical reasons. Employees are eligible if they have worked for a covered employer for at least one year, and for 1,250 hours over the previous 12 months, and if there are at least 50 employees within 75 miles.

Reasons For Taking Leave:

Unpaid leave must be granted for *any* of the following reasons:

- to care for the employee's child after birth, or placement for adoption or foster care;
- to care for the employee's spouse, son or daughter, or parent, who has a serious health condition; or
- for a serious health condition that makes the employee unable to perform the employee's job.

At the employee's or employer's option, certain kinds of *paid* leave may be substituted for unpaid leave.

Advance Notice and Medical Certification:

The employee may be required to provide advance leave notice and medical certification. Taking of leave may be denied if requirements are not met.

- The employee ordinarily must provide 30 days advance notice when the leave is "foreseeable."
- An employer may require medical certification to support a request for leave because of a serious health condition, and may require second or third opinions (at the employer's expense) and a fitness for duty report to return to work.

Job Benefits and Protection:

- For the duration of FMLA leave, the employer must maintain the employee's health coverage under any "group health plan."

- Upon return from FMLA leave, most employees must be restored to their original or equivalent positions with equivalent pay, benefits, and other employment terms.
- The use of FMLA leave cannot result in the loss of any employment benefit that accrued prior to the start of an employee's leave.

Unlawful Acts By Employers:

FMLA makes it unlawful for any employer to:

- interfere with, restrain, or deny the exercise of any right provided under FMLA;
- discharge or discriminate against any person for opposing any practice made unlawful by FMLA or for involvement in any proceeding under or relating to FMLA.

Enforcement:

- The U.S. Department of Labor is authorized to investigate and resolve complaints of violations.
- An eligible employee may bring a civil action against an employer for violations.

FMLA does not affect any Federal or State law prohibiting discrimination, or supersede any State or local law or collective bargaining agreement which provides greater family or medical leave rights.

For Additional Information:

Contact the nearest office of the Wage and Hour Division, listed in most telephone directories under U.S. Government, Department of Labor.

U.S. Department of Labor
Employment Standards Administration
Wage and Hour Division
Washington, D.C. 20210

WH Publication 1420
June 1993

U S G.P.O.: 353-608

Executive Order
11375 Executive order which added sex-based discrimination to Executive Order 11246.

Executive Order
11478 Superseded parts of Executive Order 11246 stating that employment practices in the federal government must be based on merit and must prohibit discrimination based on race, color, religion, sex, national origin, political affiliation, marital status, or physical disability.

followed by **Executive Order 11375**, which added sex-based discrimination to the above criteria. In 1969, President Richard Nixon issued **Executive Order 11478** to supersede part of Executive Order 11246. It stated that employment practices in the federal government must be based on merit and must prohibit discrimination based on race, color, religion, sex, national origin, political affiliation, marital status, or physical disability.

These orders cover all organizations that have contracts of $10,000 or more with the federal government. Additionally, those organizations with 50 or more employees and/or $50,000 in federal grants must have a written active affirmative

EXHIBIT 3-3
*Employer Communication
Requirements Under FMLA*

- The FMLA poster must be placed in an easy-to-see location.
- The employee handbook (or some other form of policy communication mechanism) must state the employee's rights and obligations under FMLA. This is to be reissued to an employee the first time an employee requests leave under FMLA in any given six-month period. The policy must also include:
  - That the leave will be counted against the employee's FMLA leave.
  - An explanation regarding whether or not a medical certification is required; and if it is and the employee fails to provide such information, what consequences the employee may face.
  - An explanation to employees regarding how health insurance premiums are to be paid, if any, to maintain health insurance coverage; and under what circumstances coverage may be discontinued for lack of payment.
  - Information pertaining to medical certification to return to work.
  - An explanation, where appropriate, when the employee's job is considered exempt from FMLA, and the subsequent possibility that returning to one's job may not exist.
  - Information regarding the repayment of employer-paid health insurance premiums if the employee does not return to work at the end of the leave period.

Source: Based on material by Marcia Haight, "Final FMLA Rule Require More Communication,"*HR News* (March 1995), p. 8.

Office of Federal Contract Compliance Programs The government office that administers the provisions of Executive Order 11246.

action program. The **Office of Federal Contract Compliance Program (OFCCP)** administers the order's provisions and provides technical assistance. We'll return to the OFCCP shortly when we discuss the enforcement aspects of equal employment opportunities.

The Civil Rights Act of 1991

Civil Rights Acts of 1991 Employment discrimination law that nullified selected Supreme Court decisions. Reinstated burden of proof by the employer, and allowed for punitive and compensatory damage through jury trials.

The **Civil Rights Act of 1991** was one of the most hotly debated civil rights laws since the 1964 act. The impetus for this legislation stemmed from a number of Supreme Court decisions in the late 1980s that diminished the effect of the *Griggs* decision. Proponents of the 1964 legislation quickly banded together in an attempt to issue new legislation aimed at restoring the provisions lost in these Supreme Court rulings.

The Civil Rights Act of 1991 prohibits discrimination on the basis of race and prohibits racial harassment on the job; returns the burden of proof that discrimination did not occur back to the employer; reinforces the illegality of employers who make hiring, firing, or promoting decisions on the basis of race, ethnicity, sex, or religion; and permits women and religious minorities to seek punitive damages in intentional discriminatory claims. Additionally, this Act also included the Glass Ceiling Act—establishing the Glass Ceiling Commission, whose purpose is to study a variety of management practices in organizations.

What impact did this legislation have on employers? The issue dealing with punitive damages may prove to be the most drastic change to have taken place. For the first time, individuals claiming they have been intentionally discriminated against are able to sue for damages. The amount of these compensatory and punitive charges, however, is prorated based on number of employees in the organization.[40]

DEALING WITH THE LEGAL SIDE OF HRM

T HERE ARE NOW A VARIETY OF software and Internet-based applications that have been created to help organizations deal with many of the legal issues in HRM. The following are a few highlights of these applications.

■ *Desktop Employment Law CD-Rom* (Glasser LegalWorks: www.legalwks.com/dcroms/desktop/front.shtml). Developed by a San Francisco attorney, this software application provides "source text, forms, and checklists on 22 of the most pressing legal issues facing HR departments."[41] The base price for this software is about $895 but will vary based on number of site licenses ordered.

■ *Preventing Sexual Harassment* (New Media Learning: www.new medialearning.com). This software program permits customization for

an organization to more properly reflect its issues. Software includes a number of "test" questions to reinforce concepts on the software. Feedback on these test questions is immediately provided. The software program costs $795 for one user, and prices vary depending on the number of site licenses granted.

■ *Sexual Harassment CD-ROM* (Corvus Digital Solutions: www.corvisdigital.com). This CD-based software application assists organizational members by providing a series of training scenarios for them to better understand how to deal with sexual harassment matters.[42] The CD package is somewhat expensive ($4,000), but does provide an excellent self-paced opportunity for organizational members to review individually or as part of a group training program.

GUARDING AGAINST DISCRIMINATION PRACTICES

Facing a number of laws and regulations, it's critical for HRM to implement practices that are nondiscriminatory. Although it is hoped that senior management has established an organizational culture that encourages equal employment opportunity, discrimination does happen.[43] Recall from our earlier discussion that employment discrimination may stem from a decision that is based on factors other than those relevant to the job. Should that occur frequently, the organization may face charges that it discriminates against some members of a protected group. Determining what constitutes discrimination, however, typically requires more than one individual being adversely affected.

Determining Potential Discriminatory Practices

To determine if discrimination possibly occurred, one of four tests can be used. These are the 4/5ths rule, restricted policies, geographic comparisons, and the McDonnell-Douglas Test. Remember, however, that each of these tests is simply an indicator that risky practices may have occurred. It is up to some judicial body to make the final determination.

The 4/5ths Rule One of the first measures of determining potentially discriminatory practices is to use a rule of thumb called the **4/5ths rule**. Issued by the EEOC in its Uniform Guidelines on Employee Selection Procedures, the 4/5ths rule serves as a basis for determining whether an adverse impact has occurred. Of course, the 4/5ths rule is not a definition of discrimination. It is, however, a "practical device to keep the attention of the enforcement agencies on serious discrepancies in hiring and promotion rates, or other employment decisions."[44] Moreover, in applying the 4/5ths rule, the Supreme Court ruled in *Connecticut v. Teal* (1984) that decisions in each step of the selection process must conform to the 4/5ths rule.[45]

4/5ths Rule A rough indicator of discrimination, this rule requires that the number of minority members that a company hires must be at least 80 percent of the majority members in the population hired.

To see how the 4/5ths rule works, suppose we have two pools of applicants for jobs as management information systems analysts. Our applicants' backgrounds reflect the following: 40 applicants are classified in the majority, while 15 applicants are classified as members of a minority population.[46] After we go through a testing process and an interview, the following number of people are hired: 22 majority and 8 minority members. Is the organization in compliance? Exhibit 3-4 provides the analysis. In this case, we find that the company is in compliance; that is, the ratio of minority to majority members is 80 percent or greater (the 4/5ths rule). Accordingly, even though fewer minority members were hired, no apparent discrimination has occurred. Exhibit 3-4 also shows the analysis of an organization not in compliance.

Remember, whenever the 4/5ths rule is violated, it only indicates that discrimination may have occurred. Should the analysis show that the percentage is less than 80 percent, then more elaborate statistical testing is needed to confirm or reject that there was an adverse impact. That is because many factors can enter in the picture. For instance, if Company A finds a way to keep most minority group members from applying in the first place, it will only have to hire a few of them to meet its 4/5ths rule-of-thumb measure. Conversely, if Company B actively seeks numerous minority group applicants and hires more than Company A, it still may not meet the 4/5ths rule.

Restricted Policy   An HRM policy that results in the exclusion of a class of individuals.

Restricted Policy   A restricted policy infraction occurs whenever an enterprise's HRM activities result in the exclusion of a class of individuals. For instance, assume a company is restructuring and laying off an excessive number of employees who are over age 40. Simultaneously, however, the company is recruiting for selected positions on college campuses only. Because of economic difficulties, this company wants to keep salaries low by hiring people just entering the work force. Those over age 39, who were making higher salaries, are not given the opportunity to even apply for these new jobs. By these actions, a

EXHIBIT 3-4
Applying the 4/5ths Rule

IN COMPLIANCE

Majority Group (MAJ) = 40 applicants			Minority Group (Min) = 15 applicants			
Item	Number	Percent	Item	Number	Percent	%Min/%Maj
Passed test	30	75%	Passed test	11	73%	73%/75% = 97%
Passed interview	22	73%	Passed interview	8	72%	72%/73% = 98%
Hired	22	100%	Hired	8	100%	100%/100% = 100%
Analysis	22/40 =	55%	Analysis	8/15 =	53%	
Ratio of minority/majority 53%/55% = 96%						

NOT IN COMPLIANCE

Majority Group (MAJ) = 40 applicants			Minority Group (Min) = 15 applicants			
Item	Number	Percent	Item	Number	Percent	%Min/%Maj
Passed test	30	75%	Passed test	11	73%	73%/75% = 97%
Passed interview	22	86%	Passed interview	4	36%	36%/86% = 41%
Hired	26	100%	Hired	4	100%	100%/100% = 100%
Analysis	26/40 =	65%	Analysis	4/15 =	26%	
Ratio of minority/majority 26%/65% = 40%						

restricted policy may have occurred. That is, through its hiring practice (intentional or not), a class of individuals (in this case, those protected by age discrimination legislation) has been excluded from consideration.

Geographical Comparisons A third means of supporting discriminatory claims is through the use of a geographic comparison. In this instance, the characteristics of the potential qualified pool of applicants in an organization's hiring market are compared to the characteristics of its employees. If the organization has a proper mix of individuals at all levels in the organization that reflects its recruiting market, then the company is in compliance. Additionally, that compliance may assist in fostering diversity in the organization. The key factor here is the qualified pool according to varying geographic areas.

McDonnell-Douglas Corp. v. Green A four-part test used to determine if discrimination has occurred.

McDonnell-Douglas Test Named for the *McDonnell-Douglas Corp. v. Green* 1973 Supreme Court case,[47] this test provides a means of establishing a solid case.[48] It has four components that must exist. These are:[49]

1. The individual is a member of a protected group.
2. The individual applied for a job for which he or she was qualified.
3. The individual was rejected.
4. The enterprise, after rejecting this applicant, continued to seek other applicants with similar qualifications.

If these four conditions are met, an allegation of discrimination is supported. It is up to the company to refute the evidence by providing a reason for such action. Should that explanation be acceptable to an investigating body, the protected group member must then prove that the reason used by the company is inappropriate. If any of the preceding four tests are met, the company might find itself having to defend its practices. In the next section, we'll explain how an enterprise can do that.

Providing a Response to an EEO Charge

If an adverse impact results from the HRM practices in an organization, there are a few remedies for the employer dealing with valid allegations. First, the employer should discontinue the practice. Only after careful study should the practice, or a modified version, be reinstated. However, even if enough evidence exists, an employer may choose to defend its practices. Generally, three defenses can be used when confronted with an allegation. These are job relatedness or business necessity; bonafide occupational qualifications; and seniority systems.

Business Necessity An organization has the right to operate in a safe and efficient manner. These are business necessities, without which organizational survival could be threatened. A major portion of business necessity involves job-relatedness factors, or having the right to expect employees to perform successfully. This means that employees are expected to possess the required skills, knowledge, and abilities needed to perform the essential elements of the job. Job-relatedness criteria are substantiated through the validation process. We'll return to this topic in Chapter 7.

Bonafide Occupational Qualifications Job requirements that are "reasonably necessary to meet the normal operation of that business or enterprise."

Bonafide Occupational Qualifications The second defense against discriminatory charges is a **bonafide occupational qualification (BFOQ)**. Under Title VII, a BFOQ was permitted where such requirements were "reasonably necessary to meet the normal operation of that business or enterprise." As originally worded, BFOQs could be used only to support sex discrimination. Today, BFOQ coverage is extended to other categories covered. BFOQs cannot, however, be used in cases of race or color.

It is important to note that while BFOQs are "legal" exceptions to Title VII, they are very narrowly defined. Simply using a BFOQ as the response to a charge of discrimination is not enough; it must be directly related to the job. Let's look at some examples.

Just a few decades ago, airlines used BFOQs as a primary reason for hiring female flight attendants. The airlines' position was that most of their passengers were male and preferred to see stewardesses. The courts, however, did not hold the same view. As a result, it is now common to see both sexes today as flight attendants. Using sex as a criterion for a job is difficult to prove. Even the classic washroom attendant case has seen a change: many fine restaurants have members of the opposite sex working in washroom facilities. However, under certain circumstances sex as a BFOQ has been supported. In some healthcare jobs, sex may be used as a determining factor to "protect the privacy interests of patients, clients, or customers."[50]

A religious BFOQ may have similar results. To be an ordained minister in a church, religion may be used as a differentiating factor; but a faculty member doesn't have to be Catholic to teach at a Jesuit college. An organization under certain circumstances may refuse to hire individuals whose religious observances fall on days that the enterprise normally operates. And if the organization demonstrates that it cannot reasonably accommodate these religious observances, then a BFOQ may be permissible.[51] But it's getting harder to demonstrate an inability to make a reasonable accommodation.[52] For example, pizza delivery establishments cannot refuse to hire, or terminate, an employee who has facial hair—like that in the Hindu tradition. HRM managers must understand that some of their "traditional" policies may have to change to reflect the religious diversity of the work force.[53] At FedEx, for instance, a policy that prohibits employees who have customer contact from having beards may be a violation of the Civil Rights Act. Accordingly, the company may have to change its policy to accommodate religious traditions.[54]

In terms of national origin, BFOQs have become rarer. However, if an organization can show that nationality plays a role in a person's being able to perform successfully on the job, then a BFOQ may prevail.

Individuals were once told by their employers that they either had to be clean shaven or lose their jobs. The difficulty arose when one factored in the realization that facial hair for some individuals was a religious custom. Many pizza establishments now recognize the legal ruling and no longer include clean-shaven faces as a requirement of initial or continued employment.

Our last area of BFOQ is age. With subsequent amendments to the Age Discrimination in Employment Act, age BFOQs are very hard to support. As we mentioned in our discussion of age discrimination, there are times when age can be used as a determining factor. However, aside from pilots and a select few key management executives in an organization, age as a BFOQ is limited.

Seniority Systems   Finally, the organization's bonafide seniority system can serve as a defense against discrimination charges. So long as employment decisions, like layoffs, are the function of a well-established and consistently applied seniority system, decisions that may adversely affect protected group members may be permissible. However, an organization using seniority as a defense must be able to demonstrate the "appropriateness" of its system.

Although means are available for organizations to defend themselves, the best approach revolves around job-relatedness. BFOQ and seniority defenses are often subject to great scrutiny, and at times, are limited in their use.

SELECTED RELEVANT SUPREME COURT CASES

In addition to the laws affecting discriminatory practices, HRM must be aware of decisions rendered in the Supreme Court. Many of these cases help to further define HRM practices, or indicate activities that are permissible. While it is impossible to discuss every applicable Supreme Court case, we have chosen a few of the more critical ones for what they have meant to the field.

Cases Concerning Discrimination

Let's return to one of the most important legal rulings affecting selection procedures. In the 1971 *Griggs v. Duke Power Company* decision, the U.S. Supreme Court adopted the interpretive guidelines set out under Title VII: that is, tests must fairly measure the knowledge and skills required in a job in order not to discriminate unfairly against minorities. This action single-handedly made invalid any employment test or diploma requirement that disqualified African-Americans at a substantially higher rate than whites (even when this was not intended) if this differentiation could not be shown to be job-related. Such action was said to create an adverse (disparate) impact.[55]

The *Griggs* decision had even wider implications. It made illegal most intelligence and conceptual tests used in hiring unless there was direct empirical evidence that the tests employed were valid. This crucial decision placed the burden of proof on the employer. Based on this decision, it was now the responsibility of the employer to provide adequate support that any test used did not discriminate on the basis of non-job-related characteristics. For example, if an employer requires all applicants to take an IQ test, and the results of that test will be used in making the hiring decision, it is the employer's responsibility to prove that individuals with higher scores will outperform on the job those individuals with lower scores. Nothing in the Court's decision, however, precludes the use of testing or measuring procedures. What it did was to place the burden of proof on management to demonstrate, if challenged, that the tests used provided a reasonable measure of job performance.

Although companies began a process of validating these tests, requiring all job applicants to take them raised further questions. In 1975, the Supreme Court decision in the case of ***Albemarle Paper Company v. Moody*** (1975) clarified the methodological requirements for using and validating tests in selection.[56] In the

Albermarle Paper Company v. Moody   Supreme Court case that clarified the requirements for using and validating tests in selection processes.

case, four African-American employees challenged their employer's use of tests for selecting candidates from the unskilled labor pool for promotion into skilled jobs. The Court endorsed the EEOC guidelines by noting that Albemarle's selection methodology was defective because:

- The tests had not been used solely for jobs on which they had previously been validated.
- The tests were not validated for upper-level jobs alone but were also used for entry-level jobs.
- Subjective supervisory ratings were used for validating the tests, but the ratings had not been done with care.
- The tests had been validated on a group of job-experienced white workers, whereas the tests were given to young, inexperienced, and often non-white candidates.

In addition to these two landmark cases, other Supreme Court rulings have had an effect on HRM practices. We have identified some of the more important ones and their results in Exhibit 3-5. During the late 1980s, however, we began to see a significant change in the Supreme Court's perception of EEO. One of the most notable cases during this period was ***Wards Cove Packing Company v. Antonio*** (1989).[57] Wards Cove operates two primary salmon canneries in Alaska. The issue in this case stemmed from different hiring practices for two types of jobs. Noncannery jobs that were viewed as unskilled positions were predominately filled by nonwhites (Filipinos and native Alaskans). On the other hand, cannery jobs were seen as skilled administrative/engineering positions and were held by a predominately white group. Based on the ruling handed down in *Griggs v. Duke Power,* an adverse (disparate) impact could be shown by the use

Wards Cove Packing Company v. Antonio A notable Supreme Court case that had the effect of potentially undermining two decades of gains made in equal employment opportunities.

EXHIBIT 3-5
Summary of Selected Supreme Court Cases Affecting EEO

Case	Ruling
Griggs v. Duke Power (1971)	Tests must fairly measure the knowledge or skills required for a job; also validity of tests.
Albemarle Paper Company v. Moody (1975)	Clarified requirements for using and validating test in selection.
Washington v. Davis (1976)	Job-related tests are permissible for screening applicants.
Connecticut v. Teal (1984)	Requires all steps in a selection process to meet the 4/5ths rule.
Firefighters Local 1784 v. Stotts (1984)	Layoffs are permitted by seniority despite effects it may have on minority employees.
Wyant v. Jackson Board of Education (1986)	Layoffs of white workers to establish racial or ethnic balances are illegal; however, reaffirmed the use of affirmative action plans to correct racial imbalance.
United States v. Paradise (1986)	Quotas may be used to correct significant racial discrimination practices.
Sheetmetal Workers Local 24 v. EEOC (1987)	Racial preference could be used in layoff decisions only for those who had been subjected to previous race discrimination.
Johnson v. Santa Clara County Transportation Agency (1987)	Reaffirmed the use of preferential treatment based on sex to overcome problems in existing affirmative action plans.

of statistics (the 4/5ths rule). However, in the decision, the Court ruled that statistics alone could not support evidence of discrimination. Consequently, the burden of proof shifted from the employer to the individual employee.

The *Wards Cove* decision had the effect of potentially undermining two decades of gains made in equal employment opportunities. This case could have struck a significant blow to affirmative action. Inasmuch as the potential was there, businesses appeared to be unwilling to significantly deviate from the affirmative action plans that had developed over the years. Of course, it's now a moot point, as the Civil Rights Bill of 1991 nullified many of these Supreme Court rulings.

Cases Concerning Reverse Discrimination

Reverse Discrimination A claim made by white males that minority candidates are given preferential treatment in employment decisions.

Affirmative action programs are necessary to assure continued employment possibilities for minorities and women. Programs to foster the careers of these two groups have grown over the decades. But while this voluntary action may have been needed to correct past abuses, what about the white male—who at some point is becoming a minority in the work force? Some white males feel that affirmative action plans work against them—leading to charges of **reverse discrimination.** Although reverse discrimination cases exist, two specific cases of reverse discrimination have been noteworthy: the *Allen Bakke* and the *Brian Weber* cases.

In 1978, the Supreme Court handed down its decision in the case of *Bakke v. The Regents of the University of California at Davis Medical School.*[58] Allen Bakke was an applicant to the Davis Medical School for one of the 100 first-year seats. At that time, U.C. at Davis had a self-imposed quota system to promote its affirmative action plan: that is, of the 100 first-year seats, 16 were set aside for minority applicants. Bakke's charge stemmed from those 16 reserved seats. His credentials were not as good as those gaining access to the first 84 seats, but were better than those of minorities targeted for the reserved seats. The issue that finally reached the Supreme Court was, Could an institution impose its own quota to correct past imbalances between whites and minorities? The Supreme Court ruled that the school could not set aside those seats, for doing so resulted in "favoring one race over another."[59] Consequently, Bakke was permitted to enter Davis Medical School.

The Supreme Court's decision in the case of the *United Steelworkers of America v. Weber* (1979) appeared to have important implications for organizational training and development practices and for the larger issue of reverse discrimination. In 1974, Kaiser Aluminum and the United Steelworkers Union set up a temporary training program for higher-paying skilled trade jobs, such as electrician and repairer, at a Kaiser plant in Louisiana. Brian Weber, a white employee at the plant who was not selected for the training program, sued on the grounds that he had been illegally discriminated against. He argued that African Americans with less seniority were selected over him to attend the training due solely to their race. The question facing the Court was: Is it fair to discriminate against whites in order to help African Americans who have been long-time victims of discrimination? The Justices said that Kaiser could choose to give special job preference to African Americans without fear of being harassed by reverse discrimination suits brought by other employees. The ruling was an endorsement of voluntary affirmative action efforts—goals and timetables for bringing an organization's minority and female work force up to the percentages they represent in the available labor pool.

Despite the press coverage that both cases received, many questions remained unanswered. Just how far was a company permitted to go regarding preferential treatment (see "Ethical Issues in HRM")? In subsequent cases, more information became available. In 1984, the Supreme Court ruled in *Firefighters Local 1784 v. Stotts*[60] (1984) that when facing a layoff situation, affirmative action may not take precedence over a seniority system: that is, the last in (often minorities) may be the first to go. This decision was further reinforced in *Wyant v. Jackson Board of Education*[61] (1986), when the Supreme Court ruled that a collective bargaining agreement giving preferential treatment to preserve minority jobs in the event of a layoff was illegal. On the contrary, in *Johnson v. Santa Clara County Transportation* (1987) the Supreme Court did permit affirmative action goals to correct worker imbalances as long as the rights of nonminorities were protected. This ruling had an effect of potentially reducing reverse discrimination claims.

The implications of these cases may be somewhat confusing. The conclusion one needs to draw from these is that *any HRM practice may be challenged by anyone*. HRM must be able to defend its practices if necessary, and to explain the basis and the parameters on which the decisions were made. Failure to document or to base the decisions on business necessities may lead to serious challenges to the action taken.

ENFORCING EQUAL EMPLOYMENT OPPORTUNITY

Two U.S. government agencies are primarily responsible for enforcing equal employment opportunity laws. They are the Equal Employment Opportunity Commission (EEOC) and the Office of Federal Contract Compliance Programs (OFCCP).

The Role of the EEOC

Any charge leveled against an enterprise regarding discrimination based on race, religion, color, sex, national origin, age, qualified disabilities, or wages due to sex falls under the jurisdiction of the EEOC.[64] That is, the EEOC is the en-

ethical issues in HRM

ENGLISH-ONLY RULES

CAN AN ORGANIZATION REQUIRE ITS EMPLOYEES to speak only English on the job? The answer is an unquestionable "maybe."[62] At issue here are several items. On the one hand, employers have identified the need to have a common language spoken at the work site. Employers must be able to communicate effectively with all employees, especially when safety or productive efficiency matters are at stake. This, they claim, is a business necessity. Consequently, if it is a valid requirement of the job, the practice could be permitted. Furthermore, an employer's desire to have one language also stems from the fact that some workers may use bilingual capabilities to harass and insult other workers in a language they could not understand. With today's ever-increasing concern with protecting employees, especially women, from hostile environments, English-only rules serve as one means of reasonable care.

A counterpoint to this English-only rule firmly rests with the work-force diversity issue. Workers in today's organizations come from all nationalities and speak different languages. More than 30 million workers in the United States speak a language other than English. What about these individuals' desire to speak their language, to communicate effectively with their peers, and to maintain their cultural heritage? To them, English-only rules are discriminatory in terms of national origin in that they create an adverse impact for non-English-speaking individuals.[63]

Should employers be permitted to require that only English be spoken in the workplace? What if it is necessary for successful performance or to prevent a safety or health hazard? Should the Supreme Court view this as a discriminatory practice, or render a decision that would create a single, nationwide standard on English-only? What do you think about this issue?

forcement arm for Title VII of the 1964 Civil Rights Act, the Equal Pay Act,[65] the Age Discrimination in Employment Act, the Vocational Rehabilitation Act of 1973, the Americans with Disabilities Act,[66] and the Civil Rights Act of 1991. The EEOC requires that charges typically be filed within 180 days of an alleged incident,[67] and that these charges be written and sworn under oath. Once the charges have been filed, the EEOC may progress (if necessary) through a four-step process:[68]

1. The EEOC will notify the organization of the charge within 10 days of its filing and then begin to investigate the charge to determine if the complaint is valid. The company may simply settle the case here, and the process stops.

2. The EEOC will notify the organization in writing of its findings within 120 days. If the charge is unfounded, the EEOC's process stops, the individual is notified of the outcome, and informs the individual that he or she may still file charges against the company in civil court (called a right-to-sue notice). The individual has 90 days upon receipt of the right-to-sue notice to file his or her suit.

   If there is justification to the charge, the EEOC will attempt to correct the problem through informal meetings with the employer. Again, the company, recognizing that discrimination may have occurred, may settle the case at this point.

3. If the informal process is unsuccessful, the EEOC will begin a formal settlement meeting between the individual and the organization (called a *mediation meeting*). The emphasis here is to reach a voluntary agreement between the parties.

4. Should Step 3 fail, the EEOC may file charges in court.

It's important to note that while acting as the enforcement arm of Title VII, the EEOC has the power to investigate claims, but it does not have the power to force organizations to cooperate.

The EEOC is staffed by five presidentially appointed commissioners and staff counsels. It is generally well known that the EEOC is quite understaffed. And as a result, more than 40,000 cases are backlogged.[69] Consequently, the EEOC began prioritizing cases in 1995, attempting to spend more of its time on cases that initially appear to have merit. Furthermore, its enforcement plans are prioritized—with those cases that "raise issues appropriate for widespread or class relief" receiving the highest priority.[70] But even then, the EEOC may decide not to file suit. If conciliation efforts are unsuccessful, the EEOC may simply issue a "right-to-sue" letter to the complainant and reallocate its resources on other cases. Under these new EEOC directions, it's more important than ever for HRM to investigate the complaints internally, to communicate openly with the EEOC regarding the priority level of the complaint, and even to seek alternative means to resolve the dispute with the individual.[71]

The EEOC prioritizes its cases to spend more time on those that have the greatest significance.

The relief that the EEOC tries to achieve for the individual is regulated by Title VII. If the allegation is substantiated, the EEOC attempts to make the individual whole. That is, under the law, the EEOC attempts to obtain lost wages or back pay, job reinstatement, and other rightfully due employment factors (e.g., seniority or benefits). The individual may also recover attorney fees. However, if the discrimination was intentional, other damages may be awarded. Lastly, under no circumstances may the enterprise retaliate against an individual filing charges—whether or not the person remains employed by the organization.[72] The EEOC monitors that no further adverse action against that individual occurs.

Office of Federal Contract Compliance Program (OFCCP)

In support of Executive Order 11246, the OFCCP enforces the provisions of this order (as amended), as well as Section 503 of the Vocational Rehabilitation Act of 1973 and the Vietnam Veterans Readjustment Act of 1974.[73] Provisions of the OFCCP apply to any organizations, including universities, that have a federal contract or act as a subcontractor on a federal project. The OFCCP operates within the U.S. Department of Labor. Similar to the EEOC, the OFCCP investigates allegations of discriminatory practices and follows a similar process in determining and rectifying wrongful actions. One notable difference is that the OFCCP has the power to cancel an enterprise's contract with the federal government if the organization is not in compliance with EEO laws.

CURRENT ISSUES IN EMPLOYMENT LAW

EEO today continues to address two important issues affecting female employees. These are sexual harassment in the workplace and the glass ceiling initiative. Let's take a closer look at both of these.

Sexual Harassment

Sexual Harassment Anything of a sexual nature where it results in a condition of employment, an employment consequence, or creates a hostile or offensive environment.

Sexual harassment is a serious issue in both public and private sector organizations. More than 15,000 complaints are filed with the EEOC each year.[74] Not only have settlements in these cases incurred a substantial cost to the companies in terms of litigation, it is estimated that this is the single biggest financial risk facing companies today—and results in upwards of a 30 percent drop in a company's stock price.[75] At Mitsubishi, for example, the company paid out more than $34 million to 300 women for the rampant sexual harassment they were exposed to.[76] But it's more than just jury awards. Sexual harassment results in millions lost in "absenteeism, low productivity, and turnover."[77] Sexual harassment, furthermore, is not just a U.S. phenomenon. It's a global issue. For instance, sexual harassment charges have been filed against employers in such countries as Japan, Australia, Netherlands, Belgium, New Zealand, Sweden, Ireland, and Mexico.[78] While discussions of sexual harassment cases often focus on the large awards granted by a court, there are other concerns for employers. Sexual harassment creates an unpleasant work environment for organization members and undermines their ability to perform their job. But just what is sexual harassment?

Sexual harassment can be regarded as any unwanted activity of a sexual nature that affects an individual's employment. It can occur between members of the opposite or of the same sex, between employees of the organization, or involve an employee and a nonemployee.[79] Although such an activity was generally protected under Title VII (sex discrimination), in recent years this problem has gained more recognition. By most accounts, prior to the mid-1980s this problem was generally viewed as an isolated incident, with the individual committing the act being solely responsible (if at all) for his or her actions.[80] By the beginning of the new millennium, however, charges of sexual harassment continue to appear in the headlines on an almost regular basis.

Much of the problem associated with sexual harassment is determining what constitutes this illegal behavior. In 1993, the EEOC cited three situations in which sexual harassment can occur. These are instances where verbal or physical conduct toward an individual (1) creates an intimidating, offensive, or hostile environment; (2) unreasonably interferes with an individual's work; or (3) adversely affects an employee's employment opportunities.

For many organizations, it's the offensive or hostile environment issue that is problematic.[81] Just what constitutes such an environment? Challenging hostile environment situations gained much support from the Supreme Court case of *Meritor Savings Bank v. Vinson*.[82] This case stemmed from a situation in which Ms. Vinson initially refused the sexual advances of her boss. However, out of fear of reprisal, she ultimately conceded. But according to court records, it did not stop there. Vinson's boss continued to hassle Vinson, subjecting her to severe hostility, which affected her job performance.[83] In addition to supporting hostile environment claims, the *Meritor* case also identified employer liability: that is, in sexual harassment cases, an organization can be held liable for sexual harassment actions by its management team, employees, and even customers![84]

Although the *Meritor* case has implications for organizations, how do organizational members determine if something is offensive? For instance, does sexually explicit language in the office create a hostile environment? How about off-color jokes or pictures of women totally undressed? The answer is: it could! It depends on the people in the organization and the environment in which they work. What does this tell us? The point here is that we all must be attuned to what makes fellow employees uncomfortable—and if we don't know, then we should ask! Organizational success entering the new millennium will, in part, reflect how sensitive each employee is toward another in the company.[85] At DuPont, for example, the corporate culture and diversity programs are designed to eliminate sexual harassment through awareness and respect for all individuals.[86] This means understanding one another and, most importantly, respecting others' rights. Similar programs exist at Federal Express, General Mills, and Levi-Strauss.

If sexual harassment carries with it potential costs to the organization, what can a company do to protect itself (see HRM Skill, p. 84)?[87] The courts want to know two things—did the organization know about, or should it have known about, the alleged behavior; and what did management do to stop it? With the number and dollar amounts of the awards against organizations today, there is even greater need for management to educate all employees on sexual harassment matters and have mechanisms available to monitor employees (see Workplace Issues). Furthermore, "victims" no longer have to prove that their psychological well-being is seriously affected. The Supreme Court ruled in 1993 in the case of *Harris v. Forklift Systems, Inc.* "that victims do not have to suffer substantial mental distress in order to be awarded jury awards."[88]

Furthermore, in June 1998, the Supreme Court ruled that sexual harassment may have occurred even if the employee had not experienced any "negative" job repercussions.[89] In this case, Kimberly Ellerth, a marketing assistant at Burlington Industries, filed harassment charges against her boss because he "touched her, suggested she wear shorter skirts, and told her during a business trip that he could make her job 'very hard or very easy.'" When Ellerth refused, the harasser never "punished" her; in fact, Kimberly even received a promotion during the time the harassment was ongoing. What the Supreme Court's decision in this case indicates is that "harassment is defined by the ugly behavior of the manager, not by what happened to the worker subsequently."[90]

Finally, whenever involved in a sexual harassment matter, one must remember that the harasser may have rights, too.[91] This means that no action should be taken against someone until a thorough investigation has been conducted. Furthermore, the results of the investigation should be reviewed by an independent and objective individual before any action against the alleged

IF IT'S OFFENSIVE . . .

SEXUALLY EXPLICIT LANGUAGE. SEXUAL JOKING. SEXUALLY suggestive remarks. Inappropriate touching. Displaying a questionable pin-up photo or drawing. Some employees would find some or all behaviors on that list offensive. The fact that some people are offended by some or all of the above can place those actions squarely under the heading of "sexual harassment."

While offering or demanding sexual favors in return for rewards in the workplace clearly qualifies as sexual harassment or sex discrimination, there's a harder-to-recognize kind of harassment defined by the Equal Employment Opportunity Commission; that type of sexual harassment is conduct which "has the purpose or effect of unreasonably interfering with another employee's job performance or creating an intimidating, hostile or offensive work environment." Title 7 of the 1964 Civil Rights Act prohibits sexual harassment. Any behavior that may be perceived as harassment is prohibited. Suppose someone is told that keeping his or her job, or getting a raise or plum assignment, depends on submitting to sexual advances or granting sexual favors; that's sexual harassment, pure and simple.

If it happens to you, report it immediately—to the ethics hot line, to your supervisor, or to another supervisor. The reverse situation—offering sexual favors to get a job, an assignment, or a raise—can also be sexual harassment. When an employee gains job advantages in exchange for sex, there is discrimination against other employees; that's illegal conduct as well. Everyone loses.

A hostile work environment is one where sexual conduct between coworkers is offensive to either one of them, or to an observer, and that may include the actions on our list above. Sexual harassment can have a number of negative effects on employees and on the company. It can lead to reduced productivity. An employee trapped in work areas where sexual harassment is tolerated is under stress and becomes less productive. Customers may gain an unfavorable impression of the company's professionalism if they see harassment being tolerated. Supervisors or coworkers can report sexual harassment they observe, resulting in an investigation and discipline of those involved. Knowing what is and what is not acceptable and being sensitive to others' feelings is extremely important.

But what if you feel you are being harassed? A word to the offender might be enough. That person may be unaware of your sensitivity to the behavior. If that doesn't work, report the behavior to your supervisor or another manager, to labor or employee relations, or to the president of the company if you have to.

Education and training play an important role in cultivating an environment free of harassment. Managers throughout many companies have received training in identifying and eliminating sexual harassment problems. Additional training in larger organizations is usually offered by human resources. Some people may fear that their complaints will be ignored or that reporting an incident will become a negative in their work record. Neither is the case. Companies should take all complaints of sexual harassment seriously and investigate each thoroughly and discreetly. Both sides are considered, and disciplinary action is often taken against proven violators, as well as those who make false accusations.

---

harasser is taken. Even then, the harasser should be given an opportunity to respond to the allegation, and have a disciplinary hearing if desired. Additionally, an avenue for appeal should also exist for the alleged harasser—an appeal heard by someone in a higher level of management who is not associated with the case.

The Glass Ceiling Initiative

In decades past, many jobs were formally viewed as being male- or female-oriented. For example, positions such as librarian, nurse, and elementary schoolteacher were considered typical jobs for women; by contrast, police officers, truck drivers, and top management positions were regarded as the domain of men. Historically, this attitude resulted in the traditional female-oriented jobs paying significantly less than the male-oriented positions. This differentiation led to concerns over gender-based pay systems, commonly referred to as the **comparable worth** issue. For instance, a nurse may be judged to have a comparable job to

Comparable Worth Equal pay for similar jobs, jobs similar in skills, responsibility, working conditions, and effort.

that of a police officer. Both must be trained, both are licensed to practice, both work under stressful conditions, and both must exhibit high levels of effort. But they are not typically paid the same; male-dominated jobs have traditionally been paid more than female-oriented jobs. Under comparable worth, estimates of the importance of each job are used in determining and equating pay structures. While the 1963 Equal Pay Act requires that workers doing essentially the same work must initially be paid the same wage (later wage differences may exist due to performance, seniority, merit systems, and the like), the act is not directly applicable to comparable worth. Comparable worth proponents want to take the Equal Pay Act one step further. Under such an arrangement, factors present in each job (e.g., skills, responsibilities, working conditions, effort) are evaluated. A pay structure is based solely on the presence of such factors on the job. The result is that dissimilar jobs equivalent in terms of skills, knowledge, and abilities are paid similarly.

The point of the comparable worth issue revolves around the economic worth of jobs to employers. If jobs are similar, even though they involve different occupations, why shouldn't they be paid the same? The concern here is one of pay disparities: women still earn less than men. While the disparity is lessening, the fact remains that although significant progress has been made in terms of affirmative action for women, it appears they have reached a plateau in the organization. That is, while laws prohibit organizations from keeping qualified women out of high-paying positions, there appears to be a "glass ceiling" holding them down.

The **glass ceiling** is a term used to reflect why women and minorities aren't more widely represented at the top of today's organizations. The glass ceiling is not, however, synonymous with "classic" discrimination. Rather, the glass ceiling, according to the Glass Ceiling Commission, is indicative of "institutional and psychological practices, and the limited advancement and mobility of men and women of diverse racial and ethnic backgrounds."[92] It appears that while significant gains have been made by minorities and women in gaining entry to organizations, less than 12 percent of senior management positions are held by women and minorities.[93] Although the percentage is low, around the globe it's even worse. For example, in Europe, women hold approximately 5 percent of the top slots; in Japan and Germany, fewer than 3 percent of women are top executives.[94]

To begin to correct this invisible barrier, the OFCCP is expanding its audit compliance reviews. In these reviews, the auditors look to see if government contractors do indeed have training and development programs operating to provide career growth to the affected groups. Should these be lacking, the OFCCP may take legal action to ensure compliance. For example, as a result of an audit of the Coca-Cola Company, several violations were noted. Consequently, Coke, while admitting no wrongdoing, made several internal changes to improve the career opportunities of both women and minorities.[95] Beyond those organizations covered under the OFCCP, several—like Deloitte & Touche—are implementing policies and changing the organization's culture to enhance opportunities for women and minorities.[96] With such practices over the past few years, for example, more than 7 million women are now in "full-time executive, administrative, or managerial positions."[97] Similar progress for minorities has been noted, too.[98]

Glass Ceiling   The invisible barrier that blocks females and minorities from ascending into upper levels of an organization.

The glass ceiling is being smashed. Women such as Carly Fiorina, CEO of Hewlett-Packard, have broken through this invisible barrier and are seeing opportunities for women at the very top of organizations becoming a reality. Fiorina's position at H-P is the highest level ever held by a woman at a Dow 30 company.

HANDLING SEXUAL HARASSMENT MATTERS

ABOUT THE SKILL: SEXUAL HARASSMENT is a major issue for today's organizations. Given the rulings at all court levels, there are a number of things organizations can do to limit their liability. Below are recommended steps that should be taken.[99]

1. *Issue a sexual harassment policy describing what constitutes sexual harassment and what is inappropriate behavior.* Just stating that sexual harassment is unacceptable at your organization is not enough. In this policy, specific behaviors that are unacceptable must be identified. The more explicit these unacceptable behaviors, the less chance of misinterpretation later on.

2. *Institute a procedure (or link to an existing one) to investigate sexual harassment charges.* Employees, as well as the courts, need to understand what avenue is available for an employee to levy a complaint. This too, should be clearly stated in the policy and widely disseminated to employees.

3. *Inform all employees of the sexual harassment policy.* Educate these employees (via training) about the policy and how it will be enforced. Don't assume that the policy will convey the information simply because it is a policy. It must be effectively communicated to all employees. Some training may be required to help in this understanding.

4. *Train management personnel in how to deal with sexual harassment charges and in what responsibility they have to the individual and the organization.* Poor supervisory practices in this area can open the company up to a tremendous liability. Managers must be trained in how to recognize signs of sexual harassment and where to go to help the victim. Because of the magnitude of the issue, a manager's performance evaluation should reinforce this competency.

5. *Investigate all sexual harassment charges immediately.* All means *all* — even those that you suspect are invalid. You must give each charge of sexual harassment your attention and investigate it by searching for clues, witnesses, and so on. Investigating the charge is also consistent with our societal view of justice. Remember, the alleged harasser also has rights. These, too, must be protected by giving the individual the opportunity to respond. You may also want to have an objective party review the data before implementing your decision.

6. *Take corrective action as necessary.* Discipline those doing the harassing and "make whole" the harassed individual. If you find that the charge can be substantiated, you must take some corrective action, including up to dismissing the individual. If the punishment does not fit the crime, you may be reinforcing or condoning the behavior. The harassed individual should also be given whatever was taken away. For example, if the sexual behavior led to an individual's resignation, making the person whole would mean reinstatement, with full back pay and benefits.

7. *Continue to follow up on the matter to ensure that no further harassment occurs or that retaliation does not occur.* One of the concerns that individuals have in coming forward with sexual harassment charges is that there may be some retaliation against them — especially if the harasser has been disciplined. You must continue to observe what is affecting these individuals — through follow-up conversations with them.

8. *Periodically review turnover situations to determine if a potential problem may be arising.* (This may be EEO audits, exit interviews, and the like.) There may be a wealth of information at your disposal that may indicate a problem. For example, if only females are resigning in a particular department, that may indicate that a serious problem exists. Pay attention to your regular reports and search for trends that may be indicated.

9. *Don't forget to privately recognize individuals who bring these matters forward.* Without their courageous effort, the organization might have been faced with tremendous liability. These individuals took a risk in coming forward. You should show your appreciation for that risk. Besides, if others know that such risk is worthwhile, they may feel more comfortable in coming to you when any type of problem exists.

HRM WORKSHOP

SUMMARY

(This summary relates to the Learning Outcomes identified on p. 60.)

After reading this chapter, you should be able to:

1. **Identify the groups protected under the Civil Rights Act of 1964, Title VII.** The Equal Employment Opportunity Act of 1972 is an important amendment to the Civil Rights Act of 1964, as it granted the EEOC enforcement powers to police the provisions of the Act. The Civil Rights Act of 1964, Title VII, gives individuals protection on the basis of race, color, religion, sex, and national origin. In addition to those protected under the 1964 Act, amendments to the Act, as well as subsequent legislation, give protection to the disabled, veterans, and individuals over age 40. In addition, state laws may supplement this list and include categories like marital status.

2. **Discuss the importance of the Equal Employment Opportunities Act of 1972.** The Equal Employment Opportunity Act of 1972 is an important amendment to the Civil Rights Act of 1964 as it granted the EEOC enforcement powers to police the provisions of the Act.

3. **Describe affirmative action plans.** Affirmative action plans are good-faith efforts by organizations to actively recruit and hire protected group members, and to show measurable results. Such plans are voluntary actions by an organization.

4. **Define what is meant by the terms *adverse impact, adverse treatment*, and *protected group members*.** An adverse impact is any consequence of employment that results in a disparate rate of selection, promotion, or termination of protected group members. Adverse treatment occurs when members of a protected group receive different treatment than other employees. A protected group member is any individual who is afforded protection under discrimination laws.

5. **Identify the important components of the Americans with Disabilities Act of 1990.** The Americans with Disabilities Act of 1990 provides employment protection for individuals who have qualified disabilities. The Act also requires organizations to make reasonable accommodations to provide qualified individuals access to the job.

6. **Explain the coverage of the Family and Medical Leave Act of 1993.** The Family and Medical Leave Act grants up to 12 weeks of unpaid leave for family or medical matters. Fetal protection laws were overturned because they created an adverse impact for women.

7. **Discuss how a business can protect itself from discrimination charges.** A business can protect itself from discrimination charges first by having HRM practices that do not adversely affect protected groups, through supported claims of job relatedness, bonafide occupational qualifications, or a valid seniority system.

8. **Specify the HRM importance of the *Griggs v. Duke Power* case.** *Griggs v. Duke Power* was one of the most important Supreme Court rulings as it pertains to EEO. Based on this case, items used to screen applicants had to be related to the job. Additionally, post-*Griggs*, the burden was on the employer to prove discrimination did not occur.

9. **Define what constitutes sexual harassment in today's organizations.** Sexual harassment is a serious problem existing in today's enterprises. Sexual harassment is defined as any verbal or physical conduct toward an individual that (1) creates an intimidating, offensive, or hostile environment; (2) unreasonably interferes with an individual's work; or (3) adversely affects an employee's employment opportunities.

10. **Discuss what is meant by the term *glass ceiling*.** The glass ceiling is an invisible barrier existing in today's organizations that is keeping minorities and women from ascending to higher levels in the workplace.

DEMONSTRATING COMPREHENSION: *Questions for Review and Discussion*

1. What is the Civil Rights Act of 1964 and who does it protect?
2. What are the *Griggs v. Duke Power* implications for HRM?
3. What is an adverse impact? How does it differ from adverse treatment?
4. What is meant by reasonable accommodation as it pertains to the Americans with Disabilities Act of 1990?
5. What is "business necessity" as it applies to equal employment opportunity? How can HRM provide supporting documentation for business necessity?
6. Identify and explain how organizations can use BFOQs or seniority systems to defend charges of discrimination.
7. What is sexual harassment? Identify and describe the three elements which may constitute sexual harassment.
8. "Affirmative action does not work. When you're hired

under an affirmative action program, you're automatically labeled as such and are rarely viewed for the value that you can bring to an organization." Do you agree or disagree with the statement? Defend your position.

9. What are the arguments for a "glass ceiling" existing in today's organizations?

10. "Sexual harassment occurs between two people only. The company should not be held liable for the actions of a few wayward supervisors." Do you agree or disagree with this statement? Explain.

CASE APPLICATION: *TEAM FUN!*

Tony, the new Director of Human Resources, and Edna, the Compensation and Benefits Manager, are hanging employment legislation posters in RETREAT, the TEAM FUN! employee cafeteria. Edna offers, "I remember some woman who applied for a job to advertise men's baseball gear, and sued when she didn't get the job. The EEOC said she had no case. A couple of years ago we moved Fred from fitness demos to stock management because he couldn't do the treadmill or lift the big weights anymore. There was talk about an age discrimination case because he was 57, but that never went anywhere."

Tony asks, "Do you realize that all of the warehouse workers are male and all the RETREAT workers are female?"

Edna replies, "What's your point?" Tony waves his hand at the EEOC information they displayed. Edna shrugs, "This is the best job I ever had. If you ask anyone else who works here, they will say the same thing."

Questions:

1. What is the probable defense for the baseball gear job? (BFOQ, 4/5 rule, glass ceiling) Explain.
2. Why didn't Fred's age discrimination case go anywhere?
3. IS TEAM FUN! open to discrimination charges in other areas?
4. What should be done to protect TEAM FUN! from discrimination charges?

WORKING WITH A TEAM: *What's Your Perception?*

Could these situations demonstrate sexual harassment or prohibitive behaviors? Answer *true* or *false* to each question. Make whatever assumptions you need to make to form your opinion. Form into groups of three or four students and discuss each of your responses. Where differences exist, come to some consensus on the situation. Then, you can look at the footnote for suggested responses.[100]

1. A female supervisor frequently praises the work of a highly competent male employee.
2. A male employee prominently posts a centerfold from a female pornographic magazine.
3. A female employee voluntarily accepts a date with her male supervisor.
4. A male employee is given favored work assignments in exchange for arranging dates for his boss.
5. A female employee is offered a job promotion in exchange for sex.
6. A client pressures a female salesperson for dates and sex-

ual favors in exchange for a large purchase.

7. A female requests that her male assistant stay in her hotel room to save on expenses while out of town at a conference and holds acceptance as a job condition for continued employment.
8. A male has asked two female coworkers to stop embarrassing him by telling jokes of a sexual nature and sharing their sexual fantasies, but they continue, telling him a "real man wouldn't be embarrassed."
9. Although he has shared with his coworker that rubbing his shoulders and arms, calling him "Babe" in front of his coworkers, and pinching him is offensive, she continues to touch him in a way that makes him feel uncomfortable.
10. Al tells Marge an offensive joke, but when Marge says "Al, I don't appreciate your nasty jokes," Al responds, "I'm sorry, Marge, you're right, I shouldn't have told that one at work."

ENHANCING YOUR WRITING SKILLS

1. Several Supreme Court cases relating to sexual harassment were decided in the late 1990s. Visit the Supreme Court's web site <http://www.supremecourtus.gov> and research these cases. Then provide a three- to five-page writeup regarding the implications these cases had on same-sex harassment, responsibilities of management in

sexual harassment matters, and the determination of harassment even when an implied threat is not carried out.

2. Contact your local EEO office (may be called Human Rights Commission or Fair Employment Practice Agencies). Determine what equal employment opportunity laws exist in your state that go beyond those required

under federal law. Provide a two- to three-page writeup of your findings.
3. Visit your college's EEO/Affirmative Action officer. Find out what specific EEO requirements exist on your campus affecting students, faculty, and staff in matters such as recruiting, promotion, sexual harassment, and so on. Provide a two- to three-page writeup of your findings.

www.wiley.com/college/decenzo

$\mathcal{E}$NDNOTES

1. This vignette based on Joann Muller, "Ford: The High Cost of Harassment," *Business Week* (November 15, 1999), pp. 94–96; and Jeffrey Ball, "Judge Says Women at Two Ford Plants Can Proceed with Harassment Lawsuit," *Wall Street Journal* (October 20, 1999), p. B-11.
2. Jess Bravin, "Courts Open Alternative Route to Extend Job-Bias Laws to Homosexuals," *Wall Street Journal* (September 22, 2000), p. B-1; and Society of Human Resource Management, "Sexual Orientation Complaints Are Small Part of Dockets in 11 States with Gay Rights Laws," *BNA Labor Report* (January 2000), p. 1. The eleven states are California, Connecticut, Hawaii, Massachusetts, Minnesota, Nevada, New Hampshire, New Jersey, Rhode Island, Vermont, and Wisconsin. The District of Columbia also has similar legislation.
3. SIECUS, "World Discrimination: Laws and Policies Based on Sexual Orientation," *Fact Sheet* (2000), www.siecus.org/ pubs/fact/fact0014.html, pp. 1–5. The countries include Canada, Denmark, Finland, France, Iceland, Ireland, Israel, The Netherlands, New Zealand, Norway, Slovenia, South Africa, Spain, and Sweden.
4. Cases filed under this act could be heard by a jury. Such opportunity was unavailable under the Civil Rights Act of 1964.
5. Under the Civil Rights Act of 1964, the only remedy is back pay.
6. *Patterson v. McLean Credit Union,* 87 U.S. Supreme Court, 107 (1989).
7. Ibid.
8. Another stipulation is receiving $50,000 or more of government monies. Thus, a two-person operation that has a government contract for more than $50,000 is bound by Title VII.
9. See, for example, Arthur P. Brief, Robert T. Buttram, Robin M. Reisenstein, S. Douglas Pugh, Jodi D. Callahan, Richard L. McCline, and Joel B. Vaslow, "Beyond Good Intentions: The Next Steps Toward Racial Equality in the American Workplace," *Academy of Management Executive,* Vol. 11, No. 4 (November 1997), pp. 59–71.
10. *Washington Metropolitan Police Department v. Davis,* 422 U.S. Supreme Court, 229 (1976).
11. The EEOA of 1972 amended Title VII in several ways, including expanding the definition of employer to include state and local government agencies and educational institutions; reduced the minimum number of employees in private sector organizations from 25 to 15; and gave more power to the EEOC to file suit against alleged violators of Title VII.
12. R. Roosevelt Thomas, Jr., "From Affirmative Action to Affirming Diversity," *Harvard Business Review* (March–April 1990), p. 107.
13. See, for example, Marian N. Ruderman, "Affirmative Action: Does It Really Work?" *Academy of Management Executive,* Vol. 10, No. 3 (November 1996), pp 64–66.
14. For an interesting view on this subject, see Alison M. Konrad and Frank Linnehan, "Formalized HRM Structures: Coordinating Equal Employment Opportunity or Concealing Organizational Practices," *Academy of Management Journal,* Vol. 38, No. 3 (Fall 1995), pp. 787–820.
15. See, for instance, Harry Holzer and David Neumark, "Assessing Affirmative Action," *Journal of Economic Literature* (September 2000), pp. 483-568; and Robert J. Grossman, "Is Diversity Working?" *HRMagazine* (March 2000), pp. 46–50.
16. Thomas Sowell, "The 'Q' Word," *Forbes* (April 10, 1995), p. 61.
17. Steven V. Roberts, "Affirmative Action on the Edge," *U.S. News & World Report* (February 13, 1995), pp. 32–38.
18. Ibid.; and Dinesh D'Souza, "Damned If You Do, Damned If You Don't," *Forbes* (September 25, 1995), pp. 50–56.
19. See, for example, Bill McConnell, "Stay or No Stay, EEO's Here to Stay," *Broadcasting & Cable* (April 17, 2000), p. 22; Arthur A. Fletcher, "Business and Race: Only Halfway There," *Fortune* (March 6, 2000), pp. F-76 – F-78; Jonathan Kaufam, "White Men Shake Off That Losing Feeling on Affirmative Action," *Wall Street Journal* (September 5, 1996), p. A-1; and James P. Pinkerton, "Why Affirmative Action Won't Die," *Fortune* (November 13, 1995), p. 191.
20. Adverse impact refers to an employment practice that results in a disparate selection, promotion, or firing of a class of protected group members, whereas adverse treatment affects one or more individuals.
21. ADEA is afforded to all individuals age 40 and older who are employed in organizations with 20 or more employees.
22. Executive and high policy-making employees of an organization may still be required to retire. Three conditions must be met, however. These are as follows: they are at least 65 years of age, will receive a pension from the organization of at least $44,000, and have been in

this executive or high policy-making position for the previous two years.

23. Equal Employment Opportunity Commission, "Employers and Other Entities Covered by EEO Laws," http://www.eeoc.gov.facts/qanda.html (December 10, 1998).

24. Ray Scippa, "Retired Pilots Take to the Skies—Again," *Profiles* (*Continental Airlines* magazine) (October 1995), p. 65.

25. The age 60 issue is currently being debated. Questions regarding on whom medical research was conducted (e.g., private pilots, not commercial ones) have raised many concerns. However, at this time, mandatory retirement for pilots attaining age 60 is still in force.

26. See *Price v. Maryland Casualty Co.,* 561 F.2d 609, 612 (C.A. 5th Cir., 1977).

27. See, for instance, Charles J. Muhl, "Preferential Treatment and Pregnancy," *Monthly Labor Review* (January 1999), pp. 48–49; Lynn Atkinson, "No Bias in Treating Work and Non-Work Illnesses Differently," *HR Focus* (July 1998), p. 15; and D. Diane Hatch and James E. Hall, "Pregnancy Does Not Require Preferential Treatment," *Workforce* (July 1998), p. 83.

28. This act defines a disability as any condition that curtails one or more major life activities for an individual.

29. Stephen P. Sonnenberg, "Mental Disabilities in the Workplace," *Workforce* (June 2000), pp. 142–146; and Wray Herbert, "Troubled at Work," *U.S. News & World Report* (February 9, 1998), pp. 62–64.

30. "Accommodation Will Be the Next ADA Issue," *HR Focus* (March 2000), p. 2.

31. An undue hardship under the Americans with Disabilities Act refers to a situation in which an organization, in making accommodations, would incur significant expenses or difficulties that would severely impact the organization's finances or its operations.

32. Robert LaGow, "Supreme Court Says HIV-Infection Is a Disability under ADA," *HR News* (August 1998), p. 14.

33. Employees covered under the FMLA are individuals who have worked for an employer for at least 1250 hours in the previous 12-month period.

34. The Department of Labor has defined just what counts toward the 50-employee threshold. Specifically, temporary employees and those on permanent layoff do not count toward the 50 minimum. Furthermore, under certain circumstances, and in compliance with company policy, the employee or the employer may substitute paid personal leave or accrued vacation time for the unpaid leave. The paid leave portion of the Act, however, has several limitations and qualifiers. See also "DOL Regs Requiring Designation of FMLA Leave Are Invalid," *HR Focus* (September 2000), p. 2.

35. Susan E. Long, "Employee on FMLA Leave Must Be Offered Similar Position," *HR Focus* (April 1999), p. 3.

36. See, for instance, Jane Waldfogel, "Family Leave Coverage in the 1990s," *Monthly Labor Review* (October 1999), pp. 13–21.

37. Bill Leonard, "FMLA Does Create Hardships for Employers," *HRMagazine* (August 2000), p. 28; and Milton Zall, "The Family and Medical Leave Act: An Employer Perspective," *Strategic Finance* (February 2000), pp. 46–

50; and "FMLA Does Create Hardships for Employers," *HRMagazine* (August 2000), p. 28.

38. Chicago Legal Net, "What Is a Serious Health Condition under FMLA?" www.chicagolegalnet.com/FMLA.htm (1998); and "Ear Infection Not a Serious Health Condition under FMLA," *HR News* (March 1995), p. 5.

39. Based on *Seidle v. Provident Mutual Life Insurance Co.* (CA No. 94-3306 E.D. Penn., 12/19/94).

40. For example, with 15–100 employees, the maximum damage award is $50,000; 101–200 employees, $100,000; 201–500 employees, $200,000; and more than 500 employees, $300,000. See Barbara Gutek, "Workplace Sexual Harassment Law: Principles, Landmark Devlopments, and Framework for Effective Risk Management," *Personnel Psychology* (Autumn 2000), p. 746.

41. Jim Meade, "Desktop Employment Law: An HR Attorney in Your PC," *HRMagazine* (October 1999), p. 116.

42. Lynn Monaco, "Harassment CD," *Training and Development* (January 2000), p. 59.

43. Michael A. Verespej, "Zero Tolerance," *Industry Week* (January 6, 1997), pp. 24–28.

44. *Federal Register,* pp. 38, 290.

45. *Connecticut v. Teal,* U.S. Supreme Court, 102, Docket No. 2525 (1982).

46. We must note here that the 4/5ths rule, as established, does not recognize specific individuals' requirements: That is, a minority could be any group. For example, when airlines hired only females as flight attendants, males were the minority.

47. *McDonnell-Douglas Corp. v. Green,* 411 U.S. 792, 80 (U.S. 1973).

48. Such a case is frequently referred to as a *prima facie* case. In such a situation, there is enough evidence to support the charge, and will be considered sufficient evidence unless refuted by the organization.

49. *McDonnell-Douglas Corp. v. Green,* 411 U.S. 792, 80 (U.S. 1973).

50. Jillian B. Berman, "Defining the 'Essence of the Business': An Analysis of Title VII's Privacy Controls After Johnson Controls," *University of Chicago Law Review* (Summer 2000), p. 749.

51. Reasonable accommodation here is a difficult area not to support. If through the use of personal leave an individual can be accommodated, then no BFOQ exists. Also, the courts may view how an enterprise treats traditional Christian holidays in viewing reasonable accommodation. See Tracey I. Levy, "Religion in the Workplace," *Management Review* (February 2000), pp. 38–40.

52. See, for example, Karen C. Cash, George R. Gray, and Sally A. Rood, "A Framework for Accommodating Religion and Spirituality in the Workplace: Executive Commentary," *Academy of Management Executive* (August 2000), pp. 124–134; and Peter J. Petesch, "Are the Newest ADA Guidelines Reasonable?" *HRMagazine* (June 1999), pp. 54–58.

53. Maureen Minehan, "Time to Promote Religious Tolerance," *HRMagazine* (January 1996), p. 144.

54. "FedEx Faces Lawsuit Citing Religious Bias Against an Ex-Driver," *Wall Street Journal* (March 20, 2000), p. B-17.

55. A disparate impact occurs when an HRM practice eliminates a group of individuals from job considerations. Dis-

parate treatment exists when an HRM practice eliminates an individual from employment consideration.

56. *Albemarle Paper Company v. Moody,* 422 U.S. Supreme Court (U.S. 1975).

57. *Wards Cove Packing Co., Inc., v. Atonio,* U.S. Supreme Court, Docket No. 87-1387, June 5, 1989.

58. *Bakke v. Regents of the University of California,* 438 U.S. 265 (1978).

59. Terence J. Pell, "Does Diversity Justify Quotas? The Courts Say No," *Wall Street Journal* (November 24, 1998), p. A22.

60. *Firefighters Local 1784 v. Stotts,* 467 Supreme Court, 561 (1984).

61. *Wyant v. Jackson Board of Education,* 106 Supreme Court, 842 (1986).

62. Jana Howard Carey and Larry R. Seegull, "Beware the Native Tongue: National Origin and English-Only Rules," *HR Legal Report* (Spring 1995), pp. 1–4.

63. See, for instance, U.S. Equal Employment Opportunity Commission, "EEOC Reaches Landmark 'English-Only' Settlement: Chicago Manufacturer to Pay over $190,000 to Hispanic Workers," www.eeoc.gov/press/9-1-00.html (September 1, 2000), pp. 1–2; and Lisa Girion, "13 Phone Operators Win Record $709,284 in English-Only Suit," *Los Angeles Times* (September 20, 2000), p. C-1.

64. It is important to note that individuals are not required to file charges against the organization through the EEOC. They may, at their discretion, use a state agency (like a Human Rights Commission) or proceed on their own. However, the outcomes of these other avenues are not binding to the EEOC. Additionally, charges may be filed by the individual, his or her representative (e.g., union), or the EEOC itself.

65. We'll look at the Equal Pay Act in Chapter 11 as it relates to compensation plans.

66. Under the Americans with Disabilities Act, the EEOC enforces Titles I and V of the Act.

67. In *EEOC v. Commercial Office Products,* U.S. Supreme Court Docket No. 86-1696 (1988), the Court ruled that if a work-sharing arrangement exists between the EEOC and a state or local agency, then the time limit increases to 300 days.

68. Adapted from the 1981 *Guidebook to Fair Employment Practices,* pp. 123–161; unpublished manuscript by Stanley Mazaroff, Esquire, "A Management Guide to Responding to a Charge of Discrimination Filed with the EEOC" (Baltimore, MD: Venable, Baetjer, and Howard, Attorneys-at-Law, 1994), p. 1. It should also be noted that the EEOC automatically refers all claims to the appropriate state agency. If, however, the state agency defers it back to the EEOC, it will proceed with the case. See also Maria Greco Danaher, "EEOC Allowed to Pursue Discrimination Claim on Behalf of Pregnant Nurse," *HR News* (October 2000), p. 6.

69. Bureau of National Affairs, "EEOC Identifies Enforcement Strategies and Priorities Covering the Next Five Years," *Daily Labor Report* (September 2000), pp. 1–3; and Jess Bravin, "For This First-Grader, Cutting Red Tape Just Wouldn't Be Fair Play," *Wall Street Journal* (July 13, 2000), p. B-1.

70. Ibid.

71. Ibid., p. 122; Michael A. Verespej, "Sidestepping Court Costs," *Industry Week* (February 2, 1998), pp. 68–72; and Edward R. Silverman, "He Who Arbitrates," *Working Woman* (October 1997), p. 71.

72. "Title VII Does Bar Post-Employment Retaliation," *HR News* (August 1996), p. 26.

73. Under Section 503 of the Vocational Rehabilitation Act, those organizations that have a contract or subcontract in the amount of $2,500 must have affirmative action plans to hire the disabled. For the Vietnam Veterans Readjustment Act, the amount is $10,000.

74. U.S. Equal Employment Opportunity Commission, "Sexual Harassment Charges EEOC and FEPAs Combines: FY 1992–FY 1999," EEOC (January 12, 2000) http://www.eeoc.gov/stats/harass.html; and Gerald E. Calvasina, Richard V. Calvasina, and Eugene J. Calvasina, "Management and the EEOC," *Business Horizons* (July–August 2000), p. 3.

75. Norman F. Foy, "Sexual Harassment Can Threaten Your Bottom Line," *Strategic Finance* (August 2000), pp. 56–57.

76. "Federal Monitors Find Illinois Mitsubishi Unit Eradicating Harassment," *Wall Street Journal* (September 7, 2000), p. A-8.

77. Liberty J. Munson, Charles Hulin, and Fritz Drasgow, "Longitudinal Analysis of Dispositional Influences and Sexual Harassment: Effects on Job and Psychological Outcomes," *Personnel Psychology* (Spring 2000), p. 21; and "Cost of Sexual Harassment in the U.S.," *Manpower Argus* (January 1997), p. 5.

78. See, for instance, Gerald L. Maatman, Jr., "A Global View of Sexual Harassment," *HR Magazine* (July 2000), pp. 151–158; Glenda Strachan and Suzanne Jamieson, "Equal Opportunity in Australia in the 1990s," *New Zealand Journal of Industrial Relations* (October 1999), p. 319; "Mexico: Sexual Harassment in the Workplace," *Manpower Argus* (March 1997), p. 8; Susan Webb, *The Webb Report: A Newsletter on Sexual Harassment* (Seattle, WA: Premier Publishing, Ltd., January 1994), pp. 4–7, and (April 1994), pp. 2–5.

79. Adam Jack Morrell, "Non-Employee Harassment," *Legal Report* (January–February 2000), p. 1.

80. While the male gender was referred to here, it is important to note that sexual harassment may involve either sex sexually harassing another or the same sex harassing another individual. (See, for instance, *Oncale v. Sundowner Offshore Service, Inc.,* 118 S. Ct. 998.)

81. Richard L. Wiener and Linda E. Hurt, "How Do People Evaluate Social Sexual Conduct at Work? A Psychological Model," *Journal of Applied Psychology* (February 2000), p. 75.

82. *Meritor Savings Bank v. Vinson,* U.S. Supreme Court 106, Docket No. 2399 (1986).

83. Robert D. Lee and Paul S. Greenlaw, "Employer Liability for Employee Sexual Harassment: A Judicial Policy-Making Study," *Public Administration Review* (March–April 2000), p. 127.

84. Ibid. See also Diana L. Deadrick, Scott W. Kezman, and Bruce McAfee, "Harassment by Nonemployees: How

Should Employers Respond?" *HRMagazine* (December 1996), p. 108; Frank Clancy, "When Customer Service Crosses the Line," *Working Woman* (December 1994), pp. 36–39; 77.

85. Anne Field, "Trial by Hire," *Working Woman* (April 1998), p. 66.

86. "You and DuPont: Diversity," DuPont Company Documents (1999–2000); www.dupont.com/careers/you/diverse.html; and "DuPont Announces 2000 Dr. Martin Luther King, Jr., Days of Celebration," DuPont Company Documents (January 11, 2000), www.dupont.com/corp/whats-news/releases/00/001111.html.

87. See Jonathan A. Segal, "The Catch-22s of Remedying Sexual Harassment Complaints," *HRMagazine* (October 1997), pp. 111–117; Steven C. Bahls and Jane Easter Bahls, "Hands-Off Policy," *Entrepreneur* (July 1997), pp. 74–76; Jonathan A. Segal, "Where Are We Now?" *HRMagazine* (October 1996), pp. 69–73; Bruce McAfee and Diana L. Deadrick, "Teach Employees to Just Say No," *HRMagazine* (February 1996), pp. 86–89; Gerald D. Bloch, "Avoiding Liability for Sexual Harassment," *HRMagazine* (April 1995), pp. 91–97; and Jonathan A. Segal, "Stop Making Plaintiffs' Lawyers Rich," *HRMagazine* (April 1995), pp. 31–35. Also, it should be noted here that under the Title VII and the Civil Rights Act of 1991, the maximum award that can be given, under the Federal Act, is $300,000. However, many cases are tried under state laws which permit unlimited punitive damages.

88. Anne Fisher, "After All This Time, Why Don't People Know What Sexual Harassment Means?" *Fortune* (January 12, 1998), p. 156; and *Harris v. Forklift Systems* (92-1168), 510 U.S. 17 (1993).

89. Aline Sullivan, "Harassment on Trial," *Working Woman* (June 1998), p. 18.

90. Milton Zall, "Workplace Harassment and Employer Liability," *Fleet Equipment* (January 2000), p. B-1; and Marianne Lavelle, "The New Rules of Sexual Harassment," *U.S. News and World Report* (July 6, 1998), pp. 30–31.

91. See, for instance, Peter W. Dorfman, Anthony T. Cobb, and Roxanne Cox, "Investigations of Sexual Harassment Allegations: Legal Means Fair—Or Does It?" *Human Resource Management* (Spring 2000), pp. 33–39.

92. Cornel University, School of Industrial and Labor Relations, Glass Ceiling Commission, "About the Glass Ceiling," *Glass Ceiling Commission* (2000), pp. 1–2.

93. Genaro C. Armas, "Glass Ceiling Shows Some Cracks," *Associated Press* (April 23, 2000), pp. 1–2; Michelle Conlin and Wendy Zellner, "The CEO Still Wears Wingtips," *Business Week* (November 22, 1999), pp. 89–90; and Belle Rose Ragins, Bickley Townsend, and Mary Mattis, "Gender Gap in the Executive Suite: CEOs and Female Executives Report on Breaking the Glass Ceiling," *Academy of Management Executive* (February 1998), pp. 28–42.

94. Colin James, "Breaking Glass?" *Far Eastern Economic Review* (September 28, 2000), p. 26; Janet Guyon, "The Global Glass Ceiling and Ten Women Who Broke Through It," *Fortune* (October 12, 1998), p. 102; "Female Executives Are Rare in Japan," *Manpower Argus* (November 1996), p. 3; and "Workplace Equality in Japan Still Faces Barriers," *Manpower Argus* (October 1996), p. 6.

95. "Federal Investigation into Coca-Cola Shifts to Pay-Bias Concerns," *Wall Street Journal* (June 16, 2000), p. B-8.

96. Charlene Marmer Solomon, "Cracks in the Glass Ceiling," *Workforce* (September 2000), pp. 86–94.

97. "Women Rise in Workplace But Wage Gap Continues," *Wall Street Journal* (April 25, 2000), p. A-12.

98. Robyn D. Clarke, "Has the Glass Ceiling Really Been Shattered?" *Black Enterprise* (February 2000), p. 145.

99. Adapted from Marshall H. Tanick, "No Rhyme for the 'Seinfeld' Firing," *National Law Journal* (August 18, 1997), p. A-19; Anne B. Fisher, "Sexual Harassment: What to Do," *Fortune* (August 23, 1993), pp. 84–88; Clifford M. Koen, Jr., "Sexual Harassment Claims Stem from a Hostile Work Environment," *Personnel Journal* (August 1990), pp. 97–98.

100. 1-false; 2-true; 3-false; 4-true; 5-true; 6-true; 7-true; 8-true; 9-true; and 10-false.

4

EMPLOYEE RIGHTS

LEARNING OUTCOMES

AFTER READING THIS CHAPTER, YOU WILL BE ABLE TO:

1. Explain the intent of the Privacy Act of 1974 and its effect on HRM.
2. Discuss the HRM implications of the Drug-Free Workplace Act of 1988 and the Polygraph Protection Act of 1988.
3. Describe the provisions of the Worker Adjustment and Retraining Notification Act of 1988.
4. Identify the pros and cons of employee drug testing.
5. Explain why honesty tests are used in hiring.
6. Discuss the implications of the employment-at-will doctrine.
7. Identify the five exceptions to the employment-at-will doctrine.
8. Define discipline and the contingency factors that determine the severity of discipline.
9. Describe the general guidelines for administering discipline.
10. Identify how employee counseling can be used to assist a poorly performing employee.

Technological advances in computer hardware and software have made the process of managing an organization much easier. But technological advancements have also provided employers a means of sophisticated employee monitoring. Although most of this monitoring is designed to enhance worker productivity, it could be, and has been, a source of concern over worker privacy. These advantages have also brought with them difficult questions regarding what managers have the right to know about employees and how far they can go in controlling employee behavior both on and off the job.

What can your employer find out about you and your work? You might be surprised by the answers! Employers can, among other things: read your e-mail (even confidential messages), tap your work telephone, monitor your activities by computer, and monitor you anywhere on company property.[1] Consider the following:

- The mayor of Colorado Springs, Colorado, read the electronic mail messages that city council members sent to each other from their homes. He defended his actions by saying he was making sure that their e-mail to each other was not being used to circumvent his state's "open meeting" law that requires most council business to be conducted publicly.

■ The U.S. Internal Revenue Service's internal audit group monitors a computer log that shows employee access to taxpayers' accounts. This monitoring activity allows management to check and see what employees are doing on their computers.

■ American Express has an elaborate system for monitoring telephone calls. Daily reports are provided to supervisors that detail the frequency and length of calls made by employees, as well as how quickly incoming calls are answered.

■ Management at Midland Bank's branch in Newark, New Jersey, has defined 48 everyday tasks that employees do, and each task has a spot on every employee's computer screen. Every time workers complete a task, they make a record of it by touching the appropriate box on the screen. Custom software then tabulates reports for management that classify which tasks people do and exactly how long it takes to do them.

■ Just how much control should a company have over the private lives of its employees? Where should an employer's rules and controls end? Does the boss have the right to dictate what you do on your own free time and in your own home? Could, in essence, your boss keep you from engaging in riding a motorcycle, skydiving, smoking, drinking alcohol, or eating junk food? Again, the answers may surprise you. What's more, employer involvement in employees' off-work lives has been going on for decades. For instance, in the early 1900s, Ford Motor Company would send social workers to employees' homes to determine whether their off-the-job habits and finances were deserving of year-end bonuses. Other firms made sure employees regularly attended church services. Today, many organizations, in their quest to control safety and health insurance costs, are once again delving into their employees' private lives.

Although controlling employees' behaviors on and off the job may appear unjust or unfair, nothing in our legal system prevents employers from engaging in these practices. Rather, the law is based on the premise that "if employees don't like the rules, they have the option of quitting." Managers, too, typically defend their actions in terms of ensuring quality, productivity, and proper employee behavior. For instance, an IRS audit of its southeastern regional offices found that 166 employees took unauthorized looks at the tax returns of friends, neighbors, and celebrities.

When does management's need for information about employee performance cross over the line and interfere with a worker's right to privacy? Is any action by management acceptable as long as employees are notified ahead of time that they will be monitored? And what about the demarcation between monitoring work and nonwork behavior? When employees do work-related activities at home during evenings and weekends, does management's prerogative to monitor employees remain in force? Answers to questions such as these have become increasingly relevant as technology has redefined management's ability to monitor the most minute details of employees' behavior.

INTRODUCTION

Employee rights has become one of the more important issues for human resource management to deal with. Individuals are guaranteed certain rights based on amendments to the U.S. Constitution. For instance, the Fourth Amendment prohibits illegal searches and seizures by the government or its agents. However, this does not mean that those outside the government, like businesses, cannot perform such an activity.[2] This has led to the question: Are employers all-powerful in this arena? The answer is no! In fact, in more and more situations—such as terminating an employee or maintaining health files on employees for insurance purposes—such organizational practices may be more constrained.[3] Consequently, various laws and Supreme Court rulings are establishing guidelines for employers dealing with employee privacy and other matters. Let's now turn to these laws.

EMPLOYMENT RIGHTS LEGISLATION AND ITS HRM IMPLICATIONS

Over the past few decades, a number of federal laws have given specific protection to employees. These laws are the Privacy Act of 1974, the Drug-Free Workplace Act of 1988, the Employee Polygraph Protection Act of 1988, and the Worker Adjustment and Retraining Notification Act of 1988.

The Privacy Act of 1974

Privacy Act of 1974 Requires federal government agencies to make available information in an individual's personnel file.

When an organization begins the hiring process, it establishes a personnel file for that person—a file that is maintained throughout a person's employment. Any pertinent information, like the completed application, letters of recommendation, performance evaluations, or disciplinary warnings, is kept in the file. The contents of these files often were known only to those who had access to the files—often only managers and HRM personnel. The **Privacy Act of 1974** sought to change that imbalance of information. This act, while applicable to only federal government agencies, requires that an employee's personnel file be open for inspection.[4] This means that employees are permitted to review their files periodically to ensure that the information contained within is accurate. The Privacy Act also gives these federal employees the right to review letters of recommendation written on their behalf.

Even though this act applies solely to the federal worker, it provided the impetus for state legislatures to pass similar laws governing employees of state- and private-sector enterprises. This legislation is often more comprehensive and includes protection regarding how employers disseminate information on past and current employees. For human resource management, a key question is: How should employees be given access to their files? Although the information contained within rightfully may be open for inspection, certain restrictions must be addressed. First, any information for which the employee has waived his or her right to review must be kept separate. For instance, job applicants often waive their right to see letters of recommendation written for them. When that happens, human resources is not obligated to make that information available to the employee. Second, an employee can't simply demand to immediately see his or her file; there is typically a 24-hour turnaround time. Consequently, organizations frequently establish special review procedures. For example, whether the employee can review the file alone or only in the presence of an HRM representative is up to each organization. In either case, personnel files generally are not permitted to leave the HRM area. And although an individual may take notes about the file's contents, copying the file often is not permitted.

The increasing use of computers in human resource management has complicated the issue of file reviews. Because much of this information is now stored in computerized employee data systems, access has been further constrained. Yet although computerization of HRM files is a more complicated system, appropriate access to this information should not be any different than when using a paper file; employees still have a right to see the information about themselves, regardless of where it is kept. Gaining entry into computerized information, however, can be a more time-consuming process. Many times, such access requires certain security clearances to special screens—clearance that is not available to everyone. However, as technology continues to improve, HRM will be better able to implement procedures to give employees access, while simultaneously protecting the integrity of the system.

Fair Credit Reporting Act of 1971   Requires an employer to notify job candidates of its intent to check into their credit.

Companies are also being held accountable to the **Fair Credit Reporting Act of 1971,** an extension to the Privacy Act. In many organizations, the employment process includes a credit check on the applicant.[5] The purpose of such checks is to obtain information about the individual's "character, general reputation,"[6] and various other personal characteristics. Typically, companies can obtain this information by using two different approaches. The first is through a credit reporting agency, similar to the type that is used when you apply for a loan. In this instance, the employer is required to notify the individual that a credit report is being obtained. However, if an applicant is rejected based on information in the report, the individual must be provided a copy of the credit report, as well as a means for how to appeal the accuracy of the findings.[7] The second type of credit report is obtained through a third-party investigation. Under this arrangement, not only is one's credit checked, but people known to the applicant are interviewed regarding the applicant's lifestyle, spending habits, and character. For an organization to use this type of approach, the applicant must be informed of the process in writing, and as with the credit report, must be notified of the report's details if the information is used to negatively affect an employment decision. Keep in mind, however, that how the information is used must be job relevant. If, for example, an organization denies employment to an individual who once filed for bankruptcy and this information has no bearing on the individual's ability to do the job, the organization may be opening itself up to a challenge in the courts.

Credit report information used in employment decisions must be job relevant.

The Drug-Free Workplace Act of 1988

Drug-Free Workplace Act of 1988   Requires specific government-related groups to ensure that their workplace is drug free.

The **Drug-Free Workplace Act of 1988** was passed to help keep the problem of substance abuse from entering the workplace. Under the act, government agencies, federal contractors, and those receiving federal funds ($25,000 or more) are required to actively pursue a drug-free environment. In addition, the act requires employees of companies regulated by the Department of Transportation (DOT) and the Nuclear Regulatory Commission who hold certain jobs to be subjected to drug tests.[8] For example, long-haul truck drivers, regulated by the DOT, are required to take drug tests.

For all organizations covered under this act, other stipulations are included. For example, the enterprise must establish its drug-free work environment policy and disseminate it to its employees. This policy must spell out what is expected of employees in terms of being substance free, and detail the penalties regarding infractions of the policy. In addition, the organization must provide substance-abuse awareness programs to its employees.

There's no doubt that this act has created difficulties for organizations. To comply with the act, they must obtain information about their employees. The whole issue of drug testing in today's companies is a major one, and we'll come back to its applications later in this chapter.

The Polygraph Protection Act of 1988

As a security specialist applicant for the National Security Administration (NSA), you are asked to submit to a polygraph test as a condition of employment. Unsure of what is going to transpire, you agree to be tested. During the examination, you are asked if you have ever used Ecstasy. You respond that you never have, but the polygraph records that you are not telling the truth. Because suspicion of substance use is grounds for disqualification from the job, you are removed from consideration. Can this organization use the polygraph information against you? In the case of a job involving security operations, it can!

However, the **Polygraph Protection Act of 1988**[9] prohibits employers in the private sector[10] from using polygraph tests (often referred to as lie-detector tests) in all employment decisions. Based on the law, companies may no longer use these tests to screen all job applicants.[11] The act was passed because polygraphs were used inappropriately. In general, polygraph tests have been found to have little job-related value, and as such their effectiveness is questionable.[12] However, the Employee Polygraph Protection Act did not eliminate their use in organizations altogether. There are situations where the law permits their use, such as when there has been a theft in the organization, but this process is regulated, too. The polygraph cannot be used as a "witch-hunt." For example, suppose that there has been a theft in the organization. The Employee Polygraph Protection Act prohibits employers from testing all employees in an attempt to determine the guilty party. However, if an investigation into the theft points to a particular employee, then the employer can ask that employee to submit to a polygraph. Even in this case, however, the employee has the right to refuse to take a polygraph test without fear of retaliation from the employer. And in cases in which one does submit to the test, the employee must receive, in advance, a list of questions that will be asked. Furthermore, the employee has the right to challenge the results if he or she believes the test was inappropriately administered.[13] Exhibit 4-1 contains the Department of Labor's Notice of Polygraph Testing explaining employee rights.

Worker Adjustment and Retraining Notification Act of 1988

In the mid-1990s, General Motors announced its plan to sell its car rental firm, National Car Rental Systems, to Vestar Equity Partners.[14] GM had been looking to divest itself of diversified activities in an effort to reinforce its automotive business. But had GM been unable to find a buyer, and just decided to close the car rental business, could GM's management have immediately closed the business unit and terminated the 6,400 National employees without prior notification? No![15] Why? Because of the **Worker Adjustment and Retraining Notification (WARN) Act of 1988**.[16] Sometimes called the Plant Closing Bill, this act places specific requirements on employers considering significant changes in staffing levels. Under WARN, an organization employing 100 or more individuals must notify workers 60 days in advance if it is going to close its facility or lay off 50

Polygraph Protection Act of 1988 Prohibits the use of lie detectors in screening all job applicants. Often referred to as "lie-detector" test.

Worker Adjustment and Retraining Notification Act of 1988 Federal law requiring employers to give 60 days' notice of pending plant closing or major layoff.

EXHIBIT 4-1
Polygraph Protection Notice

NOTICE
EMPLOYEE POLYGRAPH PROTECTION ACT

The Employee Polygraph Protection Act prohibits most private employers from using the detector tests either for pre-employment screening or during the course of employment.

PROHIBITIONS

Employers are generally prohibited from requiring or requesting any employee or job applicant to take a lie detector test, and from discharging, disciplining, or discriminating against an employee or prospective employee for refusing to take a test or for exercising other rights under the act.

EXEMPTIONS*

The law does not apply to tests given by the federal government to certain private individuals engaged in national security-related activities.

The act permits *polygraph* (a kind of lie detector) tests to be administered in the private sector, subject to restrictions, to certain prospective employees of security service firms (armored car, alarm, and guard), and of pharmaceutical manufacturers, distributors and dispensers.

The act also permits polygraph testing, subject to restrictions, of certain employees of private firms who are reasonably suspected of involvement in a workplace incident (theft, embezzlement, etc.) that resulted in economic loss to the employer.

EXAMINEE RIGHTS

Where polygraph tests are permitted, they are subject to numerous strict standards concerning the conduct and length of the test. Examinees have a number of specific rights, including the right to a written notice before testing, the right to refuse or discontinue a test, and the right not to have test results disclosed to unauthorized persons.

ENFORCEMENT

The Department of Labor may bring court actions to restrain violations and assess civil penalties up to $10,000 against violators. Employees or job applicants may also bring their own court actions.

ADDITIONAL INFORMATION

Additional information may be obtained, and complaints of violations may be filed, at local offices of the Wage and Hour Division, which are listed in the telephone directory under U.S. Government, Department of Labor, Employment Standards Administration.

The Law Requires Employers to Display This Poster Where Employees and Job Applicants Can Readily See It.

*The law does not preempt any provision of any state or local law or any collective bargaining agreement that is more restrictive with respect to lie detector tests.
Source: The U.S. Department of Labor, WH Publication, 1462 (September 1988), Employment Standards Administration, Wage and Hour Division, Washington, D.C. 20210.

or more individuals. Should a company fail to provide this advance notice, it is subject to a penalty not to exceed "one day's pay and benefits to each employee for each day's notice that should have been given."[17]

However, the law does recognize that under certain circumstances, advance notice may be impossible. Assume, for example, a company is having financial difficulties and is seeking to raise money to keep the organization afloat. If these

EXHIBIT 4-2
*Summary of Laws Affecting
Employee Rights*

Law	Effect
Fair Credit Reporting Act	Requires employers to notify individuals that credit information is being gathered and may be used in the employment decision.
Privacy Act	Requires government agencies to make information in their personnel files available to employees.
Drug-Free Workplace Act	Requires government agencies, federal contractors, and those who receive government monies to take steps to ensure that their workplace is drug free.
Employee Polygraph Protection Act	Prohibits the use of lie-detector tests in screening all job applicants. Permits their use under certain circumstances.
Worker Adjustment and Retraining Notification Act	Requires employers with 100 or more employees contemplating closing a facility or laying off 50 or more employees to give 60 days' notice of the pending action.

efforts fail and creditors foreclose on the company, no advance notice is required. For example, when Fair Lanes, Inc. (of bowling alley fame) was unable to meet its debt obligation, it filed for bankruptcy. Although filing for bankruptcy permitted the bowling alleys to remain open, had they closed immediately,[18] WARN would not have applied.

Plant closings, similar to the employee rights issues raised previously, continue to pose problems for human resource management. These laws have created specific guidelines for organizations to follow. None precludes the enterprise from doing what is necessary. Rather, the laws exist to ensure that whatever action the organization takes is done in such a way that employee rights are protected. A summary of these laws is presented in Exhibit 4-2.

Current Issues Regarding Employee Rights

Recently, emphasis has been placed on curtailing specific employer practices, as well as addressing what employees may rightfully expect from their organizations. These basic issues are drug testing, honesty tests, and employee monitoring.

Drug Testing   Previously in our discussion of the Drug-Free Workplace Act, we mentioned the legislation applicable to certain organizations. However, because of the severity of substance abuse in our organizations, many organizations not covered by this 1988 Act have voluntarily begun a process of drug testing. Why? Let's look at some facts. It is estimated that a fairly large percentage of the U.S. work force may be abusing some substance (e.g., drugs or alcohol).[19] Moreover, nearly half of all on-the-job injuries and work-related deaths are attributed to substance abuse. And if that weren't enough, it has been estimated that U.S. companies lose well over $246 billion due to "health-care expenditures, premature death, impaired productivity, automobile accidents, crime and welfare."[20]

As a result of the "numbers," many private employers began to implement programs to curb substance-related problems in their organizations.[21] For instance, Home Depot and Motorola test all current employees as well as job applicants. In fact, walk into any Home Depot and you'll see prominently displayed at the entrance a sign that says something to the effect that "the employees of this store are drug free. Applicants who cannot pass a drug screening test should not apply." The intent of drug testing is to identify the abusers and either help them to overcome their problem (current employees) or not hire them in the first place (applicants). It is in this arena that many issues arise. For example, what happens if an individual refuses to take the drug test? What happens if the test is positive? Let's look at some possible answers.

A major concern for opponents of drug testing is how the process works and how the information will be used. **Drug testing** in today's organizations should be conducted to eliminate drugs in the workplace, not to catch those doing drugs.[22] For instance, drug testing may make better sense when there is "reasonable suspicion of substance abuse by an employee, or after an accident has occurred."[23] Although many might say that the same outcome is achieved, it's the process, and how employees view the process, that matters. In some organizations, individuals who refuse the drug test are terminated immediately.[24] Although this treatment appears harsh, the ill effect of employing a substance abuser is perceived as too great. But what if that person took the drug test and failed it? Many organizations place these individuals into a rehabilitation program, where they can get help—and the intent here is to help these workers. However, if they don't accept the help, or later fail another test, then they can be terminated.[25]

Applicants, on the other hand, present a different story. If an applicant tests positive for substance abuse, that applicant is generally no longer considered. The company's liability begins and ends there—they are not required to offer those applicants any help. But that needn't imply that applicants can't "straighten" out and try again. For example, the Red Lion Hotels and Inns organization requires all applicants to submit to a drug test. Should they test positive, their application is rejected; however, after a 90-day period, these individuals may reapply, as if nothing occurred previously.[26] It is recommended that employers conduct applicant drug testing only after a conditional job offer is made. That is, the job offer is contingent on the applicant passing a drug test. Why a drug test at this stage? To properly administer the test, questions about one's health and medication record need to be addressed. Posing such questions before a conditional offer is made may be viewed as a violation of the Americans with Disabilities Act.[27]

From all indications, drug testing can work in achieving its goals of lessening the effect of drugs and alcohol on job-related activities like lower productivity, higher absenteeism, and job-related accidents.[28] Nonetheless, until individuals believe that the tests are administered properly and employees' dignity is respected, criticism of drug testing is likely to continue.[29] There have been many instances where the drug test gave a false reading or the specimen was improperly handled. It is estimated that many of the results may be false—that is, attributed to legitimate medication or the food one eats.[30] To help with this concern, companies are moving toward more precise tests—ones that do not involve body fluids[31] (see Exhibit 4-3) and some that involve computers.[32]

As we move forward in drug-testing methodologies, the process should continue to improve. However, we must not forget individuals' rights—especially their privacy. Most employees recognize why companies must drug test, but expect to be treated humanely in the process; they also want safeguards built into the process to challenge false tests. And if there is a problem, many may want help, not punishment. For organizations to create this positive atmosphere,

Drug Testing The process of testing applicants/employees to determine if they are using illicit drugs.

Many organizations today remind all of us, applicants, current employees, and customers, that the store supports a drug-free and violence-free work environment.

EXHIBIT 4-3
*Alternatives to Body Fluid
Testing*

PUPILLARY-REACTION TEST

A trained professional can determine if a subject is under the influence of drugs or alcohol by examining the subject's eyes. The pupil will react differently to light (a flashlight is used) if the subject is under the influence of drugs. Follow-up tests by body fluid testings are usually needed.
Positive features: Noninvasive.
Negative features: Must be administered by a trained professional. Some medical conditions may give a false positive result. Follow-up tests are needed.

HAIR ANALYSIS

Hair samples are examined using radioimmunoassay, then confirmed by gas chromatography or mass spectrometry. The same techniques are used to test urine samples. Chemicals—drugs, legal or illegal—are left behind in hair follicles and provide a record of past drug use. Type of drug, frequency and duration of use can be determined. Because hair grows about half an inch per month, a relatively small sample can provide a long record of drug use.
Positive features: Accepted by courts in criminal trials. Detailed record of drug use. Cannot be avoided as easily as urinalysis. Less embarrassing than urinalysis.
Negative features: Highly invasive.

VIDEO-BASED EYE–HAND COORDINATION TEST

One company has begun marketing a video-based test of eye–hand coordination. The test takes less than a minute to complete and is self-administered. The test determines only impairment and the employee is actually tested against their own normal performance. Lack of sleep, illness, stress, drugs, or alcohol could cause an employee to fail.
Positive features: Can be used immediately before employee begins work. Noninvasive. Does not make lifestyle judgments. Self-administered. Low cost.
Negative features: So far only implemented at test sites. Follow-up tests necessary.

Source: Reprinted with permission of *HR Magazine*, published by the Society for Human Resource Management, Alexandria, VA: Michael R. Carroll and Christina Heavrin, "Before You Drug Test," *HR Magazine* (June 1990), p. 65.

several steps must be taken. This is where human resource management comes into play. HRM must issue its policies on substance abuse and communicate that message to every employee. That policy must state what is prohibited, under what conditions an individual will be tested, the consequences of failing the test, and how the process of testing will be handled. By making clear what is expected, as well as what the company intends to do, the emotional aspect of this process can be reduced.[33] Where such a policy exists, questions of legality and employee privacy issues are reduced.[34] Additionally, where drug testing is related to preventing accidents and actual job performance, tests have been shown to be more positively viewed.[35]

Honesty Tests   How would you respond to the question: How often do you tell the truth?[36] All the time? Sorry, we can't hire you because everyone has stretched the truth at some point in life. So you must be lying, and therefore are not the honest employee we desire. Most of the time? Sorry again! We can't afford to hire someone who may not have the highest ethical standards. Sound like a Catch-22? Welcome to the world of **honesty tests** (sometimes referred to as integrity tests). Although polygraph testing has been significantly curtailed in the

Honesty Tests A specialized paper-and-pencil test designed to assess one's honesty.

hiring process, employers have found another mechanism that supposedly provides similar information.[37]

Much of the intent of these tests is to get applicants to provide information about themselves that otherwise would be hard to obtain. These "integrity" tests tend to focus on two particular areas—theft and drug use. But the tests are not simply indicators of what has happened; typically, they assess an applicant's past dishonest behavior and that individual's attitude toward dishonesty.[38] One would anticipate that applicants would try to answer these questions to avoid "being caught," or would even lie; however, research findings suggest otherwise. That is, individuals frequently perceive that "dishonesty is okay as long as you are truthful."[39] As such, applicants discuss questions in such a way that the tests do reveal the information intended. These tests frequently are designed with multiple questions covering similar topic areas, to assess consistency. If consistency in response is lacking, the test may indicate that an individual is being dishonest.[40]

Because of the effectiveness of these tests, coupled with their lower costs than those of other types of investigations, a number of companies have begun using them in their selection process. In fact, it was estimated that over 5,000 organizations are using some variation of honesty tests to screen applicants, testing some 5 million individuals each year.[41] Surprisingly, however, companies using these tests seldom reveal that they do. The large use of these tests has provoked questions about their validity and their potential for adverse impact. Research to date is promising.[42] Although instances have been recorded that indicate that individuals have been wrongly misclassified as dishonest,[43] other studies have indicated that they do not create an adverse impact against protected group members.[44] Based on the evidence, our conclusion is that these tests may be useful for providing more information about applicants but should not be used as the sole criterion in the hiring decision.

Honesty tests focus on two areas: theft and drug abuse.

Whistle-Blowing   Over the past few years, more emphasis has been placed on companies being good corporate citizens. Incidents like tobacco-industry whistle-blowing[45] have fueled interest in the area. One aspect of being responsible to the community at large is permitting employees to challenge management's practice without fear of retaliation. This challenge is often referred to as whistle-blowing.

Whistle-blowing A situation in which an employee notifies authorities of wrongdoing in an organization.

Whistle-blowing occurs when an employee reports the organization to an outside agency for what the employee believes is an illegal or unethical practice. In the past, these employees were often subjected to severe punishment for doing what they believed was right.[46] For instance, several years ago, an employee in General Electric's nuclear fuel facility operation complained that "radioactive spills in the work setting were not properly cleaned up."[47] As the employee attempted to document her case, she was subjected to personnel actions by the company. The company believed that the employee, instead of leaving the "mess" for all to see, should have cleaned it up. This employee was ultimately terminated,[48] and unfortunately no federal law protected her.

Although federal legislation is lacking (except for a federal law passed in 1989 that covers public employees), state laws may be available in some jurisdictions. However, the extent of these laws, and how much protection they afford, differ greatly.[49] Nonetheless, many firms have voluntarily adopted policies to permit employees to identify problem areas.[50] The thrust of these policies is to have an established procedure whereby employees can safely raise these concerns

EXHIBIT 4-4
Ten Steps to an Effective
Whistle-Blowing Policy

1. Develop the policy in written form.
2. See input from top management in developing the policy, and obtain their approval for the finished work.
3. Communicate the policy to employees using multiple media. Inclusion in the employee handbook is not sufficient. Active communication efforts such as ethics training, departmental meetings and employee seminars will increase awareness of the policy and highlight the company's commitment to ethical behavior.
4. Provide a reporting procedure for employees that does not require them to go to their supervisor first. Instead, designate a specific office or individual to hear initial employee complaints. Streamline the process and cut the red tape. Make it easy for the employees to use the procedure.
5. Make it possible for employees to report anonymously, at least initially.
6. Guarantee employees who report suspected wrongdoing in good faith that they will be protected from retaliation from any member of the organization. Make this guarantee stick.
7. Develop a formal investigative process and communicate to employees exactly how their reports will be handled. Use this process to investigate all reported wrongdoings.
8. If the investigation reveals that the employee's suspicions are accurate, take prompt action to correct the wrongdoing. Employees will quickly lose confidence in the policy if disclosed wrongdoing is allowed to continue. Whatever the outcome of the investigation, communicate it quickly to the whistle-blowing employee.
9. Provide an appeals process for employees dissatisfied with the outcome of the initial investigation. Provide an advocate (probably from HRM) to assist the employee who wishes to appeal an unfavorable outcome.
10. Finally, a successful whistle-blowing policy requires more than a written procedure. It requires a commitment from the organization, from top management down. This commitment must be to create ethical work environment.

Source: Timothy R. Barrett and Daniel S. Cochran, "Making Room for the Whistleblower." *HRMagazine*, (January 1991), p. 59. Reprinted with permission of *HRMagazine*, published by the Society for Human Resource Management, Alexandria, Virginia.

and the company can take corrective action. A suggested whistle-blower policy is presented in Exhibit 4-4.

Employee Monitoring and Workplace Security

Technology, enhanced in part by improvements in computers, has done some wonderful things in our work environment. It has allowed us to be more productive, to work smarter, not harder, and to bring about efficiencies in organizations that were not possible two decades ago. It has also provided us a means of **employee monitoring**—what some would call spying on our employees![51]

Employee Monitoring An activity whereby the company is able to keep informed of its employees' activities.

Workplace security has become a critical issue for employers (see Ethical Issues in HRM). Workplace security can be defined as actions on behalf of an employer to ensure that the employer's interests are protected: that is, workplace security focuses on protecting the employer's property and its trade business.[52] Without a doubt, employers must protect themselves. Employee theft, revealing trade secrets to competition, or using the company's customer database for personal gain could be damaging to the company. But how far can this protection extend? Don't we need to consider employees' rights too? Obviously the answer is yes, but how is that balance created?

Consider what happened to Alana Shorts.[53] Arriving at work at Epson America one morning, Alana noticed her boss reading her electronic mail. Although company managers verbally stated that electronic mail messages were private, the company's written policy was different. It was her employer's contention that it owned the system and accordingly had the right to see what was going on. And they were right! In fact, employers can even film you in the restroom. But whatever employers deem fair game, they should explain for employees in terms of a company policy.[54]

Part of the problem here goes back to the balance of security. Abuses by some employees—for instance, employees using the company's computer system for gambling purposes, running their own businesses,[56] playing computer games, or pursuing personal matters—have resulted in companies implementing a more "policing" role. This can extend, too, to Internet sites, ensuring that employees are not logging on to adult-oriented web sites.[57]

As employee-monitoring issues become more noticeable, keep a few things in mind. Employers, as long as they have a policy regarding how employees are monitored, will continue to check on employee behavior.[58] Specifically targeted for this monitoring are system computers, electronic mail, and the telephone.[59] In fact, it's estimated that more than "20 million employees have their computer files monitored each year."[60] In companies like Gateway, Continental Airlines, and UPS, employees are continually told that they may be monitored. Undoubtedly, the debate regarding the necessity of this action will continue. Nonetheless, only when employees understand what the company expects and how it will gather its information will their rights be safeguarded.

ethical issues in HRM

EMPLOYEE MONITORING

IF YOU WORKED FOR NISSAN MOTORS in most of their many jobs and used their e-mail system, how would you feel if your supervisor routinely read your computer messages (especially if in the past you've called your supervisor derogatory terms in e-mail messages to colleagues)? Or how would you feel as a loyal employee of the Boston Sheraton Hotel about you and a friend being secretly videotaped in the men's room at the hotel—even if the videotaping is designed to monitor behavior in hopes of ridding from the premises substance abusers and drug dealers? Technology today makes it possible, even easy, for companies to monitor their employees. And many do so in the hopes that it will help both you and them become more productive and more quality oriented.

The appropriate question for employee rights is, when does such employee snooping become unethical?

Just how pervasive is this practice of monitoring employees? Exact numbers are simply not known, although guesstimates in the millions appear reasonable. For example, call most 800-customer-service numbers, like that of Gateway 2000, and you'll likely hear a message that calls are monitored for quality. Or recognize that networked computer stations can be monitored from a central location to assess "real-time" productivity. Under such an arrangement, however, employers should issue an "employee monitoring" policy, which details what is monitored, when, and how the information is used. In such instances, employees appear more tolerant of being monitored. Yet, these same employees appear to exhibit more stress-related symptoms than employees who are not monitored.

Are employers overstepping the bounds of decency and respect for employees?[55] Consider that it is almost kids' play to monitor cellular phone conversations or to intercept and copy fax transmissions. At Olivetti, employees wear "smart badges" so their movements can be tracked. That can be helpful in having messages transferred to their location, but also means that Olivetti managers may know exactly your every move.

Sure, employee monitoring can help enhance performance and provide valuable feedback to both the employer and the employee. But at what point does the organization's need for that information violate an employee's right to privacy? What's your opinion.?

Other Employee Rights Issues

Although we have addressed a number of employee rights issues, two additional concerns deserve some brief discussion. These are monitoring of office romances (sometimes called legislating love) and sexual orientation rights.

Legislating Love   Company guidelines on how personal relationships may exist at work.

Legislating Love   Legislating love in our companies today is a direct result of potential discrimination or sexual harassment issues facing our organizations.[61] The workplace has long been a place to develop romantic interests; many individuals have met their mates or significant others through work or organizational contacts. But what happens when this organizational love reaches another plateau? What if your significant other is now your boss or has moved on to work for a competitor? Many organizations typically find such situations unacceptable.[62] As a result, they try to avoid possible conflicts of interest that may arise. To do so, they have issued various guidelines on how—if at all—relationships at work may exist. Exhibit 4-5 lists the policies of several companies.

Some companies, on the other hand, like Mitchell Energy and Development, Interstate Bakeries, and Microsoft, are seeing this dilemma differently.[63] Top management in these organizations views office romance, and possible marriage between their employees, as having a positive effect on employee morale and productivity. For Bill Gates, the CEO of Microsoft, relationships were hard to start and maintain given his 18-hour workdays. If a legislating-love policy had existed, it might have prevented Gates from marrying his marketing executive, Melinda French, in January 1994. And for a company like DEC, permitting romantic relationships between employees has helped to foster their "company-centered family."[64]

Exhibit 4-5
Selected Companies: Policies on Organizational Romance

AT&T

"Our attitude toward corporate romance is one of benign neglect," says corporate spokesperson Burke Stinson. The company, which is noted for its strong policy on sexual harassment, has never issued formal guidelines against dating, but it discourages direct supervisor–subordinate relationships, and forbids spouses from reporting to each other. "Until the 1980s," says Stinson, "all types of office romance were frowned upon. But the whole environment of corporate America has become a mini-*Love Boat*." Nationwide, there are an estimated 7,500 married couples at the company.

PRUDENTIAL

After the Clarence Thomas Supreme Court nomination hearing, the company issued a memo to its employees restating its long-standing policy on sexual harassment and went on to warn that romantic relationships can "influence the quality of decisions and can potentially hurt other people."

"We certainly can't forbid dating," says Don Mann, the company's senior vice president of human resources. "Hundreds of couples met at the company, including the chairman and his wife. The main concern we have is about chain-of-command relationships. A transfer is the typical solution."

DU PONT

The company has one of the most extensive sexual-harassment prevention and education programs in the country, including a 24-hour hot line, seminars, and, when necessary, a team of harassment investigators. Dating, however, is allowed, provided that it's not a boss–subordinate relationship. In that case, one person is reassigned.

Source: Ellen Rapp, "Legislating Love," *Working Woman* (February 1992), p. 61.

Sexual Orientation Rights   When one considers the laws and court rulings presented in Chapter 3, one begins to appreciate what has occurred over the past few decades. Remember that in Chapter 3 we mentioned that discrimination against an individual based on sexual orientation currently does not come under the jurisdiction of Title VII (although some state and local laws do exist). As a result, discriminating in hiring, firing, or promoting on the basis of sexual orientation may exist. Some organizations have even gone a step further. For instance, Cracker Barrel is a retail chain known for its cheese products. If you walk around its stores, you will notice some very fine products. You should also know that no homosexuals work there, at least none who are open about their sexual preference.[65] In the early 1990s, Cracker Barrel management began questioning certain employees about their sexual preference. This action was based on a number of factors in response to an informal survey asking customers if they preferred not to patronize an establishment that hires homosexual workers (how they would know is uncertain). Some employees had a choice—lie and keep their jobs, turning their backs on their significant others, or tell the truth and be fired. Although the company denies many of these allegations, gay and lesbian support groups have targeted Cracker Barrel and other "like" companies and have held rallies in support of employees—but federal law has not yet changed regarding sexual orientation in the workplace.

Actions such as those witnessed at Cracker Barrel are not representative of all organizations. Companies like Apple, Disney, Lotus, and Du Pont have policies and programs in place that are gay-friendly—like domestic partner benefits, and training programs designed to help employees accept one another.

THE ROLE OF THE EMPLOYMENT-AT-WILL DOCTRINE

Background

Employment-at-Will Nineteenth-century common law that permitted employers to discipline or discharge employees at their discretion.

The concept of the **employment-at-will doctrine** is rooted in nineteenth-century common law, which permitted employers to discipline or discharge employees at their discretion. The premise behind this doctrine is to equalize the playing field. If employees can resign at any time they want, why shouldn't an employer have the same right?

Workers at a company like Disney work hard at learning to accept one another. In the organization, straight and gay employees meet periodically to discuss issues that affect their work relationship. Additionally, not only does Disney offer sensitivity training to its employees, the company also provides employee benefits to same-sex partners.

Under the employment-at-will doctrine, an employer can dismiss an employee "for good cause, for no cause, or even for a cause morally wrong, without being guilty of a legal wrong."[66] Of course, even then, you can't fire on the basis of race, religion, sex, national origin, age, or disability.[67] Although this doctrine has existed for over 100 years, the courts, labor unions, and legislation have attempted to lessen the use of this doctrine.[68] In these instances, jobs are being likened to private property. That is, individuals have a right to these jobs unless the organization has specified otherwise. Employees today are challenging the legality of their discharge more frequently. When firing without cause occurs, employees may seek the assistance of the courts to address their wrongful discharge.[69] Most states permit employees to sue their employers if they believe their termination was unjust.[70] At issue in these suits is that through some action on the part of the employer, exceptions to the employment-at-will doctrine exist.

Exceptions to the Doctrine

While employment-at-will thrives in contemporary organizations, there are five exceptions under which a wrongful discharge suit can be supported. These are through a contractual relationship, statutory considerations, public policy violation, implied contracts, and a breach of good faith.[71] Let's take a closer look at these.

Contractual Relationship   A contractual relationship exists when employers and employees have a legal agreement regarding how employee issues are handled. Under such contractual arrangements, discharge may occur only if it is based on just cause. Inasmuch as a distinct definition of just cause does not exist, there are guidelines derived from labor arbitration of collective-bargaining relationships (we'll look at discipline in labor-management relationships in Chapter 15) under which just cause can be shown, as follows:

- Was there adequate warning of consequences of the worker's behavior?
- Are the rules reasonable and related to safe and efficient operations of the business?
- Before discipline was rendered, did a fair investigation of the violation occur?
- Did the investigation yield definite proof of worker activity and wrongdoing?
- Have similar occurrences, both prior and subsequent to this event, been handled in the same way and without discrimination?
- Was the penalty in line with the seriousness of the offense and in reason with the worker's past employment record?[72]

Statutory Considerations   In addition to this contractual relationship, federal legislation may also play a key role. Discrimination laws such as those discussed in the previous chapter may further constrain an employer's use of at-will terminations. For example, an organization cannot terminate an individual based on his or her age just because such action would save the company some money.

Public Policy Violation   Another exception to the employment-at-will doctrine is the public policy violation. Under this exception, an employee cannot be terminated for failing to obey an order from an employer that can be construed as an illegal activity. Additionally, should an employee refuse to offer a bribe to a public official to increase the likelihood of the organization obtaining a contract, that employee is protected. Furthermore, employers cannot retaliate against an employee for exercising his or her rights (like serving on a jury). Accordingly, employees cannot be justifiably discharged for exercising their rights in accordance with societal laws and statutes.

Implied Employment Contract   The third exception to the doctrine is the **implied employment contract.** An implied contract is any verbal or written statement made by members of the organization that suggests organizational guarantees or promises about continued employment.[73] These implied contracts, when they exist, typically take place during employment interviews or are included in an employee handbook.

One of the earlier cases reaffirming implied contracts was the case of *Toussaint v. Blue Cross and Blue Shield of Michigan.*[74] In this case, Toussaint claimed that he was improperly discharged, for unjust causes, by the organization. He asserted that he was told "he'd be with the company until age 65 as long as he did his job."[75] The employee's handbook also clearly reinforced this tenure with statements reflective of discharge for just cause. Even if just cause arose, the discharge could occur only after several disciplinary steps (we'll look at the topic of discipline in the next section) had been taken.[76] In this case, the court determined that the discharge was improper[77] because the permanence of his position was implied by the organization.

The issue of implied contracts is changing how human resource management operates in several of its functions. For instance, interviewers are increasingly cautious, avoiding anything that could conjure up a contract. Something as innocent as discussing an annual salary may cause problems, for such a comment implies at least 12 months on the job.[78] To avoid this, salaries are often communicated in terms of the amount of pay for each pay period. Many organizations, because management wants to maintain employment-at-will, have listed disclaimers such as, "This handbook is not a contract of employment," or "Employment in the organization is at the will of the employer," on the covers of their employee handbooks and manuals to reinforce their employment-at-will policy. Yet caution is warranted, as a supervisor's statements may override the printed words.

Breach of Good Faith   The final exception to the employment-at-will doctrine is the breach of good faith. Although this is the most difficult of the exceptions to prove, there are situations where an employer may breach a promise. In one noteworthy case, an individual employed over 25 years by the National Cash Register Company (NCR) was terminated shortly after completing a major deal with a customer.[79] The employee claimed that he was fired to eliminate NCR's liability to pay him his sales commission. In the case, the court ruled that this individual acted in good faith in selling the company's product and reasonably expected his commission. Although NCR had an employment-at-will arrangement with its employees, the court held that his dismissal, and their failure to pay commissions, was a breach of good faith.

DISCIPLINE AND EMPLOYEE RIGHTS

The exceptions to the employment-at-will doctrine mentioned above may lead you to think that employers cannot terminate employees, or are significantly limited in their action. That's not the point of the discussion. Rather, where exceptions

Implied Employment Contract   Any organizational guarantee or promise about job security.

exist, there may be a requirement that such an employment action follow a specific process.[80] That process, and how it works, are embedded in the topic we call discipline.

What Is Discipline?

Discipline A condition in the organization when employees conduct themselves in accordance with the organization's rules and standards of acceptable behavior.

The term **discipline** refers to a condition in the organization where employees conduct themselves in accordance with the organization's rules and standards of acceptable behavior. For the most part, employees discipline themselves by conforming to what is considered proper behavior because they believe it is the reasonable thing to do. Once they are made aware of what is expected of them, and assuming they find these standards or rules to be reasonable, they seek to meet those expectations.

But not all employees will accept the responsibility of self-discipline. There are some employees who do not accept the norms of responsible employee behavior. These employees, then, require some degree of extrinsic disciplinary action. It is this need to impose extrinsic disciplinary action that we will address in the following sections.

Factors to Consider When Disciplining

Before we review disciplinary guidelines, we should look at the major factors that need to be considered if we are to have fair and equitable disciplinary practices. The following seven contingency factors can help us analyze a discipline problem:[81]

1. *Seriousness of the Problem.* How severe is the problem? As noted previously, dishonesty is usually considered a more serious infraction than reporting to work 20 minutes late.

2. *Duration of the Problem.* Have there been other discipline problems in the past, and over how long a time span? The violation does not take place in a vacuum. A first occurrence is usually viewed differently than a third or fourth offense.

3. *Frequency and Nature of the Problem.* Is the current problem part of an emerging or continuing pattern of disciplinary infractions? We are concerned with not only the duration but also the pattern of the problem. Continual infractions may require a different type of discipline from that applied to isolated instances of misconduct. They may also point out a situation that demands far more severe discipline in order to prevent a minor problem from becoming a major one.

4. *Extenuating Factors.* Are there extenuating circumstances related to the problem? The student who fails to turn in her term paper by the deadline because of the death of her grandfather is likely to have her violation assessed more leniently than will her peer who missed the deadline because he overslept.

5. *Degree of Socialization.* To what extent has management made an earlier effort to educate the person causing the problem about the existing rules and procedures and the consequences of violations? Discipline severity must reflect the degree of knowledge that the violator holds of the organization's standards of acceptable behavior. In contrast to the previous item, the new employee is less likely to have been socialized to these standards than the 20-year veteran. Additionally, the organization that has formalized, written rules governing employee conduct is more justified in aggressively enforcing

violations of these rules than is the organization whose rules are informal or vague.

6. *History of the Organization's Discipline Practices.* How have similar infractions been dealt with in the past within the department? within the entire organization? Has there been consistency in the application of discipline procedures? Equitable treatment of employees must take into consideration precedents within the unit where the infraction occurs, as well as previous disciplinary actions taken in other units within the organization. Equity demands consistency against some relevant benchmark.

7. *Management Backing.* If employees decide to take their case to a higher level in management, will you have reasonable evidence to justify your decision? Should the employee challenge your disciplinary action, it is important that you have the data to back up the necessity and equity of the action taken and that you feel confident that management will support your decision. No disciplinary action is likely to carry much weight if violators believe that they can challenge and successfully override their manager's decision.

How can these seven items help? Consider that there are many reasons for why we might discipline an employee. With little difficulty, we could list several dozen or more infractions that management might believe require disciplinary action. For simplicity's sake, we have classified the most frequent violations into four categories: attendance, on-the-job behaviors, dishonesty, and outside activities. We've listed them and potential infractions in Exhibit 4-6. However, these

EXHIBIT 4-6
Specific Disciplinary
Problems

TYPE OF PROBLEM	INFRACTION
Attendance	Tardiness
	Unexcused absence
	Leaving without permission
On-the-job behaviors	Malicious destruction of organizational property
	Gross insubordination
	Carrying a concealed weapon
	Attacking another employee with intent to seriously harm
	Drunk on the job
	Sexually harassing another employee
	Failure to obey safety rules
	Defective work
	Sleeping on the job
	Failure to report accidents
	Loafing
	Gambling on the job
	Fighting
	Horseplay
Dishonesty	Stealing
	Deliberate falsification of employment record
	Clock-punching another's timecard
	Concealing defective work
	Subversive activity
Outside activities	Unauthorized strike activity
	Outside criminal activities
	Wage garnishment
	Working for a competing company

infractions may be minor or serious given the situation or the industry in which one works. For example, while concealing defective work in a hand-power tool assembly line may be viewed as minor, the same action in an aerospace manufacturing plant is more serious. Furthermore, recurrence and severity of the infraction will play a role. For instance, employees who experience their first minor offense might generally expect a minor reprimand. A second offense might result in a more stringent reprimand, and so forth. In contrast, the first occurrence of a serious offense might mean not being allowed to return to work, the length of time being dependent on the circumstances surrounding the violation.

Disciplinary Guidelines

All human resource managers should be aware of disciplinary guidelines. In this section, we will briefly describe them.

- *Make Disciplinary Action Corrective Rather Than Punitive.* The objective of disciplinary action is not to deal out punishment.[82] The objective is to correct an employee's undesirable behavior. While punishment may be a necessary means to that end, one should never lose sight of the eventual objective.
- *Make Disciplinary Action Progressive.* Although the type of disciplinary action that is appropriate may vary depending on the situation, it is generally desirable for discipline to be progressive.[83] Only for the most serious violations will an employee be dismissed after a first offense. Typically, progressive disciplinary action begins with a verbal warning and proceeds through a written warning, suspension, and, only in the most serious cases, dismissal. More on this in a moment.
- *Follow the "Hot-Stove" Rule.* Administering discipline can be viewed as analogous to touching a hot stove (hence, the **hot-stove rule**).[84] While both are painful to the recipient, the analogy goes further. When you touch a hot stove, you get an immediate response; the burn you receive is instantaneous, leaving no question of cause and effect. You have ample warning; you know what happens if you touch a red-hot stove. Furthermore, the result is consistent: every time you touch a hot stove, you get the same response—you get burned. Finally, the result is impersonal; regardless of who you are, if you touch a hot stove, you will get burned. The comparison between touching a hot stove and administering discipline should be apparent, but let us briefly expand on each of the four points in the analogy.

Hot-stove Rule Discipline should be immediate, provide ample warning, be consistent, and be impersonal.

The impact of a disciplinary action will be reduced as the time between the infraction and the penalty's implementation lengthens. The more quickly the discipline follows the offense, the more likely it is that the employee will associate the discipline with the offense rather than with the manager imposing the discipline. As a result, it is best that the disciplinary process begin as soon as possible after the violation is noticed. Of course, this desire for immediacy should not result in undue haste. If all the facts are not in, managers may invoke a temporary suspension, pending a final decision in the case. The manager has an obligation to give advance warning prior to initiating formal disciplinary action. This means the employee must be aware of the organization's rules and accept its standards of behavior. Disciplinary action is more likely to be interpreted as fair by employees when there is clear warning that a given violation will lead to discipline and when it is known what that discipline will be.[85]

MANAGER SHOULD BE PREPARED BEFORE DISCIPLINING EMPLOYEES

I N A PERFECT WORLD, THERE WOULD be no disciplining, no policies or procedures to misinterpret or ignore. Each employee would check his or her own work and contribute ways to cut costs, reduce waste, and improve quality and service to both internal and external customers. Lunch hours would be held to agreed-upon limits, and personal business and/or phone calls would not be conducted on company time or with company resources, equipment, or personnel. Computers, equipment, managers, the company, or "someone else" would not be blamed for work not completed or completed late or incorrectly. Managers would involve, train, and listen to employees, building teamwork through empowerment and trust. In a perfect world!

In a slightly less perfect but more exciting and challenging world, managers occasionally have to discipline employees. As a pleasurable managerial task, it ranks right after terminating someone. Dealing with the effects of the mistakes and masking anger, resentment, disappointment, and disgust to create these teaching moments can test even the most patient manager. The challenge is to keep employees focused on their behavior and how to correct or improve it, not on how they're being treated. Following these guidelines should help:

- *Cool off, but don't wait too long.* Even though you might like to ignore the problem and hope that it will go away, don't kid yourself. Any problem has a tendency to escalate from a minor to a major issue. It's not worth it. Get comfortable with positively confronting situations, mutually identifying problems, and agreeing on solutions and follow-up plans. Failing to address issues undermines your credibility and ability to do what it is you get paid to do: manage.
- *Think before you speak.* Stay calm. It may be tempting to sound off, but how you handle it may be as important as the issue. Your goal should be to correct the situation, not to further impede the working relationship. You may wish to ask the employee to consider possible so-

lutions and bring one or two to the meeting if appropriate.
- *Always discipline in private, one-on-one.* Consider using a conference room, if added privacy is needed.
- *Follow company disciplinary procedures to ensure fairness and consistency.* If in doubt, take the time to check the policy manual, boss, or personnel officer first. If you don't, you may be the next person in line to be disciplined for not following procedures.
- *Be prepared to hear a variety of both imaginative and worn-out excuses.* These can range from "I was stuck in traffic" to "Somebody made that up" to "The other department takes one-hour-45-minute lunches" to "Everybody else does it."
  - *Prepare in order to avoid nervousness.* No one likes to discipline, but it's part of the job. Before the meeting, think about objections or issues that may be raised. Rehearse in your mind, outline your comments—whatever it takes to resolve the issue in a win-win manner.
  - *Prepare by comparing the actual to the desired situation.* Then state what action is necessary, why it is necessary, and its impact.
  - *Clarify expectations and contingencies for specific actions and timetables.* Make sure that the employee understands by asking for a summarization—something beyond just a grunt of agreement.
- *Ask employees for feedback.* How can you best help or support them in making the necessary changes? What suggestions do they have? How can problems be prevented in the future?
- *Let it go.* There is no need to ignore employees, stare at them, or use any other of a variety of cruel and unusual (and immature) punishments.

Imagine an environment that tolerated no mistakes because it tolerated no risks, no changes, no tests. A less-than-perfect world looks good after all.

Fair treatment of employees also demands that disciplinary action be consistent. When rule violations are enforced in an inconsistent manner, the rules lose their impact. Morale will decline and employees will question the competence of management. Productivity will suffer as a result of employee insecurity and anxiety. All employees want to know the limits of permissible behavior, and they look to the actions of their managers for such feedback. If, for example, Barbara is reprimanded today for an action that she took last week, for which nothing was said, these limits become blurry. Similarly, if Bill and Marty are both goofing off at their desks and Bill is reprimanded while Marty is not, Bill is likely to question the fairness of the action. The point, then, is that discipline should be consistent. This need not result in treating everyone exactly alike, because that ignores the contingency factors we discussed earlier, but it does put the responsibility on management to clearly justify disciplinary actions that may appear inconsistent to employees.

The last guideline that flows from the hot-stove rule is: keep the discipline impersonal. Penalties should be connected with a given violation, not with the personality of the violator. That is, discipline should be directed at what employees have done, not the employees themselves. As a manager, you should make it clear that you are avoiding personal judgments about the employee's character. You are penalizing the rule violation, not the individual, and all employees committing the violation can expect to be penalized. Furthermore, once the penalty has been imposed, you as manager must make every effort to forget the incident; you should attempt to treat the employee in the same manner as you did prior to the infraction.

Disciplinary Actions

As mentioned earlier, discipline generally follows a typical sequence of four steps: written verbal warning, written warning, suspension, and dismissal[86] (see Exhibit 4-7). Let's briefly review these four steps.

Written Verbal Warning   The first formal step in the disciplinary process.

Written Verbal Warning   The mildest form of discipline is the written verbal warning. Yes, the term is correct. A **written verbal warning** is a temporary record of a reprimand that is then placed in the manager's file on the employee. This written verbal warning should state the purpose, date, and outcome of the interview with the employee. This, in fact, is what differentiates the written verbal warning from the verbal warning. Because of the need to document this step in the process, the verbal warning must be put into writing. The difference, however, is that this warning remains in the hands of the manager; that is, it is not forwarded to HRM for inclusion in the employee's personnel file.[87]

The written verbal reprimand is best achieved when completed in a private and informal environment. The manager should begin by clearly informing the employee of the rule that has been violated and the problem that this infraction has caused. For instance, if the employee has been late several times, the manager would reiterate the organization's rule that employees are to be at their desks by 8:00 A.M., and then proceed to give specific evidence of how violation of this rule has resulted in an increase in workload for others and has lowered departmental morale. After the problem has been made clear, the manager should then allow the employee to respond. Is he aware of the problem? Are there extenuating circumstances that justify his behavior? What does he plan to do to correct his behavior?

EXHIBIT 4-7
The Progressive Discipline Process

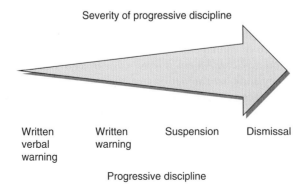

Severity of progressive discipline

Written verbal warning   Written warning   Suspension   Dismissal

Progressive discipline

After the employee has been given the opportunity to make his case, the manager must determine if the employee has proposed an adequate solution to the problem. If this has not been done, the manager should direct the discussion toward helping the employee figure out ways to prevent the trouble from recurring. Once a solution has been agreed upon, the manager should ensure that the employee understands what, if any, follow-up action will be taken if the problem recurs.

If the written verbal warning is effective, further disciplinary action can be avoided. If the employee fails to improve, the manager will need to consider more severe action.

Written Warning   First formal step of the disciplinary process.

Written Warning   The second step in the progressive discipline process is the **written warning.** In effect, it is the first formal stage of the disciplinary procedure. This is because the written warning becomes part of the employee's official personnel file. This is achieved by not only giving the warning to the employee but sending a copy to HRM to be inserted in the employee's permanent record. In all other ways, however, the procedure concerning the writing of the warning is the same as the written verbal warning; that is, the employee is advised in private of the violation, its effects, and potential consequences of future violations. The only difference is that the discussion concludes with the employee being told that a formal written warning will be issued. Then the manager writes up the warning—stating the problem, the rule that has been violated, any acknowledgment by the employee to correct her behavior, and the consequences from a recurrence of the deviant behavior—and sends it to HRM.

Suspension   A period of time off from work as a result of a disciplinary process.

Suspension   A **suspension** or layoff would be the next disciplinary step, usually taken only if the prior steps have been implemented without the desired outcome. Exceptions—where suspension is given without any prior verbal or written warning—occasionally occur if the infraction is of a serious nature.

A suspension may be for one day or several weeks; disciplinary layoffs in excess of a month are rare. Some organizations skip this step completely because it can have negative consequences for both the company and the employee. From the organization's perspective, a suspension means the loss of the employee for the layoff period. If the person has unique skills or is a vital part of a complex process, her loss during the suspension period can severely impact her department or the organization's performance if a suitable replacement cannot be located. From the employee's standpoint, a suspension can result in the employee returning in a more unpleasant and negative frame of mind than before the layoff.

Then why should management consider suspending employees as a disciplinary measure? The answer is that a short layoff is potentially a rude awakening to problem employees. It may convince them that management is serious and may move them to accept responsibility for following the organization's rules.

Dismissal   A disciplinary action that results in the termination of an employee.

Dismissal   Management's ultimate disciplinary punishment is dismissing the problem employee. **Dismissal** should be used only for the most serious offenses. Yet it may be the only feasible alternative when an employee's behavior seriously interferes with a department or the organization's operation.

A dismissal decision should be given long and hard consideration. For almost all individuals, being fired from a job is an emotional trauma. For employees who have been with the organization for many years, dismissal can make it difficult to obtain new employment or may require the individual to undergo extensive retraining. In addition, management should consider the possibility that

Rich Cronin was the head of Nick-at-Nite and TV Land cable networks for Viacom. Planning to leave Viacom when his employment contract expired in June 1998 to head Fox Kids Broadcasting's Family Channel, Cronin let his employer know of his intention about six months early. But the reaction he received was not the one he expected. He was fired immediately. He has since filed claims that he was fired without cause.

a dismissed employee will take legal action to fight the decision.[88] Recent court cases indicate that juries are cautiously building a list of conditions under which employees may not be lawfully discharged.

Positive Discipline: Can It Work?

The concept of positive discipline was first reported at Union Carbide Corporation.[89] In its design, positive discipline attempts to integrate the disciplinary process with the performance management system. When problems arise, rather than promptly responding with a written verbal warning (punitive), positive discipline attempts to get the employee back on track by helping to "convince the individual to abide by company performance standards."[90] That is, in using positive discipline, attempts are made to reinforce the good work behaviors of the employee, while simultaneously emphasizing to the employee the problems created by the undesirable performance. The basis of positive discipline is presented in Exhibit 4-8.

EMPLOYEE COUNSELING

Employee Counseling A process whereby employees are guided in overcoming performance problems.

Whenever an employee exhibits work behaviors that are inconsistent with the work environment (i.e., fighting, stealing, unexcused absences, and so forth) or is unable to perform his or her job satisfactorily, a manager must intervene. In many cases, this is done through a process called **employee counseling**. But before any intervention can begin, it is imperative for the manager to identify the prob-

EXHIBIT 4-8
Steps in Positive Discipline

Step 1: An Oral Reminder	Notice here that the word *warning* is removed. The **oral reminder,** supported by written documentation, serves as the initial formal phase of the process to identify to the employee what work problems he or she is having. This reminder is designed to identify what is causing the problem and attempts to correct it before it becomes larger.
Step 2: A Written Reminder	If the oral reminder was unsuccessful, a more formalized version is implemented. This **written reminder** once again reinforces what the problems are and what corrective action is necessary. Furthermore, specific timetables that the employee must accept and abide by, and the consequences for failing to comply, are often included.
Step 3: A Decision-making Leave	Here, employees are given a **decision-making leave**—time off from work, usually with pay—to think about what they are doing and whether or not they desire to continue to work with the company. This "deciding day" is designed to allow the employee an opportunity to make a choice—correct the behavior, or face separation from the company.

lem. If as managers we realize that the performance problem is ability related, our emphasis becomes one of facilitating training and development efforts.[91] This type of intervention, then, is more closely aligned to mentoring or coaching (see Chapter 8). However, when the performance problem is desire related, where the unwillingness is either voluntary or involuntary, employee counseling is the next logical approach.[92]

> *In employee counseling, the manager must attack the inappropriate behavior, not the person.*

Although employee counseling processes differ, some fundamental steps should be followed when counseling an employee. As a prerequisite, a manager must have good listening skills.[93] The purpose of employee counseling is to uncover the reason for the poor performance, a response that must be elicited from the employee. A manager who dominates the meeting by talking may destroy the benefits of an effective counseling session.

In employee counseling, the manager must attack the inappropriate behavior, not the person. Although they appear difficult to separate, we must deal with only objective performance data. For instance, telling an employee he or she is a poor worker is only asking for emotions to run high and for confrontation to arise. Instead, stating that he or she has been late four times this past month, which has caused a backlog of shipping receivables, is better understood and dealt with. In doing so, the manager is dealing with performance-related behaviors. Accordingly, the manager and the employee are in a better position to deal with the problem as adults.

The manager must probe the employee to determine why the performance is not acceptable. It is important to note that the manager is not attempting to be a psychologist; he or she is interested only in the behaviors that affect performance. If the problem is personal, under no circumstances should the man-

GUIDELINES FOR COUNSELING EMPLOYEES

ABOUT THE SKILL: COUNSELING EMPLOYEES involves a number of activities that go beyond disciplinary actions. While no one set procedure is available in counseling employees, we offer the following nine guidelines that you should consider following when faced with the need to counsel an employee.[95]

1. Document all problem performance behaviors. Document specific job behaviors, like absenteeism, lateness, and poor quality, in terms of dates, times, and what happened. This provides you with objective data.

2. Deal with the employee objectively, fairly, and equitably. Treat each employee similarly. That means that one should not be counseled for something that another person did, and nothing was mentioned. Issues discussed should focus on performance behaviors.

3. Confront job performance issues only. Your main focus is on those things that affect performance. Even though it may be a personal problem, you should not try to psychoanalyze the individual. Leave that to the trained specialists! You can, however, address how these behaviors are affecting the employee's job performance.

4. Offer assistance to help the employee. Just pointing the finger at an employee serves little useful purpose. If the employee could "fix" the problem alone, he or she probably would have. Help might be needed—yours and the organizations. Offer this assistance where possible.

5. Expect the employee to resist the feedback and become defensive. It is human nature to dislike constructive or negative feedback. Expect that the individual will be uncomfortable with the discussion. Make every effort, however, to keep the meeting calm such that the message can get across. Documentation, fairness, focusing on job behaviors, and offering assistance help to reduce this defensiveness.

6. Get the employee to own up to the problem. All things said, the problem is not yours; it's the employee's. The employee needs to take responsibility for his or her behavior, and begin to look for ways to correct the problems.

7. Develop an action plan to correct performance. Once the employee has taken responsibility for the problem, develop a plan of action designed to correct the problem. Be specific as to what the employee must do (e.g., what is expected and when it is expected), and what resources you are willing to commit to assist.

8. Identify outcomes for failing to correct problems. You're there to help, not carry a poor performer forever. You need to inform the employee about what the consequences will be if he or she does not follow the action plan.

9. Monitor and control progress. Evaluate the progress the employee is making. Provide frequent feedback on what you're observing. Reinforce good efforts.

ager attempt to "fix" it. Rather, the well-informed manager, when recognizing a personal problem, will refer the employee to an appropriate place in or outside the organization (like the company's employee assistance program—we'll look at these in Chapter 13).[94] Irrespective of where the problem lies, the manager must get the employee to accept the problem. Until the employee has such an understanding, little hope exists for correcting the problem. When the employee accepts the problem, the manager should work with the employee to find ways to correct it. At this point, the manager may offer whatever assistance he or she can. Assistance aside, the employee must understand that it is his or her sole responsibility to make the change; failure to do so will only result in disciplinary procedures.

HRM WORKSHOP

*S*UMMARY

(This summary relates to the Learning Outcomes identified on p. 92.)

After having read this chapter, you should be able to:

1. **Explain the intent of the Privacy Act of 1974 and its effect on HRM.** The intent of the Privacy Act of 1974 was to require government agencies to make available to employees information contained in their personnel files. Subsequent state laws have afforded the same ability to nongovernment agencies. For HRM, they will need to ensure that policies exist and are disseminated to employees regarding access to their personnel files.

2. **Discuss the HRM implications of the Drug-Free Workplace Act of 1988 and the Polygraph Protection Act of 1988.** The implications of the Drug-Free Act of 1988 were to require government agencies, federal contractors, and those who receive more than $25,000 in government money to take various steps to ensure that their workplace is drug free. Nongovernment agencies with less than $25,000 in government grants are exempt from this law. The Polygraph Protection Act of 1988 prohibits the use of lie-detector tests in screening all job applicants. The act, however, does permit selective use of polygraphs under specific circumstances.

3. **Describe the provisions of the Worker Adjustment and Retraining Notification Act of 1988.** The Worker Adjustment and Retraining Notification Act of 1988 requires employers with 100 or more employees contemplating closing a facility or laying off 50 or more workers to provide 60 days' advance notice of the action.

4. **Identify the pros and cons of employee drug testing.** Drug testing is a contemporary issue facing many organizations. Because of the problems associated with substance abuse in our society, and our organizations specifically, companies test employees. The costs in terms of lost productivity and the like support such action. On the other hand, however, comes the issue of privacy. Does the company truly have the right to know what employees do on their own time? Additionally, validity of drug tests as well as proper procedures are often cited as reasons for not testing.

5. **Explain why honesty tests are used in hiring.** Honesty testing in hiring has been used to capture the information now unavailable from a polygraph in screening applicants. Many companies use these paper-and-pencil tests to obtain information on one's potential to steal from the company, as well as to determine whether an employee has stolen before. Validity of honesty tests has some support, and their use as an additional selection device appears reasonable.

6. **Discuss the implications of the employment-at-will doctrine.** The employment-at-will doctrine permits employers to fire employees for any reason, justified or not. Although based on nineteenth-century common law, exceptions to employment-at-will have curtailed employers' use of the doctrine.

7. **Identify the five exceptions to the employment-at-will doctrine.** The five exceptions to the employment-at-will doctrine are contractual relationships, statutory considerations, public policy violations, implied employment contracts, and a breach of good faith by the employer.

8. **Define discipline and the contingency factors that determine the severity of discipline.** Discipline is a condition in the organization when employees conduct themselves in accordance with the organization's rules and standards of acceptable behavior. Whether discipline is imposed and how severe is the action chosen should reflect such contingencies as the seriousness of the problem, duration of the problem, frequency and nature of the problem, the employee's work history, extenuating circumstances, degree of orientation, history of the organization's discipline practices, implications for other employees, and management backing.

9. **Describe the general guidelines for administering discipline.** General guidelines in administering discipline include making disciplinary actions corrective, making disciplinary actions progressive, and following the hot-stove rule—be immediate, provide ample warning, be consistent, and be impersonal.

10. **Identify how employee counseling can be used to assist a poorly performing employee.** Employee counseling can be used to assist a poorly performing employee by helping the employee make behavior changes. It is an effort to correct performance declines, and to take corrective action before more serious disciplinary action is taken.

DEMONSTRATING COMPREHENSION: *Questions for Review and Discussion*

1. What should an organization do to make employees' personnel files available to them?
2. "Employees should not be permitted to see their personnel files. Allowing them access to review the file constrains realistic observations by managers. Accordingly, as long as the information is not used against an employee, these files should be off limits." Do you agree or disagree with the statement? Explain.
3. What are the pros and cons of giving workers advance notice of a major layoff or plant closing?
4. "The goals of 'consistency' and having the punishment 'fit the crime' are incompatible with just-cause termination." Do you agree or disagree with the statement? Explain.
5. Do you believe drug testing is necessary for most organizations? Why or why not? Defend your position.
6. What are the pros and cons of using honesty tests to screen job applicants?
7. What are the advantages and disadvantages of having organizational policies that "legislate love"?
8. What is positive discipline, and how does it differ from the traditional disciplinary process?
9. What is the hot-stove rule?
10. "Whistle-blowers who go outside the organization to correct abuses in the company should be disciplined for insubordination." Do you agree or disagree? Defend your position.

CASE APPLICATION: *TEAM FUN!*

Tony, the new Director of Human Resources, Joe, the general manager and Ray, the Comptroller are in conference (in the HUDDLE) about an inventory problem with Kenny and Norton, the owners of TEAM FUN!, a sporting goods manufacturer and retail outlet. They see Roberto, an employee who works in the manufacturing plant, walk past the HUDDLE, bragging about his self-appointed "bonus" and stock shelves of uniforms. He just bought a new expensive car. During the last few months, the uniform production and sales count has been very low. The problem could be bad material and quality control from the material source, or problems with the machine operators in the production process, an accounting error, or something else. At news of Roberto's comment, Kenny explodes, "I can't believe Roberto stole all those uniforms! Maybe he just borrowed them."

Norton: "Maybe he isn't involved in this at all. What about Chris and that other guy we hired?"

Kenny: "Get all three of them in here to talk about it. Can we do a lie detector test on them? Let's do that today."

Tony: "We can do a polygraph on all the employees in the warehouse. And while we are working on security measures, I think we should institute drug testing for all employees who demo equipment. And what do the two of you think about getting smart cards for everyone?"

Kenny: "I hate this stuff. If we do anything, everyone will be grouchy for a couple of months and no work will get done. We'd have to change our name to TEAM NOFUN!"

Norton frowns in agreement and adds, "What's a smart card?"

Tony says, "Let me see your employee discipline policy. I couldn't find one in the employee manual. Consistent discipline should get good reactions. Everyone knows what's expected and what's out of bounds."

Kenny and Norton both stare at him and say, "What?"

Questions:

1. Inform Kenny and Norton about the pros and cons of a polygraph test. Is Tony's suggestion legal?
2. Is drug testing legal at TEAM FUN!? What policies should be instituted regarding drug testing?
3. Explain smart cards to Kenny and Norton. Would instituting smart card security be a good measure for TEAM FUN!?
4. Outline the general guidelines for administering discipline to Kenny and Norton.
5. Should the employee handbook have a section on employee discipline? Why?
6. What organizational culture issues are relevant to this discussion?

Working with a Team: *Dealing in Gray Areas*

Below are several scenarios and several alternatives. After reading each scenario, select the alternative you feel best handles the situation. After completing the exercise, discuss your selections with a group of four to five students. Note where differences lie in your selections.

■ A coworker, Brad, invites you to share a pizza for lunch on the outside picnic tables the company recently installed. After eating pizza, Brad lights a marijuana cigarette and asks if you would like your own or a share of his. Although you know that having or consuming drugs at the worksite is a violation of policy and law, you must decide whether to:
   a. Inform Brad's supervisor, safety coordinator, or human resource manager of the incident.
   b. Tell Brad he shouldn't smoke dope at work and encourage him to seek help such as the Employee Assistance Program in the human resource department.
   c. Say nothing, excuse yourself, and hope that when Brad returns to work, his reflexes aren't slowed, mental powers and perceptions aren't lessened, or that he won't become more forgetful and injure himself or someone else.
   d. Join Brad in prohibited behavior.
   e. Other (specify).

■ You are completing an honesty test for a potential employer. The question, "Have you ever knowingly stolen any item from an employer," is a tough one because you remember the time when you were working as a cashier in a grocery store and at break you and other cashiers would eat pieces of fruit which did not meet quality requirements of store policy. You would:
   a. Check yes.
   b. Check no, rationalizing fruit consumption as an employee benefit.
   c. Reconsider working for a company that asks such questions on tests.
   d. Other (specify).

■ A coworker shares that she recently logged into the database, printed the customer mailing list, then sold it to various list subscribers for her "petty cash fund since she didn't get the raise increase she deserved." You:
   a. Tell a human resources staff member.
   b. Tell other coworkers.
   c. Wish she hadn't told you and say nothing.
   d. Other (specify).

■ You know that a coworker uses, sells, and distributes drugs to other coworkers. You:
   a. Tell human resources.
   b. Call the company security or the local police.
   c. Leave an anonymous message.
   d. Other.

In addition to considering these situations from the employee view, in your group, consider management's perspective—that is, how management can lower the probability that these types of questionable employee behaviors would occur at work; and what actions management would like their employees to take if faced with any of these scenarios.

Enhancing Your Writing Skills

1. Develop a two- to three-page report on how drug testing and drug information programs at work may discourage the sale and use of drugs in the workplace.
2. Conduct some research on employee monitoring. In a three- to five-page writeup, describe ways that employers can monitor on-site employee behaviors. In your research, cite the benefits and drawbacks companies have had from implementing such a practice.
3. In two to three pages, develop arguments for and against using honesty tests in the hiring process. Describe how such tests can be a valid measure of employee values and behaviors.

 www.wiley.com/college/decenzo

Endnotes

1. The examples of these vignettes are adapted from Stephen P. Robbins, *Management Today, 2.0* (Upper Saddle River, NJ: Prentice-Hall, 2000), pp. 187–188. Also see Sarah Boehle, "They're Watching You," *Training* (August 2000), pp. 68–72; Sandy Naiman, "Porn Patrol Companies Wrestle with Workplace Cybersex," *Toronto Sun* (September 28, 2000), p. 69; R. Behar, "Drug Spies," *Fortune* (September 6, 1999), pp. 231–246; and "Pot Smokers See Job Offers Go Up in Smoke," *HRMagazine* (April 1999), p. 30.

2. George D. Webster, "Privacy in the Work Place," *Association Management*, Vol. 43, No. 4 (November 1990), pp. 36–37.
3. See, for example, Stephanie Overman, "A Delicate Balance Protects Everyone's Rights," *HRMagazine*, Vol. 35, No. 1 (November 1990), pp. 36–37.
4. Glenn R. Simpson, "U.S. Web Sites Violate Rules, GAO Maintains," *Wall Street Journal* (September 12, 2000), p. A-12.

5. Sherry Kuczynski, "Conflicts with State Laws May Limit Improvements to FCRA," *HR News* (February 1999), pp. 1–2; Scott F. Cooper, "The Fair Credit Reporting Act—Time for Employers to Change Their Use of Credit Information," *Employee Relations Law Journal* (Summer 1998), pp. 57–71; and Kerry Hannon, "How to Pass the Secret Credit Test," *Working Woman* (July–August 1996), pp. 30–32.

6. Wayne F. Casio, *Applied Psychology in Personnel Management,* 4th ed. (Englewood Cliffs, NJ: Prentice Hall, 1991), p. 37.

7. Jane Bryant, "Many Bosses Peeking at Workers' Credit Reports," *Baltimore Sun* (March 24, 1997), p. 11c.

8. See, for example, Commerce Clearing House, *Government Implementation for the Drug-Free Workplace Act of 1988, Part 2* (Chicago: Commerce Clearing House, 1990), p. 17.

9. Public Law 100-347.

10. This act applies to all private-sector organizations except those organizations the secretary of labor deems too small (e.g., family-owned businesses).

11. See, for example, Jeffrey Ghannam, "Truth Be Told," *ABA Journal* (September 2000), p. 17; Mary-Kathryn Zachary, "Labor Law for Supervisors: Union Campaigns Prove Sensitive for Supervisory Employees," *Supervision* (May 2000), pp. 23–26; Lois R. Wise and Steven J. Charuat, "Polygraph Testing in the Public Sector: The Status of State Legislation," *Public Personnel Management,* Vol. 19, No. 4 (Winter 1990), pp. 381–390.

12. However, in cases when they are job related (requiring someone who has fiduciary responsibilities in an organization), they may be used.

13. Commerce Clearing House, "Polygraph Testing," *Human Resource Management: Ideas and Trends,* No. 173 (July 12, 1988), p. 105.

14. Gabriella Stern and Jeffrey A. Tannenbaum, "GM Plans to Sell Car Rental Unit to Buyout Firm," *Wall Street Journal* (September 23, 1994), p. A-3.

15. Of course, GM could do just that; if it did, however, it would be in violation of WARN, and subjected to the penalties imposed under the act.

16. Worker Adjustment and Retraining Notification Act, Public Law 100-379.

17. Commerce Clearing House, "Plant Closing," *Human Resources Management: Ideas and Trends,* No. 175 (August 9, 1988), p. 129.

18. Fair Lanes was able to keep operating by filing for Chapter 11 (bankruptcy) status. See Martin C. Brook, "What Happens When the WARN Act and the Bankruptcy Code Converge?" *Employee Relations Law Journal* (Spring 1999), pp. 103–121; Charles J. Muhl, "WARN Act," *Monthly Labor Review* (April 1999), p. 45; and Jay Hancock, "Fair Lanes Emerges from Bankruptcy," *Baltimore Sun* (September 21, 1994), p. 8-C.

19. Janet Gemignani, "Substance Abusers: Terminate or Treat?" *Business and Health* (June 1999), pp. 32–38.

20. Ibid. See also "An Alternative to Drug Testing?" *Inc.* (April 1995), p. 112.

21. "Fewer Employers Are Currently Conducting Psych and Drug Tests," *HR Focus* (October 2000), p. 78. It is important to note that drug testing may be constrained by collective bargaining agreements, or state laws. See Erica Gordon Sorohan, "Making Decisions about Drug Testing," *Training and Development* (May 1994), pp. 111–117.

22. "Narc in a Can," *Executive Female* (November–December 1990), p. 24; and Edward J. Miller, "Investing in a Drug Free Workplace," *HRMagazine,* Vol. 36, No. 5 (May 1991), p. 48.

23. Jonathan A. Segal, "Urine or You're Out," *HRMagazine* (December 1994), pp. 33, 35.

24. See also, Susan E. Long, "No Comp for Employee Who Refuses Drug Test," *HR Focus* (June 1999), p. 3.

25. Ibid., and "Narc in a Can," p. 24.

26. Leslee Jaquette, "Red Lion Pleased with Drug-Testing Program," *Hotel and Motel Management,* Vol. 206, No. 3 (February 25, 1991), p. 3.

27. See Jane Easter Bahls, "Dealing with Drugs: Keep It Legal," *HRMagazine* (March 1998), pp. 104–116; and Commerce Clearing House, "The ADA Changes the Rules," *Human Resources Management: Ideas and Trends* (July 11, 1994), p. 111.

28. Debra R. Comer, "Employees' Attitude Toward Fitness-for-Duty Testing," *Journal of Managerial Issues* (Spring 2000), p. 61; J. Michael Walsh, "Is Workplace Drug-Testing Effective," *HR News* (April 1996), p. 5; and Jonathan A. Segal, "Urine or You're Out," *HRMagazine* (December 1994), pp. 30–38.

29. See Jane H. Philbrick, Barbara D. Bart, and Marcia E. Hass, "Pre-Employment Screening: A Decade of Change," *American Business Review* (June 1999), p. 75.

30. See, for example, Holtford Kent, MD, *Urine Trouble* (Scottsdale, AZ: Vandalay Press, 1997). See also Brenda Paik Sunoo, "Top-10 Ways Employees Disguise Drug Abuse," *Workforce* (May 1998), p. 16.

31. Ken Kunsman, "Oral Fluid Testing Arrives," *Occupational Health and Safety* (April 2000), pp. 28–34. Stephanie Overman, "Splitting Hairs," *HRMagazine* (August 1999), pp. 42–48. Also, for an interesting review of hair sampling, for example, see Pascal Kintz (ed.), *Drug Testing in Hair* (Boca Raton, FL: CRC Press, 1996).

32. "An Alternative to Drug Testing," *Inc.* (April 1995), p. 112.

33. Dianna L. Stone and Debra A. Kotch, "Individuals' Attitudes Toward Organizational Drug Testing Policies and Practices," *Journal of Applied Psychology,* Vol. 74, No. 3 (1989), p. 521.

34. Ibid., and Michael R. Carroll and Christina Heavrin, "Before You Drug Test," *HRMagazine* (June 1990), p. 64.

35. See, for example, Kevin R. Murphy, George C. Thornton III, and Kristin Prue, "Influence of Job Characteristics on the Acceptability of Employee Drug Testing," *Journal of Applied Psychology,* Vol. 76, No. 3 (1991), pp. 447–453.

36. This question comes from an article citing actual questions on an honesty test. See Michael P. Cronin, "This Is a Test," *Inc.* (August 1993), p. 67.

37. Deniz S. Ones and Chockalingam Viswesvaran, "Gender, Age, and Race Differences on Overt Integrity Tests: Results Across Four Large Scale Job Applicants, Data Sets," *Journal of Applied Psychology* (February 1998), pp. 35–42.

38. Ibid.

39. Ed Bean, "More Firms Use Attitude Tests to Keep Thieves Off the Payroll," *Wall Street Journal* (February 27, 1987), p. A-19.

40. Ibid.

41. Matthew Budman, "The Honest Business," *Across the Board* (November–December 1993), pp. 313–337.

42. See, for example, H. John Bernardin and Donna K. Cooke, "Validity of an Honesty Test in Predicting Theft Among

Convenience Store Employees," *Academy of Management Journal,* Vol. 38, No. 5 (Fall 1993), pp. 1097–1108.

43. Ibid.

44. Casio, p. 268.

45. See, for instance, Richard Lacayo, "Truth & Consequence," *Time* (November 1, 1999), pp. 92–98; Janet P. Near and Marcia P. Miceli, "Effective Whistle-Blowing," *Academy of Management Review,* Vol. 20, No. 3 (Summer 1995), pp. 679–708.

46. Hal Lancaster, "Workers Who Blow the Whistle on Bosses Often Pay a High Price," *Wall Street Journal* (July 18, 1995), p. B-1; and "A Whistle-Blower Gets His Reward," *Business Week* (August 28, 1995), p. 38.

47. Commerce Clearing House, "Whistleblower Can Sue for Emotional Distress, Supreme Court Rules," *Human Resources Management: Ideas and Trends,* No. 223 (June 13, 1990), pp. 97–98.

48. Ibid.

49. Kenneth L. Sovereign, *Personnel Law,* 3rd ed. (Englewood Cliffs, NJ: Prentice-Hall, 1994), p. 177.

50. Timothy R. Barnett and Daniel S. Cochran, "Making Room for the Whistleblower," *HRMagazine* (January 1991), p. 58.

51. James D. Vigneau, "To Catch a Thief . . . and Other Workplace Investigations," *HRMagazine* (January 1995), pp. 90–95.

52. See, for example, Michael F. Rosenblum, "Security v. Privacy: An Emerging Employment Dilemma," *Employee Relations Law Journal,* Vol. 17, No. 1 (Summer 1991), pp. 81–101.

53. Adapted from Glenn Rifkin, "Do Employees Have a Right to Electronic Privacy?" *New York Times* (December 8, 1991), Sections 3–8. See also, "Electronic Monitoring," *Society of Human Resource Management: Government Affairs* (September 2000), pp. 1–3; and Anne Fisher, "Is Your Office Romance the Company's Business?" *Fortune* (September 6, 1999), p. 296.

54. Lee Smith, "What the Boss Knows about You," *Fortune* (August 9, 1993), p. 89.

55. Mike France and Dennis K. Berman, "Big Brother Calling," *Business Week* (September 25, 2000), pp. 92–98.

56. Ibid.

57. Michael A. Verespej, "Internet Surfing," *Industry Week* (February 7, 2000), pp. 59–64; and Lauren M. Bernardi, "The Internet at Work: An Employment Danger Zone," *Canadian Manager* (Summer 2000), pp. 17–18.

58. Jeffrey A. Van Dorn, "Monitoring E–Mail? Better Have a Policy," *HR News* (February 1996), p. 2.

59. Michael Underhill, and Thomas A. Linthorst, "E-Mail in the Workplace: How Much Is Private?" *Society for Human Resource Management: Legal Report* (Winter 1996), p. 1; Raju Narisetti, "E-Mail Snooping Is OK in the Eyes of the Law," *Wall Street Journal* (March 20, 1996), p. A-1; and Carl Quintanilla, "Employee Monitoring Accelerates as Technology Improves," *Wall Street Journal* (June 11, 1996), p. A-1.

60. Dana Hawkins, "Who's Watching Now?" *U.S. News & World Report* (September 15, 1997), pp. 56–58; and Rochelle Sharpe, "Workers' Privacy Concerns Grow as Electronic Snooping, Urine Testing Increase," *Wall Street Journal* (September 10, 1996), p. A-1.

61. See, for example, Chianti C. Cleggett, "How Do I Love Thee? Let Me Check Our Consensual Relationship Contract," *Daily Record* (July 22, 2000), p. 1; Judy Greenwald,

"Office Romances May Court Trouble," *Business Insurance* (February 14, 2000), p. 3; Brenda Park Sunoo, "Flirting: Red Flag or Lost Art?" *Workforce* (June 2000), pp. 128–133; Dennis M. Powers, "Consensual Workplace Relationships: The Stereotypes, Policies, and Challenges," *Compensation and Benefits Review* (Summer 1999), pp. 20–32; and "Frisky Business," *Psychology Today* (March–April 1995), pp. 36–41, 70; and Alex Markels, "Employers' Dilemma: Whether to Regulate Romance," *Wall Street Journal* (February 14, 1995), pp. B-1, B-13.

62. Dennis M. Powers, "Consensual Workplace Relationships: The Stereotypes, Policies, and Challenges," *Compensation and Benefits Management* (Summer 1999), pp. 20–32; Gary W. Yunker and Barbara D. Yunker, "The Office Romance: Playing With Fire Without Getting Burned," *Personnel Psychology* (Winter 1999), pp. 1084–1086; William C. Symonds, Steve Hamm, and Gail DeGeorge, "Sex on the Job," *Business Week* (February 16, 1998), pp. 30–31; and Jonathan A. Segal, "The World May Welcome Lovers," *HRMagazine* (June 1996), pp. 170–179.

63. "Love Contracts," *Training* (August 1999), p. 19; Anne B. Fisher, "Getting Comfortable with Couples in the Workplace," *Fortune* (October 3, 1994), pp. 139–144.

64. Ibid., p. 142.

65. See, for example, Jason A. Cecil, "Taking the "Cracker" Out of Cracker Barrel," *Juris Publici: Opinion Editorial* (November 1999), pp. 1–4; Susan Kerlinger, "Company Policy Disputed in Cracker Barrel Protest," *Miscellany News* (April 16, 1999), pp. 1–3; and Jack Hayes, "Cracker Barrel Comes Under Fire for Ousting Gays," *Nation's Restaurant News,* Vol. 25 (March 4, 1991), p. 1.

66. *Payne v. Western and Atlantic Railroad Co.,* 812 Tenn. 507 (1884). See also Paul Falcone, "A Legal Dichotomy?" *HRMagazine* (May 1999), pp. 110–120.

67. Jane Easter Bahls, "Playing with Fire," *Entrepreneur* (October 1994), p. 66.

68. *Payne v. Western and Atlantic Railroad Co.,* 812 Tenn. 507 (1884). See also Paul Falcone, "A Legal Dichotomy?" *HRMagazine* (May 1999), pp. 110–120.

69. See, for instance, "Employees from Hell," *Inc.* (January 1995), p. 54.

70. Commerce Clearing House, *Topical Law Reports* (Chicago: Commerce Clearing House, 1989), p. 2773.

71. Paul Falcone, "A Legal Dichotomy?" *HRMagazine* (May 1999), pp. 110–120; and Deborah A. Ballam, "Employment-at-Will: The Impending Death of a Doctrine," *American Business Law Journal* (Summer 2000), pp. 653–687.

72. Adapted from Carroll R. Daugherty, *Enterprise Wire Co.* 46 LA 359 (1966).

73. See, for example, John J. Meyers, David V. Radack, and Paul M. Yenerall, "Making the Most of Employment Contracts," *HRMagazine* (August 1998), p. 106; Kenneth L. Sovereign, *Personnel Law,* 3rd ed. (Englewood Cliffs, NJ: Prentice Hall, 1994), p. 178.

74. *Toussaint v. Blue Cross and Blue Shield of Michigan,* 408 Michigan, 529, 292 N.W. 2d 880 (1980).

75. Sovereign, p. 180.

76. Ibid.

77. Ibid., p. 179.

78. Ibid.

79. *Fortune v. National Cash Register,* 364 373 Massachusetts 91, 36 N.E. 2d 1251 (1977).

80. For another view of means of "reclaiming" employment-at-will practices, see Theresa Donahue Egler, "A Manager's Guide to Employment Contracts," *HRMagazine* (May 1996), pp. 28–33.

81. See Dennis L. Johnson, Christie A. King, and John G. Kurutz, "A Safe Termination Model for Supervisors," *HRMagazine* (May 1996), pp. 73–78; and Wallace Wohlking, "Effective Discipline in Employee Relations," *Personnel Journal* (September 1975), pp. 491–492.

82. Martin Levy, "Discipline for Professional Employees," *Personnel Journal* (December 1990), pp. 27–28.

83. Paul Falcone, "Adopt a Formal Approach to Progressive Discipline," *HRMagazine* (November 1998), pp. 55–59; and Paul Falcone, "The Fundamentals of Progressive Discipline," *HRMagazine* (February 1997), pp. 90–94.

84. Robert McGarvey, "Lords of Discipline," *Entrepreneur* (January 2000), pp. 127–129; and Walter Kiechel, "How to Discipline in the Modern Age," *Fortune* (May 7, 1990), pp. 179–180.

85. See for instance, John E. Lyncheski, "Mishandling Terminations Causes Legal Nightmares," *HRMagazine* (May 1995), pp. 25–30.

86. It is true that two other disciplinary actions may be used—pay cuts or demotion—but they are rare.

87. Paul Falcone, "Letters of Clarification: A Disciplinary Alternative," *HRMagazine* (August 1999), p. 134.

88. See also Jeffrey C. Connor, "Disarming Terminated Employees," *HRMagazine* (January 2000), pp. 113–116; and Michael A. Verespej, "Wrongful Demotion," *Industry Week* (February 5, 1996), p. 18.

89. A. B. Chimezie, Osigweh Yg, and William R. Hutchinson, "To Punish or Not to Punish? Managing Human Resources Through Positive Discipline," *Employee Relations* (March 1990), pp. 27–32. See also Herff L. Moore and Helen Moore, "Discipline + Help = Motivation," *Credit Union Management* (August 1998), p. 33.

90. A. B. Chimezie, Osigweh Yg, and William R. Hutchinson, "Positive Discipline," *Human Resource Management* (Fall 1989), p. 367.

91. Michael Scott, "7 Pitfalls for Managers When Handling Poor Performers and How to Overcome Them," *Manage* (February 2000), pp. 12–13.

92. Ibid.

93. Gerald D. Cook, "Employee Counseling Session," *Supervision* (August 1989), p. 3.

94. See James Greiff, "When an Employee's Performance Slumps," *Nation's Business* (January 1989), pp. 44–45.

95. Adapted from Commerce Clearing House, "The Do's and Don'ts of Confronting a Troubled Employee," *Topical Law Reports* (Chicago, IL: Commerce Clearing House October 1990), pp. 4359–4360; Gerald D. Cook, "Employee Counseling Session," *Supervision* (August 1989), p. 3; and Andrew E. Schuartz, "Counseling the Marginal Performer," *Management Solutions* (March 1988), p. 30.

5

EMPLOYMENT PLANNING AND JOB ANALYSIS

LEARNING OUTCOMES

AFTER READING THIS CHAPTER, YOU WILL BE ABLE TO:

1. Describe the importance of employment planning.
2. Define the steps involved in the employment planning process.
3. Explain what Human Resource Information Systems are used for.
4. Define what is meant by the term *job analysis.*
5. Identify the six general techniques for obtaining job analysis information.
6. Describe the steps involved in conducting the job analysis.
7. Explain the difference between job descriptions, job specifications, and job evaluations.
8. Describe how job analysis permeates all aspects of HRM.

K risten Schaffner-Irvin is an individual who sees opportunities in the changing world.[1] A native of Huntington Beach, California, Kristen was a stay-at-home mom. But money was short in the family, and Schaffner-Irvin felt that she had to go to work. She wanted to find a job that would allow her to care for her children while simultaneously bringing some extra income into the household. Having grown up in a family-owned fuel business, Kristen knew the ins and outs of the fuel-delivery industry. However, she didn't want to go to work for her father. Instead, she wanted to make it on her own—fulfilling a lifelong dream of being her own boss, in her own company. So with just a laptop computer and a telephone, she started Team Petroleum in 1992.

Having worked in the industry, Schaffner-Irvin recognized that a more efficient fuel-delivery system was possible. Although she doesn't own any oil wells, fuel depots, or even fuel trucks, she felt that her company could be successful if she could demonstrate that Team Petroleum added value to its customers. Kristen envisioned this happening by buying fuel for her customers from suppliers and having it delivered to them. But delivery alone would not be sufficient to add value. She offered her customers a special service that her competitors didn't. She has her fuel tanks linked to her computer system. This system monitors the customer's fuel consumption, and automatically transmits to Schaffner-Irvin's office when another delivery is needed. With some 80 fuel suppliers nationwide in her network, she is able to schedule fuel deliveries more effectively and efficiently than if her customers did this themselves with their own staff. And she offers this service and makes scheduled deliveries on a 24/7 basis.

Since 1992, Kristen Schaffner-Irvin has nurtured a thriving business. She now employs eight people in her business and has revenues in excess of $34 million. Her desire, focus, and ability to plan effectively, to use technology, and to have the right people working for her has turned Kristen's opportunity into a reality. She also now has more time to be with her children and her husband and to enjoy the lifestyle that her income provides!

INTRODUCTION

Kristen Schaffner-Irvin realized that changes do occur in organizations. But adapting to these changes requires all organizational members to understand where the organization is going and to support what the enterprise is about to do. Individuals like Schaffner-Irvin understand that before you can depart on a journey, you have to know your destination. Just think about the last time you took a vacation. For example, if you live in Memphis, Tennessee, and decide to go to a Florida beach for two weeks in the summer, you need to decide specifically what beach—Daytona or Fort Lauderdale—you want to go to and the best route you can take to get you there. In an elementary form, this is what planning is all about—knowing where you are going and how you are going to get there. The same holds true for human resource management.

Whenever an organization is in the process of determining its human resource needs, it is engaged in a process we call **employment planning.** Employment planning is one of the most important elements in a successful human resource management program,[2] because it is a process by which an organization ensures that it has the right number and kinds of people, at the right place, at the right time, capable of effectively and efficiently completing those tasks that will help the organization achieve its overall strategic objectives.[3] Employment planning, then, ultimately translates the organization's overall goals into the number and types of workers needed to meet those goals. Without clear-cut planning, and a direct linkage to the organization's strategic direction, estimations of an organization's human resource needs are reduced to mere guesswork.

This means that employment planning cannot exist in isolation. It must be linked to the organization's overall strategy.[4] Thirty-five years ago, outside of possibly the firm's top executives, few employees in a typical firm really knew about the company's long-range objectives. The strategic efforts were often no more than an educated guess in determining the organization's direction. But things are different today. Aggressive domestic and global competition, for instance, has made strategic planning virtually mandatory. Although it's not our intention to go into every detail of the strategic planning process in this chapter, senior HRM officials need to understand it because they're playing a more vital role in the strategic process. It's often HRM's responsibility to lead the entire management team in "showing the best way to take charge of the new workplace."[5] Let's look at a fundamental strategic planning process in an organization.

Employment Planning
Process of determining an organization's human resource needs.

AN ORGANIZATIONAL FRAMEWORK

The strategic planning process in an organization is both long and continuous.[6] At the beginning of the process, the organization's main emphasis is to determine what business it is in. This is commonly referred to as developing the **mission statement.** At Oticon Holding A/S of Hellerup, Denmark, company officials set their sights on becoming the world's premier hearing-aid manufacturer. Why is the mission statement important? Achieving that mission "drives the business, mobilizes the workers, and gets the high-quality product to the market."[7] Take, for instance, a part of Black & Decker's mission statement—to be the premier manufacturer and marketer of tools. What that statement does is clarify for all organizational members what exactly the company is about. Accordingly, the company specifies clearly why it exists and sets the course for company operations. That is, a sound mission statement facilitates the decision-making process.

Mission Statement The reason an organization is in business.

The decision to focus on the DeWalt tool line of products was made by Black & Decker management to focus on a core competency in the tool manufacturing market.

SWOT Analysis A process for determining an organization's strengths, weaknesses, opportunities, and threats.

Strengths Things that an organization does well.

Core Competency Those organizational strengths that represent unique skills or resources.

Weaknesses Those resources that an organization lacks or does not do well.

For example, Black & Decker's decision to sell industrial hand tools and enter that market with its DeWalt line of products is a decision that is within the boundaries set by the mission. However, these same managers would know that any effort to expand the company's product lines to include home appliances is not consistent with the mission. That's why, when Black & Decker in the late 1990s reformulated its mission statement to reflect its core business (tools), company officials decided to sell off its home appliance division—the coffee makers, toaster ovens, mixers, and so on.[8] This discussion is not meant to say that mission statements are written in stone; at any time, after careful study and deliberation, they can be changed. For example, the March of Dimes was originally created to facilitate the cure of infantile paralysis (polio). When polio was essentially eradicated in the 1950s, the organization redefined its mission as seeking cures for children's diseases. Nonetheless, the need to specifically define an organization's line of business is critical to its survival.

After reaching agreement on what business the company is in and who its consumers are, senior management then begins to set strategic goals.[9] During this phase, these managers define objectives for the company for the next five to twenty years. These objectives are broad statements that establish targets the organization will achieve. After these goals are set, the next step in the strategic planning process begins—the corporate assessment. During this phase, a company begins to analyze its goals, its current strategies, its external environment, its strengths and weaknesses, and its opportunities and threats, in terms of whether they can be achieved with the current organizational resources. Commonly referred to as a "gap or **SWOT** (strengths, weaknesses, opportunities, and threats) **analysis,**" the company begins to look at what skills, knowledge, and abilities are available internally, and where shortages in terms of people skills or equipment may exist (see Ethical Issues in HRM).

This analysis forces management to recognize that every organization, no matter how large and powerful, is constrained in some way by the resources and skills it has available. An automobile manufacturer, such as Ferrari, cannot start making minivans simply because its management sees opportunities in that market. Ferrari does not have the resources to successfully compete against the likes of DaimlerChrysler, Ford, Toyota, and Nissan. On the other hand, Renault and a Peugeot Fiat partnership can, and they may begin expanding their European markets by selling minivans in North America.[10]

The SWOT analysis should lead to a clear assessment of the organization's internal resources—such as capital, worker skills, patents, and the like. It should also indicate organizational departmental abilities such as training and development, marketing, accounting, human resources, research and development, and management information systems. Internal resources that are available or things that the organization does well are called its **strengths.** And any of those strengths that represent unique skills or resources that can determine the organization's competitive edge are called its **core competency.** Calgary's Big Rock Brewery has built a core competency simply by creating a special flavor for its beers and giving them "ugly names like Warthog and Grasshopper."[11] On the other hand, those resources that an organization lacks or activities that the firm does not do well are its **weaknesses.** This SWOT Analysis phase of the strategic planning process cannot be overstated; it serves as the link between the organization's goals and ensuring that the company can meet its objectives—that is, establishes the direction of the company through strategic planning.

The company must determine what jobs need to be done, and how many and what types of workers will be required. In management terminology, we call

COMPETITIVE INTELLIGENCE

ONE OF THE FASTEST-GROWING AREAS of a SWOT analysis is competitive intelligence.[12] It seeks basic information about competitors: Who are they? What are they doing? How will what they are doing affect us? One individual who has closely studied **competitive intelligence** suggests that 95 percent of the competitor-related information an organization needs to make crucial strategic decisions is available and accessible to the public.[13] In other words, competitive intelligence isn't organizational espionage. Advertisements, promotional materials, press releases, reports filed with government agencies, annual reports, want ads, newspaper reports, information placed on the Internet, and industry studies are examples of readily accessible sources of information. Specific information on an industry and associated organizations is increasingly available through electronic databases. Managers can literally tap into a wealth of competitive information through purchasing access to databases sold by companies such as Nexus and Knight-Ridder or obtained free through information contained on corporate or Securities and Exchange Commission web sites. Trade shows and the debriefing of your own sales staff can be other good sources of information on competitors. Many organizations even regularly buy competitors' products and have their own employees evaluate them to learn about new technical innovations.

The techniques and sources listed above can reveal a number of issues and concerns that can affect an organization. But in a global business environment, environmental scanning and obtaining competitive intelligence become more complex.[14] Because global scanning must gather information from around the world, many of the previously mentioned information sources may be too limited. One means of overcoming this difficulty is for management to subscribe to news services that review newspapers and magazines from around the globe and provide summaries to client companies.

Knowing as much as you can about your competition is simply good business sense. But how far can you go to obtain that information? It's clear that over the past few years competitive intelligence activities have increased—but sometimes these same well-intended actions have crossed the line to corporate spying.[15] For example, when a company pays for information that was obtained by someone who hacked a company's computer system, receiving that data is illegal. By the late 1990s, nearly 1,500 U.S. companies had been victims of some type of corporate espionage, resulting in more than $300 billion in losses for these organizations.[16]

Most individuals do understand the difference between what is legal and what's not. That's not the issue. Rather, while some competitive intelligence activities may be legal, are they ethical? Consider the following scenarios:

1. You obtain copies of lawsuits and civil cases that have been filed against a competitor. Although the information is public, you use some of the surprising findings against your competitor in bidding for a job.
2. You pretend to be a journalist who's writing a story about the company. You call company officials and seek responses to some specific questions regarding the company's plans for the future. You use this information in designing a strategy to compete better with this company.
3. You apply for a job at one of your competitors. During the interview you ask specific questions about the company and its direction. You report what you've learned back to your employer.
4. You dig through a competitor's trash and find some sensitive correspondence about a new product release. You use this information to launch your competing product before your competitor's.
5. You purchase some stock in your competitor's company so that you'll get the annual report and other company information that is sent out. You use this information to your advantage in developing your marketing plan.

Which, if any, of these actions are unethical? Defend your position. What ethical guidelines would you suggest for competitive intelligence activities? Explain.

Competitive Intelligence
Seeking basic information about competitors.

this *organizing*. Thus, establishing the structure of the organization assists in determining the skills, knowledge, and abilities required of jobholders. It is only at this point that we begin to look at people to meet these criteria. And that's where human resource management comes in to play an integral role. To determine what skills are needed, HRM conducts a job analysis. Exhibit 5-1 is a graphic representation of this process. The key message in Exhibit 5-1 is that all jobs in the organization ultimately must be tied to the company's mission and strategic direction. Unless jobs can be linked to the organization's strategic goals, these goals become a moving target. It's no wonder, then, that employment planning has become more critical in organizations. Let's look at how human resource planning operates within the strategic planning process.

EXHIBIT 5-1
*The Strategic Direction—
Human Resource Linkage*

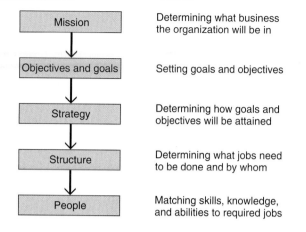

EXHIBIT 5-1
*The Strategic Direction—
Human Resource Linkage*

Mission	Determining what business the organization will be in
Objectives and goals	Setting goals and objectives
Strategy	Determining how goals and objectives will be attained
Structure	Determining what jobs need to be done and by whom
People	Matching skills, knowledge, and abilities to required jobs

LINKING ORGANIZATIONAL STRATEGY TO EMPLOYMENT PLANNING

To ensure that appropriate personnel are available to meet the requirements set during the strategic planning process, human resource managers engage in employment planning. The purpose of this planning effort is to determine what HRM requirements exist for current and future supplies and demands for workers. For example, if a company has set as one of its goals to expand its production capabilities over the next five years, such action will require that skilled employees be available to handle the jobs. After this assessment, employment planning matches the supplies and demands for labor, supporting the people component.[17]

How Do You Assess Current Human Resources?

Assessing current human resources begins by developing a profile of the organization's current employees. This is an internal analysis that includes information about the workers and the skills they currently possess. In an era of sophisticated computer systems, it is not too difficult for most organizations to generate an effective and detailed human resources inventory report. The input to this report would be derived from forms completed by employees and then checked by supervisors. Such reports would include a complete list of all employees by name, education, training, prior employment, current position, performance ratings, salary level, languages spoken, capabilities, and specialized skills.[18] For example, if internal translators were needed for suppliers, customers, or employee assistance, a contact list could be developed.

From a planning viewpoint, this input is valuable in determining what skills are currently available in the organization. The inventory serves as a guide for supporting new organizational pursuits or in altering the organization's strategic direction. This report also has value in other HRM activities, such as selecting individuals for training and development, promotion, and transfers. The completed profile of the human resources inventory can also provide crucial information for identifying current or future threats to the organization's ability to successfully meets its goals. For example, the organization can use the information from the inventory to identify specific variables that may have a particular relationship to training needs, productivity improvements, and succession

EMPLOYEE DATABASE REQUIREMENTS

OBTAINING INFORMATION ON JOB REQUIREMENTS AND BUILDING a database on employee skills and job requirements have been enhanced with technology. There are now alernatives to massive, expensive systems. Here are some opportunities that technology has offered to HRM practitioners.

O*Net OnLine: Online database (www.onetcenter.org) providing information on "critical information on essential elements of job performance." This site provides information on worker characteristics, worker requirements, experience requirements, occupational requirements, occupation characteristics, and occupation specific information. O*Net is the replacement for the Department of Labor's *Dictionary of Occupational Titles*. Materials can be accessed free on the Internet. Requires Adobe software.

SOAR: Part of the Job Accommodation Network (JAN: www.jan.wvu.edu); specializes in providing information on job accommodations. SOAR (Searchable Online Accommodation Resource) is "designed to

let users explore various accommodation options for persons with disabilities in the work setting (www.jan.wvu.edu/soar/ index.html). This is a free service.

HR Task Counselor: A comprehensive HRIS system that "stores all critical employee information, tracks salary history, training, and EEO status, stores vital benefit information," and gathers data and prints relevant government reporting forms. HR Task Counselor (www.hrpress-software.com/hrtask.html) is available from HR Press, and is available in software or network versions. Prices start at $495 and vary based on the format used and size of the company.

Staff Files: Staff Files (HR Press, $195 CD version; www.hrpress-software.com/staffile.html) permits tracking of a wide variety of employee information such as general employee data (name, address, Social Security number, etc.), emergency numbers, wages, performance evaluations, as well as separation information.

planning. A characteristic like technical obsolescence, or workers who are not trained to function with new computer requirements, can, if it begins to permeate the entire organization, adversely affect the organization's performance.

Human Resource Information System A computerized system that assists in the processing of HRM information.

Human Resource Information Systems   To assist in the HR inventory, organizations have implemented a **human resource information system (HRIS).** The HRIS (sometimes referred to as a human resource management system [HRMS]) is designed to quickly fulfill the human resource management informational needs of the organization.[19] The HRIS is a database system that keeps important information about employees in a central and accessible location—even information on the global work force.[20] When such information is required, the data can be retrieved and used to facilitate employment planning decisions. Its technical potential permits the organization to track most information about employees and jobs, and to retrieve that information when needed.[21] An HRIS may also be used to help track EEO data.[22] Exhibit 5-2 is a listing of typical information tracked on an HRIS.

HRISs have grown significantly in popularity in the past two decades. This is essentially due to the recognition that management needs timely information on its people; moreover, new technological breakthroughs have significantly cut the cost of these systems.[23] Additionally, HRISs are now more "user-friendly" and provide quick and responsive reports, especially when linked to the organization's management information system.[24]

At a time when quick analysis of an organization's human resources is critical, the HRIS is filling a void in the human resource planning process.[25] With

EXHIBIT 5-2
*Information Categories of
Human Resource
Management Systems*

Group 1 Basic Nonconfidential Information
   Employee name
   Organization name
   Work location
   Work phone number
Group 2 General Nonconfidential Information
   Information in the previous category, plus:
   Social Security number
   Other organization information (code, effective date)
   Position-related information (code, title, effective date)
Group 3 General Information with Salary
   Information in the previous category, plus:
   Current salary, effective date, amount of last change, type of last change and
      reason for last change)
Group 4 Confidential Information with Salary
   Information in the previous category, plus:
   Other position information (EEO code, position ranking and FLSA)
   Education data
Group 5 Extended Confidential Information with Salary
   Information in the previous category, plus:
   Bonus information
   Projected salary increase information
   Performance evaluation information

Source: Joan E. Goodman, "Does Your HRIS Speak English?" *Personnel Journal* (March 1990), p. 81. Used with permission.

information readily available, organizations are in a better position to quickly move forward in achieving their organizational goals.[26] Additionally, the HRIS is useful in other aspects of human resource management, providing data support for compensation and benefits programs, as well as providing a necessary link to corporate payroll.[27]

Replacement Charts   In addition to the computerized HRIS system, some organizations also generate a separate senior management inventory report. This report, called a **replacement chart,** typically covers individuals in middle-to-upper-level management positions. In an effort to facilitate succession planning[28]—ensuring that another individual is ready to move into a position of higher responsibility—the replacement chart highlights those positions that may become vacant in the near future due to retirements, promotions, transfers, resignations, or death of the incumbent. But not all companies use replacement charts, and this can create confusion, or even worse.[29] The gravity of having replacement charts was truly witnessed in April 1996 when U.S. Commerce Secretary Ronald Brown's plane crashed while on a trip to the Balkans. On board with Brown were 30 executives from U.S. companies. Those organizations without replacement charts were at a loss for a substantial period of time.[30]

Replacement Charts HRM organizational charts indicating positions that may become vacant in the near future and the individuals who may fill the vacancy.

Against this list of positions is placed the individual manager's skills inventory to determine if there is sufficient managerial talent to cover potential future vacancies. This "readiness" chart then gives management an indication of time frames for succession, as well as helping to spot any skill shortages.[31] Should skill shortages exist, human resource management can either recruit new employees or intensify employee development efforts (see Chapter 8).

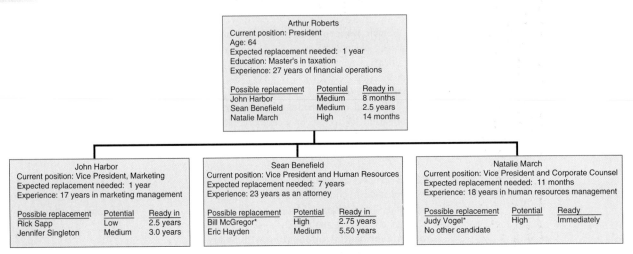

* Denotes minority

EXHIBIT 5-3
A sample Replacement Chart

Replacement charts look very similar to traditional organizational charts. With the incumbents listed in their positions, those individuals targeted for replacement are listed beneath with the expected time in which they will be prepared to take on the needed responsibility. We have provided a sample replacement chart in Exhibit 5-3.

How Does One Determine the Demand for Labor?

Once an assessment of the organization's current human resources situation has been made and the future direction of the organization has been considered, a projection of future human resource needs can be developed. It will be necessary to perform a year-by-year analysis for every significant job level and type. In effect, the result is a human resource inventory covering specified years into the future. These pro-forma inventories obviously must be comprehensive, and therefore complex. Organizations usually require a diverse mix of people. That's because employees are not perfectly substitutable for one another within an organization. For example, a shortage of actuaries in an insurance company cannot be offset by transferring employees from the purchasing area where there is an oversupply. If accurate estimates are to be made of future demands in both qualitative and quantitative terms, more information is needed than just to determine that, for example, in the next 24 months, we will have to hire another 85 individuals. Instead, it is necessary to know what types of employees, in terms of skills, knowledge, and abilities, are required. Remember, these skills, knowledge, and abilities are determined based on the jobs required to meet the strategic direction of the organization. Accordingly, our forecasting methods must allow for the recognition of specific job needs as well as the total number of vacancies.

Can We Predict the Future Supply of Labor?

Estimating changes in internal supply requires HRM to look at those factors that can either increase or decrease its employee base. As previously noted in the discussion on estimating demand, forecasting of supply must also concern itself with the micro, or unit, level. For example, if one individual in Department X is transferred to a position in Department Y, and an individual in Department Y is transferred to a position in Department X, the net effect on the organization is zero. However, if only one individual is initially involved—say, promoted and sent to another location in the company—it is only through effective human resource planning that a competent replacement will be available to fill the position vacated by the departing employee. An increase in the supply of any unit's human resources can come from a combination of four sources: new hires, contingent workers, transfers-in, or individuals returning from leaves.[32] The task of predicting these new inputs can range from simple to complex.

Decreases in the internal supply can come about through retirements, dismissals, transfers-out of the unit, layoffs, voluntary quits, sabbaticals, prolonged illnesses, or deaths.[33] Some of these occurrences are obviously easier to predict than others. The easiest to forecast are retirements, assuming that employees typically retire after a certain length of service, and the fact that most organizations require some advance notice of one's retirement intent. Given a history of the organization, HRM can predict with some accuracy how many retirements will occur over a given time period. Remember, however, that retirement, for the most part, is voluntary. Under the Age Discrimination in Employment Act, an organization cannot force most employees to retire.

At the other extreme, voluntary quits, prolonged illnesses, and deaths are difficult to predict—if they can be at all. Deaths of employees are the most difficult to forecast because they are often unexpected. Although Southwest Airlines or Nissan Motors can use probability statistics to estimate the number of deaths that will occur among its employee population, such techniques are useless for forecasting in small organizations or estimating the exact positions that will be affected in large ones. Voluntary quits can also be predicted by utilizing probabilities when the population size is large. In a company like Microsoft, managers can estimate the approximate number of voluntary quits during any given year. In a department consisting of two or three workers, however, probability estimation is essentially meaningless. Weak predictive ability in small units is unfortunate, too, because voluntary quits typically have the greatest impact on such units.

In between the extremes—transfers, layoffs, sabbaticals, and dismissals—forecasts within reasonable limits of accuracy can be made. Since all four of these types of action are controllable by management—that is, they are either initiated by management or are within management's veto prerogative—each type can be reasonably predicted. Of the four, transfers out of a unit, such as lateral moves, demotions, or promotions, are the most difficult to predict because they depend on openings in other units. Layoffs are more controllable and anticipated by management, especially in the short run. Sabbaticals, too, are reasonably easy to forecast, since most organizations' sabbatical policies require a reasonable lead time between request and initiation of the leave. For example, at the McDonald's Corporation,[34] employees with ten years of continuous service are eligible for an eight-week sabbatical. The sabbatical can be taken during any eight continuous weeks, but with advanced approval of management. This gives the corporation ample time to find a replacement if needed.

Dismissals, based on inadequate job performance, can usually be forecasted with the same method as voluntary quits, using probabilities where large numbers of employees are involved. Additionally, performance evaluation reports are usually a reliable source for isolating the number of individuals whose employment might have to be terminated at a particular point in time due to unsatisfactory work performance.

Where Will We Find Workers?

The previous discussion on supply considered internal factors. We will now review those factors outside the organization that influence the supply of available workers. Recent graduates from schools and colleges expand the supply of available human resources. This market is vast and includes high-school and college graduates, as well as those who received highly specialized training through an alternative supplier of job skills training. Entrants to the work force from sources other than schools may also include men and women seeking full or part-time work; students seeking work to pay for their education or support themselves while in school; employees returning from military service; job seekers who have been recently laid off; and so on. Migration into a community may also increase the number of individuals who are seeking employment opportunities and accordingly represent another source for the organization to consider as potential additions to its labor supply.

It should be noted that consideration of only these supply sources just identified tends to understate the potential labor supply because many people can be retrained through formal or on-the-job training. Therefore, the potential supply can differ from what one might conclude by looking only at the obvious sources of supply. For example, with a minimal amount of training, a journalist can become qualified to perform the tasks of a book editor; thus, an organization that is having difficulty securing individuals with skills and experience in book editing should consider those candidates who have had recent journalism or similar experience and are interested in being editors. In similar fashion, the potential supply for many other jobs can be expanded.

How Do We Match the Demand and Supply of Labor?

The objective of employment planning is to bring together the forecasts of future demand for workers and the supply for human resources, both current and future. The result of this effort is to pinpoint shortages both in number and in kind; to highlight areas where overstaffing may exist (now or in the near future); and to keep abreast of the opportunities existing in the labor market to hire qualified employees—either to satisfy current needs or to stockpile potential candidates for the future.

Special attention must be paid to determining shortages. Should an organization find that the demand for human resources will be increasing in the future, then it will have to hire or contract with additional staff or transfer people within the organization, or both, to balance the numbers, skills, mix, and quality of its human resources. An often-overlooked action, but one that may be necessary because of inadequate availability of human resources, is to change the organization's objectives. Just as inadequate financial resources can restrict the growth and opportunities available to an organization, the unavailability of the right types of employees can also act as such a constraint, even leading to changing the organization's objectives.

When dealing with employment planning, another outcome is also likely: the existence of an oversupply. When this happens, human resource management must undertake some difficult steps to sever these people from the organization— a process referred to as *decruitment*. There was a time in Corporate America when organizations followed a relatively simple rule. In good times you hire employees; in bad times, you fire them. Since the late 1980s that "rule" no longer holds true, at least for most of the largest companies in the world. Throughout the 1990s, for instance, most Fortune 500 companies made significant cuts in their overall staff. IBM cut staff by 122,000 workers, and 83,000 employees were let go at AT&T. Boeing reduced its staff by 61,000, Sears cut 50,000 jobs, and Eastman Kodak reduced its work force by more than 34,000 positions.[35] This **downsizing** phenomenon is not going on just in the United States. Jobs are be-

Downsizing An activity in an organization aimed at creating greater efficiency by eliminating certain jobs.

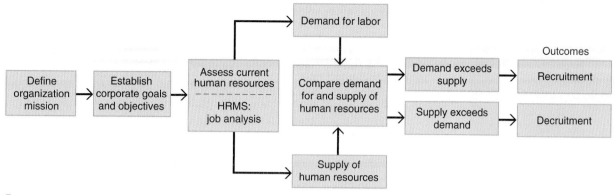

EXHIBIT 5-4
Employment Planning and the Strategic Planning Process

ing eliminated in almost all industrialized nations. For example, Peugeot (France) cut nearly 10 percent of its work force over a five-year period; Renault (France) eliminated 17 percent of its jobs; and Volkswagen (Germany) eliminated about 30,000 jobs and cut the remaining employees' pay by 16 percent.[36] In Japan, Sony eliminated 17,000 workers, NEC cut 15,000 jobs, and Toyo Engineering eliminated 29 percent of its work force.[37]

Why this trend for downsizing? Organizations are attempting to increase their flexibility to better respond to change. Continuous improvement and work process engineering are creating flatter structures and redesigning work to increase efficiency. The result is a need for fewer employees. Are we implying that big companies are disappearing? Absolutely not! It is how they are operating that is changing. Big isn't necessarily inefficient. Companies such as PepsiCo, Home Depot, and Motorola manage to blend large size with agility by dividing their organization into smaller, more-flexible units.

Rightsizing Linking employee needs to organizational strategy.

Downsizing as a strategy is here to stay. It's part of a larger goal of balancing staff to meet changing needs.[38] When organizations become overstaffed, they will likely cut jobs. At the same time, they are likely to increase staff when doing so adds value to the organization. A better term for this organizational action, then, might be **rightsizing.** Rightsizing involves linking staffing levels to organizational goals. For example, in one recent year, AT&T cut 8000 jobs—mostly operators being replaced by voice-recognition technology—while at the same time, adding staff in marketing and network systems. Accordingly, rightsizing promotes greater use of outside firms for providing necessary products and services, called **outsourcing,** in an effort to remain flexible and responsive to the ever-changing environment.[39]

Outsourcing Sending work "outside" the organization to be done by individuals not employed full time with the organization.

Corporate strategic and employment planning are two critically linked processes; one cannot survive without the other. Accordingly, to perform both properly requires a blending of activities. We have portrayed these linkages in Exhibit 5-4.

DETERMINING ESSENTIAL SKILLS, KNOWLEDGE, AND ABILITIES

Vital Resources (VR), a corporate strategic development firm, has been working with a client that has experienced a 65 percent turnover of sales professionals over the past 18 months. An analysis of the resignations indicated that the average length of stay has been only 9 months. Perplexed by this dilemma and the

What skills, knowledge, and abilities does this employee need to be successful in her job as a network specialist? The answer to that question lies in the job analysis. Information for the job analysis is used to develop job descriptions and job specifications, which detail the duties of the job and the performance expectations as well as what personal characteristics the employee must possess to be a successful performer.

A job analysis involves identifying and describing what is happening on a job.

Job Analysis Provides information about jobs currently being done and the knowledge, skills, and abilities that individuals need to perform the jobs adequately.

Observation Method A job analysis technique in which data are gathered by watching employees work.

resulting loss to productivity and revenue, consultants from VR recommended an investigation to find out why such high turnover levels exist.

The investigation, while much more complex, involved contacting most of the individuals who resigned to ask them why they quit. The responses were that what they were hired to do and what they were required to do were often two different things. The latter required different skills and aptitudes. Feeling frustrated and bored, and not wanting to jeopardize their career records, they quit. Unfortunately, the company's training costs these past three years had run approximately 300 percent over budget. When one of the senior managers was asked what it was about the jobs that made it so difficult to properly match the job requirements with people skills, she did not have an answer. It appeared that no one in the organization had taken the time to find out what the jobs were all about. In other words, the job analysis process was lacking.

What Is Job Analysis?

A **job analysis** is a systematic exploration of the activities within a job. It is a technical procedure used to define the duties, responsibilities, and accountabilities of a job. This analysis "involves the identification and description of what is happening on the job . . . accurately and precisely identifying the required tasks, the knowledge, and the skills necessary for performing them, and the conditions under which they must be performed."[40] Let's explore how this can be achieved.

Job Analysis Methods

The basic methods that HRM can use to determine job elements and the essential knowledge, skills, and abilities for successful performance include the following:

Observation Method Using the **observation method,** a job analyst watches employees directly or reviews films of workers on the job. Although the observation method provides firsthand information, workers often do not function most efficiently when they are being watched, and thus distortions in the job analysis can occur. This method also requires that the entire range of activities be observable. This is possible with some jobs, but impossible for many—for example, most managerial jobs.

Individual Interview Method Using the **individual interview method,** a team of job incumbents is selected and extensively interviewed. The results of these interviews are combined into a single job analysis. This method is effective for assessing what a job entails, and involving employees in the job analysis is essential.

Group Interview Method The **group interview method** is similar to the individual interview method except that a number of job incumbents are interviewed simultaneously. Accuracy is increased in assessing jobs, but group dynamics may hinder its effectiveness.

Structured Questionnaire Method Under the **structured questionnaire method,** workers are sent a specifically designed questionnaire on which they check or rate items they perform on their job from a long list of possible task items. This technique is excellent for gathering information about jobs. However, exceptions to a job may be overlooked, and there is often no opportunity to ask follow-up questions or to clarify the information received.

Technical Conference Method A job analysis technique that involves extensive input from the employee's supervisor.

Diary Method A job analysis method requiring job incumbents to record their daily activities.

Technical Conference Method The **technical conference method** uses supervisors with extensive knowledge of the job. Here, specific job characteristics are obtained from the "experts." Although a good data-gathering method, it often overlooks the incumbent workers' perceptions about what they do on their job.

Diary Method The **diary method** requires job incumbents to record their daily activities. The diary method is the most time consuming of the job analysis methods and may have to extend over long periods of time—all adding to its cost.

These six methods are not meant to be viewed as mutually exclusive; no one method is universally superior. Even obtaining job information from the incumbents can create a problem, especially if these individuals describe what they think they should be doing rather than what they actually do. The best results, then, are usually achieved with some combination of methods—with information provided by individual employees, their immediate supervisors, a professional analyst, or an unobtrusive source such as filmed observations.

In the Learning an HRM Skill section of this chapter, we've described several steps involved in conducting the job analysis (see Exhibit 5-5).

Structured Job Analyses Techniques

Now that we realize that job analysis data can be collected in a number of ways, and that there's a process that we can follow to do the work, let us consider other notable job analysis processes. These are the Department of Labor's Job Analysis Process and the Position Analysis Questionnaire.

Individual Interview Method Meeting with an employee to determine what his or her job entails.

Group Interview Method Meeting with a number of employees to collectively determine what their jobs entail.

Structured Questionnaire Method A specifically designed questionnaire on which employees rate tasks they perform on their jobs.

The Department of Labor's Job Analysis Process The *Department of Labor's Job Analysis Process* describes what a worker does by having someone observe and interview the employee. This information is standardized and cataloged into three general functions that exist in all jobs: data, people, and things (see Exhibit 5-6). An employment interviewer, for example, might be found to analyze data, speak to people, and handle things; the job would be coded 2, 6, 7. Exhibit 5-7 shows the listing for the employment interviewer's position. This type of coding of key elements has already been done for thousands of job titles listed in the *O**Net OnLine, which is readily available online (see Technology Corner). Use of this service may significantly reduce HRM's burden of gathering information on jobs for its organization. Additionally, the DOL job codes are supplemented with

EXHIBIT 5-5
Steps in a Job Analysis

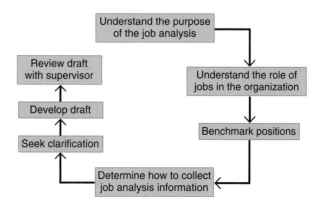

Exhibit 5-6
Department of Labor Job Analysis Process

Work Functions		
Data	**People**	**Things**
0 Synthesizing	0 Mentoring	0 Setting up
1 Coordinating	1 Negotiating	1 Precision working
2 Analyzing	2 Instructing	2 Operating–controlling
3 Compiling	3 Supervision	3 Driving–operating
4 Computing	4 Diverting	4 Manipulating
5 Copying	5 Persuading	5 Tending
6 Comparing	6 Speaking–signaling	6 Feeding–offbearing
	7 Serving	7 Handling
	8 Taking instructions–helping	

Source: U.S. Department of Labor, *Dictionary of Occupational Titles,* 4th ed. revised (Washington, DC: Government Printing Office, 1997), p. xix.

Exhibit 5-7
Excerpts from a Department of Labor Job Narrative

(O*Net 21508)   Employment Interviewer

Regular evaluation of employee job skills is an important part of the job for interviewers working in temporary help services companies. Initially, interviewers evaluate or test new employees' skills to determine their abilities and weaknesses. The results are kept on file and referred to when filling job orders. In some cases, the company trains employees to improve their skills, so interviewers periodically reevaluate or retest employees to identify any new skills they may have developed.

The duties of employment interviewers in job service centers differ somewhat from those in personnel supply firms because applicants may lack marketable skills. An employment interviewer reviews these forms and asks the applicant about the type of job sought and salary range desired.

Applicants may also need help identifying the kind of work for which they are best suited. The employment interviewer evaluates the applicant's qualifications and either chooses an appropriate occupation or class of occupations or refers the applicant for vocational testing. After identifying an appropriate job type, the employment interviewer searches the file of job orders seeking a possible job match and refers the applicant to the employer if a match is found. If no match is found, the interviewer shows the applicant how to use listings of available jobs.

Besides helping individuals find jobs, employment interviewers help firms fill job openings. The services they provide depend on the company or type of agency they work for and the clientele it serves.

A private industry employment interviewer must also be a salesperson. Counselors pool together a group of qualified applicants and try to sell them to many different companies. Often a consultant will call a company that has never been a client with the aim of filling their employment needs. Maintaining good relations with employers is an important part of the employment interviewer's job because this helps assure a steady flow of job orders. Being prepared to fill an opening quickly with a qualified applicant impresses employers most and keeps them as clients.

Source: Bureau of Labor Statistics, U.S. Department of Labor, *Occupational Outlook Handbook,* 2000-2001 Edition (Bulletin 2520) (Washington, DC: Government Printing Office, 2000), pp. 37–39.

a detailed narrative. So the information regarding the employment interviewer's job would tell us what the jobholder's main functions are, with whom the jobholder speaks, and which things are handled. The DOL technique allows managers to group jobs into job families that require similar kinds of worker behavior. Candidates for these jobs, therefore, should hold similar worker skills.

A variation of the Department of Labor's methodology was developed by a U.S. Employment Service employee, Sidney Fine. Fine developed a process that further described those items listed by the DOL, called the Functional Job Analysis (FJA) (see Exhibit 5-8). In so doing, the FJA provides a more accurate picture of what the jobholder does.[41]

Position Analysis Questionnaire

A job analysis technique that rates jobs in 194 elements in six activity categories.

Position Analysis Questionnaire Developed by researchers at Purdue University, the **Position Analysis Questionnaire (PAQ)** generates job requirement information that is applicable to all types of jobs. In contrast to the DOL approach, the PAQ presents a more quantitative and finely tuned description of jobs. The PAQ procedure involves "194 elements that are grouped within six major divisions and 28 sections"[42] (see Exhibit 5-9).

The PAQ allows HRM to scientifically and quantitatively group interrelated job elements into job dimensions. This, in turn, should allow jobs to be compared with each other. However, research on the usefulness of the PAQ is suspect. For the most part, it appears to be more applicable to higher-level, professional jobs.[43]

Purpose of Job Analysis

No matter what method is used to gather data, the information amassed and written down from the job analysis process generates three outcomes: job descriptions, job specifications, and job evaluation. It is important to note that these are the tangible products of the work—not the job analysis, which is the conceptual, analytical process or action from which we develop these outcomes. Let's look at them more closely.

EXHIBIT 5-8
Fine's Functional Job Analysis (FJA) Scale

Data	People	Things
1. Comparing	1a. Taking instruction 1b. Serving	1a. Handling 1b. Feeding/off-bearing 1c. Tending
2. Copying	2. Exchanging information	2a. Manipulating 2b. Operating/controlling 2c. Driving/controlling
3a. Computing 3b. Compiling	3a. Coaching 3b. Persuading 3c. Diverting	3a. Precision work 3b. Setting up
4. Analyzing	4a. Consulting 4b. Instructing 4c. Treating	
5a. Innovating 5b. Coordinating 6. Synthesizing	5. Supervising	
	6. Negotiating 7. Mentoring	

Source: A. S. Fine, *Functional Job Analysis Scales: A Desk Aid* (Kalamazoo, MI: W.E. Upjohn Institute for Employment Research, 1973). Used with permission.

Exhibit 5-9
*Categories and Their Number
of Job Elements of the PAQ*

Category	Number of Job Elements
1. *Information input* Where and how does the worker get the information he or she uses on the job?	35
2. *Mental Processes* What reasoning, decision making, Planning, etc., are involved in the job?	14
3. *Work output* What physical activities does the worker perform and what tools or devices are used?	49
4. *Relationships with other people* What relationships with other people are required in the job?	36
5. *Job context* In what physical and social contexts is the work performed?	19
6. *Other job characteristics* What special attributes exist on this job (e.g., schedule, responsibilities, pay).	41

Source: Reprinted with permission from the Position Analysis Questionnaire, Copyright 1969, Purdue Research Foundation.

Job Description   A written statement of what the jobholder does, how it is done, and why it is done.

Job Descriptions

Job Descriptions   A **job description** is a written statement of what the jobholder does, how it is done, under what conditions it is done, and why it is done. It should accurately portray job content, environment, and conditions of employment. A common format for a job description includes the job title, the duties to be performed, the distinguishing characteristics of the job, environmental conditions, and the authority and responsibilities of the jobholder. An example of a job description for a Benefits Manager is provided in Exhibit 5-10.

When we discuss employee recruitment, selection, and performance appraisal, we will find that the job description acts as an important resource for: (1) describing the job (either verbally by recruiters and interviewers or in written advertisements) to potential candidates; (2) guiding newly hired employees in what they are specifically expected to do; and (3) providing a point of comparison in appraising whether the actual activities of a job incumbent align with the stated duties. Furthermore, under the Americans with Disabilities Act, job descriptions have taken on an added emphasis in identifying essential job functions.

Job Specifications   Statements indicating the minimal acceptable qualifications incumbents must possess to successfully perform the essential elements of their jobs.

Job Specifications

Job Specifications   The **job specification** states the minimum acceptable qualifications that the incumbent must possess to perform the job successfully. Based on the information acquired through job analysis, the job specification identifies the knowledge, skills, education, experience, certification, and abilities needed to do the job effectively. Individuals possessing the personal characteristics identified in the job specification should perform the job more effectively than those lacking these personal characteristics. The job specification, therefore, is an important tool in the selection process, for it keeps the selector's attention on the list of qualifications necessary for an incumbent to perform the job and assists in determining whether candidates are essentially qualified.

Job Evaluation   Specifies the relative value of each job in the organization.

Job Evaluations

Job Evaluations   In addition to providing data for job descriptions and specifications, job analysis is also valuable in providing the information that makes comparison of jobs possible. If an organization is to have an equitable compensation program, jobs that have similar demands in terms of skills, knowledge, and abilities should be placed in common compensation groups. **Job evaluation** contributes toward that end by specifying the relative value of each job in the organization. Job evaluation, therefore, is an important part of compensation

EXHIBIT 5-10
Example of a Job Description

Job Title: Benefits Manager **Occupational code:** 166.167.018
Reports To: Director, Human Resources **Job No.** 1207
Supervises: Staff of Three **Date:** February 2001
Environmental Conditions: None
Functions: Manages Employee benefits program for organization
Duties and Responsibilities:

- Plans and directs implementation and administration of benefits programs designed to insure employees against loss of income due to illness, injury, layoff, or retirement;
- Directs preparation and distribution of written and verbal information to inform employees of benefits programs, such as insurance and pension plans, paid time off, bonus pay, and special employer sponsored activities;
- Analyzes existing benefits policies of organization, and prevailing practices among similar organizations, to establish competitive benefits programs;
- Evaluates services, coverage, and options available through insurance and investment companies, to determine programs best meeting needs of organization;
- Plans modification of existing benefits programs, utilizing knowledge of laws concerning employee insurance coverage, and agreements with labor unions, to ensure compliance with legal requirements;
- Recommends benefits plan changes to management; notifies employees and labor union representatives of changes in benefits programs;
- Directs performance of clerical functions, such as updating records and processing insurance claims;
- May interview, select, hire, and train employees.

Job Characteristics:

- Successful incumbent will have knowledge of policies and practices involved in personnel/human resource management functions—including recruitment, selection, training, and promotion regulations and procedures; compensation and benefits packages; labor relations and negotiations strategies; and human resource information systems.
- Excellent written and verbal communications skills as well as deductive and inductive reasoning skills are critical.

Sources: Adapted from Bureau of Labor Statistics, *Occupational Outlook Handbook*, 2000–2001 (Washington, DC: Government Printing Office, 2000), p. 58; and O*Net, Human Resource Management; Compensation and Benefits Managers, 2000 (www.online.onetcenter.org/cgi-bin/jdo?1179+5)

administration, as will be discussed in detail in Chapter 11. In the meantime, you should keep in mind that job evaluation is made possible by the data generated from job analysis.

The Multifaceted Nature of Job Analysis

One of the overriding questions about job analysis is: Is it being conducted properly, if at all? The answer to this question varies, depending on the organization. Generally, most organizations do conduct some type of job analysis. This job analysis extends further, however, than meeting the federal equal employment opportunity requirement. Almost everything that HRM does is directly related to the job analysis process (see Exhibit 5-11). Recruiting, selection, compensation, and performance-appraising activities are most frequently cited as being directly affected by the job analysis. But there are others. Employee training and career development are assisted by the job analysis process by identifying necessary skills, knowledge, and abilities. Where deficiencies exist, training

EXHIBIT 5-11
The Multifaceted Nature of the Job Analysis

Traditional job analysis may not accurately reflect what workers in some organizations do. For instance, the Medium Speed Configuration Team at Unisys requires a different set of skills because they manage themselves. The flexibility needed to achieve their team goals isn't always reflected in a traditional job analysis process.

Job Morphing Readjusting skills to match job requirements.

and development efforts can be used. Similar effects can also be witnessed in determining safety and health requirements, and labor relations processes, if a union exists. Accordingly, this often-lengthy and complex job analysis process cannot be overlooked.

We cannot overemphasize the importance of job analysis, as it permeates most of an organization's activities. If an organization doesn't do its job analysis well, it probably doesn't perform many of its human resource activities well. If employees in the organization understand human resource activities, they should understand the fundamental importance of job analysis. The job analysis, then, is the starting point of sound human resource management. Without knowing what the job entails, the material covered in the following chapters may be merely an effort in futility.

The Job Analysis and the Changing World of Work

We leave this chapter with a few words, revisiting the changing world of work and the importance of employment planning. Globalization, quality initiatives, telecommuting, and teams, for example, are requiring organizations to rethink the components of their jobs. When jobs are designed around individuals, job descriptions frequently clarify employee roles.[44] Jobs today frequently go beyond the individual, however, requiring the activities and collaboration of a team.

To be effective, teams need to be flexible and continually making adjustments. Effective work teams require competent individuals. Team members must have the relevant technical skills and abilities to achieve the desired corporate goals and the personal characteristics required to achieve excellence while working well with others. These same individuals must also be capable of readjusting their work skills—called **job-morphing**—to fit the needs of the team.[45] It's important not to overlook the personal characteristics. Not everyone who is technically competent has the skills to work well as a team member. Accordingly, employment planning requires finding team members who possess both technical and interpersonal skills. As such, team members must have excellent communication skills. Team members must be able to convey messages among each other in a form that is readily and clearly understood. This includes nonverbal as well as spoken messages. Good communication is also characterized by a healthy dose of feedback from team members and management.[46] This helps to guide team members and to correct misunderstandings. Team members must be able to quickly and efficiently share ideas and feelings.

CONDUCTING THE JOB ANALYSIS

ABOUT THE SKILL: RECOGNIZING THAT the job analysis is the cornerstone of HRM activities, it's important to understand how the activity is performed. Below are suggested steps in conducting the job analysis (an elaboration of Exhibit 5-5).

1. *Understand the purpose of conducting the job analysis.* Before embarking on a job analysis, one must understand the nature and purpose of conducting the investigation. Recognize that job analyses serve a vital purpose in such HRM activities as recruiting, training, setting performance standards, evaluating performance, and compensation. In fact, nearly every activity in HRM revolves around the job analysis.

2. *Understand the role of jobs and values in the organization.* Every job in the organization should have a purpose. Before conducting the job analysis, one must understand the linkage that the job has to the strategic direction of the organization. In essence, one must answer why the job is needed. If an answer cannot be determined, then maybe the job is not needed.

3. *Benchmark positions.* In a large organization, it would be impossible to evaluate every job at one time. Accordingly, by involving employees and seeking their input, selected jobs can be chosen based on how well they represent other, similar jobs in the organization. This information, then, will be used as a starting point in later analysis of the other positions.

4. *Determine how you want to collect the job analysis information.* Proper planning at this stage permits one to collect the data desired in the most effective and efficient manner. This means developing a process for collecting the data. Several combined methods—such as structured questionnaires, group interviews, and technical conferences—should be used. Select the ones, however, that best meet your job analysis goals and timetables.

5. *Seek clarification, wherever necessary.* Some of the information collected may not be entirely understood by the job analyst. Accordingly, when this occurs, one must seek clarification from those who possess the critical information. This may include the employee and the supervisor. Failure to understand and comprehend the information will make the next step in the job analysis process—writing the job description—more difficult.

6. *Develop the first draft of the job description.* Although there is no specific format that all job descriptions follow, most include certain elements. Specifically, a job description contains the job title, a summary sentence of the job's main activities, the level of authority and accountability of the position, performance requirements, and working conditions. The last paragraph of the job description typically includes the job specifications, or those personal characteristics the job incumbent should possess to be successful on the job.

7. *Review draft with the job supervisor.* Ultimately, the supervisor of the position being analyzed should approve the job description. Review comments from the supervisor can assist in determining a final job description document. When the description is an accurate reflection, the supervisor should sign off, or approve the document.

HRM WORKSHOP

SUMMARY

(This summary relates to the Learning Outcomes identified on p. 124.)

After having read this chapter, you should be able to:

1. **Describe the importance of employment planning.** Employment planning is the process by which an organization ensures that it has the right number and kinds of people capable of effectively and efficiently completing those tasks that are in direct support of the company's mission and strategic goals.

2. **Define the steps involved in the employment planning process.** The steps in the employment planning process include mission formulating, establishing corporate goals and objectives, assessing current human resources, estimating the supplies and demand for labor, and matching demand with current supplies of labor. The two outcomes of this process are recruitment and decruitment.

3. **Explain what human resource information systems are used for.** A human resource information system is useful for quickly fulfilling human resource management information needs by tracking employee information and having that information readily available when needed.

4. **Define what is meant by the term** *job analysis.* Job analysis is a systematic exploration of the activities surrounding and within a job. It defines the job's duties, responsibilities, and accountabilities.

5. **Identify the six general techniques for obtaining job analysis information.** The six general techniques for obtaining job information are observation method, indi-

vidual interview method, group interview method, structured interview method, technical conference method, and diary method.

6. **Describe the steps involved in conducting the job analysis.** The steps involved in conducting the job analysis include: (a) understanding the purpose of conducting the job analysis; (b) understanding the role of jobs in the organization; (c) benchmarking positions; (d) determining how you want to collect job analysis information; (e) seeking clarification, wherever necessary; (f) developing the first draft of the job description; and (g) reviewing the draft with the job supervisor.

7. **Explain the difference between job descriptions, job specifications, and job evaluations.** Job descriptions are written statements of what the jobholder does (duties and responsibilities); job specifications identify the personal characteristics required to perform successfully on the job; and job evaluation is the process of using job analysis information in establishing a compensation system.

8. **Describe how job analysis permeates all aspects of HRM.** Job analysis permeates all aspects of HRM in that almost everything that HRM does is directly related to the job analysis process. Recruiting, selection, compensation, and performance-appraising, employee training and career activities, and safety and health requirements, for example, are affected by the job analysis in terms of identifying necessary skills, knowledge, and abilities.

DEMONSTRATING COMPREHENSION: *Questions for Review and Discussion*

1. Define employment planning. Why is it important to organizations?

2. What is involved in the employment planning process?

3. How can an organization's human resources supply be increased?

4. What is a job analysis?

5. Identify the advantages and disadvantages of the observation, structured questionnaire, and diary methods of conducting a job analysis.

6. Explain what is meant by the terms *job description, job specification,* and *job evaluation.*

7. Describe the employment planning implications when an organization is in a downsizing mode.

8. "More emphasis should be placed on the external supply of employees for meeting future needs because these employees bring new blood into the organization. This results in more innovative and creative ideas." Do you agree or disagree with this statement? Explain your response.

9. "Job analysis is just another burden placed on organizations through EEO legislation." Do you agree or disagree with this statement? Defend your position.

10. "Although systematic in nature, a job description is still at best a subjective process." Build an argument for and against this statement.

CASE APPLICATION: *TEAM FUN!*

Tony has been director of human resources at TEAM FUN!, a sporting goods manufacturer and retailer for 3 months. He is constantly amazed that the company does so well, considering that everything is so loose. Nothing is documented about job roles and responsibilities. People apparently have been hired because Kenny and Norton, the owners and founders, like them or their relatives. Tony is lunching with Mary, a friend from college who now manages the human resource function for a large financial investor. Tony tells Mary, "I don't know if I should quit or what. They both got mad at me last week when I suggested smart cards for security. The employee handbook looks like a scrapbook from their kids' high school football days . . . No, their high school football days. No one has job descriptions. I don't get it. Everyone likes working there. The job does get done. Am I the one with the problem?"

Mary replies, "Couldn't be you! It does sound like a great place to work. Has it grown fast in the last few years?"

Tony: "Unbelievably. It had 25 employees 5 years ago, now we have nearly 150."

Mary: "That's probably part of it. Remember how Dr. DeCenzo said in his class that you could get by without a formal human resource structure up to about 100 employees?"

Tony: "Yeah. That was a great class! I met my wife in that class! We did lots of team exercises and projects."

Mary: "Anyway, maybe you could start with writing your own job description. That would be a start."

Tony: "Then I could talk about formal job evaluation processes. That's a great idea. Have you used QUICKHR, the new software tool?"

Mary: "No, but a package is a good idea. What's your current HRIS like?" Tony laughed until he couldn't get his breath. Mary continues, "OK. That's another place you could start."

Questions:
1. Help Tony write his job description.
2. What techniques should he use to gather data?
3. How should he conduct the job analysis?
4. What should he say to Kenny and Norton to get their buy-in on this project?
5. How will job descriptions change the organization?
6. Give Tony some pointers on software packages and HRIS.

WORKING WITH A TEAM: *Job Analysis Information*

Research the technical, people, conceptual knowledge, and skills required to perform the tasks of a human resources manager effectively. Describe your findings and compare them with the results of members of your group.

You may obtain samples directly from a company's manager, with permission, interview a human resources manager, or use any of the related web sites such as www.hrq.com and www.shrm.org. Discuss what values will be important for the human resources manager to personally possess and how these will be demonstrated in that role.

Finally, based on the information you've obtained, write a brief description of the job. What challenges did you experience in coming to a consensus on job responsibilities and in choosing the correct words for inclusion in the job description?

ENHANCING YOUR WRITING SKILLS

1. Develop a two- to three-page response to the following statement: "Formal employment planning activities reduce flexibility and may hinder success." Present both sides of the argument and include supporting data. Conclude your paper by defending and supporting one of the two arguments you've presented.
2. Over the past few years we've witnessed a few mega-mergers of organizations like DaimlerBenz and Chrysler or Travelers Insurance and Citicorp. These organizations have used mergers as a growth strategy. But with mergers comes the potential duplication of personnel. Describe what you believe to be the benefits and the potential drawbacks of mergers to the employment planning process.
3. Select a job (or position in an organization) that you have an interest in. Visit the O*Net OnLine web site (www.onetcenter.org) and locate all relevant information about the position. Write a two- to three-page analysis of what the job entails, highlighting the job description and job specification data.

ENDNOTES

1. "The Top 500 Women-Owned Businesses," *Working Woman* (June 1999), pp. 52–54.
2. See, for example, Max Messmer, "Strategic Staffing for the 90s," *Personnel Journal* (October 1990), p. 92.
3. See also Bill Roberts, "Pick Employees' Brains," *HRMagazine* (February 2000), p. 175.
4. Patrick M. Wright, Dennis L. Smart, and Gary C. McMahan, "Matches Between Human Resources and Strategy Among NCAA Basketball Teams," *Academy of Management Journal*, Vol. 38, No. 4 (Winter 1995), pp. 1052–1074; Martin J. Plevel, Sandy Nells, Fred Lane, and Randall S. Schuler, "AT&T Global Business Communications Systems: Linking HR with Business Strategy," *Organizational Dynamics* (1994), pp. 59–71. See also Randall S. Schuler, "Strategic Human Resources Management: Linking the People with the Strategic Needs of the Business," *Organizational Dynamics* (1992), pp. 18–32.
5. Messmer, p. 96.
6. As previous users have concurred, while strategic planning cannot be oversimplified in a two-page discussion, a quick overview is in order. With respect to the strategic nature of business, we recommend for a comprehensive review of strategic planning: James Brian Quinn, Henry Mintzberg, and Robert M. James, *The Strategic Process* (Englewood Cliffs, NJ: Prentice-Hall, 1988).
7. P. LaBarre, "Knowledge Brokers," *Industry Week* (April 1, 1996), p. 52.
8. Amy Barrett and Gail DeGeorge, "Home Improvement at Black & Decker," *Business Week* (May 11, 1998), pp. 54–56.
9. Goals that are established are a function of a number of factors. Such issues as the economy, government influences, market maturity, technological advances, company image, and location will factor into the analysis.
10. A. Taylor III, "New Ideas from Europe's Automakers," *Fortune* (March 21, 1994), pp. 159–172.
11. "Sounds Awful, Tastes Great," *Canadian Business* (December 1995), p. 79.
12. B. Gilad, "The Role of Organized Competitive Intelligence in Corporate Strategy," *Columbia Journal of World Business* (Winter 1989), pp. 29–35; B. D. Gelb, M. J. Saxton, G. M. Zinkhan, and N. D. Albers, "Competitive Intelligence: Insights from Executives," *Business Horizons* (January–February 1991), pp. 43–47; L. Fuld, "A Recipe for Business Intelligence," *Journal of Business Strategy* (January–February 1991), pp. 12–17; G. B. Roush, "A Program for Sharing Corporate Intelligence," *Journal of Business Strategy* (January–February 1991), pp. 4–7; and R. S. Teitelbaum, "The New Role for Intelligence," *Fortune* (November 2, 1992), pp. 104–107.
13. M. Robichaux, "'Competitor Intelligence': A Grapevine to Rivals' Secrets," *Wall Street Journal* (April 12, 1989), p. B2.
14. W. H. Davidson, "The Role of Global Scanning in Business Planning," *Organizational Dynamics* (Winter 1991), pp. 5–16.
15. See, for example, W. J. Holstein, "Corporate Spy Wars, *U.S. News & World Report* (February 23, 1998), pp. 46–52; E. A. Robinson, "China's Spies Target Corporate America,"

Fortune (March 30, 1998), pp. 118–122; and A. Farnham, "Spy vs. Spy: Are Your Company Secrets Safe?" *Fortune* (February 17, 1997), p. 136.
16. W. J. Holstein, "Corporate Spy Wars," p. 46.
17. See, for instance, John E. Delery and D. Harold Doty, "Modes of Theorizing in Strategic Human Resource Management: Tests of Universalistic Contingency and Configurational Performance Predictions," *Academy of Management Journal*, Vol. 38, No. 4 (August 1996), pp. 802–835.
18. Joan E. Goodman, "Does Your HRIS Speak English?" *Personnel Journal* (March 1990), p. 81.
19. William A. Minneman, "Strategic Justification for an HRIS that Adds Value," *HRMagazine* (December 1996), pp. 35–38.
20. Sandra E. O'Connell, "Systems Issues of International Business," *HRMagazine* (March 1997), pp. 36–41.
21. Jeffrey B. Arthur, "Effects of Human Resource Systems on Manufacturing Performance and Turnover," *Academy of Management Journal*, Vol. 37, No. 3 (Summer 1994), pp. 670–687.
22. See, for example, Jim Meade, "One-Stop HRIS Strong on Reports," *HRMagazine* (March 2000), pp. 137–139; and Jim Meade, "Affordable HRIS Strong on Benefits," *HRMagazine* (April 2000), pp. 132–134.
23. Jim Mead, "Web-Based HRIS Meets Multiple Needs," *HRMagazine* (August 2000), pp. 129–133; Robert H. Elliott and Siriwal Tevavichulada, "Computer Literacy and Human Resource Management: A Public/Private Sector Comparison," *Public Personnel Management* (Summer 1999), pp. 259; and Bill Roberts, "The New HRIS: Good Deal or a $6 Million Paperweight," *HRMagazine* (February 1998), pp. 40–46.
24. See Joel Lapointe and Judy Parker-Matz, "People Make the Systems Go . . . Or Not," *HRMagazine* (September 1998), pp. 28–36.
25. See, for instance, Kenneth A. Kovach and Charles E. Cathcart, Jr., "Human Resource Information Systems (HRIS): Providing Business with Rapid Data Access, Information Exchange, and Strategic Advantage," *Public Personnel Management* (Summer 1999), pp. 275–282; and Bill Roberts, "Focus on Making Employee Data Pay," *HRMagazine* (November 1999), pp. 86–96.
26. Jim Mead, "New Functions Upgrade a Familiar Product, *HRMagazine* (January 2000), pp. 105–108.
27. Ibid.
28. Pamela L. Moore and Diane Brady, "Running the House That Jack Built," *Business Week* (October 2, 2000); pp. 130–131; Wendy Zellner, "Earth to Herb: Pick a Co-Pilot," *Business Week* (August 16, 1999), p. 70; John A. Byrne and Jennifer Reingold, "Who Will Step into Jack Welch's Shoes," *Business Week* (December 21, 1998), pp. 37–38; David Greising, "What Other CEOs Can Learn from Goizueta," *Business Week* (November 3, 1997), p. 38; and Jennifer Wing, "Succession Planning Smooths Return to Business-as-Usual," *HR News* (May 1996), p. 11.
29. John A. Byrne, Jennifer Reingold, and Richard A. Melcher, "Wanted: A Few Good CEOs," *Business Week* (August 11, 1997), pp. 64–70.

30. Jennifer Wing, "Co-Workers Absorb Loss of Leaders in Plane Crash," *HR News* (May 1996), pp. 1, 10.

31. "Succession: Are You Prepared?" *HRMagazine* (November 1996), p. 19.

32. See, for example, Courtney von Hippel, Stephen L. Mangum, David B. Greenberger, Robert L. Heneman, and Jeffrey D. Skoglind, "Temporary Employment: Can Organizations and Employees Both Win?" *Academy of Management Executive* (February 1997), pp. 93–103; Thomas C. Greble, "A Leading Role for HR in Alternative Staffing," *HRMagazine* (February 1997), pp. 99–103; Michael A. Verespej, "Skills on Call," *Industry Week* (June 3, 1996), pp. 46–51; Richard A. Melcher, "Manpower Upgrades Its Resume," *Business Week* (June 10, 1996), pp. 81–82; Glenn Burkins, "Temporary Employment Is Growing in Popularity, Some Schools Report," *Wall Street Journal* (June 4, 1996), p. A-1; Lucy A. Newton, "Stiff Competition for Talented Temps," *HRMagazine* (May 1996), pp. 91–94; "Rent-a-Worker," *Profiles* (October 1995), p. 15; and Paul Klebnikov, "Focus, Focus, Focus," *Forbes* (September 11, 1995), pp. 42–44.

33. Mark Henricks, "Time Out," *Entrepreneur* (October 1995), pp. 70–74.

34. Commerce Clearing House, "Sabbaticals: A Good Investment for McDonald's," *Human Resources Management: Ideas and Trends* (May 11, 1994), pp. 77, 84.

35. See A. Bernstein, "Who Says Job Anxiety Is Easing?" *Business Week* (April 7, 1997), p. 38; and "Loser Layoffs," *U.S. News and World Report* (November 25, 1996), pp. 73–81; and "Happy Labor Day," *Time,* September 4, 1995, p. 21.

36. A. Taylor III, "New Ideas from Europe's Automakers," *Fortune* (March 21, 1994), p. 166; see also D. Woodruff, I. Katz, and K. Naughton, "VW's Factory of the Future," *Business Week* (October 7, 1996), p. 52–54; and D. Woodruff, "Is VW Revving Too High?" *Business Week,* March 30, 1998, pp. 48–49.

37. I. M. Kunii, E. Thornton, and J. Rae-Dupree, "Sony's Shakeup," *Business Week* (March 22, 1999), pp. 52–53.

38. See, for example, W. F. Casio, C. E. Young, J. R. Morris, "Financial Consequences of Employment-Change Decisions in Major U.S. Corporations," *Academy of Management Journal* (October 1997), pp. 1175–1189.

39. S. Leibs, "Outsourcing's No Cure-All," *Industry Week* (April 6, 1998), pp. 20–38.

40. See Richard Henderson, *Compensation Management in a Knowledge-Based World,* 8th ed. (Englewood Cliffs, NJ: Prentice Hall, 2000).

41. Sidney A. Fine, *Functional Job Analysis Scales: A Desk Aid, No. 7* (Kalamazoo, MI: W.E. Upjohn Institute for Employment Research, 1973).

42. See Richard Henderson, *Compensation Management in a Knowledge-Based World,* 8th ed. (Englewood Cliffs, NJ: Prentice Hall, 2000).

43. See Wayne Casio, *Managing Human Resources,* 5th ed. (Boston, MA: Irwin McGraw-Hill, 1998), p. 145.

44. See also Linda K. Stroh, Sven Grasshoff, Andre Rude, and Nancy Carter, "Integrated HR Systems Help Develop Global Leaders," *HRMagazine* (April 1998), pp. 14–17.

45. "Job Morphing," *Wall Street Journal* (June 29, 1995), p. A1.

46. See, for example, "Effects of Distribution of Feedback in Work Groups," *Academy of Management Journal,* Vol. 37, No. 3 (1994), pp. 635–641.

6

RECRUITING

LEARNING OUTCOMES

AFTER READING THIS CHAPTER, YOU WILL BE ABLE TO:

1. Define what is meant by the term *recruiting*.
2. Identify the dual goals of recruiting.
3. Explain what constrains human resource managers in determining recruiting sources.
4. Identify the principal sources involved in recruiting employees.
5. Describe the advantages and disadvantages of employee referrals.
6. Identify three important variables that affect response rates to job advertisements.
7. Explain what distinguishes a public employment agency from a private employment agency.
8. Describe the benefits of cyberspace recruiting.
9. Explain what is meant by the concept of employee leasing and the organizational benefits of such an arrangement.

After having established its strategic direction and developed a corresponding employment plan, an organization must turn its attention to getting the right people. The jobs that have been identified, and their associated skills, point to very specific types of employees that are required. But these employees don't just magically appear—nor do they frequently come knocking on the organization's door. Instead, the company must embark on an employment process of finding and hiring qualified people.

That process starts when the organization notifies the public that openings exist. The organization wants to get its information out such that a large number of potentially qualified applicants respond. Then, hopefully, after several interactions with the most promising of these candidates, employees are hired. These candidates will best demonstrate the skills, knowledge, and abilities to successfully perform the job. The keyword today is *hopefully*!

It isn't breaking news that we have a labor shortage in the United States as we enter this new millennium. All types of jobs—from high-tech to service jobs—

are getting more difficult to fill. For example, in the information technology (IT) arena, consider the following. There was an estimated need to fill more than 1.6 million IT jobs in 2000 alone.[1] If every person who has any IT skill and experience were hired, there would still be more than 800,000 jobs unfilled. That's a nightmare for organizations. But more importantly, what about the 800,000 that *are* hired? Competition for them is unbelievable. Compounding this is the realization that in areas where high-tech work flourishes, unemployment is well below 2 percent—about half the national average. So how do you locate these potential applicants and entice them to join *your* organization? Let's look at what some companies have done.[2]

- A number of companies in the Silicon Valley area flash job-opening advertisements on movie screens just before the main-attraction film starts;
- Microsoft, in an effort to attract and retain its IT workers, significantly raised the salaries of their positions;
- Interwoven lures engineers to the job by offering new hires a 2-year lease on a BMW Z3;
- OnLink Technology hires an airplane to fly above rush-hour traffic in southern California carrying banners advertising jobs;
- Some organization recruiters show up at people's homes, offering them the corporate jet for a weekend to fly somewhere to think about joining the company;
- Dot.com companies advertise at college career fairs advocating that joining the company now gets the new hire in pre-IPO;
- Cisco has gone into the high schools, replacing shop class with a "new economy" course on inputting computer codes. Some of these high school students may end up with jobs approaching $70,000 annually after graduating. Cisco is also doing the same with individuals in homeless shelters.

The use of creativity in searching for job candidates will continue to gain momentum. Whenever labor shortages exist, recruiting efforts take on new proportions. It's also safe to say that a competitive advantage can be gained by targeting good talent and encouraging them to apply—and to always be looking. Quite possibly that is what the CEO of Acteva, Inc., must have thought when she hired the driver of the automobile who just rear-ended her car. Impressed with how the driver reacted to this stressful event, the CEO talked about a job opening she had, and offered the job on the spot, and it was accepted. Impressed with the company, the driver's significant other also joined the company two weeks later. In this case, the recruiting effort was no accident!

INTRODUCTION

Successful employment planning is designed to identify an organization's human resource needs. Once these needs are known, an organization will want to do something about meeting them. The next step, then, in the staffing function—assuming, of course, that demand for certain skills, knowledge, and abilities is greater than the current supply—is recruiting. This activity makes it possible for a company to acquire the people necessary to ensure the continued operation of the organization. **Recruiting** is the process of discovering potential candidates for actual or anticipated organizational vacancies. Or, from another perspective, it is a linking activity—bringing together those with jobs to fill and those seeking jobs.

> **Recruiting**   The process of discovering potential job candidates.

In this chapter, we'll explore the activities surrounding sourcing for employees. We'll do this by looking at the fundamental activities surrounding the recruiting process. We'll end this chapter by providing you with some insight and guidance in preparing your resume and cover letter that may enhance your chances of making it through this first step of the hiring process.

RECRUITING GOALS

For the recruiting process to work effectively, there must be a significant pool of candidates to choose from—and the more diversity within that group the better. Achieving a satisfactory pool of candidates, however, may not be that easy, especially in a tight labor market. For example, CDI, the largest engineering-services firm in the United States, was having difficulty filling such jobs as product designer and computer modeler. As an incentive to boost the number of applicants, the company offered a drawing for a multipurpose vehicle, or a Caribbean cruise for two, to those qualified individuals who sent resumes.[3] The first goal of recruiting, then, is to communicate the position in such a way that job seekers respond. Why? The more applications received, the better the recruiter's chances for finding an individual who is best suited to the job requirements.

Simultaneously, however, the recruiter must provide enough information about the job that unqualified applicants can select themselves out of job candidacy. For instance, when Ben & Jerry's was searching for a new CEO a few years ago, someone with a conservative political view, and with a classical, bureaucratic perspective of management, would not have wanted to apply because that individual wouldn't fit the renowned countercultural ways of the company. Why is having potential applicants remove themselves from the applicant pool important to human resource management? Typically, when applications are received, the company acknowledges their receipt. That acknowledgment costs time and money. Then there are the application reviews, and a second letter is sent, this time rejecting the applications. Again, this incurs some costs. Accordingly, whenever possible, applications from those who are unqualified must be discouraged. A good recruiting program should attract the qualified, and not the unqualified. Meeting this dual objective will minimize the cost of processing unqualified candidates.

What Factors Affect Recruiting Efforts?

Although all organizations will, at one time or another, engage in recruiting activities, some do so to a much larger extent than others. Obviously, size is one factor; an organization with 100,000 employees will find itself recruiting continually. So, too, will fast-food firms, smaller-service organizations, as well as firms that pay lower wages. Certain other variables will also influence the extent of recruiting. Employment conditions in the community where the organization is located will influence how much recruiting takes place. The effectiveness of past recruiting efforts will show itself in the organization's historical ability to locate and keep people who perform well. Working conditions and salary and benefit packages offered by the organization will influence turnover and, therefore, the need for future recruiting. Organizations that are not growing, or those that are actually declining, may find little need to recruit. On the other hand, organizations that are growing rapidly, like Home Depot, Nucor, and U.S. Healthcare, will find recruitment a major human resource activity.[4]

The more applications received, the better the recruiter's chances for finding an individual who is best suited to the job requirements.

Recruitment efforts, even in these growing companies, are no easy task. Recall in Chapter 1 the discussion of skill deficiencies. Quality workers are becoming harder to locate. Unemployment in the new millennium is at a 30-year low. Therefore, HRM will have to develop new strategies to locate and hire those individuals possessing the skills the company needs.[5] United Parcel Service (UPS), for example, found a creative way to locate talented people.[6] Having problems finding workers in its three New Jersey facilities, UPS met with a local public employment agency that offered, among other services, employment counseling. Through having UPS describe the type of employee it was seeking, this agency sought to match its clients with UPS needs. This cooperation effort resulted in about 1,500 new employees for the company.

Are There Constraints on Recruiting Efforts?

Constraints on Recruiting Efforts Factors that can affect maximizing outcomes in recruiting.

While the ideal recruitment effort will bring in a satisfactory number of qualified applicants who will take the job if it is offered, the realities cannot be ignored. For example, the pool of qualified applicants may not include the "best" candidates; or the "best" candidate may not want to be employed by the organization. These and other **constraints on recruiting efforts** limit human resource recruiters' freedom to recruit and select a candidate of their choice. However, we can narrow our focus by suggesting five specific constraints.

Image of the Organization We noted that a prospective candidate may not be interested in pursuing job opportunities in the particular organization. The image of the organization, therefore, should be considered a potential constraint. If that image is perceived to be low, the likelihood of attracting a large number of applicants is reduced.[7] Many college graduates know, for example, that the individuals who occupy the top spots at Disney earn excellent salaries, are given excellent benefits, and are greatly respected in their communities. Among most college graduates, Disney has a positive image. The hope of having a shot at one of its top jobs, being in the spotlight, and having a position of power results in Disney having little trouble in attracting college graduates into entry-level positions. Microsoft, too, enjoys a positive image—to the point where the company receives more than 12,000 resumes a month![8] But not all graduates hold a positive image of some large organizations. More specifically, their image of some organizations is pessimistic. In a number of communities, local firms have a reputation for being in a declining industry; engaging in practices that result in polluting the environment, poor-quality products, and unsafe working conditions; or being indifferent to employees' needs. Such reputations can and do reduce these organizations' abilities to attract the best personnel available.[9]

Attractiveness of the Job   If the position to be filled is an unattractive job, recruiting a large and qualified pool of applicants will be difficult. In recent years, for instance, many employers have been complaining about the difficulty of finding suitably qualified individuals for manual labor positions. In a job market where unemployment rates are low, and where a wide range of opportunities exists creating competition for these workers, a shortage results. Moreover, any job that is viewed as boring, hazardous, anxiety-creating, low-paying, or lacking in promotion potential seldom will attract a qualified pool of applicants. Even during economic slumps, people have refused to take many of these jobs.[10]

Internal Organizational Policies   Internal organizational policies, such as "promote from within wherever possible," may give priority to individuals inside the organization. Such policies, when followed, typically ensure that all positions, other than the lowest-level entry positions, will be filled from within the ranks. Although this is promising once one is hired, it may reduce the number of applications.[11]

Government Influence   The government's influence in the recruiting process should not be overlooked. An employer can no longer seek out preferred individuals based on non-job-related factors such as physical appearance, sex, or religious background. An airline wishing to staff all its flight attendant positions with attractive females will find itself breaking the law if comparably qualified male candidates are rejected on the basis of sex—or female candidates are rejected on the basis of age (see Diversity and HRM).

diversity issues in HRM

JOB ADVERTISEMENTS AND EEO

RECALL IN CHAPTER 3 THE DISCUSSION OF adverse impact. In essence, an adverse impact occurs when protected group members are treated differently from others. Although most organizations will make statements that they are an equal employment opportunity employer, sometimes their actions may indicate differently. For instance, here are a few vignettes that reflect job advertisements which ended up in the hands of the EEOC.[13]

1. An advertisement that appeared in a newspaper for a cashier in a grocery store: "Applicant must be young and energetic . . . and be required to stand for long periods of time."

2. An advertisement that appeared for an advertising firm: "Young-thinking, 'new wave' progressive advertising firm has openings for entry level graphic artist with no more than three years' experience."

3. An advertisement for a part-time employee in a Laundromat: "Opening for a person seeking to supplement pension . . . retired persons preferred."

   What's potentially wrong with these ads? Let's take a look. In the first ad, the word *young* indicated a preference for someone under age 40.

Therefore, those 40 and older might be deterred from applying for the job. In the second ad, while not as clear-cut as the language in the first advertisement, the problems arise with the implication that older workers might not be "young thinking." Furthermore, "with no more than three years' experience" also points to someone younger. Had it stated, "young-thinking individuals of any age, and at least three years' experience," the ad would have been acceptable.

   The third ad is somewhat unique. Indicating a retirement preference might be viewed as acceptable. But retirement usually doesn't come prior to age 55 and is more likely closer to age 65. Thus, while the ad focuses on older workers, those individuals age 40 to 55 (or 65) might be excluded from this recruiting pool. Accordingly, an adverse impact may be occurring.

   What lessons can we learn from these vignettes? The primary lesson should reflect that while we may hold ourselves as an equal opportunity employer, our choice of words in our communication to the public may indicate otherwise. The bottom line is that whatever we communicate in HR, we must make sure that the language is proper.

   What do you think of situations like this?

Recruiting Costs   The last constraint, but certainly not lowest in priority, is one that centers on recruiting costs. Recruiting efforts by an organization are expensive—costing as much as $7,000 per position being filled.[12] Sometimes continuing a search for long periods of time is not possible because of budget restrictions. Accordingly, when an organization considers various recruiting sources, it does so with some sense of effectiveness in mind—like maximizing its recruiting travel budget by first interviewing employees over the phone or through videoconferencing.

RECRUITING FROM A GLOBAL PERSPECTIVE

When beginning to recruit for overseas positions, the first step, as always, is to define the relevant labor market.[14] For international positions, however, that market is the whole world.[15] Organizations must decide if they want to send an American overseas, recruit in the host country where the position is, or ignore nationality and do a global search for the best person available.[16] Thus, the possibilities are to select someone from the United States, the host country, or a third country. It's important to make a proper choice, if for no other reason than it's estimated that the cost of failure in an international assignment approximates $250,000.[17]

To some extent, this basic decision depends on the type of occupation and its requirements, as well as the stage of national and cultural development of the overseas operations. Although production, office, and clerical occupations are rarely filled beyond a local labor market, executive and sometimes scientific, engineering, or professional managerial candidates may be sought in national or international markets. If the organization is searching for someone with extensive company experience to launch a very technical product in a country where it has never sold before, it will probably want a home-country national. This approach is often used when a new foreign subsidiary is being established and headquarters wants to control all strategic decisions, but technical expertise and experience are needed. It is also appropriate where there is a lack of qualified host-country nationals in the work force.

In other situations it might be more advantageous to hire a **host-country national (HCN)**, assuming there is a choice. For an uncomplicated consumer product it may be a wise corporate strategic decision to have each foreign subsidiary acquire its own distinct national identity.[18] Clothing has different styles of merchandising, and an HCN may have a better feel for the best way to market the sweaters or jeans of an international manufacturer.

Sometimes the choice may not be entirely left to the corporation. In some countries, such as most African nations, local laws control how many **expatriates** a corporation can send. There may be established ratios, such as that 20 host-country nationals must be employed for every American granted working papers. Using HCNs eliminates language problems and avoids problems of expatriate adjustment and the high cost of training and relocating an expatriate with a family. It also minimizes one of the chief reasons international assignments fail—the family's inability to adjust to their new surroundings.[19] Even when premiums are paid to lure the best local applicants away from other companies, the costs of maintaining the employee are significantly lower than with sending an American overseas. In some countries, where there are tense political environments, an HCN is less visible and can somewhat insulate the U.S. corporation from hostilities and possible terrorism.

Host-country National   Hiring a citizen from the host country to perform certain jobs in the global village.

Expatriates   Individuals who work in a country in which they are not citizens of that country.

The third option, recruiting regardless of nationality, develops an international executive cadre with a truly global perspective. On a large scale this type of recruiting may reduce national identification of managers with particular organizational units. For example, automobile manufacturers may develop a Taiwanese parts plant, Mexican assembly operations, and a U.S. marketing team, creating internal status difficulties through its different treatment of each country's employees.

RECRUITING SOURCES

Recruiting is more likely to achieve its objectives if recruiting sources reflect the type of position to be filled. For example, an ad in the business employment section of the *Wall Street Journal* is more likely to be read by a manager seeking an executive position in the $150,000-to-$225,000-a-year bracket than by an automobile assembly-line worker seeking to find employment. Similarly, an interviewer who is seeking to fill a management training position and visits a two-year vocational school in search of a college graduate with undergraduate courses in engineering and a master's degree in business administration is looking for "the right person in the wrong place." Moreover, the Internet is rewriting all the rules. Jobs at all levels can be advertised on the Internet, and access to literally millions of people is possible.

Certain recruiting sources are more effective than others for filling certain types of jobs. As we review each source in the following sections,[20] the strengths and weaknesses in attempting to attract lower-level and managerial-level personnel will be emphasized.

Sourcing for candidates has been significantly enhanced with the use of the Internet. Organizations like Recruiters Online Network are able to advertise job openings and reach many more individuals than was thought possible. And an online recruiting effort can reach more potential job candidates at a lower cost.

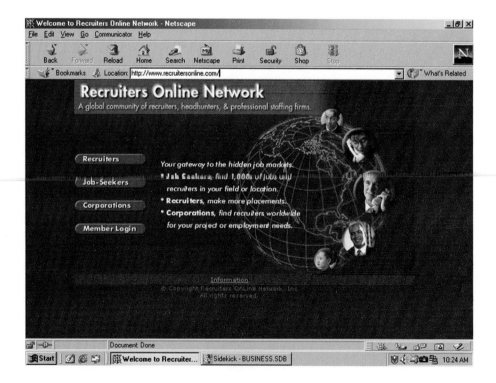

The Internal Search

Internal Search A promotion-from-within concept.

Many large organizations will attempt to develop their own employees for positions beyond the lowest level. These can occur through an **internal search** of current employees, who have either bid for the job, been identified through the organization's human resource management system, or even been referred by a fellow employee. The advantages of such searches—a promote-from-within-wherever-possible policy—are:[21]

- It is good public relations.
- It builds morale.
- It encourages good individuals who are ambitious.
- It improves the probability of a good selection, since information on the individual's performance is readily available.
- It is less costly than going outside to recruit.
- Those chosen internally already know the organization.
- When carefully planned, promoting from within can also act as a training device for developing middle- and top-level managers.

There can be distinct disadvantages, however, to using internal sources. It can be dysfunctional to the organization to utilize inferior internal sources only because they are there, when excellent candidates are available on the outside. However, an individual from the outside, in contrast with someone already employed in the organization, may appear more attractive because the recruiter is unaware of the outsider's faults. Internal searches may also generate infighting among the rival candidates for promotion, as well as decreasing morale levels of those not selected.

The organization should also avoid excessive inbreeding. Occasionally it may be necessary to bring in some new blood to broaden the current ideas, knowledge, and enthusiasm, and to question the "we've-always-done-it-that-way" mentality. As noted in the discussion of human resource inventories in Chapter 5, the organization's HRM files should provide information as to which employees might be considered for positions opening up within the organization. Most organizations can utilize their computer information system to generate an output of those individuals who have the desirable characteristics to potentially fill the vacant position.

In many organizations, it is standard procedure to post any new job openings and to allow any current employee to apply for the position. This action, too, receives favorable marks from the EEOC. The posting notification can be communicated on a central "positions open" bulletin board in the plants or offices, in the weekly or monthly organization newsletter, or, in some cases, in a specially prepared posting sheet from human resources outlining those positions currently available. Even if current employees are not interested in the position, they can use these notices to give to other individuals who may seek employment within the organization—the employee referral.

Employee Referrals/Recommendations

One of the best sources for individuals who will perform effectively on the job is a recommendation from a current employee.[23] Why? Because employees rarely recommend someone unless they believe that the individual can perform adequately. Such a recommendation reflects on the recommender, and when someone's reputation is at stake, we can expect the recommendation to be based on

"BEST PRACTICE" IDEAS APPLICABLE TO RECRUITMENT AND HIRING[22]

WHAT ARE THE EEOC RECOGNIZED BEST practices for private-sector organizations? Below are the things that the "best of the best" do when recruiting.

- Establish a policy for recruitment and hiring, including criteria, procedures, responsible individuals, and applicability of diversity and affirmative action.
- Engage in short-term and long-term strategic planning.
- Identify the applicable barriers to equal employment opportunity.
- Ensure that there is a communication network notifying interested persons of opportunities, including advertising within the organization and, where applicable, not only with the general media, but with minority, persons with disabilities, older persons, and women-focused media.
- Communicate the competencies, skills, and abilities required for available positions.
- Communicate about family-friendly and work-friendly programs.
- Where transportation is an issue, consider arrangements with the local transit authority.
- Participate in career and job fairs and open houses.
- Work with professional associations, civic associations, and educational institutions with attractive numbers of minorities, women, persons with disabilities, and/or older persons to recruit.
- Use recruiter, referral, and search firms with instructions to present diverse candidate pools to expand search networks.
- Partner with organizations that have missions to serve targeted groups.
- Use internship, work/study, co-op, and scholarship programs to attract interested persons and to develop interested and qualified candidates.
  - Develop and support educational programs and become more involved with educational institutions that can refer a more diverse talent pool.
  - Ensure that personnel involved in the recruitment and hiring process are well trained in their equal employment opportunity responsibilities.
  - Explore community involvement options so the company's higher profile may attract more interested persons.
- Eliminate practices which exclude or present barriers to minorities, women, persons with disabilities, older persons, or any individual.
- Include progress in equal employment opportunity recruitment and hiring as factors in management evaluation.

Employee Referral A recommendation from a current employee regarding a job applicant.

considered judgment. **Employee referrals** also may have acquired more accurate information about their potential jobs. The recommender often gives the applicant more realistic information about the job than could be conveyed through employment agencies or newspaper advertisements. This information reduces unrealistic expectations and increases job survival. As a result of these preselection factors, employee referrals tend to be more acceptable applicants, to be more likely to accept an offer if one is made, and, once employed, to have a higher job survival rate. Additionally, employee referrals are an excellent means of locating potential employees in those hard-to-fill positions. For example, because of the difficulty in finding IT professionals, computer programmers, engineers, or nurses with specific skills required by the organization, some organizations have turned to their employees for assistance. In many of these organizations, these specifically identified hard-to-fill positions include a reward if an employee referral candidate is hired—referral bonuses of $10,000 or more are not unusual in these fields.[24] In doing so, both the organization and the employee benefit; the employee receives a monetary reward and the organization receives a qualified candidate without the major expense of an extensive recruiting search.

There are, of course, some potentially negative features of employee referral. For one thing, recommenders may confuse friendship with job performance competence. Individuals often like to have their friends join them at their place of employment for social and even economic reasons; for example, they may be able to share rides to and from work. As a result, a current employee may recommend a friend for a position without giving an unbiased consideration to the friend's job-related competence. Employee referrals may also lead to nepotism, that is, hiring individuals who are related to persons already employed by the organization. Although such actions may not necessarily align with the objective of hiring the most qualified applicant, interest in the organization and loyalty to it may be long-term advantages. Finally, employee referrals may also minimize an organization's desire to add diversity to the workplace.[25]

Employee referrals are an excellent means of locating potential employees for those hard-to-fill positions.

Employee referrals do, however, appear to have universal application. Lower-level and managerial-level positions can be, and often are, filled by the recommendation of a current employee. In higher-level positions, however, it is more likely that the referral will be a professional acquaintance rather than a friend with whom the recommender has close social contact. In jobs where specialized expertise is important, and where employees participate in professional organizations that foster the development of this expertise, it can be expected that current employees will be acquainted with, or know about, individuals they think would make an excellent contribution to the organization.

The External Searches

In addition to looking internally for candidates, it is customary for organizations to open up recruiting efforts to the external community. These efforts include advertisements (including Internet postings), employment agencies, schools, colleges and universities, professional organizations, and unsolicited applicants.

Advertisements   The sign outside the construction location reads: "Now Hiring—Framers." A newspaper advertisement reads:

> Telemarketing Sales. We are looking for someone who wants to assume responsibility and wishes to become part of the fast-growing cellular telephone business. No previous sales experience required. Salary to $35,000. For appointment, call Mr. Reynolds at 1-888-555-0075.

And more sophisticated Internet job search engines can provide us with a richness of data about the job and the company, and link us to several other web sites that provide additional information.

Most of us have seen these kinds of advertisements. When an organization wishes to communicate to the public that it has a vacancy, advertisement is one of the most popular methods used. However, where the advertisement is placed is often determined by the type of job. Although it is not uncommon to see blue-collar jobs listed on placards outside the plant gates, we would be surprised to find a vice presidency listed similarly. The higher the position in the organization, the more specialized the skills, or the shorter the supply of that resource in the labor force, the more widely dispersed the advertisement is likely to be. The search for a top executive might include advertisements in national publications—like the *Wall Street Journal*—or be posted on executive-search firm web sites. On the other hand, the advertisement of lower-level jobs is usually confined to the local daily newspaper, regional trade journal, or broad-based Internet job sites.

A number of factors influence the response rate to advertisements. There are three important variables: identification of the organization, labor market conditions, and the degree to which specific requirements are included in the advertisement. Some organizations place what is referred to as a **blind-box ad,**

Blind-box Ad   An advertisement in which there is no identification of the advertising organization.

one in which there is no specific identification of the organization. Respondents are asked to reply to a post office box number or to an employment firm that is acting as an agent between the applicant and the organization. Large organizations with a national reputation seldom use blind advertisements to fill lower-level positions; however, when the organization does not wish to publicize the fact that it is seeking to fill an internal position, or when it seeks to recruit for a position where there is a soon-to-be-removed incumbent, a blind-box advertisement may be appropriate.

Although blind ads can assist HRM in finding qualified applicants, many individuals may be reluctant to answer them. Obviously, there is the fear, sometimes justified, that the advertisement has been placed by the organization in which the individual is currently employed. Also, the organization itself is frequently a key determinant of whether the individual is interested; therefore, potential candidates may be reluctant to reply. Further deterrents are the bad reputation that advertisements have received because of organizations that place ads when no position exists in order to test the supply of workers in the community, to build a backlog of applicants, or to identify those current employees who are interested in finding a new position; or to satisfy affirmative action requirements when the final decision, for the greater part, has already been made.

The job analysis process is the basic source for the information placed in the ad (see HRM Skills, p. 168). A decision must be made as to whether the ad will focus on descriptive elements of the job (job description) or on the applicant (job specification). The choice made will often affect the number of replies received. If, for example, you are willing to sift through 1,000 or more responses, you might place a national ad in the *New York Times,* the Chicago *Tribune,* or a regional newspaper's employment section, or on a web site like Monster.com (see Exhibit 6-1). However, an advertisement in these locations that looks like Exhibit 6-2 might attract less than a dozen replies.

The difference between Exhibits 6-1 and 6-2 is obvious. Exhibit 6-1 uses more applicant-centered criteria to describe the successful candidate. Most individuals perceive themselves as having confidence and seeking high income. More important, how can an employer measure these qualities? The response rate should therefore be high. In contrast, Exhibit 6-2 describes a job requiring precise abilities and experience. The requirements of at least "2+ years research experience in speech/language technology" are certain to limit the respondent pool.

Employment Agencies   We will describe three forms of employment agencies: public or state agencies, private employment agencies, and management consulting firms. The major difference between these three sources is the type of clientele served. All states provide a public employment service. The main function of these agencies is closely tied to unemployment benefits, since benefits in some states are given only to individuals who are registered with their state employment agency. Accordingly, most public agencies tend to attract and list individuals who are unskilled or have had minimum training. This, of course, does not reflect on the agency's competence, but rather reflects on the image of public agencies. State agencies are perceived by prospective applicants as having few high-skilled jobs, and employers tend to see such agencies as having few high-skilled applicants. Therefore public agencies tend to attract and place predominantly low-skilled workers. The agencies' image as perceived by both applicants and employers thus tends to result in a self-fulfilling prophecy; that is, few high-skilled individuals place their names with public agencies, and, similarly, few employers seeking individuals with high skills list their vacancies or inquire about applicants at state agencies.

EXHIBIT 6-1
*Advertisement with General
Information*

US-LA-New Orleans-Investment Representative

Be in business for yourself, but not by yourself!

- Be your own boss—you are the office manager.
- Control your own future.
- Determine your own income.

As an Edward Jones Investment Representative, you have that opportunity. You build a business and run it from your branch office in a location of your choice. You build relationships with clients and help them reach their financial goals by recommending appropriate investments and services.

Requirements: Edward Jones, an equal opportunity employer, is looking for candidates who have a strong desire to succeed and the ability to work in a self-sufficient manner. Confidence, persistence and excellent communication skills are necessary. The candidate must also believe that customer satisfaction is No. 1. Although sales experience and a business degree are preferred, they are not required. Training and marketing materials are provided.

To learn more about details and apply directly online, please visit our website at http://www.jonesopportunity.com/us or contact us at recrecruit@edwardjones.com. Don't hesitate, apply today for your opportunity with the 7th Best Company in America to Work For (as rated by *Fortune* Magazine). You could be opening the next Edward Jones office. If you are an accountant, teacher or lawyer, visit our website to find out why this might be the alternative career opportunity for you.

EXHIBIT 6-2
*Advertisement with Specific
Information*

US-MA-Boston-Computational Linguist-Speech Synthesis

You will be working with the industry leading Speechify TTS system—based on AT&T's speech synthesis technology—to improve the quality, robustness and performance of the text processing engine. You will develop the engine to support a range of additional languages and develop additional features and functionality to enhance performance of the TTS engine and related products in future applications.

Responsibilities:

- Architectural design of a multilingual, highly configurable, and robust text processing engine
- Robust morphology and syntax for TTS
- Prosody generation
- Working as part of a team of speech technology experts

Requirements:

- 2+ years research experience in speech/language technology
- Desire and ability to work as part of a team
- Familiarity with XML authoring and tools
- Strong C/C++ programming skills
- Fluency in UNIX or NT (ideally both)
- Excellent oral and written communications skills in English—additional languages are a bonus
- MSCS or MA (or equivalent experience)
- Be able to work with a minimum amount of direct supervision
- Instill confidence in your abilities
- Identify functionality versus schedule tradeoffs under pressure
- Work well with other technical experts in speech technology and application development.

Yet this image may not always be the case. For example, a nationwide computer network at the Employment Security Commission acts as a clearinghouse for professional-level jobs. In this case, a public agency may be a good source for such applicants.

How does a private employment agency, which has to charge for its services, compete with state agencies that give their service away? They must do something differently from what the public agencies do, or at least give that impression.[26] The major difference between public and private employment agencies is their image; that is, private agencies are believed to offer positions and applicants of a higher caliber. Private agencies may also provide a more complete line of services. They may advertise the position, screen applicants against the criteria specified by the employer, and provide a guarantee covering six months or a year as protection to the employer should the applicant not perform satisfactorily. The private employment agency's fee can be totally absorbed by either the employer or the employee, or it can be split. The alternative chosen usually depends on the demand-supply situation in the community involved.

The third agency source consists of management consulting, **executive search,** or "headhunter" firms. Agencies of this type—such as Korn/Ferry International in New York, Heidrick & Struggles in Chicago, Ray & Berndtson in Fort Worth, and Cypress International in Tampa—are actually specialized private employment agencies. They specialize in middle-level and top-level executive placement,[27] as well as hard-to-fill positions such as actuaries or IT specialists. In addition to the level at which they recruit, the features that distinguish executive search agencies from most private employment agencies are their fees, their nationwide contacts, and the thoroughness of their investigations. In searching for an individual of vice-president caliber, whose compensation package may be far in excess of $250,000 a year, the potential employer may be willing to pay a very high fee to locate exactly the right individual to fill the vacancy. A fee up to 35 percent of the executive's first-year salary is not unusual as a charge for finding and recruiting the individual.[28]

Executive search firms canvass their contacts and do preliminary screening. They seek out highly effective executives who have the skills to do the job, can effectively adjust to the organization, and most important, are willing to consider new challenges and opportunities. Possibly such individuals are frustrated by their inability to move up in their current organization at the pace at which

Executive Search   Private employment agency specializing in middle- and top-level placements.

Charging upwards of 35 percent of a manager's first-year's salary means that excellent services must be provided to an organization. Executive search firms, like Tampa, Florida-based Sterling-Sharpe, do just that. In essence, they perform most of the "recruiting" activities for an organization for a specific position, and present a slate of qualified candidates for final selection by client members.

they are capable, or they recently may have been bypassed for a major promotion. The executive search firm can act as a buffer for screening candidates and, at the same time, keep the prospective employer anonymous.[29] In the final stages, senior executives in the prospective firm can move into the negotiations and determine the degree of mutual interest.

Schools, Colleges, and Universities Educational institutions at all levels offer opportunities for recruiting recent graduates. Most educational institutions operate placement services where prospective employers can review credentials and interview graduates. Most also provide employers an opportunity to witness a "prospective employee's" performance through cooperative arrangements and internships.[30]

Whether the educational level required for the job involves a high-school diploma, specific vocational training, or a college background with a bachelor's, master's, or doctoral degree, educational institutions are an excellent source of potential employees.[31]

High schools or vocational-technical schools can provide lower-level applicants; business or secretarial schools can provide administrative staff personnel; and two- and four-year colleges and graduate schools can often provide professional and managerial-level personnel. While educational institutions are usually viewed as sources for inexperienced entrants to the work force, it is not uncommon to find individuals with considerable work experience using an educational institution's placement service. They may be workers who have recently returned to school to upgrade their skills, or former graduates interested in pursuing other opportunities.

Professional Organizations Many professional organizations, including labor unions, operate placement services for the benefit of their members. The professional organizations include such varied occupations as industrial engineering, psychology, accounting, legal, and academics. These organizations publish rosters of job vacancies and distribute these lists to members. It is also common practice to provide placement facilities at regional and national meetings where individuals looking for employment and companies looking for employees can find each other—building a network of employment opportunities.

Professional organizations, however, can also apply sanctions to control the labor supply in their discipline. For example, although the law stipulates that unions cannot require employers to hire only union members, the mechanisms for ensuring that unions do not break this law are poorly enforced. As a result, it is not unusual for labor unions to control supply through their apprenticeship programs and through their labor agreements with employers. Of course, this tactic is not limited merely to blue-collar trade unions. In those professional organizations where the organization placement service is the focal point for locating prospective employers, and where certain qualifications are necessary to become a member (such as special educational attainment or professional certification or license), the professional organization can significantly influence and control the supply of prospective applicants.

Unsolicited Applicants Unsolicited applications, whether they reach the employer by letter, e-mail, telephone, or in person, constitute a source of prospective applicants. Although the number of unsolicited applicants depends on economic conditions, the organization's image, and the job seeker's perception of the types of jobs that might be available, this source does provide an excellent supply of stockpiled applicants. Even if there are no particular openings when the applicant contacts the organization, the application can be kept on file for later needs. Unsolicited applications made by unemployed individuals, however, generally have a short life. Those individuals who have adequate skills and who would be prime candidates for a position in the organization if a position were currently available usually find employment with some other organization that does have an opening. However, in times of economic stagnation, excellent prospects are often unable to locate the type of job they desire and may stay actively looking in the job market for many months.

Cyberspace Recruiting

Newspaper advertisements and employment agencies may be on their way to extinction as primary sources for identifying job candidates. The reason: Internet recruiting.[32]

Nearly four out of five companies currently use the Internet to recruit new employees—increasingly by adding a recruitment section to their web site.[33] As almost every organization—small as well as large—creates its own web site, these become natural extensions for finding new employees. Organizations planning to do a lot of Internet recruiting often develop dedicated sites specifically designed for recruitment. They have the typical information you might find in an employment advertisement—qualifications sought, experienced desired, benefits provided. But they also allow the organization to showcase its products, services, corporate philosophy, and mission statement. This information increases the quality of applicants, as those whose values don't mesh with the organization tend to select themselves out. The best designed of those web sites include an online response form, so applicants don't need to send a separate resume by mail, e-mail, or fax. Applicants need only fill in a resume page and hit the "submit" button. A company like Cisco Systems, Inc., for example, receives more than 80 percent of its resumes electronically.[34]

Facilitating the growth of Internet recruitment are commercial job-posting services that provide essentially electronic classified ads.[35] We've listed the 100 most popular of these, by category, in Exhibit 6-3.

Aggressive job candidates are also using the Internet. They set up their own web pages—frequently called **websumes**—to "sell" their job candidacy. When they learn of a possible job opening, they encourage potential employers to "check me out at my web site." There, applicants have standard resume information, supporting documentation, and sometimes a video where they introduce themselves to potential employers. These same websumes are also frequently searched by recruiting firms that scan the Internet in search of viable job candidates.

Internet recruiting provides a low-cost means for most businesses to gain unprecedented access to potential employees worldwide.[36] For example, a job posted online for the San Francisco-based Joie de Vivre Hospitality organization cost $50. Had company officials used the more traditional local paper advertisement, the same ad would have cost $2,000.[37] It's also a way to increase diversity and find people with unique talents.[38] For example, job-posting services create subgroup categories for employers looking to find bilingual workers, female attorneys, or African-American engineers.

Finally, Internet recruiting won't be merely the choice of those looking to fill high-tech jobs. As computer prices fall, access costs to the Internet decrease, and the majority of working people become comfortable with the Internet, online recruiting will be used for all kinds of nontechnical jobs—from those paying thousands of dollars a week to those paying $7 an hour.

Websumes Web pages that are used as resumes.

Exhibit 6-3
Top 100 Electronic Recruiters Quick Views Site Map

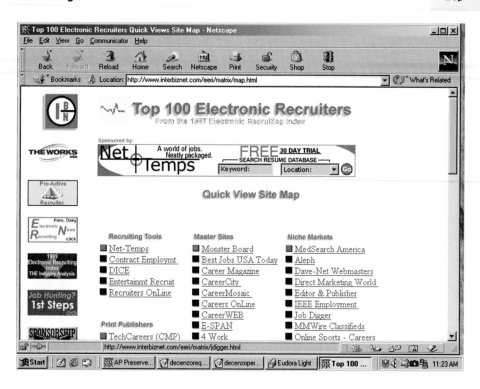

Recruitment Alternatives

Much of the previous discussion on recruiting sources implies that these efforts are designed to bring into the organization full-time, permanent employees. However, economic realities, coupled with management trends such as rightsizing, have resulted in a slightly different focus. More and more companies today are looking at hiring temporary help (including retirees), leasing employees, and using the services of independent contractors.[39]

Temporary Help Services   Organizations like the Kelly Temporary Services, Accountemps, and Temp-Force, Inc. can be a source of employees when individuals are needed on a temporary basis. Temporary employees are particularly valuable in meeting short-term fluctuations in HRM needs.[40] While traditionally developed in the office administration area, the temporary staffing service has expanded its coverage to include a broad range of skills. It is now possible, for example, to hire temporary nurses, computer programmers, accountants, librarians, drafting technicians, secretaries, even CEOs.[41]

In addition to specific temporary help services, another quality source of temporary workers is older workers, those who have already retired or have been displaced by rightsizing in many companies.[42] An aging work force and some individuals' desire to retire earlier have created skill deficiencies in some disciplines. Older workers bring those skills back to the job. In fact, at Monsanto, the company has capitalized on this rich skill base by establishing its own temporary, in-house employment agency, the Retiree Resource Corps (RRC).[43] Then, when there is a need for temporary help somewhere in the organization, the RRC provides the needed talent pool. For Monsanto, such a temporary work force is saving the company almost $2 million a year. While the reasons many of these older workers wish to continue to work vary,[44] they bring with them several advantages. These include "flexibility in scheduling, low absenteeism, high motivation, and mentoring abilities for younger workers."[45] It was these very attributes that the first ten sales representatives of Everyday Learning Company, the Evanston, Illinois, publishing organization specializing in elementary school math curriculum books, brought to the job.[46] By their fifth year, they had helped the founder, Jo Anne Schiller, build a business that generates more than $2 million annually and has its books in over 2,000 schools.

Leased Employees Individuals who are hired by one firm and sent to work in another for a specific duration of time.

Employee Leasing   Whereas temporary employees come into an organization for a specific short-term project, **leased employees** typically remain with an organization for longer periods of time. Under a leasing arrangement, individuals work for the leasing firm.[47] When an organization has a need for specific employee skills, it contracts with the leasing firm to provide a certain number of trained employees. For example, consider Robert Half International. As a leasing firm, Robert Half has on its staff fully trained accountants ready to meet an organization's accounting needs. If tax season requires additional tax accountants, Robert Half can supply them; the same holds true for other accounting areas. One reason for leasing's popularity is cost.[48] The acquiring organization pays a flat fee for the employees. The company is not responsible for benefits or other costs, like Social Security payments, it would incur for a full-time employee. This is because leased employees are, in fact, employees of the leasing firm. Furthermore, when the project is over, employees are returned to the leasing company, thus eliminating any cost associated with layoffs or discharge.

Leased employees are also well-trained individuals. They are screened by the leasing firm, trained appropriately, and often go to organizations with an unconditional guarantee. Thus, if one of these individuals doesn't work out, the company can get a new employee, or make arrangements to have its fee returned. There are also benefits from the employee's point of view. Some of today's workers prefer more flexibility in their lives. Working with a leasing company and being sent out at various times allow these workers to work when they want, for the length of time they desire.

Our discussion in Chapter 1 regarding professional employee organizations (PEOs) is precisely what employee leasing is about. As more and more organizations—especially smaller organizations—move toward PEOs, we can expect the trend of employee leasing to increase significantly.[49] When that happens, the effort expended by organizational members on recruiting will be significantly reduced.

Organizations like McDonald's have found that employing the elderly is a win-win situation. For McDonald's, they are able to more efficiently staff their restaurants with individuals who have a positive work ethic and good work habits. For such individuals, these jobs give them a few extra dollars each week and an opportunity to be involved in a productive activity that helps keep their spirits up.

Independent Contractors   Another means of recruiting is the use of independent contractors. Often referred to as consultants, independent contractors are taking on a new meaning. Companies may hire independent contractors to do very specific work at a location on or off the company's premises. For instance, claims-processing or medical and legal transcription activities can easily be done at one's home and forwarded to the employer on a routine basis. With the continuing growth of personal computers, fax machines, and voice mail, employers can ensure that home work is being done in a timely fashion.

Independent contractor arrangements benefit both the organization and the individual. Because the company does not have to regard this individual as an employee, it saves costs associated with full- or part-time personnel, like Social Security taxes and workers' compensation premiums. Additionally, such opportunity is also a means of keeping good individuals associated with your company. Suppose an employee wants to work, but also to be at home when the kids are home. This cannot be done through typical work arrangements, but allowing the individual to work at home, on his or her time, can be a win-win solution to the problem.

GETTING INTO THE ORGANIZATION

So far in this chapter we've introduced you to the recruiting activities of organizations. When recruiters make a decision to hire employees, information is often sent out announcing the job in some format. Seeing that announcement, and feeling like there's a potential match between what you can offer and what the organization wants, you need to throw your hat into the "hiring ring."

One of the more stressful situations you will face happens when you apply for a job. This occurs because generally there are no specific guidelines to follow to guarantee you success. However, several tips can be offered that may increase your chances of finding employment. Even though getting a job interview should be one of your major goals in the hiring process, being offered an interview opportunity requires hard work. You should view getting a job as your job at the moment.[50]

Competition for most good jobs is fierce—even in times of low unemployment.[51] As such, you can't wait until the last minute to enter the job market. Your job hunt must start well in advance of when you plan to start work. So, for seniors in college who plan to graduate in May, is starting in the fall helpful? There are two advantages. First, it shows that you are taking an interest in your career and that you are planning. You're not waiting until the last minute to begin, and this reflects favorably on you. Second, starting in the fall coincides with many companies' recruiting cycles. If you wait until March to begin the process, some job openings are likely to already have been filled. For specific information regarding the company recruiting cycles in your area, visit your college's career development center.

For specific information regarding company recruiting cycles in your area, visit your college's career development center.

How Do You Prepare Your Resume?

All job applicants need to have information circulating that reflects positively on their strengths. That information needs to be sent to prospective employers in a format that is understandable and consistent with the organization's hiring practices. In most instances, this is done through the resume.

No matter who you are or where you are in your career, you need a current resume. Your resume is typically the only information source that a recruiter will use in determining whether to grant you an interview. Therefore, your resume must be a sales tool; it must give key information that supports your candidacy, highlights your strengths, and differentiates you from other job applicants. An example of the type of information that should be included is shown in Exhibit 6-4. Notice, too, that the volunteer experience this individual has is noted on the resume. Anything that distinguishes you from other applicants should be included. It shows that you are well rounded, committed to your community, and willing to help others.

It is important to pinpoint a few key themes regarding resumes that may seem like common sense but are frequently ignored. If you are making a paper copy of your resume, it must be printed on a quality printer. The style of font should be easy to read (e.g., Courier or Times New Roman type fonts). Avoid any style that may be hard on the eyes, such as a script or italic font. A recruiter

EXHIBIT 6-4
A Sample Resume

CHRIS WILLIAMS
1690 West Road
Charlotte, NC 56013

CAREER OBJECTIVE:	Seeking employment in an investment firm that provides a challenging opportunity to combine exceptional interpersonal and computer skills.
EDUCATION:	Pembroke Community College A.A., Business Administration (May 1998) Winthrop University B.S., Finance (May 2001)
EXPERIENCE:	Winthrop University
12/99 to present	Campus Bookstore, Assistant Bookkeeper *Primary Duties*: Responsible for coordinating book purchases with academic departments; placing orders with publishers; invoicing, receiving inventory, pricing, and stocking shelves. Supervised four student employees. Managed annual budget of $45,000.
9/96 to 9/98	Pembroke Community, College Student Assistant, Business Administration *Primary Duties*: Responsible for routine administrative matters in an academic department—including answering phones, word processing faculty materials, and answering student questions.
10/93 to 6/96	High Point High School Yearbook Staff *Primary Duties*: Responsible for coordinating marketing efforts in local community. Involved in fund raising through contacts with community organizations.
SPECIAL SKILLS:	Experienced in Microsoft Excel and Word, Netscape, D-Base, and powerpoint presentation software. Some programming experience in C++. Fluent in speaking and writing Spanish. Certified in CPR.
SERVICE ACTIVITIES:	Secretary/Treasurer, Student Government Association President, Finance Club Volunteer, Special Olympics Volunteer, Meals-On-Wheels
REFERENCES:	Available on request.

who must review 100 or more resumes a day is not going to look favorably at difficult-to-read resumes. So use an easy-to-read font and make the recruiter's job easier.

It is also important to note that many companies today are using computer scanners to make the first pass through resumes.[52] They scan each resume for specific information like key job elements, experience, work history, education, or technical expertise.[53] The use of scanners, then, has created two important aspects for resume writing.[54] First, the computer matches keywords in a job description. Thus, in creating a resume, typical job description phraseology should be used. Second (and this goes back to the issue of font type), the font used should be easily read by the scanner. If it can't be, your resume may be put in the rejection file.

BUILDING A RESUME

RECRUITING IN ORGANIZATIONS BRINGS WITH IT two certainties—resumes that people submit and the need to track what's been sent in.[55] Software on the market today can help in both of these areas—helping someone design an effective resume, and helping the organization track applicant information.

Resume Expert: Resume Expert is a computer software program that is widely used on college campuses. You may want to check with your college's career center to see if they subscribe to Resume Expert. The typical Resume Expert fee is $25, and sometimes is paid by your student fees, or charged to you individually for registering for its use. Resume Expert is designed to help you build several resumes that can be tailored to specific audiences. Moreover, with Resume Expert, your information is placed into a database which can be accessed by client organizations who can search through the database looking for matches. You also can obtain a paper copy as well as an electronic file copy.

Resume Maker: Resume Maker (Individual Software, Inc., $49.95; www.resumemaker.com) provides sample resume designs, recommended resume phrases (keywords), and sample cover letters. Resume Maker also provides an opportunity for you to develop and submit an electronic resume to several career web sites, such as Monster.com. You can also develop a web page of your resume with Resume Maker.

Applicant Tracking/HR Tools: (For the employer, Applicant Tracker) HR Press, $495, provides a paperless environment in which to track applicant information. The software permits user-defined fields that can be tailored to the specific needs of the organization. Applicant Tracking/HR Tools tracks such information as skills, education, EEO classification, job applied for, and salary requested. The software also builds a database of relevant applicant information that enables the HR practitioner to send customized letters to the applicant, or merge data (like name and address) into other word processing software.

Your resume should be copied on good-quality white or off-white paper (no off-the-wall colors). There are certain types of jobs—like a creative artist position—where this suggestion may be inappropriate. But these are the *exceptions*. You can't go wrong using a 20-bond-weight paper that has some cotton content (about 20 percent). By all means, don't send standard duplicating paper—you don't want it to look as if you are mass-mailing resumes (even if you are).

Much of what we stated in the last few paragraphs also hold true if you are producing an electronic resume. That is, the style should be similar, fonts should be easy to read, and the like. But it's important to note that in today's technology-rich companies, many of these organizations are requiring electronic resumes. That means that rather than mailing a printed version of your resume to the company, you are asked to e-mail it in an attached file to the organization. Accordingly, you'll need to be able to e-mail an attachment, and ensure that your electronically attached resume is properly formatted and in a word processing format that is readable. Whether an electronic resume is required will often be designated in the advertisement you've read, or there will be directions in the Internet recruiting site in which you have seen the job opening.

Our last point regarding resumes—irrespective of whether it's a paper or an electronic version—relates to proofreading. Because the resume is the only representation of you the recruiter has, a sloppy resume can be deadly. If it contains misspelled words or is grammatically incorrect, your chances for an interview will be significantly reduced. Proofread your resume, and if possible, let others proofread it, too.

In addition to your resume, you need a cover letter. Your cover letter should contain information that tells the recruiter why you should be considered for the job. You need to describe why you'd be a good job candidate. This means having a cover letter that highlights your greatest strengths and indicates how these strengths can be useful to the company. Your cover letter should also contain

WRITING A JOB ADVERTISEMENT

ABOUT THE SKILL: How DO you get individuals to pay attention to your job opening? Get them interested in your organization? Give them enough information so that those who are not qualified do not respond? The answer to these questions lies in the job advertisement.[56] The more effective your advertisement, the more likely you will be to achieve the dual goal of recruiting.

1. *Tell enough about the job.* Your goal here is to provide enough information about the job so potential applicants can determine whether they are interested or qualified.

2. *Give the relevant information about the job.* This includes providing a job title and a description of job duties. This information should be drawn directly from the job description.

3. *List the minimum qualities a successful job incumbent needs.* This includes specific requirements a job incumbent is required to possess. This may reflect educational levels, prior experience, and specific competencies or skills. Again, much of this information should be readily available from the job-specification component of the job description.

4. *Be specific about unique aspects of the job.* Disclose any pertinent information about the job that an applicant should know about. For example, if the job requires extensive traveling, state so. If experience on specific equipment, technology applications, and so forth, is required, this too, should be stated.

5. *Check the advertisement for correctness.* Make sure the advertisement is properly written, contains no grammatical or punctuation errors, and is easy to read. Whenever possible, avoid using jargon and abbreviations that may be confusing. Checking for correctness also means reviewing each word to ensure that no terms used may be deemed inappropriate or potentially create an adverse impact.

some information citing why the organization getting your resume is of interest to you. Cover letters should be carefully tailored to each specific organization. This shows that you've taken some time and given some thought to the job you're applying for.

Cover letters should be addressed to a real name. Don't send anything out "To Whom It May Concern." These letters frequently tell the recruiter that you are on a fishing expedition—mass mailing resumes in hopes that some positive response is generated. This technique seldom works in job hunting. You may not always have the recruiter's name and title, but with some work you can get it. Telephone the company in question and ask for it; most receptionists in an employment office will give out the recruiter's name and title. If you just can't get a name, go to the organization's web site and search for the information you're looking for. If this is unsuccessful, you can always resort to the traditional standby—the reference section of a library (you may also find this information on the Internet)—and locate a copy of a publication like the *Standard & Poor's Register Manual,* or *Moody's.* These publications usually list the names and titles of officers in the organization. If everything else fails, send your resume to one of the officers, preferably the officer in charge of employment or administration, or even to the president of the organization.

Like the resume, the cover letter should be flawless—whether it's sent in a paper version or electronically. Proofread this as carefully as you do the resume. Finally, if you're using a paper version, sign each cover letter individually.

HRM WORKSHOP

SUMMARY

(This summary relates to the Learning Outcomes identified on p. 148.)

After having read this chapter, you should be able to:

1. **Define what is meant by the term** *recruiting*. Recruiting is the discovering of potential applicants for actual or anticipated organizational vacancies. It involves searching and sourcing for viable job candidates.

2. **Identify the dual goals of recruiting.** The two goals of recruiting are to generate a large pool of applicants from which to choose while simultaneously providing enough information for individuals to self-select out of the process.

3. **Explain what constrains human resource managers in determining recruiting sources.** Influences that constrain HRM in determining recruiting sources include image of the organization, attractiveness and nature of the job, internal policies, government requirements, and the recruiting budget.

4. **Identify the principal sources involved in recruiting employees.** The principal sources of recruiting employees include internal search, advertisements, employee referral/recommendations, employment agencies, temporary rental services, schools, colleges, universities, professional organizations, the Internet (or cyberspace recruiting), and casual or unsolicited applicants. Employee leasing, temporary employees, and independent contractors continue to be a good source of employees.

5. **Describe the advantages and disadvantages of employee referrals.** The advantages of employee referrals include access to individuals who possess specific skills, having job applicants with more complete job and organization information, and a universal application to all levels in the organization. The disadvantages of employee referrals include the potential of confusing friendship with job performance, the potential for nepotism, and a potential for minimizing the organization's desire to add diversity to the organization's employee mix.

6. **Identify three important variables that affect response rates to job advertisements.** The three important variables are identification of the organization, labor market conditions, and the degree to which specific requirements are included in the advertisement.

7. **Explain what distinguishes a public employment agency from a private employment agency.** The major difference between public and private employment agencies often lies in their image. Private employment agencies are believed to offer positions and applicants of a higher caliber. Private agencies may also provide a more complete line of services in that they advertise the position, screen applicants against the criteria specified by the employer, and

provide a guarantee covering six months or a year as protection to the employer should the applicant not perform satisfactorily. Public employment agencies are more closely linked to unemployment benefits. Accordingly, the image of most public agencies (while not completely accurate) is that they tend to attract and list individuals who are unskilled or have had minimum training.

8. **Describe the benefits of cyberspace recruiting.** Internet recruiting provides a low-cost means for many businesses to gain unprecedented access to potential employees worldwide. Cyberspace recruiting is also a way to increase diversity and find people with unique talents.

9. **Explain what is meant by the concept of employee leasing and the organizational benefits of such an arrangement.** Employee leasing refers to a situation whereby individuals employed in an organization actually work for the leasing firm. One reason for leasing's popularity is cost. The acquiring organization pays a flat fee for the employees. The company is not responsible for benefits or other costs, like Social Security payments, it would incur for a full-time employee. This is because leased employees are, in fact, employees of the leasing firm.

DEMONSTRATING COMPREHENSION: *Questions for Review and Discussion*

1. What is the "dual objective" of recruiting?
2. What factors influence the degree to which an organization will engage in recruiting?
3. What specific constraints might prevent an HR manager from hiring the best candidate?
4. What are the advantages and disadvantages of recruiting through an internal search?
5. What are the pros and cons of using employee referrals for recruiting workers?
6. Describe the differences one may encounter when recruiting globally.
7. "A job advertisement that generates 1,000 responses is always better than one that gets 20 responses." Build an argument supporting this statement and an argument against this statement.
8. "An organization should follow a promote-from-within policy." Do you agree or disagree with this statement? Explain.
9. When you go looking for a job after graduation, what sources do you expect to use? Why?
10. "The emphasis on leased or temporary employees in an organization will only lead to a decrease in employee morale. These employees come in, do their jobs, then leave it up to the full-timers to handle the details." Build an argument supporting this statement, and an argument against this statement.

CASE APPLICATION: *TEAM FUN!*

Kenny and Norton, owners of TEAM FUN!, a sporting goods manufacturer and retailer, are in the OFFICE, looking at the model of their organization on the wall. Norton comments, "I think it's great that your daughter, Gloria, is getting married again. And I agree that we'll give Bobby, your new son-in-law, a manager job at a branch. But we have all the branch managers we need."

Kenny grins, "I think this would be a great time to open a Florida store. They could live there; run the place in the summer. We go down there in the winter and make sure everything is going fine. It will be great."

Norton groans, "Maybe. Hey, Tony!" He yells to the Director of Human Resources who is walking by, "Come in here for a minute. We need to hire 20–30 people in the Fort Myers, Florida, area to work in our new branch. How long will it take you to get that together?"

Meanwhile, Kenny picks up the phone, "Ray, remember that mall area by the new golf course in Punta Gorda we played last year? Find out if we can lease 30–40,000 square feet of it by. . . ." He puts his hand over the receiver and looks at Tony. "How long 'til you get the people?"

Tony gulps and says, "Six months, probably. Who do I take from here?"

Kenny continues on the phone with Ray, the Comptroller, "By. . . What is this? June? By September–October 1. That gives us about 60 to 90 days to redo the inside. We can open TEAM FUN! SOUTH in time for a Christmas rush! Sure. Sure. Whatever you need. Get back to me." He hangs up, obviously well pleased.

As Tony slumps into a side chair, Norton says to him, "Now that you did all those job descriptions, I'm amazed you think it will take 5 months. We know lots of people along the Gulf Coast. Let me find you some names." He and Kenny both paw through a huge rolodex and laugh at certain names and memories as they pull cards for Tony.

Tony sighs, "Good thing I've got that intern starting next week. I'll turn him/her loose on this."

Questions:
(You are Tony's intern.)
Make a recruiting plan for TEAM FUN! Identify at least four principal sources to use for recruiting for the new store. Be sure to discuss the pros and cons of each of your suggestions.

Working with a Team: *A Question of Effective Recruiting*

Alan Carlson is an impatient, results-oriented, innovative, hard-working, focused entrepreneur, who likes to be surrounded with aggressive, highly creative, skilled, focused team players who are flexible, change driven, informed, cutting-edge-skilled professionals much like himself in work ethic, but come from diverse groups. He believes that professionals with varied backgrounds, culture, race, national origin, and other factors contribute to better solutions and creativity. He wants only those who are as committed as he is to growing a company that produces the industry standard that will become the benchmark in intranet and software technology. That means being willing to work 60 or 90 hours a week if the project requires, and dedication to and passion for customers, HI-5-TECH, and the project team.

Mr. Carlson may start people out with slightly below-industry-average salaries, but you know he rewards performance and tenure. He's reputed to double a salary when a developer exceeds expectations. He also contributes his company's stock to the employees' benefit package, subject to their length of employment, and at the current rate, a person might retire a millionaire if he or she can withstand the pace.

Interested? Discuss why or why not, comparing responses with your paired team member. Also, here are some guiding questions for you and your partner to consider:

1. What web sites would you use to recruit from an international perspective?
2. Would you consider being an expatriate; why or why not?
3. What ideas do you have on developing an employee-referral system that provides some type of incentives or rewards for those hired that remain six months or more because "likes attract"?

Enhancing Your Writing Skills

1. Using the job description of the benefits manager from Exhibit 5-10 (Chapter 5, p. 141), write a job advertisement for this position to be placed in a national newspaper like the *Wall Street Journal*.
2. Develop a two- to three-page response to the following question: What are the pluses and minuses for an organization in using temporary employees as a pool from which to select permanent employees? Are there pluses from the employee's standpoint?
3. Visit three different cyberspace-recruiting job sites (as listed in Exhibit 6-3). Describe the similarities and differences you noticed among the three. Which job site did you prefer? Explain why?

www.wiley.com/college/decenzo

Endnotes

1. See, for example, Robert J. Grossman, "Robbing the Cradle?" *HRMagazine* (September 2000), pp. 41–45.
2. Based on Kevin Ferguson, "Cisco High," *Business Week E-Biz* (June 5, 2000), pp. EB102–EB104; Joan O'C. Hamilton, "The Panic over Hiring," *Business Week E-Biz* (April 3, 2000), EB130–EB132; and "Book It," *Entrepreneur* (May 2000), p. 44.
3. Justin Martin, "One Company's Hiring Binge," *Fortune* (February 7, 1994), p. 14.
4. See, for example, Wendy Zellner, Robert D. Hof, Richard Brandt, Stephen Baker, and David Greising, "Go-Go Goliaths," *Business Week* (February 13, 1995), pp. 80–81; and Cora Daniels, "To Hire a Lumber Expert, Click Here," *Fortune* (April 3, 2000), pp. 267–270.
5. Andrew S. Bargerstock and Gerald Swanson, "Four Ways to Build Cooperative Recruitment Alliances," *HRMagazine* (March 1991), p. 49.
6. Ibid., pp. 50–51.
7. "Code Words," *Wall Street Journal* (September 12, 1995), p. A-1.
8. "Wired for Hiring: Microsoft's Slick Recruiting Machine," *Fortune* (February 5, 1996), p. 123.
9. See, for instance, Daniel B. Turban and Daniel W. Greening, "Corporate Social Performance and Organizational Attractiveness to Prospective Employers," *Academy of Management Journal*, Vol. 40, No. 3 (June 1997), pp. 658–672.
10. See, for example, Stephen J. Holoviak and David A. DeCenzo, contributing eds., "Service Industry Seeks Summer Help," *Audio Human Resource Report*, Vol. 1, No. 9 (October 1990), p. 5.

11. Ken Jordan, "Play Fair and Square When Hiring from Within," *HRMagazine* (January 1997), pp. 49–51.

12. See, for instance, Ruth E. Thaler-Carter, "EMA Model Defines Cost-Per-Hire as Part of Staffing Performance," *HRMagazine* (December 1997), p. 4.

13. Vignettes adapted from CCH Business Owner's Toolkit, "Case Study—Discrimination in Ads," SOHO Guidebook [www.lycos.com/business/cch/guidebook.html?1pv=1&docNumber=P05-0683] (2000), pp. 1–4.

14. Linda Micco, "Global Recruiting Called Essential for Many Firms," *HR News* (May 1998), p. 15.

15. See, for instance, Sarah Cuthill, "Guest Column: Managing HR Across International Borders," *Compensation and Benefits* (Summer 2000), pp. 43–45; "Global Recruiting," *Practical Accountant* (October 2000), p. 6; Donna Fenn, "International: Opening Up and Overseas Operation," *Inc.* (June 1995), p. 89; and Pamela Sebastian, "Expatriate Employees," *Wall Street Journal* (March 9, 1995), p. A-1.

16. See, for instance, Clair Poole, "The New Nationalization," *Latin Trade* (June 1998), pp. 71–72; and "Hire Power," *Canadian Business* (December 1996), p. 56.

17. C. Grove, "An Ounce of Prevention: Supporting International Job Transitions," *Employment Relations Journal*, Vol. 17, No. 2 (Spring 1990), p. 111.

18. Robert J. Grossman, "HR in Asia," *HRMagazine* (July 1997), p. 106.

19. See, for example, Barbara Fitzgerald-Turner, "Myths of Expatriate Life," *HRMagazine* (June 1997), p. 65.

20. See, for example, Michelle Neely Martinez, "Looking for Young Talent? Inroads Helps Diversify Efforts," *HRMagazine* (March 1996), pp. 73–75.

21. Jack Stack, "The Next in Line," *Inc.* (April 1998), p. 43.

22. The U.S. Equal Employment Opportunity Commission, *Best Practices of Private Sector Employers* (December 27, 1997).

23. Thomas A. Stewart, "In Search of Elusive Tech Workers," *Fortune* (February 16, 1998), p. 171; Andy Bargerstock and Hank Engle, "Six Ways to Boost Employee Referral Programs," *HRMagazine* (December 1994), pp. 72–79.

24. Julekha Dash, "Filling Slots with Inside Referrals," *Computerworld* (July 10, 2000), p. 35; and Keith Swenson, "Maximizing Employee Referrals," *HR Focus* (January 1999), pp. 9–10.

25. Kathryn Tyler, "Employees Can Help Recruit New Talent," *HRMagazine* (September 1996), p. 60.

26. See, for example, Clyde J. Scott, "Recruitment: Employing a Private Employment Firm," *Personnel Journal* (September 1989), pp. 78–83.

27. See, for example, *Executive Recruiting News* (November 1999), p. 1 [www.kennedyinfo.com/er/ern.html], and Jennifer Reingold and Nicole Harris, "Casting for a Different Set of Characters," *Business Week* (December 8, 1997), pp. 38–39.

28. Ibid.; and Perri Capbell, "When a Recruiter Comes Knocking, Be Ready to Respond," *Wall Street Journal* (August 6, 1996), p. B-1.

29. Gayle Sato Stodder, "Getting Personnel," *Entrepreneur* (October 1995), p. 94.

30. Christopher Caggiano, "Beyond Campus Recruiting," *Inc.* (April 1998), p. 115.

31. Linda Thornburg, "Employers and Graduates Size Each Other Up," *HRMagazine* (May 1997), pp. 76–79; and Robert W. Thompson. "Job-Hunting Students Seek Balance," *HR News* (May 1997), p. 2.

32. This section based on information from R. Maynard, "Casting the Net for Job Seekers," *Nation's Business* (March 1997), pp. 28–29; V. Pospisil, "Recruitment Added to Web Sites," *Industry Week* (April 21, 1997), p. 12; E. I. Schwartz, "A New Reality," *Business Week* (February 9, 1998), p. ENT 7; and J. Martin, "Changing Jobs? Try the Net," *Fortune* (March 2, 1998), pp. 205–208.

33. Michelle Neely Martinez, "Get Job Seekers to Come to You," *HRMagazine* (August 2000), pp. 42–52.

34. Ibid., p. 50.

35. See, for example, Bill Leonard, "Online and Overwhelmed," *HRMagazine* (August 2000), pp. 37–42; Pat Curry, "Long On for Recruits," *Industry Week* (October 16, 2000), pp. 46–54; Rachel Emma Silverman, "Your Career Matters: Raiding Talent Via the Web—Personal Pages, Firms's Sites Are Troves of Information for Shrewd Headhunters," *Wall Street Journal* (October 3, 2000), p. B-1; and Michelle Neely Martinez, "Get Job Seekers to Come to You," *HRMagazine* (August 2000), pp. 45–52.

36. Milton Zall, Internet Recruiting," *Strategic Finance* (June 2000), p. 66; and Steven L. Thomas and Katherine Ray, "Recruiting and the Web: High-Tech Hiring," *Business Horizons* (May–June 2000), p. 43.

37. Marty Whitford, "Hi-Tech HR, Hotel," *Hotel and Motel Management* (October 16, 2000), p. 49.

38. Candee Wilde, "Recruiters Discover Diverse Value in Web Sites," *Informationweek* (February 7, 2000), p. 144

39. Patricia W. Hamilton, "Staffing on a Shoestring," *Executive Female* (July–August 1995), pp. 32–34; and John Ross, "Effective Ways to Hire Contingent Personnel," *HRMagazine* (February 1991), pp. 52–53.

40. Kent Blake, "She's Just a Temporary," *HRMagazine* (August 1998), p. 45.

41. Jerry Useem, "Treating Temporary Work as a Permanent Fixture," *Inc.* (September 1997), p. 28.

42. See, for example, American Association of Retired Persons, *How to Recruit Older Workers* (Washington, DC: American Association of Retired Persons, 1993).

43. Lee Phillion and John R. Brugger, "Encore! Retirees Give Top Performance as Temporaries," *HRMagazine* (October 1994), pp. 74–77.

44. Reasons cited by the American Association of Retired Persons include the need to make money, to get health insurance coverage, to develop skills, to use their time more productively, to feel useful, to make new friends, to provide some structure to their daily lives, or to have a sense of achievement. See "How to Recruit Older Workers," p. 27.

45. American Association of Retired Persons and the Society for Human Resource Management, *The Older Workforce: Recruitment and Retention* (Washington, DC: American Association of Retired Persons, 1993), p. 1.

46. Susan Greco, "Recruiting the Newly Retired," *Inc.* (August 1993), p. 23.

47. Caution is warranted regarding for whom an individual works. Generally, the employee is the responsibility of the leasing company. But under certain circumstances, like long-term duration of the lease, the acquiring organization may be the employer of record, with the leasing company handling a variety of HRM associated paperwork.

48. Bargerstock and Swanson, p. 50.

49. Carolyn Hirschman, "For PEOs, Business Is Booming," *HRMagazine* (February 2000), p. 23–28.

50. See, for instance, R. D. Clarke, "Getting a Job! . . . After College," *Black Enterprise* (February 1998), pp. 135–138.

51. N. Munk, "Finished at Forty," *Fortune* (February 1999), pp. 50–64.

52. William H. Baker, Kirsten DeTeinne, and Karl L. Smart, "How Fortune 500 Companies Are Using Electronic Resume Management Systems," *Business Communication Quarterly* (September 1998), pp. 8–19.

53. See, for example, J. Lawlor, "Scanning Resumes: The Impersonal Touch," *USA Today* (October 7, 1991), p. 7B.

54. T. Mullins, "How to Land a Job," *Psychology Today* (September–October 1994), pp. 12–13.

55. Jim Meade, "Where Did They Go?" *HRMagazine* (September 2000), pp. 81–84, and "Manage Hiring Steps with Web-Based Aid," *HRMagazine* (February 2000), pp. 121–124.

56. This skill vignette is based on information provided in CCC Business Owner's Toolkit, "Information to Include in Job Ads," *SOHO Guidebook* (2000), p. 1.

7

FOUNDATIONS OF SELECTION

LEARNING OUTCOMES

AFTER READING THIS CHAPTER, YOU WILL BE ABLE TO:

1. Describe the selection process.
2. Identify the primary purpose of selection activities.
3. Discuss why organizations use application forms.
4. Explain the primary purposes of performance simulation tests.
5. Discuss the problems associated with job interviews and means of correcting them.
6. Specify the organizational benefits derived from realistic job previews.
7. Explain the purpose of background investigations.
8. List three types of validity.
9. Explain how validity is determined.

———————◼———————

Truth is often said to be stranger than fiction. While this adage could be debated, when it comes to employment selection, it appears to hold true. That's because anyone who's ever worked in the screening process—especially reviewing cover letters, resumes, or interviewing—typically has some fascinating story to tell. Like what? Well, consider the following items that have been taken from events in actual interview situations.[1] For your convenience, we've italicized the points of concern.

- Candidate *fell asleep* during the interview.
- Would you hire this applicant with *WordPurpose* and *Locust* skills?
- Candidate explained that he didn't finish high school because he was *kidnaped and kept in a closet.*
- Imagine the embarrassment this applicant must have felt when he proofread his cover letter and noticed that he had written "*As indicted,* I have five years of analyzing investments.
- Of course, this applicant was correct when she noted that this was just a "*ruff draft* of her resume."

- How about the applicant who was dressed to the "9's" for an interview at a well-known "conservative" organization — tailored dark-blue pinstriped Armani suit, white spread-collar Egyptian-broadcloth shirt, a red power tie, black polished cap-toe shoes, *and multiple facial-piercing, including four in each ear, his tongue, one in his left nostril.*
- The job applicant challenged the interviewer to *an arm wrestling match.*

Wouldn't it be nice if the selection process were this clear cut? It sure would make things easier! Of course, these are exaggerations. HR practitioners usually are not this lucky to have their decisions handed to them on silver platters. Yet, all selection activities exist for the purpose of making effective selection decisions—seeking to predict which job applicants will be successful job performers if hired.

INTRODUCTION

A recent Marketing graduate went on her first interview in an upstart dot-com company specializing in managing web sales.[2] Not knowing what to expect, she prepared as best she could. She was exquisitely dressed in a new navy pinstriped suit and was carrying her new black leather Tumi briefcase. As she entered the human resource management office, she encountered two doors. On the first door was "Marketing Majors." On the second was "All Other Majors." She entered door 1, which opened up to two more doors. On door 1 was, "3.55 or Better GPA"; door 2, "All Other GPAs." Having a 3.83 GPA, she once again entered door 1, and found herself facing yet two more choices. Door 1 stated, "Took E-Business Marketing Course," and door 2, "Didn't Take E-Business Marketing." Because this course was not offered in her major, she went through door 2. Upon opening the door, she found a box with preprinted letters saying, "Your qualifications did not meet the expectations of the job. Thanks for considering our organization. Please exit to the right."

A lot of careful planning and careful thought is required for selection activities to be successful. The selection process is composed of a number of steps. Each of these steps provides decision makers with information that will help them predict whether an applicant will prove to be a successful job performer.[3] One way to conceptualize this is to think of each step as a higher hurdle in a race. The applicant able to clear all the hurdles wins the race—victory being the receipt of a job offer. And how long this takes varies. The process may take weeks, or as in the case of Toyota U.S., the selection process could take almost two years (see Exhibit 7-1)![4]

THE SELECTION PROCESS

Selection activities typically follow a standard pattern, beginning with an initial screening interview and concluding with the final employment decision. The selection process typically consists of eight steps: (1) initial screening interview, (2) completing the application form, (3) employment tests, (4) comprehensive interview, (5) background investigation, (6) a conditional job offer; (7) medical or physical examination, and (8) the permanent job offer. Each step represents a decision point requiring some affirmative feedback for the process to continue. Each step in the process seeks to expand the organization's knowledge about the applicant's background, abilities, and motivation, and it increases the information from which decision makers will make their predictions and final choice. However, some steps may be omitted if they do not yield data that will aid in predicting success, or if the cost of the step is not warranted. Applicants should also be advised what specific screening will be done, such as credit checks, reference checking, and drug tests. The flow of these activities is depicted in Exhibit 7-2. Let's take a closer look at each.

Initial Screening

Initial Screening The first step in the selection process whereby inquiries about a job are screened.

As a culmination of our recruiting efforts, we should be prepared to initiate a preliminary review of potentially acceptable candidates. This **initial screening** is, in effect, a two-step procedure: (1) the screening of inquiries and (2) the provision of screening interviews.

HRM WORKSHOP

Summary

(This summary relates to the Learning Outcomes identified on p. 174.)

After having read this chapter, you should be able to:

1. **Describe the selection process.** The selection process would include the following: initial screening interview, completion of the application form, employment tests, comprehensive interview, background investigation, conditional job offer, physical or medical examination, and the permanent job offer. In the discrete selection process, each step acts as a standalone predictor—failing to pass any of these discrete steps means disqualification from the job. In the comprehensive approach, candidates are taken through most of the steps before a final decision about them is rendered.

2. **Identify the primary purpose of selection activities.** Selection devices provide managers with information that will help them predict whether an applicant will prove to be a successful job performer. The primary purpose of selection activities is to predict which job applicant will be successful if hired. During the selection process, candidates are also informed about the job and organization. Proper selection can minimize the costs of replacement and training, reduce legal challenges, and result in a more productive work force.

3. **Discuss why organizations use application forms.** The application form is effective for acquiring hard biographical data—data that can ultimately be verified.

4. **Explain the primary purposes of performance simulation tests.** Performance simulation tests require the applicant to engage in specific behaviors that have been demonstrated to be job related. Work sampling and the assessment center, which are performance simulations, receive high marks for their predictive capability.

5. **Discuss the problems associated with job interviews, and means of correcting them.** Interviews consistently achieve low marks for reliability and validity. These, however, are more the result of interviewer problems as opposed to the interview itself. Interviewing validity can be enhanced by using a structured process.

6. **Specify the organizational benefits derived from realistic job previews.** Realistic job previews reduce turnover by giving the applicant both favorable and unfavorable information about the job.

7. **Explain the purpose of background investigations.** Background investigations are valuable when they verify hard data from the application; they tend, however, to offer little practical value as a predictive selection device.

8. **List three types of validity.** There are three validation strategies. These are content, construct, and criterion-related validity.

9. **Explain how validity is determined.** Validity is determined either by discovering the extent to which a test represents actual job content, or through statistical analyses that show the test used relates to an important job-related trait, or to performance on the job.

Demonstrating Comprehension: *Questions for Review and Discussion*

1. Describe the seven-step selection process.
2. What is meant by a "reliable and valid" selection process? What is a legal employee selection process?
3. What is a weighted application form? How does it work?
4. Contrast work samples with the assessment center.
5. What are the major problems of the interview as a selection device? What can HRM do to reduce some of these problems?
6. What effect should a realistic job preview have on a new hire's attitude and behavior?
7. Why should a background investigation be done?
8. What do you think of realistic job previews? Would you be more likely to choose a position where recruiters emphasized only the positive aspects of the job?
9. Define the concepts of reliability and validity. What are the three types of validity? Why are we concerned about reliability and validity?
10. "Because of the law regarding employment questions, application forms provide limited information. Accordingly, they should not be used." Do you agree or disagree with this statement? Explain.
11. "Even though interviews have been widely criticized, they are heavily used." Discuss why this selection device still rates very highly when it is known that it can provide unreliable information.

CASE APPLICATION: *TEAM FUN!*

Tony, the Director of Human Resources for TEAM FUN!, a sporting goods manufacturer and retailer, is meeting with Kenny and Norton, the owners and founders. He is ready to go to South Florida to select people for the new store that will be opening in a few months. Tony says, "We had over a thousand people interested in the newspaper ad: 200 for the sales representatives; 300 for the stockroom people; 200 for the cashiers; 100 for cleanup; and, 500 for manager. We need to prescreen some of these people. I thought I'd only go down for two weeks to hire everyone."

Kenny: "That's a great response! Wonder if they have all heard about us? Bobby (Kenny's son in law who will manage the operation) can go down week after next. I think he should hire the managers. That should take a load off you. And just pick the best few out of the rest to talk to."

Norton: "What about all that EEO stuff that Tony has been telling us about? Do we have to keep records of all these inquiries?"

Tony: "We do need an applicant pool profile. I can do that when I go there for the selection process. Could we agree on a few guidelines for me to cut the numbers down to size?"

Kenny: "Sure. Put some ideas together. We'll go over it tomorrow."

Tony: "I thought some performance simulation tests would be a good idea, especially for the cashiers and the sales people. Maybe lifting and stacking for the stockroom, too."

Norton: "Sure. Put some tests together. We'll go over them tomorrow."

Tony: "What about drug testing and background checks."

Kenny and Norton both glare at him until he walks out of the room.

Questions:

You are Tony's intern. Help him get ready for the meeting with Kenny and Norton tomorrow.

1. Devise a screening mechanism for each job category.
2. What kinds of performance simulation tests would be appropriate?
3. Set up an interview protocol for each job category.
4. Should Bobby select the managers himself? Should Bobby select all the other employees?
5. If you want Tony to try again with background checks and drug testing, prepare a carefully worded statement for him to present to Kenny and Norton. If you don't think these steps are desirable, explain your position.

WORKING WITH A TEAM: *Preparing for the Interview*

Using the job description you developed for the Benefits Manager (Chapter 5) and the ad you wrote (Chapter 6), develop a list of interview questions you'd ask of job candidates. Forming into groups of two or three compare your interview questions and reach a consensus on the questions you'd ask. Then based on those questions, develop a list of evaluation metrics (how you'll evaluate a candidate's responses). Share your team's responses with other teams in the class.

What are the similarities and differences noted? If time permits, you may want to have a mock interview. One of you play the role of the interviewer, one the job candidate, and one the observer. Ask the candidate your questions, and make an evaluation of the information obtained. The observer's job is to critique the interview. When you are finished, change roles and redo the mock interview.

ENHANCING YOUR WRITING SKILLS

1. Develop a two- to three-page response to the following statement: "Graphology as a selection criterion is not a valid selection device. Accordingly, it should not be used in determining whether or not to hire a job candidate." Present both sides of the argument and include supporting data. Conclude your paper by defending and supporting one of the two arguments you've presented.

2. Visit your college's career center and obtain a copy of the 50 most frequently asked questions in an interview. Reviewing the questions, which ones do you believe would pose the greatest difficulty for you? Which ones would be easier for you? In a two- to three-page writeup, discuss *why* the questions you've identified as difficult would be difficult for you, and what you can do to help overcome this difficulty.

3. Search the Internet for software packages that can be used to assist HRM in the selection process. Identify three different software packages that can be purchased by the public. State the benefits of the software package to the HRM practitioner, and the costs associated with purchasing the product. Based on your limited search, which of the three software packages would you recommend? Write a two-page memo to your boss requesting permission to purchase your selected software. Remember to include in your memo a comparison of the software packages and the reasons for your recommendation.

ENDNOTES

1. Employment situations are based on vignettes cited in Stephen Mraz, "Job Interview Weirdness," *Machine Design* (September 7, 2000), p. 152; Vivian Pospisil, "Resume Gaffes," *Industry Week* (March 1996), p. 10; Rochelle Sharpe, "Checkoffs," *Wall Street Journal* (August 8, 1995), p. A-1; and Tom Washington, "Selling Yourself in Job Interviews," *National Business Employment Weekly* (Spring–Summer 1993), p. 30.

2. This story was influenced by an example in Arthur Sloan, *Personnel: Managing Human Resources* (Englewood Cliffs, NJ: Prentice-Hall, 1983), p. 127.

3. For an interesting view on selection, see Orlando Behling, "Employee Selection: Will Intelligence and Conscientiousness Do the Job?" *Academy of Management Executive*, Vol. 12, No. 1 (January 1998), pp. 77–86.

4. Micheline Maynard, "Toyota Devises Grueling Workout for Job Seekers," *USA Today* (August 11, 1997), p. 3B.

5. Karl O. Magnusen and K. Galen Kroeck, "Videoconferencing Maximizes Recruiting," *HRMagazine* (August 1995), pp. 70–71.

6. See also Matthew T. Miklave and A. Jonathan Trafimow, "Ask Them If They Were Fired, But Not When They Graduated," *Workforce* (August 2000), pp. 90–93; Timothy S. Bland and Sue S. Stalcup," "Build a Legal Employment Application," *HRMagazine* (March 1999), pp. 129–133; and Elizabeth Bahnsen, "Questions to Ask, and Not to Ask, Job Applicants,"*HR News* (November 1996), pp. 10–11.

7. Saundra Jackson and Nan McGrane, "Get Application Form Before Offering Job," *HR News* (June 1996), p. 13.

8. See, for instance, Scott R. Kaak, Hubert S. Feild, William F. Giles, and Dwight R. Norris, "The Weighted Application Blank," *Cornell Hotel and Restaurant Administration Quarterly* (April 1998), pp. 18–24.

9. The seven items were not specifically identified so that the competitive edge the hotel had in hiring practices would not be weakened.

10. See the *Albemarle Paper Company* reference in Chapter 3.

11. See, for example, Joshua Harris Prager, "Nasty or Nice: 56-Question Quiz," *Wall Street Journal* (February 22, 2000), p. A-4; and E. James Randall and Cindy H. Randall, "Review of Salesperson Selection Techniques and Criteria: A Managerial Approach," *International Journal of Research in Marketing*, Vol. 7, No. 2 (December 1990), pp. 81–95.

12. Gilbert Nicholsen, "Screen and Glean: Good Screening and Background Checks Help Make the Right Match for Every Open Position," *Workforce* (October 2000), pp. 70, 72.

13. John A. Parnel, "Improving the Fit Between Organizations and Employees," *SAM Advanced Management Journal* (Winter 1998), pp. 35–42; and Jerry Flint, "Can You Tell Applesauce from Pickles?" *Forbes* (October 9, 1995), p. 108.

14. See, for instance, Rudy M. Yandrick, "Employers Turn to Psychological Tests to Predict Applicants' Work Behavior," *HR News* (November 1995), pp. 2, 13; and Wade Lambert, "Flunking Grade: Psychological Tests Designed to Weed Out Rogue Cops Get a 'D'," *Wall Street Journal* (September 11, 1995), p. A-1.

15. Jonathan A. Segal, "Take Applicants for a Test Drive," *HRMagazine* (December 1996), pp. 120–122.

16. "Mind Your P's and Q's," *Successful Meetings* (February 2000), p. 33.

17. Jonathan A. Segal, "Mirror, Mirror on the Wall," *HRMagazine* (March 1996), pp. 29–34.

18. Ronald Henkoff, "Finding, Training, and Keeping the Best Service Workers," *Fortune* (October 3, 1994), p. 118.

19. Clifford E. Montgomery, "Organizational Fit Is Key to Job Success," *HRMagazine* (January 1996), pp. 94–96; and Donna Fenn, Promoting "Getting the Right Fit," *Inc.* (February 1995), p. 111.

20. "Footnotes," *Business Week* (May 10, 1999), p. 8; and Stephenie Overman, "Bizarre Questions Aren't the Answer," *HRMagazine* (April 1995), p. 56.

21. Steven D. Maurer and Thomas W. Lee, "Situational Interview Accuracy in a Multiple Rating Context," *Academy of Management Best Papers Proceedings*, Lloyd N. Dosier and J. Bernard Keys, eds. (August 8–13, 1997), pp. 149–153; and Steven D. Maurer and Thomas W. Lee, "Toward a Resolution of Contrast Error in the Employment Interview: A Test of the Situational Interview," *Academy of Management Best Papers Proceedings*, Dorothy P. Moore, ed. (August 14–17, 1994), pp. 132–136.

22. For a discussion on fit and its appropriateness to the interviewing process, see "The Right Fit," *Small Business Reports* (April 1993), p. 28.

23. Gary N. Powell, and Laurel R. Goulet, "Recruiters' and Applicants' Reactions to Campus Interviews and Employment Decisions," *Academy of Management Journal*, Vol. 39, No. 6 (December 1996), pp. 1619–1640; and Robert C. Dipboye, *Selection Interviews: Process Perspectives* (Cincinnati: Southwestern Publishing, 1992), pp. 6–9.

24. For a more detailed discussion of impression management, see Nicholas L. Vasilopoulos, Richard R. Reilly, and Julia A. Leaman, "The Influences of Job Familiarity and Impression Management on Self-Report Measure Scales and Response Latencies," *Journal of Applied Psychology* (February 2000), pp. 50–64; Donna R. Pawlowski and John Hollwitz, "Work Values, Cognitive Strategies, and Applicant Reactions in a Structured Pre-Employment Interview for Ethical Integrity," *Journal of Business Communication* (January 2000), pp. 58–76; Amy L. Kristof and Cynthia Kay Stevens, "Applicant Impression Management Tactics: Effects on Interviewer Evaluations and Interview Outcomes," *Academy of Management Best Papers Proceedings*, Dorothy P. Moore, ed. (August 14–17, 1994), pp. 127–131.

25. Herbert M. Greenberg and Patrick J. Sweeney, "Hiring Expertise: How to Find the Right Fit," *HR Focus* (October 1999), p. 6.

26. Reported in Robert E. Carlson, Paul W. Thayer, Eugene C. Mayfield, and Donald A. Peterson, "Improvements in the Selection Interview," *Personnel Journal* (April 1971), p. 272.

27. Dipboye, p. 201.

28. Ibid.

29. A. Phillips and R. L. Dipboye, "Correlation Tests of Predictions from a Process Model of the Interview," *Journal of Applied Psychology,* Vol. 74 (1989), pp. 41–52; M. Ronald Buckley and Robert W. Edner, "B. M. Springbett and the Notion of the 'Snap Decision' in the Interview," *Journal of Management,* Vol. 14, No. 1 (March 1988), pp. 59–67.

30. See, for example, Dipboye, pp. 39–45.

31. For an interesting discussion on this topic, see P. Gregory Irving and John E. Meyer, "On Using Residual Differences Scores in the Measurement of Congruence: The Case of Met Expectations Research," *Personnel Psychology* (Spring 1999), pp. 85–95; and Robert D. Bretz, Jr., and Timothy A. Judge, "Realistic Job Previews: A Test of Adverse Self-Selection Hypothesis," *Journal of Applied Psychology* (April 1998), pp. 330–337.

32. Bruce M. Meglino and Angelo S. DeNisi, "Realistic Job Previews: Some Thoughts on Their More Effective Use in Managing the Flow of Human Resources," *Human Resources Planning,* Vol. 10, No. 3 (Fall 1987), p. 157.

33. See, for example, "What Personnel Offices Really Stress in Hiring," *Wall Street Journal* (March 6, 1991), p. A-1.

34. Paul Falcone, "Getting Employers to Open Up on a Reference Check," *HRMagazine* (July 1995), pp. 58–63; Michael A. McDaniel, "Biographical Constructs for Predicting Employee Suitability," *Journal of Applied Psychology,* Vol. 74, No. 6 (December 1989), pp. 964–970; and Michael Tadman, "The Past Predicts the Future," *Security Management,* Vol. 33, No. 7 (July 1989), pp. 57–61.

35. Jill Hecht Maxwell, "Of Resumes and Rap Sheets," *Inc.* (June 13, 2000), p. 9; Commerce Clearing House, *Human Resources Management: Ideas and Trends* (May 17, 1992), p. 85.

36. Paul W. Barada, "Reference Checking Is More Important Than Ever," *HRMagazine* (November 1996), p. 49.

37. Frances A. McMorris, "Ex-Bosses Face Less Peril Giving Honest Job References," *Wall Street Journal* (July 8, 1996), p. B-1; Elizabeth Bahnsen and Adrienne Loftin, "Handle Reference Requests Consistently; Stick to Facts, " *HR News* (December 1995), p. 16; and Bill Leonard, "Reference-Checking Laws: Now What?" *HRMagazine* (December 1995), p. 57.

38. Paul W. Barada, "Reference Checking Is More Important Than Ever," p. 49.

39. John Gibeaut, "Performance Review," *ABA Journal* (October 1997), p. 38.

40. See, for example, Theresa Donahue Egler, "White Lies Limit Employee Recovery in Discrimination Lawsuits," *HRMagazine* (November 1994), pp. 30–32.

41. Edward A. Robinson, "Beware — Job Seekers Have No Secrets," *Fortune* (December 29, 1997), p. 285.

42. See, for instance, "Hiring: Measure of Success," *Industry Week* (February 1996), p. 11.

43. See David E. Bowen, Gerald E. Ledford, Jr., and Barry R. Nathan, "Hiring for the Organization, Not the Job," *Academy of Management Executive,* Vol. 5, No. 4 (November 1991), pp. 35–51.

44. See, for example, Sara L. Rynes, Robert D. Bretz, and Barry Gerhart, "The Importance of Recruitment in Job Choice: A Different Way of Looking," *Personnel Psychology,* Vol. 44, No. 3 (Autumn 1991), pp. 487–521.

45. See, for example, Charles A. O'Reilly III, David I. Caldwell, and Richard Mirable, "A Profile Comparison Approach to Person vs. Job Fit: More Than a Mirage," in Jerry L. Wall and Lawrence R. Jauch, eds., *Academy of Management Best Papers Proceedings,* Las Vegas (August 9–12, 1992), pp. 237–242.

46. See, for example, Thomas F. Casey, "Making the Most of a Selection Interview," *Personnel* (September 1990), pp. 41–43.

47. Kathryn Tyler, "The Art of Saying No,"*HRMagazine* (January 1999), pp. 8–11.

48. Donna Fenn, "Hiring: Employees Take Charge," *Inc.* (October 1995), p. 111.

49. Dale E. Yeatts, Martha Hipskind, and Debra Barnes, "Lessons Learned from Self-Managed Work Teams," *Business Horizons* (July–August 1994), pp. 11–18.

50. Carol Hymowitz, "In the Lead: How to Avoid Hiring the Prima Donnas Who Hate Teamwork," *Wall Street Journal* (February 15, 2000), p. B-1; "How to Form Hiring Teams," *Personnel Journal* (August 1994), pp. 14–17.

51. See, for example, Alexander Mikalachki, "Creating a Winning Team," *Business Quarterly* (Summer 1994), pp. 14–22.

52. "How to Form Hiring Teams," p. 14.

53. As one reviewer correctly pointed out, there are several methods of determining reliability. These include equivalent form, test-retest method, and internal consistency forms of reliability. Their discussion, however, goes well beyond the scope of this text.

54. See, for example, Wayne Casio, *Applied Psychology in Personnel Management* (Englewood Cliffs, NJ: Prentice-Hall, 1991), pp. 151–154.

55. For an interesting perspective on the use of construct validity, see Linn Van Dyne and Jeffrey A. LePine, "Helping and Voice Extra-Role Behaviors: Evidence of Construct and Predictive Validity," *Academy of Management Journal* (February 1998), pp. 108–119.

56. A limitation of concurrent validity is the possibility of restricting the range of scores in testing current employees. This occurs because current employees may have been in the upper range of applicants. Those not hired were undesirable for some reason. Therefore, these scores theoretically should represent only the top portion of previous applicant scores.

57. A specific correlation coefficient for validation purposes is nearly impossible to pinpoint. There are many variables that will enter into the picture, such as the sample size, the power of the test, and what is measured. However, for EEO purposes, correlation coefficients must be indicative of a situation where the results are predictive of performance that is greater than one where chance alone dictated the outcomes.

58. Cut scores are determined through a set of mathematical formulas—namely, a regression analysis and the equation of a line. We refer you to any good introductory statistics text for a reminder of how these formulas operate.

59. Frank L. Schmidt and John E. Hunter, "Developing a General Solution to the Problem of Validity Generalization," *Journal of Applied Psychology,* Vol. 62, No. 5 (October 1977), pp. 529–539.

60. See, for instance, Cheri Ostroff and David A. Harrison, "Meta-analysis, Level of Analysis, and Best Estimates of Population Correlations: Cautions for Interpreting Meta-analytic Results in Organizational Behavior," *Journal of Applied Psychology* (April 1999), pp. 260–270; Calvin C. Hoffman, "Generalizing Physical Ability Test Validity: A Case Study Using Test Transportability, Validity Generalization, and Construct-Related Validation Evidence," *Personnel Psychology* (Winter 1999), pp. 1019–1041; Nambury S. Raju, Tobin V. Anselmi, Jodi S. Goodman, and Adrian Thomas, "The Effect of Correlated Artifacts and True Validity on the Accuracy of Parameter Estimation in Validity Generalization," *Personnel Psychology* (Summer 1998), pp. 453–465; Lauress L. Wise, Jeffrey McHenry, and John P. Campbell, "Identifying Optimal Predictor Composites and Testing for Generalizability Across Jobs and Performance Factors," *Personnel Psychology*, Vol. 43, No. 2 (Summer 1990), pp. 355–366.

61. Frank L. Schmidt, Kenneth Pearlman, John E. Hunter, and Hannah Rothstein Hirsh, "Forty Questions About Validity Generalization and Meta-Analysis," *Personnel Psychology*, Vol. 38, No. 4 (Winter 1985), pp. 697–822.

62. See, for instance, Irene F. H. Wong, and Lai Phooi-Ching, "Chinese Cultural Values and Performance at Job Interviews: A Singapore Perspective," *Business Communication Quarterly* (March 2000), pp. 9–22.

63. See, for example, Kathy B. Strawn and Steven P. Nurney, "Outsource Expatriate Support for High Quality, Low Costs," *HRMagazine* (December 1995), pp. 65–69.

64. Michelle Neely Martinez, "Myths About Women Expatriates Bad for Business," HR *News* (February 1996), p. B-3.

65. Michael A. O'Neil, "How to Implement Relationship Management Strategies," *Supervision* (July 2000), p. 3.

66. For an interviewee's perspective on small talk, see Jack Wolfe, "The Power of Babble," *Men's Health* (November 1996), pp. 74–76.

67. "Interviewing: It's How You Play the Game," *Inc.* (December 1995), p. 120.

68. Robert McGarvey, "Good Questions," *Entrepreneur* (January 1996), p. 87.

8

SOCIALIZING, ORIENTING, AND DEVELOPING EMPLOYEES

LEARNING OUTCOMES

AFTER READING THIS CHAPTER, YOU WILL BE ABLE TO:

1. Define socialization
2. Identify the three stages of employee socialization.
3. Identify the key personnel involved in orientation.
4. Explain why employee training is important.
5. Define training.
6. Describe how training needs evolve.
7. Indicate what is meant by the term *organizational development* and the role of the change agent.
8. Describe the methods and criteria involved in evaluating training programs.
9. Explain issues critical to international training and development.

Imagine spending nearly $1,500 a year to maintain a daily latte and scone habit. Millions of individuals do at Starbucks. This coffee company, with more than 2,600 locations and more opening each day, plans on turning the world on to "triple-tall nonfat mochas." But it can't do that without the skilled effort of its employees.[1]

What's the secret to Starbucks' amazing success? A quality product and an organization culture focused on customer service. Every one of Starbucks' 20,000+ employees has gone through a set of formal classes during his or her first six weeks with the company. By the time this socialization process is complete, employees have become coffee experts.

The Starbucks indoctrination begins with a history of the company. It's followed by a session on what customers need to know to brew a perfect cup of coffee at home. These include purchasing new beans weekly, the right type of water to use, and tips like never letting coffee sit on a hotplate for more than 20 minutes. The specific techniques for drink making are learned in an eight-hour class on retail skills. Here, new employees learn such varied skills as how to steam milk for latte, how to clean an espresso machine, and the proper way to fill one-pound sacks with coffee. There are also classes that teach new employees how to explain Starbucks' Italian drink names to baffled customers and coffee-tasting classes so employees understand why Sanani is described as "winey" and Costa Rica as "tangy and bright."

Starbucks' socialization program turns out employees who are steeped in the company's culture and understand management's obsession with "elevating the coffee experience," as the company's senior vice president of marketing put it.

Comprehensive training, pay that exceeds most entry-level food service jobs, and comprehensive benefits (including health insurance, even for part-timers, and stock options) have produced a skilled and loyal work force. As a result, annual turnover among Starbucks employees is nearly one-third less than the industry average within the fast-food business. And for Starbucks, that has translated into revenues approaching $2 billion and $100 million in profit.

INTRODUCTION

When we talk about socializing, orienting, and developing employees, we are referring to a process of helping new employees adapt to their new organizations and work responsibilities. These programs are designed to assist employees to fully understand what working is about in the organization and to get them to become fully productive as soon as possible. In essence, it's about learning the ropes! This means that employees understand and accept the behaviors that the organization views as desirable, and that when exhibited, will result in each employee attaining his or her goals.[2]

In this chapter, we'll explore the arena of socializing, orientating, and developing employees. We'll first look at the socialization process, and what organizations should do when employees first join them. We'll then proceed to explore their training and later development efforts designed to ensure a supply of highly skilled employees.

THE INSIDER-OUTSIDER PASSAGE

Socialization A process of adaption that takes place as individuals attempt to learn the values and norms of work roles.

When we talk about **socialization,** we are talking about a process of adaptation. In the context of organizations, the term refers to all passages undergone by employees. For instance, when you begin a new job, accept a lateral transfer, or get a promotion, you are required to make adjustments. You must adapt to a new environment—different work activities, a new boss, a different and most likely a diverse group of coworkers, and probably a different set of standards for what constitutes good performance.[3] Although we recognize that this socialization will go on throughout our careers—within an organization as well as between organizations—the most profound adjustment occurs when we make the first move into an organization: the move from being an outsider to being an insider. The following discussion, therefore, is limited to the outsider-insider passage, or what is more appropriately labeled organization-entry socialization.

What Is Socialization?

Do you remember your first day in college? What feelings did you experience? Anxiety over new expectations? Uncertainty over what was to come? Excitement at being on your own and experiencing new things? Fear based on all those things friends said about how tough college courses were? Stress over what classes to take, and what professors to get? Well, you probably experienced many of these things. And entry into a job is no different. For organizations to assist in the adjustment process, a few matters must be understood. We'll call these the assumptions of employee socialization.[4]

What Are the Assumptions of Employee Socialization?

Several assumptions underlie the process of socialization. The first is that socialization strongly influences employee performance and organizational stability. Also, new members suffer from anxiety; socialization does not occur in a vacuum; and the way in which individuals adjust to new situations is remarkably similar. Let's look a little closer at each of these assumptions.

Socialization Strongly Influences Employee Performance and Organizational Stability   Your work performance depends to a considerable degree on knowing what you should or should not do. Understanding the right way to do a job indicates proper socialization.[5] Furthermore, the appraisal of your performance includes how well you fit into the organization. Can you get along with your coworkers? Do you have acceptable work habits? Do you demonstrate the right attitude? These qualities differ among jobs and organizations. For instance, on some jobs you will be evaluated higher if you are aggressive and outwardly indicate that you are ambitious. On another job, or on the same job in another organization, such an approach might be evaluated negatively. As a result, proper socialization becomes a significant factor in influencing both your actual job performance and how it is perceived by others.[6]

Organizational Stability Is Also Increased Through Socialization[7]
When, over many years, jobs are filled and vacated with a minimum of disruption, the organization will be more stable. Its objectives will be more smoothly transferred between generations. Loyalty and commitment to the organization should be easier to maintain because the organization's philosophy and objectives will appear consistent over time. Given that most managers value high employee performance and organizational stability, the proper socialization of employees should be important.

New Members Suffer from Anxiety   The outsider-insider passage is an anxiety-producing situation. Stress is high because the new member feels a lack of identification—if not with the work itself, certainly with a new superior, new coworkers, a new work location, and a new set of rules and regulations. Loneliness and a feeling of isolation are not unusual. This anxiety state has at least two implications. First, new employees need special attention to put them at ease. This usually means providing an adequate amount of information to reduce uncertainty and ambiguity. Second, the existence of tension can be positive in that it often acts to motivate individuals to learn the values and norms of their newly assumed role as quickly as possible.[8] We can conclude, therefore, that the new member is anxious about the new role but is motivated to learn the ropes and rapidly become an accepted member of the organization.

Loneliness and a feeling of isolation are not unusual for new employees —they need special attention to put them at ease.

Socialization Does Not Occur in a Vacuum   The learning associated with socialization goes beyond the formal job description and the expectations that may be held by people in human resources or by the new member's manager. Socialization is influenced by subtle and less subtle statements and behaviors offered up by colleagues, management, employees, clients, and other people with whom new members come in contact.

The Way in Which Individuals Adjust to New Situations Is Remarkably Similar   This holds true even though the content and type of adjustments may vary. For instance, as pointed out previously, anxiety is high at entry and the new member usually wants to reduce that anxiety quickly. The information obtained during the recruitment and selection stages is always incomplete and usually distorted. New employees, therefore, must alter their understanding of their role to fit more complete information they get once they are on the job.

The point is that there is no instant adjustment—every new member goes through a settling-in period that tends to follow a relatively standard pattern.

How Does the Socialization Process Operate?

Socialization can be conceptualized as a process made up of three stages: prearrival, encounter, and metamorphosis.[9] The first stage encompasses the learning the new employee has gained before joining the organization. In the second stage, the new employee gets an understanding of what the organization is really like, and deals with the realization that the expectations and reality may differ. In the third stage, lasting change occurs. Here, new employees become fully trained in their jobs, perform successfully, and fit in with the values and norms of coworkers.[10] These three stages ultimately affect new employees' productivity on the job, their commitment to the organization's goals, and their decision to remain with the organization.[11] Exhibit 8-1 is a graphic representation of the socialization process.

Prearrival Stage The socialization process stage that recognizes individuals arrive in an organization with a set of organizational values, attitudes, and expectations.

The **prearrival stage** explicitly recognizes that each individual arrives with a set of organizational values, attitudes, and expectations. These may cover both the work to be done and the organization. For instance, in many jobs, particularly high-skilled and managerial jobs, new members will have undergone a considerable degree of prior socialization in training and in school.[12] Part of teaching business students is to socialize them to what business is like, what to expect in a business career, and what kind of attitudes professors believe will lead to successful assimilation in an organization. Prearrival socialization, however, goes beyond the specific job. The selection process is used in most organizations to inform prospective employees about the organization as a whole. In addition, of course, interviews in the selection process also act to ensure the inclusion of the "right type"—determining those who will fit in![13] "Indeed, the ability of individuals to present the appropriate face during the selection process determines their ability to move into the organization in the first place. Thus, success depends on the degree to which aspiring members have correctly anticipated the expectations and desires of those in the organization in charge of selection."[14]

Encounter Stage The socialization stage where individuals confront the possible dichotomy between their organizational expectations and reality.

Upon entry into the organization, new members enter the **encounter stage**. Here the individuals confront the possible dichotomy between their expectations—about their jobs, their coworkers, their supervisors, and the organization in general—and reality. If expectations prove to have been more or less accurate, the encounter state merely provides a reaffirmation of the perceptions generated earlier. However, this is often not the case. Where expectations and reality differ, new employees must undergo socialization that will detach them from their previous assumptions and replace these with the organization's pivotal standards.[15] Socialization, however, cannot solve all the expectation differences. At

EXHIBIT 8-1
A Socialization Process

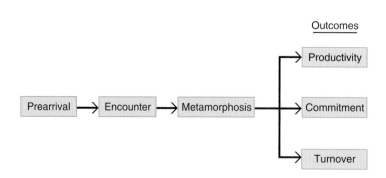

the extreme, some new members may become totally disillusioned with the actualities of their jobs and resign. It's hoped that proper selection, including the realistic job preview, would significantly reduce this latter occurrence.

Finally, the new member must work out any problems discovered during the encounter stage. This may mean going through changes—hence we call this the **metamorphosis stage.** But what is a desirable metamorphosis? Metamorphosis is complete—as is the socialization process—when new members have become comfortable with the organization and their work teams. In this situation, they will have internalized the norms of the organization and their coworkers; and they understand and accept these norms.[16] New members will feel accepted by their peers as trusted and valued individuals. They will become confident that they have the competence to complete their jobs successfully. They will have gained an understanding of the organizational system—not only their own tasks but the rules, procedures, and informally accepted practices as well. Finally, they will know how they are going to be evaluated. That is, they've gained an understanding of what criteria will be used to measure and appraise their work. They'll know what is expected of them and what constitutes a good job. Consequently, as Exhibit 8-1 shows, successful metamorphosis should have a positive effect on new employees' productivity and the employee's commitment to the organization, and should reduce the likelihood that the employee will leave the organization any time soon.[17]

If HRM recognizes that certain assumptions hold for new employees entering an organization and that they typically follow a three-staged socialization process, they can develop a program to begin helping these employees adapt to the organization. Let's turn our attention, then, to this aspect of organizational life—socializing our new employees through the new-employee orientation process.

Metamorphosis Stage The socialization stage whereby the new employee must work out inconsistancies discovered during the encounter stage.

$\mathcal{T}$HE PURPOSE OF NEW-EMPLOYEE ORIENTATION

New-employee **orientation** covers the activities involved in introducing a new employee to the organization and to his or her work unit. It expands on the information received during the recruitment and selection stages, and helps to reduce the initial anxiety we all feel when beginning a new job. For example, an orientation program should familiarize the new member with the organization's objectives, history, philosophy, procedures, and rules; communicate relevant HRM policies such as work hours, pay procedures, overtime requirements, and company benefits; review the specific duties and responsibilities of the new member's job; provide a tour of the organization's physical facilities; and introduce the employee to his or her manager and coworkers. Exhibit 8-2 illustrates a generic new-employee orientation agenda used in one organization.

Who is responsible for orienting the new employee? This can be done by either the new employee's supervisor, the people in HRM, or some combination thereof. In many medium-sized and most large organizations, HRM takes charge of explaining such matters as overall organizational policies and employee benefits. In other medium-sized and most small firms, new employees will receive their entire orientation from their supervisor. Exhibit 8-2 demonstrates a situation where the process is shared between the HRM staff and the new employee's supervisor. Of course, the new employee's orientation may not be formal at all. For instance, in many small organizations, orientation may mean the new member reports to her supervisor, who then assigns the new member to

Orientation The activities involved in introducing new employees to the organization and their work units.

EXHIBIT 8-2
Sample Orientation Agenda

NEW EMPLOYEE: Karen Bradley
B.S. in Finance
University of Delaware, 1999.

JOB TITLE:	Financial Analyst
DEPARTMENT:	Accounting and Finance
8:15 a.m.	Report to Human Resources:
	Receive new-employee package, including brochures describing the organization's history, products, and philosophy.
8:15–8:30	Welcome by company president.
8:30–9:00	Mr. Reynolds, Employment:
	Review Employment policies and practices.
9:00–10:00	Ms. Bateman, Training and Development:
	Review Training, Development, and Career Development Program offerings.
10:00–10:20	Break
10:20–10:50	Mr. Caldwell, Compensation:
	Overview and philosophy of company pay practices.
10:50–12:00	Ms. Reed, Benefits:
	Overview and enrollment for eligible benefits.
12:00–12:30	Mr. Wright, Employee Relations:
	Overview of safety, health, and communications programs.
12:30–1:30	Lunch with Mr. Haight (new employee's supervisor).
1:30–3:00	Supervisory Orientation.
	Provides a detailed tour of the Finance Department. Reviews the Department's overall structure. Discusses daily job routine and department policies and rules. Explains job expectations. Introduces new employee to her coworkers.
3:00–4:00	Tour of physical plant.
4:00–5:00	New employee is on her own to familiarize herself with and set up her office.

another employee who will introduce her to those persons with whom she will be working closely.[18] This may then be followed by a quick tour to show her where the lavatory is, how to make her way to the cafeteria, and how to find the coffee machine. Then the new employee is shown to her desk and left to fend for herself.

Although these programs may function differently, it is our contention that new-employee orientation requires much more. For instance, in today's dynamic organizations, it is imperative that new employees understand what the organization is about.[19] More specifically, these individuals need to understand the organization's culture.

Learning the Organization's Culture

Every organization has its own unique culture. This culture includes longstanding, and often unwritten, rules and regulations; a special language that facilitates communication among members; shared standards of relevance as to the critical aspects of the work that is to be done; matter-of-fact prejudices; standards for social etiquette and demeanor; established customs for how members should relate to peers, employees, bosses, and outsiders; and other traditions that clarify what is appropriate and "smart" behavior within the organization and what

Every organization has its own culture.

is not.[20] An employee who has been properly socialized to the organization's culture, then, has learned how things are done, what matters, and which work-related behaviors and perspectives are acceptable and desirable and which ones are not. In most cases, this involves input from many individuals.

The CEO's Role in Orientation

Prior to the mid-1980s, new-employee orientation operated, if at all, without any input from the company's executive management. But that began to change, due in part to management consultants advocating that senior management become more accessible to employees. What this meant was that senior managers become highly visible in the organization, meeting and greeting employees, and listening to employee concerns. At the same time, these individuals were given the opportunity to talk about the company—where it is going and how it is going to get there. In management terminology, this was called *visioning*. As more and more successful companies began to be cited in business literature for their leaders' ability to be involved in the work force, one question arose. If it appeared to work well for existing employees, what would it do for new employees joining the organization? The answer appears to be a lot.[21]

One of the more stressful aspects of starting a new job is the thought of entering the unknown. Although a previous organization may have done something that made you leave—like having no upward mobility—at least you knew what you had. But starting a new job is frightening. Did you do the right thing, make the right choice? Having the CEO present from day one addressing new employees helps to allay some of those fears. The CEO's first responsibility is to welcome new employees aboard and talk to them about what a good job choice they made.[22] In fact, this segment of new-employee orientation can be likened to a cheerleading pep rally. The CEO is in a position to inspire these new employees by talking about what it is like to work for the organization. In addition, the CEO is in a position to begin to discuss what really matters in the company—an indoctrination to the organization's culture.[23]

When a CEO is present, the company is sending the message that it truly cares for its employees. Employee satisfaction concepts are sometimes thrown around an organization to such an extent that they are nothing more than ruses to pay lip service to the idea. But this senior company official's presence validates that the company really is concerned—the CEO's commitment to making the first day special is evidenced by his or her presence. And even when scheduling conflicts may arise, companies can use previously prepared videos, or some other electronic means of carrying the same message.

HRM's Role in Orientation

In our introductory comments we stated that the orientation function can be performed by HRM, line management, or a combination of the two. Inasmuch as Exhibit 8-2 indicates a preference for a combination strategy, it is our contention that HRM plays a major role in new-employee orientation—the role of coordination, which ensures that the appropriate components are in place. In addition, HRM also serves as a participant in the program. Consequently, it is important to recognize what HRM must do. For example, in our discussion of making the job offer (Chapter 7), we emphasized that the offer should come from human resources. This was necessary to coordinate the administrative activities surrounding a new hire. The same holds true for new-employee orientation. Depending on the recruiting that takes place, there should be a systematic schedule of when new employees join a company.

As job offers are made and accepted, HRM should instruct the new employee when to report to work. However, before the employee formally arrives, HRM must be prepared to handle some of the more routine needs of these individuals; for example, new employees typically have a long list of questions about benefits. More proactive organizations like AT&T prepare a package for new employees. This package generally focuses on the important decisions that a new employee must make—decisions like the choice of health insurance, institutions for direct deposit of paychecks, and tax-withholding information. By providing this information a few weeks before an individual starts work, the HRM unit in these companies gives new hires ample time to make a proper choice—quite possibly a choice that must be made in conjunction with a working spouse's options. Furthermore, forms often require information that most employees do not readily keep with them—for example, Social Security numbers of family members and medical histories. Accordingly, having that information before the new-employee orientation session saves time.[24] HRM's second concern revolves around its role as a participant in the process. Most new employees' exposure to the organization thus far has been with HRM, but after the hiring process is over, HRM quickly drops out of the picture unless there is a problem. Therefore, HRM must spend some time in orientation addressing what assistance it can offer to employees in the future. This point cannot be minimized. HRM provides an array of services, like career guidance and training, to other areas of the company. Although these areas generally are unable to go outside the organization for their HRM needs, HRM cannot become complacent. They must continue to provide their services to the employees and departments of the organization. And one means of affecting this service is to let these new employees know what else HRM can do for them.

diversity issues in $\mathcal{HRM}$

TRAINING AND EEO

MUCH OF OUR PREVIOUS DISCUSSIONS OF EEO have centered on the selection process. Undoubtedly, equal employment opportunities are most prevalent in the hiring process, but its application to training cannot be overlooked. Remember that under the definition of adverse impact, we referenced any HRM activity that adversely affects protected group members in hiring, firing, and promoting. So how does training fall into the EEO realms?[25] Let's briefly take a look.

Training programs may be required for promotions, job bidding (especially in unionized jobs), or salary increases. Under any of these scenarios, it is the responsibility of the organization to ensure that training selection criteria are related to the job. Furthermore, equal training opportunities must exist for all employees. Failure at something as simple as the schedule of training programs being well advertised to all employees could raise suspicions regarding how fair the training programs are.

Organizations should also pay close attention to training-completion rates. If protected group members fail to pass training programs more frequently than the "majority group," this might indicate dissimilarities in the training that is offered. Once again, organizations should monitor these activities and perform periodic audits to ensure full compliance with EEO regulations.

EMPLOYEE TRAINING

Every organization, like Starbucks, needs to have well-adjusted, trained, and experienced people to perform the activities that must be done. As jobs in today's dynamic organizations have become more complex, the importance of employee education has increased. When jobs were simple, easy to learn, and influenced to only a small degree by technological changes, there was little need for employees to upgrade or alter their skills. But that situation rarely exists today. Instead, rapid job changes are occurring, requiring employee skills to be transformed and frequently updated. In organizations, this takes place through what we call employee training.

Training is a learning experience in that it seeks a relatively permanent change in an individual that will improve the ability to perform on the job. We typically say training can involve the changing of skills, knowledge, attitudes, or behavior. It may mean changing what employees know, how they work, their attitudes toward their work, or their interaction with their coworkers or supervisor. For our purposes, we will differentiate between **employee training** and **employee development** for one particular reason. Although both are similar in the methods used to affect learning, their time frames differ. Training is more present-day oriented; its focus is on individuals' current jobs, enhancing those specific skills and abilities to immediately perform their jobs.[26] For example, suppose you enter the job market during your senior year of college, pursuing a job as a marketing representative. Although you have a degree in Marketing, when you are hired, some training is in order. Specifically, you'll need to learn the company's policies and practices, product information, and other pertinent selling practices. This, by definition, is job-specific training, or training that is designed to make you more effective in your current job.

Employee development, on the other hand, generally focuses on future jobs in the organization. As your job and career progress, new skills and abilities will be required. For example, if you become a sales territory manager, the skills needed to perform that job are quite different from those required for selling the products. Now you will be required to supervise a number of sales representatives, requiring a broad-based knowledge of marketing and very specific management competencies like communication skills, evaluating employee performance, and disciplining problem individuals. As you are groomed for positions of greater responsibility, employee development efforts can help prepare you for that day.

Irrespective of whether we are involved in employee training or employee development, the same outcome is required. That is, we are attempting to help individuals learn! Learning is critical to everyone's success, and it's something that will be with us throughout our working lives. But learning for learning's sake does not happen in a vacuum. Rather, it is a function of several events that occur, with the responsibility for learning being a shared experience between the teacher and the learner (see Exhibit 8-3).

Determining Training Needs

Now that we have a better understanding of what training is, we can look at a more fundamental question for organizations. That is, how does an organization assess whether there is a need for training? We propose that HRM can determine this following a process depicted in Exhibit 8-4.[27]

Employee Training
Present-oriented training, focusing on individuals' current jobs.

Employee Development
Future-oriented training, focusing on the personal growth of the employee.

EXHIBIT 8-3
Principles of Learning

Learning Is Enhanced When the Learner Is Motivated.	An individual must want to learn. When that desire exists, the learner will exert a high level of effort. There appears to be valid evidence to support the adage, "You can lead a horse to water, but you can't make him drink."
Learning Requires Feedback.	Feedback, or knowledge of results, is necessary so that learners can correct their mistakes. Feedback is best when it is immediate rather than delayed; the sooner individuals have some knowledge of how well they are performing, the easier it is for them to compare performance to goals and correct their erroneous actions.
Reinforcement Increases the Likelihood That a Learned Behavior Will Be Repeated.	The principle of reinforcement tells us that behaviors that are positively reinforced (rewarded) are encouraged and sustained. When the behavior is punished, it is temporarily suppressed but is unlikely to be extinguished. What is desired is to convey feedback to the learners when they are doing what is right to encourage them to keep doing it.
Practice Increases a Learner's Performance.	When learners actually practice what they have read or seen, they gain confidence and are less likely to make errors or to forget what they have learned.
Learning Begins Rapidly, Then Plateaus.	Learning rates can be expressed as a curve that usually begins with a sharp rise, then increases at a decreasing rate until a plateau is reached. Learning is very fast at the beginning, but then plateaus as opportunities for improvement are reduced.
Learning Must Be Transferable to the Job.	It doesn't make much sense to perfect a skill in the classroom and then find that you can't successfully transfer it to the job. Therefore, training should be designed for transferability.

EXHIBIT 8-4
Determining Training Needs

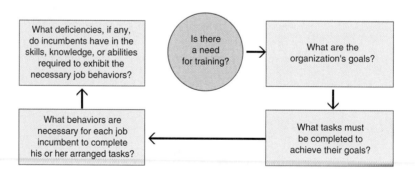

Recall from Chapter 5 that these questions demonstrate the close link between employment planning and the determination of training needs. Based on our determination of the organization's needs, the type of work to be done, and the type of skills necessary to complete this work, our training programs should follow naturally.[28] Once we can identify where deficiencies lie, we have a grasp of the extent and nature of our training needs.

What kinds of signals can warn employee supervisors that employee training may be necessary? The more obvious ones relate directly to productivity—especially inadequate job performance or a drop in productivity. The former is likely to occur in the early months on a new job. When a supervisor sees evidence of inadequate job performance, assuming the individual is making a satisfactory effort, attention should be given to raising the worker's skill level.[29] When a supervisor is confronted with a drop in productivity, it may suggest that skills need to be fine-tuned. Of course it could be related to other factors, too—like a lack of resources or equipment malfunctions. That's why it's imperative to pinpoint the problem precisely.

In addition to productivity measures, a high reject rate or larger-than-usual scrappage may indicate a need for employee training. A rise in the number of accidents reported can also suggest some type of retraining is necessary.[30] Furthermore, the changes that are being imposed on workers as a result of a job redesign or a technological breakthrough demand training.

A word of caution on training, however, is in order. If deficiencies in performance are uncovered, it doesn't necessarily follow that the manager should take corrective action. It is important to put training into perspective. Training may be costly, and it should not be viewed as a cure-all for what ails the organization.[31] Rather, training should be judged by its contribution to performance, where performance is a function of skills, abilities, motivation, and the opportunity to perform. Managers must also compare the value received from the increase in performance that can be attributed to training with the costs incurred in that training.

Once it has been determined that training is necessary, training goals must be established. Management should explicitly state what results are sought for each employee. It is not adequate merely to say the change in employee knowledge, skills, attitudes, or behavior is desirable; we must clarify what is to change and by how much. These goals should be tangible, verifiable, timely, and measurable. They should be clear to both the supervisor and the employee. For instance, a firefighter might be expected to jump from a moving fire truck traveling at 15 miles per hour, successfully hook up a four-inch hose to a hydrant, and turn on the hydrant, all in less than 40 seconds. Such explicit goals ensure that both the supervisor and the employee know what is expected from the training effort.

Training Approaches

The most popular training and development methods used by organizations can be classified as either on-the-job or off-the-job training.[32] In the following pages, we will briefly introduce the better-known techniques of each category.

On-the-Job Training   The most widely used training methods take place on the job. The popularity of these methods can be attributed to their simplicity and the impression that they are less costly to operate. On-the-job training places the employees in actual work situations and makes them appear to be immediately productive. It is learning by doing. For jobs that either are difficult to simulate or can be learned quickly by watching and doing, on-the-job training makes sense.

One of the drawbacks of on-the-job training can be low productivity while the employees develop their skills. Another drawback can be the errors made by the trainees while they learn. However, when the potential problems trainees can create are minimal, where training facilities and staffs are limited or costly, or where it is desirable for the workers to learn the job under normal working conditions, the benefits of on-the-job training frequently offset the drawbacks. Let's look at two types of on-the-job training: apprenticeship programs and job instruction training.

People seeking to enter skilled trades—to become, for example, heating/air conditioning/ventilation technicians, plumbers, or electricians—are often required to undergo apprenticeship training before they are elevated to master-mechanic status. Apprenticeship programs put the trainee under the guidance of a master worker. The argument for apprenticeship programs is that the required job knowledge and skills are so complex as to rule out anything less than a period of time where the trainee understudies a skilled master.[33] During World War II, a systematic approach to on-the-job training was developed to prepare supervisors to train employees. This approach was called **job instruction training (JIT)**. JIT proved highly effective and became extremely popular. JIT consists of four basic steps:

Job Instruction Training
A systematic approach to on-the-job training consisting of four baisc steps.

1. Preparing the trainees by telling them about the job and overcoming their uncertainties;
2. Presenting the instruction, giving essential information in a clear manner;
3. Having the trainees try out the job to demonstrate their understanding;
4. Placing the workers in the job, on their own, with a designated resource person to call upon should they need assistance.[34]

Job instruction training applications can achieve impressive results.[35] By following these steps, studies indicate that employee turnover can be reduced.[36] Higher levels of employee morale have been witnessed, as well as decreases in employee accidents.[37]

Individuals who desire to make a career in the trades (like this television cable stringer), frequently must go through an extensive apprenticeship training program often lasting for several years. The training this individual receives is more appropriately referred to as job instruction training.

Off-the-Job Training   Off-the-job training covers a number of techniques—classroom lectures, films, demonstrations, case studies and other simulation exercises, and programmed instruction. The facilities needed for each technique vary from a small, makeshift classroom to an elaborate development center with large lecture halls, supplemented by small conference rooms with sophisticated instructional technology equipment. We have summarized the majority of these methods in Exhibit 8-5. Because of its growing popularity in today's technology-oriented organizations, however, programmed instruction warrants a closer look.

The **programmed instruction** technique can be in the form of programmed tests and manuals, video displays, or some type of computer-based training. All programmed instruction approaches have a common characteristic. They condense the material to be learned into highly organized, logical sequences that require the trainee to respond. The ideal format provides for nearly instantaneous feedback that informs the trainee if his or her response is correct.

Programmed Instruction
Material is learned in a highly organized, logical sequence that requires the individual to respond.

For example, popular today with the purchase of computer software is an accompanying tutorial program. This tutorial walks the user through the software application, giving the individual opportunities to experiment with the program. These tutorials, then, form one basis of programmed instruction.

Interactive Video Disks
Videos that permit the user to make changes/selections.

As technology continues to evolve, we can expect programmed instruction to become more dominant. Two noticeable versions, **interactive video disks (IVDs)** and **virtual reality,** are gaining momentum in corporate training. Interactive video disks (sometimes referred to as multimedia technology) allow users to interact with a personal computer while simultaneously being exposed to multimedia elements.[38] This "motion picture" enables the trainee to experience the effect of his or her decision in real-time mode.[39] In the past few years, the Internet, along with the advances in multimedia presentations, has taken this concept to an even higher plateau. A number of companies, such as Pitney Bowes, Applied Learning, and IBM, have begun using IVDs.[40]

Virtual Reality   A process whereby the work environment is simulated by sending messages to the brain.

EXHIBIT 8-5
Off-the-job Training Methods

Classroom Lectures	Lectures designed to communicate specific interpersonal, technical, or problem-solving skills.
Videos and Films	Using various media productions to demonstrate specialized skills that are not easily presented by other training methods.
Simulation Exercises	Training that occurs by actually performing the work. This may include case analysis, experiential exercises, role playing, or group decision making.
Computer-Based Training	Simulating the work environment by programming a computer to imitate some of the realities of the job.
Vestibule Training	Training on actual equipment used on the job, but conducted away from the actual work setting—a simulated work station.
Programmed Instruction	Condensing training materials into highly organized, logical sequences. May include computer tutorials, interactive video disks, or virtual reality simulations.

Virtual reality is a newer concept in corporate training.[41] Virtual-reality systems simulate actual work activities by sending various messages to the brain. For example, one type of virtual reality requires an individual to place a helmet over his or her head. Inside this helmet are sensors that display both visual and audio simulations of an event. For instance, skiers can be taught to ski through virtual reality. Under the system, an individual standing on dry land can be made to feel like he or she is actually skiing downhill, with the speed, obstacles, and weather being simulated. This sophisticated simulation allows for individuals to interact with their environment as if they were really there.

EMPLOYEE DEVELOPMENT

Employee development, by design, is more future oriented and more concerned with education than employee job-specific training. By education we mean that employee development activities attempt to instill sound reasoning processes—to enhance one's ability to understand and interpret knowledge—rather than imparting a body of facts or teaching a specific set of motor skills. Development, therefore, focuses more on the employee's personal growth. Successful employees prepared for positions of greater responsibility have analytical, human, conceptual, and specialized skills. They are able to think and understand. Training, per se, cannot overcome an individual's inability to understand cause-and-effect relationships, to synthesize from experience, to visualize relationships, or to think logically. As a result, we suggest that employee development be predominantly an education process rather than a training process.[42]

It is important to consider one critical component of employee development: all employees, regardless of level, can be developed. Historically, development was reserved for potential management personnel. Although it is critical for individuals to be trained in specific skills related to managing—like planning, organizing, leading, controlling, and decision making—time has taught us that these skills are needed by nonmanagerial employees as well. The use of work teams, reductions in supervisory roles, allowing workers to participate in setting the goals of their jobs, and a greater emphasis on quality and customers have changed the way developing employees is viewed. Accordingly, organizations now

All employees, no matter at what level, can be developed.

require new employee skills, knowledge, and abilities. Thus, as we go through the next few pages, note that those methods used to develop employees in general are the same as those used to develop future management talent.

Employee Development Methods

Some development of an individual's abilities can take place on the job. We will review several methods, three popular on-the-job techniques (job rotation, assistant-to positions, and committee assignments) and three off-the-job methods (lecture courses and seminars, simulation exercises, and outdoor training).

Job Rotation   Moving employees horizontally or vertically to expand their skills, knowledge, or abilities.

Job Rotation   Job rotation involves moving employees to various positions in the organization in an effort to expand their skills, knowledge, and abilities. Job rotation can be either horizontal or vertical. Vertical rotation is nothing more than promoting a worker into a new position. In this chapter, we will emphasize the horizontal dimension of job rotation, or what may be better understood as a short-term lateral transfer.

Job rotation represents an excellent method for broadening an individual's exposure to company operations and for turning a specialist into a generalist. In addition to increasing the individual's experience and allowing him or her to absorb new information, it can reduce boredom and stimulate the development of new ideas. It can also provide opportunities for a more comprehensive and reliable evaluation of the employee by his or her supervisors.

Assistant-To Positions   Employees with demonstrated potential are sometimes given the opportunity to work under a seasoned and successful manager, often in different areas of the organization. Working as staff assistants or, in some cases, serving on special boards, these individuals perform many duties under the watchful eye of a supportive coach (see Workplace Issues). In doing so, these employees get exposure to a wide variety of management activities and are groomed for assuming the duties of the next higher level.

Committee Assignment   Committee assignments can provide an opportunity for the employee to share in decision making, to learn by watching others, and to investigate specific organizational problems. When committees are of a temporary nature, they often take on task-force activities designed to delve into a particular problem, ascertain alternative solutions, and make a recommendation for implementing a solution. These temporary assignments can be both interesting and rewarding to the employee's growth.

Appointment to permanent committees increases the employee's exposure to other members of the organization, broadens his or her understanding, and provides an opportunity to grow and make recommendations under the scrutiny of other committee members. In addition to the on-the-job techniques described above, we will briefly discuss three of the more popular ones: lecture courses and seminars, simulations, and outdoor training.

Lecture Courses and Seminars   Traditional forms of instruction revolved around formal lecture courses and seminars. These offered an opportunity for individuals to acquire knowledge and develop their conceptual and analytical abilities. For many organizations, they were offered in-house by the organization itself, through outside vendors, or both.

Today, however, technology is allowing for significant improvements in the training field. A growing trend at companies is to provide lecture courses and seminars revolving around what we call distance learning.[43] Through the use of digitized computer technology, a facilitator can be in one location giving a lecture, while simultaneously being transmitted over fiber-optic cables, in real time, to several other locations. For example, the Memphis, Tennessee-based specialty chemicals manufacturer, Buckman Laboratories, uses distance learning to train all its employees.[44] With more than 1,200 employees located in 80 different countries, the opportunity to receive training has been made more cost effective and more "learner" friendly because of distance learning.

Over the past few years, we've witnessed an expansion of lecture courses and seminars for organizational members. This has been in the form of returning to college classes,[45] either for credit toward a degree or by way of "continuing education" courses. Either way, the outcome is the same. Employees are taking the responsibility to advance their skills, knowledge, and abilities in an effort to enhance their value-addedness to their current, or future employer.

PLAYING COACH

INCREASINGLY, MANAGERS MUST ASSUME THE ROLE of coach. In fact, some organizations officially have changed the title from MANAGER to COACH. Changing titles doesn't change abilities, but with training and practice, managers—by whatever name—can learn to coach and counsel their employees more effectively.

With the change toward teamwork, empowerment, and managing by influence, acquiring such skills is imperative for the success of both corporations and their employees. Coaching and counseling improves efficiency and productivity and prevents situations from escalating, while enhancing job satisfaction and confidence when attitude or performance problems occur.[46] Some managers suffer from the Ostrich Syndrome—hiding their heads in the sand in the hope that the problem or employee will go away. Too pressed for time, afraid that they may give the wrong advice and be blamed for it, or just not having any solutions for a particular situation, managers may avoid counseling/coaching.

But as managers, we must accept coaching and counseling as a part of our jobs, however uncomfortable it may be. It means regularly providing employees with feedback about their performance—not just at appraisal time; providing appropriate ongoing training, support, and encouragement; viewing them as partners in the process; giving credit when deserved; and providing information about the company and its goals, as well as their role, responsibilities, and expectations in meeting them.

If you have employees blocked from career opportunities, dissatisfied with their jobs, needing help setting priorities, or feeling stressed, burned out, and insecure, your counseling skills are going to be tested. Employees may not tell you initially that they have a problem, but they will give you an assortment of clues, such as missed deadlines, absenteeism, and decreased quality and productivity. They may show less initiative or interest, or become irritable or withdrawn. Your job is to find out why their attitude or performance is waning; could it be that they were not recognized for some work or they are frustrated because of a lack of time, training, or feedback? After all, most employees believe that their managers either can or should read minds.

Maybe it's time to reassess what's happening. For example, have you as a manager taken time to explain expectations, directions, and priorities, and have you removed obstacles and reinforced performance? When it's time to practice your new coaching/counseling insights, carefully plan what you are going to say in advance, then allow enough time without distractions or interruptions to discuss how the situation is affecting performance, to listen without becoming defensive, and to obtain enough information to develop an action plan of improvement. Invite the employee to propose solutions or alternatives. Be prepared to have a follow-up session to review progress and to reinforce improvements.

Sometimes even the best coaches/counselors have to cut their losses if and when performance continues to decline, which may call for more severe measures such as probation, demotion, transfer, termination, or disciplinary action if alternatives such as transfer, retraining, or restructuring a job are impossible. But on the optimistic side, if the coaching or counseling session is effective, everybody wins—the company, employee, and manager. Attitude or performance improves, communication lines up, and both managers and employees can build on the situation.

Think about the alternatives—not saying anything, not taking action. But don't wait too long. The problem may persist, even if the opportunity to fill the job doesn't.

Simulations

Simulations Any artificial environment that attempts to closely mirror an actual condition.

Simulations were previously cited in Exhibit 8-5 as a training technique. While critical in training employees on actual work experiences, simulations are probably even more popular for employee development. The more widely used simulation exercises include case studies, decision games, and role plays.

The case-study-analysis approach to employee development was popularized at the Harvard Graduate School of Business. Taken from the actual experiences of organizations, these cases represent attempts to describe, as accurately as possible, real problems that managers have faced. Trainees study the cases to determine problems, analyze causes, develop alternative solutions, select what they believe to be the best solution, and implement it. Case studies can provide stimulating discussions among participants, as well as excellent opportunities for individuals to defend their analytical and judgmental abilities. It appears to be a rather effective method for improving decision-making abilities within the constraints of limited information.

Simulated decision games and role-playing exercises put individuals in the role of acting out supervisory problems. Simulations, frequently played on a computer program, provide opportunities for individuals to make decisions and to witness the implications of their decisions for other segments of the organization. Airlines, for instance, find that simulations are a much more cost-effective means of training pilots—especially in potentially dangerous situations. And should the trainee's decision be a poor one, there typically would be no adverse effects on the learner—other than an explanation of why his or her choice was not a good one. Role playing allows the participants to act out problems and to deal with real people. Participants are assigned roles and are asked to react to one another as they would have to do in their managerial jobs.

The advantages of simulation exercises are the opportunities to attempt to "create an environment" similar to real situations managers face, without the high costs involved should the actions prove to be undesirable. Of course, the disadvantages are the reverse of this: it is difficult to duplicate the pressures and realities of actual decision making on the job, and individuals often act differently in real-life situations than they do in a simulated exercise.

Outdoor Training   A trend in employee development has been the use of outdoor (sometimes referred to as wilderness or survival) training. The primary focus of such training is to teach trainees the importance of working together, of gelling as a team.[47] Outdoor training typically involves some major emotional and physical challenge. This could be white-water rafting, mountain climbing, paint-ball games, or surviving a week in the "jungle." The purpose of such training is to see how employees react to the difficulties that nature presents to them. Do they face these dangers alone? Do they "freak"? Or are they controlled and successful in achieving their goal? The reality is that today's business environment does not permit employees to stand alone. This has reinforced the importance of working closely with one another, building trusting relationships, and succeeding as a member of a group.[48]

*O*RGANIZATION DEVELOPMENT

Although our discussion so far has been related to the people side of business, it is important to recognize that organizations change from time to time. With the changes experienced with respect to continuous improvements, diversity, and

Organization Development
The part of HRM that deals with facilitating systemwide change in the organization.

work process engineering, it is necessary to move the organization forward through a process we call **organization development (OD)**. OD has taken on a renewed importance today. Brought about by continuous-improvement goals, many organizations have drastically changed the way they do business.[49]

Whenever change occurs, four areas are usually affected: the organization's systems, its technology, its processes, and its people. No matter what the change is, or how minor it may appear, understanding the effect of the change is paramount for it to be supported and lasting. That is where OD comes in to play. OD efforts are designed to support the strategic direction of the business. For instance, if work processes change, people will need to learn new production methods and procedures, and maybe obtain new skills. OD becomes instrumental in bringing about the change. How so? Whenever change occurs, the effect of that change becomes an organizational culture issue. Accordingly, OD efforts must be expended to ensure that all organizational members support the new culture and provide whatever assistance is needed to bring the new culture to fruition.

The basis of organizational development, then, is to help people adapt to change. Although there are different perspectives on how that change should occur, one of the best descriptions of the change process was illustrated by Kurt Lewin.[50] According to Lewin, change occurs over three stages. These include the unfreezing of the status quo, the change to the new state, and refreezing to ensure that the change becomes permanent. We have graphically portrayed this process in Exhibit 8-6.

What Lewin identified was the movement in the organization away from the status quo. Portraying the status quo in Exhibit 8-6 as circles, the change effort helps the organization move in the direction of the squares. Through OD efforts, the intervention can take place, with the change effort supported by continual reinforcement to make it permanent.

Of course change doesn't always happen in a nicely predicted way. Moreover, in today's dynamic environments, change has taken on unprecedented proportions—likened to "rafting in white waters." The **"white water" metaphor** takes into consideration that environments are both uncertain and dynamic. To get a feeling for what managing change might be like when you have to continually maneuver in uninterrupted rapids, consider attending a college that had the following curriculum. Courses vary in length. Unfortunately, when you sign up, you don't know how long a course will last. It might go for 2 weeks or 30 weeks. Furthermore, the instructor can end a course any time he or she wants, with no prior warning. If that isn't bad enough, the length of the class changes each time it meets—sometimes it lasts 20 minutes, while other times it runs for three hours—and determination of the time of the next class meeting is set by the instructor during the previous class. Oh yes, there's one more thing. The exams are all unannounced, so you have to be ready for a test at any time. To succeed positively and proactively in this college, you would have to be incredibly

White-Water Metaphor
Organizational change reflecting uncertain and dynamic environments.

EXHIBIT 8-6
Lewin's Change Process

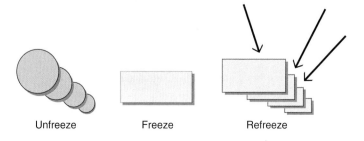

Unfreeze   Freeze   Refreeze

flexible and be able to respond quickly to every changing condition. Students who are too structured or unable to adjust may not survive.

A growing number of employees and managers are coming to accept that their jobs are much like what these students would face in such a college. The stability and predictability of Lewin's model don't frequently exist. Disruptions in the status quo are not occasional and temporary, followed by a return to equilibrium. Most of today's professionals never get out of the rapids. They face constant change, bordering on chaos. These managers are being forced to play a game they've never played before, which is governed by rules that are created as the game progresses.[51] Is the "white water" metaphor merely an overstatement? No! Take the case of Harry Quadracci, founder and president of Quad/Graphics, Inc., a commercial printing firm based in Pewaukee, Wisconsin.[52] Founded in 1971, the company is one of the largest and fastest-growing printers in the United States. It prints such magazines as *Time, People,* and *Architectural Digest.* The company now employs more than 3,000 people and has sales in excess of $800 million a year. Quadracci attributes his company's success to its ability to act fast when opportunities arise. Change and growth are among the few constants at Quad/Graphics. He encourages his people to "act now, think later." The company has no budgets because it is moving too fast—its annual growth rate during the past decade has been an astounding 40 percent! As Quadracci points out, when every department looks 30 percent different every six months, budgets aren't much use. Instead of budgets, each of the company's ten divisions is measured against its own previous performance.

OD Methods

Development efforts in human resource management go beyond the individual. There are instances, like changing an organization's culture, where systemwide change and development are required. Organizational development techniques have been created to change the values and attitudes of people and the structure of organizations in order to make them more adaptive. Included among the more popular OD techniques are three approaches that rely heavily on group interactions, participation, and collaboration. These are climate surveys, team building, and third-party intervention.[53]

Climate Survey Assessment of employees' perceptions and attitudes about their jobs organization.

Climate Surveys One tool for assessing attitudes held by organizational members, identifying discrepancies among member perceptions, and solving these differences is the **climate survey**. Organization members may be asked to respond to a set of specific questions or may be interviewed to determine what issues are relevant. A questionnaire (see Exhibit 8-7) typically asks members for their perceptions and attitudes on a broad range of topics, such as decision-making practices; leadership; communication effectiveness; coordination between units; and satisfaction with the organization, job, coworkers, and their immediate supervisor.

The data from this questionnaire are tabulated. These data then become the springboard for identifying problems and clarifying issues that may be creating difficulties for people (see the Technology Corner). Addressing these difficulties hopefully will result in the group agreeing on commitments to various actions that will remedy the problems that have been identified.

Team Building Organizations are composed of people working together to achieve a common end. Since people are frequently required to work in groups, considerable attention has been focused on OD for team building.

EXHIBIT 8-7
A Sample Climate Survey

Rate each of the following statements using the following scale:

1 = strongly agree
2 = agree
3 = undecided
4 = disagree
5 = strongly disagree

1. The environment in this organization is conducive to productive work.	5	4	3	2	1
2. Getting ahead in this organization is strictly a function of one's performance.	5	4	3	2	1
3. My salary is fair and competitive.	5	4	3	2	1
4. Employee benefits are appropriate and meet my personal needs.	5	4	3	2	1
5. I have the opportunity to make decisions about my job for those things that affect it.	5	4	3	2	1
6. I have an open and trusting relationship with my boss.	5	4	3	2	1
7. Clear work expectations exist for my job.	5	4	3	2	1
8. My job challenges me to use my skills, knowledge, and abilities.	5	4	3	2	1
9. The organization encourages a team environment.	5	4	3	2	1
10. Managers of this organization have a clear direction for the next ten years.	5	4	3	2	1

Team Building Activities associated with helping employees come together and work as a team.

Team building can be applied within groups or at the intergroup level where activities are interdependent. For our discussion, we will emphasize the intragroup level. The activities included in team building typically include goal setting, development of interpersonal relations among team members, role analysis to clarify each member's role and responsibilities, and team process analysis. Of course, team building may emphasize or exclude certain activities depending on the purpose of the development effort and the specific problems with which the team is confronted. Basically, however, team building attempts to use high interaction among group members to increase trust and openness.

Third-Party Intervention Using an outsider to assist employees in a group to change their attitudes, stereotypes or perceptions about one another.

Third-Party Intervention Third-party intervention seeks to change the attitudes, stereotypes, and perceptions that groups have of each other. For example, in one company, the marketing representatives saw HRM as having a bunch of "smiley-types who sit around and plan company picnics." Such stereotypes have an obvious negative impact on the coordinating efforts between the departments that leads to conflict.

Conflict Resolution Attempts to get both parties to see the similarities and differences that exist between them, and look for ways to overcome the differences.

Although there are a number of approaches for third-party intervention, **conflict resolution** strategies are often dominant.[54] In conflict resolution, the OD practitioner attempts to get both parties to see the similarities and differences existing between them, and focus on how the differences can be overcome. Achieving some movement toward reducing these differences is often gained through consensus building—or finding a solution that is acceptable to both parties.

The Role of Change Agents

No matter what role OD takes in an organization, it requires facilitation by an individual well versed in organization dynamics. In HRM terms, we call this person a **change agent**.[55] Change agents are responsible for fostering the environment in which change can be made, working with the affected employees to help them adapt to the change that is taking place. To achieve this goal, change agents must possess two critical skills—the ability to take risk and outstanding communication skills.[56] Change agents may be either internal employees, often associated with the training and development function of HRM, or external consultants.

Change Agent   Individual responsible for fostering the change effort and assisting employees in adapting to the changes.

A Special OD Case: The Learning Organization

Imagine you've just entered the grand ballroom of the Loews Anatole in Dallas, and your senses are picking up some strange occurrences. There are several hundred people gathered, milling around with the constant drone of a beating drum in the background. Bird and other animal sounds permeate the air every so often, as your eyes glance at the seaside sunset on the giant projection screen in front of the room. Have you just walked into a religious experience, or a seminar on the latest diet fad? No! You've just been exposed to a seminar on the learning organization.

Based on research by MIT Professor Peter Senge, the **learning organization** attempts to promote change—change that will result in the organization radically transforming itself. Senge describes the learning organization as one that "values, and thinks competitive advantages derive from, continued learning." The learning organization attacks the premise that the status quo is good enough. It then fosters an environment where open, trusting work relationships abound—resulting in the revitalization of the organization.[57]

Learning Organization   An Organization that values continued learning and believes a competitive advantage can be derived from it.

The learning organization fosters an environment of open, trusting work relationships.

Learning organizations possess five characteristics. These are *systems thinking, personal mastery, mental models, shared vision,* and *team learning.* As *Fortune* magazine writer Brian Dumaine summarizes, to fully develop the learning organization, "people

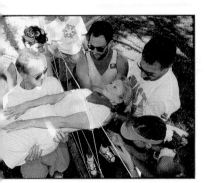

Being a fully functioning team member requires a lot of trust. At wilderness training camps, individuals like this executive learn to trust one another, and they learn that their success is dependent on the help of others. Together, there's no obstacle a team can't overcome.

need to put aside their old ways of doing thinking (mental models), learn to be open with others (personal mastery), understand how their company really works (systems thinking), for a plan everyone can agree on (shared vision), and then work together to achieve that vision (team learning)."[58] How widespread is the belief in the learning organization as a means of creating an OD transformation? Organizations subscribing to the learning organization concept read like a *Who's-Who* in Corporate America—including Ford, Federal Express, Intel, AT&T, and Motorola.

EVALUATING TRAINING AND DEVELOPMENT EFFECTIVENESS

Any training or development implemented in an organization effort must be cost effective. That is, the benefits gained by such programs must outweigh the costs associated with providing the learning experience. Only by analyzing such programs can effectiveness be determined. It is not enough to merely assume that any training an organization offers is effective; we must develop substantive data to determine whether our training effort is achieving its goals—that is, if it's correcting the deficiencies in skills, knowledge, or attitudes that were assessed as needing attention.[59] Note, too, that training and development programs are expensive—in the billions of dollars. The costs incurred alone justify evaluating the effectiveness.

How Do We Evaluate Training Programs?

It is easy to generate a new training program, but if the training effort is not evaluated, it becomes possible to rationalize any employee-training efforts. It would be nice if all companies could boast returns on investments in training as do Motorola executives, who claim they receive $30 in increased productivity for every dollar spent on training,[60] as well as a 139 percent increase in sales productivity.[61] But such a claim cannot be made without properly evaluating training.

Can we generalize how training programs are typically evaluated? The following is probably generalizable across organizations: Several managers, representatives from HRM, and a group of workers who have recently completed a training program are asked for their opinions. If the comments are generally positive, the program may get a favorable evaluation and the organization will continue it until someone decides, for whatever reason, it should be eliminated or replaced.

The reactions of participants or managers, while easy to acquire, are the least valid; their opinions are heavily influenced by factors that may have little to do with the training's effectiveness—things like difficulty, entertainment value, or personality characteristics of the instructor. However, trainees' reactions to the training may in fact provide feedback on how worthwhile the participants viewed the training. Beyond general reactions, training must also be evaluated in terms of how much the participants learned, how well they are using their new skills on the job (did their behavior change?), and whether the training program achieved its desired results (reduced turnover, increased customer service, etc.).[62]

Performance-based Evaluation Measures

We'll explore three popular methods of evaluating training programs. These are the *post-training performance method*, the *pre-post-training performance method*, and the *pre-post-training performance with control group method*.

Post-Training Performance Method   The first approach is referred to as the **post-training performance method.** Participants' performance is measured after attending a training program to determine if behavioral changes have been made. For example, assume we provide a week-long seminar for HRM recruiters on structured interviewing techniques. We follow up one month later with each participant to see if, in fact, the techniques addressed in the program were used, and how. If changes did occur, we may attribute them to the training. But caution must be in order, for we cannot emphatically state that the change in behavior was directly related to the training. Other factors, like reading a current HRM journal or attending a presentation at a local Society of Human Resource Management, may have also influenced the change. Accordingly, the post-training performance method may overstate the benefits of training.

Pre-Post-Training Performance Method   In the **pre-post-training performance method,** each participant is evaluated prior to training and rated on actual job performance. After instruction—of which the evaluator has been kept unaware—is completed, the employee is reevaluated. As with the post-training performance method, the increase is assumed to be attributed to the instruction. However, in contrast to the post-training performance method, the pre-post-performance method deals directly with job behavior.

Pre-Post-Training Performance with Control Group Method   The most sophisticated evaluative approach is the **pre-post-training performance with control group method.** Under this evaluation method, two groups are established and evaluated on actual job performance. Members of the control group work on the job but do not undergo instruction. On the other hand, the experimental group is given the instruction. At the conclusion of training, the two groups are reevaluated. If the training is really effective, the experimental group's performance will have improved, and its performance will be substantially better than that of the control group. This approach attempts to correct for factors, other than the instruction program, that influence job performance.

Although a number of methods for evaluating training and development programs may exist, these three appear to be the most widely recognized. Furthermore, the latter two methods are preferred, because they provide a stronger measure of behavioral change directly attributable to the training effort.

𝓘NTERNATIONAL TRAINING AND DEVELOPMENT ISSUES

Important components of international human resource management include both cross-cultural training and a clear understanding of the overseas assignment as part of a manager's development.

Training

Cross-cultural training is necessary for expatriate managers and their families before, during, and after foreign assignments.[63] It is crucial to remember that when the expatriates arrive, they are the foreigners, not the host population. Before the employee and family are relocated to the overseas post, it is necessary to provide much cultural and practical background.[64] Language training is essential for everyone in the family.

Although English is the dominant business language worldwide, relying on English puts the expatriate at a disadvantage. The expatriate will be unable to

---

Post-Training Performance Method   Evaluating training programs based on how well employees can perform their jobs after they have received the training.

Pre-Post-Training Performance Method   Evaluating training programs based the difference in performance before and after one receives training.

Pre-Post-Training Performance with Control Group Method   Evaluating training by comparing pre- and post-training results with individuals who did not receive the training.

read trade journals and newspapers, which contain useful business information, and will be reliant on translators, which at best only slow down discussions and at worst "lose things" in the process. Even if an expatriate manager is not fluent, a willingness to try communicating in the local language makes a good impression on the business community—unlike the insistence that all conversation be in English. Foreign-language proficiency is also vital for family members to establish a social network and accomplish the everyday tasks of maintaining a household. Americans may be able to go to the produce market and point at what they recognize on display, but if the shop has unfamiliar meats or vegetables, it helps to be able to ask what each item is and it's even better to understand the answers!

But cross-cultural training is much more than just language training. It should provide an appreciation of the new culture, including details of its history and folklore, economy, politics (both internal and its relations with the United States), religion, social climate, and business practices. It is easy to recognize that religion is highly important in daily life in the Middle East, but knowledge of the region's history and an understanding of the specific practices and beliefs is important to avoid inadvertently insulting business associates or social contacts.

All this training can be carried out through a variety of techniques. Language skills are often provided through classes and tapes, while cultural training utilizes many different tools. Lectures, reading materials, videotapes, and movies are useful for background information, while cultural sensitivity is more often taught through role playing, simulations, and meetings with former international assignees,[65] as well as natives of the countries now living in the United States.

While all this training in advance of the overseas relocation is important, cultural learning takes place during the assignment as well. One American corporation provides some of the following suggestions for adapting to a foreign environment: forget the word *foreign*. Learn how things get done: at work, at home, at schools, at social gatherings. Watch television, even if you don't understand it yet. Read newspapers, as many as possible. Visit parks, museums, and zoos. Make friends with local people and learn from them. Plan vacations and day trips in the new country.[66]

After the overseas assignment has ended and the employee has returned, more training is required for the entire family. All family members must reacclimate to life in the United States. The family must face changes in the extended family, friends, and local events that have occurred in their absence. Teenagers find reentry particularly difficult, as they are ignorant of the most recent jargon and the latest trends, but often are more sophisticated and mature than their local friends. The employee also must adjust to organizational changes, including the inevitable promotions, transfers, and resignations that have taken place during his or her absence. Returnees are anxious to know where they fit in, or if they have been gone for so long that they no longer are on a career path.

When a U.S. organization sends a U.S. citizen to another country to work, a lot of things have to happen. The employee (and family members, if they are sent, too) must be well prepared for the overseas assignment. This requires extensive training and development efforts to ensure that the employee will be able to acclimate to the new culture, and perform the job properly with as few problems as possible.

Development

In the current global business environment, the overseas assignment should be a vital component in the development of top-level executives. However, so far this is truer in Europe and Japan than it is in the United States. Many American managers return with broader experiences than what appears on paper, having been relatively independent of headquarters. Particularly, mid-level managers have experienced greater responsibilities than others at their level, having frequently acquired greater sensitivity and flexibility to alternative ways of doing things. Unfortunately they are often ignored and untapped after their return.

One survey showed that although 70 percent of international assignments were presented as career opportunities, only 30 percent of the sample's respondents were told anything about their career after returning. Only 23 percent reported being promoted upon their return, while 18 percent reported being demoted. Only 54 percent reported there was a specific job waiting for them.[67] It is vital for the organization to make the overseas assignment part of a career development program. In the absence of such a developmental program, two negative consequences often occur. First, the recently returned manager who is largely ignored or underutilized becomes frustrated and leaves the organization. This is extremely costly, because the investment in developing this individual is lost and the talent the individual has will likely be recruited by a competitor, either at home or overseas.

Second, when overseas returnees are regularly underutilized or leave out of frustration, other potential expatriates become reluctant to accept overseas posts, inhibiting the organization's staffing ability. When the overseas assignment is completed, the organization has four basic options. First, the expatriate may be assigned to a domestic position, beginning the repatriation process. Hopefully, this new assignment will build on some of the newly acquired skills and perspectives. Second, the return may be temporary, with the goal of preparing for another overseas assignment. This might be the case where a manager has successfully opened a new sales territory and is being asked to repeat that success in another region. Third, the expatriate may seek retirement, either in the United States or in the country in which she or he spent the last few years. Finally, employment may be terminated, either because the organization has no suitable openings or because the individual has found opportunities elsewhere.

All of these options involve substantial expenses or a loss in human investment. A well-thought-out and organized program of employee development is necessary to make overseas assignments a part of the comprehensive international human resource management program.[68]

HRM WORKSHOP

SUMMARY

(This summary relates to the Learning Outcomes identified on p. 206.)

After having read this chapter, you should be able to:

1. **Define socialization.** Socialization is a process of adaptation. Organization-entry socialization refers to the adaptation that takes place when an individual passes from outside the organization to the role of an inside member.

2. **Identify the three stages of employee socialization.** The three stages of employee socialization are the prearrival, the encounter, and the metamorphosis states.

3. **Identify the key personnel involved in orientation.** The key people in orientation are the CEO and the representatives from HRM. The CEO's role is to welcome the new employees, reaffirm their choice of joining the com-

pany, and discuss the organization's goals and objectives while conveying information about the organization's culture. Each function in HRM has a specific role in orientation to discuss what employee services they can offer in the future.

4. **Explain why employee training is important.** Employee training has become increasingly important as jobs have become more sophisticated and influenced by technological and corporate changes.

5. **Define training.** Training is a learning experience that seeks a relatively permanent change in individuals that will improve their ability to perform on the job.

6. **Describe how training needs evolve.** An organization's training needs will evolve from seeking answers to these

COACHING EMPLOYEES

ABOUT THE SKILL: EFFECTIVE MANAGERS are increasingly being described as coaches rather than bosses. Just like coaches, they're expected to provide instruction, guidance, advice, and encouragement to help team members improve their job performance. Here are some suggestions to make that happen.

1. *Analyze ways to improve the team's performance and capabilities.* A coach looks for opportunities for team members to expand their capabilities and improve performance. How? You can use the following behaviors. Observe your team members' behavior on a day-to-day basis. Ask questions of them: Why do you do a task this way? Can it be improved? What other approaches might be used? Show genuine interest in team members as individuals, not merely as employees. Respect them individually. Listen to each employee.

2. *Create a supportive climate.* It's the coach's responsibility to reduce barriers to development and to facilitate a climate that encourages personal performance improvement. How? You can use the following behaviors. Create a climate that contributes to a free and open exchange of ideas. Offer help and assistance. Give guidance and advice when asked. Encourage your team. Be positive and upbeat. Don't use threats. Ask "What did we learn from this that can help us in the future?" Reduce obstacles. Assure team members that you value their contribution to the team's goals. Take personal responsibility for the outcome, but don't rob team members of their full responsibility. Validate the team members' efforts when they succeed. Point to what was missing when they fail. Never blame team members for poor results.

3. *Influence team members to change their behavior.* The ultimate test of coaching effectiveness is whether an employee's performance improves. You must encourage ongoing growth and development. How can you do this? Try the following behaviors. Recognize and reward small improvements and treat coaching as a way of helping employees to continually work toward improvement. Use a collaborative style by allowing team members to participate in identifying and choosing among improvement ideas. Break difficult tasks down into simpler ones. Model the qualities that you expect from your team. If you want openness, dedication, commitment, and responsibility from your team members, you must demonstrate these qualities yourself.

questions: (a) What are the organization's goals? (b) What tasks must be completed to achieve these goals? (c) What behaviors are necessary for each job incumbent to complete his or her assigned tasks? and (d) What deficiencies, if any, do incumbents have in the skills, knowledge, or attitudes required to perform the necessary behaviors?

7. **Indicate what is meant by the term** *organizational development* **and the role of the change agent.** Organization development is the process of affecting change in the organization. This change is facilitated through the efforts of a change agent.

8. **Describe the methods and criteria involved in evaluating training programs.** Training programs can be evaluated by post-training performance, the pre-post-training performance, or the pre-post-training performance with control group methods. In the evaluation, focus is placed on trainee reaction, what learning took place, and how appropriate the training was to the job.

9. **Explain issues critical to international training and development.** International issues in training and development include cross-cultural training, language training, and economic issues training.

DEMONSTRATING COMPREHENSION: *Questions for Review and Discussion*

1. What benefits can socialization provide for the organization?
2. What benefits can socialization provide for the new employee?
3. What might a socialization program look like if management desired employees who were innovative and individualistic?
4. Describe the role HRM plays in orientation. Describe the CEO's role.
5. "Proper selection is a substitute for socialization." Do you agree or disagree with this statement? Explain.
6. What kinds of signals can warn a manager that employee training may be necessary?
7. Why is the evaluation of training effectiveness necessary?
8. Why is cultural training critical for employees embarking on an overseas assignment?
9. Training programs are frequently the first items eliminated when management wants to cut costs. Why do you believe this occurs?
10. Describe how selection and training are related. Describe how socialization and training are related.

CASE APPLICATION: *TEAM FUN!*

Kenny and Norton, owners of a sporting goods manufacturing and retail operation are meeting with Tony, the Director of Human Resources and Bobby (the manager of a new store). Twenty-five employees have just been hired and the new store in South Florida is scheduled to open in a month. Norton thunders, "No way am I going to bring all those socialist bozos up here for a week! What's the matter with you! Why did you hire a bunch of socialists?"

Kenny calms him, "He said to socialize them, not that they were socialists. But why should they come here for a party? We should go to South Florida! And I think an opening party is a great idea. Bobby, that's your idea, right?"

Bobby smiles and Tony says, "I don't mean party. I mean get them used to the way things run at TEAM FUN! They need to know the rules, what's expected of them, how to treat the customers and each other, that sort of thing."

Kenny asks, "What did you do when you interviewed them? I thought they'd know what to expect day 1."

Norton adds, "I know as soon as I meet someone if they should work at TEAM FUN! Anyway, people just all work out or quit right away—first day, usually. New people just start one day, follow someone around for a week, and then they are fine."

Tony looks helplessly at both of them until Norton finally says, "Oh, I get it. There is no one down there for a new person to follow around. Everyone will be new!" Tony nods his head. So does Kenny. Norton continues, "That's still a lot of bozo airfaire. I thought you said they were mostly family people. Do we have to bring all their kids and dogs up here, too? Find another way."

Kenny offers, "Dogs don't usually like to fly. I don't know. Remember that video we did for Christmas last year? Ginny followed everyone around at work for 5 minutes with her video camera. I think I'm the only one who watched the whole thing. Most everyone only wanted their part and the rest of the crew they worked with. Tony, could we send the video to Florida with a few key people to run everyone through their paces a week or so before we open? Would that be socialization?"

Norton frowns, "We just started working when we opened this store. What's the big deal?"

Tony: "That was just the two of you, and you'd known each other all your lives."

Norton: "So?"

Questions:

1. Explain to Kenny and Norton why employee socialization is necessary (or not necessary) for the new TEAM FUN! store.

2. What orientation activities do you recommend? Who should be involved?

3. What training needs should be considered?

WORKING WITH A TEAM: *Orienting Employees*

Identify, call, and ask the human resource manager if you may observe part or all of an upcoming orientation or training program of your college or university, employer, nonprofit organization, or a company, as a part of class assignment.

1. Summarize your orientation experience in a one- or two-page report, then share your experience with your class or team.

2. What guidelines, policies, or standards did your organization practice regarding orientation?

3. Discuss and compare.

ENHANCING YOUR WRITING SKILLS

1. Do a search of articles on learning organizations. Summarize in a two- to three-page article how organizations become learning organizations and what benefits a learning organizations provides for a company.

2. Visit the following web page at the Society of Human Resource Management (http://www.shrm.org/hrmagazine/articles/0898trab.htm). Develop a two-page writeup on the cost of developing a training program. Discuss how companies may find ways to make training programs more cost effective.

3. Write a two-page summary of the type of organization culture you would prefer to work in. In your discussion, describe how you anticipate locating such an organization with the type of preferred culture you identified.

www.wiley.com/college/decenzo

ENDNOTES

1. Vignette based on Karyn Strauss, "Howard Schultz: Starbucks' CEO Serves a Blend of Community, Employee Commitment," *Nation's Restaurant News* (January 2000), pp. 162–163; and J. Reese, "Starbucks: Inside the Coffee Cult," *Fortune* (December 9, 1996), pp. 190–200.

2. See, for instance, Blake E. Ashforth and Alan M. Saks, "Socialization Tactics: Longitudinal Effects on Newcomer Adjustment," *Academy of Management Journal*, Vol. 39, No. 1 (February 1996), pp. 149–178; and Cheryl L. Adkins, "Previous Work Experience and Organizational Socialization: A Longitudinal Examination," *Academy of Management Journal*, Vol. 38, No. 3 (October 1995), pp. 839–862.

3. See, for example, Jitendra M. Mishra and Pam Strait, "Employee Orientation: The Key to Lasting and Productive Results," *Health Care Supervisor* (March 1993), pp. 19–29; Henry L. Tosi, *Organizational Behavior and Management: A Contingency Approach* (Boston, MA: PWS Kent Publishing, 1990), pp. 233–235; also John Van Maanen, "People Processing: Strategies of Organizational Socialization," in Henry L. Tosi's *Organizational Behavior and Management: A Contingency Approach*, pp. 65–66.

4. See, for instance, R. L. Falcione and C. E. Wilson, "Socialization Process in Organizations," in G. M. Goldhar and G. A. Barnett (eds.), *Handbook of Organizational Communication* (Norwood, NJ: Ablex Publishing, 1988), pp. 151–170; N. J. Allen and J. P. Meyer, "Organizational Socialization Tactics: A Longitudinal Analysis of Links to Newcomers' Commitment and Role Orientation," *Academy of Management Journal* (December 1990), pp. 847–858; V. D. Miller and F. M. Jablin, "Information Seeking During Organizational Entry: Influences, Tactics, and a Model of Process," *Academy of Management Review* (January 1991), pp. 92–120; and J. A. Chatam, "Matching People and Organizations: Selection and Socialization in Public Accounting Firms," *Administrative Science Quarterly* (September 1991), pp. 459–484.

5. Silva Gherardi, Davide Nicolini, and Francesca Odella, "Toward a Social Understanding of How People Learn in Organizations," *Management Learning* (September 1998), pp. 273–298.

6. Shirley A. Hopkins and Willie E. Hopkins, "Organizational Productivity 2000: A Work Force Perspective," *SAM Advanced Management Journal* (Autumn 1991), pp. 44–48.

7. See, for example, Sandra L. Robinson and Elizabeth Wolfe, "The Development of Psychological Contract Breech Violation: A Longitudinal Study," *Journal of Organizational Behavior* (August 2000), pp. 525–546.

8. Coy A. Jones and William R. Crandall, "Determining the Source of Voluntary Employee Turnover," *SAM Advanced Management Journal* (March 22, 1991), p. 16.

9. John Van Maanen and Edgar H. Schein, "Career Development," in J. Richard Hackman and J. Lloyd Suttle (eds.), *Improving Life at Work* (Santa Monica, CA: Goodyear, 1977), pp. 58–62. See also J. P. Wanous, A. E. Reichers, and S. D. Malik, "Organizational Socialization and Group Development," *Academy of Management Review,* Vol. 9 (1992), pp. 670–683.

10. D. C. Feldman, "The Multiple Socialization of Organization Members," *Academy of Management Review* (April 1981), p. 310.

11. For a thorough discussion of these issues, see Jennifer A. Chatman, "Matching People and Organizations: Selection and Socialization in Public Accounting Firms," *Administrative Science Quarterly* (September 1991), pp. 459–485.

12. For example, see Gary Blau, "Early-Career Job Factors Influencing the Professional Commitment of Medical Technologies," *Academy of Management Journal* (December 1999), pp. 687–699; and Lisa K. Gundry, "Fitting into Technical Organizations: The Socialization of Newcomer Engineers," *IEEE Transactions of Engineering Management* (November 1993), p. 335.

13. For an interesting viewpoint on selection fit and socialization, see Isaiah O. Ugboro, "Loyalty, Value Congruency, and Affective Organizational Commitment: An Empirical Study," *Mid-American Journal of Business* (Fall 1993), pp. 29–37.

14. Ibid., p. 59.

15. See Timothy J. Fogarty, "Socialization and Organizational Outcomes in Large Public Accounting Firms," *Journal of Managerial Issues* (Spring 2000), pp. 13–33; Rabindra N. Kanungo and Jay A. Conger, "Promoting Altruism as a Corporate Goal," *Executive* (August 1993), pp. 37–48; Elizabeth Wolfe Morrison, "Longitudinal Study of the Effects of Information Seeking on Newcomer Socialization," *Journal of Applied Psychology* (April 1993), pp. 173–183; and Laurie K. Lewis and David R. Seinbold, "Innovation Modification During Intraorganizational Adoption," *Academy of Management Review* (April 1993), pp. 322–354.

16. See, for instance, Thomas G. Reio, Jr., and Albert Wiswell, "Field Investigations of the Relationship Among Adult Curiosity, Workplace Learning, and Job Performance," *Human Resource Development Quarterly* (Spring 2000), p. 5.

17. Max Messmer, "Orientation Programs Can Be Key to Employee Retention," *Strategic Finance* (February 2000), pp. 12–14; Cheryl Mahaffey, "The First 30 Days: The Most Critical Time to Influence Employee Success," *Employment Relations Today* (Summer 1999), pp. 53–60; and Tayla N. Bauer and Stephen G. Green, "Effect of Newcomer Involvement in Work-Related Activities: A Longitudinal Study of Socialization," *Journal of Applied Psychology* (April 1994), pp. 211–223.

18. David K. Lindo, "New Employee Orientation Is Your Job!" *Supervision* (August 1999), pp. 6–9; and Robert D. Ramsey, "A Supervisor's Check-List for Helping New Employees Succeed," *Supervision* (July 1998), pp. 3–5.

19. See, for example, Alice M. Starcke, "Building a Better Orientation Program," *HRMagazine* (November 1996), pp. 107–113; and H. Eugene Baker III and Daniel C. Feldman, "Linking Organizational Socialization Tactics with Corporate Human Resource Management Strategies," *Human Resource Management Review,* Vol. 1, No. 3 (Fall 1991), pp. 193–202.

20. Howard J. Klein and Natasha A. Weaver, "The Effectiveness of an Organizational-Level Orientation Training Program in the Socialization of New Hires," *Personnel Psychology* (Spring 2000), pp. 47–66; John Van Maanen and Edgar H. Schein, "Toward a Theory of Organizational Socialization," in *Research in Organizational Behavior,* Barry M. Staw (ed.) (Greenwich, CT:JAI Press, 1979), p. 210. See also, "New Employee Orientation: Ensuring a Smooth Transition," *Small Business Report,* Vol. 13, No. 7 (July 1988), pp. 40–43.

21. Adapted from Richard F. Federico, "Six Ways to Solve the Orientation Blues," *HRMagazine,* Vol. 36, No. 5 (May 1991), p. 69.

22. See, for example, Sabrina Hicks, "Successful Orientation Programs," *Training and Development* (April 2000), pp. 59–60; and Nancy K Austin, "Giving New Employees a Better Beginning," *Working Woman* (July 1995), pp. 20–22; 74.

23. Martha I. Finney, "Employee Orientation Programs Can Help Introduce Success," *HR News* (October 1995), p. 2; and Andre Nelson, "New Employee Orientation: Are They Really Worthwhile?" *Supervision,* Vol. 51, No. 11 (November 1990), p. 6.

24. See, for example, Joseph F. McKenna, "Training: Welcome Aboard," *Industry Week,* Vol. 238, No. 21 (November 6, 1989), pp. 31–38.

25. "Are Your Training Programs Legal Time Bombs," *HR Focus* (July 2000), pp. 6–7.

26. Larry Cole and Michael Cole, "Bring New Employees Up to Speed Fast for Top Performance," *Communication World* (December 1999–January 2000), pp. 31–32.

27. Commerce Clearing House, "Interview with George Odiorne," *Human Resource Management: Ideas and Trends,* No. 165 (March 22, 1988), p. 45.

28. Carla Joinson, "A Return to Good Manners," *HRMagazine* (February 1997), p. 88; Candice Harp, "Link Training to Corporate Mission," *HRMagazine* (August 1995), p. 65; Teresa L. Smith, "Job-Related Materials Reinforce Basic Skills," *HRMagazine* (July 1995), p. 84; Michael Dulworth and Robert Shea, "Six Ways Technology Improves Training," *HRMagazine* (May 1995), p. 33; and Gale Cohen Ruby, "Basic Training," *Entrepreneur* (December 1994), p. 129.

29. Frederick Kuri, "Basic-Skills Training Boosts Productivity," *HRMagazine* (September 1996), p. 73.

30. Neville C. Tompkins, "Lessons in Many Languages," *HRMagazine* (March 1996), pp. 94–96.

31. See, for example, Jack Stack, "The Training Myth," *Inc.* (August 1998), pp. 41–42.

32. See, for example, Lakewood Research and Training Magazine, "Instructional Methods: Charting the Top 10," in Carla Joinson, "Make Your Training Stick," *HRMagazine* (May 1995), p. 55.

33. Beth Rogers, "The Making of a Highly Skilled Worker," *HRMagazine* (July 1994), p. 62.

34. Leslie A. Bryan, Jr., "An Ounce of Prevention for Workplace Accidents," *Training and Development Journal,* Vol. 44, No. 7 (July 1990), p. 101.

35. William J. Rothwell and H. C. Kazanas, "Planned OJT Is Productive OJT," *Training and Development Journal,* Vol. 44, No. 10 (October 1990), pp. 53–56.

36. Kathryn Tyler, "Tips for Structuring Workplace Literacy Programs," *HRMagazine* (October 1996), p. 112.

37. Ibid., p. 55, and Bryan, Jr., p. 102.

38. Sandra E. O'Connell, "CD-ROMs Offer Practical Advantages for HR," *HRMagazine* (November 1996), pp. 35–38.

39. Richard P. Lookatch, "How to Talk to a Talking Head," *Training and Development Journal*, Vol. 44, No. 9 (September 1990), pp. 63–65.

40. See Jo McHale and David Flegg, "Training Extra: Screentest," *Personnel Management*, Vol. 23, No. 6 (June 1991), p. 69; and Patricia A. Galagan, "IBM Faces the Future Again," *Training and Development Journal*, Vol. 44, No. 3 (March 1990), p. 36.

41. See, for example, Samuel Greengard, "'Virtual' Training Becomes Reality," *Industry Week* (January 19, 1998), p. 72; Tom Simmons, "Virtual Reality," *Inc.* (October 1995), p. 23; and Gene Bylinsky, "The Marvels of Virtual Reality," *Fortune* (June 3, 1991), p. 138.

42. Debra Eller, "Motorola Trains VPs to Become Growth Leaders," *HRMagazine* (June 1995), pp. 82–87.

43. Ibid.

44. Samuel Greengard, "Going the Distance," *Industry Week* (May 4, 1998), p. 22.

45. James Bredin, "Broadening Horizons," *Industry Week* (October 1997), p. 68.

46. Daniel C. Feldman, William R. Folks, and William H. Turnley, "Mentor-Protege Diversity and Its Impact on International Internship Relationships," *Journal of Organizational Behavior* (September 1999), pp. 597–611.

47. Mark Henricks, "Excellent Adventures," *Entrepreneur* (July 1995), p. 58; and Keith Green, "Leadership Program a Life-Altering Experience," *HR News* (March 1995), p. 4.

48. See, for example, "Survival Training for Employees," *ABC World News Tonight/American Agenda* (July 21, 1993).

49. Sabrina Hicks, "What Is Organization Development?" *Training and Development* (August 2000), p. 65.

50. Kurt Lewin, *Field Theory in Social Science* (New York: Harper & Row, 1951).

51. See, for instance, Tom Peters, *Thriving on Chaos* (New York: Alfred A. Knopf, 1987).

52. Phyllis Berman, "Harry's a Great Story Teller," *Forbes* (February 27, 1995), pp. 112–116; Janet Bamford, "Changing Business as Usual," *Working Woman* (November 1993), p. 62; and "Interview with Harry V. Quadracci," *Business Ethics* (May–June 1993), pp. 19–21.

53. R. Wayne Pace, Phillip C. Smith, and Gordon E. Mills, *Human Resource Development* (Englewood Cliffs, NJ: Prentice-Hall, 1991), p. 131.

54. Ibid.

55. See Billy O. Fireman, "Characteristics of Change Agents," *Vital Speeches of the Day* (December 15, 1998), pp. 152–154.

56. Gib Akin and Ian Palmer, "Putting Metaphors to Work for a Change in Organizations," *Organizational Dynamics* (Winter 2000), pp. 67–79.

57. Marc Adams, "Training Employees as Partners," *HRMagazine* (February 1999), pp. 65–70; Eileen M. Garger, "Goodbye Training, Hello Learning," *Workforce* (November 1999), pp. 35–42; and Dominic Bencivenga, "Learning Organizations Evolve in New Directions," *HRMagazine* (October 1995), pp. 69–73.

58. Brian Dumaine, "Mr. Learning Organization," *Fortune* (October 17, 1994), pp. 147–157.

59. Kathryn Tyler, "Focus on Training: Hold On to What You've Learned," *HRMagazine* (May 2000), pp. 94–102; and Maureen Minehan, "Skills Shortage in Asia," *HRMagazine* (March 1996), p. 152.

60. Ronald Henkoff, "Companies That Train Best," p. 62.

61. Linda Grant, "A School for Success," *U.S. News & World Report* (May 22, 1995), p. 53.

62. See, for example, R. E. Catalano and D. L. Kirkpatrick, "Evaluating Training Programs—The State of the Art," *Training and Development Journal* (May 1968), pp. 2–9.

63. Susanne Taylor, "When Workers Travel Abroad, Caution Is Advisable," *HR News* (April 1999), p. 13.

64. See, for example, Joseph W. Weiss and Stanley Bloom, "Managing in China: Expatriate Experiences in Training," *Business Horizons*, Vol. 33, No. 3 (May–June 1990), pp. 23–29.

65. S. Ronen, "Training the International Assignee," in I. L. Goldstein & Associates (eds.), *Training and Development in Organizations* (San Francisco: Jossey-Bass, 1989), pp. 417–453.

66. From an undated Bristol-Myers handout.

67. G. Oddou, teaching note in "The Overseas Assignment: A Practical Look," *International Human Resource Management*, M. Mendenhall and G. Oddou (eds.) (Boston: PWS-Kent Publishing, 1991), pp. 259–269.

68. See, for instance, Michael Harvey and Danielle Wiese, "Global Dual-Career Couple Mentoring: A Phase Model Approach," *Human Resource Planning* (February 1998), pp. 33–48; and Ellen Van Velsor and Jean Brittain Leslie, "Why Executives Derail: Perspectives Across Time and Cultures," *Academy of Management Executive*, Vol. 9, No. 4 (May 1995), pp. 62–72.

9

Managing Careers

LEARNING OUTCOMES

After reading this chapter, you will be able to:

1. Explain who is responsible for managing careers.
2. Describe what is meant by the term *career*.
3. Discuss the focus of careers for both the organization and individuals.
4. Describe how career development and employee development are different.
5. Explain why career development is valuable to organizations.
6. Identify the five traditional stages involved in a career.
7. List the Holland Vocational Preferences.
8. Describe the implications of Personality Typologies and jobs.
9. Identify several suggestions that you can use to manage your career more effectively.

Eric N. Watson thought he had his life in total control—even from a very early age. By fourth grade, being the tallest person in his class, he became a star basketball player. Throughout the next few years he would demonstrate his talent on the court, leading his team to numerous victories. But basketball wasn't Eric's only concern. He also knew he had to do well in the classroom. His academic ability, coupled with his basketball prowess, earned him an academic/athletic scholarship to Livingston College. But his athletic career was soon about to end. Eric, who grew quickly in his childhood to 5'7", never grew another inch. Being height challenged, he recognized a career in basketball was not probable. Accordingly, he left the team, focusing his talents on academics.[1]

Shortly after graduating from college, Watson accepted a position with the St. Paul Companies. He worked for St. Paul for years in the claims division. But his upbringing taught him something—that there was good in all people, but sometimes you had to help others find it. This attitude and his desire to help others led to his appointment as the company's director of diversity. Shortly thereafter, after a few years of excellent performance, he was promoted to vice president for global diversity. His work as vice president included staff development programs, leadership training,

have careers. The concept is as relevant to transient, unskilled laborers as it is to engineers and physicians. For our purposes, therefore, any work, paid or unpaid, pursued over an extended period of time, can constitute a career. In addition to formal job work, careers can include schoolwork, homemaking, or volunteer work. Furthermore, career success is defined not only objectively, in terms of promotion, but also subjectively, in terms of satisfaction.

Individual versus Organizational Perspective

The study of careers takes on a very different orientation, depending on whether it is viewed from the perspective of the organization or of the individual. A key question in career development, then, is, "With whose interests are we concerned?" From an organizational or HRM viewpoint, career development involves tracking career paths and developing career ladders.[7] HRM seeks information to direct and to monitor the progress of special groups of employees, and to ensure that capable professional, managerial, and technical talent will be available to meet the organization's needs (see Technology Corner). Career development from the organization's perspective is also called *organizational career planning*.

In contrast, individual career development, or career planning, focuses on assisting individuals to identify their major goals and to determine what they need to do to achieve these goals. Note that in the latter case the focus is entirely on the individual and includes his or her life outside the organization, as well as inside. So while organizational career development looks at individuals filling the needs of the organization, individual career development addresses each individual's personal work career and other lifestyle issues.[8] For instance, an excellent employee, when assisted in better understanding his or her needs and aspirations through interest inventories, life-planning analysis, and counseling, may even decide to leave the organization if it becomes apparent that career aspirations can be best achieved outside the employing organization. Employee expectations today are different from employee expectations a generation ago. Sex-role stereotypes are crumbling as people are less restricted by gender-specific occupations. Additionally, our lifestyles are more varied, with, for example, more dual-career couples today than ever before.[9] Both career approaches (individual and organizational) have value. This chapter blends the interests of both the individual within the organization and the organization itself. However, since the primary focus of human resource management is the interest of careers to the organization, we will primarily emphasize this area. However, at the end of the chapter we will take a special look at how you can better manage your career.

Career Development versus Employee Development

Given our discussions in Chapter 8 on employee development, you may be wondering what, if any, differences there are between career development and employee development. These topics have a common element,[11] but there is one distinct difference—the time frame.

Career development looks at the long-term career effectiveness and success of organizational personnel. By contrast, the kinds of development discussed in the last chapter focused on work effectiveness or performance in the immediate or intermediate time frames. These two concepts are closely linked; employee training and development should be compatible with an individual's career development in the organization. But a successful career program, in attempting to

TRACKING CAREER PATHS

KEEPING TRACK OF CAREER PATHS FOR individuals can be better facilitated through technology. Here are a couple of software packages that can assist in this activity.[10]

Workforce Vision: Workforce Vision (Criterion Inc., www.criterioninc.com) helps an organization link its succession planning strategies with career planning. The software "identifies talent based on performance, competency profiles and professional networks instead of simplistic skills checklists or job progression ladders." Workforce Vision also "pulls together essential facts about employee performance, education, competencies, training, development, career paths, succession plans, job requirements, and reporting relationships." This software is somewhat expensive and is probably better aimed at medium to large organizations.

SkillView: SkillView (SkillView Technologies, www.skillview.com) software is touted as an "easy-to-use assessment, which allows employees to record and track their competencies and to perform comparative analysis against their job position as well as other positions in the organization." SkillView software can be useful in "individual skill profiling, personal development and career planning." Costs for this, and other SkillView Software programs, are on a per user per month basis.

---

match individual abilities and aspirations with the needs of the organization, should develop people for the long-term needs of the organization and address the dynamic changes that will take place over time.

Career Development: Value for the Organization

Assuming that an organization already provides extensive employee development programs, why should it need to consider a career development program as well? A long-term career focus should increase the organization's effectiveness in managing its human resources. More specifically, we can identify several positive results that can accrue from a well-designed career development program.

Ensures Needed Talent Will Be Available   Career development efforts are consistent with, and are a natural extension of, strategic and employment planning. Changing staff requirements over the intermediate and long term should be identified when the company sets long-term goals and objectives. Working with individual employees to help them align their needs and aspirations with those of the organization will increase the probability that the right people will be available to meet the organization's changing staffing requirements.[12]

Improves the Organization's Ability to Attract and Retain Highly Talented Employees   Outstanding employees will always be scarce, and there is usually considerable competition to secure their services. Such individuals may give preference to employers who demonstrate a concern for their employees' future. If already employed by an organization that offers career advice, these people may exhibit greater loyalty and commitment to their employer. Importantly, career development appears to be a natural response to the rising concern by employees for the quality of work life and personal life planning. As more individuals seek jobs that offer challenge, responsibility, and opportunities for advancement, realistic career planning becomes increasingly necessary. Additionally, social values have changed so that more members of the work force no longer look at their work in isolation. Their work must be compatible with their personal and family interests and commitments. Again, career development should result in a better individual-organization match for employees and thus lead to less turnover.

Ensures That Minorities and Women Get Opportunities for Growth and Development   As discussed in previous chapters, equal employment opportunity legislation and affirmative-action programs have demanded that minority groups and women receive opportunities for growth and development that will prepare them for greater responsibilities within the organization. The fair employment movement has served as a catalyst to career development programs targeted for these special groups. Recent legislation, such as the Americans with Disabilities Act, offers an even greater organizational career challenge. Furthermore, courts frequently look at an organization's career development efforts with these groups when ruling on discrimination suits.

Reduces Employee Frustration   Although the educational level of the work force has risen, so, too, have their occupational aspirations. However, periods of economic stagnation and increased concern by organizations to reduce costs have also reduced opportunities. This has increased frustration in employees who often see a significant disparity between their aspirations and actual opportunities. When organizations cut costs by downsizing, career paths, career tracks, and career ladders often collapse.[13] Career counseling can result in more realistic, rather than raised, employee expectations.

Enhances Cultural Diversity   The work force in the next decade will witness a more varied combination of race, nationality, sex, and values in the organization.[14] Effective organizational career development provides access to all levels of the organization for more varied types of employees. Extended career opportunities make cultural diversity, and the appreciation of it, an organizational reality.[15]

Marion Manigo-Truell is quite typical of individuals in today's dynamic market. That is, she has followed what once would be considered an unusual career path. She's worked in a bank, a hotel, and in the investment field. Each step of the way, she learned new skills—all of which have helped her earn bigger job titles and more money.

Promotes Organizational Goodwill   If employees think their employing organizations are concerned about their long-term well-being, they respond in kind by projecting positive images of the organization into other areas of their lives (e.g., volunteer work in the community).[16] For instance, Larry works for a long-distance phone carrier. He also coaches clinic basketball with other parents in the community. When he expresses his trust of the phone company, because of their expressed career interest, his friends might consider proposed rate hikes with greater tolerance.

Career Development: Value for the Individual

Effective career development is also important for the individual. In fact, as we've previously mentioned, it is more important today than ever. Because the definitions of careers and what constitutes success have changed, the value of individual career development programs has expanded. Career success may no longer be measured merely by an employee's income or hierarchical level in an organization. Career success may now include using one's skills and abilities to face expanded challenges, or having greater responsibilities and increased autonomy in one's chosen profession.[17] Intrinsic career development, or "psychic income," is desired by contemporary workers who are seeking more than salary and security from their jobs.[18] Contemporary workers seek interesting and meaningful work; such interest and meaning are often derived from a sense of being the architect of one's own career.[19]

External Career   Involves the properties or qualities of an occupation.

Careers are both external and internal. The **external career** involves properties or qualities of an occupation or an organization.[20] For example, a career in business might be thought of as a sequence of jobs or positions held during the life of the individual: undergraduate degree in business; sales representative for a construction supply house; graduate training in business; district manager in a "Do-It-Yourself" hardware chain; president of a small housing inspection and appraisal firm; retirement. External careers may also be characterized by such things as career ladders within a particular organization (employment recruiter, employment manager, HRM director, vice president HRM).

The individual career encompasses a variety of individual aspects or themes: accumulation of external symbols of success or advancement (bigger office with each promotion);[21] threshold definition of occupational types (i.e., physicians have careers, dog catchers have jobs);[22] long-term commitment to a particular occupational field (i.e., career soldier);[23] a series of work-related positions;[24] and, work-related attitudes and behaviors.[25]

With careers being the pattern of work-related experiences that span the course of a person's life, we must understand that both personal relationships and family concerns are also intrinsically valued by employees. Subjective and objective elements, then, are necessary components of a theoretical perspective, which captures the complexity of career.[26] Success can then be defined in external terms. For example, if after five years at the same company you get a promotion, and Rick, a colleague who was hired the same day you were for the same type of job, has not yet been promoted, then you may view yourself as more successful than Rick. The external definition also states that a certified public accountant is more successful than a dog catcher. However, if you consider the subjective, internal valuation of success, the story may be different. A dog catcher who defines his job as protecting children and others in the community from danger, who goes home proud at night because he has successfully and compassionately captured dogs that day, is successful in his career. Compare that to a CPA who works only to buy a new sports car so she can escape from the

Exhibit 9-1
*Internal and External Events
and Career Stages*

Stage	External Event	Internal Event
Exploration	Advice and examples of relatives, teachers, friends, and coaches	Development of self-image of what one "might" be, what sort of work would be fun
	Actual successes and failures in school, sports and hobbies	Self-assessment of own talents and limitations
	Actual choice of educational path—vocational school, college, major, professional school	Development of ambitions, goals, motives, dreams
		Tentative choices and commitments, changes
Establishment	Explicit search for a job	Shock of entering the "real world"
	Acceptance of a job	Insecurity around new tasks of interviewing, applying, being tested, facing being turned down
	Induction and orientation	
	Assignment to further training or first job	Making a "real" choice; to take a job or not; which job; first commitment
	Acquiring visible job and organizational membership trappings (ID card, parking sticker, uniform, organizational manual)	Fear of being tested for the first time under *real* conditions, and found out to be a fraud
	First job assignment, meeting the boss and coworkers	Reality shock—what the work is really like, doing the "dirty work"
	Learning period, indoctrination	Forming a career strategy, how "to make it"—working hard, finding mentors, conforming to an organization, making a contribution
	period of full performance—"doing the job"	
		This is "real," what I'm doing matters
		Feeling of success or failure—going uphill, either challenging or exhausting
		Decision to leave organization if things do not look positive
		Feeling of being accepted fully by the organization, "having made it"—satisfaction of seeing "my project"
Mid-Career	Leveling off, transfer, and/or promotion	Period of settling in or new ambitions based on self-assessment
	Entering a period of maximum productivity	More feeling of security, relaxation, but danger of leveling off and stagnation
	Becoming more of a teacher/mentor than a learner	Threat from younger, better trained, more energetic, and ambitious persons—"Am I too old for my job?"
	Explicit signs from boss and coworkers that one's progress has plateaued	Possible thoughts of "new pastures" and new challenges—"What do I really want to do?"
		Working through mid-life crisis toward greater acceptance of oneself and others
		"Is it time to give up on my dreams? Should I settle for what I have?"
Late Career	Job assignments drawing primarily on maturity of judgment	Psychological preparation for retirement
		Deceleration in momentum
	More jobs involving teaching others	Finding new sources of self-improvement off the job, new sources of job satisfaction through teaching others
Decline	Formal preparation for retirement	Learning to accept a reduced role and less responsibility
	Retirement rituals	Learning to live a less structured life
		New accommodations to family and community

Source: Adapted from John Van Maanen and Edgar H. Schein, "Career Development," in *Improving Life at Work*, eds. J. Richard Hackman and J. Lloyd Suttle (Santa Monica, CA: Goodyear, 1977), pp. 55–57; and D. Levinson, *The Seasons of a Man's Life*.

drudgery of her day-to-day office life of dealing with clients, accounting forms, and automated systems. Is she more or less successful than the dog catcher?

This differentiation of internal from external is important to the manager who wants to motivate employees (Exhibit 9-1). Different employees may respond to different motivational tools. For instance, Darin is working as a consultant for you, looking to earn enough money to purchase a time-share in a condo in Florida. Diane, your newest software developer, joined the company with the expectation that within four years she will have obtained her Master's degree and be in a supervisory position in the company. Would they respond equally to the opportunity to be trained in interpersonal skills? Would both of them be as likely to accept (or reject) a transfer to another city? Probably not, because both have different drives. Thus, we can say that internal and external career events may be parallel, but result in different outcomes. We have displayed these events in Exhibit 9-1. They are discussed in the context of career stages, the topic discussed in the next section.

Mentoring and Coaching

It has become increasingly clear over the years that employees who aspire to higher management levels in organizations often need the assistance and advocacy of someone higher up in the organization.[27] These career progressions often require having the favor of the dominant in-group, which sets corporate goals, priorities, and standards.[28]

Mentoring or Coaching
Actively guiding another individual.

When a senior employee takes an active role in guiding another individual, we refer to this activity as **mentoring or coaching.** Just as baseball coaches observe, analyze, and attempt to improve the performance of their athletes, "coaches" on the job can do the same. The effective coach, whether on the diamond or in the corporate hierarchy, gives guidance through direction, advice, criticism, and suggestion in an attempt to aid the employee's growth.[29] These individuals offer to assist certain junior employees in terms of providing a support system. This system, in part, is likened to the passing of the proverbial baton—that is, the senior employee shares his or her experiences with the protege, providing guidance on how to make it in the organization. Accordingly, in organizations such as The Washington Post, J&L Peaberry's Coffee & Tea Company, Prudential, and Wal-Mart that promote from within, employees who aspire to succeed must have the corporate support system[30] in their favor. This support system, guided by a mentor, vouches for the candidate, answers for the candidate in the highest circles within the organization, makes appropriate introductions, and advises and guides the candidate on how to effectively move through the system.

The technique of senior employees coaching individuals has the advantages that go with learning by doing, particularly the opportunities for high interaction and rapid feedback on performance. Unfortunately, its two strongest disadvantages are: (1) its tendencies to perpetuate the current styles and practices in the organization; and (2) its heavy reliance on the coach's ability to be a good teacher. In the same way that we recognize that all excellent Hall-of-Fame baseball players don't make outstanding baseball coaches, we cannot expect all excellent employees to be effective coaches. An individual can become an excellent performer without necessarily possessing the knack of creating a proper learning environment for others to do the same; thus, the effectiveness of this technique relies on the ability of the coach. Coaching of employees can occur at any level and can be most effective when the two individuals do not have any type of reporting relationship.

Recall from Chapter 3 the discussion of the glass ceiling. One of the main reasons for its existence is that women previously didn't have many role models sitting at top levels in the organization who could help them through the system.[31] Although there was no excuse for this situation, there may be some explanation. Mentors sometimes select their proteges on the basis of seeing themselves, in their younger years, in the employee.[32] Since men rarely can identify with younger women, many appeared unwilling to play the part of their mentor. Of course, as women have battled their way into the inner circle of organizational power, some success is being witnessed. Additionally, organizations are beginning to explore ways of advocating cross-gender mentoring. This revolves around identifying the problems associated with such an arrangement,[33] deciding how they can be handled effectively, and providing organizational support.[34]

TRADITIONAL CAREER STAGES

One traditional way to analyze and discuss careers is to consider them in stages or steps.[35] Progression, from a beginning point through growth and decline phases to a termination point, is typically a natural occurrence in one's work life. Most of us begin to form our careers during our early school years. Our careers begin to wind down as we reach retirement age. We can identify five career stages that are typical for most adults, regardless of occupation: exploration, establishment, mid-career, late career, and decline. These stages are portrayed in Exhibit 9-2. The age ranges for each stage in Exhibit 9-2 are intended *only* to show general guidelines. For some individuals pursuing certain careers, this model may be too simplistic. The key is, however, to give your primary attention to the stages rather than the age categories. For instance, someone who makes a dramatic change in career to undertake a completely different line of work at age 45 will have many of the same establishment-stage concerns as someone starting at age 25. On the other hand, if the 45-year-old started working at 25, he or she now has 20 years of experience, as well as interests and expectations that differ from those of a peer who is just starting a career at middle age. Of course, if the 45-year-old individual is a newly admitted college student who starts college once her children have grown, she will have more in common—career-stage-wise—with the 23-year-old sitting next to her than she will with the 45-year-old full professor who is teaching the class. So don't get hung-up on the age generalizations in Exhibit 9-2. They're presented simply for points of reference.

EXHIBIT 9-2
Career Stages

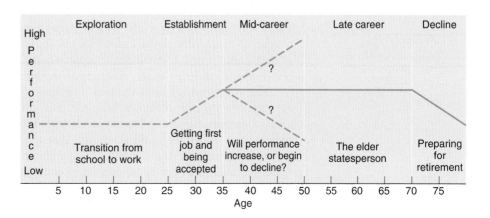

Exploration

Many of the critical choices individuals make about their careers are made prior to entering the work force on a paid basis. What we hear from our relatives, teachers, and friends, what we see on television, in the movies, or on the Internet, helps us to narrow our career choice alternatives, leading us in certain directions. Certainly, the careers, interests, and aspirations of family members and financial resources will be heavy factors in determining our perception of what careers are available or what schools, colleges, or universities we might consider.

The **exploration period** ends for most of us as we make the transition from formal education programs to work. From an organizational standpoint, this stage has the least relevance, since it occurs prior to employment. It is, of course, not irrelevant. The exploration period is a time when a number of expectations about one's career are developed, many of which are unrealistic. Such expectations may lie dormant for years and then pop up later to frustrate both employee and employer.

Successful career exploration strategies involve trying a lot of potential fields to see what you like or don't like. The college internships and cooperative education programs are excellent exploration tools. You are given the opportunity to see your future coworkers firsthand and to do, day in and day out, a "real" job. Some successful internships lead to job offers. From a career-stage perspective, an internship that helps you realize that you're bored to death with the work is also a successful one. In the exploration stage we form our attitudes toward work (doing homework, meeting deadlines, taking or avoiding shortcuts, attendance), and our dominant social relationship patterns (easygoing, domineering, indifferent, likable, obnoxious). Therefore, exploration is preparation for work.

Establishment

The **establishment period** begins with the search for work and includes getting your first job, being accepted by your peers, learning the job, and gaining the first tangible evidence of success or failure in the real world.[36] It begins with uncertainties and anxieties, and is, indeed, dominated by two problems: "finding a niche" and "making your mark."[37]

Finding the right job takes time for many of us. In fact, you may know a 37-year-old who has held a series of seemingly unrelated jobs (for instance, after high school, clerk in a sporting goods store, three years; Navy, six years; police dispatcher, four years; small business owner, three years; over-the-road truck driver, now). This person has looked for a niche—or attempted to establish one—for nearly 20 years! A more typical pattern is to recognize that we may not change as frequently as the individual above. On the other hand, your first real job probably won't be with the company from which you retire. Thorough career exploration helps make this part of establishment an easier step.

The second problem of the establishment stage, making your mark, is characterized by making mistakes, learning from those mistakes, and assuming increased responsibilities.[38] However, individuals in this stage have yet to reach their peak productivity, and rarely are they given work assignments that carry great power or high status. As shown in Exhibit 9-2, this stage is experienced as "going uphill." The career takes a lot of time and energy. There is often a sense of growth, of expectation, or anticipation, such as a hiker feels when approaching a crest, waiting to see what lies on the other side. And, just as a hiker "takes" a hill when she stands at the crest, the establishment stage has ended when you

Exploration Period A career stage that usually ends in one's mid-twenties as one makes the transition from school to work.

When you establish your career, you are trying to find your niche and make your mark.

Establishment Period A career stage in which one begins to search for work. It includes getting one's first job.

have "arrived" (made your mark). Of course, at this time you're considered a seasoned veteran. Consequently, you're now responsible for your own mistakes.

Mid-Career

Mid-career Stage A career stage marked by a continuous improvement in performance, leveling off in performance, or the beginning of deterioration of performance.

Many people do not face their first severe career dilemmas until they reach the **mid-career stage**.[39] This is a time when individuals may continue their prior improvements in performance, level off, or begin to deteriorate. Therefore, although the challenge of remaining productive at work after you're "seasoned" is a major challenge of this career stage, the pattern ceases to be as clear as it was for exploration and establishment. Some employees reach their early goals and go on to even greater heights. For instance, a worker who wants to be the vice president of HRM by the time he's 35 to 40 years old might want to be CEO by the time he's 55 to 60 if he has achieved the prior goal. Continued growth and high performance are not the only successful outcomes at this stage. Maintenance, or holding onto what you have, is another possible outcome of the mid-career stage. These employees are plateaued, not failed. **Plateaued mid-career** employees can be very productive.[40] They are technically competent—even though some may not be as ambitious and aggressive as the climbers. They may be satisfied to contribute a sufficient amount of time and energy to the organization to meet production commitments; they also may be easier to manage than someone who wants more. These employees are not deadwood, but good, reliable employees and "solid citizens." An example would be the same HRM vice president who decides at 40 to not go for the next promotion, but to enjoy other aspects of his life more—pursuing his hobbies—while still performing well on the job.

Plateauing A condition of stagnating in one's current job.

The third option for mid-career deals with the employee whose performance begins to deteriorate. This stage for this kind of employee is characterized by loss of both interest and productivity at work.[41] Organizations are often limited to relegating such individuals to less conspicuous jobs, reprimanding them, demoting them, or severing them from the organization altogether. The same HRM vice president could become less productive if, by 42, he realizes that he will never be CEO and tries to "wait it out" for 13 years until he can take early retirement. Fortunately, some affected individuals can be reenergized by moving them to another position in the organization. This can work to boost their morale and their productivity.[42]

Late Career

Late-career Stage A career phase in which individuals are no longer learning about their jobs, nor is it expected that they should be trying to outdo levels of performance from previous years.

For those who continue to grow through the mid-career stage, the **late-career stage** is usually a pleasant time when one is allowed the luxury to relax a bit and enjoy playing the part of the elder statesperson. It is a time when one can rest on one's laurels and bask in the respect given by less experienced employees. Frequently during the late career, individuals are no longer expected to outdo their levels of performance from previous years. Their value to the organization typically lies heavily in their judgment, built up over many years and through varied experiences. They can teach others based on the knowledge they have gained.[43]

For those who have stagnated or deteriorated during the previous stage, on the other hand, the late career brings the reality that they will not have an everlasting impact or change the world as they once thought. Employees who decline in mid-career may fear for their jobs. It is a time when individuals recognize that they have decreased work mobility and may be locked into their current job. One begins to look forward to retirement and the opportunities of doing something different. Mere plateauing is no more negative than it was during mid-career. In fact, it is expected at late career. The marketing vice president who didn't make it to executive vice president might begin delegating more to her next in line. Life off the job is likely to carry far greater importance than it did in earlier years, as time and energy, once directed to work, are now being redirected to family, friends, and hobbies.

Decline (Late Stage)

Decline or Late Stage The final stage in one's career, usually marked by retirement.

The **decline or late stage** in one's career is difficult for just about everyone but, ironically, is probably hardest on those who have had continued successes in the earlier stages. After decades of continued achievements and high levels of performance, the time has come for retirement. These individuals step out of the limelight and relinquish a major component of their identity. For those who have seen their performance deteriorate over the years, it may be a pleasant time; the frustrations that have been associated with work are left behind. For the plateaued, it is probably an easier transition to other life activities.

Adjustments, of course, will have to be made regardless of whether one is leaving a sparkling career or a hopeless job. The structure and regimentation that work provided will no longer be there. Work responsibilities are generally fewer, and life is often less structured due to the absence of work. As a result, it is a challenging stage for anyone to confront.

However, as we live longer, healthier lives, coupled with laws removing age-related retirement requirements, 62 or 65 ceases to be a meaningful retirement demand. Some individuals shift their emphasis from one type of work to another—either paid or volunteer work. Oftentimes, the key element in this decision is the financial security one has. Those who have adequate funds to "maintain their lifestyles in retirement" are more likely to engage in activities that they desire. Unfortunately, those less financially secure may not be able to retire when they want, or find that they have to seek gainful employment in some capacity to supplement their retirement income.

How has technology changed traditional career paths? Just ask Mark Rabe. After returning to Duke's Fuqua School of Business for an MBA degree, Mark turned down jobs from such traditional and successful companies as Coca-Cola, Gillette, and Clorox. Instead, he decided to go to work for About.com (an Internet Media Company) in hopes that he'd have some opportunity to influence the company's work environment. Many others from some of the best business schools in the United States have followed suit.

CAREER CHOICES AND PREFERENCES

The best career choice is the choice that offers the best match between what you want and what you need. Good career choice outcomes for any of us should result in a series of positions that give us an opportunity for good performance, make us want to maintain our commitment to the field, and give us high work satisfaction. A good career match, then, is one in which we are able to develop a positive self-concept and to do work that we think is important.[44] Let's look at some of the existing research that can help you discover which careers may provide the best match for your skills.

Holland Vocational Preferences

Holland Vocational Preference An individual occupational personality as it relates to vocational themes.

One of the most widely used approaches to guide career choices is the **Holland vocational preferences model**.[45] This theory consists of three major components. First, Holland found that people have varying occupational preferences; we do not all like to do the same things. Second, his research demonstrates that if you have a job where you can do what you think is important, you will be a more productive employee. Personality of workers may be matched to typical work environments where that can occur. Third, you will have more in common with people who have similar interest patterns and less in common with those who don't. For instance, assume Karen hates her job; she thinks it is boring to waste her time packing and unpacking trucks on the shipping dock of a manufacturing firm, and would rather be working with people in the recruiting area. Pat,

EXHIBIT 9-3
*Holland's General
Occupational Themes*

Realistic   Rugged, robust, practical, prefer to deal with things rather than people mechanical interests. Best matches with jobs that are Agriculture, Nature, Adventure, Military, Mechanical.

Investigative   Scientific, task-oriented, prefer abstract problems, prefer to think through problems rather than to act on them, not highly person-oriented, enjoy ambiguity. Corresponding jobs are Science, Mathematics, Medical Science, Medical Service.

Artistic   Enjoy creative self-expression, dislike highly-structured situations, sensitive, emotional, independent, original. Corresponding jobs are Music/Dramatics, Art, Writing.

Social   Concerned with the welfare of others, enjoy developing and teaching others, good in group settings, extroverted, cheerful, popular. Corressponding jobs are Teaching, Social Service, Athletics, Domestic Arts, Religious Activities.

Enterprising   Good facility with words, prefer selling or leading, energetic, extroverted, adventurous, enjoy persuasion. Corresponding jobs are Public Speaking, Law/Politics, Merchandising, Sales, Business Management.

Conventional   Prefer ordered, numerical work, enjoy large organizations, stable, dependable. Corresponding job is Office Practices.

Source: Adapted from *Making Vocational Choices*, 2nd edition, Psychological Assessment Resources, Inc., Copyright 1973, 1985, 1992. All Rights reserved.

on the other hand, enjoys the routine of her work; she likes the daily rhythm and the serenity of loading and unloading the warehouse. Do Karen and Pat get the same satisfaction from their jobs? There's a good chance that they don't. Why? Their interests, expressed as occupational interests, are not compatible.

The Holland vocational preferences model identifies six vocational themes (realistic, investigative, artistic, social, enterprising, conventional) presented in Exhibit 9-3. An individual's occupational personality is expressed as some combination of high and low scores on these six themes. High scores indicate that you enjoy those kinds of activities. Although it is possible to score high or low on all six scales, most people are identified by three dominant scales. The six themes are arranged in the hexagonal structure shown in Exhibit 9-4. This scale model represents the fact that some of the themes are opposing, while others have mutually reinforcing characteristics.

For instance, Realistic and Social are opposite each other in the diagram. A person with a realistic preference wants to work with things, not people. A person with a social preference wants to work with people, no matter what else they

EXHIBIT 9-4
*Structure of Holland's
Themes*

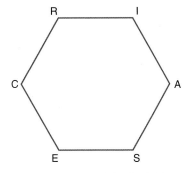

Letters connected by the line indicate reinforcing themes; letters not connecte represent opposing themes

do. Therefore, they have opposing preferences about working alone or with others. Investigative and Enterprising are opposing themes, as are Artistic and Conventional preferences.

An example of mutually reinforcing themes is the Social-Enterprising-Conventional (SEC) vocational preference structure. Sally, for example, likes working with people, being successful, and following ordered rules. That combination is perfect for someone willing to climb the ladder in a large bureaucracy. What about Bob? He's Realistic-Investigative-Artistic, preferring solitary work to large groups, asking questions to answering them, and making his own rules instead of following someone else's. How does Bob fit into a large bureaucracy? Some may see his preferred actions labeling him as a troublemaker. Where would he fit better? Possibly in a research lab! Both the preference of the scientist and the environment of the research lab are characterized by a lack of human interruptions and a concentration on factual material. That's consistent with the Realistic-Investigative-Artistic profile.

The Schein Anchors

Edgar Schein has identified anchors, or personal value clusters, that may be satisfied or frustrated by work. When a particular combination of these personal value clusters (technical-functional competence, managerial competence, security-stability, creativity, and autonomy-independence) is held by the worker and characteristically offered by the organization, that person is "anchored" in that job, organization, or industry.[46] Most people have two or three value clusters that are important to them. If an organization satisfies two out of three, that is considered a stable match. For instance, Donny is a recent college graduate. He wants to use his human resources degree. His father was laid off when his organization downsized last year, and he never wants to have to deal with that type of uncertainty. Schein would describe Donny's anchors as technical competence and security-stability. His current job choices are marketing on a commission basis for a new credit card company, or recruiting for an established and growth-oriented computer firm. Which job should he take? Based on his combination of value clusters, at this time the recruiting job appears to better match Donny's preferences.

Jung and the Myers-Briggs Typologies

Myers-Briggs Type Indicator   Uses four dimensions of personality to identify 16 personality types.

One of the more widely used methods of identifying personalities is the **Myers-Briggs Type Indicator (MBTI)®**.*[47] Building on the works of the early psychologist, Carl Jung, the MBTI uses four dimensions of personality to identify 16 different personality types—for example, ISTJ, ENFP, and so on—based on one's responses to an approximately 100-item questionnaire (see Exhibit 9-5). More than 2 million individuals each year in the United States alone take the MBTI. It's also used in such companies as Apple, AT&T, Exxon, and 3M, as well as many hospitals, educational institutions, and the U.S. armed forces.[48] These personality dimensions can be matched to work environments, much as Holland vocational preferences are used. People with different personality attributes express different job skills and are compatible with other workers with similar personality structures.

The EI dimension measures an individual's orientation toward the inner world of ideas (I) or the external world of the environment (E). The sensing-

---

*The Myers-Briggs Type Indicator and MBTI are registered trademarks of Consulting Psychologists Press, Inc.

Exhibit 9-5
*Characteristics Frequently
Associated with Myers-Briggs
Types*

		Sensing Types S		Intuitive Types N	
		Thinking T	Feeling F	Feeling F	Thinking T
Introverts I	Judging J	**ISTJ** Quiet, serious dependable, practical matter-of-fact. Value traditions and loyalty.	**ISFJ** Quiet, friendly, responsible, thorough, considerate. Strive to create order and harmony.	**INFJ** Seek meaning and connection in ideas. Committed to firm values. Organized and decisive in implementing vision.	**INTJ** Have original minds and great drive for their ideas. Skeptical and independent, have high standards of competence for self and others.
Introverts I	Perceiving P	**ISTP** Tolerant and flexible. Interested in cause and effect. Value efficiency.	**ISFP** Quiet, friendly, sensitive. Like own space. Dislike disagreements and conflicts.	**INFP** Idealistic, loyal to their values. Seek to understand people and help them fulfill their potential.	**INTP** Seek logical explanations. Theoretical and abstract over social interactions. Skeptical, sometimes critical. Analytical.
Extroverts E	Perceiving P	**ESTP** Flexible and tolerant. Focus on here and now. Enjoy material comforts. Learn best by doing.	**ESFP** Outgoing, friendly. Enjoy working with others. Spontaneous. Learn best by trying a new skill with other people.	**ENFP** Enthusiastic, imaginative. Want a lot of affirmation. Rely on verbal fluency and ability to improvise.	**ENTP** Quick, ingenious, stimulating. Adept at generating conceptual possibilities and analyzing them strategically. Bored by routine.
Extroverts E	Judging J	**ESTJ** Practical, realistic, matter-of-fact, decisive. Focus on getting efficient results. Forceful in implementing plans.	**ESFJ** Warmhearted, cooperative. Want to be appreciated for who they are and for what they contribute.	**ENFJ** Warm, responsive, responsible. Attuned to needs of others. Sociable, facilitate others, provide inspirational leadership.	**ENTJ** Frank, decisive, assume leadership. Enjoy long-term planning and goal setting. Forceful in presenting ideas.

intuitive dimension indicates an individual's reliance on information gathered from the external world (S) or from the world of ideas (I). Thinking-feeling reflects one's preference to evaluate information in either an analytical manner (T) or based on values and beliefs (F). Lastly, the judging-perceiving index reflects one's attitude toward the external world, which is either task-completion oriented (J) or information-seeking (P). Using this information, then, let's describe someone who is identified as an INFP (introvert-intuitive-feeling-perceptive). Under Myers-Briggs, the INFP individual would be someone who is quiet and reserved and generally in deep thought, sees the "big picture," is flexible and adaptable, likes a challenge, looks for complete information before making a decision, and cares for others.[49]

Just as each individual has a psychological typology, so too do jobs. As such, this body of work would indicate that employees will be better performers if they are appropriately matched to the job. For example, consider the job of a computer programmer. This job requires an individual to work with details, to work autonomously much of the time, and to complete complex programs according to a set schedule. Using the Myers-Briggs profiles, this job would be viewed as having characteristics of introversion, sensing, thinking, judging (ISTJ). Would the description of the INFP person above be a good match for this job? Probably not—it may not provide what the INFP is looking for. Accordingly, to be better matched to the job, research would suggest that the employee share the same personality type.

*M*ANAGING YOUR CAREER

The career is dead—long live the career. A play on words or an insight into today's careers? Maybe it's a little bit of both. Nonetheless, it's also the title of Douglas T. Hall's book.[50] For several decades, Douglas Hall has been highly regarded for his research about people's careers. And similar to what we've previously discussed, careers are changing. The greatest difference is that you, the individual, are responsible for developing and managing your career.[51] We'll look at suggestions to help you in developing your career—whatever your field of interest.

Making Your Career Decision

The best career choice is the one that offers the best match between what you want out of life and what you need (see Workplace Issues). Good career choice outcomes should result in a series of positions that give you an opportunity to be a good performer, make you want to maintain your commitment to your career, lead to highly satisfying work, and give you the proper balance between work and personal life. A good career match, then, is one in which you are able to develop a positive self-concept, to do work that you think is important, and to lead the kind of life you desire.[52] Identifying this is referred to as *career planning* (see HRM Skills).

Achieving Your Career Goals

We wish we had a foolproof process to give you. Nothing would make our jobs easier than if we could say emphatically, "Follow these steps and you'll be guaranteed career success." Of course, we all know that such a guarantee could never be given. But that's not to imply that achieving your career goals is left simply to chance. Instead, there are suggestions on how to "survive" in most organizations, as well as techniques that you might use to make inroads toward building a successful career (see Exhibit 9-6).

CAREERS

workplace issues

SUSAN HAS WORKED IN THE SAME position as an executive assistant for 12 years and has reached the top grade level for her career path in her company. Becoming bored and disenchanted with the lack of challenge and opportunities, she fears "burnout" as well as boredom. Nevertheless, she does not want to leave the company regardless of the lack of openings in the company due to recent downsizing. Lately, she has realized that her feelings of powerlessness and frustration are affecting her attitude and consequently her performance.

Susan is experiencing feelings and a work-state common to those who experience rapid company downsizing, specialized careers, or employment in smaller companies with shorter career ladders. Regardless of the situation, Susan and others experiencing symptoms of career burnout, boredom, or blockage do have a number of options. To overcome burnout, boredom, or blockage, recharge your career by taking responsibility and accountability for enriching your own position and maximizing your career potential. For example, before quitting, talk with your manager. Although Susan has been with the company for 12 years, she has not had a raise in three years and does not believe she will be given another raise or opportunity without going into management. She does not want to go into management and sees no other alternative than to stay and be miserable, and since misery loves company, make what coworkers are left miserable too.

Susan, like so many others, needs to have a chat with her manager rather than assuming or reading minds. What is the worst thing that could happen if the situation was discussed and the manager had an opportunity to respond, possibly support a plan of action? What could be gained? Frequently situations continue unresolved until a termination or resignation is the only option. However, taking charge of your own career destiny can prevent many terminations and resignations, as well as bring renewed fulfillment by choosing from the following strategies:

1. Take books home and read the operations manuals, annual reports, training materials, trade journals, product information, newsletters—anything and everything to learn new information and gain a new perspective.
2. Volunteer to start or join teams or committees to meet fresh faces and potential career contacts.

3. Review your current job description, highlighting the task or responsibilities you prefer to perform the best. Write your dream job description—how do they compare? Is it possible to incorporate more of the dream job into your current job? If not, what would it take to get that dream job?
4. Enroll in seminars and courses. It's back to school time—why not you? Countless opportunities for internal, public, computer—online and tutorials courses as well as vocational, nontraditional and academic offerings abound. Stagnation and obsolescence is a personal choice. Consider unique course opportunities such as the Fast-Track Management Program at Texas Woman's University which offers a series of five, three-weekend credit courses in courses such as leadership, management, communication, and relations, and supervision.
5. Soul search. What would you really like to be or do when you grow up, considering that you still want to grow? What skills, contacts, credentials, and abilities will you need, and are you willing to pay the price?
6. Network—join clubs, organizations, church groups, to gain the contacts, role models, support and learning opportunities and to do the same for someone else.
7. Tap your internal and external resources as well as human resources or personnel department. They may be delighted to assist someone positively, a refreshing change from personnel problems and paperwork. After all, people can't help you if they do not know what you need.
8. Reassess your needs, values and set some goals—share them with your boss or tell someone who cares. If no one seems to, then start a new list. Look into your own crystal ball, your heart, mind or your consciousness—among the confusion is that inner guiding voice, and so far betting on yourself may be your best bet.

And Susan . . . finally got the courage to talk with her manager who encouraged her to delegate and reassign tasks to free her to develop computer and customer service skills in order to qualify for the upcoming promotion and raise. True story. . . . Really.

The following discussion provides a dozen suggestions based on proven tactics that many individuals have used to advance their careers.[53]

Select Your First Job Judiciously All first jobs are not alike. Where individuals begin in the organization has an important effect on their subsequent career. Specifically, evidence suggests that if you have a choice, you should select a powerful department as the place to start your management career.[54] A *power department* is one in which crucial and important organizational decisions are made. If you start out in departments that are high in power within the organization, you're more likely to advance rapidly.

EXHIBIT 9-6
Steps in Managing Your Career

Develop a network

Acquire and continue upgrading your skills

Participate in an internship

Think laterally

Stay mobile

Support your boss

Find a mentor

Don't stay too long

Stay visible

Gain control of organizational resources

Learn the power structure

Present the right image

Do good work

Select your job judiciously

Participate in an Internship Although it's currently a seller's market, and unemployment rates are relatively low in the United States, the competition for the select positions in an organization is tremendous. Companies often want individuals who have some experience and who show some initiative. One of the better ways of demonstrating these attributes is through an internship. Many universities today not only offer internships as part of their curriculum, they require some type of job experience to fulfill their degree prerequisites. Internships offer you a chance to see what the work is really like, to get a better understanding of an organization's culture, and to see if you fit well into the organization. And although no guarantees are given, many organizations use internships as a means of developing their applicant pool—often extending job offers to outstanding interns.

Even if a job offer at the end of an internship is not available, the internship is not wasted. The work experience the intern gets and the realistic preview of his or her profession of choice are invaluable. Furthermore, internship experience also enables an individual to list work experience on a resume—something that recruiters view very favorably. If an internship is not possible, consider part-time employment in your field of choice while you pursue your education. Like internships, part-time work in entry-level positions provides you with a sound foundation that reflects well on you when you seek full-time employment in the near future.

Do Good Work   Good work performance is a necessary (but not sufficient) condition for career success. The marginal performer may be rewarded in the short term, but his or her weaknesses are bound to surface eventually and cut off career advancement. Your good work performance is no guarantee of success, but without it, a successful long-term career is unlikely.[55]

Present the Right Image   Assuming that your work performance is in line with that of other successful employees, the ability to align your image with that sought by the organization is certain to be interpreted positively. You should assess the organization's culture so that you can determine what the organization wants and values.[56] Then you need to project that image in terms of style of dress, organizational relationships that you do and do not cultivate, risk-taking or risk-averse stance, leadership style, attitude toward conflict, the importance of getting along well with others, and so forth.

Learn the Power Structure   The authority relationships defined by the organization's formal structure as shown by an organizational chart explain only part of the influence patterns within an organization. It's of equal or greater importance to know and understand the organization's power structure. You need to learn who's really in charge, who has the goods on whom, what are the major debts and dependencies—all things that won't be reflected in neat boxes on the organizational chart. Once you have this knowledge, you can work within the power structure with more skill and ease.

Gain Control of Organizational Resources   The control of scarce and important organizational resources is a source of power. Knowledge and expertise are particularly effective resources to control. They make you more valuable to the organization and therefore more likely to gain job security and advancement.

Stay Visible   Because the evaluation of your effectiveness can be very subjective, it's important that your boss and those in power in the organization be made aware of your contributions. If you're fortunate enough to have a job that brings your accomplishments to the attention of others, taking direct measures to increase your visibility might not be needed. But your job may require you to handle activities that are low in visibility, or your specific contribution may be indistinguishable because you're part of a group endeavor. In such cases, without creating the image of a braggart, you'll want to call attention to yourself by giving progress reports to your boss and others. Other tactics include being seen at social functions, being active in your professional associations, and developing powerful allies who speak positively of you.

Don't Stay Too Long in Your First Job   Evidence has shown that given a choice between staying in your first job until you've "really made a difference" or accepting an early transfer to a new job assignment, you should go for the early transfer.[57] By moving quickly through different jobs, you signal to others that you're on the fast track. This, then, often becomes a self-fulfilling prophecy. Start fast by seeking early transfers or promotions from your first management job.

Find a Mentor   It has become increasingly clear over the years that employees who aspire to higher levels in organizations often need the assistance and advocacy of someone higher up in the organization (see Ethical Issues in HRM).[58] These career progressions often require the favor of the dominant in-group that sets corporate goals, priorities, and standards. It's also interesting to note that when a good mentoring and protege relationship exists, employee stress is decreased.[59]

Support Your Boss   Your immediate future is in the hands of your current boss. He or she evaluates your performance, and you are unlikely to have enough power to successfully challenge this manager. Therefore, you should make the effort to help your boss succeed, be supportive if your boss is under siege from other organizational members, and find out how he or she will be assessing your work effectiveness. Don't undermine your boss or speak negatively of your boss to others. If your boss is competent and visible and possesses a power base, he or she is likely to be on the way up in the organization. If you are perceived as supportive, you might find yourself pulled along, too. If your boss's performance is poor and his or her power is negligible, you need to transfer to another unit. A mentor may be able to help you arrange a transfer. It's hard to have your competence recognized or your positive performance evaluation taken seriously if your boss is perceived as incompetent.

---

ethical issues in HRM

SPECIAL MENTORING PROGRAMS FOR WOMEN AND MINORITIES

WE HAVE BEEN WITNESSING MANY DISCUSSIONS lately regarding how more women and minorities can break through the glass ceiling. There is no doubt that these groups are underrepresented at the top echelons of organizations. Several reasons have been well documented detailing why this occurred. One of those reasons centers around the issue of mentoring.

Finding, or getting, a mentor to support you is rarely easy. In fact, more often than not, a mentor approaches you to begin the relationship. In the past, many of these individuals happened to be white males; and historically, women and minorities found it difficult to gain the favor of these mentors simply because mentors preferred someone more like them.

With the changing work-force composition, employment legislation, and changing societal views of women and minorities in the workplace, mentoring relationships for this group are occurring more frequently. But it is not, as yet, fully ingrained in the minds and hearts of some managers. Consequently, a number of organizations have developed special mentor-

ing programs for women and minorities—formalizing a practice that typically naturally evolved. In some respects, this may be the best way at this time to help further advance these two groups. Leaving it up to nature just doesn't work well. The prevalence of the glass ceiling dilemma attests to that. On the other hand, can a mentoring relationship be forced and regulated? The crux of these relationships is for an individual to become very close to his or her protégé in an effort to further one's career. Won't forcing these people together—two individuals who have not come together naturally—lead to a constrained relationship? Given the degree of conflict that may arise between the two, it's possible more harm than good for the protégé's career may result.

Should women and minorities be given special treatment in the mentoring relationship by having organizational policies dictating who will mentor and how it will be handed? Should there be special guidelines to ensure that mentoring for women and minorities occurs? And what about the white male? Is he being left out? What do you think?

Employees in organizations are continually reminded that a coach or mentor can provide valuable assistance. Mary Bradford surely understands that. With the help of a good coach, she was able to increase her team's sales nearly 60 percent. At Met Life, that put her in a bright spotlight!

Stay Mobile   You're likely to advance more rapidly if you indicate your willingness to move to different geographical locations and across functional lines within the organization. Career advancement may also be facilitated by your willingness to change organizations. Working in a slow-growth, stagnant, or declining organization should make mobility even more important to you.

Think Laterally   Lateral thinking acknowledges the changing world of management. Because of organizational changes, there are fewer rungs on the promotion ladder in many large organizations. To survive in this environment, you should think in terms of lateral career moves. It's important to recognize that lateral movers in the 1960s and 1970s were presumed to be mediocre performers. That presumption doesn't hold today. Lateral shifts are now a viable career consideration. They give you a wider range of experiences, which enhances your long-term mobility. In addition, these moves can energize you by making your work more interesting and satisfying. So if you're not moving ahead in your organization, consider a lateral move internally or a lateral shift to another organization.

Keep Your Skills Current   Organizations need employees who can readily adapt to the demands of the rapidly changing marketplace. Focusing on skills that you currently have and continuing to learn new skills can establish your value to the organization. It's the employees who don't add value to an organization whose jobs (and career advancement) are in jeopardy. College graduation is not an end. Rather, it's the beginning of a continued lifelong learning journey. And remember, it's your responsibility to manage your career.

College graduation is not an end. Rather, it's the beginning of a continued lifelong learning journey.

Develop a Network   Our final suggestion is based on the recognition that a network of friends, colleagues, neighbors, customers, suppliers, and so on can be a useful tool for career development. If you spend some time cultivating relationships and contacts throughout your industry and community, you'll be prepared if your current job is eliminated. Even if your job is in no danger of being cut, a network can prove beneficial in getting things done.

Some Final Words of Wisdom

Have you ever pondered the freight-train career ride of the Baby Boom generation that occurred from the 1960s through the 1980s? Did you ever wonder what climate existed that promoted some of these meteoric career heights in such a quick period? Were the Baby Boomers smarter than the Generation Xers or the dot-com'ers; or were they just luckier? A precise answer is difficult to pinpoint, but clearly luck played a major role. How so? Consider that during the 1960s, organizations in the United States experienced unprecedented growth. This meant new markets opened up, bringing along with them many new jobs.[60] Organizations during this period became overly hierarchical, which translated into the creation of managerial positions for almost any task that existed.

Undoubtedly, many of the Baby Boomers were in the right place, at the right time. But don't chalk it up solely to luck. The Baby Boomers were better educated than the generation preceding them, and they brought an aggressive trait to the work force that was rarely witnessed before. Furthermore, accepting almost any challenging assignment, being willing to relocate, and having the support of mentors all fostered a career boom. Unfortunately, this prosperity didn't last forever. In fact, many of these Baby Boomers who skyrocketed to the top in their first 10 to 15 years on the job were the ones hardest hit by the downsizing that began in the late 1980s. For them, and those that have followed, fast-tracked career progression may be a thing of the past. Our organizations just cannot afford to promote workers in droves as they once did. And, many of the jobs that served as stepping-stones to careers may be lost forever.

What, then, can you do to keep your career alive in today's dynamic organizations? The answer may lie in the acronym DATA.[61]

The *D* stands for *Desire*. Although experience was once perceived as the best preparation for the future, past experience may actually be a hindrance. The past may promote a status-quo mentality—one that is ill-fitted to a dynamic environment. Instead, your desire will be a key factor in your career growth. If you desire to be the best in your field, continually strive to excel, and perform under a variety of difficult situations, you'll have an advantage over those who don't possess this trait.

You must have the *Ability* to perform the required work. This means that you can never sit back on your laurels and bask in that glory. Rather, you must continually upgrade your skills, knowledge, and abilities in order to become the best at your job. This also means looking closely at yourself and identifying your strengths and weaknesses, capitalizing on the strengths and working to develop the weaknesses. You must also have an appropriate *Temperament*. The security of yesterday's jobs is gone.[62] You are on your own in many circumstances. And when the job is done, so, too, might be your association with the organization. That being the case, you must have a disposition that easily adjusts to an ever-changing work situation. Rigidity and the desire for security may be the ultimate killers of your career. Finally, you must possess a variety of *Assets*. This means that whatever resources the job requires, you must be able to provide them. This may be networking contacts, equipment, or even time commitments—all resources that contribute to a successful performer.

Succeeding in today's organizations needn't be a hopeless cause. You must recognize that yesterday's career paths don't exist everywhere. But with proper preparation and a positive mindset, you can open the doors to career growth.[63] This time, however, it will be solely your responsibility.

HRM WORKSHOP

*S*UMMARY

(This summary relates to the Learning Outcomes identified on p. 236.)

After having read this chapter, you should be able to:

1. **Explain who is responsible for managing careers.** The responsibility for managing a career belongs to the individual. The organization's role is to provide assistance and information to the employee, but it is not responsible for growing an employee's career.

2. **Describe what is meant by the term *career*.** A career is a sequence of positions occupied by a person during the course of a lifetime.

3. **Discuss the focus of careers for both the organization and individuals.** Career development from an organizational standpoint involves tracking career paths and developing career ladders. From an individual perspective, career development focuses on assisting individuals in identifying their major career goals and in determining what they need to do to achieve these goals.

4. **Describe how career development and employee development are different.** The main distinction between career development and employee development lies in their time frames. Career development focuses on the long-range career effectiveness and success of organizational personnel. Employee development focuses on more of the immediate and intermediate time frames.

5. **Explain why career development is valuable to organizations.** Career development is valuable to an organization because it (1) ensures needed talent will be available; (2) improves the organization's ability to attract and retain high-talent employees; (3) ensures that minorities and women get opportunities for growth and development; (4) reduces employee frustration; (5) enhances cultural diversity; (6) assists in implementing quality; and (7) promotes organizational goodwill.

6. **Identify the five traditional stages involved in a career.** The five stages in a career are exploration, establishment, mid-career, late-career, and decline.

7. **List the Holland Vocational Preferences.** The Holland Vocational Preferences are realistic, investigative, artistic, social, enterprising, and conventional.

8. **Describe the implications of Personality Typologies and jobs.** Typology focuses on personality dimensions including extroversion-introversion; sensing-intuition; thinking-feeling; and judging-perceiving. These four pairs can be combined into 16 different combination profiles. With this information, personality of jobs can be matched to personality of individuals.

9. **Identify several suggestions that you can use to manage your career more effectively.** Some suggestions for managing your career include: (1) select your first job judiciously; (2) do good work; (3) present the right image; (4) learn the power structure; (5) gain control of organizational resources; (6) stay visible; (7) don't stay too long in your first job; (8) find a mentor; (9) support your boss; (10) stay mobile; (11) think laterally; (12) think of your career in terms of skills you're acquiring and continue upgrading those skills; and (13) work harder than ever at developing a network.

MAKING A CAREER CHOICE

ABOUT THE SKILL: CAREER PLANNING is designed to assist you in becoming more knowledgeable of your needs, values, and personal goals. This can be achieved through the following three-step, self-assessment process.[64]

1. *Identify and organize your skills, interests, work-related needs, and values.* The best place to begin is by drawing up a profile of your educational record. List each school attended from high school on. What courses do you remember liking most and least? In what courses did you score highest and lowest? In what extracurricular activities did you participate? Are there any specific skills that you acquired? Are there other skills in which you have gained proficiency? Next, begin to assess your occupational experience. List each job you have held, the organization you worked for, your overall level of satisfaction, what you liked most and least about the job, and why you left. It's important to be honest in covering each of these points.

2. *Convert this information into general career fields and specific job goals.* By completing step 1, you should now have some insights into your interests and abilities. What you need to do now is look at how these can be converted into the kind of organizational setting or field of endeavor with which you will be a good match. Then you can become specific and identify distinct job goals. What fields are available? In business? In government? In nonprofit organizations? Your answer can be broken down further into areas such as education, financial, manufacturing, social services, or health services. Identifying areas of interest is usually far easier than pinpointing specific occupations. When you are able to identify a limited set of occupations that interest you, you can start to align these with your abilities and skills. Will certain jobs require you to move? If so, would this be compatible with your geographic preferences? Do you have the educational requirements necessary for the job? If not, what additional schooling will be needed? Does the job offer the status and earning potential that you aspire to? What is the long-term outlook for jobs in this field? Does the career suffer from cyclical employment? Since no job is without its drawbacks, have you seriously considered all the negative aspects? When you have fully answered questions such as these, you should have a relatively short list of specific job goals.

3. *Test your career possibilities against the realities of the organization or the job market.* The final step in this self-assessment process is testing your selection against the realities of the marketplace. This can be done by going out and talking with knowledgeable people in the fields, organizations, or jobs you desire. These informational interviews should provide reliable feedback as to the accuracy of your self-assessment and the opportunities in the fields and jobs that interest you.

DEMONSTRATING COMPREHENSION: *Questions for Review and Discussion*

1. Which career perspective is more relevant to HRM managers—the individual or the organizational? Defend your position.
2. Contrast employee development with career development. How are they alike? Different?
3. How might a formal career development program be consistent with an organization's affirmative action program?
4. Contrast the external and internal dimensions of a career. Which do you believe is more relevant in determining an employee's work behavior?
5. Do you think a person's age and career stage evolve together? Why or why not?
6. Which of the five traditional career stages is probably least relevant to HRM? Defend your position.

7. Which of the 16 Myers-Briggs Typologies do you believe are most consistent with the behaviors needed in (a) a sales position; (b) a computer programmer; and (c) an HRM recruiter? Support your selections.
8. "Women and minorities require more career attention than do white males." Do you agree or disagree with the statement? Why or why not?
9. "Investments in career development do not provide an organization a viable return on its investment. It simply raises employee expectations, and then, if not fulfilled, employees leave. Accordingly, the organization has trained employees for its competitors." Take a position in support of this statement, and one against it.
10. What is a mentor and how do you go about finding one?

CASE APPLICATION: *TEAM FUN!*

Tony, the Director of Human Resources for TEAM FUN!, and Bobby, the store manager for the new Florida branch store are sitting on the beach, sipping a cold one and watching the sun set over the Gulf of Mexico. Tony salutes his bottle to Bobby, "We had a great first week!"

Bobby agrees, "Kenny and Norton couldn't have done it better themselves! They're proud of us, I think."

Tony leans back in his chair, "Great guys. I can't believe they only stayed down here two days before turning us loose on our own. How did they start this? How did they get this way?"

Bobby, Kenny's son-in-law, says, "Gloria (Kenny's daughter) tells a good story. Seems Kenny and Norton have known each other since grade school. They played baseball, football, basketball, stickball. They went fishing, camping and exploring caves together. They loved all the games. Both had to have other people around to admire them, to be with them. Kenny was happy as long as everyone played. Norton was happy when they won, especially when they won big. They kept in touch through college and wives (both married their high school sweethearts) and kids. They played on community teams and were big in Little League coaching, stuff like that.

When they were about 45 years old, they had all the fame and fortune they wanted and decided to give their childhood another try. Kenny left a job as a radio-television marketing and promotions manager. Norton was a structural engineer for an auto manufacturer. They first started TEAM FUN! as a sporting equipment store and used equipment swap for middle school and high school teams. That's when their own kids were that age. Gloria remembers getting used softball equipment from the old store."

Tony stares at the water. "Wonder what I'll be doing when I hit the big 4 0? I could see myself still at TEAM FUN! I like all the people, and I think people are really important. Sports, fitness, balance, are all part of what is important to me. I'm ok with not alot of money. What about you?"

Bobby looks at him, "I think I'll own the business by then. I know how it could be more profitable. We could give leaner commissions and cut some of the benefits. I think it could be a lot bigger. Take on the major franchises. I'd like that. Maybe change the name to BOBBY TEAM FUN!

Questions:

1. Define career and success for Bobby, Tony, Kenny and Norton.
2. Trace career stages for each of them.
3. What career and employee development activities should Kenny and Norton provide for Bobby and Tony?
4. Identify Holland Vocational Preferences for Bobby, Tony, Kenny and Norton.
5. Suggest several career management strategies that Bobby and Tony could utilize.

WORKING WITH A TEAM: *Career Insights*

Imagine that you enter the elevator on your way to an interview for an entry-level job at the company for which you would most like to work. You are on the elevator with two other individuals. As you are heading to your floor, the elevator stalls, and it will be another 20 minutes before the mechanics are able to get the elevator moving. Not wanting to waste time, you and the two other individuals begin to talk, introduce yourselves, and find that each of you is in the building for an interview. You decide to pose questions to one another.

Take turns responding to the following questions—noting similarities and differences in your responses.

- Who do you think is responsible for your career?
- What are your plans to continue your education?
- Why did you pick your chosen career?
- What phase of your career development are you in?
- How would you match what you want out of life and your career? Career goals? Job goals?

- What are your skills, interests, work-related needs, and values?
- What courses do you like best and least? Which are most challenging and most difficult?
- Have you ever had a mentor? Share that experience.

Enhancing Your Writing Skills

1. Using the material presented earlier in HRM Skills, develop a two- to three-page response to your skills, interests, work-related needs, and values.

2. Visit America Online's career and work web page (on AOL, type key words *career* and *work*). Select careers, and work through the career guidance survey. After completing the survey, write up a two- to three-page analysis of the results you received. End the paper with some insight into what the survey indicated to you.

3. Write a two- to three-page paper on "Where I want to be in 10 years." Describe how you intend to get there, and what you'll have to do to increase your chances of attaining this goal.

www.wiley.com/college/decenzo

Endnotes

1. Based on the story by Patricia A. Galagan and Jennifer J. Salopek, "Thinking Differently About Difference," *Training and Development* (May 2000), pp. 52–54.

2. Daniel C. Feldman and Carrie R. Leana, "What Ever Happened to Laid-Off Executives?: A Study of Reemployment Challenges After Downsizing," *Organizational Dynamics* (Summer 2000), pp. 64–75; Sanford M. Jacoby, "Are Career Jobs Headed for Extinction?" *California Management Review* (Fall 1999), pp. 123–145; and Patricia Buhler, "Managing Your Career: No Longer Your Company's Responsibility," *Supervision* (November 1997), pp. 23–26.

3. Kristi Heim, "With Layoffs Up and Stock Prices Down at High-Tech Firms, Unions Step Up Their Quest for Power in the New Economy," *San Jose Mercury News* (December 28, 2000), p. A-1; "Three Million U.S. Jobs Cut in Seven Years, *Manpower Argus* (March 1996), p. 3; Manuel London, "Redeployment and Continuous Learning in the 21st Century: Hard Lessons and Positive Examples from the Downsizing Era," *Academy of Management Executive*, Vol. 10, No. 4 (November 1996), pp. 67–78; "New Paths to Success," *Fortune* (June 12, 1995), p. 90; and Bill Leonard, "Downsized & Out: Career Survival in the '90s" *HRMagazine* (June 1995), pp. 89–92.

4. Carolyn Griffith, "Building a Resilient Work Force," *Training* (Winter 1998), pp. 54–60.

5. Douglas T. Hall, *Careers in Organizations* (Santa Monica, CA: Goodyear Publishing, 1976); and J. Van Maanen and E. H. Schein, "Career Development," in J. R. Hackman and J. L. Suttle (eds.), *Improving Life at Work: Behavioral Sciences Approaches to Organizational Change* (Santa Monica, CA: Goodyear Publishing, 1977), pp. 341–355.

6. Jeffrey H. Greenhaus, *Career Management* (New York: Dryden Press, 1987), p. 6.

7. See, for instance, Ron MacLean, "My Start-Up, Myself," *Inc.* (October 17, 2000), pp. 210–211.

8. See, for instance, E. P. Cook, "1991 Annual Review: Practice and Research in Career Counseling and Development, 1990," *Career Development Quarterly* (February 1991), pp. 99–131.

9. Diane Cyr, "Life at the Top," *Working Mother* (March 2000), p. 75; and "What Gender Gap?" *Working Mother* (April 1999), p. 8; Valerie Frazee, "Expert Help for Dual-Career Couples," *Workforce* (March 1999), p. 18.

10. For write-ups on these two software packages, see Jim Meade, "Boost Careers and Succession Planning," *HRMagazine* (October 2000), pp. 175–178; and Jim Meade, "Self-Assessment Tool Helps Target Training," *HRMagazine* (May 2000), pp. 167–170.

11. For an interesting overview of the similarities, see Thomas A. Stewart, "Planning a Career in a World Without Managers," *Fortune* (March 20, 1995), pp. 72–80.

12. Donna Fenn, "Homegrown Employees," *Inc.* (July 1995), p. 93.

13. Justin Martin, "Employees Are Fighting Back," *Fortune* (August 8, 1994), p. 12.

14. See M. Koden and J. B. Rousener, *Workforce America: Managing Employee Diversity as a Vital Resource* (Homewood, IL: Irwin Publishing, 1991).

15. "Promoting a Development Culture in Your Organization: Using Career Development as a Change Agent," *HRMagazine* (February 1998), pp. 132–133; Kenneth Labich, "Making Diversity Pay," *Fortune* (September 9,

1996), p. 177; Rose Mary Wentling, "Breaking Down Barriers to Women's Success," *HRMagazine* (May 1995), pp. 79, 81.

16. R. S. Bangar, "Human Resource Development—Career and Skill," *Employment News* (January 17/23, 1998), p. 1.

17. Hal Lancaster, "Professionals Try Novel Way to Assess and Develop Skills," *Wall Street Journal* (August 2, 1995), p. B-1.

18. D. Yankelovich and J. Immerwahl, "The Emergence of Expressivism Will Revolutionize the Contract Between Workers and Employers," *Personnel Administrator* (December 1983), pp. 34–39, 114.

19. See B. B. Grossman and R. J. Blitzer, "Choreographing Careers," *Training and Development* (November 1991), pp. 68–89; R. Chanick, "Career Growth for Baby Boomers," *Personnel Journal* (January 1992), pp. 40–44.

20. Van Maanen and Schein.

21. Ibid.

22. Douglas T. Hall, *Careers in Organizations* (Santa Monica, CA: Goodyear Publishing, 1976).

23. Van Maanen and Schein.

24. See M. London and S. A. Stumpf, *Managing Careers* (Reading, MA: Addison Wesley, 1982); and A. S. Miner, "Organizational Evolution and the Social Ecology of Jobs," *American Sociological Review* (Fall 1991), pp. 772–785.

25. Cook, p. 99.

26. Greenhaus, p. 6.

27. Susan Caminiti, "Straight Talk," *Working Woman* (September 1999), pp. 66–69; Bennett J. Tepper, "Upward Maintenance Tactics in Supervisory Mentoring and Nonmentoring Relationships," *Academy of Management Journal*, Vol. 38, No. 4 (May 1995), p. 1191; Patricia Schiff Estess, "A Few Good Mentors," *Entrepreneur* (September 1995), p. 83; and Commerce Clearing House, "Should Your Company Encourage Mentoring?" *Human Resources Management: Ideas and Trends* (July 20, 1994), p. 122.

28. Betsy Morris, "So You're a Player: Do You Need a Coach?" *Fortune* (February 21, 2000), pp. 144–154.

29. See, for example, B. Rose Ragins and J. Cotton, "Mentoring Functions and Outcomes: A Comparison of Men and Women in Formal and Informal Mentoring Relationships," *Proceedings of the Fifty-Eighth Annual Meeting of the Academy of Management* (August 7–12, 1998), p. CAR-A1; J. A. Wilson and N. S. Elman, "Organizational Benefits of Mentoring," *Academy of Management Executive*, Vol. 4, No. 4 (November 1990), pp. 88–94.

30. "Work/Family Balance: News, Opinion, Child Care," *Working Woman* (April 1999), p. 8; and E. O. Wells, "The Mentors," *Inc.* (June 1998), p. 47, 52.

31. Charlene Marmer Solomon, "Cracks in the Glass Ceiling," *Workforce* (September 2000), p. 86.

32. Jonathan A. Segal, "Mirror-Image Mentoring," *HRMagazine* (March 2000), pp. 157–165. For another view on this topic, see Tammy Allen, Mark L. Poteet, and Joyce E. A. Russel, "Protege Selection by Mentors: What Makes the Difference?" *Journal of Organizational Behavior* (May 2000), pp. 271–282.

33. Ibid.

34. See Monica C. Higgins, Lloyd Trotter, Steven Luria Ablon, Stuart Pearson, and Mohan Mohan, "What Should C.J. Do?" *Harvard Business Review* (November–December

2000), pp. 43–52; Jennifer Hutchins, "Getting to Know You," *Workforce* (November 2000), pp. 44–48; Rochele Sharpe, "As Leaders, Women Rule," *Business Week* (November 20, 2000), pp. 74–84; Charles Benabou and Raphael Benabou, "Establishing a Formal Mentoring Program for Organizational Success," *National Productivity Review* (Autumn 2000), pp. 1–8; and Dave Zeilinski, "Mentoring Up," *Training* (October 2000), pp. 136–140.

35. See, for example, Donald E. Super, *The Psychology of Careers* (New York: Harper & Row, 1957); Edgar Schein, *Career Dynamics: Matching Individual and Organizational Needs* (Reading, MA: Addison Wesley, 1978); and Daniel J. Levinson, C. N. Darrow, E. B. Klein, M. H. Levinson, and B. McKee, *A Man's Life* (New York: Knopf, 1978).

36. For an interesting account of career failures and the success that can follow, see Patricia Sellers, "So You Fail, Now Bounce Back," *Fortune* (May 1, 1995), pp. 48–66.

37. See, for instance, "Career Management," *Black Enterprise* (November 1998), p. 143.

38. See Anne Fisher, "Six Ways to Supercharge Your Career," *Fortune* (January 13, 1997), pp. 46–48.

39. Betsy Morrie, "Executive Women Confront Mid-Life Crisis," *Fortune* (September 18, 1995), pp. 60–86; and Jaclyn Fierman, "Beating the Mid-Life Career Crisis," *Fortune* (September 6, 1993), p. 51.

40. See Max Messmer, "Moving Beyond a Career Plateau," *National Public Accountant* (September 2000), pp. 20–21; Louis Lemire, Tania Saba, and Yves-Chantal Gagnon, "Managing Career Plateauing in the Quebec Public Sector," *Public Personnel Management* (Fall 1999), pp. 375–391; Janice Baker Corzine, Gabriel F. Buntzman, and Edgar T. Busch, "Machiavellianism in U. S. Bankers," *International Journal of Organizational Analysis* (January 1999), pp. 72–83; Mary Beth Regan, "Your Next Job," *Business Week* (October 13, 1997), pp. 64–72; Frederic M. Hudson, "When Careers Turn Stale," *Next* (Lakewood, CA: American Association of Retired Persons, 1994), p. 3; and Julie Connelly, "Have You Gone as Far as You Can Go?" *Fortune* (December 26, 1994), p. 231.

41. Harvey Schachter, "Careers," *Canadian Business* (April 1997), p. 70; Shari Caudron, "Downshifting Yourself," *Industry Week* (May 20, 1996), p. 126; Ronald Henkoff, "So You Want to Change Your Job," *Fortune* (January 15, 1996), p. 52; and Shari Caudron, "Pursue Your Passion," *Industry Week* (September 2, 1996), p. 27.

42. Adele Scheele, "Moving Over Instead of Up," *Working Woman* (November 1993), pp. 75–76.

43. See, for instance, Belle Rose Ragins, "Diversified Mentoring Relationships in Organizations: A Power Perspective," *Academy of Management Review*, Vol. 22, No. 2 (April 1997), pp. 482–521.

44. D. E. Super, "A Life-span Life Space Approach to Career Development," *Journal of Vocational Behavior*, Vol. 16 (Spring 1980), pp. 282–298. See also E. P. Cook, pp. 99–131, and M. Arthur, *Career Theory Handbook* (Englewood Cliffs, NJ: Prentice-Hall, 1991). See also Louis S. Richman, "The New Worker Elite," *Fortune* (August 22, 1994), pp. 56–66.

45. John Holland, *Making Vocational Choices*, 2nd ed. (Englewood Cliffs, NJ: Prentice-Hall, 1985).

46. For an interesting discussion of Schein anchors, see Edgar H. Schein, "Career Anchors Revisited: Implications for Career Development in the 21st Century," *Academy of Man-

agement Journal, Vol. 10, No. 1 (January 1996), pp. 80–88; and Daniel C. Feldman and Mark C. Bolino, "Career Patterns of the Self-Employed: Career Motivations and Career Outcomes," *Journal of Small Business Management* (July 2000), pp. 53–67.

47. Isabel Briggs-Myers, *Introduction to Type* (Palo Alto, CA: Consulting Psychologists Press, 1980).

48. Robert P. Hanlon, Jr., "The Use of Typology in Financial Planning," *Journal of Financial Planning* (July 2000), pp. 96–112; and Stephen P. Robbins, *Organizational Behavior,* 9th ed. (Upper Saddle River, NJ: Prentice-Hall, 2001), p. 95.

49. Ibid., pp. 7–8.

50. D. T. Hall and Associates, *The Career Is Dead—Long Live the Career: A Relational Approach to Careers* (San Francisco, CA: Jossey-Bass, 1996). See also Douglas T. Hall, "Protean Careers of the 21st Century," *Academy of Management Journal,* Vol. 10, No. 4 (November 1996), pp. 8–16; and Hal Lancaster, "A New Social Contract to Benefit Employer and Employee," *Wall Street Journal* (November 29, 1994), p. B-1.

51. Hal Lancaster, "Managing Your Career: You, and Only You, Must Stay in Charge of Your Employability," *Wall Street Journal* (November 15, 1994), p. B-1.

52. D. E. Super, "A Life-span Life Space Approach to Career Development," *Journal of Vocational Behavior,* Vol. 16 (Spring 1980), pp. 282–298; E. P. Cook, pp. 99–131; M. Arthur, *Career Theory Handbook* (Englewood Cliffs, NJ: Prentice Hall, 1991); L. S. Richman, "The New Worker Elite," *Fortune* (August 22, 1994), pp. 56–66; Lynne Cusack, "Is It Time for a Career Change?" *Working Mother* (April 1998), p. 31; T. S. Price, "Surviving Job Change," *Industry Week* (February 19, 1996), p. 57; and Julie Connelly, "How to Choose Your Next Career," *Fortune* (February 6, 1995), p. 145.

53. A. N. Schoonmaker, *Executive Career Strategy* (New York: American Management Association, 1971); A. J. DuBrin, *Fundamentals of Organizational Behavior: An Applied Perspective,* 2nd ed. (Elmsford, NY: Pergamon Press, 1978), Chapter 5; E. E. Jennings, "Success Chess," *Management of Personnel Quarterly* (Fall 1980), pp. 2–8; and R. Henkoff, "Winning the New Career Game," *Fortune* (July 12, 1993), pp. 46–49.

54. J. E. Sheridan, J. W. Slocum Jr., R. Buda, and R. C. Thompson, "Effects of Corporate Sponsorship and Departmental Power on Career Tournaments," *Academy of Management Journal* (September 1990), pp. 578–602.

55. See also Sheila J. Henderson, "Follow Your Bliss: A Process for Career Happiness," *Journal of Counseling and Development* (Summer 2000), pp. 305–315.

56. Stanley Bing, "How to Succeed in Business," *Fortune* (May 1, 2000), p. 81.

57. Ibid.

58. E. O. Wells, "The Mentors," *Inc.* (June 1998), pp. 49–61; B. J. Tepper, "Upward Maintenance Tactics in Supervisory Mentoring and Nonmentoring Relationships," *Academy of Management Journal,* Vol. 38, No. 4 (May 1995), p. 1191; P. S. Estess, "A Few Good Mentors," *Entrepreneur* (September 1995), p. 83; and Commerce Clearing House, "Should Your Company Encourage Mentoring?" *Human Resources Management: Ideas and Trends* (July 20, 1994), p. 122.

59. John J. Sosik and Veronica M. Godshalk, "Leadership Styles, Mentoring Functions Received, and Job-Related Stress: A Conceptual Model and Preliminary Study," *Journal of Organizational Behavior* (June 2000), p. 365.

60. Carole L. Jurkiewicz and Roger G. Brown, "GenXers vs. Boomers vs. Matures: Generational Comparisons of Public Employee Motivation," *Review of Public Personnel Administration* (Fall 1998), pp. 18–37.

61. William Bridges, "The End of the Job," *Fortune* (September 19, 1994), p. 72; and Patricia Sellers, "Don't Call Me Slacker!" *Fortune* (December 12, 1994), pp. 181–182.

62. See Betsy Morris, "MBAs Get .Com Fever," *Fortune* (August 2, 1999), pp. 60–66; and Louis S. Richman, "Getting Past Economic Insecurity," *Fortune* (April 17, 1995), pp. 161–168.

63. See, for instance, John H. Sheridan, "Selling Skills, Not Experience," *Industry Week* (January 8, 1996), pp. 15–18; Hal Lancaster, "Managers Beware: You're Not Ready for Tomorrow's Jobs," *Wall Street Journal* (January 24, 1995), p. B-1.

64. I. R. Schwartz, "Self-Assessment and Career Planning: Matching Individuals and Organizational Goals," *Personnel* (January–February 1979), p. 48.

10

EVALUATING EMPLOYEE PERFORMANCE

LEARNING OUTCOMES

AFTER READING THIS CHAPTER, YOU WILL BE ABLE TO:

1. Identify the three purposes of performance management systems and who is served by them.
2. Explain the six steps in the appraisal process.
3. Discuss what is meant by absolute standards in performance management systems.
4. Describe what is meant by relative standards in performance management systems.
5. Discuss how MBO can be used as an appraisal method.
6. Explain why performance appraisals might be distorted.
7. Identify ways to make performance management systems more effective.
8. Describe what is meant by the term *360-degree appraisal*.
9. Discuss how performance appraisals may differ in the global village.

I to-Yokado Co., the majority owner of 7-Eleven, is shipping the performance system it uses in its more than 5,700 Japanese stores across the Pacific to the United States. And American managers at these 7-Elevens aren't too thrilled with how their performance is going to be evaluated; nor with the organizational changes implemented during the past few years.[1] That's because over the past decade (since Ito-Yokado purchased 7-Eleven from the Texas-based Southland Corporation in 1991) U.S. 7-Elevens have had to change to their owner's performance requirements.

For example, the system new to the U.S. has been in place in Japan's 7-Elevens for several decades. Toshifumi Suzuki, Ito-Yokado's CEO, credits the performance management system with doubling unit sales in Japan and dramatically cutting inventory costs for the company. Specifically, the average Japanese store currently turns over its inventory every 7 days, down from 25 days in the 1970s. Now Suzuki wants to bring his performance management system to the U.S. to improve the efficiency of the company's American operations.

What must U.S. 7-Eleven managers do? Essentially, their stores will be computer linked to headquarters in Tokyo and every point of sales will be recorded. This system will now schedule 7-Eleven's managers' activities. It will monitor how much time they spend using analytical tools built into the cash registers to track product sales. They will be evaluated on how they review this sales data, demographic trends, and local weather forecasts graphed out on the computer screen in each store.

The premise behind these requirements is to help store managers fine-tune orders to a daily deadline. Based on sales, store managers will receive deliveries up to three times a day. The precise timing of the reports ensures that sandwiches, deli dishes, and other perishables will be fresh and that none is wasted. Undoubtedly, the performance requirements impose a strict regimen on store managers. Headquarters staff rank stores by how often store personnel use the computers. In one case, for example, a manager of one 7-Eleven was cited for using the computer to check on an average of 600 products a week. He was told to "shape up and use the computer more." For this owner, he feels his performance is not truly of his own desire—rather, it's like being under 24-hour surveillance.

INTRODUCTION

Every year, most employees experience an evaluation of their past performance. This may take the form of a five-minute informal discussion between employees and their supervisors, or a more elaborate, several-week process involving many specific steps. Irrespective of their formality, however, employees generally see these evaluations as having some direct effect on their work lives. They may result in increased pay, a promotion, or assistance in personal development areas for which the employee needs some training. As a result, any evaluation of employees' work can create an emotionally charged event. Because the performance evaluation is not the simple process it once was, it is now more critical to perform one while simultaneously focusing on key activities of the job. For example, should an employee's body language in terms of interactions with other employees and customers become part of the employee's performance evaluation? How about how well a manager serves as a mentor to her employees? Moreover, should a supervisor's employees have input into their boss's effectiveness at work? Should employee ability to perform tasks in a timely and accurate manner matter in an evaluation of their work? Questions like these cannot be overlooked. If we want to know how well our employees are doing, we've got to measure their performance—not necessarily an easy task. Many factors go into the performance evaluation process, such as why do we do them, who should benefit from the evaluation, what type of evaluation should be used, and what problems we might encounter. This chapter seeks answers to these and several other important factors in the performance-appraisal process.

Before beginning this chapter, however, recognize that no performance appraisal system is perfect. There are a lot of reasons for completing them properly, but sometimes that simply doesn't happen. That may be a function of poor appraisal training or obsolete measures. It could also be the result of the dynamic environment in which employees work. That is, the job changes so frequently that it's almost impossible to properly define what an employee is supposed to do over the next 12 months. As a result, performance appraisals have come under attack.[2]

Regardless of the potential problems that may exist, one can expect performance management systems to survive in some format. Accordingly, understanding the foundations of performance management systems, the way appraisals might be constructed, as well as the potential problems that one may encounter, is beneficial to anyone involved in contemporary organizations.

PERFORMANCE MANAGEMENT SYSTEMS

Performance management systems involve a number of activities. They are more than simply reviewing what an employee has done. These systems must fulfill several purposes.[3] Moreover, they are often constrained by difficulties in how they operate. Let's look at these two primary areas.

What Are the Purposes of a Performance Management System?

Nearly three decades ago, performance evaluations were designed primarily to tell employees how they had done over a period of time and to let them know what pay raise they would be getting. This was the "feedback" mechanism in place. Although this may have served its purpose then, today there are additional factors that must be addressed. Specifically, performance evaluations should also address development and documentation concerns.[4]

Performance appraisals must convey to employees how well they have performed on established goals. It's also desirable to have these goals and performance measures mutually set between the employee and the supervisor. Without proper two-way feedback about one's effort and its effect on performance, we run the risk of decreasing an employee's motivation. However, equally important to feedback is the issue of development.[5] By development, we are referring to those areas in which an employee has a deficiency or weakness, or an area that simply could be better if some effort was expended to enhance performance. For example, suppose a college professor demonstrates extensive knowledge in his or her field and conveys this knowledge to students in an adequate way. Although this individual's performance may be regarded as satisfactory, his or her peers may indicate that some improvements could be made. In this case, then, development may include exposure to different methods of teaching, such as bringing into the classroom more experiential exercises, real-world applications, Internet applications, case analyses, and so forth.[6]

Without proper two-way feedback about one's effort and its effect on performance, we run the risk of decreasing an employee's motivation.

Documentation Used as a record of the performance appraisal process outcomes.

Finally comes the issue of **documentation**. A performance evaluation system would be remiss if it did not concern itself with the legal aspects of employee performance. Recall in Chapter 3 the discussion about EEO and the need for job-related measures. Those job-related measures must be performance-supported when an HRM decision affects current employees. For instance, suppose a supervisor has decided to terminate an employee. Although the supervisor cites performance matters as the reason for the discharge, a review of recent performance appraisals of this employee indicates that performance was evaluated as satisfactory for the last two review periods. Accordingly, unless this employee's performance significantly decreased (and assuming that proper methods to correct the performance deficiency were performed), personnel records do not support the supervisor's decision. This critique by HRM is absolutely critical—to ensure that employees are fairly treated and that the organization is "protected." Additionally, in our discussion of sexual harassment in Chapter 3, we addressed the need for employees to keep copies of past performance appraisals. If retaliation (such as termination or poor job assignments) for refusing a supervisor's advances occurs, existing documentation can show that the personnel action was inappropriate (see Ethical Issues in HRM). That's because it may not be consistent with past performance—but attributable to something else, like the harassment!

Because documentation issues are prevalent in today's organizations, HRM must make the effort to ensure that the evaluation systems used support the legal needs of the organization. However, even though the performance appraisal process is geared to serve the organization, we should also recognize two other important players in the process: employees and their appraisers. Through timely and accurate feedback and development we can better serve employees' needs. In doing so, we may also be in a better position to show the effort-performance linkage.

Next, we should keep in mind the needs of the appraiser. If feedback, development, and documentation are to function effectively, appraisers must have a performance system that is appropriate for their needs—a system that facilitates giving feedback and development information to their employees, and one that allows for employee input. For example, if appraisers are required to evaluate their employees using inappropriate performance measures, or answer questions about employees that have little bearing on the job, then the system may not provide the same benefits as one where such negatives are removed. In contrast to evaluations used decades ago, it's acceptable, and absolutely necessary, for the evaluation criteria used to be different for some jobs. Tailoring the evaluation process to the job analysis and the organization's and employee's goals is the difference between an evaluation system that is satisfactory and one that is an integral part of the HRM process.

To create the performance management system we desire, however, we must recognize that difficulties in the process may exist. We must look for ways to either overcome these difficulties or deal with them more effectively. Let's turn our attention to these challenges.

What Difficulties Exist in Performance Management Systems?

When you consider that three constituencies coexist in this process—employees, appraisers, and organizations—coordinating the needs of each may cause problems. By focusing on the difficulties, we can begin to address them in such a way that we can reduce their overall consequence in the process. In terms of difficulties, two primary categories can be addressed: (1) the focus on the individual, and (2) the focus on the process.

Focus on the Individual   Do you remember the last time you received a graded test from a professor and felt that something was marked incorrect that wasn't wrong, or that your answer was too harshly penalized? How did you feel about that? Did you accept the score and leave it at that, or did you question the instructor? Whenever performance evaluations are administered (and tests are one form of performance evaluation), we run into the issue of having peo-

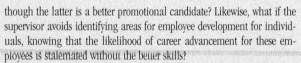

THE INACCURATE PERFORMANCE APPRAISAL

MOST INDIVIDUALS RECOGNIZE THE IMPORTANCE OF effective performance management systems in an organization. Not only are they necessary for providing feedback to employees and for identifying personal development plans, they serve an important legal purpose. Furthermore, organizations that fail to accurately manage employee performance often find themselves facing difficult times in meeting their organizational goals.[7]

Most individuals would also agree that performance appraisals must meet Equal Employment Opportunity requirements. That is, they must be administered in such a way that they result in a fair and equitable treatment for the diversity that exists in the workplace. Undeniably, this is an absolute necessity. But what about those gray areas—instances where an evaluation meets legal requirements, but verges on a questionable practice? For example, what if a manager deliberately evaluates a favored employee higher than one he likes less, even

though the latter is a better promotional candidate? Likewise, what if the supervisor avoids identifying areas for employee development for individuals, knowing that the likelihood of career advancement for these employees is stalemated without the better skills?

Supporters of properly functioning performance appraisals point to two vital criteria that managers must bring to the process—sincerity and honesty. Yet, there are no legislative regulations, like EEO laws, that enforce such ethical standards. Thus, they may be, and frequently are, missing from the evaluation process.

Can an organization have an effective performance-appraisal process without sincerity and honesty dominating the system? Can organizations develop an evaluation process that is ethical? Should we expect companies to spend training dollars to achieve this goal? What do you think?

ple seeing "eye-to-eye" on the evaluation. Appraising individuals is probably one of the more difficult aspects of a supervisor's job. Why? Because emotions are involved, and sometimes supervisors just don't like to do appraisals.[8] We all think we are performing in an outstanding fashion, but that may very well be *our* perception. And although our work is good, and a boss recognizes it, it may not be seen as outstanding. Accordingly, in evaluating performance, emotions may arise.[9] And if these emotions are not dealt with properly (we'll look at ways to enhance performance evaluations later in this chapter), they can lead to greater conflict. In fact, consider the aforementioned test example, assuming you confronted the professor. Depending on the encounter, especially if it is aggressive, both of you may become defensive. And because of the conflict, nothing but ill feelings may arise. For appraisers, the same thing applies. You both differ on the performance outcomes.[10]

When that occurs, it may lead to a situation in which emotions overcome both parties. This is not the way for evaluations to be handled. Accordingly, our first concern in the process is to remove the emotion difficulty from the process. When emotions do not run high in these meetings, employee satisfaction of the process increases,[11] and additionally, this satisfaction carries over into future job activities, where both the employee and supervisor have opportunities to have ongoing feedback in an effort to fulfill job expectations.[12]

Focus on the Process   Wherever performance evaluations are conducted, there is a particular structure that must be followed. This structure exists to facilitate the documentation process that often allows for some sort of a quantifiable evaluation. Additionally, HRM policies often exist that dictate performance outcomes. For example, if a company ties performance evaluations to pay increases, consider the following potential difficulty. Sometime during spring, managers develop budgets for their units—budgets that are dictated and approved by upper management. Now in this budget for the next fiscal year, each manager's salary budget increases by 4 percent. As we enter the new fiscal year, we evaluate our employees. One in particular has done an outstanding job and is awarded a 6 percent raise. What does this do to our budget? To average 4 percent, some employees will get less than the 4 percent salary increase. Consequently, company policies and procedures may present barriers to a properly functioning appraisal process.[13]

Furthermore, to get these numbers to balance means that rather than accentuating the positive work behaviors of some employees, an appraiser focuses on the negative.[14] This can lead to a tendency to search for problems, which can ultimately lead to an emotional encounter. We may also find from the appraiser's perspective some uncertainty about how and what to measure, or how to deal with the employee in the evaluation process.[15] Frequently, appraisers are poorly trained in how to evaluate an employee's performance. Because of this lack of training, appraisers may make errors in their judgment, or permit biases to enter into the process. We'll talk more about these problems later.

Because difficulties may arise, we should begin to develop our performance appraisal process so that we can achieve maximum benefit from it. This maximum benefit can be translated into employee satisfaction with the process. Such satisfaction is achieved by creating an understanding of the evaluation criteria used, permitting employee participation in the process, and allowing for development needs to be addressed.[16] To begin doing so requires us to initially understand the appraisal process.

PERFORMANCE APPRAISALS AND EEO

Performance evaluations are an integral part of most organizations. Properly developed and implemented, the performance appraisal process can help an organization achieve its goals by developing productive employees. Although there are many types of performance evaluation systems, each with its own advantages and disadvantages, we must be aware of the legal implications that arise.

EEO laws require organizations to have HRM practices that are bias free. For HRM, this means that performance evaluations must be objective and job related. That is, they must be reliable and valid! Furthermore, under the Americans with Disabilities Act, performance appraisals must also be able to measure "reasonable" performance success. To assist in these matters, two factors arise: (1) The performance appraisal must be conducted according to some established intervals; and (2) appraisers must be trained in the process.[17] The reasons for this become crystal clear when you consider that any employee action, like a promotion or termination, must be based on valid data—data prescribed from the performance evaluation document.[18] These objective data often support the legitimacy of employee actions.[19]

THE APPRAISAL PROCESS

The appraisal process (Exhibit 10-1) begins with the establishment of performance standards in accordance with the organization's strategic goals. These should have evolved out of the company's strategic direction—and, more specifically, the job analysis and the job description discussed in Chapter 5.[20] These performance standards should also be clear and objective enough to be understood and measured. Too often, these standards are articulated in ambiguous phrases that tell us little, such as "a full day's work" or "a good job." What is a "full day's work" or a "good job"? The expectations a supervisor has in terms of work performance by her employees must be clear enough in her mind so that she will be able to, at some later date, communicate these expectations to her employees, mutually agree to specific job performance measures, and appraise their performance against these established standards.

EXHIBIT 10-1
The Appraisal Process

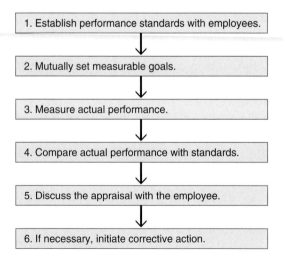

1. Establish performance standards with employees.

↓

2. Mutually set measurable goals.

↓

3. Measure actual performance.

↓

4. Compare actual performance with standards.

↓

5. Discuss the appraisal with the employee.

↓

6. If necessary, initiate corrective action.

One of the primary reasons for having an effective performance management system in an organization is that it can help reduce emotional confrontations. Everyone needs to recognize that emotions may run high during a performance evaluation session. However, with a properly designed system and effective implementation (including effective appraiser training) emotional outbursts can be significantly reduced.

Once performance standards are established, it is necessary to communicate these expectations; it should not be part of the employees' job to guess what is expected of them. Too many jobs have vague performance standards, and the problem is compounded when these standards are set in isolation and do not involve the employee.[21] It is important to note that communication is a two-way street: mere transference of information from the supervisor to the employee regarding expectations is not communication! The third step in the appraisal process is the measurement of performance. To determine what actual performance is, it is necessary to acquire information about it. We should be concerned with how we measure and what we measure.

Four common sources of information are frequently used by managers regarding how to measure actual performance: personal observation, statistical reports, oral reports, and written reports. Each has its strengths and weaknesses; however, a combination of them increases both the number of input sources and the probability of receiving reliable information. What we measure is probably more critical to the evaluation process than how we measure, since the selection of the wrong criteria can result in serious, dysfunctional consequences. And what we measure determines, to a great extent, what people in the organization will attempt to excel at. The criteria we measure must represent performance as it was mutually set in the first two steps of the appraisal process.

The fourth step in the appraisal process is the comparison of actual performance with standards. The point of this step is to note deviations between standard performance and actual performance so that we can proceed to the fifth step in the process—the discussion of the appraisal with the employee. As we mentioned previously, one of the most challenging tasks facing appraisers is to present an accurate assessment to the employee. Appraising performance may touch on one of the most emotionally charged activities—the evaluation of another individual's contribution and ability.[22] The impression that employees receive about their assessment has a strong impact on their self-esteem and, very importantly, on their subsequent performance. Of course, conveying good news is considerably less difficult for both the appraiser and the employee than conveying the bad news that performance has been below expectations. In this context, the discussion of the appraisal can have negative as well as positive motivational consequences.

The final step in the appraisal is the identification of corrective action where necessary. Corrective action can be of two types: one is immediate and deals predominantly with symptoms, and the other is basic and delves into causes. Immediate corrective action is often described as "putting out fires," whereas basic corrective action gets to the source of deviation and seeks to adjust the difference permanently. Immediate action corrects something right now and gets things back on track. Basic corrective action asks how and why performance deviated. In some instances, appraisers may rationalize that they do not have the time to take basic corrective action and therefore must be content to "perpetually put out fires." Good supervisors recognize that taking a little time to analyze the problem today may prevent the problem from getting worse tomorrow.

APPRAISAL METHODS

The previous section described the appraisal process in general terms. In this section we will look at specific ways in which HRM can actually establish performance standards and devise instruments that can be used to measure and appraise an employee's performance. Three different approaches exist for doing appraisals: employees can be appraised against (1) absolute standards, (2) relative standards, or (3) objectives. No one approach is always best; each has its strengths and weaknesses.[23]

In What Ways Can One Evaluate Absolute Standards?

Our first group of appraisal methods uses **absolute standards**. This means that employees are compared to a standard; and their evaluation is independent of any other employee in a work group. Included in this group are the following methods: the essay appraisal, the critical incident appraisal, the checklist, the adjective rating scale, forced choice, and behaviorally anchored rating scales. Let's look at each of these, focusing on their strengths and weaknesses.

Absolute Standards Measuring an employee's performance against some established standards.

The Essay Appraisal   Probably the simplest method of appraisal is to have the appraiser write a narrative describing an employee's strengths, weaknesses, past performance, potential, and suggestions for improvement. The strength of the **essay appraisal** lies in its simplicity. It requires no complex forms or extensive training to complete. The essay appraisal is also valuable in providing specific information, much of which can be easily fed back and understood by the employee.

However, inherent in this method are several weaknesses. Because the essays are unstructured, they are likely to vary widely in terms of length and content. This makes it difficult to compare individuals across the organization. And, of course, some raters are better writers than others. So a "good" or "bad" evaluation may be determined as much by the rater's writing skill as by the employee's actual level of performance. This method also provides only qualitative data. HRM decisions generally improve when useful quantitative data is obtained because it enables employees to be compared and ranked more objectively.

In spite of its inherent weaknesses, the essay appraisal is a good start. It's also very beneficial if used in conjunction with other appraisal methods.

Essay Appraisal A performance appraisal method whereby an appraiser writes a narrative about the employee.

The Critical Incident Appraisal   **Critical incident appraisal** focuses the rater's attention on those critical or key behaviors that make the difference between doing a job effectively and doing it ineffectively. The appraiser writes down anecdotes describing what the employee did that was especially effective or ineffective. For example, a police sergeant might write the following critical incident about one of her officers: "Brought order to a volatile situation by calmly discussing options with an armed suspect during a hostage situation which resulted in all hostages being released, and the suspect being apprehended without injury to any individual." Note that with this approach to appraisal, specific behaviors are cited, not vaguely defined individual traits. A behavior-based appraisal such as this should be more valid than trait-based appraisals because it is clearly more job related. It is one thing to say that an employee is "aggressive," "imaginative," or "relaxed," but that does not tell us anything about how well the job is being done. Critical incidents, with their focus on behaviors, judge performance rather than personalities.

The strength of the critical incident method is that it looks at behaviors. Additionally, a list of critical incidents on a given employee provides a rich set of examples from which employees can be shown which of their behaviors are desirable and which ones call for improvement. Its drawbacks are basically that: (1) appraisers are required to regularly write these incidents down, and doing this on a daily or weekly basis for all employees is time-consuming and burdensome for supervisors; and (2) critical incidents suffer from the same com-

Critical incident Appraisal A performance appraisal method that focuses on the key behaviors that make the difference between doing a job effectively or ineffectively.

	Yes	No
1. Are supervisor's orders usually followed?	___	___
2. Does the individual approach customers promptly?	___	___
3. Does the individual suggest additional merchandise to customers?	___	___
4. Does the individual keep busy when not servicing a customer?	___	___
5. Does the individual lose his or her temper in public?	___	___
6. Does the individual volunteer to help other employees?	___	___

parison problem found in essays—mainly, they do not lend themselves easily to quantification. Therefore the comparison and ranking of employees may be difficult.

Checklist Appraisal A performance appraisal type in which a rater checks off those attributes of an employee that apply.

The Checklist Appraisal In the **checklist appraisal**, the evaluator uses a list of behavioral descriptions and checks off those behaviors that apply to the employee. As Exhibit 10-2 illustrates, the evaluator merely goes down the list and checks off "yes" or "no" to each question.

Once the checklist is complete, it is usually evaluated by the HRM staff, not the appraiser completing the checklist. Therefore the rater does not actually evaluate the employee's performance; he or she merely records it. An analyst in HRM then scores the checklist, often weighing the factors in relationship to their importance to that specific job. The final evaluation can then be returned to the appraiser for discussion with the employee, or someone from HRM can provide the feedback to the employee.

The checklist appraisal reduces some bias in the evaluation process since the rater and the scorer are different. However, the rater usually can pick up the positive and negative connections in each item—so bias can still be introduced. From a cost standpoint, too, this appraisal method may be inefficient if there are a number of job categories for which an individualized checklist of items must be prepared.

Adjective Rating Scales A performance appraisal method that lists a number of traits and a range of performance for each.

The Adjective Rating Scale Appraisal One of the oldest and most popular methods of appraisal is the **adjective rating scale**.[24] An example of some rating scale items is shown in Exhibit 10-3. Rating scales can be used to assess factors such as quantity and quality of work, job knowledge, cooperation, loyalty, dependability, attendance, honesty, integrity, attitudes, and initiative. However, this method is most valid when abstract traits like loyalty or integrity are avoided, unless they can be defined in more specific behavioral terms.[25]

To use the adjective rating scale, the assessor goes down the list of factors and notes the point along the scale or continuum that best describes the employee. There are typically five to ten points on the continuum. In the design of the rating scale, the challenge is to ensure that both the factors evaluated and the scale points are clearly understood and are unambiguous to the rater. Should ambiguity occur, bias is introduced.

Why are rating scales popular? Although they do not provide the depth of information that essays or critical incidents do,[26] they are less time-consuming to develop and administer. They also provide a quantitative analysis that is useful for comparison purposes. Furthermore, in contrast to the checklist, there is more generalization of items so that comparability with other individuals in diverse job categories is possible.[27]

EXHIBIT 10-3
Sample of Adjective Rating Scale Items and Format

Performance Factor	Performance Rating				
	☐	☐	☐	☐	☐
Quality of work is the accuracy, skill, and completeness of work.	Consistently unsatisfactory	Occasionally unsatisfactory	Consistently satisfactory	Sometimes superior	Consistently superior
	☐	☐	☐	☐	☐
Quality of work is the volume of work done in a normal workday.	Consistently unsatisfactory	Occasionally unsatisfactory	Consistently satisfactory	Sometimes superior	Consistently superior
	☐	☐	☐	☐	☐
Job knowledge is information pertinent to the job that an individual should have for satisfactory job performance.	Poorly informed about work duties	Occasionally unsatisfactory	Can answer most questions about the job	Understands all phases of the job	Has complete mastery of all phases of the job
	☐	☐	☐	☐	☐
Dependability is following directions and company policies without supervision.	Requires constant supervision	Requires occasional follow-up	Usually can be counted on	Requires very little supervision	Requires absolute minimum of supervision

Forced-choice Appraisal   A type of performance appraisal method in which the rater must choose between two specific statements about an employee's work behavior.

The Forced-Choice Appraisal   Have you ever completed one of those tests that presumably gives you insights into what kind of career you should pursue? (Questions might be, for example, "Would you rather go to a party with a group of friends or attend a lecture by a well-known political figure?") If so, then you are familiar with the forced-choice format. The **forced-choice appraisal** is a special type of checklist where the rater must choose between two or more statements. Each statement may be favorable or unfavorable. The appraiser's job is to identify which statement is most (or in some cases least) descriptive of the individual being evaluated. For instance, students evaluating their college instructor might have to choose between: "(a) keeps up with the schedule identified in the syllabus; (b) lectures with confidence; (c) keeps interest and attention of class; (d) demonstrates how concepts are practically applied in today's organizations; or (e) allows students the opportunity to learn concepts on their own." All the preceding statements could be favorable, but we really don't know. As with the checklist method, to reduce bias, the right answers are not known to the rater; someone in HRM scores the answers based on the answer key for the job being evaluated. This key should be validated so HRM is in a position to say that individuals with higher scores are better-performing employees.

The major advantage of the forced-choice method is that, because the appraiser does not know the "right" answers, it reduces bias and distortion.[28] For example, the appraiser may like a certain employee and intentionally want to give him a favorable evaluation, but this becomes difficult if one is not sure which response is most preferred. On the negative side, appraisers tend to dislike this method; many dislike being forced to make distinctions between similar-sounding statements. Raters also may become frustrated with a system in which they do not know what represents a "good" or "poor" answer. Consequently, they may try to second-guess the scoring key in order to get the formal appraisal to align with their intuitive appraisal.

The Behaviorally Anchored Rating Scales An approach that has received considerable attention by academics in past years involves **behaviorally anchored rating scales (BARS)**. These scales combine major elements from the critical incident and adjective rating scale approaches. The appraiser rates the employees based on items along a continuum, but the points are examples of actual behavior on the given job rather than general descriptions or traits. The enthusiasm surrounding BARS grew from the belief that the use of specific behaviors, derived for each job, should produce relatively error-free and reliable ratings. Although this promise has not been fulfilled,[29] it has been argued that this may be partly due to departures from careful methodology in the development of the specific scales themselves rather than to inadequacies in the concept.[30] BARS, too, has also been found to be very time-consuming.

Behaviorally anchored rating scales specify definite, observable, and measurable job behavior. Examples of job-related behavior and performance dimensions are generated by asking participants to give specific illustrations of effective and ineffective behavior regarding each performance dimension; these behavioral examples are then translated into appropriate performance dimensions. Those that are sorted into the dimension for which they were generated are retained. The final group of behavior incidents are then numerically scaled to a level of performance that each is perceived to represent. The identified incidents which have high rater agreement on performance effectiveness are retained for use as anchors on the performance dimension. The results of these processes are behavioral descriptions, such as anticipates, plans, executes, solves immediate problems, carries out orders, or handles emergency situations. Exhibit 10-4 is an example of a BARS for an employee relations specialist's scale.

The research on BARS indicates that while it is far from perfect, it does tend to reduce rating errors. Possibly its major advantage stems from the dimensions generated, rather than from any particular superiority of behavior over trait anchors.[31] The process of developing the behavioral scales is valuable for clarifying to both the employee and the rater which behaviors represent good performance and which don't. Unfortunately, it, too, suffers from the distortions inherent in most rating methods.[32] These distortions will be discussed later in this chapter.

What Are the Relative Standards Methods?

In the second general category of appraisal methods, individuals are compared against other individuals. These methods are **relative standards** rather than absolute measuring devices. The most popular of the relative methods are group order ranking, individual ranking, and paired comparison.

Group Order Ranking Group order ranking requires the evaluator to place employees into a particular classification, such as "top 20 percent." This method, for instance, is often used in recommending students to graduate schools. Evaluators are asked to rank the student in the top 5 percent, the next 5 percent, the next 15 percent, and so forth. But when used by appraisers to evaluate employees, raters deal with all their employees in their area. So, for example, if a rater has 20 employees, only four can be in the top fifth; and, of course, four also must be relegated to the bottom fifth.

Behaviorally Anchored Rating Scales (BARS) A performance appraisal technique that generates critical incidents and develops behavioral dimensions of performance. The evaluator appraises behaviors rather than traits.

Relative Standards Evaluating an employee's performance by comparing the employee with other employees.

EXHIBIT 10-4
Sample BARS for an
Employee Relations Specialist

Performance dimension scale development under BARS for the dimension "Ability to Absorb and Interpret Policies for an Employee Relations Specialist."

This employee relations specialist

	9 Could be expected to serve as an information source concerning new and changed policies for others in the organization
Could be expected to be aware quickly of program changes and explain these to employees	8
	7 Could be expected to reconcile conflicting policies and procedures correctly to meet HRM goals
Could be expected to recognize the need for additional information to gain a better understanding of policy changes	6
	5 Could be expected to complete various HRM forms correctly after receiving instruction on them
Could be expected to require some help and practice in mastering new policies and procedures	4
	3 Could be expected to know that there is always a problem, but go down many blind alleys before realizing they are wrong
Could be expected to incorrectly interpret guidelines, creating problems for line managers	2
	1 Could be expected to be unable to learn new procedures even after repeated explanations

Source: Reprinted from *Business Horizons* (August 1976), Copyright 1976 by the Foundation for the School of Business at Indiana University. Used with permission.

The advantage of this group ordering is that it prevents raters from inflating their evaluations so everyone looks good or from forcing the evaluations so everyone is rated near the average—outcomes that are not unusual with the adjective rating scale. The main disadvantages surface, however, when the number of employees being compared is small. At the extreme, if the evaluator is looking at only four employees, it is quite possible that all may be excellent, yet the evaluator may be forced to rank them into top quarter, second quarter, third quarter, and low quarter! Theoretically, as the sample size increases, the validity of relative scores as an accurate measure increases; but occasionally the technique is implemented with a small group, utilizing assumptions that apply to large groups.

Another disadvantage, which plagues all relative measures, is the "zero-sum game" consideration. This means that any change must add up to zero. For example, if there are 12 employees in a department performing at different levels of effectiveness, by definition, three are in the top quarter, three are in the second quarter, and so forth. The sixth-best employee, for instance, would be in the second quartile. Ironically, if two of the workers in the third or fourth quartiles leave the department and are not replaced, then our sixth-best employee now falls into the third quarter. Because comparisons are relative, an employee who is mediocre may score high only because he or she is the "best of the worst"; in contrast, an excellent performer who is matched against "stiff" competition may be evaluated poorly, when in absolute terms his or her performance is outstanding.

Individual Ranking Ranking employees' performance from highest to lowest.

Individual Ranking The **individual ranking** method requires the evaluator merely to list the employees in order from highest to lowest. In this process, only one employee can be rated "best." If the evaluator is required to appraise 30 individuals, this method assumes that the difference between the first and second employee is the same as that between the twenty-first and the twenty-second. Even though some of these employees may be closely grouped, this method typically allows for no ties. In terms of advantages and disadvantages, the individual ranking method carries the same pluses and minuses as group order ranking. For example, individual ranking may be more manageable in a department of six employees than in one where a supervisor must evaluate the 19 employees that report to her.

Paired Comparison Ranking individuals' performance by counting the number of times any one individual is the preferred member when compared with all other employees.

Paired Comparison The **paired comparison** method is calculated by taking the total of $[N(N-1)]/2$ comparisons. A score is obtained for each employee by simply counting the number of pairs in which the individual is the preferred member. It ranks each individual in relationship to all others on a one-on-one basis. If 10 employees are being evaluated, the first person is compared, one by one, with each of the other nine, and the number of times this person is preferred in any of the nine pairs is tabulated. Each of the remaining nine persons, in turn, is compared in the same way, and a ranking is formed by the greatest number of preferred "victories." This method ensures that each employee is compared against every other, but the method can become unwieldy when large numbers of employees are being compared.

How Can Objectives Be Used to Evaluate Employees?

The third approach to appraisal makes use of objectives. Employees are evaluated on how well they accomplished a specific set of objectives that have been determined to be critical in the successful completion of their job. This approach is frequently referred to as **management by objectives** (MBO).[33] Management by objectives is a process that converts organizational objectives into individual objectives. It consists of four steps: (1) goal setting, (2) action planning, (3) self-control, and (4) periodic reviews.

Management by Objectives (MBO) A performance appraisal method that includes mutual objective setting and evaluation based on the attainment of the specific objectives.

In goal setting, the organization's overall objectives are used as guidelines from which departmental and individual objectives are set. At the individual level, the supervisor and employee jointly identify those goals that are critical to fulfilling the requirements of the job as determined by job analysis. These goals are agreed on and then become the standards by which the employee's results will be evaluated. In action planning, the means are determined for achieving the ends established in goal setting; that is, realistic plans are developed to attain the objectives. This step includes identifying the activities necessary to accomplish the objective, establishing the critical relationships between these activities, estimating the time requirements for each activity, and determining the resources required to complete each activity.

Self-control refers to the systematic monitoring and measuring of performance—ideally, by having the employee review his or her own performance.[34] Inherent in allowing employees to control their own performance is a positive image of human nature. The MBO philosophy is built on the assumption that employees can be responsible, can exercise self-direction, and do not require external controls and threats of punishment to motivate them to work toward their objectives. Finally, with periodic progress reviews, corrective action is initiated when behavior deviates from the standards established in the goal-setting phase. Again, consistent with the MBO philosophy, these supervisor-employee reviews are conducted in a constructive rather than punitive manner. Reviews are not meant to degrade the employee but to aid in future performance. These reviews should take place at least two or three times a year. What will these objectives look like? It is important that they be tangible, verifiable, and measurable. This means that, wherever possible, we should avoid qualitative objectives and substitute quantifiable statements. For example, a quantitative objective might be "to cut, each day, 3,500 yards of cable to standard five-foot lengths, with a maximum scrap of 50 yards," or "to prepare, process, and transfer to the treasurer's office, all accounts-payable vouchers within three working days from the receipt of the invoice."

MBO's advantages lie in its results-oriented emphasis.

MBO's advantages lie in its results-oriented emphasis.[35] It assists the planning and control functions and provides motivation, as well as being an approach to performance appraisal. That's because employees know exactly what is expected of them and how they will be evaluated. Moreover, employees understand that their evaluation will be based on the success in achieving mutually agreed-on objectives. Finally, it's expected that employees should have a greater commitment to the objectives they have participated in developing than to those unilaterally set by their boss.

The major disadvantage of MBO is that it is unlikely to be effective in an environment where management has little trust in its employees. This type of environment could be one where management makes decisions autocratically and relies heavily on external controls to direct employee behavior. The amount of time needed to implement and maintain an MBO process may also cause problems. Many activities must occur to set it up, such as meetings between supervisors and employees to set and monitor objectives. These meetings can be very time-consuming. Additionally, it may be difficult to measure whether the MBO activities are being carried out properly. The difficulty involved in properly appraising supervisors' efforts and performance as they carry out their MBO activities may cause it to fail.

FACTORS THAT CAN DISTORT APPRAISALS

The performance appraisal process and techniques that we have suggested present systems in which the evaluator is free from personal biases, prejudices, and idiosyncrasies.[36] This is defended on the basis that objectivity minimizes the potential arbitrary and dysfunctional behavior of the evaluator, which may be detrimental to the achievement of the organizational goals. Thus, our goal should be to use direct performance criteria where possible.

It would be naive to assume, however, that all evaluators impartially interpret and standardize the criteria upon which their employees will be appraised. This is particularly true of those jobs that are not easily programmable and for which developing hard performance standards is most difficult—if not impossible. These would include, but are certainly not limited to, such jobs as researcher, teacher, engineer, and consultant. In the place of such standards, we can expect appraisers to use nonperformance or subjective criteria against which to evaluate individuals.

A completely error-free performance appraisal is only an ideal we can aim for.[37] In reality, most appraisals fall short of this ideal. This is often due to one or more actions that can significantly impede objective evaluation.[38] We've briefly described them below (see Exhibit 10-5).

Leniency Error

Leniency Error   A means by which performance appraisal can be distorted by evaluating employees against one's own value system.

Every evaluator has his or her own value system that acts as a standard against which appraisals are made. Relative to the true or actual performance an individual exhibits, some evaluators mark high, while others mark low. The former is referred to as positive **leniency error,** and the latter as negative leniency error. When evaluators are positively lenient in their appraisal, an individual's performance becomes overstated. In doing so, the performance is rated higher than it actually should be. Similarly, a negative leniency error understates performance, giving the individual a lower appraisal.

If all individuals in an organization were appraised by the same person, there would be no problem. Although there would be an error factor, it would be applied equally to everyone.[39] The difficulty arises when we have different raters with different leniency errors making judgments. For example, assume a situation where both Jones and Smith are performing the same job for a different supervisor, with absolutely identical job performance. If Jones's supervisor tends to err toward positive leniency while Smith's supervisor errs toward negative leniency, we might be confronted with two dramatically different evaluations.

Halo Error

Halo Error   The tendency to let our assessment of an individual on one trait influence our evaluation of that person on other specific traits.

The **halo error** or effect is a "tendency to rate high or low on all factors due to the impression of a high or low rating on some specific factor."[40] For example, if an employee tends to be conscientious and dependable, we might become biased

EXHIBIT 10-5
*Factors That Distort
Appraisals*

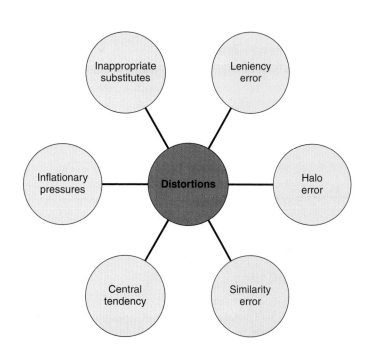

toward that individual to the extent that we will rate him or her positively on many desirable attributes.

People who design teaching appraisal forms for college students to fill out in evaluating the effectiveness of their instructor each semester must confront the halo effect. Students tend to rate a faculty member as outstanding on all criteria when they are particularly appreciative of a few things he or she does in the classroom. Similarly, a few bad habits—like showing up late for lectures, being slow in returning papers, or assigning an extremely demanding reading requirement— might result in students evaluating the instructor as "lousy" across the board.

One method frequently used to deal with the halo error is "reverse wording" the evaluation questions so that a favorable answer for, say, question 17 might be 5 on a scale of 1 through 5, while a favorable answer for question number 18 might be 1 on a scale of 1 through 5. Structuring the questions in this manner seeks to reduce the halo error by requiring the evaluator to consider each question independently. Another method, which can be used where there is more than one person to be evaluated, is to have the evaluator appraise all ratees on each dimension before going on to the next dimension.

Similarity Error

Similarity Error   Evaluating employees based on the way an evaluator perceives himself or herself.

When evaluators rate other people in the same way that the evaluators perceive themselves, they are making a **similarity error.** Based on the perception that evaluators have of themselves, they project those perceptions onto others. For example, the evaluator who perceives himself or herself as aggressive may evaluate others by looking for aggressiveness. Those who demonstrate this characteristic tend to benefit, while others who lack it may be penalized.

Low Appraiser Motivation

What are the consequences of the appraisal? If the evaluator knows that a poor appraisal could significantly hurt the employee's future—particularly opportunities for promotion or a salary increase—the evaluator may be reluctant to give a realistic appraisal. There is evidence that it is more difficult to obtain accurate appraisals when important rewards depend on the results.[41]

Central Tendency

Central Tendency   The tendency of a rater to give average ratings.

It is possible that regardless of who the appraiser evaluates and what traits are used, the pattern of evaluation remains the same. It is also possible that the evaluator's ability to appraise objectively and accurately has been impeded by a failure to use the extremes of the scale. When this happens, we call the action **central tendency.** Central tendency is "the reluctance to make extreme ratings (in either direction); the inability to distinguish between and among ratees; a form of range restriction."[42] Raters who are prone to the central tendency error are those who continually rate all employees as average. For example, if a supervisor rates all employees as 3, on a scale of 1 to 5, then no differentiation among the employees exists. Failure to rate employees as 5, for those who deserve that rating, and as 1, if the case warrants it, will only create problems, especially if this information is used for pay increases.

Inflationary Pressures

A middle manager in a large Georgia-based company could not understand why he had been passed over for promotion. He had seen his file and knew that his average rating by his supervisor was 88. Given his knowledge that the appraisal system defined "outstanding performance" at 90 or above, "good" as 80 or above, "average" as 70 or above, and "inadequate performance" as anything below 70, he was at a loss to understand why he had not been promoted—considering his near-outstanding performance appraisal. The manager's confusion was somewhat resolved when he found out that the "average" rating of middle managers in his organization was 92. This example addresses a major potential problem in appraisals—inflationary pressures. This, in effect, is a specific case of low differentiation within the upper range of the rating choices.

Inflationary pressures have always existed but appear to have increased as a problem over the past three decades. As "equality" values have grown in importance in our society, as well as fear of retribution from disgruntled employees who fail to achieve excellent appraisals, there has been a tendency for evaluation to be less rigorous and negative repercussions from the evaluation to be reduced by generally inflating or upgrading appraisals. However, by inflating these evaluations, many organizations have found themselves in a difficult position when having to defend their personnel action in the case of discharging an employee.[43]

Inappropriate Substitutes for Performance

It is the unusual job where the definition of performance is absolutely clear and direct measures are available for appraising the incumbent. In many jobs it is difficult to get consensus on what is "a good job," and it is even more difficult to get agreement on what criteria will determine performance. For a salesperson the criteria are affected by factors such as economic conditions and actions of competitors—factors outside the salesperson's control. As a result, the appraisal is frequently made by using substitutes for performance—criteria that, it is believed, closely approximate performance and act in its place. Many of these substitutes are well chosen and give a good approximation of actual performance. However, the substitutes chosen are not always appropriate. It is not unusual, for example, to find organizations using criteria such as effort, enthusiasm, neatness, positive attitudes, conscientiousness, promptness, and congeniality as substitutes for performance. In some jobs, one or more of these criteria are part of performance. Obviously, enthusiasm does enhance the effectiveness of a teacher: you are more likely to listen to and be motivated by a teacher who is enthusiastic than by one who is not; and increased attentiveness and motivation typically lead to increased learning. But enthusiasm may in no way be relevant to effective performance for many accountants, watch repairers, or copy editors. So what may be an appropriate substitute for performance in one job may be totally inappropriate in another.

Attribution Theory

There is a concept in management literature called **attribution theory**. According to this theory, employee evaluations are directly affected by a "supervisor's perceptions of who is believed to be in control of the employee's performance—the employer or the manager."[44] Attribution theory attempts to differentiate between those things that the employee controls (internal) versus those that the employee cannot control (external). For example, if an employee fails to finish a project that he has had six months to complete, a supervisor may view this negatively if he or she believes that the employee did not manage either the project or his time well (internal control). Conversely, if the project is delayed because top management requested that something else be given a higher priority, a supervisor may see the incomplete project in more positive terms (external control).

How would you rate the coaching effectiveness of former Indiana University and current Texas Tech basketball coach Bobby Knight? If you evaluate him on his win/loss record, you might come to one conclusion. If, on the other hand, you evaluate him based on off-the-court incidents, you may draw a different conclusion. The point is, depending on how you perceive the situation, your conclusions may differ. This is an example of how one particular factor may distort an appraisal.

Attribution Theory A theory of performance evaluation based on the perception of who is in control of an employee's performance.

TEAM PERFORMANCE APPRAISALS

PERFORMANCE EVALUATION CONCEPTS HAVE BEEN ALMOST exclusively developed with only individual employees in mind. This reflects the historic belief that individuals are the core building block around which organizations are built.[47] But as we've witnessed in contemporary organizations, more and more organizations are restructuring themselves around teams. In those organizations using teams, how should they evaluate performance? Four suggestions have been offered for designing an effective system that supports and improves team performance.[48]

1. Tie team's results to the organization's goals. It's important to find measures that apply to important goals that the team is supposed to accomplish.
2. Begin with the team's customers and the work process the team follows to satisfy customers' needs. The final product the customer receives can be evaluated in terms of the customer's re-

quirements. The transactions between teams can be evaluated based on delivery and quality. And the process steps can be evaluated based on waste and cycle time.

3. Measure both team and individual performance. Define the roles of each team member in terms of accomplishments that support the team's work process. Then assess each member's contributions and the team's overall performance. Remember that individual skills are necessary for team success but are not sufficient for good team performance.[49]
4. Train the team to create its own measures. Having the team define its objectives and those of each member ensures everyone understands their role on the team and helps the team develop into a more cohesive unit.

One research study found support for two key generalizations regarding attribution:[45]

- When appraisers attribute an employee's poor performance to internal control, the judgment is harsher than when the same poor performance is attributed to external factors.
- When an employee is performing satisfactorily, appraisers will evaluate the employee more favorably if the performance is attributed to the employee's own efforts than if the performance is attributed to outside forces.

While attribution theory is interesting and sheds new light on rater effects on performance evaluations, continued study of the topic is needed. Yet it does provide much insight on why unbiased performance evaluations are important. An extension of attribution theory relates to what is called **impression management**. Impression management takes into account how the employee influences the relationship with his or her supervisor. In one study, impression management was viewed as having an effect on performance ratings. In such a case, when the employee "positively impressed his or her supervisor," the outcome was seen as a higher performance rating.[46]

Impression Management: How an employee influences the relationship with a supervisor

CREATING MORE EFFECTIVE PERFORMANCE MANAGEMENT SYSTEMS

The fact that evaluators frequently encounter problems with performance appraisals should not lead us to throw up our hands and give up on the concept. There are things that can be done to make performance appraisals more effective. In this section, we offer some suggestions that can be considered individually or in combination (see Exhibit 10-6).

EXHIBIT 10-6
*Towards a More Effective
Performance Management
System*

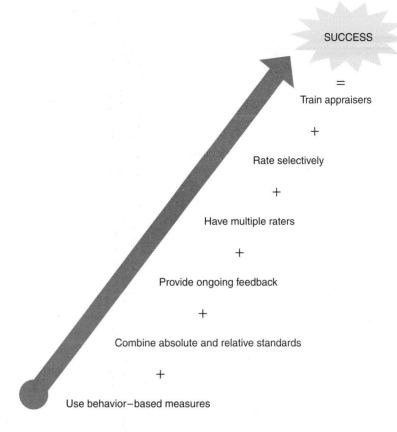

SUCCESS

=

Train appraisers

+

Rate selectively

+

Have multiple raters

+

Provide ongoing feedback

+

Combine absolute and relative standards

+

Use behavior–based measures

Use Behavior-based Measures

As we have pointed out, the evidence favors behavior-based measures over those developed around traits. Many traits often considered to be related to good performance may, in fact, have little or no performance relationship. Traits like loyalty, initiative, courage, reliability, and self-expression are intuitively appealing as desirable characteristics in employees. But the relevant question is: Are individuals who rate high on those traits higher performers than those who rate low? Of course we can't definitively answer this question. We know that there are employees who rate high on these characteristics and are poor performers. Yet, we can find others who are excellent performers but do not score well on traits such as these. Our conclusion is that traits like loyalty and initiative may be prized by appraisers, but there is no evidence to support the notion that certain traits will be adequate synonyms for performance in a large cross section of jobs.

A second weakness in traits is the judgment itself. What is "loyalty"? When is an employee "reliable"? What you consider "loyalty," we may not. So traits suffer from weak inter-rater agreement. Behavior-derived measures can deal with both of these objections. Because they deal with specific examples of performance—both good and bad—we avoid the problem of using inappropriate substitutes. Additionally, because we are evaluating specific behaviors, we increase the likelihood that two or more evaluators will see the same thing. You might consider a given employee as "friendly" while we might perceive her as "stand-offish." But when asked to rate her in terms of specific behaviors, we might both agree that in terms of specific behaviors, she "frequently says 'Good morning' to customers," "willingly gives advice or assistance to coworkers," and "always consolidates her cash drawer at the end of her work day."

Combine Absolute and Relative Standards

A major drawback to individual or absolute standards is that they tend to be biased by positive leniency; that is, evaluators lean toward packing their subjects into the high part of the rankings. On the other hand, relative standards suffer when there is little actual variability among the subjects. The obvious solution is to consider using appraisal methods that combine both absolute and relative standards. For example, you might want to use the adjective rating scale and the individual ranking method. This dual method of appraisal, incidentally, has been instituted at some universities to deal with the problem of grade inflation. Students get an absolute grade—A, B, C, D, or F—and next to it is a relative mark showing how this student ranked in the class. A prospective employer or graduate school admissions committee can look at two students who each got a B in their international finance course and draw considerably different conclusions about each when next to one grade it says "ranked 4th out of 33," while the other says "ranked 17th out of 21." Clearly, the latter instructor gave a lot more high grades!

Provide Ongoing Feedback

Several years back, a nationwide motel chain advertised, "The best surprise is no surprise." This phrase clearly applies to performance appraisals. Employees like to know how they are doing. The "annual review," where the appraiser shares the employees' evaluations with them, can become a problem. In some cases, it is a problem merely because appraisers put off such reviews. This is particularly likely if the appraisal is negative. But the annual review is additionally troublesome if the supervisor "saves up" performance-related information and unloads it during the appraisal review. This creates an extremely trying experience for both the evaluator and employee. In such instances it is not surprising that the supervisor may attempt to avoid confronting uncomfortable issues that, even if confronted, may only be denied or rationalized by the employee.[50]

The solution lies in having the appraiser share with the employee both expectations and disappointments on a frequent basis. By providing the employee with repeated opportunities to discuss performance before any reward or punishment consequences occur, there will be no surprises at the time of the formal annual review. In fact, where ongoing feedback has been provided, the formal sitting-down step shouldn't be particularly traumatic for either party. Additionally, in an MBO system that actually works, ongoing feedback is the critical element.

Have Multiple Raters

As the number of raters increases, the probability of attaining more accurate information increases.[51] If rater error tends to follow a normal curve, an increase in the number of raters will tend to find the majority clustering about the middle. If a person has had 10 supervisors, nine of whom rated him or her excellent and one poor, then we must investigate what went into that one. Maybe this rater was the one who identified an area of weakness where training is needed, or an area to be avoided in future job assignments.[52] Therefore, by moving employees about within the organization to gain a number of evaluations, we increase the probability of achieving more valid and reliable evaluations—as well as helping to support changes that may need to be made.[53] Of course, we are making the assumption that the process functions properly, and bias free![54]

Use Peer Evaluations   Have you ever wondered why a professor asks you to evaluate one another's contributions when a group or team project is used in the class? The reasoning behind this action is that the professor cannot tell what every member did on the project, but only what the overall product quality was. And at times, that may not be fair to everyone—especially if a member or two in the group left most of the work up to the remaining group members.

Similarly, supervisors find it difficult to evaluate their employees' performance because they are not observing them every moment of the work day. Unfortunately, unless they have this information, they may not be making an accurate assessment. And if their goal for the performance evaluation is to identify deficient areas and provide constructive feedback to their employees, they have been providing a disservice to these workers by not having all the information. Yet how do they get this information? One of the better means is through **peer evaluations.** Peer evaluations are conducted by the employees' coworkers—people explicitly familiar with the behaviors involved in their jobs.[55]

The main advantage of peer evaluation is that (1) there is a tendency for coworkers to offer more constructive insight to each other so that, as a unit, each will improve; and (2) their recommendations tend to be more specific regarding job behaviors. Unless specificity exists, constructive measures may be hard to obtain.[56] But caution is in order because these systems, if not handled properly, could lead to increases in halo effects and leniency errors,[57] and fear among employees.[58] Thus, along with training our supervisors to properly appraise employee performance, so too must we train peers to evaluate one another.

A slight deviation from peer assessments is a process called the **upward appraisal,** or the reverse review.[59] Used in such companies as Pratt and Whitney, Dow Chemical, CitiCorp, and AT&T, upward appraisals permit employees to offer frank and constructive feedback to their supervisors on such areas as leadership and communication skills.[60]

360-Degree Appraisals   An appraisal device that seeks performance feedback from such sources as oneself, bosses, peers, team members, customers, and suppliers has become very popular in contemporary organizations.[61] It's called the 360-degree appraisal.[62] It's being used in approximately 90 percent of the *Fortune* 1000 firms, which includes such companies as DuPont, Nabisco, Warner-Lambert, Black & Decker, Mobil Oil, Cook Children Health Care System, General Electric, and UPS.[63]

In today's dynamic organizations, traditional performance evaluations systems may be archaic. Delayering has resulted in supervisors having greater work responsibility and more employees reporting directly to them. Accordingly, in some instances, it is almost impossible for supervisors to have extensive job knowledge of each of their employees. Furthermore, the growth of project teams and employee involvement in today's companies places the responsibility of evaluation where people are better able to make an accurate assessment.[64]

The 360-degree feedback process also has some positive benefits for development concerns. Many managers simply do not know how their employees truly view them and the work they have done. For example, Jerry Wallace, GM's Saturn plant's head of personnel, viewed himself as being up-to-date on all the latest management techniques.[65] While Jerry viewed himself as open to change

Peer Evaluation   A performance evaluation situation in which coworkers provide input into the employee's performance.

360-Degree Appraisal   Performance appraisal process in which supervisors, peers, employees, customers, and the like evaluate the individual.

and flexible to new ideas, feedback from his employees indicated that Jerry was a "control freak." After some soul-searching, plus an assessment from an external leadership group, Jerry realized his employees were right. He finally understood why nobody wanted to be on a team with him and why he had to do everything himself.[66] In this case, the 360-degree feedback instrument eliminated a strong barrier to Jerry's career progression.

Research studies into the effectiveness of 360-degree performance appraisals are reporting positive results. These stem from having more accurate feedback, empowering employees, reducing the subjective factors in the evaluation process, and developing leadership in an organization.[67] Moreover, to enhance honesty and efficiency in feedback, companies like Otis Elevator have put their 360-degree feedback appraisal on the Internet.[68]

Rate Selectively

It has been suggested that appraisers should rate only in those areas in which they have significant job knowledge. If raters make evaluations on only those dimensions for which they are in a good position to rate, we can increase the inter-rater agreement and make the evaluation a more valid process. This approach also recognizes that different organizational levels often have different orientations toward ratees and observe them in different settings. In general, therefore, we recommend that, in terms of organizational level, appraisers should be as close as possible to the individual being evaluated. Conversely, the more levels separating the evaluator and employee, the less opportunity the evaluator has to observe the individual's work behavior and, not surprisingly, the greater the possibility for inaccuracies.

The specific application of these concepts results in having immediate supervisors or coworkers as the major input into the appraisal and having them evaluate those factors that they are best qualified to judge. For example, it has been suggested that when professors are evaluating secretaries within a university, they use such criteria as judgment, technical competence, and conscientiousness, whereas peers (other secretaries) use such criteria as job knowledge, organization, cooperation with coworkers, and responsibility.[69] Such an approach appears both logical and more reliable, since people are appraising only those dimensions of which they are in a good position to make judgments.

In addition to taking into account where the rater is in the organization or what he or she is allowed to evaluate, selective rating should also consider the characteristics of the rater. If appraisers differ in traits, and if certain of these traits are correlated with accurate appraisals while others are correlated with inaccurate appraisals, then it seems logical to attempt to identify effective raters. Those identified as especially effective could be given sole responsibility for doing appraisals, or greater weight could be given to their observations.

Train Appraisers

If you cannot find good raters, the alternative is to make good raters. Evidence indicates that the training of appraisers can make them more accurate raters.[70] Common errors such as halo and leniency can be minimized or eliminated in workshops where supervisors can practice observing and rating behaviors. Why should we bother to train these individuals? Because a poor appraisal is worse than no appraisal at all.[71] These negative effects can manifest themselves as demoralizing employees, decreasing productivity, and making the company "liable for wrongful termination damages."[72]

technology

c o r n e r

Evaluating Employee Performance

J UST WHERE DO YOU BEGIN IN putting together a performance appraisal system? For many smaller organizations, this question poses some difficulties. Fortunately, with the advent of technology, getting started with implementing an effective performance management system is just a simple purchase away. Here are some of the possibilities on the market today.

Performance Now: Performance Now, HR Press (www.hrpress-software.com/perfn.html, $99) is available for organizations that are looking for a way to "track, manage, and evaluate performance." Performance Now allows the user to set goals, track them, and look for legally sensitive areas. This software package also offers users some performance coaching tips and assistance.

Evalu-Aide: Evalu-Aide (Goode Enterprises, Inc., www.goode-ent.com/val-uaide.htm, $195) provides software that can be used by one supervisor, or can be set up for multiple raters. Performance traits, job activities, and so on, can be selected from a preset menu or customized to fit one's specific job.

Employee Appraiser: Employee Appraiser (Success Factors, www.successfactors.com/solutions/eap/standard.shtml, $140) was developed by HR professionals to assist managers in the performance appraisal process. With review-writing assistance, this software program assists the user in "reinforcing positive aspects of an employee's performance, offering criticism, and addressing difficult issues with sensitivity." Sample written statements come from actual appraisals used. Employee appraiser also includes a legal checker to "flag" potentially problematic areas.

*I*NTERNATIONAL PERFORMANCE APPRAISAL

In evaluating employee performance in international environments, other factors come into play. For instance, the cultural differences between the parent country and the host country must be considered. The cultural differences between the United States and England are not as great as those between the United States and China, for example. Thus, hostility or friendliness of the cultural environment in which one manages should be considered when appraising employee performance.

Who Performs the Evaluation?

There are also issues to consider regarding who will be responsible for the evaluations: the host-country management or the parent-country management. Although local management would generally be considered a more accurate gauge, it typically evaluates expatriates from its own cultural perspectives and expectations, which may not reflect those of the parent country. For example, in some countries, a participatory style of management is acceptable, while in other countries, hierarchical values make it a disgrace to ask employees for ideas. This could vastly alter a supervisor's performance appraisal.[73]

Confusion may arise from the use of parent-country evaluation forms if they are misunderstood, either because the form has been improperly translated or not translated at all, or because the evaluator is uncertain what a particular question means. The home-office management, on the other hand, is often so remote that it may not be fully informed on what is going on in an overseas office. Because they lack access and because one organization may have numerous foreign operations to evaluate, home-office managements often measure performance by quantitative indices, such as profits, market shares, or gross sales.[74] However, "simple" numbers are often quite complex in their calculations and data are not always comparable. For example, if a company has many operations in South America, it must be aware of the accounting practices in each country. Peru, for instance, counts sales on consignment as firm sales, while Brazil does not. Local import tariffs can also distort pricing schedules, which alter gross sales figures, another often-compared statistic. Even when the measurements are comparable, the comparison country will have an effect. For example, factory productivity levels in Mexico may be below those of similar plants in the United States, but American-owned plant productivity in Mexico may be above that of similar Mexican-owned plants. Depending on where the supervisor's results are compared, different outcomes may occur. Such issues complicate parent-country management performance evaluations by numerical criteria, or indices—and can add to the emotional levels in appraisals. For instance, recall the opening vignette of U.S. 7-Eleven stores. American 7-Eleven owners aren't looking forward to the performance management system imposed by their parent company. According to one New Jersey 7-Eleven owner, the performance system goes against American workers' desire for independence and reflects a deep philosophical difference between America and Japan. That is, he and many of his fellow 7-Eleven owners bristle at the idea that headquarters' staff, thousands of miles away, know what's best for them.

Which Evaluation Format Will Be Used?

Other issues surround the question of selecting the best format to use in performance appraisals. If we have an overseas operation that includes both parent-country nationals (PCNs) and host-country nationals (HCNs), we must determine if we will use the same forms for all employees. While most Western countries accept the concept of performance evaluation, some cultures interpret it as a sign of distrust or even an insult to an employee. This complicates a decision to use one instrument like an adjective rating scale for all employees. On the other hand, using different formats for PCNs and HCNs may create a dual track in the subsidiary, in turn creating other problems.

The evaluation form presents other problems. If there is a universal form for the entire corporation, an organization must determine how it will be translated accurately into the native language of each country. English forms may not be readily understood by local supervisors. For example, clerical and office jobs do not always have identical requirements in all cultures. As a result, some U.S.

Should a manager at this Wal-Mart in Mexico be required to use the corporate evaluation developed and used extensively in the United States? If so, will the evaluation need to be translated into Spanish? Questions such as these need to be addressed when evaluating employees in the global village.

multinationals may be hesitant about evaluating HCNs and TCNs (third-country nationals). In some countries, notably those that support the Communist ideology, all workers are rewarded only when the group performs—with punishment or discipline being highly limited. You'll find this, for example, in the hotel industry in the People's Republic of China. Without the ability to reward good individual performance or to punish poor performance, there is little motivation to have any evaluation at all.[75]

Although the subject of international performance appraisal continues to receive research attention, two general recommendations have been suggested, as follows.

- Modify the normal performance criteria of the evaluation sheet for a particular position to fit the overseas position and site characteristics. Expatriates who have returned from a particular site or the same country can provide useful input into revising criteria to reflect the possibilities and constraints of a given location.[76]
- Include a current expatriate's insights as part of the evaluation. This means that nonstandardized criteria, which are difficult to measure, will be included, perhaps on a different basis for each country. This creates some administrative difficulties at headquarters, but in the long run will be a more equitable system.[77]

HRM WORKSHOP

S UMMARY

(This summary relates to the Learning Outcomes identified on p. 266.)

After having read this chapter, you should be able to:

1. **Identify the three purposes of performance management systems and who is served by them.** The three purposes of performance management systems are feedback, development, and documentation. They are designed to support the employees, the appraisers, and the organization.

2. **Explain the six steps in the appraisal process.** The six-step appraisal process is to: (1) establish performance standards with employees; (2) set measurable goals (manager and employee); (3) measure actual performance; (4) compare actual performance with standards; (5) discuss the appraisal with the employee; and (6) if necessary, initiate corrective action.

3. **Discuss what is meant by absolute standards in performance management systems.** Absolute standards refer to a method in performance management systems whereby employees are measured against company-set performance requirements. Absolute standard evaluation methods involve the essay appraisal, the critical incident approach, the checklist rating, the adjective rating scale, the forced-choice inventory, and the behaviorally anchored rating scale (BARS).

4. **Describe what is meant by relative standards in performance management systems.** Relative standards refer to a method in performance management systems whereby employees' performance is compared with that of other employees. Relative standard evaluation methods include group order ranking, individual ranking, and paired comparisons.

5. **Discuss how MBO can be used as an appraisal method.** MBO is used as an appraisal method by establishing a specific set of objectives for an employee to achieve and reviewing performance based on how well those objectives have been met.

6. **Explain why performance appraisals might be distorted.** Performance appraisal might be distorted for a number of reasons, including leniency error, halo error, similarity error, central tendency, low appraiser motivation, inflationary pressures, and inappropriate substitutes for performance.

7. **Identify ways to make performance management systems more effective.** More effective appraisals can be achieved with behavior-based measures, combined absolute and relative ratings, ongoing feedback, multiple raters, selective rating, trained appraisers, peer assessment, and rewards to accurate appraisers.

8. **Describe what is meant by the term *360-degree appraisal*.** In 360-degree performance appraisals evaluations are made by oneself, supervisors, employees, team members, customers, suppliers, and the like. In doing so, a complete picture of one's performance can be assessed.

CONDUCTING THE PERFORMANCE EVALUATION

ABOUT THE SKILL: How DOES one properly conduct the performance appraisal process? We offer the following steps that can assist in this endeavor.[78]

1. Prepare for and schedule the appraisal in advance. Before meeting with employees, some preliminary activities should be performed. You should at a minimum review employee job descriptions, period goals that may have been set, and performance data on employees you may have. Furthermore, you should schedule the appraisal well in advance to give employees the opportunity to prepare their data, too, for the meeting.

2. Create a supportive environment to put employees at ease. Performance appraisals conjure up several emotions. As such, every effort should be made to make employees comfortable during the meeting, such that they are receptive to constructive feedback.

3. Describe the purpose of the appraisal to employees. Make sure employees know precisely what the appraisal is to be used for. Will it have implications for pay increases, or other personnel decisions? If so, make sure employees understand exactly how the appraisal process works, and its consequences.

4. Involve the employee in the appraisal discussion, including a self-evaluation. Performance appraisals should not be a one-way communication event. Although as supervisor, you may believe that you have to talk more in the meeting, that needn't be the case. Instead, employees should have ample opportunity to discuss their performance, raise questions about the facts you raise, and add their own data/perceptions about their work.[79] One means of ensuring that two-way communication occurs is to have employees conduct a self-evaluation. You should actively listen to their assessment. This involvement helps to create an environment of participation.[80]

5. Focus discussion on work behaviors, not on the employees. One way of creating emotional difficulties is to attack the employee. Therefore, you should keep your discussion on the behaviors you've observed. Telling an employee, for instance, that his report stinks doesn't do a thing. That's not focusing on behaviors. Instead, indicating that you believe that not enough time was devoted to proofreading the report describes the behavior that may be a problem to you.

6. Support your evaluation with specific examples. Specific performance behaviors help clarify to employees the issues you raise. Rather than saying something wasn't good (subjective evaluation), you should be as specific as possible in your explanations. So, for the employee who failed to proof the work, describing that the report had five grammatical mistakes in the first two pages alone would be a specific example.

7. Give both positive and negative feedback. Performance appraisals needn't be all negative. Although there is a perception that this process focuses on the negative, it should also be used to compliment and recognize good work. Positive, as well as negative, feedback helps employees to gain a better understanding of their performance. For example, although the report was not up to the quality you expected, the employee did do the work and completed the report in a timely fashion. That behavior deserves some positive reinforcement.

8. Ensure employees understand what was discussed in the appraisal. At the end of the appraisal, especially where some improvement is warranted, you should ask employees to summarize what was discussed in the meeting. This will help you to ensure that you have gotten your information through to the employee.

9. Generate a development plan. Most of the performance appraisal revolves around feedback and documentation. But another component is needed. Where development efforts are encouraged, a plan should be developed to describe what is to be done, by when, and what you, the supervisor, will commit to aid in the improvement/enhancement effort.

9. **Discuss how performance appraisals may differ in the global village.** Performance management systems may differ in the international spectrum in terms of who performs the evaluation and the format used. Cultural differences may dictate that changes in the U.S. performance management system are needed.

$\mathcal{D}$EMONSTRATING COMPREHENSION: *Questions for Review and Discussion*

1. To what three purposes can performance appraisal be applied, and who is served by this process?
2. Describe the appraisal process.
3. Contrast the advantages and disadvantages of (1) absolute standards and (2) relative standards.
4. What is BARS? Why might BARS be better than trait-oriented measures?
5. What is MBO? What are its advantages and disadvantages?
6. What are some of the major factors that distort performance appraisals?
7. How should performance appraisals change when teams, rather than individuals, are evaluated?

8. "Performance appraisal should be a multifaceted. Supervisors should evaluate their employees, and employees should be able to evaluate their supervisors. And customers should evaluate them all." Do you agree or disagree with this statement? Discuss.
9. "The higher the position an employee occupies in an organization, the easier it is to appraise his or her performance objectively." Do you agree or disagree with this statement? Why?
10. "Using a performance evaluation instrument that is not valid is a waste of time." Do you agree or disagree with this statement? Discuss.

$\mathcal{C}$ASE APPLICATION: *TEAM FUN!*

Kenny and Norton, owners of TEAM FUN!, a sporting goods manufacturer and retailer, are hosting their annual management retreat at a hunting lodge in central Canada. This year, the attendees are Tony, Director of Human Resources, Josephine, Comptroller, Arlien from marketing, research and production operations and the three retail branch store managers, Eric, Joe, and Bobby. They are in Day 3 of the hunting, fishing, planning, and evaluating week. settling into an afternoon of Performance Appraisal discussions, according to the soggy agendas that Tony has placed in front of them.

Kenny punches Norton in the ribs and says, "Looks like I can catch a 3–4 hour nap this afternoon. Let me know if anyone says anything funny." He turns to Tony, "Sorry about cleaning the fish on these papers of yours. Looked like fish gut paper to me! Whew. Maybe the smell will keep me awake." The group spent yesterday talking about the successes and failures of each branch for the last year. They talked about each employee, and how that individual helped or hindered overall operations. It was decided to move a few people to new assignments for the coming year.

Tony starts: "Apparently TEAM FUN! has been using a modified MBO process for all of its employees."

Eric, who had run operations since the company was founded agrees, "Yes, from what you said about MBO, we do. I know I work out with each shift and team what the goals are for each quarter. We usually have 5 or 6 goals for each person and group. If all are met, we all get a nice bonus from the profit share plan. If most are met, we get decent raises. That one year, no one got raises."

Norton shakes his head, "That was a tough time. We turned it around faster than most, though. And we didn't lay anyone off."

Bobby asks, "What would be good sales goals? My guys set goals like these, for example. Attract 10,000 customers a month by the third month of operation. Keep shrinkage/breakage under .5%. Have zero customer complaints/returns. Every cash register balances at the end of each shift. All employees will speak both Spanish and English."

Tony comments, "Bobby, you were a special case because the South Florida store just opened this year."

Josephine adds, "You all need good financial goals—for each and every employee."

Arlien snaps, "Bobby, you need to sell more. And we need to know what you are promising customers *before* they call to ask me why its late"

Kenny wakes up and asks, "What about the fun? Do you have goals for fun? Eric, what were you saying about relative and absolute standards for fun that you learned in that supervisor class that Tony sent you and Joe to?"

Tony brightens up and pulls out a chart on absolute rating scales, "Now we're talking!"

Questions:

1. Does TEAM FUN! follow the six step appraisal process?
2. Is an MBO plan good for the company? What could be done to improve it? Evaluate Bobby's goals according to MBO criteria. Suggest an alternative to their MBO exclusive performance appraisal process.
3. Comment on the overall effectiveness of the performance appraisal process at TEAM FUN!
4. Provide an outline for their discussion on absolute and relative measurement techniques for "fun."

WORKING WITH A TEAM: *The 360-Degree Performance*

As human resource management students, you and your class team have been asked to conduct a 30-minute presentation for 10 to 15 supervisors at the next supervisors' meeting, since supervisors have not adapted as well as desired by management to a change in the appraisal system.

Develop a 30-minute presentation about the purposes of the performance management systems, who benefits, and the six basic steps; clarify the difference between relative and absolute standards, with possible distortions, and introduce the 360-degree feedback system.

ENHANCING YOUR WRITING SKILLS

1. Develop a two- to three-page paper describing the relationship that exists between the job analysis and the performance evaluations. Cite specific examples where appropriate.
2. Visit the web site http://nefried.com/360/360hrmagarticle.html. This article provides some data on the pros and the cons of using a 360-degree performance appraisal in an organization. Summarize the article and end the paper with your beliefs on whether 360-degree evaluations should be used in all organizations.
3. Endnote number 2 in this chapter refers to several articles that have been recently published regarding the potential obsolescence of performance appraisals. Select two of the cited articles, summarize them, and end your report with your analysis and conclusions.

www.wiley.com/college/decenzo

ENDNOTES

1. Based on Shiba-Koen, Seven-Eleven Japan (Tokyo, Japan, November 22, 2000), p. 1156 Retail, 8183, http://profiles.wisi.com/profiles/scripts; Wendy Zellner and Emily Thornton, "How Classy Can 7-Eleven Get?" *Business Week* (September 1, 1997), p. 74; and Norihiko Shirouzu, "7-Eleven Operators Resist System to Monitor Managers," *Wall Street Journal* (June 16, 1997), pp. B-1, B-3.
2. For some interesting articles on this subject, see Bob Nelson, "Are Performance Appraisals Obsolete?" *Compensation and Benefits Review* (May–June 2000), pp. 39–42; Jonathan A. Segal, "86 Your Performance Process?" *HRMagazine* (October 2000), pp. 199–206; Dick Grote, "Performance Evaluations: Is It Time for a Makeover?" *HR Focus* (November 2000), pp. 6–7; Michael Schrage, "How the Bell Curve Cheats You," *Fortune* (February 21, 2000), p. 296; and "HR Execs Dissatisfied with Their Performance Appraisal Systems," *HR Focus* (January 2000), p. 2.
3. Suzanne S. Masterson and M. Susan Taylor, "Total Quality Management and Performance Appraisal: An Integrative Perspective," *Journal of Quality Management* (January 1996), p. 73.
4. We would like to recognize Dr. Peter F. Norlin, an organizational consultant specializing in performance management systems, for providing the framework terminology for the purposes, who is served, and inherent difficulties.
5. Robert J. Sahl, Ph.D., "Design Effective Performance Appraisals," *Personnel Journal* (October 1990), pp. 56–57.
6. See Stuart Feldman, "Amoco Keeps Its Employees in the Big Picture," *Personnel* (June 1991), p. 24.
7. Larry L. Axline, "Ethical Considerations of Performance Appraisals," *Management Review* (March 1994), p. 62.
8. Mary Mavis, "Painless Performance Evaluations," *Training and Development* (October 1994), p. 40; and Herbert H. Meyer, "A Solution to the Performance Appraisal Feedback Enigma," *Academy of Management Executive* (February 1991), p. 68.
9. Henry M. Findley, Kevin W. Mossholder, and William F. Giles, "Performance Appraisal Process and System Facets: Relationships with Contextual Performance," *Journal of Applied Psychology* (August 2000), pp. 634–640.
10. For a discussion on perception differences, see Kenneth P. Carron, Robert L. Cardy, and Gregory H. Dobbins, "Per-

formance Appraisals as Effective Management or Deadly Management Disease: Two Initial Empirical Investigations," *Group and Organizational Studies* (June 1991), pp. 143–159.

11. See, for example, Maria Castanda and Afsaneh Nahavandi, "Link of Manager Behavior to Supervisory Performance Rating and Subordinate Satisfaction," *Group and Organizational Studies* (December 1991), pp. 357–366.

12. Ibid.; and Robert B. Campbell and Lynne Moses Garfinkel, "Strategies for Success," *HRMagazine* (June 1996), p. 104.

13. See, for instance, M. Susan Taylor, Suzanne S. Masterson, Monika K. Renard, and Kay B. Tracy, "Managers' Reactions to Procedurally Just Performance Management Systems," *Academy of Management Journal* (October 1998), pp. 568–678.

14. See Gary English, "Tuning Up for Performance Management," *Training and Development Journal* (April 1991), pp. 56–60.

15. Donald W. Myers, Wallace R. Johnston, and C. Glenn Pearce, "The Role of Human Interaction Theory in Developing Models of Performance Appraisal Feedback," *SAM Advanced Management Journal* (Summer 1991), p. 28.

16. See Barry R. Nathan, Allan M. Mohrman, Jr., and John Milliman, "Interpersonal Relations as a Context for the Effects of Appraisal Interviews on Performance and Satisfaction: A Longitudinal Study," *Academy of Management Journal* (June 1991), pp. 352–363.

17. David C. Martin, Kathryn M. Bartol, and Patrick E. Kehoe, "The Legal Ramifications of Performance Appraisal: The Growing Significance," *Public Personnel Management* (Fall 2000), pp. 379–406.

18. Larry L. Axline, "Ethical Considerations of Performance Appraisals," *Management Review* (March 1994), p. 62.

19. See David C. Martin and Kathy M. Bartol, "The Legal Ramifications of Performance Appraisal: An Update," *Employee Relations Law Review* (Autumn 1991), pp. 257–286.

20. See also Jonathan A. Segal, "Performance Management for Jekyll and Hyde," *HRMagazine* (February 1999), pp. 130–135.

21. Kathryn Tyler, "Careful Criticism Brings Better Performance," *HRMagazine* (April 1997), p. 57.

22. Jack Stack, "The Curse of the Annual Performance Review," *Inc.* (May 1997), pp. 39–40; and Dick Grote, "Handling Employee Reviews," *Incentive* (October 1997), p. 32.

23. Readers might find the following article of interest. Jaesun Park and John K. S. Chong, "A Comparison of Absolute and Relative Performance Appraisal System," *International Journal of Management* (September 2000), pp. 423–429.

24. Richard Henderson, *Compensation Management: Rewarding Performance*, 6th ed. (Englewood Cliffs, NJ: Prentice-Hall, 1994), p. 433.

25. Ahron Tziner and Richard Kopelman, "Effects of Rating Format on Goal-Setting: A Field Experiment," *Journal of Applied Psychology* (May 1988), p. 323.

26. See, for example, Dennis M. Daley, "Great Expectations, or a Tale of Two Systems: Employee Attitudes Toward Graphic Rating Scales and MBO-Based Performance Appraisal," *Public Administration Quarterly* (Summer 1991), pp. 188–201.

27. Richard Henderson, *Compensation Management: Rewarding Performance*, 6th ed. (Englewood Cliffs, NJ: Prentice-Hall, 1994), p. 433.

28. Mary L. Tenopyr, "Artificial Reliability of Forced-Choice Scales," *Journal of Applied Psychology* (November 1988), pp. 750–751.

29. See Kevin R. Murphy, "Criterion Issues in Performance Appraisal Research: Behavioral Accuracy Versus Classification Accuracy," *Organizational Behavior and Human Decision Processes* (October 1991), pp. 45–50.

30. H. John Bernardin and Richard W. Beatty, *Performance Appraisal: Assessing Human Behavior at Work* (Boston: Kent Publishing, 1984), p. 86.

31. See, for example, Ahron Tziner, Christine Joanis, and Kevin R. Murphy, "A Comparison of Three Methods of Performance Appraisal with Regard to Goal Properties, Goal Perception, and Ratee Satisfaction," *Group & Organization Management* (June 2000), pp. 175–190; Kevin R. Murphy and Virginia A. Pardaffy, "Bias in Behaviorally Anchored Rating Scales: Global or Scale Specific," *Journal of Applied Psychology* (April 1989), pp. 343–346; and Michael J. Piotrowski, Janet L. Barnes-Farrell, and Francine H. Esris, "Behaviorally Anchored Bias: A Replication and Extension of Murphy and Constans," *Journal of Applied Psychology* (October 1988), pp. 827–828.

32. Ibid.

33. For an overview of MBO, see Peter F. Drucker, *The Practice of Management* (New York: Harper & Row, 1954).

34. See also Janice S. Miller and Robert L. Cardy, "Self-Monitoring and Performance Appraisal: Rating Outcomes in Project Teams," *Journal of Organizational Behavior* (September 2000, pp. 606–629.

35. See, for example, Dick Grote, "Painless Performance Appraisals Focus on Results, Behaviors," *HRMagazine* (October 1998), pp. 52–58.

36. See, for instance, Nancy E. Day, "Can Performance Raters Be More Accurate? Investigating the Benefits of Prior Knowledge of Performance Dimensions," *Journal of Managerial Issues* (Fall 1995), pp. 323–343.

37. Henderson, pp. 428–429.

38. See, for example, William H. Bommer, Jonathan L. Johnson, and Gregory A. Rich, "An Extension of Heneman's Meta-Analysis of Objective and Subjective Measures of Performance," *Academy of Management Best Papers Proceedings*, Dorothy P. Moore, ed. (August 14–17, 1994), pp. 112–116.

39. For an interesting discussion of leniency errors, see Jeffrey S. Kane, H. John Bernardin, Peter Villanova, and Joseph Peyrefitte, "Stability of Rater Leniency: Three Studies," *Academy of Management Journal*, Vol. 38, No. 4 (November 1995), pp. 1036–1051.

40. Bernardin and Beatty, p. 140.

41. Ibid., p. 270.

42. Ibid., p. 139.

43. Jonathan A. Segal, "Are Your Performance Appraisals Just and Act?" *HRMagazine* (October 1995), pp. 45–50.

44. David Kipnis, Karl Price, Stuart Schmidt, and Christopher Stitt, "Why Do I Like Thee: Is It Your Performance or My Orders?" *Journal of Applied Psychology* (June 1981), pp. 324–328.

45. Ibid.

46. See, for example, A. Montagliani and R. A. Giacalone, "Impression Management and Cross Cultural Adaption," *Journal of Social Psychology* (October 1998), pp. 598–608; Sandy J. Wayne, Isabel K. Graf, and Gerald R. Ferris, "The Role of Employee Influence Tactics in Human Resource De-

cisions," *Academy of Management Best Papers Proceedings*, Dorothy Perrin Moore, ed. (Vancouver, British Columbia, Canada, August 6–9, 1995), pp. 156–160; Sandy J. Wayne and Robert C. Liden, "Effects of Impression Management on Performance Ratings: A Longitudinal Study," *Academy of Management Journal*, Vol. 38, No. 1 (February 1995), pp. 232–260; and Sandy J. Wayne and K. Michele Kacmar, "The Effects of Impressive Management on the Performance Appraisal Process," *Organization Behavior and Human Decision Processes* (February 1991), pp. 70–88.

47. Stephen P. Robbins, *Organizational Behavior*, 9th ed. (Upper Saddle River, NJ: Prentice-Hall, 2001), p. 494.

48. J. Zigon, "Making Performance Appraisal Work for Teams," *Training* (June 1994), pp. 58–63. See also John Day, "Simple, Strong Team Ratings," *HRMagazine* (September 2000), pp. 159–161.

49. E. Salas, T. L. Dickinson, S. A. Converse, and S. I. Tannenbaum, "Toward an Understanding of Team Performance and Training," in R. W. Swezey and E. Salas (eds.), *Teams: Their Training and Performance* (Norwood, NJ: Ablex, 1992), pp. 3–29.

50. See, for example, Bernardin and Beatty, pp. 271–276.

51. An assumption has been made here. That is, these raters have specific performance knowledge of the employee. Otherwise, more information may not be more *accurate* information. For example, if the raters are from various levels in the organization's hierarchy, these individuals may not have an accurate picture of the employee's performance; thus, quality of information may decrease. See also Clive Fletcher and Caroline Baldry, "A Study of Individual Differences and Self-Awareness in the Context of Multi-source Feedback," *Journal of Occupational and Organizational Psychology* (September 2000), pp. 303–319.

52. See, for example, Hannah R. Rothstein, "Interrater Reliability of Job Performance Ratings: Growth to Asymptote Level with Increasing Opportunity to Observe," *Journal of Applied Psychology* (June 1990), pp. 322–327. See also Mary D. Zalesny, "Rater Confidence and Social Influence in Performance Appraisals," *Journal of Applied Psychology* (June 1990), pp. 274–289.

53. Susan J. Wells, "A New Road: Traveling Beyond the 360-Degree Evaluation," *HRMagazine* (September 1998), pp. 83–91.

54. For an interesting perspective on aspects to avoid when using multiple raters, see Allan H. Church, Steven G. Rogelberg, and Janine Waclawski, "Since When Is No News Good News? The Relationship Between Performance and Response Rates in Multirater Feedback," *Personnel Psychology* (Summer 2000), pp. 435–451; and Susan Haworth, "The Dark Side of Multi-Rater Assessments," *HRMagazine* (May 1998), pp. 106–114.

55. Kathleen A. Guinn, "Performance Management for Evolving Self-Directed Work Teams," *ACA Journal* (Winter 1995), pp. 74–79; Stephanie Gruner, "The Team-Building Peer Review," *Inc.* (July 1995), pp. 63–65; and Ted H. Shore, Lynn McFarlane, and George C. Thornton III, "Construct Validity of Self- and Peer Evaluations of Performance Dimensions in an Assessment Center," *Journal of Applied Psychology* (February 1992), pp. 42–54.

56. See, for example, Martin L. Ramsey and Howard Lehto, "The Power of Peer Review," *Training and Development* (July 1994), pp. 38–41.

57. See David Antonioni and Heejoon Park, "Rater-Ratee Personality Similarities Predict Peer Appraisal Ratings," in Stephen J. Havlovic (ed.), *Fifty-Eighth Annual Meeting of the Academy of Management, Academy of Management Proceedings* (August 7–12, 1998), pp. HRH1–HRH7; Jiing-Lib Farh, Albert A. Cannella, and Arthur G. Bedian, "Peer Ratings: The Impact of Purpose on Rating Quality Acceptance," *Group and Organization Studies* (December 1991), pp. 367–386.

58. Marilyn Moats Kennedy, "Where Teams Drop the Ball," *Across the Board* (September 1993), p. 9.

59. Irene H. Buhalo, "You Sign My Report Card—I'll Sign Yours," *Personnel* (May 1991), p. 23.

60. Stephanie Gruner, "Turning the Tables," *Inc.* (May 1996), p. 87; Joann S. Lublin, "Turning the Tables: Underlings Evaluate Bosses," *Wall Street Journal* (October 4, 1994), pp. B1, B11; and Jerry Baumgartner, "Give It to Me Straight," *Training and Development* (July 1994), pp. 49–51.

61. Richard Lepsinger and Antoinette D. Lucia, "360-Degree Feedback and Performance Appraisal," *Training* (September 1997), pp. 62–70; Mark R. Edwards and Ann J. Ewen, "Moving Multisource Assessment Beyond Development," *ACA Journal* (Winter 1995), pp. 82–93; and John F. Milliman, Robert A. Zawacki, Carol Norman, Lynda Powell, and Jay Kirksey, "Companies Evaluate Employees from All Perspectives," *Personnel Journal* (November 1994), p. 99.

62. Ibid., pp. 99–104.

63. Ruth E. Thaler-Carter, "Whither Global Leaders," *HRMagazine* (May 2000), p. 82; Leanne Atwater and David Waldman, "Accountability in 360-Degree Feedback," *HRMagazine* (May 1998), p. 96; Robert Hoffman, "Ten Reasons You Should Be Using 360-Degree Feedback," *HRMagazine* (April 1995), p. 82; and "Companies Where Employees Rate Executives," *Fortune* (December 27, 1993), p. 128.

64. Carol Hymowitz, "In the Lead: Do '360' Job Reviews by Colleagues Promote Honesty or Insults?" *Wall Street Journal* (December 12, 2000), p. B-1; and Phaedra Brotherton, "Candid Feedback Spurs Changes in Culture," *HRMagazine* (May 1996), pp. 47–52.

65. Brian O'Reilly, "360-Feedback Can Change Your Life," *Fortune* (October 17, 1994), p. 96.

66. Ibid.

67. See, for example, David A. Waldman, Leanne E. Atwater, and David Antonioni, "Has 360-Degree Feedback Gone Amok? *Academy of Management Journal* (February 1998), pp. 86–94; Dianne Nilsen, "Self-Observer Rating Discrepancies: Once an Overrater, Always an Overrater," *Human Resource Management* (Fall 1993), pp. 265–282; Walter W. Turnow, "Perceptions or Reality: Is Multi-Perspective Measurement a Means or an End?" *Human Resource Management* (Fall 1993), pp. 221–230; Manuel London and Richard W. Beatty, "360-Degree Feedback as a Competitive Advantage," *Human Resource Management* (Fall 1993), pp. 353–373; Robert E. Kaplan, "360-Degree Feedback PLUS: Boosting the Power of Co-Worker Rating for Executives," *Human Resource Management* (Fall 1993), pp. 299–315; and Hal Lancaster, "Performance Reviews Are More Valuable When More Join In," *Wall Street Journal* (July 9, 1996), p. B1.

68. G. Douglas Huet-Cox, Tjai M. Neilsen, and Eric Sundstrom,

"Get the Most from 360-Degree Feedback: Put it on the Net," *HRMagazine* (May 1999), pp. 92–103.

69. W. C. Borman, "The Rating of Individuals in Organizations: An Alternative Approach," *Organizational Behavior and Human Performance* (August 1974), pp. 105–124.

70. Christopher P. Neck, Greg L. Stewart, Charles C. Manz, "Thought Self-leadership as a Framework for Enhancing the Performance of Performance Appraisers," *Journal of Applied Behavior Science* (September 1995).

71. Charles Lee, "Poor Performance Appraisals Do More Harm Than Good," *Personnel Journal* (September 1989), p. 91.

72. Ibid.

73. See Peter J. Dowling, Randall S. Schuler, and Denice E. Welch, *International Dimensions of Human Resource Management*, 2d ed. (Belmont, CA: Wadsworth, 1994), pp. 103–120; and G. Oddou and M. Mendenhall, "Expatriate Performance Appraisal: Problems and Solutions," in M. Mendenhall and G. Oddou (eds.), *International Human Resource Management* (Boston: PWS Kent Publishing, 1991), pp. 364–374.

74. G. Oddou and M. Mendenhall, "Expatriate Performance Appraisal: Problems and Solutions," in M. Mendenhall and G. Oddou (eds.), *International Human Resource Management* (Boston: PWS Kent Publishing, 1991), p. 366.

75. J. S. Solomon, "Employee Relations Soviet Style," *Personnel Administrator*, Vol. 30, No. 10 (October 1985), pp. 79–86. See also "Rewarding Individuals Hinders Team Performance," *HRMagazine* (November 1996), p. 16.

76. Dowling, Schuler, and Welch, pp. 113–115; and Oddou and Mendenhall, pp. 372–374.

77. Ibid.

78. See also Paula Peters, "7 Tips for Delivering Performance Feedback," *Supervision* (May 2000), pp. 12–14.

79. See Wendy R. Boswell and John W. Boudreau, "Employee Satisfaction with Performance Appraisals and Appraisers: The Role of Perceived Appraisal Use," *Human Resource Development Quarterly* (Fall 2000), pp. 283–299.

80. Stephen M. Pollan and Mark Levine, "Maximizing Your Performance Review," *Working Woman* (December 1993), p. 74; and Elaine McShulskis, "Involve Employees in Performance Appraisals," *HRMagazine* (April 1997), p. 24.

11

ESTABLISHING REWARDS AND PAY PLANS

LEARNING OUTCOMES

AFTER READING THIS CHAPTER, YOU WILL BE ABLE TO:

1. Explain the various classifications of rewards.
2. Discuss why some rewards are considered membership based.
3. Define the goal of compensation administration.
4. Discuss job evaluation and its three basic approaches.
5. Explain the evolution of the final wage structure.
6. Describe competency-based compensation programs.
7. Discuss why executives are paid significantly higher salaries than other employees in an organization.
8. Identify what is meant by the balance sheet approach to international compensation.

Consider the following scenario. For the past several years, you have been working six to seven days a week, 12 to 14 hours a day struggling to keep your business afloat. You do everything possible to make the company succeed. But it's hard. Competition is keen, yet you know what your company can become. And then it becomes a reality. After years of keeping things alive, of waking up in the middle of the night wondering how to make payroll, it happens. Success, phenomenal growth, and an unparalleled mission. The profits are there. And what's one of the first things you'll do? If you're Wayne Coffey, President of Coffey and Company Insurance in Towson, Maryland, that answer is easy. You share the good fortune with those who helped get you there—the employees.[1]

After having worked for years as a farmer, Wayne entered the insurance business. His driving goals were to help people get through their toughest times and to be there with the assistance that could make a difficult situation a bit easier to handle. Working for someone else, however, created a bit of a concern for Coffey. Furthermore, Wayne wanted to fulfill a second passion—developing people. There were things he wanted to do, but he was constrained by organizational policies and politics. Finally, he decided to take the plunge and go out on his own, forming Coffey and Company in the early 1990s.

As a small insurance broker, Coffey realized that to be successful he had to be different from his competitors. To Wayne, this meant that he had to develop a vision and a mission for the company that made his company unique. Coffey and Company achieved this through their "commitment to the highest standards of service and integrity, an organization that embraces professionalism, integrity, and competency." Still, mission statements alone won't make that happen. Rather, it is only possible through the outstanding efforts of a team of highly energized employees under the leadership of a concerned, dedicated, community-driven leader.

Over the past several years, Coffey and Company has built a team of employees that not only embrace the company's mission, but practice it regularly. Whether it's the company's outside sales associates, or the internal administrative people, they work in concert to deliver excellent service. It has not gone unnoticed. For their efforts, the company has achieved a level of recognition in the community that is second to none. And with that have come the fruits of success.

Many organizations are successful and profitable. But it's what happens to these profits that sometimes make a difference. Clearly Coffey had every right simply to pocket every cent. After all, it's he who has had the burden the past several years, and it is Coffey who is responsible if anything should go wrong. But that's not what Wayne wanted. Instead, he recognized that sharing with his employees was not only a good thing to do, it was the right thing. It was through their team efforts that they got to this point and positioned themselves for the future. Accordingly, treating them to a special recognition luncheon in their honor, closing the company down for a team party, and awarding each employee with a surprise holiday bonus check as well as making a match to the Company's 401K including a separate 401K bonus was the least Coffey felt he could do.

Has it worked? Just ask Dolores Coffey, Dawn Wilhelm, Lisa Allender, Carol Bradely, Nat Coughlin and Chip McCuen. Each will tell you Coffey and Company is the most fulfilling and rewarding organization for which they've ever worked!

INTRODUCTION

"What's in it for me?" That is a question nearly every individual consciously or unconsciously asks before engaging in any form of behavior. Our knowledge of motivation and people's behavior at work tells us that people do what they do to satisfy some need. Before they do anything, therefore, they look for a payoff or reward.

The most obvious reward employees get from work is pay. However, rewards also include promotions, desirable work assignments, and a host of other less obvious payoffs—a smile, peer acceptance, work freedom, or a kind word of recognition. We'll spend the major part of this chapter addressing pay as a reward as well as how compensation programs are established.

TYPES OF EMPLOYEE REWARDS

There are several ways to classify rewards. We have selected three of the most typical dichotomies: *intrinsic versus extrinsic rewards, financial versus nonfinancial rewards,* and *performance-based versus membership-based rewards.* As you will see, these categories are far from being mutually exclusive, yet all share one common thread—they assist in maintaining employee commitment.

Intrinsic versus Extrinsic Rewards

Intrinsic Rewards Rewards one receives from the job itself, such as pride in one's work, a feeling of accomplishment, or being part of a team.

Intrinsic rewards are the personal satisfactions one gets from the job itself. These are self-initiated rewards, such as having pride in one's work, having a feeling of accomplishment, or being part of a work team.[2] Job enrichment, for instance (see Workplace Issues), can offer intrinsic rewards to employees by making work seem more meaningful. **Extrinsic rewards,** on the other hand, include money, promotions, and benefits.[3] Their common thread is that they are external to the job and come from an outside source, mainly management. Consequently, if an employee experiences feelings of achievement or personal growth from a job, we would label such rewards as intrinsic. If the employee receives a salary increase or a writeup in the company magazine, we would label these rewards as extrinsic. The general structure of rewards has been summarized in Exhibit 11-1.

Extrinsic Rewards Rewards one gets from the employer, usually money, a promotion, or benefits.

Financial versus Nonfinancial Rewards

Rewards may or may not enhance the employee's financial well-being. If they do, they can do this directly, for instance, through wages, bonuses, or profit sharing, or indirectly, through employer-subsidized benefits such as retirement plans, paid vacations, paid sick leaves, and purchase discounts.[4]

Nonfinancial rewards cover a smorgasbord of desirable extras that are potentially at the disposal of the organization. Their common link is that they do not directly increase the employee's financial position. Instead of enhancing the employee's finances, nonfinancial rewards emphasize making life on the job more attractive. The nonfinancial rewards that we will identify represent a few of the more obvious; however, the creation of these rewards is limited only by HRM's ingenuity and ability to use them to motivate desirable behavior.

The saying, "One person's food is another person's poison," applies to the entire subject of rewards, but specifically to the area of nonfinancial rewards. What one employee views as "something I've always wanted," another might find relatively useless. Therefore, HRM must take great care in providing the

Exhibit 11-1
Structure of Rewards

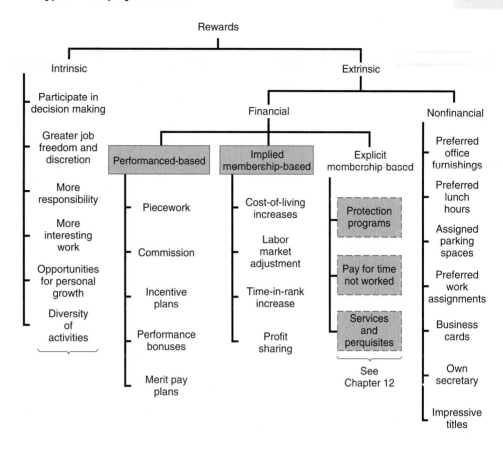

"right" nonfinancial reward for each person. Yet where selection has been done properly, the benefits by way of increased performance to the organization should be significant.

Some workers, for example, are very status conscious. A plush office, a carpeted floor, a large solid wood desk, or signed artwork may be just the office furnishing that stimulates an employee toward top performance. Similarly, status-oriented employees may value an impressive job title, their own business cards, their own administrative assistant, or a well-located parking space with their name clearly painted underneath the "Reserved" sign. In another case, the employee may value the opportunity to dress casually while at work, or even do a portion of one's job at home. Irrespective of the "incentive," these are within the organization's discretion. And when carefully used, they may provide a stimulus for enhanced performance.

Performance-based versus Membership-based Rewards

The rewards that the organization allocates can be said to be based on either performance or membership criteria. While HR representatives in many organizations will vigorously argue that their reward system pays off for performance, you should recognize that this isn't always the case. Few organizations actually reward employees based on performance—a point we will discuss later in this chapter. Without question, the dominant basis for reward allocations in organizations is membership.

Performance-based rewards are exemplified by the use of commissions, piecework pay plans, incentive systems, group bonuses, merit pay, or other forms of

Performance-based Rewards Rewards exemplified by the use of commissions, piecework pay plans, incentive systems, group bonuses, or other forms of merit pay.

JOB ENRICHMENT

THE MOST POPULARLY ADVOCATED STRUCTURAL TECHNIQUE for increasing an employee's reward potential is **job enrichment.** To enrich a job, management allows the worker to assume some of the tasks executed by his or her supervisor. Enrichment requires that workers do increased planning and controlling of their work, usually with less supervision and more self-evaluation. From the standpoint of increasing the internal motivation from doing a job, it has been proposed that job enrichment offers great potential. This comes from the increased responsibility, increased employee's freedom and independence, organized tasks so as to allow individuals to do a complete activity, and providing feedback to allow individuals to correct their own performance. In addition, we can say that these factors lead, in part, to a better quality of work life. Furthermore, job-enrichment efforts will be successful only if the individuals in the enriched jobs find the "enrichment" rewarding. If these individuals do not want increased responsibility, for example, then increasing responsibility will not have the desired effect. Successful job enrichment, then, is contingent on worker input.

A successful job enrichment program should ideally increase employee satisfaction and commitment. But since organizations do not exist to create employee satisfaction as an end, there must also be direct benefits to the organization. There is evidence that job enrichment and quality of life programs produce lower absenteeism, reduce turnover costs, and increase employee commitment, but on the critical issue of productivity, the evidence is inconclusive, or poorly measured.[5] In some situations, job enrichment has increased productivity; in others, productivity has been decreased. However, when it decreases, there does appear to be a consistently conscientious use of resources and a higher quality of product or service. In other words, in terms of efficiency, for the same input a higher quality of output is obtained; so fewer repairs could increase productivity if the measure included the number of repairs.

---

pay-for-performance plans. On the other hand, membership-based rewards include cost-of-living increases, benefits, and salary increases attributable to labor-market conditions, seniority or time in rank, credentials (such as a college degree or a graduate diploma), a specialized skill, or future potential (e.g., the recent MBA out of a prestigious university). The key point here is that membership-based rewards are generally extended regardless of an individual's, group's, or organization's performance. The difference between the two is not always obvious. In practice, performance may be only a minor determinant of rewards, despite academic theories holding that high motivation depends on performance-based rewards.

WHAT IS COMPENSATION ADMINISTRATION?

Why do regional sales managers at Moen in North Olmstead, Ohio earn more than the customer service representatives? Intuitively, you might say that the sales managers are more skilled and have greater job responsibility, so they should earn more. But how about sales managers who specialize in major accounts like Home Depot and Lowe's? Should they make more or less than the sales manager who supervises sales of faucets to much smaller hardware stores? The answers to questions such as these lie in job evaluation.

Job Evaluation Determining the worth of a job.

Job evaluation is the process whereby an organization systematically establishes its compensation program. In this process, jobs are compared in order to arrive at each job's appropriate worth within the organization. In this section we will discuss the broader topic of compensation, narrow our discussion to job evaluation methods, and conclude with a review of an increasingly controversial topic—executive compensation.

Employees exchange work for rewards. Probably the most important reward, and indeed the most obvious, is money. But all employees don't earn the same amount of money. Why? The search for this answer moves us directly into the topic of compensation administration.

Compensation Administration The process of managing a company's compensation program.

The goals of **compensation administration** are to design a cost-effective pay structure that will attract, motivate, and retain competent employees.[6] It should also be one that will be perceived as fair by employees. *Fairness* is a term that frequently arises in the administration of an organization's compensation program. Organizations generally seek to pay the least that they have to in order to minimize costs, so fairness means a wage or salary that is adequate for the demands and requirements of the job. Of course, fairness is a two-way street. Employees, too, want fair compensation. As we pointed out in our earlier discussion of motivation, if employees perceive an imbalance in the relation of their efforts-rewards ratio to some comparative standard, they will act to correct the inequity. So the search for fairness is pursued by both employers and employees.[7]

The goals of compensation administration are to design a cost-effective pay structure that will attract, motivate, and retain competent employees.

Government Influence on Compensation Administration

In Chapter 3, we described how government policies shape and influence HRM. This influence, however, is not equally felt in all areas. For example, collective bargaining and the employee selection process are heavily constrained by government rules and regulations. In contrast, this influence is less in the areas of employment planning and orientation.

Compensation administration falls into the former category. Government policies set minimum wages and benefits that employers must meet, and these policies provide protection for certain groups (see Exhibit 11-2). The laws and regulations we will discuss are not meant to comprehensively cover government's influence on compensation administration. Rather, they are presented as highlights. The point of these highlights should be to make you aware that government constraints reduce HRM's discretion on compensation decisions. An abundance of laws and regulations define the general parameters within which managers decide what is fair compensation. Let's look at some of these.

Fair Labor Standards Act Passed in 1938, this act established laws outlining minimum wage, overtime pay, and maximum hour requirements for most U.S. workers.

Fair Labor Standards Act The **Fair Labor Standards Act** (FLSA), passed in 1938, contained several provisions that affected organizations and their compensation systems. These included issues surrounding minimum wages, overtime pay, record-keeping and child labor restrictions. Nearly all organizations, except the smallest businesses, are covered by the FLSA. The Act also identified two primary categories of employees—exempt and nonexempt. Exempt employees would include, for instance, employees in professional and managerial jobs. Under the Act, jobs categorized as exempt are not required to meet FLSA standards, especially in the area of overtime pay. On the other hand, nonexempt employees receive certain protections under the FLSA. Specifically, employees in these jobs are eligible for premium pay—typically time-and-a-half—when they work more than 40 hours in a week. Moreover, these jobs must be paid at least the minimum wage, which in September 1997 was raised to $5.15 an hour.

Both federal and state governments have also enacted laws requiring employees who contract with the government to pay what are called *prevailing wage rates*. In the federal sector, the secretary of labor is required to review industry

EXHIBIT 11-2
Federal Minimum Wage

YOUR RIGHTS

Under the Fair Labor Standards Act

Federal Minimum Wage

$5.15

Minimum Wage of at least $5.15 per hour beginning September 1, 1997.

Certain full-time student learners, apprentices, and workers with disabilities may be paid less than the minimum wage under special certificates issued by the Department of Labor.

Tip credit — The tip credit which an employer may claim with respect to "Tipped Employees" is 50 percent of the applicable minimum wage.

Overtime Pay

At least $1\frac{1}{2}$ times your regular rate of pay for all hours worked over 40 in a workweek.

Child Labor

An employee must be at least sixteen years old to work in most non-farm jobs and at least eighteen to work in non-farm jobs declared hazardous by the Secretary of Labor. Youths fourteen and fifteen years old may work outside school hours in various non-manufacturing, non-mining, non-hazardous jobs under the following conditions:

No more than—

3 hours on a school day or eighteen hours in a school week;

8 hours on a non-school day or forty hours in a non-school week.

Also, work may not begin before 7 a.m. or end after 7 p.m., except from June 1 through Labor Day, when evening hours are extended to 9 p.m. Different rules apply in agricultural employment.

Enforcement

The Department of Labor may recover back wages either administratively or through court action, for the employees that have been underpaid in violation of the law. Violations may result in civil or criminal action.

Fines of up to $10,000 per minor may be assessed against employers who violate the child labor provisions of the law and up to $1,000 per violation against employers who willfully or repeatedly violate the minimum wage or overtime provisions. This law *prohibits* discriminating against or discharging workers who file a complaint or participate in any proceedings under the Act.

Note:

Certain occupations and establishments are exempt from the minimum wage and/or overtime pay provisions.

Special provisions apply to workers in Puerto Rico and American Samoa.

Where state law requires a higher minimum wage, the higher standard applies.

FOR ADDITIONAL INFORMATION, CONTACT the Wage and Hour Division office nearest you— listed in your telephone directory under United States Government, Labor Department.

The law requires employees to display this poster where employees can readily see it.

Source: U.S. Department of Labor, Employment Standards Administration, Wage and Hour Division, Washington, D.C. 20210. WH Publication 1088. Revised October 1996, U.S. Government Printing Office: 1996— 300–812.

rates in the specific locality to set a prevailing rate which becomes the minimum under the contract prescribed under the Walsh-Healy Act. Under this act, government contractors must also pay time-and-a-half for all work in excess of eight hours a day or 40 hours a week.

The Civil Rights and the Equal Pay Acts   The Civil Rights and the Equal Pay Acts, among other laws, protect employees from discrimination. Just as it is illegal to discriminate in hiring, organizations cannot discriminate in pay on the basis of race, color, creed, age, or sex.

The **Equal Pay Act of 1963** mandates that organizations compensate men and women doing the same job in the organization with the same rate of pay. The Equal Pay Act was designed to lessen the pay gap between male and female pay rates. Although progress is being made, women in general still earn roughly 75 percent of what their male counterparts earn.[8] Some of this difference is attributable to perceived male-versus-female-dominated occupations, but the Equal Pay Act requires employers to eliminate pay differences for the same job. That is, salaries should be established on the basis of skill, responsibility, effort, and working conditions. For example, if an organization is hiring customer service representatives, new employees, irrespective of their sex, must be paid the same initial salary because the attributes for the job are the same. It is important to note that the Equal Pay Act typically affects only initial job salaries. If two workers, one male and one female, perform at different levels during the course of the year, it is conceivable that if performance is rewarded, in the next period their pay may be different. This is permitted under the act!

Equal Pay Act   Passed in 1963, this act requires equal pay for equal work.

There are no jobs that are solely for males or females. That's illegal. But it's also illegal to initially pay women and men performing the same job at different pay levels. For example, hiring for these (insert type of job) requires a company to pay men and women the same when they start the job. That's precisely the requirement of the 1963 Equal Pay Act!

JOB EVALUATION AND THE PAY STRUCTURE

The essence of compensation administration is job evaluation and the establishment of a pay structure. Let's now turn our attention to the topic of job evaluation and a discussion of how it is done.

What Is Job Evaluation?

In Chapter 5, we introduced job analysis as the process of describing the duties of a job, authority relationships, skills required, conditions of work, and additional relevant information. We stated that the data generated from job analysis could be used to develop job descriptions and specifications, as well as to do job evaluations. By job evaluation, we mean using the information in job analysis to systematically determine the value of each job in relation to all jobs within the organization. In short, job evaluation seeks to rank all the jobs in the organization and place them in a hierarchy that will reflect the relative worth of each. It's important to note that this is a ranking of jobs, not people. Job evaluation assumes normal performance of the job by a typical worker. So, in effect, the process ignores individual abilities or the performance of the jobholder.

The ranking that results from job evaluation is the means to an end, not an end in itself. It should be used to determine the organization's pay structure. Note that we say *should;* in practice, we'll find that this is not always the case. External labor market conditions, collective bargaining, and individual skill differences may require a compromise between the job evaluation ranking and the actual pay structure. Yet even when such compromises are necessary, job evaluation can provide an objective standard from which modifications can be made.

Isolating Job Evaluation Criteria

The heart of job evaluation is the determination of what criteria will be used to arrive at the ranking. It is easy to say that jobs are valued and ranked by their relative job worth, but there is far more ambiguity when we attempt to state what it is that makes one job higher than another in the job structure hierarchy. Most job-evaluation plans use responsibility, skill, effort, and working conditions as major criteria,[9] but each of these, in turn, can be broken down into more specific terms. Skill, for example, is "an observable competence to perform a learned psychomotor act (like keyboarding)."[10] But other criteria can and have been used: supervisory controls, complexity, personal contacts, and the physical demands needed.[11]

You should not expect the criteria to be constant across jobs. Since jobs differ, it is traditional to separate jobs into common groups. This usually means that, for example, production, clerical, sales, professional, and managerial jobs are evaluated separately. Treating like groups similarly allows for more valid rankings within categories but still leaves unsettled the importance of criteria between categories. Separation by groups may permit us to say the position of software developer in the Development group requires more mental effort than that of a shipping supervisor, and subsequently receives a higher ranking; but it does not readily resolve whether greater mental effort is necessary for software designers than for customer service managers.

Methods of Job Evaluation

There are three basic methods of job evaluation currently in use: ordering, classification, and the point method.[12] Let's review each of these.

Ordering Method Ranking job worth from highest to lowest.

Ordering Method The **ordering method** (or ranking method) requires a committee—typically composed of both management and employee representatives—to arrange jobs in a simple rank order, from highest to lowest. No attempt is made to break down the jobs by specific weighted criteria. The committee members merely compare two jobs and judge which one is more important, or more difficult to perform. Then they compare another job with the first two, and so on until all the jobs have been evaluated and ranked.

The most obvious limitation to the ordering method is its sheer inability to be managed when there are a large number of jobs. Imagine the difficulty of trying to rank hundreds or thousands of jobs in the organization! It is virtually impossible to do the rankings correctly. Other drawbacks to be considered are the subjectivity of the method—there are no definite or consistent standards by which to justify the rankings—and the fact that because jobs are only ranked in terms of order, we have no knowledge of the distance between the ranks.

Classification Method The classification method was made popular by the U.S. Civil Service Commission, now the Office of Personnel Management (OPM). The OPM requires that classification grades be established and published in what they call their General Schedules. These classifications are created by identifying some common denominator—skills, knowledge, responsibilities—with the desired goal being the creation of a number of distinct classes or grades of jobs. Examples might include shop jobs, clerical jobs, and sales jobs, depending, of course, on the type of jobs the organization requires.

Once the classifications are established, they are ranked in an overall order of importance according to the criteria chosen, and each job is placed in its appropriate classification. This latter action is generally done by comparing each position's job description against the classification description and benchmarked jobs. At the OPM, for example, evaluators have classified both Securities and Exchange Compliance Officers and U.S. Army Audit Agency Auditors positions as GS-7 grades, while Plant Pathologists at the Animal and Plant Health Inspection Service and IRS Rating Specialists jobs have both been graded as GS-11.

The classification method shares most of the disadvantages of the ordering approach, plus the difficulty of writing classification descriptions, judging which jobs go where, and dealing with jobs that appear to fall into more than one classification. On the plus side, the classification method has proven itself successful and viable in classifying millions of kinds and levels of jobs in the civil service.

Point Method The last method we will present breaks down jobs based on various identifiable criteria (such as skill, effort, and responsibility) and then allocates points to each of these criteria. Depending on the importance of each criterion to performing the job, appropriate weights are given, points are summed, and jobs with similar point totals are placed in similar pay grades.

An excerpt from a **point method** chart for administrative assistant II positions is shown in Exhibit 11-3. Each job would be evaluated by deciding, for

Point Method Breaking down jobs based on identifiable criteria and the degree to which these criteria exist on the job.

EXHIBIT 11-3
Excerpts from a Point Method

Job Class: Clerk					
FACTOR	1ST DEGREE	2ND DEGREE	3RD DEGREE	4TH DEGREE	5TH DEGREE
Skill					
1. Education	22	44	66	88	110
2. Problem solving	14	28	42	56	70
Responsibility					
1. Safety of others	5	10	15	20	25
2. Work of others	7	14	21	28	35

2. Problem solving:
This factor examines the types of problems dealt with in your job. Indicate the one level that is most representative of the majority of your job responsibilities.

Degree 1: Actions are performed in a set order per written or verbal instruction. Problems are referred to supervisor.

Degree 2: Solves routine problems and makes various choices regarding the order in which the work is performed within standard practices. May obtain information from varied sources.

Degree 3: Solves varied problems that require general knowledge of company policies and procedures applicable within area of responsibility. Decisions made based on a choice from established alternatives. Expected to act within standards and established procedures.

Degree 4: Requires analytical judgment, initiative, or innovation in dealing with complex problems or situations. Evaluation not easy because there is little precedent or information may be incomplete.

Degree 5: Plans, delegates, coordinates, and/or implements complex tasks involving new or constantly changing problems or situations. Involves the origination of new technologies or policies for programs or projects. Actions limited only by company policies and budgets.

Source: Material reprinted with permission of The Dartnell Corporation, Chicago, IL 60640.

example, the degree of education required to perform the job satisfactorily. The first degree might require the equivalent of skill competencies associated with 10 years of elementary and secondary education; the second degree might require competencies associated with four years of high school; and so forth.

The point method offers the greatest stability of the four approaches we have presented. Jobs may change over time, but the rating scales established under the point method stay intact. Additionally, the methodology underlying the approach contributes to a minimum of rating error. On the other hand, the point method is complex, making it costly and time-consuming to develop. The key criteria must be carefully and clearly identified, degrees of factors have to be agreed upon in terms that mean the same to all raters, the weight of each criterion has to be established, and point values must be assigned to degrees. While it is expensive and time-consuming to both implement and maintain, the point method appears to be the most widely used method. Furthermore, this method can be effective for addressing the comparable worth issue (see Chapter 3).

Establishing the Pay Structure

Once the job evaluation is complete, the data generated become the nucleus for the development of the organization's pay structure.[13] This means pay rates or ranges will be established that are compatible with the ranks, classifications, or points arrived at through job evaluation.

Any of the three job evaluation methods can provide the necessary input for developing the organization's overall pay structure. Each has its strengths and weaknesses, but because of its wide use, we will use the point method to show how point totals are combined with compensation survey data to form wage curves.

Compensation
Surveys   Used to gather factual data on pay practices among firms and companies within specific communities.

Compensation Surveys   Many organizations use surveys to gather factual information on pay practices within specific communities and among firms in their industry.[14] This information is used for comparison purposes. It can tell compensation committees if the organization's wages are in line with those of other employers and, in cases where there is a short supply of individuals to fill certain positions, may be used to actually set wage levels. Where does an organization get wage salary data? The U.S. Department of Labor, through its Bureau of Labor Statistics, regularly publishes a vast amount of wage data broken down by geographic area, industry, and occupation. Many industry and employee associations also conduct **compensation surveys** and make their results available. But organizations can conduct their own surveys, and many large ones do!

It would not be unusual, for instance, for the HRM director at CitiCorp in Tampa Bay to regularly share wage data on key positions. Jobs such as maintenance engineer, electrical engineer, computer programmer, or administrative assistant would be identified, and comprehensive descriptions of these jobs would be shared with firms in the industry. In addition to the average wage level for a specific job, other information frequently reviewed includes entry-level and maximum wage rates, shift differentials, overtime pay practices, vacation and holiday allowances, the number of pay periods, and the length of the normal work day and work week.

Wage Curves   After the compensation committee arrives at point totals from job evaluation and obtains survey data on what comparable organizations are paying for similar jobs, a wage curve can be fitted to the data. An example of a wage curve is shown in Exhibit 11-4. This example assumes use of the point

EXHIBIT 11-4
A Wage Curve

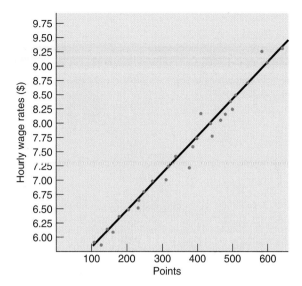

method and plots point totals and wage data. A separate wage curve can be constructed based on survey data and compared for discrepancies.

A completed wage curve tells the compensation committee the average relationship between points of established pay grades and wage base rates. Furthermore, it can identify jobs whose pay is out of the trend line. When a job's pay rate is too high, it may be identified as a "red circle" rate. This means that the pay level is frozen or below-average increases are granted until the structure is adjusted upward to put the circled rate within the normal range. Of course, there will be times when a wage rate is out of line but not red circled. The need to attract or keep individuals with specific skills may require a wage rate outside the normal range. To continue attracting these individuals, however, may ultimately upset the internal consistencies supposedly inherent in the wage structure. It also should be pointed out that a wage rate may be too low. Such undervalued jobs carry a "green circle" rate, and attempts may be made to grant these jobs above-average pay increases, or salary adjustments.

Wage Structure A pay scale showing ranges of pay within each grade.

The Wage Structure It is only a short step from plotting a wage curve to developing the organization's **wage structure.** Jobs that are similar in terms of classes, grades, or points are grouped together. For instance, pay grade 1 may cover the range from 0 to 150 points, pay grade 2 from 151 to 300 points, and so on. As shown in Exhibit 11-5, the result is a logical hierarchy of wages. The more important jobs are paid more; and as individuals assume jobs of greater importance, they rise within the wage hierarchy. Jobs may also be paid in accordance with what is commonly referred to as knowledge- or competency-based pay. We'll return to this topic shortly.

Irrespective of the determinants, notice that each pay grade has a range and that the ranges overlap. Typically, organizations design their wage structures with ranges in each grade to reflect different tenure in positions, as well as levels of performance. Additionally, while most organizations create a degree of overlap between grades, employees who reach the top of their grade can only increase their pay by moving to a higher grade. However, wage structures are adjusted every several years (if not every year) so employees who've topped-out in their pay grade aren't "maxed-out" forever.

EXHIBIT 11-5
A Sample Wage Structure

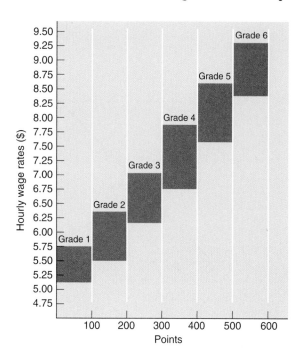

SOME SPECIAL CASES OF COMPENSATION

As organizations are rapidly changing in the dynamic world in which they exist, so, too, are compensation programs. Most notably, organizations are finding that they can no longer continue to increase wage rates by a certain percentage each year (a cost-of-living raise) without some comparable increase in performance. Subsequently, more organizations are moving to varied themes of the pay-for-performance systems. These may include incentive compensation plans, and competency and team-based compensation. Let's take a closer look at each of these.

Incentive Compensation Plans

In addition to the basic wage structure, organizations that are sincerely committed to developing a compensation system that is designed around performance will want to consider the use of incentive pay. Typically given in addition to—rather than in place of—the basic wage, incentive plans should be viewed as an additional dimension to the wage structure we have previously described. Incentives can be paid based on individual, group, or organization-wide performance—a pay-for-performance concept.

Individual Incentives   Individual incentive plans pay off for individual performances. During the 1990s, these plans had been the biggest trend in compensation administration in the United States. Popular approaches included merit pay, piecework plans, time-savings bonuses, and commissions.

Merit Pay   An increase in one's pay, usually given on an annual basis.

One popular and almost universally used incentive system is **merit pay.** Under a merit pay plan, employees who receive merit increases have a sum of money added to their base salary. Somewhat likened to a cost-of-living raise, merit pay differs in that the percentage of increase to the base wage rate is attributable solely to performance. Those who perform better generally receive more merit pay.

Piecework Plan A compensation plan whereby employees are typically paid for the number of units they actually produce.

While the merit pay plan is the most widely used, the best-known incentive is undoubtedly piecework. Under a straight **piecework plan,** the employee is typically guaranteed a minimal hourly rate for meeting some preestablished standard output. For output over this standard, the employee earns so much for each piece produced. Differential piece-rate plans establish two rates—one up to standard, and another when the employee exceeds the standard. The latter rate, of course, is higher to encourage the employee to beat the standard. Individual incentives can be based on time saved as well as output generated. As with piecework, the employee can expect a minimal guaranteed hourly rate, but in this case, the bonus is achieved for doing a standard hour's work in less than 60 minutes. Employees who can do an hour's work in 50 minutes obtain a bonus that is some percentage (say 50 percent) of the labor saved.

Salespeople frequently work on a commission basis. Added to a lower base wage, they get an amount that represents a percentage of the sales price. On toys, for instance, it may be a hefty 25 or 30 percent. On sales of multi-million-dollar aircraft or city sewer systems, commissions are frequently 1 percent or less.

Individual incentives work best where clear performance objectives can be set and where tasks are independent.[15] If these conditions are not met, individual incentives can create dysfunctional competition or encourage workers to "cut corners." Coworkers can become the enemy, individuals can create inflated perceptions of their own work while deflating the work of others, and the work environment may become characterized by reduced interaction and communications between employees. And if corners are cut, quality and safety may also be compromised. For example, when Monsanto tied workers' bonuses to plant safety, covering up accidents was encouraged.[16]

A potentially negative effect with incentive for performance is that you may "get what you pay for." Since the incentives are tied to specific goals (which are only part of the total outcomes expected from a job), people may avoid performing the unmeasured, and thus not rewarded, activities in favor of the measured, rewarded ones. For example, if your school held a colloquium and brought in a guest speaker, and your instructor decided to take your class, would you go? Your response might be contingent on whether the colloquium was a requirement, the content of which could be included on an exam, and where attendance was taken. But if it was just for your information, attending might not be as high a priority. Despite the potential negative repercussions that individual incentives can cause in inappropriate situations, they are undoubtedly widespread in practice.

Sometimes, merit pay, too, has been used as a substitute for cost-of-living raises.[17] And similar to the cost-of-living raise, merit monies accrue permanently to the base salary and become the new base from which future percentage increases can be calculated. The problem with merit pay or a cost-of-living system, then, is that pay increases may be always expected. But what if the company has a bad year, or employees don't produce what is expected of them? Under these traditional systems, wage increases still are expected. Theoretically, they should give some of their salary back!

Organizations today are looking at this latter idea. Specifically, they are requiring employees to place a percentage of their salary at risk. For example, employees at Hallmark Cards, Inc., in Kansas City, have up to 10 percent of their pay placed at risk. Depending on their productivity on such performance measures as customer satisfaction, retail sales, and profits, employees can turn the 10 percent "at-risk" pay into rewards as high as 25 percent.[18] However,

Employees at Hallmark Cards have up to 10 percent of their pay placed at risk.

failure to reach the performance measures can result in the forfeiture of the 10 percent salary placed at risk. Companies like Saturn, Steelcase, TRW, Hewlett-Packard, DuPont, Eastman Chemical, and Ameri-Tech use similar formulas where employee compensation is comprised of a base rate and reward pay.[19]

Group Incentives   Each individual incentive option we described also can be used on a group basis; that is, two or more employees can be paid for their combined performance. When are group incentives desirable? They make the most sense where employees' tasks are interdependent and thus require cooperation.

Plant-wide Incentives   An incentive system that rewards all members of the plant based on how well the entire group performed.

Plant-wide Incentives   The goal of **plant-wide incentives** is to direct the efforts of all employees toward achieving overall organizational effectiveness. This type of incentive, like that of DuPont, produces rewards for all employees based on organization-wide cost reduction or profit sharing. Kaiser Steel, for example, developed in one of its plants a cost-reduction plan that provides monthly bonuses to employees.[20] The amount of the bonus is determined by computing one-third of all increases in productivity attributable to cost savings as a result of technological change or increased effort. Additionally, Lincoln Electric has had a year-end bonus system for decades, which in some years has provided an annual bonus "ranging from a low of 55 percent to a high of 115 percent of annual earnings."[21] The Lincoln Electric plan pays off handsomely when employees beat previous years' performance standards. Since this bonus is added to the employee's salary, it has made the Lincoln Electric workers some of the highest-paid electrical workers in the United States.[22]

Scanlon Plan   An organization-wide incentive program focusing on cooperation between management and employees through sharing problems, goals, and ideas.

One of the best-known organization-wide incentive systems is the **Scanlon Plan**.[23] It seeks to bring about cooperation between management and employees through the sharing of problems, goals, and ideas. (It is interesting to note that many of the quality circle programs instituted in the 1980s were a direct outgrowth of the Scanlon Plan.[24]) Under Scanlon, each department in the organization has a committee composed of supervisor and employee representatives. Suggestions for labor-saving improvements are funneled to the committee, and, if accepted, cost savings and productivity gains are shared by all employees, not just the individual who made the suggestion. Typically, about 80 percent of the suggestions prove practical and are adopted.

IMPROSHARE   A special type of incentive plan using a specific mathematical formula for determining employee bonuses.

Another incentive plan that started in the early 1990s is called **IMPROSHARE**.[25] IMPROSHARE, which is an acronym for Improving Productivity through Sharing, uses a mathematical formula for determining employees' bonuses.[26] For example, if workers can save labor costs in producing a product, a predetermined portion of the labor savings will go to the employee. Where IMPROSHARE exists, productivity gains up to 18 percent have been identified, with most of the gains coming from reduced defects and less production downtime.[27]

Profit-sharing plans, or gainsharing plans, are also plant-wide incentives.[28] They allow employees to share in the success of a firm by distributing part of the company's profits back to the workers. For instance, employees at Chamberlin Rubber company receive 75 percent of profits in the company.[29] In essence, employees become owners of the company. The logic behind profit-sharing plans is that they increase commitment and loyalty to the organization.[30]

All the plant-wide incentives suffer from what is known as a *dilution effect*. It is hard for employees to see how their efforts result in the organization's over-

ESTABLISHING PAY PLANS

WOULDN'T IT BE NICE IF YOU could click a few buttons and your compensation system would magically appear? And it would be a system that would be consistent with the laws in your state, as well as maximizing employee rewards. Unfortunately, that dream hasn't come true yet, but there are a couple of software packages that can assist an organization in reaching that goal.

Employee Compensation: Employee Compensation in Your State (HR Press, $495, www.hrpress-software.com/comp.html) is a CD-ROM-based system that provides a wide range of compensation information—including rate ranges, compensation survey data, etc. The software also provides information regarding federal compensation laws as well as specific laws to your state. Purchase of the CD also enrolls the user into an annual subscription program which provides monthly bulletins, labor market analyses data, and changes in compensation laws that may affect your compensation program.

BLR Compensation: BLR Compensation (BLR, $99, www.blr.com/comp/online/content/index.cfm) provides a full program offering on compensation issues. These include wage and hour requirements (legal) and pay issues (as well as benefits). BLR also offers a CD-ROM product tailored to a specific state which provides an analysis of state compensation laws and compensation survey data. BLR also provides users with a monthly newsletter which discusses the latest issues in compensation administration.

all performance. These plans also tend to distribute their payoffs at wide intervals; a bonus paid in March 2001 for your efforts in 2000 loses a lot of its reinforcement capabilities. Finally, we should not overlook what happens when organization-wide incentives become both large and recurrent. When this happens, it is not unusual for the employee to begin to anticipate and expect the bonus. Employees may adjust their spending patterns as if the bonus were a certainty. The bonus may lose some of its motivating properties. When that happens, it can be perceived as a membership-based reward.

Paying for Performance

Pay-for-performance Rewarding employees based on their performance.

Pay-for-performance programs are compensation plans that pay employees on the basis of some performance measure.[31] Piecework plans, gainsharing, wage incentive plans, profit sharing, and lump sum bonuses are examples of pay-for-performance programs.[32] What differentiates these forms of pay from the more traditional compensation plans is that instead of paying an employee for time on the job, pay is adjusted to reflect some performance measures. These performance measures might include such things as individual productivity, team or work group productivity, departmental productivity, or the overall organization's profits for a given period.

Performance-based compensation is probably most compatible with demonstrating to employees that a strong relationship exists between their performance and the rewards they receive.[33] If rewards are allocated solely on nonperformance factors—such as seniority, job title, or across-the-board cost-of-living raises—then employees are likely to reduce their efforts.[34]

Pay-for-performance programs are gaining in popularity in organizations. One survey of 1,000 companies found that almost 80 percent of firms surveyed were practicing some form of pay-for-performance for salaried employees.[35] The growing popularity can be explained in terms of both motivation and cost control.[36] From a motivation perspective, making some or all of a worker's pay conditional on performance measures focuses his or her attention and effort on that measure, then reinforces the continuation of that effort with rewards. However, if the

Competency-based Compensation Programs Organizational pay system that rewards skills, knowledge, and behaviors.

Broad-banding Paying employees at preset levels based on the level of competencies they possess.

employee's, team's, or organization's performance declines, so too does the reward.[37] Thus, there is an incentive to keep efforts and motivation strong.[38,39] On the cost-savings side, performance-based bonuses and other incentive rewards avoid the fixed expense of permanent—and often annual—salary increases. The bonuses typically do not accrue to base salary, which means that the amount is not compounded in future years. As a result, they save the company money!

A recent extension of the pay-for-performance concept is called **competency-based compensation** and is used in such organizations as Amoco Corporation and Champion International.[40] A competency-based compensation program pays and rewards employees on the basis of the skills, knowledge, or behaviors employees possess.[41] These competencies may include such behaviors and skills as leadership, problem solving, decision making, or strategic planning. Pay levels are established on the basis of the degree to which these competencies exist. Pay increases in a competency-based system are awarded for growth in personal competencies as well as for the contributions one makes to the overall organization.[42] Accordingly, an employee's rewards are tied directly to how capable he or she is of contributing to the achievement of the organization's goals and objectives.

What in essence has occurred is a pay scheme based on the specific competencies an employee possesses. These may include knowledge of the business and its core competencies, skills to fulfill these core requirements, and demonstrated employee behaviors such as leadership, problem solving, decision making, and planning.[43] Based on the degree to which these competencies exist, pay levels are established. In competency-based pay plans, these preset levels are called **broad-banding.** A variety of banding programs have been witnessed—some with as few as four bands with no salary ranges, and others with as "many as 13 bands and multiple salary ranges per band."[44] For example, Exhibit 11-6 shows an eight-band compensation program that exists at Coregis Group, Inc. Broad-banding also can be used in developing wage structures on factors other than skills.

Those who possess a level of competencies within a certain range will be grouped together in a pay category. Pay increases, then, are awarded for growth in personal competencies, as well as the contribution one makes to the organization. Accordingly, career and pay advancement may not be tied to a promotion, per se, but rather to how much more one is capable of contributing to the organization's goals and objectives.

If you are making the connection back to when we discussed the point method of job evaluation, you are reading attentively. However, the point method looked specifically at the job and its worth to the company. Competency-based pay plans assess these "points" based on the value added by the employee in assisting the organization in achieving its goals. As more organizations move toward compe-

EXHIBIT 11-6
A Sample Banding

Band		Salary Range
Band	VIII:	$150,000–175,000
Band	VII:	85,000–125,000
Band	VI:	70,000–90,000
Band	V:	55,000–80,000
Band	IV:	40,000–60,000
Band	III:	25,000–45,000
Band	II:	20,000–40,000
Band	I:	15,000–25,000

Source: Based on the banding compensation program at Coregis Group, Inc., *ACA Journal* (Winter 1995), p. 53.

tency-based pay plans, HRM will play a critical role. Just as we discussed in Chapter 5 with respect to employment planning, once the direction of the organization is established, attracting, developing, motivating, and retaining competent individuals become essential. This will continue to have implications for recruiting, training and development, career development, performance appraisals, as well as pay and reward systems.[45] Not only will HRM ensure that it has the right people at the right place, but it will have assembled a competent team of employees who add significant value to the organization.

Team-based Compensation

Team-based Compensation Compensation based on how well the team performed.

You've just been handed a copy of the course syllabus for a business policy course you're taking this semester, and quickly your eyes glance at how the final grade will be calculated: two tests—a midterm and a final—and a class project. Intrigued, you read further about the class project. You and four other classmates will be responsible for thoroughly analyzing the company's operations. You are to make recommendations about the company's financial picture, human resources, product lines, competitive advantage, and strategic direction. The group is to turn in a report of no less than 50 pages, double-spaced, and make a 30-minute presentation to the class about your suggested turnaround. The report and presentation account for 75 percent of the course grade, and each member will receive the grade given by the instructor for the project. Not fair? Too much riding on the efforts of others? Welcome to the world of **team-based compensation.**

In today's dynamic organizations, much more emphasis has been placed on involving employees in most aspects of the job that affect them. When organizations group employees into teams and empower them to meet their goals, teams reap the benefits of their productive effort. That is, team-based compensation plans are tied to team-based performance. For example, at MacAllister Machinery, distributors of Caterpillar tractors in Indianapolis, bonus goals were established for its managers. If goals were achieved, they all shared in the "glory." If any of the managers failed, the entire team would not receive a dime of bonus money. How did the managers react? They pulled together and helped one another, resulting in sales increasing almost 25 percent and profits rising nearly 30 percent. Consequently, each manager received a bonus amounting to 50 percent of his or her salary.[46] The concept is now being driven down to the employee population! Similar programs also exist at DuPont, Monsanto, American Express, and General Motors.[47]

Want to have a significant influence on how a manager performs? Think about what the executives at MacAllister Machinery did. In setting goals for the company, each manager had a role in working with other managers to ensure that the goals were met. If they were, everyone would benefit—if not, all would suffer. The bottom line was that the managers worked together and helped the company increase profits. For their work, they each received about a 50 percent bonus.

Under a team-based compensation plan, team members who have worked on achieving—and in many cases, exceeding—established goals often share equally in the rewards (although, in the truest sense, teams allocate their own rewards). By providing for fair treatment of each team member, group cohesiveness is encouraged.[48] Yet, this does not occur overnight. Rather, it is a function of several key components being in place.[49] For instance, for teams to be effective, they must have a clear purpose and goals. They must understand what is expected of them and that their effort is worthwhile. Teams must also be provided the necessary resources to complete their tasks.[50] Because their livelihood may rest on accomplishing their goals, a lack of requisite resources may doom a team effort before it begins. And finally, there must be mutual trust among the team members. They must respect one another, effectively communicate with one another, and treat each member fairly and equitably. Without this, serious obstacles to teams may exist, which might defeat the purpose that group cohesiveness can foster.

EXECUTIVE COMPENSATION PROGRAMS

Executive pay is merely a special case within the topic of compensation, but it does have several twists that deserve special attention. First, the base salaries of executives are higher than those of low-level managers or operative personnel, and we want to explain why this is so. Second, executives frequently operate under bonus and stock option plans that can dramatically increase their total compensation.[51] A senior executive at American Express, General Electric, or MBNA can, in a good year, earn $10 million, $15 million, or more on top of the base salary.[52] We want to briefly look at how such compensations come about and why. Finally, executives receive perquisites (called perks) or special benefits that others do not. What are these, and how do they impact on executive motivation? These are the topics in this section on compensation.

Salaries of Top Managers

Charles Wang, CEO of Computer Associates, International, was recently awarded a salary that made people stop to check if the numbers were correct. In 1999, Wang collected more than $650 million in salary, bonuses, and stock-based incentives.[53] Wang is not alone in this high-salary category. The 10 top-paid CEOs of U.S. companies like CitiGroup, Charles Schwab, Bank of America, Compuware, and IBM earned an average of $165 million in total compensation in 1999. That's more than a 17 percent increase over their 1998 salaries. Incidentally, during this same time frame, the average worker's pay raise was in the 3 to 4 percent range.[54] Moreover, U.S. Chief Executive Officers, on average, make anywhere from 2 to 5 times the compensation of their counterparts in the global village.[55] It is interesting, however, that for the first time a woman is included in the category of the highest-paid CEO in Corporate America. That honor belongs to Carleton Fiorina, CEO of Hewlett-Packard, whose total 1999 compensation was more than $69 million.

It is well known that executives in the private sector receive considerably higher compensation than their counterparts in the public sector. Mid-level executives regularly earn base salaries of $150,000 to $225,000; the CEO of a billion-dollar corporation can expect a minimum total compensation package in excess of $25 million, while base salaries of $1 million or more are not unusual among senior management of *Fortune* 100 firms. In 1999, for instance, the average cash compensation (salary plus annual bonus, stock options, etc.) for CEOs in the *Fortune* 500 corporations was nearly $10 million.[56] How do organizations justify such extraordinary salaries for their executives? The answer is quite simple: economics and motivation.[57] In economic terms, we know that top managers are expected to demonstrate good decision-making abilities. This attribute may not be widely held by all workers. As a result, the supply of qualified senior executives is scarce, and organizations have bid up the price for this talent. They must keep their salaries in line with the competition or potentially lose an executive to another organization. High salaries also act to attract both top executives and lower-level managers. Management superstars, like superstar athletes in professional sports, are wooed with signing bonuses, interest-free loans, performance incentive packages, and guaranteed contracts. Of course, as in the case of athletes, some controversy surrounds the large dollar amounts paid to these executives (see Ethical Issues in HRM).[58]

ethical issues in HRM

ARE WE PAYING U.S. EXECUTIVES TOO MUCH?

A RE WE PAYING U.S. EXECUTIVES TOO much? Is an average salary in excess of $60 million justifiable? In any debate, there are two sides to the issue. Support for paying this amount is the fact that these executives have tremendous organizational responsibilities. They not only have to manage the organization in today's environment, they must keep it moving into the future. Their jobs are not 9-to-5 jobs, but rather six to seven days a week, often 10 to 14 hours a day. If jobs are evaluated on the basis of skills, knowledge, abilities, and responsibilities, executives should be highly paid.[59] Furthermore, there is the issue of motivation and retention. If you want these individuals to succeed and stay with the company, you must provide a compensation package that motivates them to stay. Incentives based on various measures also provide the impetus for them to excel.

On the other hand, most of the research done on executive salaries questions the linkage to performance. Even when profits are down, many executives are paid handsomely. In fact, American company executives are regarded as some of the highest-paid people in the world. On average, their salaries have increased by 6 to 10 times the average worker's salary. Additionally, when performance problems lead to dismissal, some executives are paid phenomenal severance packages. For example, ousted CEOs of Mattel and Conseco were given $50 and $49 million, respectively, as severance pay.[60] Finally, U.S. executives make two to five times the salaries of their foreign counterparts. That's an interesting comparison, especially when you consider that some executives in Japan-based organizations perform better.

Do you believe that U.S. executives are overpaid? What's your opinion?

Who's the highest-paid woman executive in the United States? That honor belongs to Carleton Fiorina, CEO of Hewlett-Packard. Her 1999 total compensation topped the $69 million mark, ranking her the 12th-highest paid of all U.S. executives in 1999.

Supplemental Financial Compensation

In 1999, the average compensation for executives in the *Fortune* 500 companies in the United States was $7.8 million.[61] This figure, as previously mentioned, includes their total compensation-base salary plus bonuses and stock options.[62] Bonuses and stock options dramatically increase the total compensation that executives receive. Much of this additional compensation is obtained through a deferred bonus—that is, the executive's bonus is computed on the basis of some formula, usually taking into account increases in sales and profits. This bonus, although earned in the current period, may be distributed over several future periods. Therefore, it is not unusual for an executive to earn a $1 million bonus but have it paid out at $50,000 a year for 20 years. The major purpose of such deferred compensation is to increase the cost to the executive of leaving the organization. In almost all cases, executives who voluntarily terminate their employment must forfeit their deferred bonuses. One of the main reasons why there are so few voluntary resignations among the ranks of senior management at General Motors is that these executives would lose hundreds of thousands of dollars in deferred income.

Interestingly, another form of bonus, the "hiring bonus," has arisen in the last decade, purposely designed to help senior executives defray the loss of deferred income. It is now becoming increasingly popular to pay senior executives a hiring bonus to sweeten the incentive for them to leave their current employer and forfeit their deferred bonuses and pension rights. These bonuses often do provide deferred income to compensate for loss of pension rights.

Stock options also have been a common incentive offered to executives. They generally allow executives to purchase, at some time in the future, a specific amount of the company's stock at a fixed price. Under the assumption that good management will increase the company's profitability and, therefore, the price of the stock, stock options are viewed as performance-based incentives.[63] It should be pointed out, however, that the use of stock options is heavily influenced by the current status of the tax laws. In recent years, tax reform legislation has taken away some of the tax benefits that could accrue through the issuance of stock options.[64] The success, however, of these IRS changes to curb CEO compensation is limited at best. Deferred pay[65] and supplemental retirement plans appear to be vehicles that skirt around the legalities of tax regulations.

Supplemental Nonfinancial Compensation: Perquisites

Perquisites Attractive benefits, over and above a regular salary, granted to executives ("perks").

Executives are frequently offered a smorgasbord of **perquisites** not offered to other employees. The logic of offering these perks, from the organization's perspective, is to attract and keep good managers and to motivate them to work hard in the organization's interest. In addition to the standard benefits offered to all employees (see Chapter 12), some benefits are reserved for privileged executives. They range from an annual physical examination (worth several hundred dollars) to interest-free loans of millions of dollars,[66] which can be worth $100,000 a year or more. Popular perks include the payment of life insurance premiums,[67] club memberships, company automobiles, liberal expense accounts, supplemental disability insurance, supplemental retirement accounts, postretirement consulting contracts, and personal financial, tax, and legal counseling. Some also may be given mortgage assistance.

Golden Parachute A protection plan for executives in the event that they are severed from the organization.

A popular benefit for top executives that gained popularity in the 1980s and continues today is the **golden parachute**. The golden parachute was designed by top executives as a means of protecting themselves if a merger or hostile takeover occurred.[68] These parachutes typically provide either a severance salary to the departing executive or a guaranteed position in the newly created (merged) operation. If in the event of a takeover, for instance, the "acquirer moves to get top executives fired even before a takeover is completed," the golden parachute automatically kicks in.[69] The concept here is to provide an incentive for the executive to stay with the company and fight the hostile takeover—rather than leave the organization.

*I*NTERNATIONAL COMPENSATION

Probably one of the most complex functions of international human resource management is the design and implementation of an equitable compensation program.[70] The first step in designing an international compensation package is to determine if there will be one policy applying to all employees or whether parent-country nationals (PCNs), host-country nationals (HCNs), and third-country nationals (TCNs) will be treated differently. Currently American PCNs and HCNs are commonly treated separately, often also differentiating among types of expatriate assignments (temporary or permanent transfer) or employee status (executive, professional, or technical). It is also necessary to thoroughly understand the statutory requirements of each country to ensure compliance with local laws. International compensation packages in the United States generally utilize the "balance-sheet approach," which considers four factors: base pay, differentials, incentives, and assistance programs.[71]

Base Pay

Ideally this is equal to the pay of employees in comparable jobs at home, but the range of pay scales in most countries is far narrower than in the United States. Thus, where a middle manager in a U.S. factory might earn $75,000 a year, the same manager in Germany might earn $110,000. However, the U.S. higher-level executive might earn $500,000 and her counterpart in Germany only $150,000 (USD). How can human resource managers satisfy the middle manager who earns a third less than the counterpart where he works, while also satisfying the German executive who earns less than her U.S. counterpart?

In addition to considerations of fairness among overseas employees, foreign currencies and laws must be considered. Should expatriates be paid in U.S. dollars, or the local currency—or a combination of the two? How will the organization deal with changes in currency values? Are there restrictions on either bringing in or taking out dollars or the local currency? If so, how will savings be handled? Should salary increases be made according to the same standards as those established for domestic employees, or according to local standards? Will the expatriate pay U.S. or foreign income taxes?

Taxation is a major factor in calculating equitable base pay rates. If there are substantial differences in tax rates, as for instance in Sweden, where income taxes are about 50 percent, will the base pay be adjusted for the actual loss of net income? While the U.S. Department of State has negotiated agreements with every country to determine where income will be taxed, the protection of income from a tax rate other than the domestic one creates new administrative requirements for the organization. Almost all multinational corporations have some tax protection plan so that the expatriate doesn't pay more in taxes than if she were in her home country.

Differentials

The cost of living is not the same around the world, although the value of the dollar to foreign currencies will affect price. For example, the average cost of a gallon of regular unleaded gasoline (in $US) in the United States is $1.48; in France, $3.48; in Germany, $3.43; and in Japan, $3.75.[72] Differentials are intended to offset the higher costs of overseas goods, services, and housing. The Department of State, which has employees in almost every country in the world, publishes a regularly updated comparison of global costs of living that is used by most multinational corporations for providing differentials to maintain the standards of living the expatriate would enjoy if he or she were home.[73]

International compensation packages generally utilize base pay, differentials, incentives, and assistance programs.

Incentives

Not all employees are willing to be separated for long periods of time from family, friends, and the comfort of home support systems. Thus, mobility inducements to go on foreign assignments are regularly offered. These may include monetary payments or services, such as housing, car, chauffeur, and other incentives. But how should a hardship premium be paid? As a percent of salary? In a lump sum payment? In the home or the foreign currency? If foreign housing is provided, what happens to the vacant home back in the United States or to the family housing situation when they eventually return? Incentives require careful planning before, during, and after the overseas assignment.[74]

Assistance Programs

As with any relocation, the overseas transfer requires a lot of expenditures for the employee's family. Some of the assistance programs commonly offered by multinational corporations include: household goods shipping and storage; major appliances; legal clearance for pets and their shipment; home sale/rental protection; automobile protection; temporary living expenses; travel, including pre-relocation visits and annual home leaves; special/emergency return leaves; education allowances for children; club memberships (for corporate entertaining); and security (including electronic systems and bodyguards).

Clearly the design of a compensation system for employees serving overseas is complex and requires enormous administrative expertise, particularly when an organization has expatriates posted in 40 or 50 different countries.

HRM WORKSHOP

SUMMARY

(This summary relates to the Learning Outcomes identified on p. 298.)
After having read this chapter, you should be able to:

1. **Explain the various classifications of rewards.** Rewards can be classified as (1) intrinsic or extrinsic, (2) financial or nonfinancial, or (3) performance-based or membership-based.

2. **Discuss why some rewards are considered membership based.** Some rewards are membership-based because one receives them for simply belonging to the organization. Employee benefits are an example of membership-based rewards, in that every employee gets them irrespective of performance levels.

3. **Define the goal of compensation administration.** Compensation administration seeks to design a cost-effective pay structure that will not only attract, motivate, and retain competent employees, but also be perceived as fair by these employees.

4. **Discuss job evaluation and its three basic approaches.** Job evaluation systematically determines the value of each job in relation to all jobs within the organization. The three basic approaches to job evaluation are: (1) the ordering method, (2) the classification method, and (3) the point method.

5. **Explain the evolution of the final wage structure.** The final wage structure evolves from job evaluation input, compensation survey data, and the creation of wage grades.

6. **Describe competency-based compensation programs.** Competency-based compensation views employees as a competitive advantage in the organization. Compensation systems are established in terms of the knowledge and skills employees possess, and the behaviors that they demonstrate. Possession of these three factors is evaluated and compensated according to a broad-banded salary range established by the organization.

7. **Discuss why executives are paid significantly higher salaries than other employees in an organization.** Executive compensation is higher than that of rank-and-file personnel and also includes other financial and nonfinancial benefits not otherwise available to operative employees. This is done to attract, retain, and motivate executives to higher performance levels.

8. **Identify what is meant by the balance sheet approach to international compensation.** The balance sheet approach to international compensation takes into account base pay, differentials, incentives, and assistance programs.

DEMONSTRATING COMPREHENSION: *Questions for Review and Discussion*

1. Contrast intrinsic and extrinsic rewards.
2. How are financial and nonfinancial rewards different from each other?
3. What is a membership-based reward? How does it differ from a performance-based reward?
4. What is compensation administration? What does it entail?
5. How do governmental influences affect compensation administration?
6. What is job evaluation? Discuss the three basic methods of job evaluation.
7. What are the advantages and disadvantages of (a) individual incentives, (b) group incentives, (c) organization-wide incentives?
8. What is broad-banding and how does it work?
9. Would you rather work for an organization where everyone knows what others are earning, or would you prefer an organization where this information is kept secret? Why?
10. "Subjectivity can be successfully removed from the compensation administration process." Build an argument for and against this statement.

PAY-FOR-PERFORMANCE GOAL SETTING

ABOUT THE SKILL: EMPLOYEES SHOULD have a clear understanding of what they're attempting to accomplish. Furthermore, as a supervisor, you have the responsibility for seeing that this task is achieved by helping your employees set work goals. While this appears to be common sense, it's not always the case. Setting pay-for-performance objectives is a skill that every manager needs to perfect. You can better facilitate this process by following these guidelines:

1. *Identify an employee's key job tasks.* Goal setting begins by defining what it is that you want your employees to accomplish. The best source for this information is each employee's job description.

2. *Establish specific and challenging goals for each key task.* Identify the level of performance expected of each employee. Specify the target for the employee to hit. Specify the deadlines for each goal. Putting deadlines on each goal reduces ambiguity. Deadlines, however, should not be set arbitrarily. Rather, they need to be realistic given the tasks to be completed.

3. *Allow the employee to actively participate.* When employees participate in goal setting, they are more likely to accept the goals. However, it must be sincere participation. That is, employees must perceive that you are truly seeking their input, not just going through the motions.

4. *Prioritize goals.* When you give someone more than one goal, it is important for you to rank the goals in order of importance. The purpose of prioritizing is to encourage the employee to take action and expend effort on each goal in proportion to its importance. Rate goals for difficulty and importance. Goal setting should not encourage people to choose easy goals. Instead, goals should be rated for their difficulty and importance. When goals are rated, individuals can be given credit for trying difficult goals, even if they don't fully achieve them.

5. *Build in feedback mechanisms to assess goal progress.* Feedback lets employees know whether their level of effort is sufficient to attain the goal. Feedback should be both self- and supervisor-generated. In either case, feedback should be frequent and recurring.

6. *Link rewards to goal attainment.* It's natural for employees to ask "What's in it for me?" Linking rewards to the achievement of goals will help answer that question.

CASE APPLICATION: *TEAM FUN!*

It's Day 4 of the Canadian retreat. Tony's newest topic is rewards and pay plans. He starts, "Edna showed me the salary figures and records for everyone. I can't find any pattern or rationale for how people are paid around here. I think we should work this out."

Kenny sends everyone but Tony and Norton out to find more firewood and looks at Tony, "No one but the four of us know how everyone is paid around here. What were you just trying to do? Start a fight?"

Norton adds, "We do fine with the system we have. Why did you think we needed to talk about compensation this week?"

Tony asks tersely, "Would you describe that system for me?"

Kenny starts, "I like a guy, want him to work for us, so I offer him whatever I made when I was his age. Or what Norton made at his age; especially, if it is a technical job, like machine design." Tony groans and holds his head.

Norton adds, "For the pros, though, we talk to them. Find out what pros are getting at other stores to demonstrate and sell the products. We pay that golf guy $10,000 each time he shows up and swings his club around the GREEN." Tony groans and holds his stomach.

Kenny counters, "Well, the pros are special cases, right?" Tony groans and sits down.

Norton asks, "Tony, you took over setting starting salaries when you got here. What have you been doing?"

Tony says, in a small voice, "Just offering what you offered the last guy in the same job. I couldn't figure out any other pattern. That's why I put compensation on the agenda for this week." Kenny and Norton groan. They all look up as the door opens and Eric comes in with a load of firewood.

Questions

Please review the TEAM FUN! case material at the end of prior chapters before answering these questions.

1. Make lists of TEAM FUN! rewards: extrinsic vs. intrinsic; financial vs. nonfinancial; performance-based vs. membership based.

2. Evaluate the appropriateness of these rewards for maintaining commitment for employees of TEAM FUN! Does the compensation system of TEAM FUN! meet the general goals of a compensation system?

3. Make three suggestions to improve the TEAM FUN! compensation system.

4. Identify three features of the compensation system that are excellent for this organization. Would they be suitable for most organizations? What types?

WORKING WITH A TEAM: *Understanding Incentive Plans*

Interview a compensation specialist in the human resources department of your employer, college, university, hospital, or other organization by asking the following questions within 15 minutes. Summarize your results in a one- to two-page typed report for your class team discussion or class 5-minute presentation. You may also want to develop a comparison chart based on your team's results, depending on your findings.

1. Could you share a job description of a compensation specialist?

2. Do you participate in wage surveys? Could you provide results of a recent survey or samples of types of questions asked?

3. What factors are considered in developing compensation surveys?

4. What types of plans, if any, are used in your organization to provide incentive to employees? How was each plan implemented, and how successful has it been?

ENHANCING YOUR WRITING SKILLS

1. Develop a two- to three-page paper on the advantages and disadvantages of competency-based compensation programs. Use specific examples where appropriate.

2. "Women executives of major U.S. corporations earn approximately 45 percent less than their male counterparts. Their average compensation in 1999 was about $900,000 as compared to approximately $1.3 million for the men."[75] Build an argument that the statement helps confirm that the glass ceiling still exists. On the contrary, show how the statement indicates that the glass ceiling has "shattered." End your paper with your conclusion supporting one side of the argument or the other.

3. Working on a team project in class is somewhat similar to working on a team in an organization. Assume your professor gave you the opportunity to develop a "team" reward (grading) procedure for your class project. Indicate what that grading procedure would look like and how you would implement it to maximize the benefits to (a) your learning and (b) your reward.

ℰNDNOTES

1. Based on "Coffey Break" (Winter Edition, 2001); and www.coffeyco.com.
2. See, for example, Claire Ginther, "Incentive Programs that Really Work," *HRMagazine* (August 2000), pp. 117–120.
3. For an interesting article on this issue, see Terrence R. Mitchell and Amy E. Mickel, "The Meaning of Money: An Individual Difference Perspective," *Academy of Management Review* (July 1999), pp. 568–578.
4. Sue Shellenbarger, "Employees Who Value Time as Much as Money Now Get Their Reward," *Wall Street Journal* (September 22, 1999), p. B-1.
5. See Ronald H. Humphrey, "How Job Characteristics Influence Prototypes and the Information Dilution Effect," *Academy of Management Best Paper Proceedings*, Dorothy Perrin Moore, ed. (Vancouver, British Columbia, Canada: August 6–9, 1995), pp. 131–135.
6. Valerie L. Williams and Jennifer E. Sunderland, "Maximize the Power of Your Reward and Recognition Strategies," *Journal of Compensation and Benefits* (September–October 1998), pp. 11–17.
7. Marc Adams, "Fair and Square," *HRMagazine* (May 1999), pp. 38–44.
8. "Closing the Pay Gap," *Business Week* (August 28, 2000), p. 38.
9. Joseph J. Martocchio, *Strategic Compensation: A Human Resource Management Approach* (Upper Saddle River, NJ: Prentice-Hall, 1998), pp. 6, 162.
10. Ibid.
11. Ibid.
12. Ibid.
13. For a thorough discussion of various methods of determining the pay structure, see Martocchio, Chapter 7, "Design a Compensation System."
14. Martocchio, p. 191; and Jerry Useem, "State-of-the-Art Compensation," *Inc.* (October 1998), p. 118.
15. For an interesting article on this topic, see Luis R. Gomez-Mejia, Theresa M. Welbourne, and Robert M. Wiseman, "The Role of Risk Sharing and Risk Taking Under Gainsharing," *Academy of Management Review* (July 2000), pp. 492–507.
16. Howard Gleckman, Sandra Atchison, Tim Smart, and John A. Byrne, "Bonus Pay: Buzzword or Bonanza?" *Business Week* (November 14, 1994), p. 62.
17. L. Kate Beatty, "Pay and Benefits Break Away from Tradition," *HRMagazine* (November 1994), p. 64.
18. Donna Fenn, "Compensation: Goal-Driven Incentives," *Inc.* (August 1996), p. 91; and Michael A. Verespej, "More Value for Compensation," *Industry Week* (June 17, 1996), p. 20.
19. Michael A. Verespej, "Top-to-Bottom Incentives," *Industry Week* (February 3, 1997), p. 30; and Stephanie Overman, "Saturn Teams Working and Profiting," *HRMagazine* (March 1995), p. 72.
20. Harold Stieglitz, "The Kaiser Steel Union Sharing Plan," *National Industrial Conference Board Studies in Personnel Policy Number 187* (New York: 1963).
21. For an interesting overview of the Lincoln Electric program, see Richard M. Hodgetts, "Discussing Incentive Compensation with Donald Hastings of Lincoln Electric," *Compensation and Benefits Review* (September–October 1997),

pp. 60–66; and Richard M. Hodgetts, "A Conversation with Donald F. Hastings of the Lincoln Electric Company," *Organizational Dynamics* (Winter 1997), pp. 68–72.
22. Ibid., p. 462
23. Ibid., pp. 455–458. See also Richard J. Long, "Gainsharing and Power: Lessons from Six Scanlon Plans," *Industrial & Labor Relations Review* (April 2000), pp. 533–535; Satish P. Deshpande, "Gainsharing and Power? Lessons from Six Scanlon Plans," *Journal of Labor Research* (Fall 1999), pp. 620–621; and Peter Cappelli, "Gainsharing and Power: Lessons from Six Scanlon Plans," *Administrative Science Quarterly* (September 1999), pp. 621–623.
24. Chris Lee, "Best Ideas That Got Lost in the Shuffle," *Training* (December 1999), pp. 35–36.
25. Roget T. Kaufman, "The Effects of IMPROSHARE on Productivity," *Industrial and Labor Relations Review* (January 1992), p. 311.
26. Ibid.
27. Ibid., pp. 319–322.
28. Ronald Recardo and Diane Pricone, "How to Determine Whether Gainsharing Is for You," *Industrial Management* (January–February 1996), pp. 12; and Robert McGarvey "Share the Wealth," *Entrepreneur* (April 1997), pp. 78–79.
29. Michael A. Verespej, "Sharing in Success," *Industry Week* (September 4, 2000), p. 9.
30. "Why Gainsharing Works Even Better Today Than in the past," *HR Focus* (April 2000), pp. 3–5.
31. R. K. Abbott, "Performance-Based Flex: A Tool for Managing Total Compensation Costs," *Compensation and Benefits Review* (March–April 1993), pp. 18–21; J. R. Schuster and P. K. Zingheim, "The New Variable Pay: Key Design Issues," *Compensation and Benefits Review* (March–April 1993), pp. 27–34; C. R. Williams and L. P. Livingstone, "Another Look at the Relationship between Performance and Voluntary Turnover," *Academy of Management Journal* (April 1994), pp. 269–298; and A. M. Dickinson and K. L. Gillette, "A Comparison of the Effects on Productivity: Piece Rate Pay versus Base Pay Plus Incentives," *Journal of Organizational Behavior Management* (Spring 1994), pp. 3–82.
32. See, for example, J. Wells, "Stock Incentives Remain Preferred Compensation Option," *HR News* (September 2000), p. 17; D. Fenn, "Compensation: Bonuses That Make Sense," *Inc.* (March 1996), p. 95; J. H. Sheridan, "Yes to Team Incentives," *Industry Week* (March 4, 1996), p. 64; and H. N. Altmansberger and M. J. Wallace Jr., "Strategic Use of Goalsharing at Corning," *ACA Journal* (Winter 1995), pp. 64–71.
33. Jeanne Bursch, "Well-Structured Employee Reward/Recognition Programs Yield Positive Results," *HR Focus* (November 1999), p. 1.
34. G. Grib and S. O'Donnell, "Pay Plans That Reward Employee Achievement," *HRMagazine* (July 1995), pp. 49–50.
35. F. Luthans and A. D. Stajkovic, "Reinforce for Performance. The Need to Go Beyond Pay and Even Rewards," *Academy of Management Executive* (May 1999), pp. 49–56.
36. "Consider Converting Merit Pay Raises to Other Rewards," *Financial Executive* (May–June 1999), p. 8.
37. "Compensation: Sales Managers as Team Players," *Inc.* (August 1994), p. 102.

38. D. Fenn, "Compensation: Goal-Driven Incentives," *Inc.* (August 1996), p. 91; and M. A. Verespej, "More Value for Compensation," *Industry Week* (June 17, 1996), p. 20.

39. S. Overman, "Saturn Teams Working and Profiting," *HRMagazine* (March 1995), p. 72.

40. D. J. Cira and E. R. Benjamin, "Competency-Based Pay: A Concept in Evolution," *Compensation and Benefits Review* (September–October 1998), pp. 22.

41. M. E. Lattoni and A. Mercier, "Developing Competency-Based Organizations and Pay Systems," *Focus: A Review of Human Resource Management Issues in Canada* (Calgary, Canada: Towers Perrin, Summer 1994), p. 18.

42. Ibid.

43. Gary I. Bergel, "Choosing the Right Pay Delivery System to Fit Banding," *Compensation and Benefits Review* (July–August 1994), pp. 34–39; and Sandra O'Neal, "Competencies: The DNA of the Corporation," *ACA Journal* (Winter 1993–94), pp. 6–12.

44. Peter V. LeBlanc and Christian M. Ellis, "The Many Faces of Banding," p. 54; and Larry Reissman, "Nine Common Myths About Broadbands," *HRMagazine* (August 1995), pp. 79–85.

45. Lattoni and Mercier, p. 7.

46. "Compensation: Sales Managers as Team Players," *Inc.* (August 1994), p. 102.

47. Howard Gleckman, Sandra Atchison, Tim Smart, and John A. Byrne, "Bonus Pay: Buzzword or Bonanza?" *Business Week* (November 14, 1994), pp. 62–64.

48. Jerry McAdmas, "The Essential Role of Rewarding Teams and Teamwork," *Compensation & Benefits Management* (Autumn 2000), pp. 15–27.

49. See Stephen P. Robbins and David A. DeCenzo, *Fundamentals of Management*, 3rd ed. (Upper Saddle River, NJ: Prentice-Hall, 2001), p. 297.

50. See, for instance, C. James Novak, "Proceed with Caution When Paying Teams," *HRMagazine* (April 1997), pp. 73–75.

51. Wany Grossman and Robert E. Hoskisson, "CEO Pay at the Crossroads of Wall Street and Main: Toward the Strategic Design of Executive Compensation," *Academy of Management Executive* (February 1998), pp. 43–57.

52. Jennifer Reingold, Richard A. Melcher, and Gary McWilliams, "Executive Pay," *Business Week* (April 20, 1998), pp. 64–70.

53. Jennifer Reingold and Fred Jespersen, "Executive Pay," *Business Week* (April 2000), p. 100.

54. See, for instance, John Mariotti, "How Much Is Too Much?" *Industry Week* (March 2, 1998), p. 68.

55. "Chief Executive Pay in 12 Countries," *Manpower Argus* (February 1997), p. 4; and "Executive Pay in Europe," *Manpower Argus* (November 1996), p. 4.

56. "Who Made the Biggest Bucks," *Wall Street Journal* (April 6, 2000), p. R-1.

57. Dawn Harris and Constance Helfat, "Specificity of CEO Human Capital and Compensation," *Strategic Management Journal* (December 1997), pp. 895–920; and Rob Norton, "Making Sense of the Boss's Pay," *Fortune* (October 3, 1994), p. 36.

58. See, for example, Louis Lavelle, "CEO Pay: The More Things Chance," *Business Week* (October 16, 2000), pp. 106–108.

59. Based on Wany Grossman and Robert E. Hoskisson, "CEO Pay at the Crossroads of Wall Street and Main: Toward the Strategic Design of Executive Compensation," *Academy of Management Executive* (February 1998), pp. 43–57; Rana Dogar, "Nineteenth Annual Salary Report," *Working Woman* (February 1998), pp. 24–25; John Mariotti, "How Much Is Too Much?" *Industry Week* (March 2, 1998), p. 68; and Sal F. Marino, "Chief Executives Are Underpaid," *Industry Week* (April 20, 1998), p. 22.

60. Louis Lavelle, "CEO Pay: Nothing Succeeds Like Failure," *Business Week* (September 11, 2000), p. 48.

61. Jennifer Reingold, "Executive Pay," p. 65.

62. For a good review of stock options and their use in organizations, see Edward O. Welles, "Stock Options," *Inc.* (February 1998), pp. 85–97; and Roger Brossy and John E. Balkcom, "Case Studies: Executive Compensation: Finding a Balance in the Quest for Value," *Compensation and Benefits Review* (January–February 1998), pp. 29–34.

63. For another perspective on stock options and their effect on profits, see Edward O. Welles, "Stock Options," *Inc.* (February 1998), p. 97; and Jack Stack, "The Problem with Profit Sharing," *Inc.* (November 1996), pp. 67–69.

64. Mark D. Fefer, "Your CEO Will Get Paid," *Fortune* (October 3, 1994), p. 18.

65. Ibid. Under IRS regulations, beginning in 1994, annual salaries paid to a company's five top officers in a publicly held firm are not tax deductible if the salaries are over $1 million. Most companies have simply ignored this new ruling, while others are deferring the excess income for these executives until retirement.

66. "In a Cost-Cutting Era, Many CEOs Enjoy Imperial Perks," *Wall Street Journal* (March 7, 1995), p. B1, B16.

67. Current tax laws require tax to be paid on that amount of premium paid on life insurance over $50,000. Furthermore, Section 89 of the IRS Tax Code requires that those perks offered to the higher-paid employees, that are not given to the average employee, be considered taxable income to the recipient.

68. Jennifer Reingold, "Where Parting Is Such a Sweet Deal," *Business Week* (March 31, 1997), pp. 42–43.

69. Debra Sparks, "The Mother of All Stock Option Plans," *Business Week* (November 23, 1998), pp. 159–159; and Gabriella Stern and Joann S. Lublin, "Chrysler Has Bold New Idea-In Parachutes," *Wall Street Journal* (July 12, 1995), pp. B1; B11.

70. For further reading on international compensation, see Elaine Ng, "Executive Pay in Asia—The Stock Option Game," *Benefits & Compensation International* (September 2000), pp. 3–6; Stephanie Overman, "In Sync," *HRMagazine* (March 2000), pp. 25–27; Calvin Reynolds, "Global Compensation and Benefits in Transition," *Compensation and Benefits Review* (January–February 2000), pp. 28–38; J. E. Richard, "Global Executive Compensation: A Look at the Future," *Compensation and Benefits Review* (May–June 2000), pp. 35–38; J. Blade Corwin, "Compensation Survey: What It Costs to Hire an Offshore Sourcing Manager," *Bobbin* (February 1998), pp. 58–59; and Peter J. Dowling, Randall S. Schuler, and Denice E. Welch, *International Dimensions of Human Resource Management*, 2nd ed. (Belmont, CA: Wadsworth, 1994), Chapter 6.

71. Edward M. Mervosh, "Managing Expatriate Compensation," *Industry Week* (July 21, 1997), pp. 13–18; and Calvin Reynolds, "Compensation of Overseas Personnel," in *Hand-*

book of *Human Resources Administration,* 2d ed., Joseph J. Famularo, ed. (New York: McGraw-Hill, 1986), pp. 56-2, 56-3.

72. Todd Pack, "Fill Up Car Now, Gas Prices Will Go Higher," *The Sentinel* (January 12, 2001), p. A-1; and International Energy Agency, "End Users Oil Production Prices for Petroleum Products," *End Users Oil Product Prices and Average Crude Oil Import Costs December 2000* (December 2000), p. 3.

73. "How Far the Paycheck Stretches," *Global Finance* (February 1998), pp. 8–9; and U.S. Department of State, *Indexes of Living Costs Abroad, Quarters, Allowances, and Hardship Differentials* (Washington, DC: Bureau of Labor Statistics, published quarterly).

74. Harold Adrion, "Rewarding the International Executive Using Stock Options: Part 2," *Benefits & Compensation International* (December 2000), pp. 13–128.

75. Gene Koretz, "The Gender Gap in Top Brass Pay," *Business Week* (November 20, 2000), p. 32.

12

EMPLOYEE BENEFITS

LEARNING OUTCOMES

AFTER READING THIS CHAPTER, YOU WILL BE ABLE TO:

1. Discuss why employers offer benefits to their employees.
2. Contrast Social Security, unemployment compensation, and workers' compensation benefits.
3. Identify and describe three major types of health insurance options.
4. Discuss the important implications of the Employee Retirement Income Security Act.
5. Outline and describe major types of retirement programs offered by organizations.
6. Explain the reason companies offer vacation benefits to their employees.
7. Describe the purpose of disability insurance programs.
8. Discuss what is meant by the term *family-friendly benefits*.
9. List the various types of flexible benefit option programs.

F ran Rogers has always believed that meeting the needs of employees required more than simply paying them and offering a slate of employee benefits. That's because she recognized that balancing the realities of one's work and personal life is difficult. More importantly, she knew that problems employees face in their personal lives will ultimately show up in their performance at work. It did for her. Having a child who suffered from asthma, Rogers wasn't about to drop her daughter off at a daycare center.[1]

One of the more critical problems is associated with finding quality child care. She believed that companies had to help their employees in this endeavor. Otherwise, productivity would be adversely affected. Helping employees, after all, was the humane thing to do. It was also a way for an organization to provide an employee benefit that employees desire.

Work/Family Directions began in 1983. Working with a client organization, IBM, Rogers attempted to help the organization's employees find quality child care in the Boca Raton, Florida, area. Rogers succeeded in helping these IBM employees—and Work/Family Directions (WFD) was off and running. Today, the company has grown to several hundred employees and has revenues of $100 million, reflecting work done on women's employment issues in over 20 countries. Its client list now boasts corporations such as Xerox, American Express, the St. Paul Companies, the Gap, and Pfizer. Interestingly, 9 out of the top 10 "100 Best Companies for Working Women" are WFD clients.

Fran Sussner Rogers may have found a secret to one aspect of employee benefits by helping companies recognize that giving something of value to employees can yield many benefits for all involved. Although she sold her business in 1998 to the Ceridan Corporation, she continues her crusade for organizations to make significant investments in work- and family-related issues. She wants organizations to do more—like helping individuals with problems they face not only with day care or elder care, but with anything that employees deal with over their life cycle.

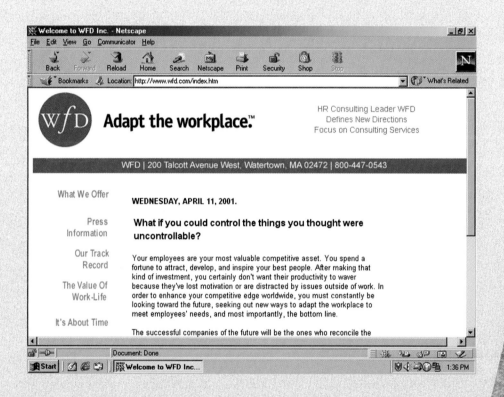

INTRODUCTION

When an organization is designing its overall compensation program, one of the critical areas of concern is what benefits should be provided. Today's workers expect more than just an hourly wage or a salary from their employer; they want additional considerations that will enrich their lives. These considerations in an employment setting are called **employee benefits.**

Employee Benefits Membership-based, nonfinancial rewards offered to attract and keep employees.

Employee benefits have grown in importance and variety over the past several decades. Once perceived as an added feature for an organization to provide its employees, employee benefit administration has transformed itself into a well-thought-out, well-organized package. Companies like Ford and Delta, for example, are providing every employee a computer and Internet access for personal use.[2] Employers realize that the benefits provided to employees have an effect on whether applicants accept their employment offers or, once employed, whether workers will continue to stay with the organization. Benefits, therefore, are necessary components of an effectively functioning compensation program.[3]

The irony, however, is that while benefits must be offered to attract and retain good workers, benefits as a whole do not directly affect a worker's performance.[4] Benefits are generally membership based, offered to employees regardless of their performance levels. While this does not appear to be a logical business practice, there is evidence that the absence of adequate benefits and services for employees contributes to employee dissatisfaction and increased absenteeism and turnover.[5] Accordingly, because the negative effect of failing to provide adequate benefits is so great, organizations spend tens of billions of dollars annually to ensure that valuable benefits are available for each worker.

Over the decades, the nature of benefits has changed drastically. The benefits offered in the early 1900s clearly were different from those offered today. In the early 1900s, much emphasis was placed on time off from work. As the first personnel departments arrived on the scene, their main emphasis was to ensure that workers were "happy and healthy." This meant that their responsibility was to administer such benefits as scheduled vacations, company picnics, and other social activities for workers. Later, around the late 1930s, the practice of having employees complete a sign-up card for some type of health insurance came about. Those days of simplicity for the organization, unfortunately, are long gone. Federal legislation, labor unions, and the changing work force have all led to growth in benefit offerings. Today's organizational benefits are more widespread, more creative, and clearly more abundant. As indicated in Exhibit 12-1, the benefits offered to employees as we enter the new millennium are designed to ensure something of value for each worker.

The Costs of Providing Employee Benefits

Most of us are aware of inflation and the effect it has had on the wages and salaries of virtually every job in the United States. It seems incredible that just 65 years ago, a worker earning $100 a week was ranked among the top 10 percent of wage earners in the United States. Although we are aware that hourly wages and monthly salaries have increased in recent years, we often overlook the more rapid growth in benefits offered to employees. Since the cost of employing workers includes both direct compensation and the corresponding benefits and services, the growth in both benefits and services has resulted in dramatic increases in labor costs to organizations. What do these dramatic cost increases mean for

EXHIBIT 12-1

Major Employee Benefits Offered (percent of employers participating)

Health Insurance:		Paid Time Off:	
Medical Care	76	Holidays	89
Dental	59	Vacations	95
Vision	26	Personal Leave	20
		Funeral Leave	81
Retirement Plans:		Military Leave	47
Defined Benefit	50	Sick Leave	56
Defined Contribution	57		
401(k)s	39	**Family Benefits:**	
Profit Sharing	13	Child Care	10
Money Purchase Plans	8	Long-Term Care	7
Stock Plans	4	Adoption Assistance	10
Health Promotion Programs:		**Miscellaneous:**	
Wellness Programs	36	Job-Related Travel	
Employee Assistance	61	Insurance	42
Fitness Center	21	Educational Assistance	67

Source: U.S. Bureau of the Census, *Statistical Abstracts of the United States, 1999* (Washington, DC: Government Printing Office, 1999), p. 449.

employers? From 1980 to 2000, the cost of providing something of value to each employee increased from $5,560 to more than $10,400 per year,[6] with the greatest cost increases coming from rising health insurance benefits premiums.[7] Today, benefit and service offerings add nearly 40 percent to an organization's payroll cost.[8] And that's comparable to benefit costs in other countries—like Russia, where the additional benefit payroll cost is 39 percent.[9]

Employers have also found that benefits present attractive areas of negotiation when large wage and salary increases are not feasible. For example, if employees were to purchase life insurance on their own, they would have to pay for it with net dollars, that is, with what they have left after paying taxes. If the organization pays for it, the benefit is nontaxable (the premiums paid on insurance up to $50,000) for each employee.[10]

Contemporary Benefits Offerings

There has been a dramatic increase in the number and types of benefits offered and an equally sensational increase in their costs. What has triggered the sweeping changes in benefits offerings that will carry us into the next millennium? The answer to that question lies, in part, in the demographic composition of the work force.

Benefits offered to employees reflect many of the trends existing in our labor force.

Benefits offered to employees reflect many of the trends existing in our labor force. As the decades have witnessed drastic changes in educational levels, family status, and employee expectations, benefits have had to be adjusted to meet the needs of the workers.[11] What specifically have we seen over the past few decades with respect to demographic changes? Let's explore a few factors to show why the benefits offered today are different from those offered 30 years ago.

Recall from Chapter 1 our discussion of the changing work force. Let's review this matter with an eye on benefits. As recently as the early 1960s, the work force was composed of a relatively homogeneous group—predominately males. This typical male had a wife who stayed home and cared for their children—

DOMESTIC PARTNER BENEFITS

TRADITIONALLY, HEALTH INSURANCE BENEFITS HAVE BEEN offered to employees and their immediate families. However, this construct of what a family is has been changing in the American society. Living arrangements, either heterosexual or homosexual, are different today that at any other time in our history. As a result, many employees are placing new demands on their employers to have the same opportunity as their married counter-

parts for medical coverage for their significant others. While many companies voluntarily offer domestic benefits to their employees, it is just that—voluntary. Companies are *not* legally required to do so, and if they do not, they are not acting in a discriminatory manner.

Should companies offer benefits to domestic partners of employees? What your opinion?

Domestic Partner Benefits
Benefits offered to an employee's "live-in" partner.

necessitating a relatively standard benefit need. That is, most of these workers required a retirement plan, sick leave, vacation time, and health insurance. Providing these to workers was customary and, for the most part, uncomplicated. However, the typical worker of the early 1960s is rare in today's work force. Dual-career couples, singles, singles with children, and individuals caring for their parents (elder care) are now widely prevalent in the work force.[12] Equally important is the topic of benefit coverage for a worker's significant other—called **domestic partner benefits**.[13] Domestic partner benefits typically include medical, dental, or vision coverage for an employee's live-in partner—whether or not that live-in partner is of the opposite sex (see Ethical Issues in HRM). More than 25 percent of all *Fortune* 500 companies offer such benefits.[14]

Today's organizations must be able to satisfy the diverse benefit needs of their employees. Consequently, organizational benefit programs are being adjusted to reflect a different focus. This is required in order to achieve the goal of "something of value" for each worker. Before we discuss some of those mechanisms, however, it's important to frame what we mean by the term *benefit administration*. In putting together a benefits package, two issues must be considered: (1) what benefits must be offered by law, and (2) what benefits and services should be offered to make the organization attractive to applicants and current workers. First, we'll explore the **legally required benefits**.

LEGALLY REQUIRED BENEFITS

U.S. organizations must provide certain benefits to their employees regardless of whether they want to or not, and they must be provided in a nondiscriminatory manner. With a few exceptions, the hiring of any employee requires the organization to pay Social Security premiums,[15] unemployment compensation, and workers' compensation. Additionally, any organization with 50 or more employees must provide Family and Medical Leave. The premium payments associated with many of these legally required benefits are either shared with employees (as in the case of Social Security), or borne solely by the organization, in an effort to provide each employee with some basic level of financial protection at retirement or termination, or as a result of injury. These benefits also provide a death benefit for dependents in case of a worker's death. Finally, employers must permit employees to take time off from work for certain personal reasons.

The United States, however, is not the only industrialized nation to have legally required benefits. Many others, like Norway, Canada, and China, have them, too. In China, for example, starting in the mid-1990s, employees in Chinese firms are provided unemployment insurance, medical insurance, and a retirement plan.[16] While it is not possible to discuss benefit offerings in the industrialized nations, it's important to understand the legally required benefits offered in the United States. Let's look at each of these.

Social Security

Social Security Retirement, disability, and survivor benefits, paid by the government to aged, former members of the labor force, the disabled, or their survivors.

A source of income for American retirees, disabled workers, and for surviving dependents of workers who have died, has been the benefits provided by Social Security insurance. **Social Security** also provides some health insurance coverage through the federal government–sponsored Medicare program. In 2000, Social Security paid out billions of dollars to the more than 150 million eligible workers in the United States.[17]

Social Security insurance is financed by contributions made by the employee and matched by the employer, computed as a percentage of the employee's earnings. In 2001, for instance, the rate was 12.4 percent (6.2 percent levied on both the employee and the employer) of the worker's earnings up to $80,400 or a maximum levy of $4,984.80. Additionally, 2.9 percent is assessed for Medicare on all earned income. Similar to Social Security, both the employer and employee split this assessment, paying 1.45 percent each in payroll taxes.[18]

To be eligible for Social Security, employees must be employed for a minimum of 40 quarters, or 10 years of work.[19] During this work period, employees must have also earned a minimum amount of money each quarter, and for the entire year. In 2001, this amounted to $830 per quarter and $3,320 for the entire year. Prior to 1983, employees became eligible for full benefits at age 65. With revisions to Social Security laws, those born in 1938 and thereafter will have to wait an additional period of time before receiving full retirement benefits.[20]

Keep in mind, however, that Social Security is not intended to be employees' sole source of retirement income. Social Security benefits vary, based on the previous year's inflation, one's additional earnings, and the age of the recipient. For 2001, the average monthly Social Security retirement check was $845. Given longer life expectancies, and a desire to maintain one's current standard of living, workers today are expected to supplement Social Security with their own retirement plans.[21] (We'll look at these shortly.) This is true whether or not Social Security will still be around in the year 2037!

Unemployment Compensation

Unemployment compensation laws provide benefits to employees who meet the following conditions: they are without a job, have worked a minimum number of weeks, submit an application for unemployment compensation to their State Employment Agency, register for available work, and are willing and able to accept any suitable employment offered them through their State Unemployment Compensation Commission. The premise behind unemployment compensation is to provide an income to individuals who have lost a job through no fault of their own (e.g., layoffs, plant closing). Being fired from a job, however, may result in a loss of unemployment compensation rights.[22]

The funds for paying unemployment compensation are derived from a combined federal and state tax imposed on the taxable wage base of the employer.

At the federal level, the unemployment tax (called FUTA) is 6.2 percent on the first $7,000 of earnings of employees. States that meet federal guidelines are given a 5.4 percent credit, thus reducing the federal unemployment tax to .08 percent, or $56 per employee.

State unemployment compensation tax is often a function of a company's unemployment experience; that is, the more an organization lays off employees, the higher its rate. Rates for employers range, for example, from 0.03 to 7.5 percent of state-established wage bases.[23] Eligible unemployed workers receive an amount that varies from state to state but is determined by the worker's previous wage rate and the length of previous employment. Compensation is provided for only a limited period—typically, the base is 26 weeks[24] but may be extended by the state another 26 weeks during times when unemployment runs excessively high.

Unemployment compensation and parallel programs for railroad, federal government, and military employees cover more than 75 percent of all members in the work force. Major groups that are excluded include self-employed workers, employees who work for organizations employing fewer than four individuals, household domestics, farm employees, and state and local government employees. As past recessions have demonstrated, unemployment compensation provides stable spending power throughout the nation. In contrast to the early 1930s, when millions of workers lost their jobs and had no compensatory income, unemployment compensation provides a floor that allows individuals to continue looking for work while receiving assistance through the transitory period from one job to the next.[25]

Workers' Compensation

Every state currently has some type of **workers' compensation** to compensate employees (or their families) for death or permanent or total disability resulting from job-related endeavors, irrespective of fault for the accident. Federal employees and others working outside the U.S. border are covered by separate

---

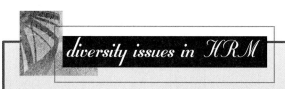

diversity issues in HRM

WHAT HAPPENS WHEN MY EMPLOYEES ARE CALLED TO ACTIVE DUTY?

MILITARY BENEFITS ARE OFTEN OVERLOOKED WITH respect to their importance to employees. The purpose of military benefits is to bridge the gap between one's military pay and one's civilian pay. Under typical conditions, many companies offer military pay to their employees who are members of the National Guard or the armed forces reserves as a means of pay continuity during the employee's two-week annual duty. That is, while the reservist or National Guard members are off work during their required training, employers usually make up the difference in their pay. But what if the company does not have a military benefit pay policy? In that case, those affected employees can use their paid time off (e.g., vacation) to attend their active duty requirement, or may choose to take a leave without pay.[26]

In either case, employees on military leave, whether it's the two weeks' annual duty, or an extended stay during a "call-up," are entitled to receive all the benefits they would have received had they not been called to active duty. That is, accrued benefits like vacation and seniority must be given to the "absent" employee. For extended stays on active duty, while the employer has the right to hire a temporary replacement, employees have the right to return to their jobs, within 31 days of being released from active duty. All HR actions that might have taken place in their absence (a promotion, salary increase, etc.) must be given to the returning military veteran upon his or her return.

legislation. The rationale for workers' compensation is to protect employees' salaries and to attribute the cost for occupational accidents and rehabilitation to the employing organization.[27] This accountability factor considers workers' compensation costs as part of the labor expenses incurred in meeting the organization's objectives.

Workers' compensation benefits are based on fixed schedules of minimum and maximum payments. For example, the loss of an index finger may be calculated at $500, or the loss of an entire foot at $5,000. When comprehensive disability payments are required, the amount of compensation is computed by considering the employee's current earnings, future earnings, and financial responsibilities.

The entire cost of workers' compensation is borne by the organization. Its rates are set based on the actual history of company accidents, the type of industry and business operation, and the likelihood of accidents occurring. The organization, then, protects itself by covering its risks through insurance. Some states provide an insurance system, voluntary or required, for the handling of workers' compensation. Some organizations may also cover their workers' compensation risks by purchasing insurance from private insurance companies. Finally, some states allow employers to be self-insurers. Self-insuring—while usually limited to large organizations—requires the employer to maintain a fund from which benefits can be paid.

Most workers' compensation laws stipulate that the injured employee will be compensated by either a monetary allocation or the payment of medical expenses, or a combination of both. Almost all workers' compensation insurance programs, whether publicly or privately controlled, provide incentives for employers to maintain good safety records. Insurance rates are computed based on the organization's accident experience; hence employers are motivated to keep accident rates low.[28]

How does an organization like the Seattle-based Starbucks Coffee Company attract and retain star employees? Very simply. Based on the philosophy of CEO Howard Schultz, all employees are provided very competitive benefits. For example, all employees are provided excellent health insurance. But there's more to this story. Part-time employees—those working at least 20 hours a week—are provided an excellent benefits package, too. They not only receive health insurance, but they get paid vacations and stock options. And what does Starbucks get for this? In a fast-food industry where turnover reaches upward of 400 percent per year, Starbucks' turnover is 80 percent less. As Starbucks' director of compensation, "People come here for the benefits, and they stay for them."

Family and Medical Leave Act

The last legally required benefit facing organizations who have 50 or more employees is the Family and Medical Leave Act of 1993. Recall from our discussion in Chapter 3 that the FMLA was passed to provide employees the opportunity to take up to 12 weeks of unpaid leave each year for family or medical reasons. Interestingly, while this is a major improvement for parents in the United States, employees in Norway have been given much superior family leave. Fathers are granted four weeks of paid leave upon the birth of a child. Mothers, on the other hand, receive either 52 weeks of leave paid at 80 percent of their salary or 42 weeks off at 100 percent of their salary.[29]

Voluntary Benefits

The voluntary benefits offered by an organization are limited only by management's creativity and budget.[30] As Exhibit 12-1 illustrates, many different benefits are offered—almost all of which carry significant costs to the employer. Some of the most common and critical ones are health insurance, retirement plans, time off from work, and disability and life insurance benefits. We will delay the discussion of benefits that deals with health issues, like employee assistance programs, until the next chapter.

Health Insurance

All individuals have health-care needs that must be met, and most organizations today offer some type of health insurance coverage to their employees. This coverage has become one of the most important benefits for employees because of the tremendous increases in the cost of health care.[31] In fact, health care costs U.S. businesses more than $174 billion annually, and the costs continue to rise.[32] Without health insurance, almost any family's finances could be depleted at any time if they had to pay for a major illness. The purpose of health insurance is to protect the employee and his or her immediate family from the catastrophes of a major illness and to minimize their out-of-pocket expenses for medical care.

Any type of health insurance offered to employees generally contains provisions for coverage that can be extended beyond the employee. Specifically, the employee, the employee's spouse, and their children may be covered. Health-care coverage generally focuses on hospital and physician care. It also typically covers major medical expenses. The specific types of coverage offered to employees will vary based on the organization's health insurance policy. Generally, three types appear more frequently than others: traditional health-care coverage, Health Maintenance Organizations (HMOs), and Preferred Provider Organizations (PPOs) (sometimes referred to as point-of-service (POS) or network plans).[33] All three are designed to provide protection for employees, but each does so in a different way. There is also increasing interest in employer-operated options such as self-funded insurance. Let's look at each of these various types.

Traditional Health Insurance   When health insurance benefits began decades ago, generally one type of health insurance was offered: the traditional membership program. The cost of this insurance to the employee, if any, was minimal. This traditional insurance generally was (and is to some extent today) provided through a Blue Cross and Blue Shield Organization.[34] However, it's not uncommon to see traditional health insurance programs being offered by such companies as Cigna, Connecticut General, or Prudential.

Since its inception in 1929, Blue Cross and Blue Shield (BC/BS) insurance has served as the dominant health-care insurer in the United States. Blue Cross and Blue Shield plans offer special arrangements to their members in return for a guarantee that medical services will be provided. **Blue Cross** organizations are concerned with the hospital end of the business. These hospitals contract with Blue Cross to provide hospital services to members, and agree to receive reimbursement from the health insurer for their fees incurred. The reimbursement is

Blue Cross A health insurer concerned with the hospital side of health insurance.

often paid on a per-diem basis for days stayed in the hospital or pays a percentage of the total bill.

Blue Shield A health insurer concerned with the provider side of health insurance.

The other component of the health insurer is the **Blue Shield** organization. Whereas Blue Cross has special arrangements with the hospitals, Blue Shield tries to achieve the same by signing up doctors to participate in Blue Shield coverage. This participation feature means that a doctor is willing to accept the payment from Blue Shield as payment in full for services rendered. These payments are generally based on what are called *usual, customary, and reasonable* (UCR) fees. The UCR fees are reflective of physician fees charged in an area.[35]

For many organizations, the costs associated with the "Cadillac" of health insurance plans have become prohibitive. Even passing these costs on to the employee has not met with much success. As such, traditional health-care coverage is rapidly being replaced by the other two plan types. Traditional insurers like Blue Cross and Blue Shield, too, have begun to offer other types of health insurance coverage options to employers in order to help contain rising health-care benefit costs.

Health Maintenance Organization Provides comprehensive health services for a flat fee.

Health Maintenance Organizations

Health Maintenance Organizations (HMOs) are designed to provide quality health care at a fixed expense for their members. People's needs have changed, and with these changing needs comes the expectation that they can obtain good health care at a reasonable cost. Under traditional coverage, preventive care is generally not covered. For instance, visiting a physician for routine baby immunizations or gynecological exams would not be paid for under the terms of traditional health insurance coverage. Accordingly, the costs of such care are borne solely by the employee.

Health Maintenance Act of 1973 Established the requirement that companies offering traditional health insurance to its employees must also offer alternative health-care options.

To meet this growing concern and provide the desired services to employees, HMOs were created. This creation stemmed from the passage of the **Health Maintenance Act of 1973,** which required employers who extended traditional health insurance to their employees to also offer alternative health-care coverage options. HMOs seek efficiencies by keeping health-care costs down; one means of achieving that goal is by providing preventive care. Approximately 80 percent of all working individuals in the United States belong to an HMO.[36]

Exhibit 12-2 is a sample of HMO coverage. The major disadvantage, however, is that under an HMO, to get full coverage, one must receive services from the service center location that is selected. Furthermore, to be seen outside of the HMO, or for other services, individuals must either receive permission from their HMO physician or incur a greater out-of-pocket expense. Accordingly, under an HMO arrangement, freedom of health-care choice is significantly limited. This limiting feature has been one of the greatest concerns some individuals have regarding using an HMO. However, for many, the cost savings far outweigh the imposed restrictions.

Preferred Provider Organizations Organization that requires using specific physicians and health-care facilities to contain the rising costs of health care.

Preferred Provider Organizations

Preferred Provider Organizations (PPOs) are health-care arrangements where an employer or insurance company has agreements with doctors, hospitals, and other related medical service facilities to provide services for a fixed fee. In return for accepting this fixed fee, the employer or the insurer promises to encourage employees to use their services. The encouragement often results in additional services being covered. PPOs often have lower premiums than traditional health insurance programs.[37] Moreover, insurance companies offering the PPO also provide valuable information to employers. Through utilization review procedures, the PPO can provide data to help the employer determine unnecessary plan use. For example, elective surgery often

EXHIBIT 12-2
Sample Health Maintenance
Organization Coverage

COVERAGE CONDITIONS	COVERAGE (HMO FACILITY ONLY)
Physician	
Primary Care	100% after $5 Co-pay
Specialists	100% after $10 Co-pay
In-Patient Care	100% (When preauthorized by Plan)
Out-Patient Care	100% (When preauthorized by Plan)
Hospital	100% (When preauthorized by Plan)
Surgery	100% (When preauthorized by Plan)
Maternity Benefits	100% (When preauthorized by Plan)
Well-Baby Care	100% after $5 Co-pay
Immunizations	100% (When preauthorized by Plan)
Dental Coverage	100%
Diagnostic	100%
Preventive	100% after $10 Co-pay
Deductibles	
Individual	None
Family	None
Out-of-Pocket Maximums	
Individual	None
Family	None

Source: State of Maryland, *Summary of Maryland State Employees Health Benefits*, 2001 (November 2000), pp. 11.

requires preauthorization, which stipulates the approved procedures and hospital stay, if any. These "checks" can act as gatekeepers designed to contain health-care costs (see Exhibit 12-3).

How can a PPO benefit the employee? Through the agreement reached between the employer and the insurance company, a PPO can provide much the same service that an HMO provides. The difference is that an individual is not required to use a specific facility—like a designated hospital. So long as a physician or the medical facility is participating in the health network, the services are covered. The individual, in the case of a participating physician, typically incurs a fixed out-of-pocket expense (defined by the agreement). In those cases, the PPO takes the form of traditional health insurance. However, if an employee decides to go elsewhere for services, then the service fee is reimbursed according to specific guidelines.

PPOs attempt to combine the best of both worlds—the HMO and traditional insurance. These networks may well be the fastest-growing form of health plans in the United States.[38]

Employer-Operated Coverage   Although the types of insurance programs mentioned above are the most popular means of health insurance today, many companies are looking for other options that will assist them in containing the rising health-care costs they incur. To this end, some companies have begun reviewing the concept of being self-insured, and in many of these instances, using the assistance of a third-party administrator (TPA).[39] A movement in health-insurance coverage witnessed in the 1980s was the formation of self-funded programs. Some organizations, such as the State of Maryland, General Motors, Motorola, and General Binding Corporation, have ventured into the insurance business to reduce health insurance costs.[40] This insurance plan is customarily established and operated under an arrangement called a *voluntary employees'*

EXHIBIT 12-3
Sample Preferred Provider Organization (Point of Service) Coverage

COVERAGE CONDITIONS	IN NETWORK	OUT OF NETWORK
Physician		
Primary Care	100% after $15 Co-pay	80% after Deductible
Specialists	100% after $20 Co-pay	80% after Deductible
In-Patient Care	100%	80% after Deductible
Out-Patient Care	100%	80% after Deductible
Hospital	100% for 365 Days	80% after Deductible
Surgery	100%	80% after Deductible
Maternity Benefits	100%	80% after Deductible
Well-Baby Care	100% after $15 Co-pay	80% after Deductible
Immunizations	100%	80% after Deductible
Dental Coverage		
Diagnostic	Not Covered	
Preventive	Not Covered	
Deductibles		
Individual	None	$250
Family	None	$500
Out-of-Pocket Maximums		
Individual	None	$3,000
Family	None	$6,000

Source: State of Maryland, *Summary of Maryland State Employees Health Benefits,* 2001 (November 2000), p. 11.

beneficiary association (VEBA). In this case, the employer typically establishes a trust fund to pay for the health benefits used.[41] For the most part, this employer trust fund has received favorable treatment from the IRS.

Health Insurance Continuation　What happens to an employee's health insurance coverage if that employee leaves the organization or is laid off? The answer to that question lies in the **Consolidated Omnibus Budget Reconciliation Act (COBRA)**. One of the main features established by the COBRA was the continuation of employee benefits for a period up to three years after the employee leaves the company.[42] Because of high unemployment rates in the early 1980s, supplemented by the downsizing of Corporate America, large numbers of individuals were out of work, and more importantly, no longer had medical insurance. To combat this problem, COBRA was enacted in 1985. When employees resign or are laid off through no fault of their own, they're eligible for a continuation of their health insurance benefits for a period of 18 months, although under certain conditions, the time may be extended to 29 months.[43] The cost of this coverage is paid by the employee. The employer may also charge the employee a small administrative fee for this service. However, COBRA requires employers to offer this benefit through the company's current group health insurance plan, which is at a rate that is typically lower than if the individual had to purchase the insurance himself or herself.

Consolidated Omnibus Budget Reconciliation Act (COBRA)　Provides for the continuation of employee benefits for a period up to three years after an employee leaves a job.

RETIREMENT PROGRAMS

Retiring from work today does not guarantee a continuation of one's standard of living. Social Security cannot sustain the lifestyle most of us grow accustomed to in our working years. Therefore, we cannot rely on the government as the sole source of our retirement income. Instead, Social Security payments must be just one component of a properly designed retirement system.[44] The other components are retirement monies we may receive from our organization and savings we have amassed over the years. Irrespective of the retirement vehicles used, it is important to recognize that retirement plans are highly regulated by the **Employee Retirement Income Security Act (ERISA)** of 1974. Let's take a brief look at ERISA before we discuss the different retirement programs.

Employee Retirement Income Security Act (ERISA) Law passed in 1974 designed to protect employee retirement benefits.

ERISA was passed to deal with one of the largest problems of the day imposed by private pension plans—employees were not getting their benefits. That was due chiefly to the design of the pension plans, which almost always required a minimum tenure with the organization before the individual had a guaranteed right to pension benefits, regardless of whether or not they remained with the company. These permanent benefits—or the guarantee to a pension when one retires or leaves the organization—are called **vesting rights.** In years past, employees had to have extensive tenures in an organization before they were entitled to their retirement benefits—if they were entitled at all. This meant, for instance, that a 60-year-old employee with 23 years of service who left the company—for whatever reason—would have no right to a pension benefit. ERISA was enacted to prevent such abuses.

Vesting rights guarantee an employee's right to a pension benefit.

Vesting Rights The permanent right to pension benefits.

ERISA requires employers who decide to provide a pension or profit sharing plan to design their retirement program under specific rules. Typically, each plan must convey to employees any information that is relevant to their retirement. Currently, vesting rights in organizations typically come after six years of service, and pension programs must be available to all employees over age 21.[45] Employees with fewer than six years of service may receive a pro-rated portion of their retirement benefit. This shorter vesting period, which came into effect with the 1986 Tax Reform Act, is crucial for employees, especially when one considers that the length of service in companies today is shorter. With this shorter vesting period, employees who leave companies after six years generally can carry their retirement rights with them. That is, ERISA enables pension rights to be portable.[46]

Pension Benefits Guaranty Corporation (PBGC) The organization that lays claim to corporate assets to pay or fund inadequate pension programs.

ERISA also created guidelines for the termination of a pension program. Should an employer voluntarily terminate a pension program, the **Pension Benefit Guaranty Corporation (PBGC)** must be notified. Similarly, the act permits the PBGC, under certain conditions (such as inadequate pension funding), to lay claim on corporate assets—up to 30 percent of net worth to pay benefits that had been promised to employees. Additionally, when a pension plan is terminated, the PBGC requires the employer to notify workers and retirees of any financial institution that will be handling future retirement programs for the organization.[47]

Summary Plan Description An ERISA requirement of explaining to employees their pension program and rights.

Another key aspect of ERISA is its requirement for a company to include what is commonly called a **Summary Plan Description (SPD)**. Summary Plan Descriptions are designed to serve as a vehicle to inform employees about the benefits offered in the company in terms the "average" employee can understand.[48] This means that employers are required to inform employees on the details of their retirement plans, including such items as eligibility requirements, and employee rights under ERISA.

Finally, it's important to note that another law has had a significant effect on ERISA. This is the 1984 Retirement Equity Act. While the Retirement Equity Act decreased plan participation from age 25 to 21, its main effect was that it "made it easier for women to earn and maintain pension and retirement benefits."[49] The Retirement Equity Act also requires plan participants to receive spouse approval before a participant is able to waive survivor benefits.

Defined Benefit Plans

Defined Benefit Plan A type of retirement program whereby a retiring employee receives a fixed amount of retirement income based on some average earnings over a period of time.

In decades past, the most popular pension was a **defined benefit plan.** This plan specifies the dollar benefit workers will receive at retirement. The amount typically revolves around some fixed monthly income for life or a variation of a lump-sum cash distribution. The amount and type of the benefit are set, and the company contributes the set amount each year into a trust fund. The amount contributed each year is calculated on an actuarial basis—considering variables such as length of service, how long plan participants are expected to live, their lifetime earnings, and how much return the trust portfolio will receive (e.g., 5 percent or 10 percent annually). The pension payout formulas used to determine retirement benefits vary widely.

Over the past two decades, defined benefit plans have received some criticism. Employees have identified a need to receive more retirement benefits and to be permitted to make their own contributions to retirement plans—giving rise to what are called *defined contribution plans.*

Defined Contribution Plans

Defined contribution plans are different from defined benefit plans in at least one very important area—no specific dollar benefits are fixed. That is, under a defined contribution plan, each employee has an individual account, to which both the employee and the employer may make contributions.[50] The plan establishes rules for contributions. For example, the Humana, Inc. defined contribution pension plan allows employees to select both a money purchase plan (described next) and a profit-sharing plan with the company matching up to 6 percent of salary. In a defined contribution plan, the money is invested and projections are offered as to probable retirement income levels. However, the company is not bound by these projections, and accordingly, unfunded pension liability problems do not occur. For this reason, defined contribution plans have become a popular trend in new qualified retirement planning. Additionally, variations in plan administration frequently allow the employee some selection in the investment choices. For instance, an employee may select bonds for security, common stocks for appreciation and an inflation hedge, or some type of money market fund.

Money Purchase Pension Plan   Money purchase pension plans are one type of defined contribution plan. Under this arrangement, the organization commits to deposit a fixed amount of money or a percentage of the employee's pay annually into a fund.[51] Under IRS regulations, however, the maximum permitted is 25 percent of worker pay. Under money purchase plans, no specific retirement dollar benefits are fixed as they are under a defined benefit plan. However, companies do make projections of probable retirement income based on various interest rates, but the company is not bound to the projection.

Profit-Sharing Plans   Profit-sharing pension plans are yet another variation of defined contribution plans. Under these plans, companies, like Fisher-Price, contribute to a trust fund account an optional percentage of each worker's pay (maximum allowed by law is 15 percent). This, of course, is guided by the profit level in the organization. The operative word in profit-sharing plans here is "optional." The company is not bound by law to make contributions every year. It should be noted, however, that although employers are not bound by law, the majority of employers feel a moral obligation to make a contribution. Often they will keep to a schedule, even in times when profits are slim or nonexistent.[52]

Individual Retirement Accounts   From 1982 to 1986, the Individual Retirement Account (IRA) was the darling of retirement planning. The law permitted each worker to defer paying taxes on up to $2,000 of earned income per year ($2,225 for employee and spouse where spouse did not work) with interest on these accounts also accumulating on a tax-deferred basis.[53] This was a tax shelter for the average person, a good way to build a nest egg. Anyone who had earned income could invest in an IRA. The purpose of an IRA was to make the individual partly responsible for his or her retirement income.

IRAs were very popular for the few years they received favorable tax status. However, with the Tax Reform Act of 1986, IRAs became significantly limited for many workers. To be eligible for deferring income to an IRA, workers now must meet specific conditions, such as not participating in a recognized retirement program at work and falling under limits on the adjusted annual income. For instance, single individuals making more than the adjusted annual income level with a company-paid pension would no longer qualify for a tax deduction from their IRA contribution. The purpose of the tax reform was to focus IRAs on lower-income workers who might not have a retirement program at their place of work, or for those who deserve to augment the one they have. That doesn't mean that the individual cannot make an IRA investment. It simply means that if he or she does, the contribution is not tax deductible.

Roth IRAs   Effective in 1998, a new version of the IRA was signed into law. This was called the Roth IRA. In a Roth IRA, an employee can contribute up to $2,000 annually to an account. However, the money is not deposited on a pre-tax basis. Instead, the money grows tax-free, and after reaching a certain age, the money can be withdrawn tax-free. As with the regular IRA, there are conditions for being eligible to contribute to a Roth IRA based on compensation.[54]

401(k)s   Under the Tax Equity and Fiscal Responsible Act (TEFRA), capital accumulation programs, more commonly known as 401(k)s or thrift-savings plans, were established. A 401(k) program is named after the IRS tax code section that created it. These programs permit workers to set aside a certain amount of their income on a tax-deferred basis through their employer.[55] In many cases, what differentiated the employer-sponsored 401(k) from an IRA was the amount permitted to be set aside, and the realization that many companies contributed an amount to the 401(k) on the employee's behalf.[56] Because of this matching feature, many companies call their 401(k) a matching-contribution plan, meaning that both the employer and the employee are jointly working to create a retirement program.

401(k) programs have been popular with employees since their inception. Both employers and employees have found that there are advantages to offering capital accumulation plans. The cost of providing retirement income for employees is lower, and employees can supplement their retirement program and often participate in investments. Employees are offered the ease of contributing to their 401(k) through payroll deductions. In some instances, the matching-contribution program may be offered to supplement the employer's noncontrib-

Exhibit 12-4
Other Retirement Plans

Plan	About the Plan
403(b)	Designed to be the 401(k) counterpart for educational and nonprofit organizations.
Simplified Employee Retirement Plans	Designed for an employer or the self-employed individual. Permits contributions up to 15 percent of net profit, or $30,000 (whichever is less).
Keogh Plans	Available to the self-employed, permits contributions of 15 percent of net profit, or $30,000 (whichever is less). The main distinction between a Keogh and an SEP lies in the annual report filing requirement of the IRS.
Stock Option Plans	Under these plans, an individual can purchase company stock through payroll deductions. The stock is generally sold at a discount to the employee, or at straight market value without the use of, or commissions for, a broker.
457	Voluntary deferred salary plans for public sector employees.

utory (defined benefit) retirement plan. Additionally, regardless of the mechanics of the program, employers are heavily regulated on offering employees investment advice.[57]

Other Retirement Vehicles While we've described the major retirement plans, we would be remiss not to mention the following retirement vehicles that are appropriate for selected groups of workers. These are 403(b)s, 457s, Simplified Employee Pension Plans (SEPs), Keogh Plans, and Stock Option Plans (ESOPS—Employee Stock Ownership Plans), Payroll-Based Stock Ownership Plans (PAYSOPS), and Tax-Benefit-based Stock Ownership Plans (TRASOPS). Exhibit 12-4 provides a summary of these retirement alternatives for certain groups of workers.

PAID TIME OFF

There are a number of benefits that provide pay for time off from work. The most popular of these are vacation and holiday leave and disability insurance, which includes sick leave and short- and long-term disability programs. Although we'll present these as separate items, some organizations today are lumping all paid time off into a single "bank." As the time is used, it is charged to one's account—regardless of whether it's used for vacation, or sick leave.[58]

Vacation and Holiday Leave

After employees have been with an organization for a specified period of time, they usually become eligible for a paid vacation. Common practice is to relate the length of vacation to the length of tenure and job classification in the organization. For example, after six months' service with an organization, an employee may be eligible for one week's vacation; after a year, two weeks; after five years, three weeks; and after 10 or more years, four weeks. It is interesting to note that U.S. workers have one of the shortest vacation periods of many industrialized nations. For example, while U.S. workers enjoy 15 to 20 days off each year, on average, employees in France, England, Germany, and Hong Kong are offered up to 30 days a year.[59]

The rationale behind the paid vacation is to provide a break in which employees can refresh themselves. This rationale is important, but is sometimes overlooked. For example, in a situation where employees accrue a certain amount of vacation time and can sell back to the company any unused vacation days, the regenerative "battery charging" intent is lost. While the cost may be the same to the employer (depending on how long vacation time can be accrued), employees who do not take a break ultimately may be adversely affected.

Holiday pay is paid time off while observing some special event—federally mandated holidays (like New Year's Day, Presidents' Day, Martin Luther King's Birthday, Memorial Day, Labor Day, Thanksgiving, and Christmas), company-provided holidays (like Christmas Eve and New Year's Eve), or personal days (days employees can take off for any reason). In the United States, employees average 10 paid holidays per year.[60] Most other countries are similar, with averages of nine paid holidays in the United Kingdom, 11 in Brazil, 17 in Japan, and a maximum of 19 in Mexico.[61]

Disability Insurance Programs

Employees today recognize that salary continuation for injuries and major illnesses is almost more important than life insurance. For most employees, there is a greater probability that they will have a disabling injury requiring an extended absence from work of more than 90 days than that they will die before

David Mason, founder of a St. Louis-based architecture and engineering firm, learned something valuable from a job candidate. Trying to "land" a highly sought-after candidate, everything appeared to be going well. That is, until the candidate stated he wanted every other Friday off. Mason thought it just might be interesting to do. Consequently, he implemented a work-schedule benefit where employees work 7:30–5:30 each day, working 81 hours over nine days—and get every other Friday off. As a result, productivity in the firm has increased, and there has been a significant increase in unsolicited job applicants. Customers, too, have found the schedule workable. As for Mason, he enjoys spending every other Friday with his family.

their retirement. Programs to address this area of need can be broken down into two broad categories—short-term and long-term disability programs.

Almost all employers offer some type of short-term disability plan. Categories under this heading include the company sick-leave policy, short-term disability programs,[62] state disability laws, and workers' compensation. The focus of each is to provide replacement income in the event of an injury or a short-term illness.[63] For many, this short-term period is defined as being six months or less in duration.

One of the most popular types of short-term disability programs is a company's sick-leave plan. Most organizations, such as General Motors and Federal Express, provide their employees with pay for days not worked because of illness. Sick leave is allocated on the basis of a specific number of days a year,[64] often accrued on a cumulative basis. In some organizations, too, the number of days may be expanded relative to years of service with the organization. Each year of employment may entitle the worker to two additional days' sick leave. Regardless of whether sick leave is used, it would continue to accumulate (usually up to some maximum number of days); those individuals who have been with the company the longest would have accumulated the most sick-leave credit.

Sick-leave abuse has often been a problem for organizations. Some research into the area indicates that "only 45 percent of sick leave days are used for personal illnesses."[65] The belief, too, that one should amass sick leave for use later in life is quickly diminishing. That belief may have been popular when a person joined an organization early in life and retired from that company, but with today's mobility, long-term focus has little meaning. This is especially alarming when we consider that sick days are not usually transferable to another organization. Thus, the "use them or lose them" concept may only hinder productivity. Attempts have been made recently to combat this potential for sick-leave abuse. This has come in the form of financial incentives to individuals who do not fully use their sick leave for the year. In a number of organizations, for example, in an effort to reward attendance, companies have what is called "well pay." Well pay focuses on providing a monetary inducement for workers not to use all of their sick leave. This incentive can be in the form of buying back the unused sick leave, lumping sick-leave days into the years of service in calculating retirement benefits, or even having special drawings for those who qualify. For instance, at Northwest Airlines, to combat absenteeism during peak production times, the airlines place names of employees who don't miss work into a drawing. Winners receive Corvettes, Ford Explorers, or cash equivalents.[66] These incentives intend to serve as a bonus and encourage judicious use of sick time.[67] It's interesting to note that in some cases, employees come to work ill when they really shouldn't so as not to lose the incentive pay. Rather than resting and taking care of themselves, they spread their germs to others. In early 1998, for instance, a virulent strain of flu ravaged many organizations. Employees exposing other employees to the flu bug resulted, at times, in nearly entire departments having to close down.

If health insurance coverage is unable to prevent a major illness from occurring, and an extended period of time off work does not provide for ample recuperation, then employees may need the benefits provided under a long-term disability program. Similar to their short-term disability counterparts, long-term disability programs are designed to provide replacement income for an employee who is no longer able to return to work and where short-term coverage has expired. The period of time before long-term disability becomes effective is usually six months. Some type of long-term disability coverage is in effect in almost all

HI-TECH BENEFIT OFFERINGS

WHAT TECHNOLOGY IS AVAILABLE IN THE open market that can assist benefits administrators? Over the past few years, several technology-based tools have hit the market. Here are just a sampling of what is available for benefits administrators to use. Some of these are PC-based, while others are Internet-based.[71] We've provided some links for you to explore these offerings:

- Atwork Technologies, Inc. www.atwork.com
- Performance Software, Inc. www.dynasuite.com
- LifeMap Communications www.lifemapcom.com
- Authoria, Inc. www.authoria.com
- Ultra Link, Inc. www.ibenefits.com
- HRPress, inc. www.hrpress-software.com/cobra.html

companies and is provided on a temporary or permanent basis. By definition, a temporary disability is one in which an individual cannot perform his or her job duties for the first 24 months after injury or illness. Permanent, long-term disability is when an individual is unable to perform in any occupation.[68]

The benefits paid to employees are customarily set between 50 and 67 percent, with 60 percent salary replacement the most common. In most plans, there is a maximum monthly payment of replacement income that lies between 70 and 80 percent of gross pay.[69] This may be as little as $2,000, or greater than $10,000. In most cases, long-term disability payments continue until the individual reaches age 65.[70]

SURVIVOR BENEFITS

To provide protection to the families of employees, many companies offer life insurance as a benefit. Life insurance programs, one of the more popular employee benefits,[72] typically come in two varieties—noncontributory and contributory policies. Our major focus in this context is on the noncontributory variety, for that is the one generally completely employer funded.

Group Term Life Insurance

When a company offers group term life insurance to its employees,[73] the standard policy provides for a death benefit of one to five times their annual rate of pay, with most including a double indemnity provision—that is, should an employee's death result from an accident, the benefit is twice the policy value. More than 90 percent of all companies provide this coverage.[74]

Death benefits offered are generally linked to one's position in the organization. Generally speaking, the more "valuable" an employee is defined in terms of his or her level in the organization, the greater the death benefit offered. Those at lower levels of the organization typically receive one to one-and-one-half their annual wage as a benefit, whereas top-level employees may receive as much as three times their salary.

Travel Insurance

Another insurance plan offered to many employees is travel insurance. Under this policy, employees' lives are covered in the event of death while traveling on company time. This insurance typically provides a lump-sum payment, from $50,000 to $1 million. Depending on any unique provisions of a policy, as long as an employee is conducting business-related activities when the death occurs, the insurance typically will be paid. For example, if a salesperson's day typically begins by traveling to a client's place of business from his or her residence, coverage begins as soon as this person gets into the car. If he or she is killed going to that location, then this insurance is activated. The key element is when death occurred. An employee who normally commutes to work would not be covered under an employer-paid travel insurance benefit if an accident happened on the way.

$\mathcal{F}$AMILY-FRIENDLY BENEFITS

Family-Friendly Benefits Flexible benefits that are supportive of caring for one's family.

In a few instances in previous chapters, we referred to something called the family-friendly organization. What makes the organization family-friendly? That answer lies in the benefits it offers. **Family-friendly benefits** are so named because they represent flexible benefits that are supportive of caring for one's family. These would include such benefits as flextime, child and elder care, dependent-care flexible spending accounts, part-time employment, relocation programs, telecommuting, summer day camp, adoption benefits,[75] and parental leave.[76] Some of the more notable companies that offer such benefits are American Express, Corning, Dow, Hoechst Celanese, Johnson & Johnson, and NationsBank.[77] At the heart of such programs, however, is a means for increasing child- and elder-care benefits.[78] While flexible spending accounts mentioned previously have assisted in affording this care, more employees are seeking ways of having quality child care and elder care in close proximity to them; this is especially true of organizations that operate in staggered shifts or around the clock.[79]

A number of societal issues are at stake here. Dual-career couples with children and/or elderly live-in parents need to have some assurance that child- or elder-care programs are available to them without major disruptions to their lives. No longer is it acceptable to assume that other family members or friends will provide this care, although in many cases that is what occurs. Nonetheless, many HRM representatives recognize that when their employees face a choice between their jobs and their families, the vast majority of employees clearly place their jobs second. For example, although sick leave is supposed to be used for the employee's illness only, when a child of that employee is sick and no child care is available, it is likely the employee will call in sick in order to care for their dependent.[80] At Johnson & Johnson, for example, absenteeism among employees who took advantage of family-friendly benefit offerings—like flexible work hours and family leaves—was 50 percent less than that for their work force as a whole.[81] While there are legal and insurance ramifications to be addressed, in locations where these programs operate, employee morale has increased. In addition, companies have also developed cooperative efforts to address this issue; for example, American Express, IBM, Work Family Directions, and Allstate Insurance have joined forces to offer quality child care at a facility that is in close proximity to all of their employees.[82] Similar to the need for child care is the need for elder care. Elder care refers to a situation in which children become more responsible for the care of an aged parent. It's estimated that approximately 12 percent of the work force have some elder-care responsibilities,[83] resulting in

Family-friendly benefits are so named because they represent benefits that are supportive of caring for one's family.

What do we mean by being creative in offering services to employees as part of their benefits package? Take the case of Chevron. The environment in the company is, at times, very stressful. To help deal with the stress, company officials decided to offer employees massage therapy. As a result, the employees of the organization are less stressed, and they have become more productive.

Flexible Benefits   A benefits program in which employees are permitted to pick benefits that most meet their needs.

significant productivity losses for their organizations.[84] The same issues arise regarding facilities, quality providers, and so forth.

The Service Side of Benefits

In addition to the benefits described above, organizations offer a wealth of services employees may find desirable. These services can be provided to the employee at no cost, or at a significant reduction from what might have been paid without the organization's support.

Services provided to employees may be such benefits as sponsored social and recreational events, employee assistance programs, credit unions, housing, tuition reimbursement, jury duty, uniforms, military pay, company-paid transportation and parking, free coffee, baby-sitting services or referrals, and even appliance repair services.[85] Companies can be as creative as they like in putting together their benefits program—many today even offer in-house massages for their employees.[86] The crucial point is to provide a package containing those benefits in which employees have expressed some interest and perceive some value in its offering.

An INTEGRATIVE PERSPECTIVE ON EMPLOYEE BENEFITS

When an employer considers offering benefits to employees, one of the main considerations is to keep costs down. Traditionally employers attempted to do this by providing a list of benefits to their employees—whether employees wanted or needed any particular benefit, or used it at all. Rising costs, and a desire to let employees choose what they want, led employers to search for alternative measures of benefits administration. The leading alternative to address this concern was the implementation of **flexible benefits.** Although flexible benefits offer greater choices to employees (and might have a motivational effect), we must understand that they are provided mainly to contain benefit costs.[87] The term *flexible benefits* refers to a system whereby employees are presented with a menu of benefits and asked to select, within monetary limits imposed, the employee benefits they desire.[88] Today, almost all major corporations in the United States offer flexible benefits. A number of types of flexible benefits exist. Specifically, three plans are popular: flexible spending accounts, modular plans, and core-plus options (see Exhibit 12-5).

Flexible Spending Accounts

Flexible spending accounts, approved and operated under Section 125 of the Internal Revenue Code (IRC), are special types of flexible benefits that permit employees to set aside up to the dollar amount offered in the plan to pay for particular services.[89] For example, Abbott Laboratories has a flexible benefit plan that enables employees to pay for such items as health-care and dental premiums under premium accounts.[90] Also, certain medical expenses (like deductibles, and dental and vision care under a medical reimbursement account) and dependent child-care expenses (up to $5,000) under a dependent-care reimbursement account can be established. By placing a specified amount into a spending account, the employee is permitted to pay for these services with monies not included in W-2 income. This can result in lower federal, state, and Social Security

EXHIBIT 12-5
Flexible Benefit Programs

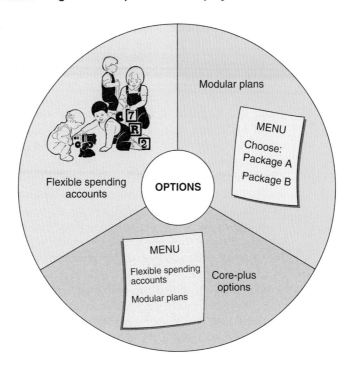

tax rates for an employee, and can increase the amount of individual spending income. Such accounts also provide Social Security tax savings for the employer.

While tax benefits exist for employees, workers must understand that flexible spending accounts are heavily regulated. Each account established must operate independently. For instance, money set aside for dependent care expenses can be used only for that purpose. One cannot decide later to seek reimbursement from one account to pay for services where no account was established, or to pay for services from another account because all monies in the designated account have been withdrawn. Additionally, money that is deposited into these accounts must be spent during the period, or forfeited. Unused monies do not revert back to the employee in terms of a cash outlay; forfeited monies typically revert back to the company. This point must be clearly communicated to employees to avoid misconception of the plan requirements.

Modular Plans

The modular plan of flexible benefits is a system whereby employees choose a predesigned package of benefits. As opposed to selecting "cafeteria style," modular plans contain "a fixed combination of benefit plans put together to meet the needs of a particular segment of the employee population." For example, suppose a company offers its employees two separate modules. Module 1 benefits consist of no dental or vision coverage, a life insurance policy at two times annual earnings, and HMO health-care insurance; this policy is provided to all employees at no cost to them. Module 2 benefits consist of dental and vision coverage, a life insurance policy of two times annual earnings, and traditional health insurance. This plan, however, requires a biweekly pretax payroll deduction of $57. While a choice does exist, it is limited to selecting either of the packages in its entirety.

Core-Plus Options Plans

A core-plus options flexible benefits plan exhibits more of a menu selection than the two programs just mentioned. Under this arrangement, employees typically are provided with coverage of core areas—typically medical coverage, life insurance at one times annual earnings, minimal disability insurance, a 401(k) program, and standard time off from work with pay.[91] With these minimum benefits in place, not only are employees provided basic coverage from which they can build more extensive packages, the core-plus option helps to keep benefit costs relatively stable.

Under the core-plus plan, employees are given the opportunity to select other benefits. These additional benefits may range from more extensive coverage of the core plan to other benefits like spending accounts. Employees are generally given credits to purchase their additional benefits. These credits are often calculated according to an employee's tenure in the company, salary, and position held. As a rule of thumb, in first-time installations, the credits given to an employee equal the amount needed to purchase the identical plan in force before flexible benefits arrived; that is, no employee should be worse off. If the employee decides to select exactly what was previously offered, the employee will be able to purchase such benefits with no added out-of-pocket expenses (copayments) other than what he or she had previously paid, with these payments now being made on a pretax basis.

HRM WORKSHOP

SUMMARY

(This summary relates to the Learning Outcomes identified on p. 326.)

After having read this chapter, you should be able to:

1. **Discuss why employers offer benefits to their employees.** Employers offer benefits to employees to attract and retain them. Benefits are expected by today's workers, and as such, must be offered in such a way that they provide meaning and value to the employees.

2. **Contrast Social Security, unemployment compensation, and workers' compensation benefits.** Social Security is an insurance program funded by current employees to provide (1) a minimum level of retirement income, (2) disability income, and (3) survivor benefits. Unemployment compensation provides income continuation to employees who lose a job through no fault of their own. Unemployment compensation typically lasts for 26 weeks. Workers' compensation provides income continuation for employees who are hurt or disabled on the job. Workers' compensation also provides compensation for work-related deaths or permanent disabilities. All three are legally required benefits.

3. **Identify and describe three major types of health insurance options.** The three major types of health insurance benefits offered to employees are traditional, health maintenance organizations, and preferred provider organizations. The latter two are designed to provide a fixed out-of-pocket alternative to health-care coverage.

4. **Discuss the important implications of the Employee Retirement Income Security Act.** The Employment Retirement Income Security Act (ERISA) has had a significant effect on retirement programs. Its primary emphasis is to ensure that employees have a vested right to their retirement monies, to ensure that appropriate guidelines are followed in the event of a retirement plan termination, and to ensure that employees understand their benefits through the Summary Plan Description.

5. **Outline and describe major types of retirement programs offered by organizations.** The most popular types of retirement benefits offered today are defined benefit pension plans, money purchase pension plans, profit-sharing plans, Social Security, individual retirement accounts, and 401(k)s. For special groups, however, 403(b)s, stock option programs, simplified employee pension plans, and Keogh plans may be used.

6. **Explain the reason companies offer vacation benefits to their employees.** The primary reason for a company to provide a vacation benefit is to allow employees a break from work in which they can refresh/reenergize themselves.

7. **Describe the purpose of disability insurance programs.**

CALCULATING A LONG-TERM DISABILITY PAYMENT

ABOUT THE SKILL: MUCH OF the work of a benefits specialist revolves around mathematics and finance calculations. Specific skills are not easily found. However, it is clear that any benefits specialist has to have excellent computer skills, especially in spreadsheet applications. To this end, here's a scenario that a benefits specialist may face, and it lends itself to the use of a spreadsheet application. To practice this skill, use the following information. We've worked through it on paper; your task is to place the information and calculations on a spreadsheet. Suppose an employee makes $36,000 per year (or $3,000) per month. Your organization offers its employees a long-term disability (LTD) insurance benefit at 65 percent of earnings, with a monthly cap at $4,000. The company's LTD is also integrated with Social Security disability payments (SSDI) such that no more than 70 percent of salary is covered. The employee has a verifiable illness, is unable to work in any occupation, and has been covered under the company's short-term disability plan for the past six months (the required time before long-term disability starts). To determine what this employee's long-term disability payment is, you need to determine the amount of SSDI monthly payment. In your research, you've found that this employee is entitled to $8,400 in SSDI payments a year ($700 a month). You now have enough data to complete this employee's LTD. After the calculations have been made, we see that this employee, given his circumstances, is eligible for a payment of $500 from SSDI and $900 from the LTD policy. Even though the LTD limit of 65 percent of the employee's salary would be $1,300, when integrated with SSDI, the employee may not receive more than $1,400 (70 percent of monthly salary). Here are the calculations.

- 65% of annual earnings/
  month = .5 　　　　　　 = $1,950 ($3000 × .65)
- 70% of monthly income
  for integration with
  Social Security 　　　　 = $2,100 ($3,000 × .70)
- SSDI benefit $8,400/12
  = $700/month 　　　　　 = $700 (given)
- Proposed total monthly
  payment without Social
  Security integration 　　 = $2,650 ($1,950 + $700)
- Proposed total monthly
  payment with Social
  Security integration 　　 = $2,100 (maximum)
- Overage 　　　　　　　 = $550 ($2,650 − $2,100)
- Actual LTD payment 　　 = $1,400 ($1,950 − $550)
  　　　　　　　　　　　　(LTD − overage)

Disability benefit programs are designed to ensure income replacement for employees in the event of a temporary or permanent disability arising from an injury or extended illness (typically originating off the job).

8. **Discuss what is meant by the term *family-friendly benefits*.** The term *family-friendly benefits* refers to a variety of benefits that are supportive of blending family and career. This may include on-site child care, flexible work schedules, dependent spending accounts, and part-time employment.

9. **List the various types of flexible benefit option programs.** Flexible benefits programs come in a variety of packages. The most popular versions existing today are flexible spending accounts, modular plans, add-on plans, and core-plus options.

DEMONSTRATING COMPREHENSION: *Questions for Review and Discussion*

1. Describe why companies provide benefits to their employees. What effect do companies expect benefits will have on employee work behaviors?

2. How does ERISA provide protection for a worker's retirement?

3. Identify and describe four legally required benefits.

4. Describe why an employee might select a PPO health insurance benefit over an HMO.

5. Describe the difference between a defined benefit pension plan and a defined contribution pension plan.

6. Describe the inherent potential for abuse in offering a sick-leave benefit.

7. Describe three types of flexible benefits programs.

8. "Social Security should serve as a foundation for employee retirement programs. Therefore, Congress should begin exploring more extensive revisions to the program to ensure that the next generation of retirees will receive the benefit." Do you agree or disagree with this statement? Explain your response.

9. "Social Security disability and survivor benefits should be the sole responsibility of each employee. A company simply cannot be responsible for the financial welfare of its employees. Additionally, legally required benefits provide some level of worker protection. Therefore, a major means of containing benefit costs should be the elimination of disability and survivor benefits." Do you agree or disagree? Explain your response.

10. "Flexible benefits programs are employer inducements to reduce benefits costs. The average employee has neither the ability nor information to make such important choices. Employees should be suspect of such programs." Do you agree or disagree? Explain your response.

CASE APPLICATION: *TEAM FUN!*

Kenny and Norton, owners of TEAM FUN!, a sporting goods manufacturer and retailer, are sitting with Tony, Director of Human Resources and Edna, Compensation and Benefits Manager. Tony comments, "You mean to tell me that no one has actually retired from TEAM FUN! and no one asked about the retirement plan before I got here?"

Norton scowls and observes, "You have been the first to bring up a whole lot of issues. And no. No retirees. No retirement questions. We always had the profit sharing and that tax shelter that Leo set up for us. Everyone does what they want."

Kenny says, "Your Mom did, Norton, after she helped us set up that bookkeeping system when we started."

Norton says, "No she didn't. We never paid her anything but free tickets to all the local pro games, so she didn't really retire."

Tony says, "I'd like to show you how to save some money for health insurance premiums. Offering everyone free full Blue coverage is really expensive. There are some other options. And I think you should consider some money saving vacation options. I never heard of anyone doing what TEAM FUN! does."

Kenny frowns, "As I recall your job interview, the vacation plan was what got you to take the job."

Tony sheepishly grins, "Four weeks to start is incredible. And earmarking one week to try out company products or services with you footing the bill sounded like a dream come true."

Norton nods, "That's what we thought. Anyone who wouldn't see it that way shouldn't work here. Why would you want to change that?"

Edna offers, "I agree that the vacation policy is great. However, we have trouble getting working moms in here. And I think that soccer moms could add a lot to us. We need more family-friendly benefits to be really attractive to them."

Tony jumps in, "Exactly! If we come up with some guidelines to let employees tailor the benefits package to their own circumstances, we will spend benefits dollars more effectively and have a happier workforce."

Kenny frowns, "How could they be any happier?"

Tony clarifies, "We'd have a more diverse workforce."

Norton, "What do you mean diverse?"

Kenny stands up and stretches and waves Norton over to the door. "Great ideas, Tony. We'll talk more tomorrow.

Come on, Norton. We've got to see the TV finals of that tournament we watched yesterday."

Questions:

1. As Tony's intern, work up a presentation chart for three major health insurance options. Make a recommendation.
2. How is TEAM FUN!'s vacation package different from

most U.S. companies? Should it be the same? Why or why not?

3. Design a flexible benefits plan for TEAM FUN!
4. Evaluate the retirement policy in light of current human resource pratices. Is it effective for this organization?
5. Is TEAM FUN! family-friendly? (Recall Edna's comment from Chapter case 1.) Expalin.

WORKING WITH A TEAM: *Benefit Selections*

Using Exhibit 12-6, determine the mix of benefits that would best fit your needs. After choosing your benefits, form into teams of three to five members and answer the following questions:

1. Explain the reasons for the choices you made. What compelled you to make those specific benefit choices?

2. Compare what benefits you have chosen with members of your team. What similarities exist? Differences?
3. Do you think that the benefits you selected will be the benefits you would select five years from now? Why or why not?

ENHANCING YOUR WRITING SKILLS

1. Discuss the pros and cons of offering benefits for the sake of being "competitive and innovative." In your discussion, address whether you believe it's possible for benefits to become fads.
2. One of the controversies surrounding benefits administration today is offering domestic partner benefits. Develop a two- to three-page paper arguing (1) why do-

mestic benefits should be offered to organizational members, and (2) why they shouldn't. End the paper with your support of one side or the argument.

3. Visit Social Security's web site (www.ssa.gov). Research the guidelines established in late 2000 regarding Social Security benefits for the disabled. Write a two- to three-page summary of your findings.

www.wiley.com/college/decenzo

ENDNOTES

1. Based on the stories by P. B. Gray, "The Rogers Revolt," *FSB* (April 2000), pp. 68–72; Jennifer J. Salopek, "The Net's Not All That," *Training and Development* (May 2000), p. 19; Michael A. Verespej, "Flexible Schedules Benefit All," *Industry Week* (August 21, 2000), p. 25; and Work/Family Directions Website www.wfd.com); Laura Factor, "HR Consulting Leader WFD Defines New Direction," *Media Release* (August 21, 2000), p. 1; and Christina Duffney, "WFD Helps Companies Achieve National Recognition for Work/Life Programs," *Media Release* (September 19, 1999), p. 1.

2. Kathleen Kerwin, Peter Burrows, and Dean Foust, "Workers of the World Log On," *Business Week* (February 21, 2001), p. 52.

3. Robert McGarvey, "Something Extra," *Entrepreneur* (May 1995), p. 70.

4. Christopher Ryan, "Employee Retention—What Can the Benefits Professional Do?" *Employee Benefits Journal* (December 2000), p. 18.

5. Frederick Herzberg, *Work and the Nature of Man* (New York: World, 1966).

6. U.S. Bureau of the Census, *Statistical Abstracts of the United States: 1999* (Washington, DC: Government Printing Office, 1999), p. 448.

7. Ibid.

8. Ibid.

9. Kevin Rubens, "Changes in Russia: A Challenge for HR," *HRMagazine* (November 1995), p. 72.

10. This assumes that the insurance policy is part of a group term plan. Should it be a single policy, other than term insurance, or if the plan discriminates in favor of the more highly paid employees, then the entire benefit would be taxable. See Elizabeth E. Vollmar, "Group Term Life Insurance," *Employee Benefits Journal* (June 2000), pp. 36–41.

11. As discussed in Chapter 3, government regulations had a major impact on the increases in employee benefits. It is

EXHIBIT 12-6
Sample Flexible Benefit Selection Sheet[1]

Name: Chris Reynolds
Annual Earnings: $38,000

Years of Service: 3
Credits to Spend[2]   6330

Health Care:[3]			**Vacation:**[4]	
HMO	Core		1 week	Core
PPO	3280		2 weeks	730
			3 weeks	1460
Life Insurance:[5]			4 weeks	2190
1 × AE		Core	**Paid Holidays:**[6]	
2 × AE		273	7 days	Core
3 × AE		546		
4 × AE		819	**Personal Days:**[7]	
			1 day	Core
Disability Insurance:			2 days	146
50% AE		Core	3 days	292
55% AE		240		
60% AE		480	**Retirement (401[k]):**	
65% AE		720	2% match	Core
			3% match	760
Dental Coverage:			4% match	1520
Dental HMO		Core	5% match	2280
Dental PPO		240	6% match	3040

[1]All cost figures represent single employee coverage only, where applicable. For additional family coverages for health insurance; see footnote #3.

[2]All flexible credits are based on 37% of annual salary (AE). Flexible spending credits are those credits available to you to spend on benefits. Credits available for spending is the difference between total flexible credits and those costs associated with core coverage. Any amount spent beyond "credits" will be deducted evenly over your 26 biweekly paychecks.

[3]Health care coverage is based on $283.33 per month for employee coverage only. Add $165 for employee plus one; and $228 for employee plus two or more per month for either coverage.

[4]Vacation costs are calculated at 1/52 of annual earnings.

[5]Life insurance is calculated at 7.20 cents per $1,000 of life insurance.

[6]Based on a 2,080-hour work week and a cost per hour rate.

[7]Based on a 2,080-hour work week and a cost per hour rate.

equally important to note that management practices and labor unions also have affected benefit offerings.

12. See, for instance, Debra Kent, "Two Men and Their Babies," *Working Mother* (June 1995), pp. 24–27.

13. Susan J. Wells, "A Benefit Built for 2," *HRMagazine* (August 1999), pp. 68–74.

14. See, for instance, "Gay Rights Group Reports More Employers Offer Health Coverage for Domestic Partners," *BNA Daily Report* (September 26, 2000), p. 1; and Kim I Mills, "GLBT Employees Make Gains in Workplaces Nationwide," *Diversity Factor* (Fall 2000), pp. 8–11.

15. Social Security here refers to FICA taxes for Old Age, Survivors, and Disability Insurance (OASDI).

16. Ames Gross and Patricia Dyson, "The Iron Rice Bowl Cracks," *HRMagazine* (July 1996), pp. 84–88.

17. Social Security Administration, "Your Taxes—What They're Paying for and Where the Money Goes," *Publication Number 05-10010* (February 2000).

18. Based on the passage of the Omnibus Budget Reconciliation Act of 1993, the 2.9% Medicare portion no longer
has a salary cap. Also, for diehard Social Security fans, Social Security taxes are actually divided into three parts: OASDI [Old Age Survivors and Disability]; HI [hospital insurance (Medicare)]; and FUTA [Federal Unemployment Tax]. OASDI and HI are combined together to form the FICA taxes deducted from employees' pay and matched by the employer. See, for example, Tom Herman, "A Special Summary and Forecast of Federal and State Tax Developments," *Wall Street Journal* (October 25, 2000), p. A-1; and Arthur Bachman and Stephen R. Leimberg, "T.D.s 8814 and 8815: A Second Look at Final Regs on FICA and FUTA Tax on Nonqualified Deferred Compensation," *Compensation and Benefits Management* (Autumn 1999), pp. 18–24.

19. Those born after 1929 need 40 credits. Those born before 1929 need fewer than 40 credits—one less credit for each year they were born prior to 1929 (e.g., if born in 1928, 39 credits; 1927, 38 credits, and so forth).

20. For specifics about retirement age extensions, year of birth, etc., see http://www.ssa.gov/pubs/10035.html#1082132.

21. Louis S. Richman, "Why Baby-Boomers Won't Be Able to Retire," *Fortune* (September 4, 1995), p. 48.

22. Susan E. Long, "No Comp for Employee Who Refuses Drug Test," *HR Focus* (June 1999), p. 3.

23. Wage bases for unemployment insurance vary. A number of states follow the federal $7,000 base, while others vary to a maximum of $22,700 in Hawaii.

24. In 1992, President George H. W. Bush signed into law a bill extending the unemployment coverage from 26 weeks to 39 weeks for those experiencing long durations of unemployment brought about by the recession in the early 1990s. This extension expired July 4, 1992. However, on July 2, 1992, President Bush again extended the coverage for an additional 20 or 26 weeks, depending on the unemployment rates in each state. This extension expired on March 6, 1993. Those who exhausted the original 39 weeks, however, were not eligible for this extended coverage.

25. Although unemployment benefits are federally mandated, that does not mean that problems will not occur. Because of the tremendous layoffs occurring in the latter part of 1990 and early 1991, a number of states had depleted their unemployment funds. Accordingly, in such states as Connecticut, Massachusetts, Ohio, Michigan, Arkansas, West Virginia, and Missouri, their rates charged to employers increased.

26. "When Duty Calls," *Entrepreneur* (March 2000), p. 127.

27. Roberto Ceniceros, "Rising Rates Have Employers Looking for Ways to Cut Costs," *Business Insurance* (October 16, 2000), pp. 3–6.

28. Mark D. Fefer, "Taking Control of Your Workers' Comp Costs," *Fortune* (October 3, 1994), pp. 131–136.

29. "Paternity Leave in Norway—Use It or Lose It," *HRMagazine* (January 1996), p. 24.

30. See, for instance, Julian Romeu, "Worldwide Business Trends Create New Leverage for Voluntary Benefits," *Employee Benefits Journal* (December 2000), p. 24.

31. "What Benefit Is Most Important to Your Employees?" *HR Focus* (December 2000), p. 11.

32. "What Are Your Priorities for 2001?" *HR Focus* (January 2001), p. 7.

33. Point-of-service or network plans are often a variation of preferred provider organizations. The main distinction typically lies in the degree of choice permitted. For example, under a preferred provider, any physician who participates can be seen by a subscriber. In a point-of-service (POS) or network, the possible physicians may be more limited. Although there are some constraints placed on choosing a physician, they are not as great as those imposed by an HMO. See also "Maximize Your Benefits: A Guide for All Employees," *Employee Benefits Journal* (December 2000), p. 53.

34. While Blue Cross and Blue Shield is the most widely known organization for traditional insurance, it is not the only one. Companies like Mutual of Omaha, New York Life, Aetna, and other commercial insurance companies all offer health-care coverage that models the BC/BS plan.

35. It is important to understand the difference between two terms that are widely used in Blue Shield contracts. These are *non-pars* and *participating physicians*. A non-par, or nonparticipating physician, will not accept Blue Shield payments as payment in full for services rendered. This means that any costs incurred above the repayment schedule set by the health insurer are the responsibility of the patient. Participating physicians, as the term implies, agree to accept Blue Shield payments as payments in full for services rendered.

36. David R. Henderson, "Sure, Visit Your Doctor, Take Your Medicine, But Who Will Pay for It?" *Wall Street Journal* (January 8, 2001), p. A30.

37. "Managed Care Lowers Health Care Costs, But Which Plan Is Best?" *HRMagazine* (May 1997), p. 26.

38. "PPOs Growing in Popularity Among Patients: Enrollment Jumps 12% in Three Years," *Health Care Strategic Management* (December 2000), p. 12.

39. "TPA Business for Self-Funded Plans Stable in 1999," *Employee Benefit Plan Review* (July 2000), pp. 12–14; James C. Spee, "Addition by Subtraction," *HRMagazine* (March 1995), p. 41; and Joey J. Barber, "Lower Health Care Costs through Direct Contracting," *HRMagazine* (September 1995), pp. 66–67.

40. See, for example, Laura Cohn, Phoebe Eliopoulos, and Arlene Weintraub, "What Comes After Managed Care?" *Business Week* (October 23, 2000), pp. 149–156.

41. It also should be noted that in some self-funding cases, organizations seek assistance from another company commonly referred to as a *third-party administrator* (TPA). The TPA's role is simply to process the health-care forms. See Allen R. Ross, "Are VEBAs Worth Another Look?" *Journal of Accountancy* (May 1999), pp. 35–40.

42. For employees who have been terminated or whose hours have been reduced, their coverage is for a period of 18 months (possibly extended to 29 months if qualifying dependents are covered).

43. The additional 11 months (19–29 months of coverage) were available to those who were disabled prior to receiving COBRA benefits. Under the Health Insurance Portability and Accountability Act of 1996, effective January 1, 1997, the 11-month extension is possible for any individual who becomes disabled within the first 60 days of COBRA coverage. See Percy Williams II, "Law Enhances Portability of Health Benefits," *HR News* (October 1996), pp. 4–5.

44. Leslie Wayne, "Pension Changes Raising Concerns," *New York Times* (August 29, 1994), pp. A-1, D-3.

45. The Retirement Equity Act of 1984 and the Tax Reform Act of 1986 modified participation ages, minimum vesting age, and vesting rights, requiring full vesting after five years, partial vesting after three years, and seven-year full vesting with plan years beginning after December 1, 1988. Those companies with a retirement plan year prior to that date were not required to go to the new lower vesting rules until December 1, 1989. It is also important to note, as will be discussed later in the chapter, that any monies contributed by employees toward their retirement are immediately 100 percent vested.

46. Portability of pension rights is a complex issue that goes beyond the scope of this book. However, depending on the company, employees may receive a permanent right to their monies, receiving a pension from the organization at retirement age, or be given a check that allows them to reinvest those monies on their own.

47. Lawrence Bivins, "Pension Treasure," *Wall Street Journal* (June 5, 2000), p. A-4.

48. Paige G. Lester, "A Checklist for Disability Plan Design," *Compensation and Benefits Review* (September–October

2000), pp. 59–61; and Robert M. McCaffery, *Employee Benefit Programs: A Total Compensation Perspective* (Boston, MA: PWS-Kent Publishing, 1992), pp. 234, 246–47.

49. The Bureau of National Affairs, "Pension Changes in Order," *Bulletin to Management,* No. 1795 (August 30, 1984), p. 1.

50. McCaffery, p. 131.

51. Ibid., p. 142.

52. Profit-sharing plans require that there be profits before a contribution can be made. When there are no profits for the period, no contributions need to be made. The only partial exception is that contributions can be made in a year in which there are no profits if there are accumulated profits from prior years. However, should this occur, further restrictions apply.

53. Legislation is moving through Congress that would increase the maximum IRA contribution from $2,000 to $5,000 over a five-year period. See Jim VandeHei and David Rogers, "House Approves Plan to Raise Limits on IRAs," *Wall Street Journal* (September 20, 2000), p. A-4.

54. See Anthony P. Curatola, "Roth IRAs Revisited," *Strategic Finance* (December 2000), pp. 18–20.

55. Joanne Cleaver, "They Want Their 401(k)s," *Workforce* (December 2000), p. 62.

56. Most companies offering matching contribution features to their 401(k) programs limit the amount of their contribution. Typically, their matching amount is set as one-half of the amount the employee contributes, with a 3 percent maximum. Thus, an employee setting aside 4 percent of his or her salary will have a 2 percent match, with up to 3 percent for a 6 percent deduction.

57. Elaine McShulskis, "Employee Benefit Specialists' New Priorities," *HRMagazine* (March 1996), p. 31.

58. Kate Walter, "Paid-Time-Off Leave Plans Experience Less Abuse," *HR News* (August 1995), p. 5.

59. Andrea C. Poe, "When in Rome," *HRMagazine* (November 1999), p. 62.

60. Bill Leonard, "The Employee's Favorite, The Employer's Quandary," *HRMagazine* (November 1994), p. 53.

61. Anita Bruzzese, "Workers Getting More Say in When, How They Take Time Off," *Carroll County Times* (July 23, 1993), p. B-5.

62. Short-term disability programs may be provided through commercial carriers or through self-funding arrangements. The more popular of the two is purchased coverage.

63. Before we proceed, an important piece of federal legislation warrants mentioning. Based on the 1978 Pregnancy Disability Act, employers that offer short-term disability insurance to their employees must include pregnancy as part of the policy's coverage. This means that in whatever capacity employers "cover" other disabilities like an extended illness, the coverage for disability due to pregnancy must be the same (see Chapter 3).

64. The number of sick days offered to employees generally varies according to their position in the organization and their length of service. Many organizations require a waiting period, approximately six months, before sick leave kicks in.

65. Rochelle Sharpe, "Workplace Epidemic: Absenteeism for Third Year in a Row," *Wall Street Journal* (February 27, 1996), p. A-1; and Elaine McShulskis, "Sick Leave Not Always for the Sick," *HRMagazine* (October 1996), p. 25.

66. Carl Quintanilla, "Calling in Sick? Some Airlines Pay Their Employees Not To," *Wall Street Journal* (September 17, 1996), p. A-1.

67. Other employers are simply doing away with sick leave and are adding the time to vacation or personal days.

68. Ibid.

69. The reason for the 70 to 80 percent of replacement income stems from the tax-free nature of some payments. (Payments from an employer LTD are generally taxable; the amount received from LTD based on employee-paid premiums is not taxable income.) If long-term payments were not reduced, it is conceivable that an employee receiving LTD and government disability payments could have a greater income than when the employee was working. This logic defeats the purpose of the program.

70. Some disability plans pay benefits for different periods if the disability is due to illness rather than injury.

71. See, for example, Joanne Wojcik, "Benefit Managers Offered New Tools to Move Online," *Business Insurance* (October 16, 2000), pp. 62–64.

72. Elaine McShulskis, "Voluntary Benefits Popular," *HRMagazine* (March 1997), p. 30.

73. Depending on company policy, there may be a time lag before a new employee's insurance policy takes effect. Waiting periods, when used, typically last about six months. Additionally, eligibility periods may be waived for management personnel.

74. U.S. Bureau of the Census, *Statistical Abstracts of the United States: 1997* (Washington, DC: Government Printing Office, 1997), p. 435.

75. Allison Kindelan, "Dependent-Care Accounts Top Family-Friendly Benefits," *HR News* (April 1996), p. 14; Shu Shu Costa, "Babies Welcome," *Working Mother* (February 1996), p. 34; and "Work-Life Initiatives Expanding at Leading Companies," *HR News* (June 1995), p. 15.

76. See, for example, Shirley Hand and Robert A. Zawacki, "Family-Friendly Benefits: More Than a Frill," *HRMagazine* (October 1994), pp. 79–84; and Sharon Nelton, "A Flexible Style of Management," *Nation's Business* (December 1993), pp. 24–31.

77. Sharon Leonard, "The Baby Gap," *HRMagazine* (June 2000), p. 368; Milton Moskowitz, "100 Best Companies for Working Mothers," *Working Mother* (October 1997), pp. 18–96; Sue Shellenbarger, "A Tangible Commitment to Work-Family Issues," *Wall Street Journal* (September 21, 1994), p. B-1; and Hand and Zawacki.

78. We group together these two issues because of similarity. Their only difference lies in the age of the individual. Obviously, child care deals with the young, and elder care deals with caring for one's elderly dependents (e.g., parents). See, for example, Sue Shellenbarger, "Family-Friendly CEOs Are Changing Cultures at More Workplaces," *Wall Street Journal* (September 15, 1999), p. B-1.

79. Susan J. Wells, "The Elder Care Gap," *HRMagazine* (May 2000), pp. 38–46. For another perspective on child care and whether or not child care benefits are fair to "single" employees, see Robert McGarvey, "Singled Out," *Entrepreneur* (March 1998), pp. 80–83.

80. See, for instance, Stacy VanDerWall, "Survey Finds Unscheduled Absenteeism Hitting Seven-Year High," *HR News* (November 1998), p. 14.

81. M. Galen, "Work & Family," *Business Week* (June 28, 1993), p. 20.

82. "Companies Team Up to Improve Quality of Their Employees' Child-care Choices," *Wall Street Journal* (October 17, 1991), p. B-1; see also Susan Gordon, "Helping Corporations Care," *Working Woman* (January 1993), p. 30.

83. Julia Lawlor, "Why Companies Should Care," *Working Woman* (June 1995), p. 38.

84. "Benefits: Get Ready for Elder Care," *Inc.* (September 1995), p. 101.

85. "Convenience Perks," *HRMagazine* (February 1995), p. 24.

86. Jacquelyn Lynn, "Rub It In," *Entrepreneur* (September 1999), p. 46; and Nancy Hatch Woodward, "Add a Refreshing Touch to Benefit Programs," *HRMagazine* (October 1998), pp. 105–110.

87. Jon J. Meyer, "The Future of Flexible Benefit Plans," *Employee Benefits Journal* (June 2000), pp. 3–7; and Christopher Caggiano, "Perks You Can Afford," *Inc.* (November 1997), p. 107.

88. Richard E. McDermott and Joan Ogden, "Five Ways to Improve Your Health Benefits Program," *HRMagazine* (August 1995), pp. 44–48.

89. Jill Andresky Fraser, "Stretching Your Benefits Dollar," *Inc.* (March 2000), pp. 123–126.

90. See, for instance, "Survey Recounts Benefits Offerings for State Employees," *Employee Benefit Plan Review* (September 2000), pp. 34–36.

91. McCaffery, p. 197.

92. This example was directly influenced by a similar example given in Jerry S. Rosenbloom and G. Victor Hallman, *Employee Benefits Planning*, 3rd ed. (Englewood Cliffs, NJ: Prentice-Hall, 1991), p. 225. See also Jerry S. Rosenbloom, *Handbook of Employee Benefits Design, Funding, and Administration*, 4th ed. (New York: McGraw-Hill Professional Book Group, 1996). Actual benefits under SSDI vary according to family status, average annual income, and the consumer price index. Therefore, SSDI given in this example is only an estimate.

13

SAFETY AND HEALTH PROGRAMS

LEARNING OUTCOMES

AFTER READING THIS CHAPTER, YOU WILL BE ABLE TO:

1. Discuss the organizational effect of the Occupational Safety and Health Act.
2. List the Occupational Safety and Health Administration's (OSHA) enforcement priorities.
3. Explain what punitive actions OSHA can impose on an organization.
4. Describe what companies must do to comply with OSHA record-keeping requirements.
5. Identify four contemporary areas for which OSHA is setting standards.
6. Describe the leading causes of safety and health accidents.
7. Explain what companies can do to prevent workplace violence.
8. Define stress and the causes of burnout.
9. Explain how an organization can create a healthy work site.
10. Describe the purposes of employee assistance and wellness programs.

*W*orkplace violence! Just the sound of the term is enough to make any HR manager squirm. What is it that makes a software tester burst into offices of the high-tech company in Massachusetts where he works and kill seven people? How about the worker that killed his colleagues at the Connecticut State Lottery office, or a former employee of Ottawa-Carleton public transit system who opened fire with a high-powered rifle, killing four people? And let's not forget shootings that have occurred in U.S. postal facilities, or even the deadly shooting at Xerox in tranquil Hawaii.[1] Fortunately, even though these events make headlines, they are not the norm. Our society and our workplaces are filled with law-abiding, compassionate people. But we know that even in the best of circumstances people exhibit behaviors that sometimes leave those witnessing the actions quite perplexed. Couple workplace violence events with a crisis and the unusual behavior is sometimes magnified. Take the case of the June 1, 1999 tragedy at Little Rock National Airport. During the evening hours of June 1, American Airlines Flight 1420 was in the last few moments of its final approach to the airport. Strong crosswinds, however, made the landing extremely difficult. Then as the plane touched down on the runway, it began to fishtail, ultimately skidding out of control, striking runway lights before coming to a stop in the Arkansas River embankment. Fire quickly erupted, trapping many of the 145 passengers and crew that were on board—ultimately leading to the untimely deaths of 11 people. But the initial crash didn't cause all of these deaths. Only three of the 11 passengers died from impact. The rest died trying to escape! In the immediate confusion, passengers started screaming. Some clawed their way over smaller, less mobile passengers. People pushed, shoved, and fought to save their own lives. Tragedy plus the desire for survival proved to be a recipe for disaster.

But while some individuals were "saving their hides," others like James Harrison rose to the challenge. Having a clear opportunity to exit the plane alive, Harrison, a college student age 21, chose to remain on board and help many other trapped passengers off the plane. Sadly, he was overcome by smoke and toxic fumes, and died at the exit door.

Is there something about the James Harrisons of the world that make them different from others? Are they naturally heroes? Maybe. On the other hand, what about the passengers who run rampant in a time of crisis? Why do they behave differently? That was a question to which researchers and aviation agencies wanted the answer. In other words, was it the tragedy itself that caused this "look-out-for-number-one" behavior? Researchers from Cranfield University in England don't think so.

Conducting a test for the Civil Aviation Authority of England and the U.S. Federal Aviation Administration, Cranfield researchers found some interesting behaviors. Boarding a "stationary" aircraft with nearly 150 people, researchers offered the first 30 passengers out of the plane 5 pounds (about US $8). What the researchers found was uncontrolled bedlam. Passengers raced to the exit doors and windows. Slower passengers were trampled; others fought at the exit doors to get out first. As one of the researchers stated, the test was simply a "mob scene" even though no one was in danger of losing his or her life. Participants in the experiment were willing to risk injury—to themselves or others—for a few bucks.

Just imagine how magnified the panic and aggressive behavior—survival of the fittest—is when life itself or something we greatly value is, or is perceived to be, on the line. For the victims of the Massachusetts shooting mentioned earlier, that something of value may have just been an IRS garnishment against the alleged shooter's pay. What a sad situation and a terrible waste of life!

INTRODUCTION

Organization officials have a legal responsibility, if not a moral one, to ensure that the workplace is free from unnecessary hazards and that conditions surrounding the workplace are not hazardous to employees' physical or mental health. Of course, accidents can and do occur, and the severity of these may astound you. There are approximately 6,000 reported work-related deaths[2] and nearly more than 5 million injuries and illnesses each year in the United States, resulting in over 90 million days lost of productive time—costing U.S. companies more than $110 billion annually.[3] Heartless as it sounds, employers must be concerned about employees' health and safety if for no other reason than that accidents cost money.

From the turn of the twentieth century through the late 1960s, remarkable progress was made in reducing the rate and severity of job-related accidents and diseases. Yet the most significant piece of legislation in the area of employee health and safety was not enacted until 1970.[4] This law is called the **Occupational Safety and Health Act.** Let's take an in-depth look at this law.

Occupational Safety and Health Act   Set standards to ensure safe and healthful working conditions and provided stiff penalties for violators.

THE OCCUPATIONAL SAFETY AND HEALTH ACT

The passage of the Occupational Safety and Health Act (OSH Act) dramatically changed the role that HRM must play in ensuring that the physical working conditions meet adequate standards. What the Civil Rights Act did to alter the organization's commitment to affirmative action, the OSH Act has done to alter the organization's health and safety programs.

OSH Act legislation established comprehensive and specific health standards, authorized inspections to ensure the standards are met, empowered the Occupational Safety and Health Administration (OSHA) to police organizations' compliance, and required employers to keep records of illness and injuries, and to calculate accident ratios. The Act applies to almost every U.S. business engaged in interstate commerce. Those organizations not meeting the interstate commerce criteria of OSH Act are generally covered by state occupational safety and health laws. The safety and health standards the OSH Act established are quite complex. Standards exist for such diverse conditions as noise levels, air impurities, physical protection equipment, the height of toilet partitions, and the correct size of ladders.[5] Furthermore, OSHA researches repetitive stress (or motion) injuries, problems associated with the eye strain that accompanies video display terminal use, and problems of needlesticks in health care activities, and develops training and education programs for businesses.

The initial OSH Act standards took up 350 pages in the *Federal Register,* and some of the annual revisions and interpretations are equally extensive. Nevertheless, employers are responsible for knowing these standards and ensuring that those that do apply to them are followed (see Exhibit 13-1).

OSHA Enforcement Priorities

Enforcement procedures of OSHA standards vary depending on the nature of the event and the organization. Typically, OSHA enforces the standards based on a five-item priority listing. These are, in descending priority: imminent danger; serious accidents that have occurred within the past 48 hours; a current employee complaint; inspections of target industries with a high injury ratio; and random inspections.

EXHIBIT 13-1
OSHA Protection

You Have a Right to a Safe and Healthful Workplace.
IT'S THE LAW!

- You have the right to notify your employer or OSHA about workplace hazards. You may ask OSHA to keep your name confidential.

- You have the right to request an OSHA inspection if you believe that there are unsafe and unhealthful conditions in your workplace. You or your representative may participate in the inspection.

- You can file a complaint with OSHA within 30 days of discrimination by your employer for making safety and health complaints or for exercising your rights under the *OSH Act*.

- You have a right to see OSHA citations issued to your employer. Your employer must post the citations at or near the place of the alleged violation.

- Your employer must correct workplace hazards by the date indicated on the citation and must certify that these hazards have been reduced or eliminated.

- You have the right to copies of your medical records or records of your exposure to toxic and harmful substances or conditions.

- Your employer must post this notice in your workplace.

The *Occupational Safety and Health Act of 1970 (OSH Act)*, P.L. 91-596, assures safe and healthful working conditions for working men and women throughout the Nation. The Occupational Safety and Health Administration, in the U.S. Department of Labor, has the primary responsibility for administering the *OSH Act*. The rights listed here may vary depending on the particular circumstances. To file a complaint, report an emergency, or seek OSHA advice, assistance, or products, call 1-800-321-OSHA or your nearest OSHA office: • Atlanta (404) 562-2300 • Boston (617) 565-9860 • Chicago (312) 353-2220 • Dallas (214) 767-4731 • Denver (303) 844-1600 • Kansas City (816) 426-5861 • New York (212) 337-2378 • Philadelphia (215) 861-4900 • San Francisco (415) 975-4310 • Seattle (206) 553-5930. Teletypewriter (TTY) number is 1-877-889-5627. To file a complaint online or obtain more information on OSHA federal and state programs, visit OSHA's website at **www.osha.gov**. If your workplace is in a state operating under an OSHA-approved plan, your employer must post the required state equivalent of this poster.

1-800-321-OSHA
www.osha.gov

U.S. Department of Labor • Occupational Safety and Health Administration • OSHA 3165

Imminent Danger   A condition where an accident is about to occur.

Imminent danger refers to a condition where an accident is about to occur. Although this is given top priority and acts as a preventive measure, imminent danger situations are hard to define. In fact, in some cases, the definition of imminent danger appears to be an accident in progress, and interpretation leaves much to the imagination. For example, suppose you were withdrawing cash at an ATM. As you remove your cash, you are grabbed by an individual who places a gun in your face and angrily demands your cash. Are you in imminent danger? Of course, most of us would say, absolutely! But, according to one interpretation of imminent danger, you may not be in "imminent" danger. That "state" would not exist until the "assailant" pulled the trigger of the weapon, and the bullet was rifling through the barrel. Tragically, by that time it is too late to worry about imminent danger. One's safety has already been threatened.

This has given rise to priority-two accidents—those that have led to serious injuries or death. Under the law, an organization must report these serious accidents to the Occupational Safety and Health Administration field office within 8 hours of occurrence. This permits the investigators to review the scene and try to determine the cause of the accident.

Priority three, employee complaints, is a major concern for any manager. If an employee sees a violation of the OSHA standards, that employee has the right to call OSHA and request an investigation. The worker may even refuse to work on the item in question until OSHA has investigated the complaint. This is especially true when there is a union. For instance, in some union contracts, workers may legally refuse to work if they believe they are in significant danger. Accordingly, they may stay off the job with pay until OSHA arrives and either finds the complaint invalid or cites the company and mandates compliance.[6]

Next in the priority of enforcement is the inspection of targeted industries. Since there are several million workplaces in the United States, inspecting each would require several hundred thousand full-time inspectors. OSHA, however, has limited resources, and its budget has been significantly cut in the past decade.[7] So, in order to have the largest effect, OSHA began to partner with state health and safety agencies, who together direct their attention to those industries with the highest injury rates—industries such as chemical processing, roofing and sheeting metal, meat processing, lumber and wood products, mobile homes and campers, and stevedoring. For instance, at Tomasco Mulciber's Columbus, Ohio facility, OSHA has inspected the premises multiple times in the past decade. That's because the company has nearly double the injury rate for hand injuries at the plant because machine guards were missing.[8]

A new rule established in 1990 also requires employers who handle hazardous waste (i.e., chemicals, medical waste) to follow strict operating procedures; any employer who handles hazardous waste is required to monitor employee exposure, develop and communicate safety plans, and provide necessary protective equipment.

The final OSHA priority is the random inspection. Originally, OSHA inspectors were authorized to enter any work area premises, without notice, to ensure that the workplace was in compliance. In 1978, however, the Supreme Court ruled in *Marshall v. Barlow's Inc.*[9] that employers are not required to let OSHA inspectors enter the premises unless the inspectors have search warrants. This decision, while not destroying OSHA's ability to conduct inspections, forces inspectors to justify their choice of inspection sites more rigorously. That is, rather than trying to oversee health and safety standards in all of their jurisdictions, OSHA inspectors often find it easier to justify their actions and obtain search warrants if they appear to be pursuing specific problem areas.[10] But don't let the

Marshall v. Barlow's, Inc.   Supreme Court case that stated an employer could refuse an OSHA inspection unless OSHA had a search warrant to enter the premises.

warrant requirement mislead you into a false sense of security. If needed, an OSHA inspector will obtain the necessary legal document. For example, when inspectors attempted to evaluate work at the Hollywood, Florida Hotel Diplomat construction site, the general contractor would not let them enter. A few days later, however, the OSHA inspectors returned with warrant in hand.[11]

Attorneys who deal with OSHA suggest that companies cooperate rather than viewing this event as confrontational. This cooperation focuses on permitting the inspection, but only after reaching consensus on the inspection process. That's not to say, however, that you can keep inspectors from finding violations. If they are found, inspectors can take the necessary action. Finally, it is recommended that any information regarding the company's safety program be discussed with the OSHA inspector, emphasizing how the program is communicated to employees, and how it is enforced.[12]

Should an employer feel that the fine levied is unjust, or too harsh, the law permits the employer to file an appeal. This appeal is reviewed by the Occupational Safety and Health Review Commission, an independently operating safety and health board. Although this commission's decisions are generally final, employers may still appeal commission decisions through the federal courts.

OSHA's Record-Keeping Requirements

To fulfill part of the requirements established under the Occupational Safety and Health Act, employers in industries where a high percentage of accidents and injuries occur must maintain safety and health records. It's important to note, however, that organizations that are exempt from record-keeping requirements—like universities and retail establishments—still must comply with the law itself; their only exception is the reduction of time spent on maintaining safety records. The basis of record-keeping for the OSH Act is the completion of OSHA Form 200 (see Exhibit 13-2). Employers are required to keep these safety records for five years.

In complying with OSHA record-keeping requirements, one issue arises for employers—that is, just what is a reportable accident or an illness? According to the Act, OSHA distinguishes between the two in the following ways. Any work-related illness (no matter how insignificant it may appear) must be reported on Form 200. Injuries, on the other hand, are reported only when they require medical treatment (besides first aid), or involve loss of consciousness, restriction of work or motion, or transfer to another job.

To help employers decide whether an incident should be recorded, OSHA offers a schematic diagram for organizations to follow (see Exhibit 13-3). By using this "decision tree," organizational members can decide if, in fact, an event should be recorded. Should that occur, the employer is responsible for recording it under one of three areas: fatality, lost workday cases, or neither fatality nor lost workdays. Part of this information is then used to determine an organization's incidence rate. An **incidence rate** reflects the "number of injuries, illnesses, or (lost) workdays related to a common exposure base rate of 100 full-time workers." This rate is then used by OSHA for determining industries and organizations that are more susceptible to injury. Let's look at the incidence rate formula and use it in an example.

Incidence Rate Number of injuries, illnesses, or lost workdays related to a common base of 100 full-time employees.

To determine the incidence rate, the formula $(N/EH) \times 200,000$ is used, where:

- N is the number of injuries and/or illnesses or lost workdays.
- EH is the total hours worked by all employees during the year.

EXHIBIT 13-2
OSHA Form 200

U.S. Department of Labor

For Calendar Year _____   Page: _____ of _____

Form Approved
O.M.B. No. 1218-0176
See OMB Disclosure
Statement on reverse.

Company Name

Establishment Name

Establishment Address

Extent of and Outcome of Injury

Fatalities / Nonfatal Injuries

Injury Related — Enter Date of death. mm/dd/yy (1)

Injuries with Lost Workdays
- (2) Enter a Check if injury involves DAYS away from work or restricted work activity or both.
- (3) Check if injury involves DAYS away from work.
- (4) Enter number of DAYS away from work
- (5) Enter number of DAYS of restricted work activity

Injuries Without Lost Workdays
- (6) Enter a Check if no entry was made in column 1 or 2 but the injury is recordable as defined above.

Type, Extent of, and Outcome of Illness

Type of Illness — CHECK Only One Column for Each Illness (See other side of form for terminations or permanent transfers) (7)
- (a) Occupational Skin Disease or Disorder
- (b) Dust Disease of the lungs
- (c) Respiratory Conditions due to toxic agents
- (d) Poisoning (systemic effects of toxic materials)
- (e) Disorders due to physical agents
- (f) Disorders associated with repeated trauma
- (g) All other occupational illnesses

Fatalities — Illness Related — (8) Enter DATE of death, mm/dd/yy

Nonfatal Illnesses

Illnesses with Lost Workdays
- (9) Enter a CHECK if illness involves DAYS away from work, or DAYS of restricted work activity or both.
- (10) Enter a CHECK if illness involves DAYS away from work.
- (11) Enter number of DAYS away from work.
- (12) Enter number of DAYS of restricted work activity

Illnesses without Lost Workdays
- (13) Enter a CHECK if no entry was made in columns 8 or 9

Certification of Annual Summary Totals by: _____   Title: _____   Date: _____

Exhibit 13-2
continued

Log and Summary of Occupational Injuries and Illnesses

NOTE: This form is required by Public Law 91-596 and must be kept in the establishment for 5 years. Failure to maintain and post can result in issuance of citations and assessment of penalties. (See posting requirements on the other side of form)

RECORDABLE CASES: You are required to record information about every occupational death; every nonfatal occupational illness; and those nonfatal occupational injuries which involve one or more of the following: loss of conciousness, restriction of work or motion, transfer to another job, or medical treatment (other than first aid) (See definitions on the other side of form)

Case or File Number	Date of Injury or Onset of Illness	Employee's Name	Occupation	Department	Description of Injury or Illness
Enter a nonduplicating number which will facilitate comparisons with supplementary records.	Enter Mo/Day	Enter first name or initial, middle initial, last name	Enter regular job title, not activity employee was performing when injury occurred or at onset of illness. In the absence of a formal title, enter a brief description of the employee's duties.	Enter department in which the employee is regularly employed or a description of normal workplace to which employee is assigned, even though temporarily working in another department at the time of injury or illness.	Enter a brief description of the injury or illness and indicate the part or parts of the body affected. Typical entries for this column might be: Amputation of 1st joint right forefinger; Strain of lower back; Contact dermatitis on both hands; Electrocution - body.
(A)	(B)	(C)	(D)	(E)	(F)
					PREVIOUS PAGE TOTALS =>
					TOTALS (Instructions on other side of form) =>

OSHA No. 200

- 200,000 is the base hour rate equivalent (100 workers × 40 hours per week × 50 weeks per year).

In using the formula and calculating an organization's accident rate, assume we have an organization with 1,800 employees that experienced 195 reported accidents over the past year. We would calculate the incidence rate as follows: (195/3,600,000) × 200,000.[13] The incidence rate, then, is 10.8. What does that 10.8 represent? That depends on a number of factors. If the organization is in the meat packing plant industry where the industry average incidence rate is 32.1,[14] then they are doing well. If, however, they are in the oil and gas extraction industry, where the industry incidence rate is 4.1,[15] then a 10.8 indicates a major concern.

OSHA Punitive Actions

An OSHA inspector has the right to levy a fine against an organization for noncompliance. While levying the fine is more complicated than described here, if an organization does not bring a red-flagged item into compliance, it can be assessed a severe penalty. As originally passed in 1970, the maximum penalty was $10,000 per occurrence, per day. However, with the Omnibus Budget Reconciliation Act of 1990, that $10,000 penalty can increase to $70,000 if the violation is severe, willful, and repetitive.[16] Although in its first 20 years questions arose regarding the value of OSH Act to workers' health and safety, such questions appear to be abating. Inroads have been made by the director of OSHA in redirecting OSHA's efforts. The agency has increased inspections and has been viewed as taking a tougher stance on workplace health and safety issues—and a number of companies have seen what that focus can mean. But fines are not

EXHIBIT 13-3
Determining Recordability of Laser under OSHA

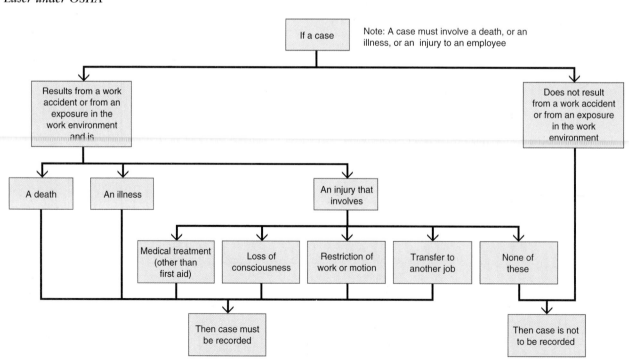

for safety violations alone. If a company fails to keep its OSH Act records properly, it can be subjected to stiff penalties.

Under the OSH Act, if an employee death occurs, executives in the company can be criminally liable. For example, three executives at Pyro Mining were sentenced to prison, and the company paid nearly $4 million in fines for the deaths of 10 miners.[17] Yet, most individuals have found the criminal penalties under the OSH Act somewhat limited—because of the death requirement. Accordingly, many state prosecutors are filing charges against company executives under general criminal statutes—and a few are having some success.[18]

OSHA: A Critique

Has the OSH Act worked? The answer is a qualified yes. In fact, the Act has had a direct and significant effect on almost every business organization in the United States. In some of the largest organizations, an additional administrator has been created who is solely responsible for safety. The impact of the OSH Act standards has made organizations more aware of health and safety. The standards may have been initially extreme in their specificity, and their red tape a nuisance, but that has been changing.[19]

What can we expect from OSHA over the next decade? Although its efforts will continue to concentrate on safety and health violations in organizations, OSHA is addressing problems associated with contemporary organizations, concentrating its efforts through the **National Institute for Occupational Safety and Health (NIOSH)** for researching, and in setting standards in such areas as bloodborne pathogens, chemical process safety (see Workplace Issues), and even focusing its attention on preventing Lyme Disease in those workers who work in areas where exposure to ticks carrying Lyme Disease is high.[20] Similarly, OSHA continues to explore motor vehicle safety, as well as focusing on fitting the work environment to the individual.[21]

First, setting standards for blood-borne pathogens is designed to protect individuals, like medical personnel, from becoming infected with such diseases as AIDS and hepatitis. In doing so, OSHA has established guidelines regarding protective equipment (like latex gloves, eye shields), and in cases where a vaccine is available, ensures that exposed workers have access to it.

Second, chemical processing standards reflect specific guidelines that must be adhered to when employees work with chemicals or other hazardous toxic substances. This requires companies to perform hazard analyses and take any corrective action required. These concerns over chemical hazards led to a number of states passing *Right-to-Know Laws*. These laws helped identify hazardous chemicals in the workplace, required employers to inform employees of the chemicals they might be exposed to, and the health risks associated with that exposure, and other policies guiding their use. Although these state laws made progress in providing information regarding workplace toxins, there were variations among the states—and some states didn't have these laws at all. Consequently, to provide some uniformity in protection, OSHA developed the Hazard Communication Standard in 1983. This policy "requires employers to communicate chemical hazards to their employees by labeling containers, and by distributing data information (called *Material Safety Data Sheet;* see Exhibit 13-4) provided by the manufacturer" to the employees. In addition, employees exposed to various hazardous chemicals must be trained in their safe handling. As enacted in 1983, this standard applied only to manufacturing industries. But by mid-1989, meeting the requirements of the Hazard Communication Standard became the responsibility of all industries.[22]

National Institute for Occupational Safety and Health(NIOSH) The government agency that researches and sets OSHA standards.

Thanks to OSHA, workers like this UPS driver are better protected in terms of their safety and health—in their trucks, as well as when they lift and deliver packages to customers.

EXHIBIT 13-4
Material Data Safety Sheet

Material Safety Data Sheet	U.S. Department of Labor
May be used to comply with OSHA's Hazard Communication Standard, 29 CFR 1910.1200. Standard must be consulted for specific requirements.	Occupational Safety and Health Administration (Non-Mandatory Form) Form Approved OMB No. 1218-0072

IDENTITY *(As Used on Label and List)*	Note: *Blank spaces are not permitted. If any item is not applicable, or no information is available, the space must be marked to indicate that.*

Section I

Manufacturer's Name	Emergency Telephone Number
Address *(Number, Street, City, State, and ZIP Code)*	Telephone Number for Information
	Date Prepared
	Signature of Preparer *(optional)*

Section II — Hazardous Ingredients/Identity Information

Hazardous Components (Specific Chemical Identity; Common Name(s))	OSHA PEL	ACGIH TLV	Other Limits Recommended	% *(optional)*

Section III — Physical/Chemical Characteristics

Boiling Point		Specific Gravity (H_2O = 1)	
Vapor Pressure (mm Hg.)		Melting Point	
Vapor Density (AIR = 1)		Evaporation Rate (Butyl Acetate = 1)	

Solubility in Water

Appearance and Odor

Section IV — Fire and Explosion Hazard Data

Flash Point (Method Used)	Flammable Limits	LEL	UEL

Extinguishing Media

Special Fire Fighting Procedures

Unusual Fire and Explosion Hazards

(Reproduce locally)   OSHA 174, Sept. 1985

Exhibit 13-4
continued

Section V — Reactivity Data

Stability	Unstable		Conditions to Avoid
	Stable		

Incompatibility (*Materials to Avoid*)

Hazardous Decomposition or Byproducts

Hazardous Polymerization	May Occur		Conditions to Avoid
	Will Not Occur		

Section VI — Health Hazard Data

Route(s) of Entry: Inhalation?   Skin?   Ingestion?

Health Hazards (*Acute and Chronic*)

Carcinogenicity: NTP?   IARC Monographs?   OSHA Regulated?

Signs and Symptoms of Exposure

Medical Conditions
Generally Aggravated by Exposure

Emergency and First Aid Procedures

Section VII — Precautions for Safe Handling and Use

Steps to Be Taken in Case Material Is Released or Spilled

Waste Disposal Method

Precautions to Be Taken in Handling and Storing

Other Precautions

Section VIII — Control Measures

Respiratory Protection (*Specify Type*)

Ventilation	Local Exhaust		Special
	Mechanical (*General*)		Other

Protective Gloves	Eye Protection

Other Protective Clothing or Equipment

Work/Hygienic Practices

☆ U.S.G.P.O.: 1986-491-529/45775

OSHA AND NEEDLESTICKS

AS MANDATED BY THE NEEDLESTICK SAFETY and Prevention Act, OSHA has revised its bloodborne pathogens standard to clarify the need for employers to select safer needle devices as they become available and to involve employees in identifying and choosing the devices. The updated standard also requires employers to maintain a log of injuries from contaminated sharps. "These changes in the OSHA bloodborne pathogens standard reaffirm our commitment to protecting health care providers who care for us all," said Labor Secretary Alexis M. Herman. "Newer, safer medical devices can reduce the risk of needlesticks and the chance of contracting deadly bloodborne diseases such as AIDS and hepatitis C. Employers need to consult their workers and use the safer devices when possible." According to the Needlestick Act, in March 2000, the Centers for Disease Control and Prevention estimated that selecting safer medical devices could prevent 62 to 88 percent of sharps injuries in hospital settings.

"Our revised bloodborne pathogen standard sets forth clearly the importance of reevaluating needle systems to identify safer devices every year. The new requirement to record all needlesticks will help employers determine the effectiveness of the devices they use and track how many needlesticks are occurring within their workplaces," said OSHA Administrator Charles N. Jeffress.

The revised OSHA bloodborne pathogen standard specifically mandates consideration of safer needle devices as part of the reevaluation of appropriate engineering controls during the annual review of the employer's exposure control plan. It calls for employers to solicit frontline employee input in choosing safer devices. New provisions require employers to establish a log to track needlesticks rather than only recording those cuts or sticks that actually lead to illness and to maintain the privacy of employees who have suffered these injuries.

Passed unanimously by Congress and signed by President Clinton in late 2000, the Needlestick Safety and Prevention Act mandated specific revisions of OSHA's bloodborne pathogens standard within six months. The legislation exempted OSHA from certain standard rulemaking requirements so that the changes could be adopted quickly. The revised bloodborne pathogens standard is scheduled for publication in the January 18 *Federal Register.* The updated rules become effective April 18, 2001.

Source: National News Release, *USDL: 01–26,* Thursday, January 18, 2001 (http://www.osha.gov/media/oshnews/jan01/national-20010118a.html).

The third area, motor vehicle safety, reflects OSHA's interest in addressing the problems associated with workers who drive substantially as part of their job duties. Nearly half of all worker deaths in any given year are attributed to motor vehicle accidents.[23] Accordingly, emphasis is placed on substance-abuse testing of drivers, safety equipment, and driver's education.

Finally, OSHA has been continuing its efforts in studying the proper design of the work environment called *ergonomics* such that it is conducive to productive work. OSHA has established an Internet web site (www.osha.gov/ergo) that helps organizations understand how ergonomics operates and how it can help. We'll come back to ergonomics later in this chapter.

JOB SAFETY PROGRAMS

If businesses are concerned with efficiency and profits, you may ask, why would they spend money to create conditions that exceed those required by law? The answer is the profit motive itself. The cost of accidents can be, and for many organizations is, a substantial additional cost of doing business. The direct cost of an accident to an employer shows itself in the organization's worker's compensation premium. This cost, as noted in the last chapter, is largely determined by the insured's accident history. Indirect costs, which generally far exceed direct costs, also must be borne by the employer. These include wages paid for time lost due to injury, damage to equipment and materials, personnel to investigate and report on accidents, and lost production due to work stoppages and personnel changeover. The impact of these indirect costs can be seen in statistics that describe the costs of accidents for American industry as a whole.

As we mentioned at the beginning of this chapter, accidents cost employers additional billions of dollars in wages and lost production. The significance of this latter figure is emphasized when we note that this cost is approximately ten times greater than losses caused by strikes, an issue that historically has received much more attention. It's also interesting to note that on average, Japanese organizations have up to seven times fewer accidents in the workplace.[24] For Japanese firms, this has positively affected productivity.

Causes of Accidents

The cause of an accident can be generally classified as either human or environmental. Human causes are directly attributable to human error brought about by carelessness, intoxication, daydreaming, inability to do the job, or other human deficiency. Environmental causes, in contrast, are attributable to the workplace and include the tools, equipment, physical plant, and general work environment. Both of these sources are important, but in terms of numbers, the human factor is responsible for the vast majority of accidents. No matter how much effort is made to create a work environment that is accident free, a low accident rate record can only be achieved by concentrating on the human element.

One of the main objectives of safety engineers is to scrutinize the work environment to locate sources of potential accidents. In addition to looking for such obvious factors as loose steps or carpets, oil on walkways, or a sharp protrusion on a piece of equipment at eye level, safety engineers will seek those that are less obvious. Standards established by OSHA provide an excellent reference to guide the search for potential hazards.

Preventative Measures

What traditional measures can we look to for preventing accidents? The answer lies in education, skills training, engineering, protection devices, and regulation enforcement. We have summarized these in Exhibit 13-5.

Ensuring Job Safety

One way HRM can be assured that rules and regulations are being enforced is to develop some type of feedback system. This can be provided by inspection of the work surroundings. HRM can rely on oral or written reports for information on enforcement. Another approach is to get firsthand information by periodically walking through the work areas to make observations. Ideally, safety personnel will rely on reports from supervisors on the floor and employees in the work areas. These are then supported by the safety inspector's personal observations.

Although safety is everyone's responsibility, it should be part of the organization's culture. Top management must show its commitment to safety by providing resources to purchase safety devices and maintaining equipment. Furthermore, safety should become part of every employee's performance goals. As we mentioned in Chapter 10 on performance evaluations, if something isn't included, there's a tendency to diminish its importance. Holding employees accountable for safety issues by evaluating their performance sends the message that the company is serious about safety.

Another means of promoting safety is to empower the action. In organizations such employee groups are called *safety committees*. Although chiefly

Exhibit 13-5
*Accident Prevention
Mechanisms*

Education	Create safety awareness by posting highly visible signs that proclaim safety slogans, placing articles on accident prevention in organization newsletters, or exhibiting a sign proclaiming the number of days the plant has operated without a lost-day accident.
Skills Training	Incorporate accident prevention measures into the learning process.
Engineering	Prevent accidents through both the design of the equipment and the design of the jobs themselves. This may also include eliminating those factors that promote operator fatigue, boredom, and daydreaming.
Protection	Provide protective equipment where necessary. This may include safety shoes, gloves, hard hats, safety glasses, and noise mufflers. Protection also includes performing preventative maintenance on machinery.
Regulation Enforcement	The best safety rules and regulations will be ineffective in reducing accidents if they are not enforced. Additionally, if such rules are not enforced, the employer may be liable for any injuries that occur.

prevalent in unionized settings, these committees serve a vital role in helping the company and its employees implement and maintain a good safety program.

A Safety Issue: Workplace Violence

Inasmuch as there is growing concern for job safety for our workers, a much greater emphasis today is being placed on the increasing violence that has erupted on the job.[25] No organization is immune from such happenstance, and the problem appears to be getting worse.[26] Shootings at a local post office by a recently disciplined employee, an upset purchasing manager who stabs his boss because they disagreed over how some paperwork was to be completed, a disgruntled

technology corner

OSHA Compliance

OSHA REPORTING GOT YOU DOWN? HOW do you get Material Data Safety Sheets? Technology can come to the rescue—below are some software packages that can assist you in handling OSHA matters.

Claimzone.com: Claimzone.com (Mountain View Software Corporation, www.mvsc.com/product_stage.html, price varies) is a reporting tool for OSHA matters. This web-based product can be used to enter, review, and submit to OSHA all first-report injuries. OSHA Form 200 reporting can also be handled with this product.

OSHA Compliance: OSHA Compliance Encyclopedia (HR Press, www.hrpress-software.com/oshacd.html, $495) can be used to develop an organization's safety program, monitor safety meetings, and provide up-to-date information on many safety and health federal regulations. Subscriptions entitle buyer to four quarterly updates.

OSHALOG: OSHALOG (HR Press, www.hrpress-software.com/oshalog.html, $199) is a compliance and injury and illness tracking software. Data from this tracking software easily completes OSHA Form 200. OSHALOG is advertised as OSHA accepted and as "the best-selling OSHA record-keeping software in the U.S."

HazCom: HazCom (Haddock HazCom, www.hazcom.net, price varies) provides its user with Hazard Communication services, such as Material Data Safety Sheets, Health Hazard Assessments, and Label Language Recommendations.

significant other enters the workplace and shoots his mate, an employee upset over having his wages garnished—incidents like these have become all too prevalent. Consider the following statistics. More than 1,000 employees are murdered, and more than 1.5 million employees are assaulted on the job each year. Homicide has become the number-two cause of work-related death in the United States.[27]

More than 1,000 employees are murdered, and more than 1.5 million employees are assaulted on the job each year.

Many individuals note that in U.S. cities, violent behaviors are spilling over into the workplace. And we're talking about much more here than homicides committed during the commission of a crime—like those horrendous events happening to cab drivers or to clerks at retail stores.[28] Two factors have contributed greatly to this trend—domestic violence and disgruntled employees.[29] The issue for companies, then, is how to prevent the violence from occurring on the job—and to reduce their liability should an unfortunate event occur.[30]

Because the circumstances of each incident are different, a specific plan of action for companies to follow is difficult to detail. However, several suggestions can be made.[31] First, the organization must develop a plan to deal with the issue.[32] This may mean reviewing all corporate policies to ensure that they are not adversely affecting employees. In fact, in many of the cases where the violent individuals caused mayhem in an office setting and didn't commit suicide, one common factor arose. That is, these employees were not treated with respect or dignity. They were laid off without any warning, or they perceived they were being treated too harshly in the discipline process. Sound HRM practices can help to ensure that respect and dignity exist for employees, even in the most difficult of issues like terminations.

Organizations must also train their supervisory personnel to identify troubled employees before the problem results in violence.[33] Employee assistance programs (EAPs) can be designed specifically to help these individuals. As we'll see shortly in our discussion of EAPs, rarely does an individual go from being happy, to committing some act of violence overnight! Furthermore, if supervisors are better able to spot the types of demonstrated behaviors that may lead to violence, then those who cannot be helped through the EAP can be removed from the organization before others are harmed. Organizations should also implement stronger security mechanisms. For example, many women who are killed at work, following a domestic dispute, die at the hands of someone who didn't belong on company premises. These individuals, as well as violence paraphernalia—guns, knives, and so on—must be kept from entering the facilities altogether.

Sadly, no matter how careful the organization is, and how much it attempts to prevent workplace violence, some will occur. In those cases, the organization must be prepared to deal with the situation and to offer whatever assistance it can to deal with the aftermath.[34]

$\mathcal{M}$AINTAINING A HEALTHY WORK ENVIRONMENT

Unhealthy work environments are a concern to us all. If workers cannot function properly at their jobs because of constant headaches, watering eyes, breathing difficulties, or fear of exposure to materials that may cause long-term health problems, productivity will decrease. Consequently, creating a healthy work environment not only is the proper thing to do, but it also benefits the employer. Often referred to as **sick buildings**, office environments that contain harmful airborne chemicals, asbestos, or indoor pollution (possibly caused by smoking) have

Sick Building An unhealthy work environment.

forced employers to take drastic steps. For many, it has meant the removal of asbestos from their buildings. Because extended exposure to asbestos has been linked to lung cancer, companies are required by various federal agencies like the EPA to remove it altogether, or at least seal it so that it cannot escape into the air. But asbestos is not the only culprit! Germs, fungi, mold, and a variety of synthetic pollutants cause problems, too.[35]

Although specific problems and their elimination go beyond the scope of this text, there are some suggestions for keeping the workplace healthy. These include:[36]

- *Making sure workers get enough fresh air.* The cost of providing it is peanuts compared with the expense of cleaning up a problem. One simple tactic: unsealing vents closed in overzealous efforts to conserve energy.
- *Avoiding suspect building materials and furnishings.* A general rule is that if it stinks, it's going to emit an odor. For instance, substitute tacks for smelly carpet glue or natural wood for chemically treated plywood.
- *Testing new buildings for toxins before occupancy.* Failure to do so may lead to potential health problems. Most consultants say that letting a new building sit temporarily vacant allows the worst fumes to dissipate.
- *Providing a smoke-free environment.* If you don't want to ban smoking entirely, then establish an area for smokers that has its own ventilation system.
- *Keeping air ducts clean and dry.* Water in air ducts is a fertile breeding ground for fungi. Servicing the air ducts periodically can help eliminate the fungi before they cause harm.
- *Paying attention to workers' complaints.* Dates and particulars should be recorded by a designated employee. Because employees are often closest to the problems, they are a valuable source of information.

While the information presented above is important to follow, one item in particular is noteworthy for us to explore a bit further. This is the smoke-free environment.

The Smoke-Free Environment

Should smoking be prohibited in a public place of business? Even, say, in a bar, where forbidding smoking could put the establishment out of business? The dangers and health problems associated with smoking have been well documented—and this is translating into increased health insurance costs. Furthermore, smokers were found to be absent more than nonsmokers, to lose productivity due to smoke breaks, to damage property with cigarette burns, to require more routine maintenance (ash/butt cleanup), and to create problems for other employees through secondhand-smoke disorders. Recognized as a means to control these maladies associated with smoking, in conjunction with society's emphasis on wellness, smoke-free policies have appeared. In fact, about 53 percent of U.S. companies have banned smoking altogether, while another 23 percent have smoking restricted to designated areas.[37]

Although many nonsmokers would agree that a total ban on smoking in the workplace is the most desirable, it may not be the most practical. For those employees who smoke, quitting immediately may be impossible. The nicotine addiction may prohibit a "cold-turkey" approach for the most ardent smoker. Accordingly, a total ban on smoking should be viewed as a phased-in approach. For example, this gradual process may begin with the involvement of representative employees to determine what the organization's smoke-free goals and

ethical issues in HRM

SAFETY AND HEALTH PROGRAMS

AS MORE AND MORE ORGANIZATIONS GO smoke-free, a major question arises. That is, what do the smokers do? In such organizations, the answer is simple. They go outside to smoke. But that raises other issues, like lost productivity while employees are outside smoking, or cleanup of ashes and butts scattered on the ground. Should smokers have rights? It has become well documented that smoking can create health problems. Accordingly, health insurance premiums, as well as other premiums like life insurance, are significantly higher for those who light up. And in most cases, employers have passed these increased premium costs on to the worker. Companies have become more stringent in developing policies on smoking, and many have banned smoking on company premises altogether. Clearly, the smoker today is disadvantaged, but how far can that go?

Can an organization refuse to hire someone simply because he or she smokes? Depending on the organization, the requirement of the job, and the state in which one lives, they might! Even so, employers may take this one step further. Companies may, in fact, be able to terminate an individual for smoking off the job—on an employee's own time. Do you believe companies have the right to dictate what you do outside of work? If an organization can take such action against employees for smoking, and justify it on the grounds that it creates a health problem, what about other things we do? Eating too much fatty food can create a health problem, so should we be susceptible to discipline for being caught eating a Big Mac? Some members of the medical community cite how one or two alcoholic drinks a day may in fact be therapeutic and prevent the onset of certain diseases. Yet, alcohol can be damaging to humans. Accordingly, should we be fired for having a glass of wine with dinner, or drinking a beer at a sporting event? What do you think? How far should we permit regulating "wellness" in our organizations?

timetables should be. This means deciding if the organization will ban smoking altogether over a period of time; or if special areas will be designated as smoking rooms. If the latter is chosen, then these rooms must be properly ventilated to keep the smoke fumes from permeating other parts of the facility.

Consequently, the organization needs to look at incentives for getting people not to smoke (see Ethical Issues in HRM). As mentioned previously, healthcare premiums—as well as life insurance policies—for smokers are significantly higher than for nonsmokers. Employers may decide to pay only the nonsmoking premium and pass the additional premium costs on to the smokers. Companies also need to have in place various options for individuals to seek help. Through various assistance programs—like smoking-cessation classes—the organization can show that it is making a deliberate commitment to eliminate the problems associated with smoking in the workplace.

Repetitive Stress Injuries

Repetitive Stress Injuries
Injuries sustained by continuous and repetitive movements of the hand.

Musculoskeletal Disorders [MSDs] Continuous motion disorders caused by repetitive stress injuries.

Carpal Tunnel Syndrome A repetitive motion disorder affecting the wrist.

Whenever workers are subjected to a continuous motion like keyboarding, without proper workstation design (seat and keyboard height adjustments), they run the risk of developing **repetitive stress injuries,** or **musculoskeletal disorders (MSDs).** These disorders, which account for nearly 40 percent of annual workplace illnesses from headaches, swollen feet, back pain, or nerve damage, cost U.S. companies several billion dollars annually and account for one-third of all worker's compensation claims.[38] The most frequent site of this disorder is in the wrist (called **carpal tunnel syndrome**). It affects more than 40,000 U.S. workers and costs companies more than $60 million annually in health-care claims.[39] Given the magnitude of problems associated with MSDs, OSHA issued its final standards in late 2000 to combat this workplace problem—standards that were to save nearly $10 billion from reduced work-related injuries.[40] However, in late March 2001, President Bush signed a Congressional resolution disapproving the bill. As such, the OSHA standard is no longer in effect.

One chief means of reducing the potential effects of cumulative trauma disorders for an organization, however, is through the voluntary use of *ergonomics*.[41] Ergonomics involves fitting the work environment to the individual. Reality tells us that every employee is different—different shape, size, height, and so forth. Expecting each worker to adjust to standard office furnishings is just not practical. Instead, recognizing and acting on these differences, ergonomics looks at customizing the work environment such that it is not only conducive to productive work, but keeps the employee healthy.[42]

When we speak of ergonomics, we are primarily addressing two main areas: the "office environment and office furniture."[43] Organizations are reviewing their office settings, their work environment, and their space utilization in an effort to provide more productive atmospheres. This means that new furniture is being purchased—furniture that is designed to reduce back strain and fatigue. Properly designed and fitted office equipment, like Pitney Bowes workstations, can also help reduce repetitive stress injuries.[44] Furthermore, companies are using colors, like the mauves and grays, that are more pleasing to the eye, and experimenting with lighting brightness as a means of lessening employee exposure to harmful eyestrain associated with today's video display terminals.

Stress

Stress A dynamic condition in which an individual is confronted with an opportunity, constraint, or demand related to what he or she desires and for which the outcome is perceived to be both uncertain and important.

Stress is a dynamic condition in which an individual is confronted with an opportunity, constraint, or demand related to what he or she desires, and for which the outcome is perceived to be both uncertain and important. Stress is a complex issue, so let us look at it more closely. Stress can manifest itself in both a positive and a negative way. Stress is said to be positive when the situation offers an opportunity for one to gain something; for example, the "psyching-up" that an athlete goes through can be stressful, but this can lead to maximum performance. It is when constraints or demands are placed on us that stress can become negative. Let us explore these two features—constraints and demands.

Constraints are barriers that keep us from doing what we desire. Purchasing a sports utility vehicle (SUV) may be your desire, but if you cannot afford

Continuous keyboarding can lead to an illness referred to as "musculoskeletal disorder." OSHA has been investigating this occurrence hoping to influence workstation designs that will reduce such injuries. To do so, OSHA issued its ergonomics standards in late 2000.

the $38,000 price, you are constrained from purchasing it. Accordingly, constraints inhibit you in ways that take control of a situation out of your hands. If you cannot afford the SUV, you cannot get it. Demands, on the other hand, may cause you to give up something you desire. If you wish to go to a movie with friends on Tuesday night but have a major examination Wednesday, the examination may take precedence. Thus, demands preoccupy your time and force you to shift priorities.

Constraints and demands can lead to potential stress. When they are coupled with uncertainty about the outcome and importance of the outcome, potential stress becomes actual stress. Regardless of the situation, if you remove the uncertainty or the importance, you remove stress. For instance, you may have been constrained from purchasing the SUV because of your budget, but if you just won one in McDonald's Monopoly game, the uncertainty element is significantly reduced. Furthermore, if you are auditing a class for no grade, the importance of the major examination is essentially nil. However, when constraints or demands have an effect on an important event and the outcome is unknown, pressure is added—resulting in stress.

While we are not attempting to minimize stress in people's lives, it is important to recognize that both good and bad personal factors may cause stress. Of course, when you consider the changes, like restructuring, that are occurring in U.S. companies, it is little wonder that stress is so rampant in today's companies. Stress-related problems are being witnessed to the tune of nearly $300 billion annually for U.S. corporations in terms of "lost productivity, increased worker compensation claims, turnover, and health care costs."[45] And stress on the job knows no boundaries.

In Japan, worker stress has been identified in 70 percent of the workers by a Fukoku Life Insurance Company study.[46] In fact, in Japan there is a concept called **karoshi,** which means death from overworking—employees who die after working more than 3,000 hours the previous year. Over 2,300 individuals die each year having karoshi listed as their cause of death.[47] Many Japanese employees literally work themselves to death—with one in six Japanese employees working more than 3,100 hours annually.[48] Employees in Germany and Britain, too, have suffered the ill effects of stress—costing their organizations more than DM 100 billion and £7 billion (US$65 billion and US$11.4 billion, respectively).[49]

Are There Common Causes of Stress?

Stress can be caused by a number of factors called **stressors.** Factors that create stress can be grouped into two major categories—organizational and personal (see Exhibit 13-6).[50] Both directly affect employees and, ultimately, their jobs.

There is no shortage of factors within the organization that can cause stress. Pressures to avoid errors or complete tasks in a limited time period, a demanding supervisor, and unpleasant coworkers are a few examples. The discussion that follows organizes stress factors into five categories: task, role, and interpersonal demands; organization structure; and organizational leadership.[51]

Task demands are factors related to an employee's job. They include the design of the person's job (autonomy, task variety, degree of automation), working conditions, and the physical work layout. Work quotas can put pressure on employees when their outcomes are perceived as excessive.[52] The more interdependence between a employee's tasks

---

Karoshi A Japanese term meaning death from overworking.

Stressor Something that causes stress in an individual.

In Japan, more than 2,300 individuals die annually from being overworked!

EXHIBIT 13-6
Major Stressors

Personal
- Personality type
- Family matters
- Financial problems

STRESS

Organizational
- Role ambiguity
- Role conflict
- Role overload
- Technological advancements
- Work process engineering
- Downsizing
- Restructuring

and the tasks of others, the more potential stress there is. *Autonomy*, on the other hand, tends to lessen stress. Jobs where temperatures, noise, or other working conditions are dangerous or undesirable can increase anxiety. So, too, can working in an overcrowded room or in a visible location where interruptions are constant.

Role demands relate to pressures placed on an employee as a function of the particular role he or she plays in the organization. **Role conflicts** create expectations that may be hard to reconcile or satisfy. **Role overload** is experienced when the employee is expected to do more than time permits. **Role ambiguity** is created when role expectations are not clearly understood and the employee is not sure what he or she is to do.

Interpersonal demands are pressures created by other employees. Lack of social support from colleagues and poor interpersonal relationships can cause considerable stress, especially among employees with a high social need.

Organization structure can increase stress. Excessive rules and an employee's lack of opportunity to participate in decisions that affect him or her are examples of structural variables that might be potential sources of stress.

Organizational leadership represents the supervisory style of the organization's company officials. Some managers create a culture characterized by tension, fear, and anxiety. They establish unrealistic pressures to perform in the short run, impose excessively tight controls, and routinely fire employees who don't measure up. This style of leadership flows down through the organization to affect all employees.

Personal factors that can create stress include family issues, personal economic problems, and inherent personality characteristics.[53] Because employees bring their personal problems to work with them, a full understanding of employee stress requires a manager to be understanding of these personal factors. There is also evidence that employees' personalities have an effect on how sus-

Role Conflicts Expectations that are difficult to achieve.

Role Overload When an employee is expected to do more than time permits.

Role Ambiguity When an employee is not sure what work to do.

ceptible they are to stress. The most commonly used descriptions of these personality traits is called Type A–Type B dichotomy.

Type A Behavior Personality type characterized by chronic urgency and excessive competitive drive.

Type B Behavior Personality type characterized by a lack of time urgency or impatience.

Type A behavior is characterized by feelings of a chronic sense of time urgency, an excessive competitive drive, and difficulty accepting and enjoying leisure time. The opposite of Type A is **Type B behavior.** Type B's never suffer from time urgency or impatience. Until quite recently, it was believed that Type A's were more likely to experience stress on and off the job. A closer analysis of the evidence, however, has produced new conclusions. It has been found that only the hostility and anger associated with Type A behavior is actually associated with the negative effects of stress. And Type B's are just as susceptible to these same anxiety-producing elements. For managers, what is important is to recognize that Type A employees are more likely to show symptoms of stress even if organizational and personal stressors are low.

What Are the Symptoms of Stress?

What signs indicate that an employee's stress level might be too high? There are three general ways that stress reveals itself: through physiological, psychological, and behavioral symptoms.

Most of the early interest in stress focused heavily on health-related, or *physiological concerns.*[54] This was attributed to the realization that high stress levels result in changes in metabolism, increased heart and breathing rates, increased blood pressure, headaches, and increased risk of heart attacks. Because detecting many of these requires the skills of trained medical personnel, their immediate and direct relevance to HRM is negligible.

Of greater importance to managers are psychological and behavioral symptoms of stress. It's these things that can be witnessed in the person. The *psychological symptoms* can be seen as increased tension and anxiety, boredom, and procrastination—which can all lead to productivity decreases. So too, can the *behaviorally related symptoms*—changes in eating habits, increased smoking or substance consumption, rapid speech, or sleep disorders.

How Can Stress Be Reduced?

Reducing stress is one thing that presents a dilemma for HRM. Some stress in organizations is absolutely necessary. Without it, there's no energy in people. Accordingly, whenever one considers stress reduction, what is at issue is reducing its dysfunctional aspects.

One of the first means of reducing stress is to make sure that employees are properly matched to their jobs—and that they understand the extent of their "authority." Furthermore, by letting employees know precisely what is expected of them, role conflict and ambiguity can be reduced. Redesigning jobs can also help ease work overload–related stressors. Employees should also have some input in those things that affect them. Their involvement and participation have been found to lessen stress.

You must recognize that no matter what you do to eliminate organizational stressors, some employees will still be stressed out. You simply have little or no control over the personal factors. You also face an ethical issue when it is personal factors causing stress. That is, just how far can you intrude on an employee's personal life? To help deal with this issue, many companies have started employee assistance and wellness programs. These employer-offered programs are designed to assist employees in areas like financial planning, legal matters, health, fitness, stress, and the like—anywhere they are having difficulties.

A Special Case of Stress: Burnout

Burnout   Chronic and long-term stress.

Worker burnout is costing U.S. industry billions of dollars. One estimate revealed that almost $20 billion is lost each year due to burnout and its related implications.[55] **Burnout** is a multifaceted phenomenon, the byproduct of both personal variables and organization variables. It can be defined as a function of three concerns: "chronic emotional stress with (a) emotional and/or physical exhaustion, (b) lowered job productivity, and (c) dehumanizing of jobs."[56] Note that none of the three concerns includes long-term boredom. While boredom is often referred to as burnout, it is not!

Causes and Symptoms of Burnout   The factors contributing to burnout can be identified as follows: organization characteristics, perceptions of organization, perceptions of role, individual characteristics, and outcomes.[57] Exhibit 13-7 summarizes these variables. While these variables can lead to burnout, their presence does not guarantee that burnout will occur. Much of that outcome is contingent on the individual's capability to work under and handle stress. Because of this contingency, stressful conditions result in a two-phased outcome—the first level being the stress itself and the second level being the problems that arise from the manifestation of this stress.

Reducing Burnout   Recognizing that stress is a fact of life and must be channeled properly, organizations must establish procedures for reducing these stress levels before workers burn out.[58] Although no clear-cut remedies are available, four techniques have been proposed:

1. *Identification.* This is the analysis of the incidence, prevalence, and characteristics of burnout in individuals, work groups, subunits, or organizations.
2. *Prevention.* Attempts should be made to prevent the burnout process before it begins.
3. *Mediation.* This involves procedures for slowing, halting, or reversing the burnout process.
4. *Remediation.* Techniques are needed for individuals who are already burned out or are rapidly approaching the end stages of this process.

The key point here is that accurate identification is first made and then, and only then, is a program tailored to meet that need. Because of the costs associ-

EXHIBIT 13-7
Variables Found to Be Significantly Related to Burnout

ORGANIZATION CHARACTERISTICS	PERCEPTIONS OF ORGANIZATION	PERCEPTIONS OF ROLE	INDIVIDUAL CHARACTERISTICS	OUTCOMES
Caseload	Leadership	Autonomy	Family/friends support	Satisfaction
Formalization	Communication	Job involvement	Sex	Turnover
Turnover rate	Staff support	Being supervised	Age	
Staff size	Peers	Work pressure	Tenure	
	Clarity	Feedback	Ego level	
	Rules and procedures	Accomplishment		
	Innovation	Meaningfulness		
	Administrative support			

Source: Baron Perlman and E. Alan Hartman, "Burnout: Summary and Future Research," *Human Relations,* Vol. 25, No. 4 (1982), p. 294.

ated with burnout, many companies are implementing a full array of programs—like employee assistance programs—to help alleviate the problem. Many of these programs are designed to do two things: increase productivity and make the job more pleasant for the worker.

THE EMPLOYEE ASSISTANCE PROGRAM

No matter what kind of organization or industry one works in, one thing is certain. At times, employees will have personal problems. Whether that problem is job stress, legal, marital, financial, or health-related, one commonality exists: if an employee experiences a personal problem, sooner or later it will manifest itself at the workplace in terms of lowered productivity, increased absenteeism, or turnover (behavioral symptoms of stress). To help employees deal with these personal problems, more and more companies are implementing **employee assistance programs (EAPs)**.[59]

A Brief History

Employee Assistance Programs (EAPs) Specific programs designed to help employees with personal problems.

EAPs, as they exist today in about half of U.S. organizations, are extensions of programs that had their birth in U.S. companies in the 1940s.[60] Companies like DuPont, Standard Oil, and Kodak recognized that a number of their employees were experiencing problems with alcohol. To help these employees, formalized programs were implemented on the company's site to educate these workers on the dangers of alcohol and to help them overcome their addiction. The premise behind these programs, which still holds today, is getting a productive employee back on the job as swiftly as possible. Let's examine this for a moment.

Throughout this text thus far, we have discussed the various aspects of HRM designed to create an environment where an employee can be productive. Emphasis was placed on finding the right employees to fit the jobs, training them to do the job, then giving them a variety of opportunities to excel. All of this takes considerable time and money. We know it takes considerable time for employees to become fully productive—a process that requires the company to make an investment in its people. As with any investment, the company expects an adequate return. Now, how does this relate to EAPs?

Suppose you have a worker, Robert, who has been with you for a number of years. Robert has been a solid performer for several years, but lately something has happened. You notice his performance declining. The quality of his work is diminishing; he has been late three times in the past five weeks, and rumor has it that Robert is having marital problems. You could, and would, have every right to discipline Robert according to the organization's discipline process. But it is doubtful discipline alone would help. Consequently, after a period of time, you may end up firing him. You've now lost a once-good performer and must fill the position with another—a process that may take 18 months to finally achieve the productivity level Robert had. However, instead of firing him, you decide to refer Robert to the organization's EAP. This confidential program[61] works with Robert to determine the cause(s) of the problems and seeks to help this employee overcome them. Although he is meeting frequently at first with the EAP counselor, you notice that after a short period of time, Robert is back on the job—with performance improving. And after four months, he is performing at the level prior to the problem getting out of hand. In this scenario, you now have your fully productive employee back in four months, as opposed to possibly 18 months had you fired and replaced Robert. As for the return on investment, it is estimated that U.S. companies spend almost $1 billion each year on EAP programs. For most, studies suggest that these companies save up to $5.00 to $16 for every EAP dollar spent.[62] That, for most of us, is a significant return on investment!

EAPs Today

Since their early focus on alcoholic employees, EAPs have ventured into new areas. One of the most notable areas is the use of EAPs to help control rising health insurance premiums, especially in the areas of mental health and substance abuse services. These cost savings accrue from such measures as managing "inpatient length of stays, outpatient treatment days, disability days, and stress-related claims."[63]

Studies suggest that for every $1 spent on EAPs, the company receives $5 to $16 return on its investment.

No matter how beneficial EAPs may be to an organization, one aspect cannot be taken for granted: employee participation. EAPs must be perceived as being worthwhile to the employee. Employees must see the EAP as an operation that is designed to help them deal with such problems as "alcohol and chemical dependency, emotional problems, stress, pre-retirement planning, marital problems, careers, finances, legal matters, or termination." In addition, EAPs are becoming more involved in helping employees who have AIDS, as well as counseling employees on cultural diversity issues.[64] For employees to accept EAPs, employees need to know about the program and understand the confidential nature of it. Accordingly, there must be extensive information given to employees regarding how the EAP works, how employees can use its services, and how confidentiality is guaranteed.[65] Furthermore, supervisors must be properly trained to recognize changes in employee behaviors and to refer them to the EAP in a confidential manner. And with the AIDS issue, confidentiality has become of even greater importance.[66] Although EAPs can help employees when problems arise, companies have given much support to finding ways to eliminate some factors that may lead to personal problems. In doing so, some organizations such as the Adolph Coors Company have promoted wellness programs.

Wellness Programs

Wellness Programs Organizational programs designed to keep employees healthy.

When we mention **wellness programs** in any organization, we are talking about any type of program that is designed to keep employees healthy. These programs are varied and may focus on such things as smoking cessation, weight control, stress management, physical fitness, nutrition education, high blood-pressure control, violence protection, work team problem intervention,[67] and so on. Wellness programs are designed to help cut employer health costs and to lower absenteeism and turnover by preventing health-related problems.[68]

It is interesting to note that, similar to EAPs, wellness programs don't work unless employees view them as having some value. Unfortunately for wellness, the numbers across the United States are not as promising. It is estimated that only about 20 percent of employees who have access to these programs actually use them.[69] To help combat this low turnout, a number of key criteria must exist. First of all, there must be top management support—without their support in terms of resources, and in personally using the programs, the wrong message may be sent to employees. Second, there appears to be a need to have the programs serve the family as well as the employees themselves. This not only provides an atmosphere where families can "get healthy together," it also reduces

More and more organizations are providing workout facilities for their employees. The reason is simple. Working out helps reduce the stress workers face and saves the company in the long run with reductions in health care insurance premiums.

possible medical costs for the dependents. And finally comes the issue of employee input. If programs are designed without considering employees' needs, even the best ones may fail. Organizations need to invite participation by asking employees what they'd use if available. Although many organization members know that exercise is beneficial, few initially addressed how to get employees involved. But after finding out that employees would like such things as on-site exercise facilities or aerobics, organizations were able to begin appropriate program development.

As wellness programs continue to expand in Corporate America, the question regarding top management support is still crucial, but questions about that support being present are lessening. Why? Because in finding out how to get senior executives involved, it was discovered that they, too, wanted a place to go for exercise. Many of these executives, as one of their perks, are provided with a membership in a health club. Whether it is executives or support staff participation, wellness or EAPs, U.S. organizations appear to be continuing their efforts to support a healthy work environment. The companies reap a good return on their investments; programs such as EAP and wellness have proven to be win-win opportunities for all involved.

INTERNATIONAL SAFETY AND HEALTH

It is important to know the safety and health environments of each country in which an organization operates.[70] Generally, corporations in western Europe, Canada, Japan, and the United States put great emphasis on the health and welfare of their employees. However, most businesses in less-developed countries have limited resources and thus cannot establish awareness or protection programs.

Most countries have laws and regulatory agencies that protect workers from hazardous work environments. It is important for American firms to learn the often-complex regulations that exist, as well as the cultural expectations of the local labor force. Manufacturers, in particular, where there are myriad potentially hazardous situations, must design and establish facilities that meet the expectations of the local employees—not necessarily those of Americans.

International Health Issues

For corporations preparing to send executives on overseas assignments, a few basic health-related items appear on every checklist. These include:

- *An up-to-date health certificate.* Often called a "shot book," this is the individual's record of vaccinations against infectious diseases such as cholera, typhoid, and smallpox. Each country has its own vaccination requirements for entry inside its borders, but in addition, the U.S. Department of State Traveler Advisories "hotline" provides alerts to specific problems with diseases or regions within a country.
- *A general first aid kit.* This should include all over-the-counter medications such as aspirin, cold and cough remedies, and so on that the employee or family members would usually take at home, but that might not be available at the overseas drugstore. In addition, any prescription drugs should be packed in twice the quantity expected to be used. In case of an accidental dunking, overheating, or other problem, it is wise to pack the

two supplies of drugs separately. It also is advisable to know the generic name—not the U.S. tradename—of any prescription drug. Finally, include special items such as disinfectant solutions to treat fresh fruit or vegetables, and water-purifying tablets, as the sanitation system of the host country warrants.

- *Emergency plans.* Upon arrival at the foreign destination, employees should check out the local medical and dental facilities and plan on what care can be expected in the host country. This might include evacuation of a sick or injured employee or family member to another city or even another country. For example, expatriates in China often prefer to go to Hong Kong even for regular medical checkups. It is always wise to take along copies of all family members' medical and dental records.

International Safety Issues

Safety for the employee has become increasingly an issue of security, both while traveling and after arrival. Again, the U.S. Department of State provides travel alerts and cautions on its web page.

But safety precautions begin before the overseas journey.[71] While it may be a matter of status and comfort to fly first class, experience with skyjacks has shown that it is safer to fly economy class. The goal is to blend into the crowd as much as possible, even if the corporation is willing to pay for greater luxury. Many corporations offer some of the following advice for traveling executives: blending in includes wearing low-key, appropriate clothing, not carrying obviously expensive luggage, avoiding luggage tags with titles like "vice president," and, if possible, traveling in small groups. Upon arrival at the airport, it is advisable to check in at the airline's ticket counter immediately and go through security checkpoints to wait in the less-public gate area. The wisdom of this advice was confirmed in Rome, Athens, and other airport bombings.

Once the expatriate family has landed, the goal remains to blend in. These individuals must acquire some local "savvy" as quickly as possible; in addition to learning the language, they also must adapt to the local customs and try to dress in the same style as the local people.

Foremost on many individuals' minds when they go abroad is security. Many corporations now provide electronic safety systems, floodlights, and the like for home and office, as well as bodyguards or armed chauffeurs—but individual alertness is the key factor. It is suggested that kidnappers select their potential targets by seeking someone who is valuable to either a government or corporation, with lots of family money or a wealthy sponsor, and where there is opportunity to plan and execute the kidnapping. This last criterion means it is important to avoid set routines for local travel and other behaviors. The employee should take different routes between home and office, and the children should vary their paths to school. The family food shopping should be done at varying times each day, or in different markets, if possible. These and other precautions, as well as a constant awareness of one's surroundings, are important for every family member.

DEVELOPING SAFETY SKILLS

ABOUT THE SKILL: THERE ARE several steps that can be recommended for developing an organization's safety and health program. Whether or not such programs are chiefly the responsibility of one individual, every supervisor must work to ensure that the work environment is safe for all employees.

1. *Involve management and employees in the development of a safety and health plan.* If neither group can see the usefulness and the benefit of such a plan, even the best plan will fail.

2. *Hold someone accountable for implementing the plan.* Plans do not work by themselves. They need someone to champion the cause. This person must be given the resources to put the plan in place, but also must be held accountable for what it's intended to accomplish.

3. *Determine the safety and health requirements for your work site.* Just as each individual is different, so, too, is each workplace. Understanding the specific needs of the facility will aid in determining what safety and health requirement will be necessary.

4. *Assess what workplace hazards exist in the facility.* Identify the potential health and safety problems that may exist on the job. By understanding what exists, preventive measures can be determined.

5. *Correct hazards that exist.* If certain hazards were identified in the investigation, fix or eliminate them. This may mean decreasing the effect of the hazard, or controlling it through other means (e.g., protective clothing).

6. *Train employees in safety and health techniques.* Make safety and health training mandatory for all employees. Employees should be instructed in how to do their jobs in the safest manner, and understand that any protective equipment provided must be used.

7. *Develop the mindset in employees that the organization is to be kept hazard free.* Often employees are the first to witness problems. Establish a means for them to report their findings, including having emergency procedures in place, if necessary. Ensuring that preventive maintenance of equipment follows a recommended schedule can also prevent breakdown of equipment from becoming a hazard.

8. *Continuously update and refine the safety and health program.* Once the program has been implemented, it must continuously be evaluated, and necessary changes must be made. Documenting the progress of the program is necessary for use in this analysis.

HRM WORKSHOP

SUMMARY

(This summary relates to the Learning Outcomes identified on p. 356.)

After having read this chapter, you should be able to:

1. **Discuss the organizational effect of the Occupational Safety and Health Act.** The Occupational Safety and Health Act (OSHA) outlines comprehensive and specific safety and health standards.

2. **List the Occupational Safety and Health Administration's (OSHA) enforcement priorities.** OSHA has an established five-step priority enforcement process consisting of imminent danger, serious accidents, employee complaints, inspection of targeted industries, and random inspections.

3. **Explain what punitive actions OSHA can impose on an organization.** OSHA can fine an organization up to a maximum penalty of $70,000 if the violation is severe, willful, and repetitive. For violations not meeting those criteria, the maximum fine is $7,000. OSHA may, at its discretion, seek criminal or civil charges against an organization's management if they willfully violate health and safety regulations.

4. **Describe what companies must do to comply with OSHA record-keeping requirements.** Companies in selected industries must complete OSHA Form 200 to record accidents, injuries, and illnesses that are job related. This information is then used to calculate the organization's incidence rate.

5. **Identify four contemporary areas for which OSHA is setting standards.** OSHA is setting standards to protect workers exposed to bloodborne pathogens, chemicals, and other work-related toxins, setting standards for motor vehicle safety, and focusing its attention on ergonomics.

6. **Describe the leading causes of safety and health accidents.** The leading causes of accidents are human or environmental factors.

7. **Explain what companies can do to prevent workplace violence.** A company can help prevent workplace violence by ensuring that its policies are not adversely affecting employees, by developing a plan to deal with the issue and by training its managers in identifying troubled employees.

8. **Define stress and the causes of burnout.** Stress is a dynamic condition in which an individual is confronted with an opportunity, constraint, or demand for which the outcome is perceived as important and uncertain. Burnout is caused by a combination of emotional and/or physical exhaustion, lower job productivity, or dehumanizing jobs.

9. **Explain how an organization can create a healthy work site.** Creating a healthy work site involves removing any harmful substance, like asbestos, germs, mold, fungi, cigarette smoke, and so forth, thus limiting employee exposure.

10. **Describe the purposes of employee assistance and wellness programs.** Employee assistance and wellness programs are designed to offer employees a variety of services that will help them to become mentally and physically healthy, which in turn helps to contain the organization's health-care costs.

DEMONSTRATING COMPREHENSION: *Questions for Review and Discussion*

1. What are the objectives of the Occupational Safety and Health Act?
2. Describe the priority of OSHA investigations.
3. Identify three methods of preventing accidents.
4. How are incidence rates calculated?
5. What is stress? How can it be positive?
6. Differentiate between physiological, psychological, and behavioral stress symptoms.
7. Describe how EAPs and wellness programs help an organization to control rising medical costs.
8. What must an organization do differently with respect to health and safety when operating in another country?
9. "Employers should be concerned with helping employees cope with stress—both job-related stress and off-the-job stress." Do you agree or disagree? Discuss.
10. Some medical experts believe that regular daily exercise results in better health, improved conditioning, and greater tolerance of stressful situations. What would you think about being employed by a company that required you to work out daily on company time? Do you think this would help or hurt the company's recruiting ability? Explain your position.

CASE APPLICATION: *TEAM FUN!*

Kenny and Norton, owners of TEAM FUN!, a sporting goods manufacturer and retailer, are meeting with Tony, Director of Human Resources, and Edna, Compensation and Benefits Manager, in the DEN, a casual area with a big screen TV, sodas and munchies on a side table. Kenny flips on the light, "We can meet here for an hour. No one shows up for break before 9am. Did you see the headlines this morning? I finally figured out what "postal" means. Wonder why those guys go nuts and shoot each other?"

Norton laughs, "Don't you remember me before we started TEAM FUN!? I was angry almost all the time. All that stupid politics. Those ridiculous schedules. Everyone stabbing each other in the back to get ahead."

Kenny frowns, "I almost forgot about you. Say, you don't think we need to do anything here for violence do you? We've got all those bows and arrows, golf clubs. Even baseball bats could be a weapon."

Tony says, "Violence is the last problem I'd expect to find here. You two have made this place very mellow for employees. You let them take play breaks during the day. Schedules and goals are posted publicly. Teams get rewarded for being teams. Customers write in and thank employees by name. Fun is a requirement of every job. You are nearly as friendly as Southwest Airlines."

Edna comments, "I think the wellness program was a natural. Hiring that nutritionist to work at the sports bar fits right in with the gear and the machines. Fit employees are less likely to overreact or burnout."

Norton nods and adds, "Nobody but Bobby ever got stressed or burned out here."

Tony says, "I think Bobby did his own burnout. But the employee assistance program should get another look."

Kenny stands up, "OK. Work something up for tomorrow. I want to try out that new paddleboat contraption in the LAGOON. See it down there? Come on, Norton. Grab a couple of beers and let our HR folks take care of our people."

Questions:

1. Do you agree with Tony's statement about workplace violence? Should TEAM FUN! take any further actions to prevent workplace violence? Identify the preventive measures that are already in place.
2. Is Tony too complacent about stress and burnout? Outline for Kenny and Norton any symptoms of stress and burnout that should be noticed.
3. What benefits would wellness programs and an employee assistance plan provide TEAM FUN!?

WORKING WITH A TEAM: *Health and Safety*

Your team may wish to role play this case for the class, then discuss what the supervisor in the scenario should do and how he should respond.

Billy Jo Rhea has been a machinist for Linco Tool and Die, a manufacturer of engine parts for large motors, for 16 years. Lately more of Billy Jo's parts have been rejected for errors; he seems preoccupied with outside matters—leaving early, asking to take days beyond sick days allowed. He has missed three work days in two weeks, and Charlie, his supervisor, wondered if he smelled alcohol on his breath after lunch yesterday. Charlie hasn't said anything yet; he doesn't want to invade his privacy. He thinks Billy Jo may just be going through a tough time, because he has been cooperative, positive, highly productive, and rarely sick or absent in the past. Besides, it has been difficult in the last month because a major shipment has required overtime, and all machinists have been asked to work 80 to 95 hours a week until the shipment is complete.

At lunch you overhear an argument between Billy Jo and a coworker, Terry, each blaming the other for a part being rejected by Quality Assurance. Billy Jo threatens him to "stay out of his way and his area" and "the next time they'll settle it outside," poking him in the chest with his finger as he states it. Billy Jo then slams a $250 gauge down on the floor, shouts profanities, and adds, "I don't care if the part falls off or if this place burns to the ground anymore; I've about had all I can take of you and this place! You know my wife left me for my best friend last week, left me with a two-year-old to raise by myself, and my other kid got expelled for possession. It just doesn't much matter to me what you think; so I'd leave me alone if I were you!" Charlie heads for the human resource office, unsure of how to proceed.

Here are some questions to guide you:

1. What should Charlie do?
2. What advice would you give Charlie as the human resource manager?
3. How should Charlie respond to the immediate situation?
4. How can you apply the assessment questions regarding violence to enable Charlie and other supervisors to handle future situations more effectively?

ENHANCING YOUR WRITING SKILLS

1. Visit OSHA's web site (www.osha.gov). Go to the web page that discusses a new release on something OSHA is doing. Provide a two- to three-page summary of the news release, focusing on what OSHA is intending to do, its effect on workers, and its effect on employers.
2. Develop a two- to three-page argument on why smoking

should and should not be prohibited on company sites. Support your position with appropriate documentation.

3. Go to the employee assistance programs provider Interlock's web site at <<http://www.interlock.org>. Research the web site for the following information: What

are the components of an EAP, and how does Interlock evaluate an EAP's success? Also identify how Interlock recommends implementing an EAP in an organization. Provide a two- to three-page summary of your findings.

www.wiley.com/college/decenzo

ℰNDNOTES

1. This opening vignette is based on Bill Leonard, "HR Staff Among Victims of Fatal Worksite Rampage," *HR News* (February 2001), p. 1; Matt Bai, "Massacre at the Office," *Newsweek* (January 8, 2001), p. 27; Lynn Miller, Karen Caldwell, and Laura C. Jackson, "When Work Equals Life: The Next Stage of Workplace Violence," *HRMagazine* (December 2000), pp. 178–180; "Xerox Cited for Violations Due to Hawaii Shootings," *Wall Street Journal* (November 8, 2000), p. C-13; Jennifer McLaughlin, "The Anger Within," *OH & S Canada* (December 2000), pp. 30–36; A. Levin and L. Parker, "Human, Mechanical Flaws Cut Off Path to Survival," *USA Today,* July 12, 1999, pp. 1A; 8A. and "Connecticut Lottery Office Swept Clean of Traces of Gunman," *The Sun* (March 11, 1998), p. 9A.

2. U.S. Department of Commerce, Bureau of the Census, *National Census of Fatal Occupational Injuries, 1999* (www.stats.bls.gov.oshome.htm, August 17, 2000); and U.S. Bureau of the Census, *Statistical Abstracts of the United States, 1999* (Washington, DC: Government Printing Office, 1999), p. 450.

3. Leon Rubis, "1995 Drop in Workplace Injuries Includes Repetitive Motion Cases," *HR News* (April 1997), p. 9.

4. The Occupational Safety and Health Act was amended in 1998.

5. See, for example, Elaine McShulskis, "Protect Employees from Hazardous Noise Levels," *HRMagazine* (April 1997), p. 22.

6. In the case of the Supreme Court case of *Whirlpool Corporation v. Marshall* [445 U.S. 1(1980)], employees may refuse to work if they perceive doing so can cause serious injury. This case has weakened termination for insubordination when the refusal stems from a safety or health issue. This refusal was further clarified in *Gateway Coal v. the United Mine Workers* [94 S. Ct. 641(1981)], where a three-part test was developed. This was where (1) the refusal is reasonable; (2) the employee was unsuccessful in getting the problem fixed; and (3) normal organizational channels to address the problem haven't worked.

7. Stephen Barlas, "Safety Last?" *Entrepreneur* (October 1995), p. 100.

8. Lisa Finnegan, "Poor Machine Guarding Expensive," *Occupational Hazards* (May 1999), p. 24.

9. *Marshall v. Barlow, Inc.,* 436 U.S., 307 (1978).

10. "Federal Court Upholds OSHA Warrant Procedure," *HR News* (April 1995), p. 19.

11. "OSHA Inspection Delay Is Legal," *ENR* (May 3, 1999), p. 21.

12. See, for example, Robert J. Grossman, "Handling Inspections: Tips from Insiders," *HRMagazine* (October 1999), pp. 40–45; and William Atkinson, "When OSHA Comes Knocking," *HRMagazine* (October 1999), pp. 34–38.

13. The number 3,600,000 is determined as follows: 1,800 employees, working 40 hour weeks, for 50 weeks a year [1,800 × 40 × 50].

14. *Statistical Abstract of the United States* (1999), p. 450.

15. Ibid.

16. For willful violation the minimum penalty is $5,000; other fines levied for violations other than willful and repetitive carry with them a $7,000 maximum.

17. "Three Men Receive Sentences, Fines in Mine Explosion," *Wall Street Journal* (June 13, 1996), p. A-4. The prosecution and fines in the Pyro Mining case stemmed from a situation where company officials allegedly lied to inspectors and failed to adhere to safety procedures. In all, 15 employees of Pyro Mining pleaded guilty, with only three executives receiving prison terms up to 18 months.

18. Jeffrey M. Rosin, "A New Twist in Enforcement Efforts," *HRMagazine* (May 1997), pp. 128–134.

19. Howard Banks, "The Agenda for Labor Law Reform," *Forbes* (January 16, 1995), p. 37.

20. U.S. Department of Labor, Occupational Safety and Health Administration, *Lyme Disease Facts* (Washington, DC: Government Printing Office, 1999), p. 1.

21. Bill Leonard, "OSHA Launches Ergonomics Page on the World Wide Web," *HRMagazine* (June 1997), p. 10.

22. See U.S. Department of Labor, Occupational Safety and Health Administration, *Hazard Communication Guidelines for Compliance* (Washington, DC: Government Printing Office, 2000).

23. *Statistical Abstracts of the United States* (1999), p. 450.

24. "Falling Behind: The U.S. Is Losing the Job Safety War to Japan, Too," *Wall Street Journal* (May 16, 1992), p. A-1.

25. Jonathan A. Segal, "When Norman Bates and Baby Jane Act Out at Work," *HRMagazine* (February 1996), p. 31.

26. Daniel Costello, "Stressed Out: Can Workplace Stress Get Worse?—Incidents of 'Desk Rage' Disrupt America's Offices—Long Hours, Cramped Quarters Produce Some Short Fuses; Flinging Phones at the Wall," *Wall Street Journal* (January 16, 2001), p. B-1.

27. U.S. Department of Labor, Occupational Safety and Health Administration, *Workplace Violence* (Washington, DC: Government Printing Office, 2000), p. 1; and Lynn Miller, Karen Caldwell, and Laura C. Lawson, "When Work Equals

Life: The Next State of Workplace Violence," *HR Magazine* (December 2000), pp. 178–180.

28. Kathryn Tyler, "Targets Behind the Counter," *HRMagazine* (August 1999), p. 106.

29. Michael Lynch, "Go Ask Alice," *Security Management* (December 2000), pp. 68–73; Joseph A. Kinney, "When Domestic Violence Strikes the Workplace," *HRMagazine* (August 1995), pp. 74–78; and John D. Thompson, "Employers Should Take Measures to Minimize Potential for Workplace Violence," *Commerce Clearing House: Ideas and Trends* (December 20, 1993), pp. 201–203, 208.

30. Edward Felsenthal, "Potentially Violent Employees Present Bosses with a Catch-22," *Wall Street Journal* (April 5, 1995), pp. B-1, B-5.

31. Ibid.

32. "Workplace Security: Preventing On-the-Job Violence," *Inc.* (June 1996), p. 116.

33. See, for example, Kate Walter, "Are Your Employees on the Brink," *HRMagazine* (June 1997), pp. 57–63; Malcolm P. Coco, Jr., "The New War Zone: The Workplace," *SAM Advanced Management Journal* (Winter 1997), pp. 15–20; Jacquelin Lynn, "Striking Back," *Entrepreneur* (June 1995), p. 56; Dennis L. Johnson, John G. Kurutz, and John B. Kiehlbauch, "Scenario for Supervisors," *HRMagazine* (February 1995), p. 63; and Commerce Clearing House, "Workplace Violence: Strategies Start with Awareness," *Human Resources Management: Ideas and Trends* (July 11, 1994), p. 109.

34. Paul Temple, "Real Danger and 'Postal' Myth," *Workforce* (October 2000), p. 8; John K. Sage, "Attack on Violence," *Industry Week* (February 17, 1997), p. 18; Rudy M. Yandrick, "Long-Term Follow-Up Urged After Workplace Disasters," *HR News* (December 1996), p. 6; and Kathleen Menda, "Defusing Workplace Violence," *HRMagazine* (October 1994), p. 113.

35. Anne Underwood, "A Hidden Health Hazard," *Newsweek* (December 4, 2000), p. 74; and Michelle Conlin and John Carey, "Is Your Office Killing You?" *Business Week* (June 5, 2000), pp. 114–128.

36. See, Conlin and Carey, "Is Your Office Killing You?" Rob Schneider, "Sick Buildings Threaten Health of Those Who Inhabit Them," *Indianapolis Star* (September 23, 2000), p. A-1; and Faye Rice, "Do You Work in a Sick Building?" *Fortune* (July 2, 1990), p. 88.

37. "Smoke-Free Workplaces Prevalent," *HRMagazine* (June 1996), p. 18; and "U.S. Employers Crack Down on Workplace Smoking But Few Provide Help," *Manpower Argus* (July 1997), p. 8.

38. U.S. Department of Labor, "Ergonomics: The Study of Work," *OSHA 3125* (Washington, DC: Government Printing Office, 2000), p. 4.

39. Kenneth J. DiLuigi, "Help for the Overworked Wrist," *Occupational Hazards* (October 2000), pp. 99–101.

40. "OSHA Issues Final Ergonomics Standards," *Healthcare Financial Management* (January 2001), p. 9; Charles Haddad, "OSHA New Regs Will Ease the Pain—For Everybody," *Business Week* (December 4, 2000), pp. 90–91; and Yochi J. Dreazen, "Ergonomic Rules Are the First in a Wave of Late Regulations," *Wall Street Journal* (November 14, 2000), p. A-4. For another view on these standards, see Phil Kuntz, "What a Pain: Proposed OSHA Rules for Workplace Injuries Make Companies Ache—Agency Stretches Data to

Fit Burgeoning Mission; Cost of Compliance Debated—Looking for 10 Pallbearers," *Wall Street Journal* (September 18, 2000), p. A-1.

41. Dominic Bencivenga, "The Economics of Ergonomics: Finding the Right Fit," *HRMagazine* (August 1996), pp. 68–75; and Linda Thornburg, "Workplace Ergonomics Makes Economic Sense," *HRMagazine* (October 1994), pp. 58–60.

42. Robina A. Gangemi, "Ergonomics: Reducing Workplace Injuries," *Inc.* (July 1996), p. 92.

43. U.S. Department of Labor, "Ergonomics: The Study of Work," *OSHA 3125* (Washington, DC: Government Printing Office, 2000), p. 1.

44. Frederick M. Spina, "Ergonomically Correct," *Risk Management* (December 2000), pp. 39–41.

45. William Atkinson, "When Stress Won't Go Away," *HRMagazine* (December 2000), p. 104.

46. This information is adapted from a newswire report by M. Yamaguchi as cited in "Stress in Japanese Business," *Audio Human Resource Report,* Vol. 2, No. 2 (March 1991), pp. 6–7.

47. "Work-Related Deaths Are on the Rise in Japan," *Manpower Argus* (April 1997), p. 11.

48. "Huge Payout by Japanese Firm for 'Karoshi,'" *Manpower Argus* (September 1996), p. 8.

49. "Stress on the Job in Germany," and "Workplace Stress Is Biggest Health Hazard in Britain," *Manpower Argus* (February 1997), p. 7.

50. For some interesting reading on organizational stress, see Elaine Wethington, "Theories of Organizational Stress," *Administrative Science Quarterly* (September 2000), p. 640; and Rob B. Briner and Shirley Reynolds, "The Costs, Benefits, and Limitation of Organizational Stress Interventions," *Journal of Organizational Behavior* (September 1999), pp. 647–664.

51. Also see J. H. Harris and L. A. Arendt, "Stress Reduction and the Small Business: Increasing Employee and Customer, Satisfaction," *SAM Advanced Management Journal* (Winter 1997), pp. 27–34.

52. See, for example, "Stressed Out: Extreme Job Stress: Survivors' Tales," *Wall Street Journal* (January 17, 2001), p. B-1.

53. For an interesting overview of this topic, see V. J. Doby and R. D. Caplan, "Organizational Stress as Threat to Reputation: Effects on Anxiety at Work and at Home," *Academy of Management Journal* (September 1995), pp. 1105–1123.

54. See, for instance, J. Schaubroeck and D. E. Merritt, "Divergent Effects of Job Control on Coping with Work Stressors: The Key Role of Self-Efficacy," *Academy of Management Journal* (June 1997), pp. 738–754.

55. Sal Marine, "The Stress Epidemic," *Industry Week* (April 7, 1997), p. 14.

56. Ibid., p. 293. See also Nico Schutte, Salla Toppinen, Raija Kalimo, and Wilmar Schaufeli, "The Factorial Validity of the Maslach Burnout Inventory—General Survey (MBI–GS) Across Occupational Groups and Nations," *Journal of Occupational and Organizational Psychology* (March 2000), pp. 3–66.

57. Sal Marine, "The Stress Epidemic," (April 7, 1997), p. 14.

58. John M. Kelly, "Getting a Grip on Stress," *HRMagazine* (February 1997), pp. 51–54. See also Joanne Cole, "De-Stressing the Workplace," *HR Focus* (October 1999), p. 1.

59. Ibid.; and Wayne Pancratz, "Employee Assistance Program a Valuable Benefit," *FDM* (December 2000), pp. 56–58; and "EAPs Adopt Broad Brush Approach to Helping Employees," *Employee Benefit Plan Review* (October 1999), pp. 44–46.

60. Fay Hansen, "Employee Assistance Programs (EAPs) Grow and Expand Their Reach," *Compensation and Benefits Review* (March–April 2000), p. 13.

61. Employee rights legislation mandates that any activity in an EAP remains confidential. This means records of who is visiting the EAP, the problems, and intervention, must be maintained separately from other personnel records.

62. William Atkinson, "Wellness, Employee Assistance Programs: Investments, Not Costs," *Bobbin* (May 2000), pp. 42–48.

63. See Meg Bryant, "Testing EAPs for Coordination," *Business and Health* (August 1991), pp. 20–24.

64. John S. McClenahen, "Working with AIDS," *Industry Week* (November 17, 1997), pp. 51–52.

65. See, for instance, Joan Hamilton, "Can Company Counselors Help You Cope?" *Business Week* (November 14, 1994), p. 141.

66. See Cynthia E. Griffin, "Crisis Control," *Entrepreneur* (August 1995), pp. 128–135.

67. Rudy M. Yandrick, "EAPs Explore Boundaries of Evolving Profession," *HR News* (August 1995), p. 1.

68. Carolyn Petersen, "Value of Complementary Care Rises, But Poses Challenges," *Managed Healthcare* (November 2000), pp. 47–48.

69. James W. Busbin and David P. Campbell, "Employee Wellness Programs: A Strategy for Increasing Participation," *Journal of Health Care Marketing,* Vol. 10, No. 4 (December 1990), p. 22.

70. Timothy Pasquarelli, "Dealing with Discomfort and Danger," *HRMagazine* (October 1996), pp. 104–110.

71. Rudy M. Yandrick, "EAPs Help Expatriates Adjust and Thrive," *HR News* (January 1995), p. B7. See also the U.S. Department of State web site (http://travel.state.gov_warnings.htm).

14

EFFECTIVE HRM COMMUNICATIONS

LEARNING OUTCOMES

AFTER READING THIS CHAPTER, YOU WILL BE ABLE TO:

1. Explain how communication serves as the foundation for HRM activities.
2. Identify the legally required communications with respect to benefit administration and safety and health.
3. Describe the purpose of HRM communications programs.
4. Discuss how corporate culture is affected by effective communication.
5. State the role of the chief executive officer promoting communications programs.
6. Specify what information employees should receive under an effective communications program.
7. Describe the purpose of the employee handbook.
8. Explain what information should be included in an employee handbook.
9. List four popular communication methods used in organizations.
10. Discuss the critical components of an effective suggestion program.

Employee handbooks have the potential to provide a wealth of information to employees—information that is important to them and is critical to their employment. Simultaneously, however, the handbook can also provide specific information that protects the organization from claims being made against it at a later date. This documentation, then, almost creates the necessity that handbooks be thorough, detailed, and "legally cleared." For management at the Fountain Valley, California, Kingston Technologies, nothing could be further from the truth.[1] Kingston Technologies was founded in 1987 by John Tu and David Sun. The company manufactures "memory, processor, networking and storage products" for the computer industry. Since its start, the company has grown to over 3,000 products, and ended 2000 with sales greater than $1.5 billion.

Management of the company recognizes that its success has not occurred in isolation. Rather, management attributes much of the success to the employees, who work in an environment that is "free of politics and mistrust." To foster this environment, Kingston's management recognized years ago the need to have in place an accurate and technically correct employee handbook. To achieve that goal, they hired a consultant to develop the manual and submit it to the company in camera-ready format for duplication and binding. Several weeks later, the company got just what it wanted. The handbook was done—another project completed. Or so the company thought! Others in the company felt, however, that the finished product was poor. It contained all significant legal jargon, which made it seem as if the company didn't trust its employees. Employees hated the manual.

Kingston Technologies operates as a wholesome company. Its founders' philosophy is to build trust and loyalty with every member of the company. Management wanted to make that statement on the first day of hiring, yet the handbook new employees left with that first day created just the opposite view. Consequently, the handbook had to be redone—not by outsiders, but by an individual in the organization who understood the philosophical underpinnings of Kingston.

Kingston's new employee handbook has been a big success. It now provides the information that employees need in a simple and straightforward manner—and in a language that employees understand! Each of the 20 pages of the handbook addresses important questions employees may have, and embellishes on the company's philosophies—courtesy, compassion, modesty, and honesty. And, as publications like *Forbes, Newsweek,* the *Wall Street Journal,* and *Inc.* have cited in feature articles about the company, as far as handbooks go, you can't get much better than this!

INTRODUCTION

Communication The transference of meaning and understanding.

For 13 chapters, we have been discussing a variety of HRM activities. Inherent in all of these activities is one common thread—effective **communication.** Although we may not have elaborated specifically on how HRM involves itself in the communication process, we have addressed its needs on several occasions. For example, in Chapter 1, the discussion of worker diversity identified the need for better communications with employees, especially those who do not speak the native language.[2] Communications in work-force diversity also means letting these individuals know that they are welcome in the corporation and that the company will make every attempt to provide them equal opportunity in the organization.

We also addressed the need to communicate with respect to the recruiting and selection process (in terms of understanding what the job entails and realistic job previews), orientation (acclimating employees to HRM activities and policies), and training (understanding how to do the job). Yet probably the most critical HRM activities emphasizing communications came in the discussion of performance evaluations, benefits, and safety and health. In performance evaluations, we highlighted the need for performance goals to be communicated— goals that will, when met, facilitate achieving organization-wide objectives. Specificity for doing so was discussed in performance evaluations and how the interaction between an employee and manager can affect performance outcomes.[3] When these outcomes are positive, individuals should be rewarded; when they are not positive, effort must be expended to correct the problem. For that, we introduced employee counseling, which relies heavily on effective communications.

For benefits and safety and health, we discussed not only the importance of informing employees of the benefits offered them, and availability of EAP and wellness programs, but the legal issues of providing certain information. That is, with respect to benefits, HRM is responsible for providing each employee with a Summary Plan Description, which describes in understandable terms employee rights under ERISA, their pension plan requirements, and updated benefits accumulations: Likewise, OSHA, under its Hazard Communication Standard, requires employers to notify employees of potential dangers and protective measures when exposed to hazardous chemicals or toxins in the workplace.[4]

We recognize that our companies will be different today, and this difference will continue well into the future. Factors like global competition and technology enhancements are making company officials rethink how they are organized. We've witnessed extensive downsizing, mergers, and acquisitions in the past. When such events occur, employee stress levels increase. One way of allaying such stress is to reduce the uncertainty that surrounds the situation—in our terms, effective communications.[5]

We know the years ahead will continue to witness change in our companies.[6] Our movement toward leaner structures, continuous improvement, employee involvement, and work teams will work best if effective communication exists.[7] And where good communications programs are operating, benefits accrue to the company.[8] With our diverse work force, this means communicating in different languages to ensure that the message is understood by all employees.

HRM COMMUNICATIONS PROGRAMS

Achieving the goals effective communications can offer is not easy. It doesn't happen by itself. Rather, it evolves after careful thought, implementation, and evaluation. For much of that, we rely on HRM. Although we've highlighted many

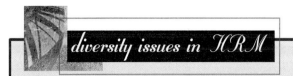

SHOULD ORGANIZATIONAL COMMUNICATIONS BE POLITICALLY CORRECT?

WHAT WORDS DO YOU USE TO describe a colleague who is confined to a wheelchair? What terms do you use in addressing female employees or female customers? How do you communicate with a brand-new client who speaks a language different from yours? The right answers to these questions can prevent the loss of a client, an employee, a lawsuit, a harassment allegation, or a job.[9]

Most of us are acutely aware of how our vocabulary has been modified to reflect political correctness. For instance, most of us have purged the words *handicapped, blind,* and *elderly* from our work vocabulary—and replaced them with terms such as *physically challenged, visually impaired,* and *senior.*

We must be sensitive to others' feelings. Certain words can and do stereotype, intimidate, or insult individuals. In an increasingly diverse work force, we must be sensitive to how words might offend others. But there's a downside to political correctness. It's shrinking our vocabulary and making it more difficult for people to communicate. To illustrate, you probably know what these three terms mean—*death, garbage,* and *quotas.* But each of these words has been found to offend one or more

groups. They've been replaced with terms such as *negative patient outcome, post-consumer waste material,* and *educational equity,*. The problem is that this latter group of terms is much less likely to convey a clear and uniform message than the words they replaced. You know what death means; I know what death means; but can we be certain that "negative patient outcome" is consistently defined by both of us? That's doubtful, as a negative patient outcome could mean that my insurance company won't pay my hospital bill.

Words are a primary means by which people communicate. When we eliminate words because they're politically incorrect, we reduce our options for conveying messages in the clearest and most accurate form. We must also be sensitive to how our choice of words might offend others. But we must not sanitize our language to the point where it clearly restricts our clarity of communications. Unfortunately, there's no simple solution to this dilemma. Effective communications, in whatever format, however, requires us to be aware of the trade-offs and to find a proper balance in our choice of words.

of these items throughout the text, there are still a few that warrant exposure. Specifically, in this chapter we want to focus on HRM's role in the communications process, look at the purpose of employee handbooks and newsletters, and close with a discussion of suggestion systems/complaint procedures that exist in companies. Let's now turn our attention to the specifics surrounding effective HRM communications programs.

What Is the Purpose of HRM Communications?

Human resource management communications programs are designed to keep employees abreast of what is happening in the organization, and knowledgeable of the policies and procedures affecting them. Whereas public relations departments are created to keep the public informed of what an organization does, HRM communications focus on the internal constituents—the employees.[10] As we mentioned in Chapter 2, regarding the role of the employee relations department in the maintenance function, communication programs serve as a basis for increasing employee loyalty and commitment. How? By building into the corporate culture a systematic means through which information is free-flowing, timely, and accurate, employees are better able to perceive that the organization values them.[11] Such a system builds trust and openness among organizational members, even assisting the sharing of "bad news."

HRM communications programs are designed to keep employees informed of organizational events, and knowledgeable of the policies affecting them.

HRM communications has the ability to bring about many positive changes in an organization. This process, by whatever means it exists, should stay focused on keeping employees informed, thereby setting the stage for enhancing employee satisfaction.[12] For employees at Challenger Electrical Equipment Corporation in Allentown, Pennsylvania, it took a union-organizing campaign before company managers realized that employees were dissatisfied with the information they had (or hadn't) been getting.[13] With this in mind, let's look at some fundamental requirements for an effective HRM communications program (see Exhibit 14-1).

Guidelines for Supporting Communications Programs

Building effective HRM communications programs involves a few fundamental elements. These include top management commitment, effective upward communication, determining what is to be communicated, allowing for feedback, and information sources. Let's look at each of these.

Top Management Commitment   Before any organization can develop and implement an internal organizational communications program, it must have the backing, support, and "blessing" of the CEO. Any activity designed to facilitate work environments must be seen by employees as being endorsed by the company's top management. In doing so, these programs are given priority and are viewed as significant components of the corporate culture. Just as it is critical for employees to see top management supporting communications, so, too, is it for them to see communications effectively operating at all levels. Effective communications does not just imply that top management sends information down throughout the company. It also implies that information flows upward as well and laterally to other areas in the organization.[14]

Effective Upward Communication   The upward flow of communication is particularly noteworthy because it is often the employees, the ones closest to the work, who may have vital information that top management should know. For instance, let's take a situation that occurs in HRM. We've recognized the ever-changing nature of this field. Legislation at any level—federal, state, or local—may add new HRM requirements for the organization. Unless top management is made aware of the implications of these requirements—like knowing how to ensure that sexual harassment charges are thoroughly investigated—severe repercussions could occur. Thus, that information must filter up in the company.

EXHIBIT 14-1
Components of Effective HRM Communication

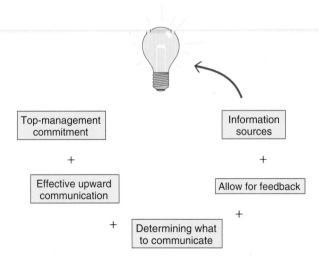

A similar point could easily be made for any part of an organization. And in keeping with the spirit of employee empowerment,[15] as employees are more involved in making decisions that affect them, that information must be communicated up the ladder. Furthermore, it's important for top management to monitor the pulse of the organization regarding how employees view working for the company. Whether that information is obtained from walking around the premises, through formal employee suggestions, or through employee satisfaction/morale surveys, such information is crucial. In fact, on the latter point, with the advances in technology, some of the employee satisfaction measures can be captured in almost real time. At IBM, for instance, such surveys are *on line*, making them easier for the employees to use, more expedient in their analysis, and more timely for company use.

Determining What to Communicate At the extreme, if every piece of information that exists in our organizations were communicated, no work would ever get done; people would be spending their entire days on information overload. Employees, while wanting to be informed, generally are not concerned with every piece of information, like who just retired, or was promoted, or what community group was given a donation yesterday. Rather, employees need *pertinent* information—addressing those things employees should know to do their jobs. This typically includes where the business is going (strategic goals), current sales/service/production outcomes, new product or service lines, and human resource policy changes.

One means of determining what to communicate is through a "what-if, so-what" test. When deciding the priority of the information to be shared, HR managers should ask themselves: What if this information is not shared? (See Ethical Issues in HRM.) Will employees be able to do their jobs as well as if it were shared? Will they be disadvantaged in some way by not knowing? If the answers show that employees will not be affected one way or the other, then that may not be a priority item. And then, the so-what test: Will employees care about the information? Or will they see it as an overload of meaningless information? If the latter is the case, then that, too, is not priority information. That's not to say this information may never be exchanged; it only means that it's not important for employees to get the information immediately.

Should HRM make it a priority to immediately communicate health insurance premium changes to its employees during its open-enrollment period? Following the what-if, so-what test, they should. That's because such a change will affect each of these employees' take-home pay. Accordingly, delaying any announcement about health insurance premium changes might have negative consequences for employee morale and productivity.

To illustrate these decision guidelines, let's consider we have two pieces of information to share. One item is that the company's health insurance premiums are significantly changing—which means that employees' payroll deductions for health insurance premiums will increase nearly 25 percent. Would this meet our what-if, so-what test? What if we didn't communicate this in a timely fashion? Would the employees be affected? You bet! When they received their first paycheck with the new deductions taken out, you'd have some inquisitive, if not upset employees. But contrast a benefit-cost change with information regarding the company officials installing a firewall security system to protect the organization's computer network from being hacked. Will employees be adversely affected if the information is delayed a day or a week? Probably not! But this delaying of information must be considered on an individual basis—that is, while many employees may not need the immediate information on security mechanisms, certain areas of the company, like management information systems and systems maintenance, would find it a necessity. Accordingly, they would need the information immediately.

Allowing for Feedback   We cannot assume that our communication efforts are achieving their goals. Consequently, we must develop into the system a means of assessing the flow of information and for fostering employee feedback. How that information is generated may differ from organization to organization. For some, it may be a casual word-of-mouth assessment. Others may use employee surveys to capture the data, or provide a suggestion box where comments can be given. For others, there is a formalized and systematic communications audit program.

Irrespective of how that information is gathered, employees must be involved. Otherwise, not only will measurement of the effectiveness of the communications program be difficult, but you may also give the perception that employee commitment is unnecessary.

Information Sources   HRM communications should serve as a conduit in promoting effective communications throughout the organization. Although HRM plays an important role in bringing this to fruition, they are not the only, or the main, source of information. For that, we have to turn to one's immediate supervisor. If successful programs can be linked to the immediate supervisor, then HRM must ensure that these individuals are trained in how to communicate properly. Even our health insurance premium change cited above, if implemented, would likely result in a number of questions for one's supervisor. Thus, HRM must make every effort to empower these supervisors with accurate data to deal with the "frontline" questions.[16] From an HRM point of view, where is information best conveyed? Although the sources for this information may be varied, there is one medium that is central to providing information to employees: the employee handbook.[17]

A GUIDE FOR EMPLOYEES: THE EMPLOYEE HANDBOOK

During the orientation of new employees, we inform them of a number of important facts regarding employment in the organization. But we must recognize that stating this information once isn't enough. There's often too much for the employee to absorb, especially during the excitement of the first day on the job. Consequently, a permanent reference guide is needed. This reference guide for employees is called the *employee handbook*.

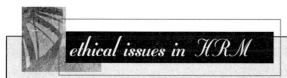

COMPLETE INFORMATION

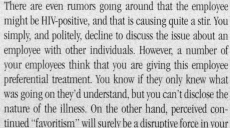

EFFECTIVE COMMUNICATIONS IN ORGANIZATIONS IS BUILT on the premise that appropriate and accurate information must be conveyed. Organization members should be afforded the respect and dignity that factual information can deliver. But at what point is it best to withhold information from employees?

We've addressed a so-what test—if it really matters to individuals, the information should be conveyed. But reality tells us that even factual information can, at times, be difficult to deliver, and may best be withheld for a number of reasons. For example, confidentiality is a must in matters that personally affect employees. Assume, then, that you have just been informed by one of your employees that he has non-Hodgkin's lymphoma, a treatable form of lymph-node cancer. Consequently, he may be absent frequently at times, especially during his chemotherapy treatments. Yet, he doesn't anticipate his attendance to be a problem, nor will it directly affect his work. After all, many of his duties involve direct computer work, so he can work at home and forward the data electronically to the appropriate people.

On several occasions, the employee has either called in sick or has had to leave early because he felt ill. Your employees are beginning to suspect something is wrong and have come to you to find out what is wrong. There are even rumors going around that the employee might be HIV-positive, and that is causing quite a stir. You simply, and politely, decline to discuss the issue about an employee with other individuals. However, a number of your employees think that you are giving this employee preferential treatment. You know if they only knew what was going on they'd understand, but you can't disclose the nature of the illness. On the other hand, perceived continued "favoritism" will surely be a disruptive force in your department. You are stumped. What do you do? Should employees be given the whole story? What if it is having an effect on their work? What's your opinion?

The Purpose of an Employee Handbook

Employee Handbook   A booklet describing the important aspects of employment an employee needs to know.

An **employee handbook** is a tool that, when developed properly, serves both employees and the employer. For employees, a well-designed handbook provides a central information source that conveys such useful information as what the company is about, its history, and employee benefits. The handbook, then, gives employees an opportunity to learn about the company and what the company provides for them—in a way that permits each employee an opportunity to understand the information at his or her own pace. By having this resource available, questions that may arise over such benefits as vacation accrual, matching contributions, and vesting can be more easily answered.[18] Serving as an easy reference guide, the employee handbook can be used by employees whenever it is warranted. Beyond just being a source of information, employee handbooks also generate some other benefits. Where they exist, it has been found that they assist in creating an atmosphere in which employees become more productive members of the organization, and increase their commitment and loyalty to the organization.[19] By being thorough in its coverage, an employee handbook will address various HRM policies and work rules, which set the parameters within which employees are expected to perform.[20] For example, the handbook may express information on discipline and discharge procedures and a means of redressing disciplinary action should the employee feel that it was administered unfairly. The handbook, then, serves to ensure that any HRM policy will be fair, equitable, and consistently applied.[21]

The handbook serves to ensure that any HRM policy will be fair, equitable, and consistently applied.

Employers, too, can benefit from using an employee handbook. In addition to any benefits accrued from having a more committed and loyal work force, handbooks can also be used in the recruiting effort. Remember, we advocated the use of realistic job previews for helping to sell recruits on the organization;

a well-written employee handbook, shown to an applicant, can be useful in providing some of the necessary information an applicant may be seeking. Although employee handbooks are designed to "educate, inform, and guide" employees in the organization, a word of caution is in order. In Chapter 4, in our discussion of employee rights and employment-at-will, we addressed the issue of implied contracts. Recall that an implied contract is anything expressed, verbally or in writing, that may be perceived by the individual to mean that she or he can't be terminated. For example, telling an employee that as long as her performance is satisfactory, she will have a job until retirement, could be construed as an implied contract. Over the years, the courts have ruled that various statements made in employee handbooks may be binding on the company. To prevent this from occurring, many legal advocates and HRM researchers recommend a careful choice of words in the handbook, and a disclaimer.[22] We have reproduced a disclaimer from one business in Exhibit 14-2.

Before we move into the specific components of a handbook, there is one other important aspect for management to consider. That is, an employee handbook is of little use if employees don't read it. To facilitate that goal, we recommend that, first of all, the handbook should be pertinent to employees' needs. Providing information that is viewed as unnecessary, or having a handbook that contains unclear wording or excessive verbiage, may diminish meeting this goal. Consequently, employers should, through feedback mechanisms, assess how employees perceive the usefulness of employee handbook information, gather their input, and make modifications where necessary. HRM should not assume that once developed and disseminated to employees, the employee handbook is final. Rather, it should be viewed as something to be updated and refined on a continuous basis. Contemporary employers are finding that putting the employee handbook on the company's intranet is an effective way of making the materials available to employees.[23] Updates, too, can be handled expeditiously. But an intranet is not the only way. The traditional loose-leaf binder system is still functional and readily allows for corrections/updates/additions.

As a second requirement, it is recommended that the handbook be well organized to make it easy to find the needed information. Just as this book has a table of contents and an index to help you find specific information more quickly, so too should the employee handbook. HRM must remember that the handbook will be helpful to employees, and it must do whatever possible to make it easy to use. To assist in achieving this goal, we have summarized some suggestions for employee handbooks in Exhibit 14-3.

Contents of an Employee Handbook

Although there are no right or wrong ways of putting together the contents of an employee handbook, we suggest the following format. As a means of facilitating this discussion, we will present an outline from an actual employee handbook (see Exhibit 14-4). Let's look at these components.

EXHIBIT 14-2
A Sample Employee Handbook Disclaimer

This handbook is not a contract, expressed or implied, guaranteeing employmet for any specific duration. Although [the company] hopes that your employment relationship with us will be long-term, either you or the company may terminate this relationship at any time, for any reason, with or without cause or notice.

EXHIBIT 14-3
Suggestions for an Employee Handbook

A well-designed, well-written employee handbook should convey such information as:

1. **What the organization expects from its employees.** Employees need to be informed of company policies. This includes such items as work hours, employee conduct, performance evaluations, disciplinary process, moonlighting, vacations, holiday, and sick and personal leave usage.
2. **What the employee can expect from the ogranization.** What benefits does the employee receive? These should be detailed enough such that the employee fully understands the "fringes" of the job. The company's HRM policies regarding salary increase, promotions, and so on, also need to be conveyed.
3. **The history of the organization.** The history section provides an opportunity to help employees understand where the organization has been and where it is heading. This section also includes the philosophy/culture of the ogranization.
4. **A glossary section.** Words have different meanings to different people and may differ depending on the context used. To eliminate confusion, the terms used in the handbook should be defined.

Source: Adapted from "The (Handbook) Handbook: A Guide to Writing the Perfect Manual for Employees You Care About," *Inc,* (November 1993), pp. 60–61.

Introductory Comments   In this section, the company conveys introductory information to the employees. Carroll Tree Service begins by having its top management send a letter of greetings to the employees, welcoming them into the organization. The purpose of this letter is to describe to employees what the company is about, its mission and goals. Furthermore, the company conveys to its employees the corporate value of customer satisfaction, and how by achieving that goal the firm can provide those things that employees may desire (e.g., job security, pay increases, better benefits).

These introductory remarks also tell new employees that they are valuable assets to the organization. By making employees feel important, and letting them know the roles they play and what the company will do to help them grow as employees, the organization fosters an environment where effective worker performance and loyalty and commitment can be realized. There is often a final component to this introductory section, that is, a brief history of the organization. Although not all employees will value this information, it does provide them with a better understanding of how the company progressed to its current state.[24]

What You Should Know   This section is designed to inform all employees of the rules and policies regarding employment in the company. Those items of importance to employees, such as attendance, work hours, and so forth, are presented so that there is no misunderstanding by employees. For example, in this company, specific information regarding the length of one's lunch period, paydays, work hours, and how employees will be evaluated is laid out in such clear terms that confusion is avoided.

In Chapter 10, on performance appraisals, we discussed the need for managers to explicitly state what is required of employees. If, for example, you expect employees on the job by 8 A.M., tell them so, and hold employees accountable for being on time. The handbook, then, reinforces those work behaviors a company expects of its employees.

EXHIBIT 14-4
Sample Employee Handbook Table of Contents

(Effective February 2000—Carroll Tree Service)

Your Benefits No matter how much value we place on the introductory remarks of any employee handbook, the section on employee benefits is probably the most widely read and perceived as most important by employees. This section should thoroughly explain the benefits employees receive, when they are eligible (if not immediately), and what, if any, costs the employee might incur. As we explained in Chapter 12 on employee benefits, although these benefits are membership-based, they are important to keep employee morale high. Therefore, we must make every effort to convey the full slate of benefits to employees in such a manner that they know what they have and how they can use them.

Your Responsibility and Safety Procedures   Just as employers are responsible for creating a safe and healthy workplace, workers must also do their part. Accordingly, this section of Carroll Tree's handbook provides information regarding company policies on reporting accidents, alcohol and substance abuse, and personal conduct, among others, explained in such terms that employees know what compliance requires. Furthermore, failure to comply with these policies and subsequent outcomes is thoroughly explained.

Other Vehicles for Employee Communications

In the spirit of finding various ways to ensure that communication takes place, there are a number of other means available besides the employee handbook. The following sections discuss the four most popular means: the bulletin board, company newsletter, company-wide meetings, and digital media. Of course, which one works best for any group of employees will depend on such factors as what the employees prefer, the organization culture, and the employees' access to technology.

Bulletin Board   A means a company uses to post information of interest to its employees.

Bulletin Board   A **bulletin board** in any organization serves several purposes in communicating with employees. Bulletin boards are generally centrally located in the organization where a majority of employees will have exposure to it. For many, these bulletin boards are found near company cafeterias (if they exist) or by the main entrance.

 The information posted on a bulletin board will vary among organizations. Job postings, upcoming company-sponsored events, new HRM policies, and the like may be posted in this highly visible location to help "get the information out." Furthermore, if employees know that important information is placed on these boards, they will be more inclined to examine them periodically. Bulletin boards also can be used for activities other than employer-related business. For instance, some organizations permit employees to post information for other employees to see—like advertising personal belongings for sale, or promoting a charitable event an employee is associated with. Although the information employees place on the bulletin board is given great latitude, most organizations require such information to have HRM approval before it is posted. By following this procedure, inappropriate or offensive information can be eliminated before any problems arise.

Company Newsletter   A means of providing information for employees in a specific recurring periodical.

Company Newsletter   The **company newsletter** or newspaper is designed to provide sound internal communication to employees regarding important information they need to know, activities happening in the organization, and anything else of interest. Just as a town's daily newspaper discusses current events, sports, and human-interest stories, so too should the company newsletter. Company newsletters provide employees with a permanent record they can keep and refer to at some future time. Furthermore, some information, like technical and detailed information, may be better communicated in this written format.

 While there is no definitive design for company newsletters, they should focus attention on activities of concern to employees of the company, problems the company may be experiencing, successes the company has enjoyed, updates on newsworthy company items (such as company-sponsored sporting events and United Way campaigns), and stories about employees (those receiving awards, recognition, retiring, etc.). Company newsletters also can be enhanced with sections devoted to questions raised by employees and answered by someone in management, and by having employees write articles. Finally, those organizations that have effective newsletters have found that they have improved employee morale.[25]

Company-Wide Meetings

Every so often, there is a need to inform all employees at once in a face-to-face encounter. Should an organization be facing a merger, going into a new product line, or changing its culture, for example, it may be useful for the CEO (or someone from senior management) to address all employees en masse. In doing so, the CEO can add emphasis to this new direction, while simultaneously answering questions and addressing concerns.

One of the most notable uses of this "town meeting" was the company-wide session held by former GM Chairman Robert Stemple. Faced with pending layoffs and restructuring, Stemple, through electronic hookups, was able to send his message to all GM employees at once, wherever the plant was located. The success of this method has been periodically repeated at GM.

In addition to opening up the channels of communications for employees, **company-wide meetings** permit all employees to have the same information at once. This, for many operations, reduces the grapevine rumors that may occur, especially when the company is facing difficult times.

The Digital Media

Technology has served organizational communications well. Whether it be the Internet, an intranet (similar to the Internet but confined solely to an organization's network), an interactive video, or having access to e-mail, technology is enhancing the effectiveness of communications.[26] And this technology is no more noteworthy than in HRM. Whenever a company wishes to provide employees with up-to-date, even real-time information regarding their pay and benefits, nothing serves that purpose better than the **digital media**.[27] Workers also can use this system to "obtain financial projections regarding future income and retirement benefits, as well as getting information on upcoming train-

Company-wide Meetings Frequently held meetings used to inform employees of various company issues.

Digital Media A form of communications that relies heavily on technology.

Digital media make it possible for employees of an organization to have instant access to employee handbook materials. By placing the information on the organization's intranet, employees can readily access a variety of policies and information sources that directly affect them. In this example, employees of Towson University can use the intranet to access a variety of HR matters.

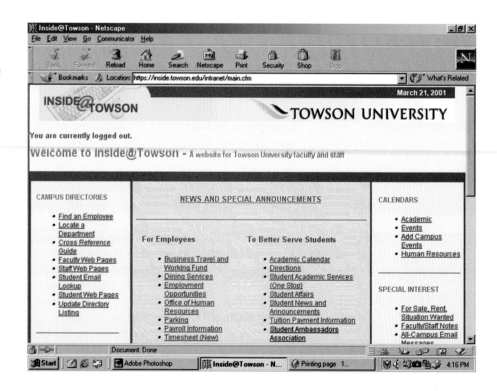

ing and development workshops."[28] Through computers, flexible benefits programs can also be better implemented, giving employees opportunities to examine what is offered to find what will best serve them.[29] Such computerized systems can be used to provide employees with personalized benefits statements. Not only do these statements provide employees information on their selections, they also reinforce the "hidden pay" they are receiving.

COMMUNICATIONS AND THE OFF-SITE EMPLOYEE

Communications in many of today's contemporary organizations no longer follow the traditional downward or upward flows so typical of hierarchical organizations. Instead, as our work changes, as well as our work force, communication mechanisms, too, must adapt. As we described in Chapter 1, one business trend today is the movement to the off-site worker. Worker needs, coupled with technology advancements, have enabled some workers to work at home. How, then, can effective communications be fostered with off-site employees? The answer typically lies in the technology that has become routine today—facsimile (fax) machines, the Internet, and e-mail (see Exhibit 14-5).

With the use of home computer systems, employees can remain in close contact with their employers, even though they are miles away. For instance, wired and wireless digital data access can be used to receive and transmit data to mainframe computers at a company location. Data downloaded to an employee can be properly manipulated, and sent back to the organization in their final form. Where electronic wires won't do, fax machines can send documents in hard copy formats almost instantaneously to anywhere in the world. E-mail allows written messages to be sent between parties that have computers that are linked together with an appropriate software. They are fast, cheap, and permit the reader to retrieve the message at his or her convenience. And let's not forget the old standby, the telephone. It has been around for decades and is still an effective way to communicate with employees.

We know that communication to our employees is important, in whatever form, but there still remains one final aspect to be addressed: Is there a mechanism in the organization that allows employees to raise their concerns? In the next section, we'll briefly look at employee complaint and suggestion systems.

EXHIBIT 14-5
Electronic Mail

Source: Scott Adams, United Feature Syndicate, Inc. 12/11/95. Used with permission.

MECHANISMS FOR EFFECTIVE UPWARD COMMUNICATIONS

Any communications system operating in an organization will only be effective if it permits information to flow upward. For HRM, enabling this process revolves around two central themes—complaint procedures and a suggestion system.

The Complaint Procedure

Complaint Procedure A formalized procedure in an organization through which an employee seeks resolution of a work problem.

An organization's **complaint procedure** is designed to permit employees to question actions that have occurred in the company and to seek the company's assistance in correcting the problem. For example, if the employee feels her boss has inappropriately evaluated her performance, or believes the behavior of the boss to be counterproductive, a complaint process allows for that information to be heard. That's important to do if for no other reason than to keep disgruntled employees from venting their complaints about the organization on the Internet.[30]

Typically under the direction of employee-relations specialists, complaints are investigated, and decisions regarding the validity of the alleged wrongdoings are made.

Complaint procedures implemented in nonunionized organizations are called by a variety of titles. Irrespective of their names, most follow a set pattern; that is, given the structure of HRM laid out in Chapter 2, a nonunionized complaint procedure may consist of the following:

1. *Employee–supervisor.* This is generally regarded as the initial step to resolve an employee problem. Here, the employee tries to address the issue with her supervisor, seeking some resolution. If the issue is resolved here, nothing further need be done. Accordingly, this is considered an informal step in the process. Furthermore, depending on the problem, this step may be skipped altogether, should the employee fear retaliation from the supervisor.

2. *Employee–employer relations.* Not getting the satisfaction desired in Step 1, the employee then proceeds to file the complaint with the employee-relations representative. As part of his or her job, the ER representative investigates the matter, including gathering information from both parties, and makes a recommendation for resolution. Although this is the first formal step, the employee may continue upward, should the recommended solution be unsatisfactory to the employee.

3. *Employee–department head.* If employee relations fails to correct the problem, or if the employee wishes to further exercise her rights, the next step in the complaint procedure is to meet with the manager of the area. Once again, an investigation will take place and a decision rendered. It is important to note, however, that if employee relations found no validity in the individual's charge, they are not responsible for providing continued assistance to the employee.

4. *Employee–president.* The final step in the process involves taking the issue to the president. Generally, although employee rights may be protected under various state laws, the president's decision is final.

Inasmuch as this is a generic portrayal of a complaint process, it is important to recognize that this serves as the foundation of an internal complaint procedure. We have graphically portrayed these steps in Exhibit 14-6. Keep in mind that in actuality, more levels of management could be included in the picture. In

EXHIBIT 14-6
*A Sample Complaint
Procedure in a Nonunionized
Work Environment*

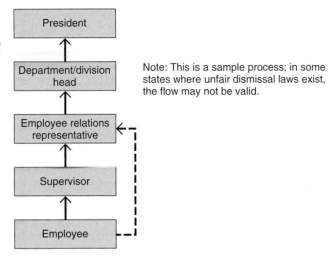

Note: This is a sample process; in some states where unfair dismissal laws exist, the flow may not be valid.

either case, however, employees must be notified that this is how the company will resolve employee complaints. And this communication should occur initially during orientation, appear in employee handbooks, and be posted throughout the company.

Finally, we mentioned that this process is generally useful in nonunionized settings. Why is it not in a unionized company? The answer to that question lies in the various labor laws that are unique to labor-management relationships. Although there is a complaint procedure, called a *grievance procedure,* its uniqueness requires us to discuss it as part of the *collective bargaining process* (Chapter 15).

The Suggestion Program

Suggestion Program A process whereby employees have the opportunity to tell management how they perceive the organization is doing.

Similar to the complaint procedure, a **suggestion program** is designed to allow employees opportunities to tell management what it is doing inefficiently and what the company should do from an employee's point of view. That is, sug-

How do organizations like the Dana Company promote innovation, creativity, and enhanced productivity? Many of them have found employee suggestion programs quite useful. Whether formalized like they are at Dana, or handled informally, most suggestion programs provide a financial reward for employees who nominate cost-saving ideas.

HANDLING WORKER CONFLICTS

IN A PERFECT WORKPLACE THERE WOULD be no conflict, just happy people with no hidden agendas, no difference in opinion, values, work ethic, wants, or needs. No finger pointing, blaming, misunderstanding, or gossiping would occur. No one would question or criticize their boss, coworkers, company, decisions, or changes—just happy little workers exceeding expectations. Noncommunicative, hostile, negative, judgmental, uncooperative people would always work somewhere else, not in your company.

How many job descriptions have you ever read that made "getting along" or "service" a requirement? Attitude may show up on the performance appraisal, but it's hard to change attitudes once or twice a year. Why shouldn't "getting along" be a job requirement? Maybe "adult behavior" won't likely be added to the next revised performance appraisal, but we can emphasize the importance of maintaining acceptable standards of cooperation and civility to reduce some conflict.

When conflicts affect performance, morale, or teamwork, they are no longer just the problems of those involved; they become the manager's problem too. As uncomfortable as such squabbling or politicking makes us, conflict resolution is a tough job, but somebody has got to do it. Conflict is normal; it's inevitable. How many courses have you taken in college that helped you deal with conflict or even address feelings? Maybe Psychology 101 or Introductory Sociology? But that clearly isn't enough.

Now more than any time in history we must not only get along with our fellow employees, we must work in the most collaborative, professional manner possible to achieve more, with fewer people and resources. Survival in this competitive environment demands unparalleled service, innovation, and quality achieved through teamwork and communication. It means putting the goals, issues, and needs of our employing organizations above our own agendas; getting along with people that we may not even like, understand, or respect; focusing on what we get paid to do; achieving the goals and objectives of our organization in the most responsive, professional manner possible. We're paid not just to deliver on time, error-free goods and services, we're also paid to respect differences, to not allow our emotions to get in the way of what's best for the company, and to honor a fellow employee's self-respect and dignity, even when we differ in values, methods, or purpose.

It's hard not to lose our tempers at times, to address a person's behavior and not their personality, to seek win-win resolutions when we find it difficult to find points of agreement, especially when we know we're right, and of course, they're wrong. Most of us could stand to learn or improve our conflict-resolution skills. If we must deal with feuding coworkers, let's try one or more of the following suggestions:

- Let them vent. Listen to each party separately without taking sides until you have both perceptions and all the facts. Just listen. You may find it helpful to ask each to write their perception of the situation down and give it to you before you meet with them to compare perceptions of both parties involved. We have worked with clients whose written descriptions of the same situation were so different it was hard to imagine it could have occurred at the same company.

  - Separate them, if needed or possible, initially from meetings or projects to allow cool-down time and to minimize damage.
  - Ask them for their perception or description of the situation, what they think, how they feel, what impact the current situation has on them, their projects, department, and so on. Ask *who, what, when, where, why,* and *how* questions. For example, what they think is the cause, who is affected or contributes to the situation, when it occurs, how often, why it occurred, etc. Most importantly, involve the parties in the resolution, ask them what they think could resolve it, what they are willing to do to bring the resolution about. Then hold them accountable for following through the resolution.

- Create a teaching moment on how to improve or prevent the situation from occurring. If others need to be included in sharing the resolution, do so, without blaming or name calling. Consider it a growth opportunity.

- Reinforce and recognize the positive efforts of the parties as they improve the situation. Nothing stays the same, and this conflict may be that golden opportunity to shake the status quo, to build rapport and ultimately morale, relations, and end results. Understanding breeds acceptance and confidence, not only in feuding parties, but in those of us who foster such resolutions.

gestion programs give employees the chance to tell management what they are doing right and what they are doing wrong.[31] In many companies, in conjunction with continuous improvement processes and employee involvement, management welcomes such suggestions.[32] In fact, as we discussed in Chapter 10, companies such as Lincoln Electric, and those that use plans such as Scanlon or IMPROSHARE, actually provide cash rewards to employees for suggestions that are implemented. The same holds true at the Dana Company, where more than 650,000 suggestions are received each year from its 45,000 employees. And more than 70 percent of the suggestions are accepted—saving the company hundreds of thousands of dollars.[33]

Although employees value the "reward," the most important aspect of a suggestion program is for individuals to witness management action.[34] That is, whether the suggestion is useful or not, employers must recognize employees submitting suggestions and inform them of their outcome.[35] Even if the idea wasn't appropriate for the company, employees still should be told what management's decision was. Failure to do so will more than likely decrease employees' willingness to make suggestions. And if the suggestion is good, in the spirit of employee communication, not only should they be rewarded, but their input should be recognized on the company's intranet[36] or in the company's next newsletter![37]

Suggestion programs give employees the chance to tell management what they are doing right and what they are doing wrong.

HRM WORKSHOP

Summary

(This summary relates to the Learning Outcomes identified on p. 390.)
After having read this chapter, you should be able to:

1. **Explain how communication serves as the foundation for HRM activities.** Effective communication surrounds the effective operations in HRM activities in that it enables understanding to occur between the organization and its employees, assists in recruiting and selection, and specifies what activities must be performed to successfully do one's job. Effective communication also implies keeping employees informed of happenings in the organization.

2. **Identify the legally required communications with respect to benefit administration and safety and health.** Communications in benefits administration and health and safety is mandated by law. In benefits administration, employers must provide employees with a summary plan description. In health and safety, employees must be given information concerning exposure to hazardous and toxic materials.

3. **Describe the purpose of HRM communications programs.** Human resources management communications programs are designed to keep current employees abreast of events occurring in the organization, including the various policies and procedures that affect them.

4. **Discuss how corporate culture is affected by effective communication.** Effective communications can affect corporate culture in that open, frank discussions indicate a culture where employees are valued.

5. **State the role of the chief executive officer promoting communications programs.** The CEO of an organization is the one individual responsible for setting the foundation from which the culture is built. If this individual promotes and practices open communications, then that activity will filter down through the company.

6. **Specify what information employees should receive under an effective communications program.** A communications program should, at the minimum, inform employees what is expected of them, what they can expect from the company, and what the various personnel policies are.

7. **Describe the purpose of the employee handbook.** The employee handbook is a tool that provides one central source of organizational information for employees regarding the company and its HRM policies.

8. **Explain what information should be included in an employee handbook.** Although employee handbooks differ, most include introductory comments about the organization, and information about what employees need to know about the workplace, their benefits, and employee responsibility.

9. **List four popular communication methods used in organizations.** Four popular communications program vehicles include bulletin boards, company newsletters, company-wide meetings, and digital media (such as e-mail, Internet, and intranet).

10. **Discuss the critical components of an effective suggestion program.** A critical component of an organizational suggestion program is the recognition that employees' suggestions will be heard. Failure to pay attention to employees' suggestions may decrease the value of the program to them.

ACTIVE LISTENING

About the skill: Active listening requires you to concentrate on what is being said. It's more than just hearing the words. It involves a concerted effort to understand and interpret the speaker's message.

1. *Make eye contact.* How do you feel when somebody doesn't look at you when you're speaking? If you're like most people, you're likely to interpret this behavior as aloofness or disinterest. Making eye contact with the speaker focuses your attention, reduces the likelihood that you will become distracted, and encourages the speaker.

2. *Exhibit affirmative nods and appropriate facial expressions.* The effective listener shows interest in what is being said through nonverbal signals. Affirmative nods and appropriate facial expressions, when added to good eye contact, convey to the speaker that you're listening.[38]

3. *Avoid distracting actions or gestures that suggest boredom.* The other side of showing interest is avoiding actions that suggest that your mind is somewhere else. When listening, don't look at your watch, shuffle papers, play with your pencil, or engage in similar distractions. They make the speaker feel that you're bored or disinterested or indicate that you aren't fully attentive.

4. *Ask questions.* The critical listener analyzes what he or she hears and asks questions. This behavior provides clarification, ensures understanding, and assures the speaker that you're listening.

5. *Paraphrase using your own words.* The effective listener uses phrases such as: "What I hear you saying is . . . " or "Do you mean . . . ?" Paraphrasing is an excellent control device to check on whether you're listening carefully and to verify that what you heard is accurate.

6. *Avoid interrupting the speaker.* Let the speaker complete his or her thought before you try to respond. Don't try to second guess where the speaker's thoughts are going. When the speaker is finished, you'll know it.

7. *Don't overtalk.* Most of us would rather speak our own ideas than listen to what someone else says. Talking might be more fun and silence might be uncomfortable, but you can't talk and listen at the same time. The good listener recognizes this fact and doesn't overtalk.

8. *Make smooth transitions between the roles of speaker and listener.* The effective listener makes transitions smoothly from speaker to listener and back to speaker. From a listening perspective this means concentrating on what a speaker has to say and practicing not thinking about what you're going to say as soon as you get your chance.

Demonstrating Comprehension: *Questions for Review and Discussion*

1. How does effective communications permeate all HRM functions?
2. In what way does a senior company officer affect corporate communication?
3. What should an organization communicate to its employees?
4. How does the employee handbook serve as a communications vehicle?
5. What types of information should be covered in an employee handbook?
6. How does a company intranet assist in fostering open communication?
7. What must a suggestion program contain for employees to view it as enhancing communication? What type of standards or support from management could be helpful to ensure that suggestions are followed up in a consistent, timely manner?
8. If you were a human resource manager would you implement a suggestion system? Why or why not?
9. "Some information should be kept from employees. It either may be too sensitive or result in an uprising in the company." Do you agree or disagree with this statement? Defend you position.
10. "Suggestion programs can become too cumbersome. If a suggestion committee has to act on every suggestion, no matter how inappropriate it may be, time will be lost that could be spent on the better suggestions. As such, only the most appropriate employee suggestions should be studied, and the rest discarded." Do you agree or disagree with this statement? Discuss.

Case Application: *TEAM FUN!*

Kenny and Norton, the owners of TEAM FUN!, a sporting goods manufacturer and retailer, run into Tony, the Director of Human Resources in the GREEN, the golf supply area. Kenny starts, "I think we need an HR communications audit. Keith, over in Springfield, had one last year and made a bunch of changes."

Norton counters, "No we don't want that kind of audition. He said it changed the culture. We don't have any culture here. That's one of the best things about TEAM FUN! Besides, what would we want to change? You're just mad because your daughter, Gloria, and her kids moved back in with you after the divorce. We should have done a Bobby audit!"

Tony asks, "Why the sudden interest in employee handbooks?"

Kenny said, "Don't start with the handbook stuff again! I'm talking about Norton and me making a new video about TEAM FUN! Maybe hiring a professional to produce it. There's lots of Hollywood guys looking for work now."

Norton: "That's a dumb idea. We have the one from last Christmas. I figured you'd want to explain the website again."

Tony: "Actually, the website is a very effective communications tool. We can do an audit next quarter if you want, but I think that TEAM FUN! does an excellent job of HR communications. I'll put my intern on it and get back to you tomorrow."

Kenny and Norton watch Tony walk off. Kenny smiles, "I think he's starting to catch on."

Questions

As Tony's intern, address the following issues:

1. Is the TEAM FUN! culture consistent with the HR communications patterns? Explain.
2. How involved should Kenny and Norton be in communications programs? Why?
3. Outline some suggestions for new employee communications.
4. Put together a communications audit for the organization. Do they need it? Why or why not?

Working with a Team: *Listening Effectively*

The objective of this exercise is to show the importance of listening skills to successful interpersonal communications. Form teams by counting off by sizes. There should be a minimum of three students to a group and a maximum of seven per group.[39]

Each team has 30 minutes to address the following four questions. The teams should begin by brainstorming answers and then narrowing their selection to the three most significant answers for each of the questions posed below. Appoint one member of the team to transcribe the answers on the board and another to tell the class why the team selected these answers.

1. How do you know when a person is listening to you?
2. Describe a situation in which you exhibited outstanding listening behaviors. How did it influence the speaker's subsequent communications with you?
3. How do you know when a person is ignoring you?
4. Describe a situation in which you ignored someone. What impact did it have on that individual's subsequent communications with you?

ENHANCING YOUR WRITING SKILLS

1. Find five companies on the Internet whose primary purpose is helping employees in organizations to improve their interpersonal communication skills. In a two- to three-page writeup, identify each company, and describe the common characteristics, if any, you found in the programs these companies offer.

2. Compare and contrast how much information you believe can be transmitted effectively using (a) face-to-face communications; (b) e-mail; (c) the company bulletin board; and (d) company newsletters.

3. The Dean of your college has asked you to provide some ideas on how the college can obtain student feedback. Develop a two- to three-page report outlining a "student suggestion" program for the Dean. Include how you envision it being implemented in your discussion.

www.wiley.com/college/decenzo

ENDNOTES

1. "Kingston Technology Company, Inc., Company Backgrounder," Kingston Technology Company, 2001 (www.kingston.com); and "The (Handbook) Handbook: A Guide to Writing the Perfect Manual for Employees You Care About," *Inc.* (November 1993), pp. 63–64.

2. Mike Hofman, "Lost in the Translation," *Inc.* (May 2000), p. 161.

3. See, for example, Donna Fenn, "Personnel Best," *Inc.* (February 2000), pp. 74–83.

4. Mark Wysong, "HazCom on the Company Intranet," *Occupational Health & Safety* (July 2000), pp. 30–32.

5. See Jonathan A. Segal, "Cybertraps for HR," *HRMagazine* (June 2000), pp. 217–231.

6. Michelle Neely Martinez, "Break the Bad Attitude Habit," *HRMagazine* (July 1997), p. 55.

7. Jill Klobucar Logan, "Retention Tangibles and Intangibles," *Training & Development* (April 2000), pp. 48–50; and Karen M. Kroll, "By the Books," *Industry Week* (July 21, 1997), pp. 47–50.

8. Gillian Flynn, "Take Another Look at the Employee Handbook," *Workforce* (March 2000), p. 132.

9. See, for instance, Dennis C. Stevenson, "How to Avoid Employee Lawsuits," *Human Resource Professional* (September–October 2000), p. 17; and J. Leo, "Language in the Dumps," *U.S. News and World Report* (July 27, 1998), p. 16.

10. Martha Finney, "Will Fiery Headlines Make Your Firm's Morale Go Up in Smoke?," *HRMagazine* (July 1997), p. 95.

11. Lloyd Corder and Jerry Thompson, "Selling Change: HR or PR's Job?" *HR Focus* (February 1999), p. 13.

12. Mark C. Johike and Dale F. Duhan, "Supervisor Communication Practices and Service Job Outcomes," *Journal of Service Research* (November 2000), p. 154.

13. Commerce Clearing House, "Challenger Meets Employee Communication Challenge with Merit Plan," *Human Resources Management: Ideas and Trends* (April 13, 1994), p. 61.

14. See, for instance, Lin Grensing-Pophal, "Follow Me," *HRMagazine* (February 2000), pp. 36–41; and Paul Sanchez, "How to Craft Successful Employee Communication in the Information Age," *Communication World* (August–September 1999), pp. 9–15.

15. Mike Hoffman, "Breaking Up the Kitchen Cabinet," *Inc.* (January 30, 2001), pp. 101–102.

16. Samuel F. Del Brocco and Robert W. Sprague, "Getting Your Supervisors and Managers in the Right Team," *Employment Relations Today* (Autumn 2000), pp. 13–27.

17. See also Thomas C. Billet and Catherine Morris, "Surfing the High-Tech Wave: How Advanced Technology Improved Health Benefits Communications at ARCO," *Compensation and Benefits Management* (Spring 1999), pp. 64–68.

18. See, for instance, David L. Barrette, "What's New," *HRMagazine* (November 2000), pp. 185–188.

19. Ibid.

20. See, for example, Robert J. Nobile, "Leaving No Doubt About Employee Leaves," *Personnel* (May 1990), pp. 54–60.

21. Ibid.

22. Segal, "Cybertraps for HR," p. 221; and Jeffrey London, "Bring Your Employee Handbook into the Millennium," *HR Focus* (January 1999), p. 6.

23. Segal, "Cybertraps for HR," p. 217; "Virtual HR," *Business Europe* (March 8, 2000), p. 1; "The Payoffs of Self-Service HR Are Significant," *HR Focus* (January 2001), p. 10; and Diane L. Prucino and Charles M. Rice," "Point-and-Click Personnel Policies: State Laws May Affect Electronic Employee Handbooks," *Employment Relations Today* (Autumn 2000), p. 111.

24. Donna Fenn, "Communication: Tell It Like It Was," *Inc.* (January 1995), p. 95.

25. Betty Sosnin, "Corporate Newsletters Improve Employee Morale," *HRMagazine* (June 1996), pp. 106–110.

26. See, for example, Martha I. Finney, "Harness the Power Within," *HRMagazine* (January 1997), pp. 69–71.

27. "Workers Want Different Information on Web," *HR Focus* (June 1999), p. 5.

28. Ibid., p. 81.

29. "Technology Can Enhance Employee Communications, Help Attract and Retain Workers," *Employee Benefit Plan Review* (June 2000), pp. 24–28.

30. Thomas E. Weber, "Worried Your E-Mail May Offend the Boss? Just Check It for Chilis," *Wall Street Journal* (September 25, 2000), p. B-1; and Bill Leonard, "Cyberventing," *HRMagazine* (November 1999), pp. 34–39.

31. Erin S. Hendriks, "Do More Than Open Doors," *HRMagazine* (June 2000), p. 171.

32. See, for example, Phyllis Kane, "Two-Way Communication Fosters Greater Commitment," *HRMagazine* (October 1996), pp. 50–52.

33. Richard Teitelbaum, "How to Harness Gray Matter," *Fortune* (June 9, 1997), p. 168.

34. Ibid., p. 158.

35. Lin Grensing-Pophal, "Talk to Me," *HRMagazine* (March 2000), p. 66; and Dale K. DuPont, "Eureka! Tools for Encouraging Employee Suggestions," *HRMagazine* (September 1999), p. 134.

36. "Forging New Employee Relationships via E-HR," *HR Focus* (December 2000), p. 13.

37. See, for example, Dale K. DuPont, "Eureka! Tools for Encouraging Employee Suggestions," *HRMagazine* (September 1999), p. 134.

38. Dr. Pierre Mornell, "The Sounds of Silence," *Inc.* (February 2001), pp. 117–118.

39. Adapted from T. Clark, "Sharing the Importance of Attentive Listening Skills," *Journal of Management Education* (April 1999), pp. 216–223.

15

LABOR RELATIONS AND COLLECTIVE BARGAINING

LEARNING OUTCOMES

AFTER READING THIS CHAPTER, YOU WILL BE ABLE TO:

1. Define what is meant by the term *unions*.
2. Discuss what effect the Wagner and the Taft-Hartley Acts had on labor-management relations.
3. Identify the significance of Executive Orders 10988 and 11491, and the Civil Service Reform Act of 1978.
4. Describe the union-organizing process.
5. Describe the components of collective bargaining.
6. Identify the steps in the collective-bargaining process.
7. Explain the various types of union security arrangements.
8. Describe the role of a grievance procedure in collective bargaining.
9. Identify the various impasse-resolution techniques.
10. Discuss how sunshine laws affect public-sector collective bargaining.

One of the fundamental issues in labor-management relationships is that both sides will come to the bargaining table and negotiate. In fact, some labor laws mandate this, as they require both unions and management to negotiate in good faith. Good-faith bargaining requires both sides to willingly work toward a settlement. That is, their efforts must be viewed as having a positive influence on the process—toward the ultimate goal of reaching an agreement. But good-faith bargaining does not guarantee that this agreement will be reached. On the contrary, serious disagreements do arise at times, resulting in negotiations breaking off. That's all part of the process. We've witnessed this occurrence countless times over the decades—with truckers, newspaper personnel, airline pilots and flight attendants, communication workers, coal miners, and even professional athletes. Even though labor-management conflicts are nothing new, they don't have to happen. Individuals like Ford's vice chairman and chief labor negotiator, Peter J. Pestillo, have made it their goal to work through even the toughest of issues.

General Motors, for example, has a long history of conflict with the United Auto Workers (UAW) union. In the late 1990s, GM was paralyzed by a 54-day strike that cost the company more than $2 billion in after-tax profits. In contrast, Ford Motor Company has excellent relations with the UAW and hasn't had a strike since 1986. Why this difference? Many industry analysts point to one chief reason, Peter Pestillo.[1]

Most auto company labor negotiators are former factory managers, with advanced business degrees, who come from middle- to upper-class roots. Not Pestillo. The son of a union machinist, his first job after high school was in a ball-bearing company where he was a dues-paying member of the UAW. After graduating from college, he worked at General Electric and B.F. Goodrich while working his way through law school. At age 38, he came to Ford Motor Company to oversee its labor policy—activities he's still performing nearly a quarter-century later.

Pestillo stands out among auto executives because of his belief in cooperation with unions. He encourages factory managers to work closely with workers and union leaders. And he's forced out factory managers who couldn't. "In the old days, they were happy to make loads of union grievances and disciplinary actions to prove how tough they were," he says. "Now we measure how effective they are." Due in no small part to Pestillo, Ford plants are now among America's best. A recent survey found that Ford ran 4 of America's 10 most productive car factories and 7 of the 10 most productive light truck factories.

Pestillo has built close personal ties with key UAW officials. He likes them and they like him. The current president of the UAW, for example, considers Pestillo a friend with whom he enjoys drinking and playing golf. This close relationship has benefited Ford. The UAW traditionally negotiates a three-year agreement with one automaker and uses that as a reference point when negotiating with the others. For most of the past 20 years, the union has gone to Ford first because of its cooperative relationship. Pestillo then used this opportunity to negotiate deals that have cut Ford's costs and done little to help its rival, GM.

INTRODUCTION

Union Organization of workers, acting collectively, seeking to protect and promote their mutual interests through collective bargaining.

A **union** is an organization of workers, acting collectively, seeking to promote and protect its mutual interests through collective bargaining. However, before we can examine the activities surrounding the collective bargaining process, it is important to have an understanding of the laws that govern the labor-management process, what unions are, and how employees unionize. While it is true that just over 13 percent of the private sector work force is unionized, the successes and failures of organized labor's activities affect most segments of the work force in two important ways. First, since major industries in the United States—such as automobile, steel, and electrical manufacturers, as well as all branches of transportation—are unionized, unions have a major effect on some of the important sectors of the economy (see Exhibit 15-1). Second, gains made by unions often spill over into other, nonunionized sectors of the economy.[2] So, the wages, hours, and working conditions of nonunion employees at a Linden, New Jersey, lumberyard may be affected by collective bargaining between the United Auto Workers and General Motors at one of the latter's North American assembly plants.

For many managers, HRM practices in a unionized organization consist chiefly of following procedures and policies laid out in the labor contract. This labor contract was agreed to by both management and the labor union, stipulating, among other things, the wage rate, the hours of work, and the terms and conditions of employment for those covered by the negotiated agreement. Decisions about how to select and compensate employees,[3] employee benefits offered, procedures for overtime, and so forth are no longer unilateral prerogatives of management for jobs that fall under the unions' jurisdiction. Such decisions are generally made at the time the labor contract is negotiated.

The concept of labor relations, and the collective-bargaining process, may mean different things to different individuals depending on their experience, background, and so on. One means of providing some focus in these areas is to have an understanding of why people join unions, and the laws that serve as the foundation of labor-management relationships.

WHY DO EMPLOYEES JOIN UNIONS?

The reasons individuals join unions are as diverse as the people themselves. Just what are they seeking to gain when they join a union? The answer to this question varies with the individual and the union contract, but the following captures the most common reasons.

Higher Wages and Benefits

There are power and strength in numbers. As a result, unions sometimes are able to obtain higher wages and benefit packages for their members than employees would be able to negotiate individually.[4] One or two employees walking off the job over a wage dispute is unlikely to significantly affect most businesses, but hundreds of workers going out on strike can temporarily disrupt or even close down a company. Additionally, professional bargainers employed by the union may be able to negotiate more skillfully than any individual could on his or her own behalf.

EXHIBIT 15-1
Union Membership by Industry Concentrations

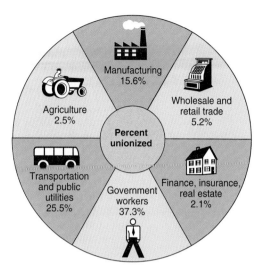

Source: Adapted from Bureau of Labor Statistics, "Union Affiliation of Employed Wage and Salary Workers by Occupation and Industry," *Union Members Survey* (January 18, 2001), Table 3.

Greater Job Security

Unions provide their members with a sense of independence from management's power to arbitrarily hire, promote, or fire.[5] The collective bargaining contract will stipulate rules that apply to all members, thus providing fairer and more uniform treatment. For example, after a lengthy strike involving the Teamsters Union and the Giant Food Company, an agreement was reached between the parties that guarantees Teamsters' union members lifelong job security—regardless of external factors affecting the company.

Influence Work Rules

Where a union exists, workers are provided with an opportunity to participate in determining the conditions under which they work, and an effective channel through which they can protest conditions they believe are unfair. Therefore, a union is not only a representative of the worker but also provides rules that define channels in which complaints and concerns of workers can be registered. Grievance procedures and rights to third-party arbitration of disputes are examples of practices that are typically defined and regulated as a result of union efforts.

Compulsory Membership

Union Security Arrangements Labor contract provisions designed to attract and retain dues-paying union members.

Many labor agreements contain statements that are commonly referred to as **union security arrangements.** When one considers the importance of security arrangements to unions—importance brought about in terms of numbers and guaranteed income—it is no wonder that such emphasis is placed on achieving a union security arrangement that best suits their goals. Such arrangements range from compulsory membership in the union to giving employees the freedom in choosing to join the union.[6] The various types of union security arrangements— the union shop, the agency shop, and the right-to-work shop, as well as some special provisions under the realm of union security arrangements—are briefly discussed below and summarized in Exhibit 15-2.

EXHIBIT 15-2
Union Security and Related
Provisions

Union Shop	The strongest of the union security arrangements. Union shops make union membership compulsory. After a given period of time, typically 30 days, a new employee must join the union or be terminated. A union shop guarantees the union that dues-paying members will become part of the union. In a right-to-work state, union shops are illegal.
Agency Shop	The second strongest union security arrangement, the agency shop, gives workers the option of joining the union or not. As such, membership is not compulsory. However, because the "gains" that are made at negotiations will benefit those not joining the union, all workers in the unit must pay union dues. However, Supreme Court decisions dictate that those individuals not members of the union, who still pay dues, have the right to have their monies used solely for collective-bargaining purposes. Like the union shop, the agency shop, too, is illegal in a right-to-work state.
Open Shop	The weakest form of a union security arrangement is the open shop. In an open shop, workers are free to join a union. If they do, they must stay in the union for the duration of the contract—and pay their dues. Those who do not wish to join the union are not required to do so—and thus pay no dues. In an open-shop arrangement, there is an escape clause at the expiration (typically two weeks) in which an individual may "quit" the union. The open shop is based on the premise of freedom of choice and is the only union security arrangement permitted under right-to-work legislation.
Maintenance of Membership	Because unions need to be able to administer their operations, in an open shop, once someone joins the union, they must maintain their union affiliation, and pay their dues, for the duration of the contract. At the end of the contract, an escape period exists in which those desiring to leave the union may do so.
Dues Checkoff	Dues checkoff involves the employer deducting union dues directly from a union member's paycheck. Under this provision, the employer collects the union dues and forwards a check to the union treasurer. Generally management does not charge an administrative fee for this service.

Union Shop Employers can hire nonunion workers, but they must become dues-paying members within a prescribed period of time.

The most powerful relationship legally available (except in right-to-work states[7]) to a union is a **union shop**. This arrangement stipulates that employers, while free to hire whomever they choose, may retain only union members. That is, all employees hired into positions covered under the terms of a collective-bargaining agreement must, after a specified probationary period of typically 30 to 60 days, join the union or forfeit their jobs.[8]

An agreement that requires nonunion employees to pay the union a sum of money equal to union fees and dues as a condition of continuing employment is

Agency Shop   A type of union security arrangement whereby employees must pay union dues to the certified bargaining unit even if they choose not to join the union.

Under a union shop arrangement, all employees in the bargaining unit must join the union or forfeit their jobs.

Open Shop   Employees are free to choose whether or not to join the union, and those who do not are not required to pay union dues.

Maintenance of Membership: If an individual chooses to join a union, that individual must remain in the union for the duration of the existing contract.

Dues Checkoff   Employer withholding of union dues from union members' paychecks.

referred to as an **agency shop.** This arrangement was designed as a compromise between the union's desire to eliminate the "free rider" and management's desire to make union membership voluntary. In such a case, if for whatever reason workers decide not to join the union (e.g., religious beliefs, values, etc.), they still must pay dues. Because workers will receive the benefits negotiated by the union, they must pay their fair share. However, a 1988 Supreme Court ruling upheld union members' claims that although they are forced to pay union dues, those dues must be specifically used for collective-bargaining purposes only—not for political lobbying.[9] In early 1992, President George Bush extended the same rights to federal-sector employees when he signed into law Executive Order 12800. Moreover, several states have adopted the Paycheck Protection Act, which requires unions "to get permission from each member before using a penny of his or her dues for political purposes."[10] In Washington State, the effect of this Act was quite evident as political use of union dues dropped from $40,000 in 1992 to $82 in 1996.[11]

The least desirable form of union security from a union perspective is the **open shop.** This is an arrangement in which joining a union is totally voluntary. Those who do not join are not required to pay union dues or any associated fees. For workers who do join, there is typically a maintenance of membership clause in the existing contract that dictates certain provisions. Specifically, a **maintenance of membership** agreement states that should employees join the union, they are compelled to remain in the union for the duration of the existing contract. When the contract expires, most maintenance of membership agreements provide an escape clause—a short interval of time, usually ten days to two weeks—in which employees may choose to withdraw their membership from the union without penalty.

A provision that often exists in union security arrangements is a process called the dues checkoff. A **dues checkoff** occurs when the employer withholds union dues from the members' paychecks. Similar to other pay withholdings, the employer collects the dues money and sends it to the union. There are a number of reasons why employers provide this service, and a reason why the union would permit them to do so. Collecting dues takes time, so a dues checkoff

One weapon that unions have to display their dissatisfaction over failure to reach an agreement with management during contract negotiations is the economic strike. These USWA members working at Kaiser Aluminum showed their solidarity and displeasure with their employers' negotiation tactics, which resulted in more than three months of strike activity and more than 600 days of lockout.

reduces the downtime by eliminating the need for the shop steward to go around to collect dues. Furthermore, recognizing that union dues are the primary source of income for the union, having knowledge of how much money there is in the union treasury can provide management with some insight as to whether or not a union is financially strong enough to endure a strike.[12] Given these facts, why would a union agree to such a procedure? Simply, the answer lies in guaranteed revenues! By letting management deduct dues from a member's paycheck, the union is assured of receiving their monies. Excuses from members that they don't have their money, or will pay next week, are eliminated!

Being Upset with Management

In spite of the reasons why employees join a union, there appears to be one common factor—management, especially the first-line supervisor. If employees are upset with the way their supervisor handles problems, upset over how a coworker has been disciplined, and so on, they are likely to seek help from a union. In fact, it is reasonable to believe that when employees vote to unionize, it's often a vote against their immediate supervisor rather than a vote in support of a particular union.[13]

$\mathcal{L}$ABOR LEGISLATION

The legal framework for labor-management relationships has played a crucial role in its development. In this section, therefore, major developments in labor law will be discussed. An exhaustive analysis of these laws and their legal and practical repercussions is not possible within the scope of this book.[14] However, we'll focus our discussion on two important laws that have shaped much of the labor relations process. We'll then briefly summarize other laws that have helped shape labor-management activities.

The Wagner Act

Wagner Act Also known as the National Labor Relations Act of 1935, this act gave employees the legitimate right to form and join unions and to engage in collective bargaining.

The National Labor Relations Act of 1935, commonly referred to as the **Wagner Act,** is the basic "bill of rights" for unions. This law guarantees workers the right to organize and join unions, to bargain collectively, and to act in concert to pursue their objectives. In terms of labor relations, the Wagner Act specifically requires employers to bargain in good faith over mandatory bargaining issues—wages, hours, and terms and conditions of employment.

National Labor Relations Board Established to administer and interpret the Wagner Act, the NLRB has primary responsibility for conducting union representation elections.

The Wagner Act is cited as shifting the pendulum of power to favor unions for the first time in U.S. labor history. This was achieved, in part, through the establishment of the **National Labor Relations Board (NLRB).** This administrative body, consisting of five members appointed by the president of the United States, was given the responsibility for determining appropriate bargaining units, conducting elections to determine union representation, and preventing or correcting employer actions that can lead to unfair labor practice charges. The NLRB, however, has only remedial and no punitive powers.

Unfair labor practices (Section 8[a]) include any employer tactics that:

- Interfere with, restrain, or coerce employees in the exercise of the rights to join unions and to bargain collectively;
- Dominate or interfere with the formation or administration of any labor organization; discriminate against anyone because of union activity;

- Discharge or otherwise discriminate against any employee because he or she filed or gave testimony under the Act; and
- Refuse to bargain collectively with the representatives chosen by the employees.

While the Wagner Act provided the legal recognition of unions as legitimate interest groups in American society, many employers opposed its purposes. Some employers, too, failed to live up to the requirements of its provisions. That's because employers recognized that the Wagner Act didn't provide protection for them from unfair union labor practices. Thus, the belief that the balance of power had swung too far to labor's side, and the public outcry stemming from post–World War II strikes, led to the passage of the Taft-Hartley Act (Labor-Management Relations Act) in 1947.

The Taft-Hartley Act

Taft-Hartley Act Also known as the Labor-Management Relations Act.

The major purpose of the **Taft-Hartley Act** was to amend the Wagner Act by addressing employers' concerns in terms of specifying unfair union labor practices. Under Section 8(b), Taft-Hartley states that it is an unfair labor practice for unions to:

- Restrain or coerce employees in joining the union, or coerce the employer in selecting bargaining or grievance representatives;
- Discriminate against an employee to whom union membership has been denied, or to cause an employer to discriminate against an employee;
- Refuse to bargain collectively;
- Engage in strikes and boycotts for purposes deemed illegal by the Act;
- Charge excessive or discriminatory fees or dues under union-shop contracts; and
- Obtain compensation for services not performed or not to be performed.

In addition, Taft-Hartley declared illegal one type of union security arrangement: the closed shop. Until Taft-Hartley's passage, the closed shop was dominant in labor contracts. The closed shop was an arrangement where a union "controlled" the source of labor. Under this arrangement, an individual would join the union, be trained by the union, and sent to work for an employer by the union. In essence, the union acted as the clearing house of employees. When an employer needed a number of employees—for whatever duration—the employer would contact the union and request that these employees start work. When the job was completed, and the employees were no longer needed on the job by the employer, they were sent back to the union. By declaring the closed shop illegal, Taft-Hartley began to shift the pendulum of power away from unions. Furthermore, in doing so, the Act enabled states to enact laws that would further reduce compulsory union membership. Taft-Hartley also included provisions that forbade secondary boycotts, and gave the president of the United States the power to issue an 80-day cooling-off period when labor-management disputes affect national security. A *secondary boycott* occurs when a union strikes against Employer A (a primary and legal strike), and then strikes and pickets against Employer B (an employer against which the union has no complaint) because of a relationship that exists between Employers A and B, such as Employer B handling goods made by Employer A. Taft-Hartley also set forth procedures for workers to decertify, or vote out, their union representatives.

Whereas the Wagner Act required only employers to bargain in good faith, Taft-Hartley imposed the same obligation on unions. Although the negotiation process is described later in this chapter, it is important to understand what is meant by the term "bargaining in good faith." This does not mean that the parties must reach agreement, but rather that they must come to the bargaining table ready, willing, and able to meet and deal, open to proposals made by the other party, and with the intent to reach a mutually acceptable agreement.

Federal Mediation and Conciliation Service A government agency that assists labor and management in settling their disputes.

Realizing that unions and employers might not reach agreement and that work stoppages might occur, Taft-Hartley also created the **Federal Mediation and Conciliation Service (FMCS)** as an independent agency separate from the Department of Labor. The FMCS's mission is to send a trained representative to assist in negotiations. Both employer and union have the responsibility to notify the FMCS when other attempts to settle the dispute have failed or contract expiration is pending. An FMCS mediator is not empowered to force parties to reach an agreement, but he or she can use persuasion and other means of diplomacy to help them reach their own resolution of differences. Finally, a fact worth noting was the amendment in 1974 to extend coverage to the health-care industry. This health-care amendment now affords Taft-Hartley coverage to for-profit and nonprofit hospitals, as well as "special provisions for the health care industry, both profit and nonprofit, as to bargaining notice requirements and the right to picket or strike."[15]

Other Laws Affecting Labor-Management Relations

While the Wagner and Taft-Hartley Acts were the most important laws influencing labor-management relationships in the United States, there are some other laws that are pertinent to our discussion. Specifically, these are the Railway Labor Act; the Landrum-Griffin Act; Executive Orders 10988 and 11491; the Racketeer Influenced and Corrupt Organizations Act of 1970; and the Civil Service Reform Act of 1978. Let's briefly review the notable aspects of these laws.

Railway Labor Act Provided the initial impetus to widespread collective bargaining.

The Railway Labor Act of 1926 The **Railway Labor Act** provided the initial impetus for widespread collective bargaining in the United States.[16] Although the Act covers only the transportation industry, it was important because work-

---

diversity issues in HRM

UNIONS AND EEO

ALTHOUGH MUCH OF THE LEGAL DISCUSSION thus far in this section has focused specifically on labor legislation, it's important to recognize that many of the laws discussed in Chapter 3 apply to labor organizations as well. For instance, the Equal Pay Act of 1963 requires that wages agreed to during collective bargaining must not be differentiated on the basis of sex. In labor relations settings, pay differentiation may exist only on the basis of skill, responsibility, accountability, seniority, or working conditions.

The Civil Rights Act of 1964 is equally relevant to labor organizations as it is to management. For unions, Title VII of the Act means that not only must unions discontinue any discriminatory practices, they must also actively recruit and give preference to minority group members. For example, if a labor union is located in a geographic area where there is a large minority population, the union must make an effort to recruit these individuals into the union's apprenticeship

programs. This means that unions have to place advertisements where such individuals will be likely to read them, visit schools they attend, and so forth. Failure to take such affirmative action steps may result in a union being found guilty of discrimination.

With regard to the Age Discrimination Act of 1967, unions are unable to mandate retirement of any of their members. They can, as a company, stop contributing to a worker's pension after the individual reaches the age of 70. Additionally, labor unions, in complying with the provisions of the Vocational Rehabilitation Act and the Americans with Disabilities Act, must take affirmative action measures to recruit, employ, and advance all qualified disabled individuals. This means that unions must make reasonable accommodations, like easy access ramps, for the disabled worker. The same holds true for abiding by the provisions of the Family and Medical Leave Act.

ers in these industries were guaranteed the right to organize, bargain collectively with employers, and establish dispute settlement procedures in the event that an agreement was not reached at the bargaining table. This dispute settlement procedure allows congressional and presidential intercession in the event of an impasse.

Landrum-Griffin Act Also known as the Labor and Management Reporting and Disclosure Act, this legislation protected union members from possible wrongdoing on the part of their unions. Its thrust was to require all unions to disclose their financial statements.

Landrum-Griffin Act of 1959

The **Landrum-Griffin Act of 1959** (Labor Management Reporting and Disclosure Act) was passed to address the public outcry over misuse of union funds and corruption in the labor movement. This Act, like Taft-Hartley, was an amendment to the Wagner Act.[17]

The thrust of the Landrum-Griffin Act is to monitor internal union activity by making officials and those affiliated with unions (e.g., union members, trustees, etc.) accountable for union funds, elections, and other business and representational matters. Restrictions are also placed on trusteeships imposed by national or international unions, and conduct during a union election is regulated. Much of this Act is part of an ongoing effort to prevent corrupt practices and to keep organized crime from gaining control of the labor movement.[18] The mechanisms used to achieve this goal are requirements for annual filing, by unions as organizations and by individuals employed by unions, of reports regarding administrative matters to the Department of Labor—reports such as their constitutions and bylaws, administrative policies, elected officials, and finances. This information, filed under forms L-M 2, L-M, or L-M 4[19] with the Department of Labor, is available to the public. Furthermore, Landrum-Griffin included a provision that allowed all members of a union to vote irrespective of their race, sex, national origin, and so forth. This provision gave union members certain rights that would not be available to the general public for another five years until the passage of the Civil Rights Act of 1964. Landrum-Griffin also required that all who voted on union matters would do so in a secret ballot, especially when the vote concerned the election of union officers.

Executive Orders 10988 and 11491

Both of these executive orders deal specifically with labor legislation in the federal sector.[20] In 1962, President Kennedy issued Executive Order 10988, which permitted, for the first time, federal government employees the right to join unions. The order required agency heads to bargain in good faith, defined unfair labor practices, and specified the code of conduct to which labor organizations in the public sector must adhere. Strikes, however, were prohibited.[21]

While this executive order was effective in granting organizing rights to federal employees, areas for improvement were identified. This was especially true regarding the need for a centralized agency to oversee federal labor relations activities. To address these deficiencies, President Richard Nixon issued Executive Order 11491 in 1969. The objectives of this executive order were to make federal labor relations more like those in the private sector and to standardize procedures among federal agencies. This order gave the assistant secretary of labor the authority to determine appropriate bargaining units, oversee recognition procedures, rule on unfair labor practices, and enforce standards of conduct on labor relations. It also established the *Federal Labor Relations Council (FLRC)* to supervise the implementation of Executive Order 11491 provisions, handle appeals from decisions of the assistant secretary of labor, and rule on questionable issues.

Both of these executive orders served a vital purpose in promoting federal-sector unionization. However, if a subsequent administration ever decided not to permit federal-sector unionization, a president would have had only to revoke a prior executive order. To eliminate this possibility, and to remove federal-sector labor relations from direct control of a president, Congress passed the Civil Service Reform Act.

Racketeering Influenced and Corrupt Organizations Act (RICO) of 1970

Racketeering Influenced and Corrupt Organizations Act (RICO)   A law designed to eliminate organized crime influence on unions.

Although this Act has far-reaching tentacles, the **Racketeering Influenced and Corrupt Organizations Act (RICO)** serves a vital purpose in labor relations. RICO's primary emphasis with respect to labor unions is to eliminate any influence exerted on unions by members of organized crime.[22] That is, it is a violation of RICO if "payments or loans are made to employee representatives, labor organizations, or officers and employees of labor organizations,"[23] where such action occurs in the form of "bribery, kickbacks, or extortion."[24] Over the past decade, RICO has been used to oust a number of labor officials in the Teamsters union who were alleged to have organized crime ties.[25]

Civil Service Reform Act of 1978

Civil Service Reform Act   Replaced Executive Order 11491 as the basic law governing labor relations for federal employees.

Title VII of the **Civil Service Reform Act** established the Federal Labor Relations Authority (FLRA) as an independent agency within the executive branch to carry out the major functions previously performed by the FLRC. The FLRA was given the authority to decide, subject to external review by courts and administrative bodies,[26] union election and unfair labor practice disputes, and appeals from arbitration awards, and to provide leadership in establishing policies and guidance. An additional feature of this act is a broad-scope grievance procedure that can be limited only by the negotiators. Under Executive Order 11491, binding arbitration had been optional. While the Civil Service Reform Act of 1978 contains many provisions similar to those of the Wagner Act, two important differences exist. First, in the private sector, the scope of bargaining includes wages and benefits, and mandatory subjects of bargaining. In the federal sector, wages and benefits are not negotiable—they are set by Congress. Additionally, the Reform Act prohibits negotiations over union security arrangements.

How Are Employees Unionized?

Employees are unionized after an extensive and sometimes lengthy process called the *organizing campaign*. Exhibit 15-3 contains a simple model of how the process typically flows in the private sector. Let's look at these elements.

Authorization Card   A card signed by prospective union members indicating that they are interested in having a union election held at their work site.

Efforts to organize a group of employees may begin by employee representatives requesting a union to visit the employees' organization and solicit members, the union itself might initiate the membership drive, or in some cases, unions are using the Internet to promote their benefits to workers.[27] Regardless, as established by the NLRB, the union must secure signed **authorization cards** from at least 30 percent of the employees it wishes to represent. Employees who sign the cards indicate that they wish the particular union to be their representative in negotiating with the employer.

Representation Certification   The election process whereby union members vote in a union as their representative.

Although a minimum of 30 percent of the potential union members must sign the authorization card prior to an election, unions are seldom interested in bringing to vote situations in which they merely meet the NLRB minimum.[28] Why? The answer is simply a matter of mathematics and business: to become the certified bargaining unit, the union must be accepted by a majority of those eligible voting workers.[29] Acceptance in this case is determined by a secret-ballot election. This election held by the NLRB, called a **representation certification (RC)**, can occur only once in a 12-month period; thus, the more signatures on the authorization cards, the greater the chances for a victory.

EXHIBIT 15-3
Union Organizing Process

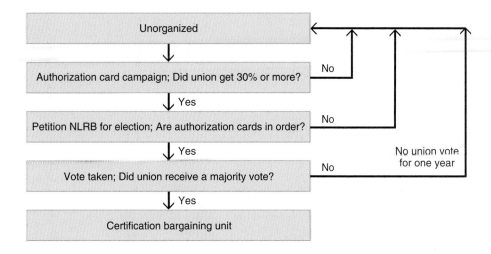

Even when a sizable proportion of the workers sign authorization cards, the victory is by no means guaranteed. Management often is not passive during the organization drive (see Workplace Issues). Although there are laws governing what management can and cannot do, management of the organization may attempt to persuade the potential members to vote no. Union organizers realize that some initial signers might be persuaded to vote no, and thus unions usually require a much higher percentage of authorization cards so they can increase their odds of obtaining a majority. When that majority vote is received, the NLRB certifies the union and recognizes it as the exclusive bargaining unit. Irrespective of whether the individual in the certified bargaining union voted for or against the union, each worker is covered by the negotiated contract and must abide by its governance. Once a union has been certified, is it there for life? Certainly not. On some occasions, union members may become so dissatisfied with the union's actions in representing them that they may want to turn to another union or return to their nonunion status. In either case, the rank-and-file members petition the NLRB to conduct a **representation decertification (RD)**. Once again, if a majority of the members vote the union out, it is gone. However, once the election has been held, no other action can occur for another 12-month period. This grace period protects the employer from employees decertifying one union today and certifying another tomorrow.

Finally, and even more rare than an RD, is a representation decertification initiated by management, or RM. The guidelines for the RM are the same as for the RD, except that it is the employer who is leading the drive. Although RDs and RMs are ways of decertifying unions, it should be pointed out that most labor agreements bar the use of either decertification election during the term of the contract.

Unions' organizing drives may be unsuccessful, but when they do achieve their goal to become the exclusive bargaining agent, the next step is to negotiate the contract. In the next section, we'll look at the specific issues surrounding collective bargaining.

Representation Decertification The election process whereby union members vote out their union as the representative.

Collective Bargaining The negotiation, administration, and interpretation of a written agreement between two parties, at least one of which represents a group that is acting collectively, that covers a specific period of time.

COLLECTIVE BARGAINING

The term **collective bargaining** typically refers to the negotiation, administration, and interpretation of a written agreement between two parties that covers a specific period of time. This agreement, or contract, lays out in specific terms the conditions of employment—that is, what is expected of employees and what

workplace issues

THE UNION DRIVE

WHAT CAN MANAGEMENT DO WHEN THEY learn that a union-organizing drive has begun in their organization? Under labor laws, while they are permitted to defend themselves against the union campaign, they must do so properly. Here are some guidelines for what to do and what not to do during the organizing drive.[30]

- If your employees ask for your opinion on unionization, respond in a natural manner. For example, "I really have no position on the issue. Do what you think is best."
- You can prohibit union-organizing activities in your workplace during work hours only if they interfere with work operations. This may apply to the organization's e-mail, too.
- You can prohibit outside union organizers from distributing union information in the workplace.
- Employees have the right to distribute union information to other employees during breaks and lunch periods.
- Don't question employees publicly or privately about union-organizing activities—for example, "Are you planning to go to that union rally this weekend?" But if an employee freely tells you about the activities, you may listen.
- Don't spy on employees' union activities—for example, by standing in the cafeteria to see who is distributing pro-union literature.
- Don't make any threats or promises that are related to the possibility of unionization—for example, "If this union effort succeeds, upper management is seriously thinking about closing down this plant. But if it's defeated, they may push through an immediate wage increase."
- Don't discriminate against any employee who is involved in the unionization effort.
- Be on the lookout for efforts by the union to coerce employees to join its ranks. This activity by unions is an unfair labor practice. If you see this occurring, report it to your boss or to human resources. Your organization may also want to consider filing a complaint against the union with the NLRB.

limits there are in management's authority. In the following discussion, we will take a somewhat larger perspective—we will also consider the organizing, certification, and preparation efforts that precede actual negotiation.

Most of us only hear or read about collective bargaining when a contract is about to expire or when negotiations break down. When a railroad contract is about to expire, we may be aware that collective bargaining exists in the transportation industry. Similarly, teachers' strikes in Cleveland, workers striking Verizon Communications, or baseball players striking against major-league baseball owners remind us that organized labor deals with management collectively. In fact, collective-bargaining agreements cover about half of all state and local government employees and one-ninth of employees in the private sector. The wages, hours, and working conditions of these unionized employees are negotiated for periods of usually two or three years at a time. Only when these contracts expire and management and the union are unable to agree on a new contract are most of us aware that collective bargaining is a very important part of HRM.

The Objective and Scope of Collective Bargaining

The objective of collective bargaining is to agree on an acceptable contract—acceptable to management, union representatives, and the union membership. But what is covered in this contract? The final agreement will reflect the problems of the particular workplace and industry in which the contract is negotiated.[31]

Irrespective of the specific issues contained in various labor contracts, four issues appear consistently throughout all labor contracts. Three of the four are mandatory bargaining issues, which means that management and the union must negotiate in good faith over these issues. These mandatory issues were defined by the Wagner Act as wages, hours, and terms and conditions of employment. The fourth issue covered in almost all labor contracts is the grievance procedure, which is designed to permit the adjudication of complaints. Before we progress further into collective bargaining, let's inspect our cast of characters.

Collective Bargaining Participants

Collective bargaining was described as an activity that takes place between two parties. In this context, the two parties are labor and management. But who represents these two groups? Given our previous discussion, would it be erroneous to add a third party—the government?

Management's representation in collective bargaining talks tends to depend on the size of the organization. In a small firm, for instance, bargaining is probably done by the president. Since small firms frequently have no specialist who deals only with HRM issues, the president of the company often handles this. In larger organizations, there is usually a sophisticated HRM department with full-time industrial relations experts. In such cases, we can expect management to be represented by the senior manager for industrial relations, corporate executives, and company lawyers—with support provided by legal and economic specialists in wage and salary administration, labor law, benefits, and so forth.

On the union side, we typically expect to see a bargaining team made up of an officer of the local union, local shop stewards, and some representation from the international/national union.[32] Again, as with management, representation is modified to reflect the size of the bargaining unit. If negotiations involve a contract that will cover 50,000 employees at company locations throughout the United States, the team will be dominated by international/national union officers, with a strong supporting cast of economic and legal experts employed by the union. In a small firm or for local negotiations covering special issues at the plant level for a nationwide organization, bargaining representatives for the union might be the local officers and a few specially elected committee members.

Watching over these two sides is a third party—government. In addition to providing the rules under which management and labor bargain, government provides a watchful eye on the two parties to ensure the rules are followed, and it stands ready to intervene if an agreement on acceptable terms cannot be reached, or if the impasse undermines the nation's well-being.

Are there any more participants? No, for the most part, with one exception—financial institutions.[33] Most people are unaware of the presence of the financial institution's role in collective bargaining. Although not directly involved in negotiations, these "banks" set limits on the cost of the contract. Exceeding that amount may cause the banks to call in the loans that had been made to the company. This results in placing a ceiling on what management can spend. While we can show that there are more groups involved in collective bargaining, our discussion will focus on labor and management. After all, it is the labor and management teams that buckle down and hammer out the contract.

Most people are unaware of the presence of the financial institution's role in collective bargaining.

The Collective Bargaining Process

Let's now consider the actual collective-bargaining process. Exhibit 15-4 contains a simple model of how the process typically flows in the private sector—which includes preparing to negotiate, actual negotiations, and administering the contract after it has been ratified.

EXHIBIT 15-4
The Collective-Bargaining Process

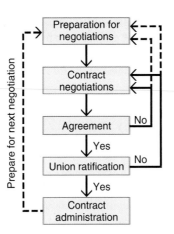

Preparing to Negotiate   Once a union has been certified as the bargaining unit, both union and management begin the ongoing activity of preparing for negotiations. We refer to this as an *ongoing* activity because ideally it should begin as soon as the previous contract is agreed upon or union certification is achieved. Realistically, it probably begins anywhere from one to six months before the current contract expires. We can consider the preparation for negotiation as composed of three activities: fact gathering, goal setting, and strategy development.

Information is acquired from both internal and external sources. Internal data include grievance and accident records; employee performance reports; overtime figures; and reports on transfers, turnover, and absenteeism. External information should include statistics on the current economy, both at local and national levels; economic forecasts for the short and intermediate terms; copies of recently negotiated contracts by the adversary union to determine what issues the union considers important; data on the communities in which the company operates—cost of living; changes in cost of living, terms of recently negotiated labor contracts, and statistics on the labor market; and industry labor statistics to see what terms other organizations, employing similar types of personnel, are negotiating.

With homework done, information in hand, and tentative goals established, both union and management must put together the most difficult part of the bargaining preparation activities—a strategy for negotiations. This includes assessing the other side's power and specific tactics.

Negotiating at the Bargaining Table   Negotiation customarily begins with the union delivering to management a list of "demands." By presenting many demands, the union creates significant room for trading in later stages of the negotiation; it also disguises the union's real position, leaving management to determine which demands are adamantly sought, which are moderately sought, and which the union is prepared to quickly abandon. A long list of demands, too, often fulfills the internal political needs of the union. By seeming to back numerous wishes of the union's members, union administrators appear to be satisfying the needs of the many factions within the membership.

While both union and management representatives may publicly accentuate their differences, the real negotiations typically go on behind closed doors. Each party tries to assess the relative priorities of the other's demands, and each begins to combine proposals into viable packages. What takes place, then, is the attempt to get management's highest offer to approximate the lowest demands that the union is willing to accept. Hence, negotiation is a form of compromise. When an oral agreement is achieved, it is converted into a written contract. Negotiation finally concludes with the union representatives submitting the contract for ratification or approval from rank-and-file members. Unless the rank-and-file members vote to approve the contract, negotiations must resume. That's precisely what happened when Federal Express and the Air Line Pilots Association representing FedEx pilots saw their long-negotiated agreement rejected by the pilots—even though union leadership supported the agreement.[34]

Contract Administration   Once a contract is agreed upon and ratified, it must be administered. In terms of contract administration, four stages must be carried out: (1) getting the information agreed to out to all union members and management personnel; (2) implementing the contract; (3) interpreting the contract and grievance resolution; and (4) monitoring activities during the contract period.[35]

In terms of providing information to all concerned, both parties must ensure that changes in contract language are spelled out. For example, the most obvious would be hourly rate changes; HRM must make sure its payroll system is adjusted to the new rates as set in the contract. But it goes beyond just pay: changes in work rules, hours, and the like must be communicated. If both sides agree to mandatory overtime, something that was not in existence before, all must be informed of how it will work. Neither the union nor the company can simply hand a copy of the contract to each organization member and expect it to be understood. It will be necessary to hold meetings to explain the new terms of the agreement.

The next stage of contract administration is ensuring that the agreement is implemented. All communicated changes now take effect, and both sides are expected to comply with the contract terms. One concept to recognize during this phase is something called *management rights*. Typically, management is guaranteed the right to allocate organizational resources in the most efficient manner; to create reasonable rules; to hire, promote, transfer, and discharge employees; to determine work methods and assign work; to create, eliminate, and classify jobs; to lay off employees when necessary; to close or relocate facilities with a 60-day notice; and to institute technological changes. Of course, good HRM practices suggest that whether the contract requires it or not, management would be wise to notify the union of major decisions that will influence its membership.

Probably the most important element of contract administration relates to spelling out a procedure for handling contractual disputes.[36] Almost all collective-bargaining agreements contain formal procedures to be used in resolving grievances of the interpretation and application of the contract. These contracts have provisions for resolving specific, formally initiated grievances by employees concerning dissatisfaction with job-related issues.

Grievance procedures are typically designed to resolve grievances as quickly as possible and at the lowest level possible in the organization (see Exhibit 15-5).[37] The first step almost always has the employee attempt to resolve the grievance with his or her immediate supervisor.[38] If it cannot be resolved at this stage, it is typically discussed with the union steward and the supervisor. Failure at this stage usually brings in the individuals from the organization's industrial relations department and the chief union steward. If the grievance still

Grievance Procedures   A complaint-resolving process contained in union contracts.

EXHIBIT 15-5
*A Sample Grievance
Procedure*

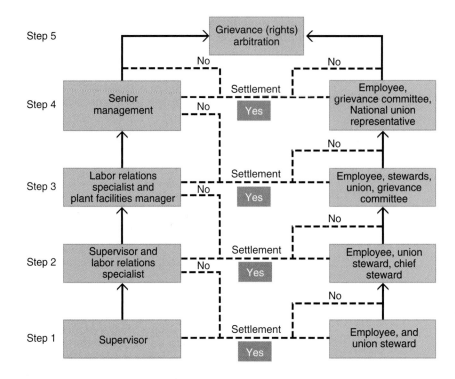

cannot be resolved, the complaint passes to the facilities' manager, who typically discusses it with the union grievance committee. Unsuccessful efforts at this level give way to the organization's senior management and typically a representative from the national union. Finally, if those efforts are unsuccessful in resolving the grievance, the final step is for the complaint to go to arbitration—called *grievance (rights) arbitration.*

In practice, we find that almost all collective-bargaining agreements provide for grievance (rights) arbitration as the final step to an impasse. Of course, in small organizations these five steps described tend to be condensed, possibly moving from discussing the grievance with the union steward to taking the grievance directly to the organization's senior executive or owner, and then to arbitration, if necessary.

Finally, in our discussion of preparation for negotiations, we stated that both company and union need to gather various data. One of the most bountiful databases for both sides is information kept on a current contract. By monitoring activities, company and union can assess how effective the current contract was, when problem areas or conflicts arose, and what changes might need to be made in subsequent negotiations.[39]

When Agreement Cannot Be Reached

Although the goal of contract negotiations is to achieve an agreement that is acceptable to all concerned parties, sometimes that goal is not achieved. Negotiations do break down, and an impasse occurs. Sometimes these events are triggered by internal issues in the union, the desire to strike against the company, the company's desire to lock out the union, or its knowledge that striking workers can be replaced. Let's explore some of these areas.

Traditional union strongholds included in the manufacturing industries. Yet, as they've declined in the information age, unions have attempted to organize nontraditional workers. In hospitals in California, for example, this has meant more focused organizing campaigns—such as organizing nurses at St. Vincent Medical Center in Los Angeles and Mercy Healthcare in Sacramento.

Economic Strike An impasse that results from labor and management's inability to agree on the wages, hours, terms, and conditions of a "new" contract.

Wildcat Strike An unauthorized and illegal strike that occurs during the terms of an existing contract.

Strikes versus Lockouts There are only two possible preliminary outcomes from negotiations. First, and obviously preferable, is agreement. The other alternative, when no viable solution can be found to the parties' differences, is a strike or a lockout.

There are several types of strikes. The most relevant to contract negotiations is the economic strike. An **economic strike** occurs when the two parties cannot reach a satisfactory agreement before the contract expires. When that deadline passes, the union leadership will typically instruct its members not to work—thus leaving their jobs.[40] Although in today's legal climate, replacement workers can be hired, no disciplinary action can be taken against workers who participate in economic strike activities (see Ethical Issues in HRM).

Another form of strike is the **wildcat strike**. A wildcat strike generally occurs when workers walk off the job because of something management has done. For example, if a union employee is disciplined for failure to call in sick according to provisions of the contract, fellow union members may walk off the job to demonstrate their dissatisfaction with management action. It is important to note that these strikes happen while a contract is in force—an agreement that usually prohibits such union activity. Consequently, wildcat strikers can be severely disciplined or terminated. In the past, the most powerful weapon unions in the private sector had was the economic strike. By striking, the union was, in essence, withholding labor from the employer, thus causing the employer financial hardships. For instance, U.S. organizations lost more than 5.1 million workdays to strike activity in 1998.[41]

Today, however, the strike weapon is questioned.[42] Strikes are not only expensive, but public sentiment supporting their use by unions is not very strong. And management hasn't been sitting by idly, for today it is more inclined to replace striking workers. Although strikes fell to a near record low in 1999,[43] worker dissatisfaction with some management practices may increase strike activity in the years ahead. That's one of the key components of the United Steelworkers of America's complaint against Kaiser Aluminum Corporation, which led to a 3½ month strike and a 613-day lockout.[44]

Lockout A situation in labor–management negotiations whereby management prevents union members from returning to work.

In contemporary times, we have also witnessed an increase in management's use of the lockout. A **lockout,** as the name implies, occurs when the organization denies unionized workers access to their jobs during an impasse. A lockout, in some cases, is management's predecessor to hiring replacement workers. In others, it's management's effort to protect their facilities and machinery and other employees at the work site. But while lockouts have been used more frequently over the past decade, their use in the early 2000s has not been successful for some companies. That's because with the tight labor markets that exist, finding replacement workers has become more difficult.[45]

In either case, the strategy is the same. Each side is attempting to apply economic pressure on its opponent in an effort to sway negotiations in its own direction. And when it works, negotiations are said to reach an impasse. When that happens, impasse-resolution techniques are designed to help.

Impasse-Resolution Techniques   When labor and management in the private sector cannot reach a satisfactory agreement themselves, they may need the assistance of an objective third-party individual. This assistance comes in the form of *conciliation and mediation, fact-finding,* or *interest arbitration.*

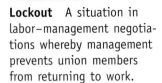

THE STRIKER REPLACEMENT DILEMMA

INHERENT IN COLLECTIVE-BARGAINING NEGOTIATIONS IS an opportunity for either side to generate a power base that may sway negotiations in its favor. For example, when labor shortages exist, or when inventories are in short supply, a strike by the union could have serious ramifications for the company. Likewise, when the situation is reversed, management has the upper hand and could easily lock out the union to achieve its negotiation goals. In fact, both the Wagner and Taft-Hartley Acts saw to it that the playing field was to be as fair as possible, by requiring both sides to negotiate in good faith, and permit impasses if they should be warranted.

For decades, this scenario played itself out over and over again. Timing of a contract's expiration proved critical for both sides. For example, in the coal industry, having a contract expire just before the winter months— when coal is needed in greater supply for heating and electricity—worked to the union's advantage, unless the coal companies stockpiled enough coal to carry them through a lengthy winter strike. This game, although serious to both sides, never appeared to be anything more than bargaining strategy—one that could show how serious both sides were. And even though a Supreme Court case from 1938, *NLRB v. MacKay Radio,* gave employers the right to hire replacement workers for those engaged in an economic strike, seldom was that used. In fact, often to settle

a strike, and for the organization to get back its skilled work force, one stipulation would be that all replacement workers be let go.

But in the early 1980s, that began to change. When President Ronald Reagan fired striking air-traffic controllers and hired their replacements, businesses began to realize the weapon they had at their disposal. As their union-busting attempts materialized, some organizations, like Caterpillar, the National Football League, and John Deere, realized that using replacement workers could be to their advantage. The union members either came back to work on management's terms, or they simply lost their jobs— period.

Undoubtedly, in any strike situation, management has the right to keep its doors open and to keep producing what it sells. Often that may mean using supervisory personnel in place of striking workers, or in some cases, bringing in replacements. But does a law that permits replacement workers undermine the intent of national labor law? Does it create an unfair advantage for management in that it could play hardball just to break the union? Should a striker replacement bill (which would prevent permanent replacement workers from being hired) be passed? Should striking workers' jobs be protected while they exercise their rights under the Wagner Act? What's your opinion?

Conciliation and mediation are two very closely related impasse-resolution techniques. Both are techniques whereby a neutral third-party attempts to get labor and management to resolve their differences. Under conciliation, however, the role of the third party is to keep the negotiations ongoing. In other words, this individual is a go-between—advocating a voluntary means through which both sides can continue negotiating. Mediation, on the other hand, goes one step further. The mediator attempts to pull together the common ground that exists and make settlement recommendations for overcoming the barriers that exist between the two sides. A mediator's suggestions, however, are only advisory. That means that the suggestions are not binding on either party.

Fact-finding is a technique whereby a neutral third-party individual conducts a hearing to gather evidence from both labor and management. The fact-finder then renders a decision as to how he or she views an appropriate settlement. Similar to mediation, the fact-finder's recommendations are only suggestions—they, too, are not binding on either party.

The final impasse-resolution technique is called **interest arbitration.** Under interest arbitration, generally a panel of three individuals—one neutral and one each from the union and management—hears testimony from both sides. After the hearing, the panel renders a decision on how to settle the current contract negotiation dispute. If all three members of the panel are unanimous in their decision, that decision may be binding on both parties.

With respect to public-sector impasse-resolution techniques, some notable differences do exist. For instance, in many states that do permit public-sector employee strikes, some form of arbitration is typically required. The decisions rendered through arbitration are binding on both parties. Moreover, in the public sector, a particular form of arbitration is witnessed. Called *final-offer arbitration,* both sides present their recommendations, and the arbitrator is required to select one party's offer in its entirety over the other. There is no attempt in final-offer arbitration to seek compromise.

Fact-finder A neutral third-party individual who conducts a hearing to gather evidence and testimony from the parties regarding the differences between them.

Interest Arbitration An impasse-resolution technique used to settle contract negotiation disputes.

CRITICAL ISSUES FOR UNIONS TODAY

As the percentage of the unionized work force has declined throughout the past few decades, several questions arise. Why has union membership declined? Can labor and management find a way to work together more harmoniously? Is public-sector unionization different from that in the private sector? And where are unions likely to focus their attention in the next decade? In this section, we'll look at these issues.

Union Membership: Where Have the Members Gone?

The birth of unionization in the United States can be traced back to the late 1700s. Although there was labor strife for about 200 years, it was not until the passage of the Wagner Act in 1935 that we began to witness significant union gains. In fact, by the early 1940s, union membership in the United States reached its pinnacle of approximately 36 percent of the work force.[46] Since that time, however, there's been nothing more than a steady decline (see Exhibit 15-6). What accounted for this phenomenon? There is no single answer to this question. However, major contributing factors can be identified.

In the early to mid-1970s, many unionized workers, especially in the private sector, were able to join the ranks of the middle class as a result of their unions' success at the bargaining table. This often meant that they were more concerned

EXHIBIT 15-6
Trends in Union Membership

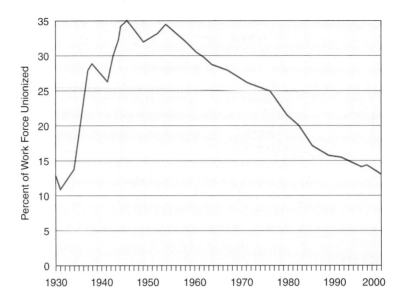

with taxes than with ideological and social issues or with support for legislation that favored the union movement. Furthermore, the private-sector labor movement had difficulty accepting into its ranks public- and federal-sector workers, women, African Americans, and the rising tide of immigrants.

The 1970s was also the decade in which predictions about the postindustrial age came to pass and manufacturing was replaced by service as the dominant industry in the American economy. As a consequence, the most rapid growth in employment was in wholesale and retail trade, service industries including high technology, and white-collar jobs. These are areas where unions either had not previously focused organizing efforts or were largely unsuccessful for a variety of reasons.

Double-digit inflation, beginning in the mid-1970s, was also a factor. High rates of inflation resulted in the first massive layoffs in both the private and public sectors, which radically diminished the financial resources of numerous unions to represent members and to engage in organizing and political activities. Additionally, the emergence of global competition caught much of American business by surprise. The primary response was to try to restore their financial positions by demanding concessions from workers (concession bargaining) and/or by reducing the work force. Both of these responses have had an enormous effect on the unions at the workplace. Fueled by these pressures, the latter half of the 1970s ushered in the strongest anti-union movement since the post–World War II era. And "outsourcing"[47] of production and assembly operations to foreign countries such as the Pacific Rim, Mexico, Brazil, Hong Kong, Taiwan, and parts of Africa was another means that originated in the late 1970s.

The 1980s and early 1990s witnessed an even more dramatic decline in union membership and power. Massive layoffs had ripped through the ranks of such unions as the United Automobile Workers (UAW), the United Steelworkers of America (USWA), the United Mine Workers (UMW), the Rubber Workers, and the Communications Workers, so that their numbers were significantly less than at the beginning of the decade. The cumulative effects of factors identified in the 1970s had even harsher consequences during the next 15 years. Union busting and avoidance were no longer sideline issues for management consultants, but were a thriving and lucrative enterprise in their own right. Worker replacement became a management weapon. If the union would not accept management's best offer, the company simply hired new workers to replace those on strike. The 1980s also witnessed a legislative sentiment that began to turn against unions. In such an environment, the role of the strike also took on new meaning. The transition began in 1981, when nationwide attention focused on President Ronald Reagan's firing of illegally striking air-traffic controllers. Important here was the message this action sent to employers across the country: the strike is no longer a union weapon, but rather a management weapon to push workers out of their jobs in an effort to bust the union and/or to gain concessions from workers that they might not otherwise have given.[48]

The picture for unions in the 1990s was just as bleak. Union-avoidance and -busting tactics, delayering of Corporate America, dejobbed organizations, technology advancements, the contingent work force, replacement workers, and so on, all contributed to a continual decline in membership. From their heyday of almost 36 percent in the early 1940s to their current 13.5 percent in 2000, unions appear not to be the force they once were.[49] But don't count unions down and out. Unions are changing some of their organizing tactics, and public sentiment might be changing to support and sympathize with union causes. Unions have also posted some major victories, like winning elections at AT&T Cellular.[50] Unions have also found that recruiting members in the service sectors—with a fair amount of success in Las Vegas, as well as with university graduate students—has been rewarding.[51]

Labor-Management Cooperation

Historically, the relationship between labor and management was built on conflict. The interests of labor and management were seen as basically at odds— each treating the other as the opposition. But times have somewhat changed. Management, and people like Peter Pestillo at Ford, have become increasingly aware that successful efforts to increase productivity, improve quality, and lower costs require employee involvement and commitment. Similarly, some labor unions have come to recognize that they can help their members more by cooperating with management rather than fighting them.[52]

Unfortunately, current U.S. labor laws, passed in an era of mistrust and antagonism between labor and management, may have become a barrier to both parties becoming cooperative partners. As a case in point, the National Labor Relations Act was passed to encourage collective bargaining and to balance workers' power against that of management.[53] That legislation also sought to eliminate the then-widespread practice of firms setting up company unions for the sole purpose of undermining efforts of outside unions organizing their employees. So the law prohibits employers from creating or supporting a "labor organization." For instance, the National Labor Relations Board ruled in the Electromation Inc. case that it was an unfair labor practice for the employer to set up employee committees in "order to impose its own unilateral form of bargaining on employees."[54] Furthermore, Electromation's actions were also viewed as a means of thwarting a Teamsters Union organizing campaign which began in its Elkhart, Indiana plant. The Electromation case and a few others have indicated that companies must ensure that their quality circle programs, quality of work life, and other employee involvement programs are legal under federal labor laws.[55]

Although this issue has been the subject of Congressional debate,[56] the current legal environment doesn't prohibit employee-involvement programs in the United States. Rather, to comply with the law, management is required to give its employee-involvement programs independence. That is, when such programs become dominated by management, they're likely to be interpreted as groups that perform some functions of labor unions but are controlled by management. What kinds of actions would indicate that an employee-involvement program is not dominated by management? Some examples might include choosing program members through secret-ballot elections, giving program members wide latitude in deciding what issues to deal with, permitting members to meet apart from management, and specifying that program members are not susceptible to dissolution by management whim. The key theme labor laws appear to be conveying is that where employee-involvement programs are introduced, members must have the power to make decisions and act independently of management.

Public-Sector Unionization

Unionizing government employees, either in the federal sector or in state, county, and municipal jurisdictions, has proven to be very lucrative for unions.[57] Significant gains have been made in these sectors, as unions increased membership from 11 percent in 1970 to 37 percent in 2000.[58] But labor relations in the government sector is not identical to its counterpart in the private sector. For example, in the federal sector, wages are nonnegotiable. Likewise, compulsory membership in unions is prohibited. At the state, county, and local levels, laws must be passed to grant employees in any jurisdiction the right to unionize—and more importantly, the right to strike.[59] Yet, probably the most notable difference lies in determining "who's the boss."

In a private company, management is the employer. This, however, is not the case in government sectors. Instead, a president, a governor, a mayor, a county executive, and so forth is responsible for the government's budget. These are *elected* officials, who have fiduciary responsibilities to their citizenry. Who, then, "owns" the government? Of course, it's the people. Accordingly, unionized employees in the public sector are actually negotiating against themselves as taxpayers. And even if some agreement is reached, the negotiated contract cannot be binding, even though the union members support it, until some legislative body has approved it.

Finally, because these negotiations are a concern to the general public, citizens have the right to know what is going on. This is handled through what are called *sunshine laws*.[60] The intent of these laws is to require the parties in public-sector labor relations to make public their negotiations; that is, contract negotiations are open to the public. This freedom of information is based on the premise that the public-sector negotiations directly affect all taxpayers, and thus, they should have direct information regarding what is occurring. However, while information is important, sunshine laws have been questioned by labor relations personnel. Their contention is, for those who do not understand what happens in negotiations, what the public may see or hear during open negotiations may ultimately differ from the final contract. As such, the public may gain a false sense of negotiation outcomes.

Unionizing the Nontraditional Employee

The strength of unionization in years past resided in the manufacturing industries of the U.S. economy. Steel, tires, automobiles, and transportation were major industries that dominated every aspect of American life—and the world. In each of these industries, there was a common element. That element was the presence of unions. Over the past few decades, however, the United States has changed gears. While once a manufacturing giant, the United States has become a service economy. Unfortunately for unions, the service sector previously had not been one of their targeted areas for organizing employees. But that, too, is

Union survival depends on their reaching out and fulfilling the needs of nontraditional employees.

changing, as survival for unions depends on their reaching out and fulfilling the needs of nontraditional employees. Who are they? Nontraditional employees could be classified as anyone who is not in the manufacturing and related industries. Such people include government workers, nurses, secretaries, professional and technical employees, dot-com employees, and even some management members. Most notably, unions like the United Food and Commercial Workers have targeted companies like Wal-Mart, Target, and K-mart as excellent union-organizing grounds.[61]

As the world of work continues to radically evolve, it is safe to assume that unions will target an even broader group of employees. The same things that unions sold 50 years ago to get people interested in the union cause—wages, benefits, job security, and having a say in how employees are treated at work—are the same things that concern employees as we enter the early years of the new millennium. Restructuring, delayering, and the dejobbing of Corporate America have forced affected workers to pay closer attention to what the unions promise. For the health-care professionals, for example, who voted to be represented by unions, this has resulted in more job security, and wages and benefits above their nonunion counterparts.[62] And with the recent problems experienced by workers at technology companies as many of these upstart organizations began shedding thousands of employees, unions are targeting the high-tech field for their next organizing emphasis.[63]

Is history repeating itself? Only time will tell. But remember, the decline in union membership—especially in the traditional industries in the 1970s—was brought about, in part, by people achieving their middle-class status. As organizational changes threaten this social class rank, there is every reason to believe that workers will present a unified, mutual front to the employer. In some cases, that is best achieved through union activities.

Unionization is not limited to the United States. It's a worldwide phenomenon. Workers in other countries also have found the need to fight for better wages, benefits, and working conditions. Here, these Hyundai are just a few of the millions of global workers who have been confronting their management with issues that directly affect them.

INTERNATIONAL LABOR RELATIONS

Labor relations practices, and the percent of the work force unionized, are different in every country (see Exhibit 15-7). Nowhere is employee representation exactly like that in the United States. In almost every case, the relationships among management, employees, and unions (or other administrative bodies) are the result of long histories. The business approach to unionism, or emphasizing economic objectives, is uniquely American. In Europe, Latin America, and elsewhere, unions have often evolved out of a class struggle, resulting in labor as a political party. The Japanese Confederation of Shipbuilding and Engineering Workers' Union only recently began dropping its "class struggle" rhetoric and slogans to pursue a "partnership" with management. The basic difference in perspective sometimes makes it difficult for U.S. expatriates to understand how the labor relations process works because even the same term may have very different meanings. For example, in the United States, "collective bargaining" implies negotiations between a labor union and management. In Sweden and Germany, it refers to negotiations between the employers' organization and a trade union for the entire industry.[64] Furthermore, arbitration in the United States usually refers to the settlement of individual contractual disputes, while in Australia arbitration is part of the contract bargaining process.

Not only does each country have a different history of unionism, each government has its own view of its role in the labor relations process. This role is often reflected in the types and nature of the regulations in force. While the U.S. government generally takes a hands-off approach toward intervention in labor-management matters, the Australian government, to which the labor movement has very strong ties, is inclined to be more involved. Thus, not only must the multinational corporate industrial relations office be familiar with the separate laws of each country, it also must be familiar with the environment in which those statutes are implemented. Understanding international labor relations is vital to an organization's strategic planning. Unions affect wage levels, which in turn affect competitiveness in both labor and product markets. Unions and labor

EXHIBIT 15-7
Unionization Around the World

Country	Percent of Employees Unionized
Sweden	91%
Italy	44%
Canada	37%
United Kingdom	30%
Germany	25%
Japan	24%
Australia	26%
Spain	18%
United States	13%
France	9%

Sources: Murray Cranston, "The Terminal Decline of Australian Trade Union Membership," *Review—Institute of Public Affairs* (December 2000), p. 26; Marc Champion, "U. K. Unions Long Battered, Stage a Rebound," *Wall Street Journal* (June 28, 2000), p. B-13; Cecilie Rohwedder, "Paying Dues: Once the Big Muscle of German Industry, Unions See It All Sag—Membership and Clout Slip as Country Rues the Cost of Labor Inflexibility—At Infineon, East Meets West," *Wall Street Journal* (November 29, 1999), p. A-1; [http://parsons.iww.org/~iw/sep1998/stories/UKUNION.html] and [http://www.ilo.org/public/english/bureau/inf/pkits/wlr97.htm].

laws may limit employment-level flexibility through security clauses that tightly control layoffs and terminations (or redundancies). This is especially true in such countries as England, France, Germany, Japan, and Australia, where various laws place severe restrictions on employers.

Differing Perspectives Toward Labor Relations

If labor relations can affect the strategic planning initiatives of an organization, it is necessary to consider the issue of headquarters' involvement in host-country international union relations. The organization must assess whether the labor relations function should be controlled globally from the parent country, or whether it would be more advantageous for each host country to administer its own operation. There is no simple means of making this assessment; frequently, the decision reflects the relationship of the product market at home to that of the overseas product market. For instance, when domestic sales are larger than those overseas, the organization is more likely to regard the foreign office as an extension of the domestic operations. This is true for many U.S. multinational organizations because the home market is so vast. Thus, American firms have been more inclined to keep labor relations centrally located at corporate headquarters. Many European countries, by contrast, have small home markets with comparatively larger international operations; thus, they are more inclined to adapt to host-country standards and have the labor relations function decentralized.

Another divergence among multinational companies in their labor relations is the national attitude toward unions. Generally, American multinational corporations view unions negatively at home and try to avoid unionization of the work force. Europeans, on the other hand, have had greater experience with unions, are accustomed to a larger proportion of the work force being unionized, and are more accepting of the unionization of their own workers.[65] In Japan, as in other parts of Asia, unions are often closely identified with an organization.[66]

The European Community

The European Community brings together a dozen or more individual labor relations systems. For both the member nations and other countries doing business in Europe, like the United States and Japan, it is important to understand the dynamics of what will necessarily be a dramatically changing labor environment.[67]

Legislation about workers' rights is continually developing,[68] which has far-ranging implications for all employers. While the French and Germans lean toward strong worker representation in labor policy, reflecting their cultural histories, the United Kingdom and Denmark oppose it. Many basic questions remain to be answered with the implementation of the free trade of labor across national boundaries. For example, with the increase in production that accompanies the opening of this market, workers and their union representatives are going to want their fair share. And what is this fair share? For starters, European unions want a maternity package that provides 80 percent of salary for a 14-week period. They are also seeking premium pay for night work, full benefits for workers who are employed more than eight hours a week, participation on companies' boards of directors, and an increase in the minimum wage level to two-thirds of each country's average manufacturing wage. Some of these inducements will be difficult to obtain, but companies doing business overseas must be aware of what is happening in pending labor legislation, and fully understand and comply with the host country's laws and customs.

NEGOTIATION SKILLS

ABOUT THE SKILL: THE ESSENCE of effective negotiation can be summarized in the following six recommendations.[69]

1. *Research your opponent.* Acquire as much information as you can about your opponent's interests and goals.[70] What people must he or she appease? What is his or her strategy? This information will help you to better understand your opponent's behavior, to predict his or her responses to your offers, and to frame solutions in terms of his or her interests.

2. *Begin with a positive overture.* Research shows that concessions tend to be reciprocated and lead to agreements. As a result, begin bargaining with a positive overture—perhaps a small concession—and then reciprocate your opponent's concessions.

3. *Address problems, not personalities.* Concentrate on the negotiation issues, not on the personal characteristics of your opponent. When negotiations get tough, avoid the tendency to attack your opponent. It is your opponent's ideas or position that you disagree with, not him or her personally. Separate the people from the problem, and don't personalize differences.

4. *Pay little attention to initial offers.* Treat an initial offer as merely a point of departure. Everyone has to have an initial position, and initial positions tend to be extreme and idealistic. Treat them as such.

5. *Emphasize win-win solutions.* If conditions are supportive, look for an integrative solution. Frame options in terms of your opponent's interests and look for solutions that can allow your opponent, as well as yourself, to declare a victory.

6. *Be open to accepting third-party assistance.* When stalemates are reached, consider the use of a neutral third party—a mediator, an arbitrator, or a conciliator. Mediators can help parties come to an agreement, but they don't impose a settlement. Arbitrators hear both sides of the dispute, then impose a solution. Conciliators are more informal and act as a communication conduit, passing information between the parties, interpreting messages, and clarifying misunderstandings.

HRM WORKSHOP

*S*UMMARY

(This summary relates to the Learning Outcomes identified on p. 412.)
After having read this chapter, you should be able to:

1. **Define what is meant by the term *unions*.** A union is an organization of workers, acting collectively, seeking to promote and protect their mutual interests through collective bargaining.

2. **Discuss what effect the Wagner and the Taft-Hartley Acts had on labor-management relations.** The Wagner (National Labor Relations) Act of 1935 and the Taft-Hartley (Labor-Management Relations) Act of 1947 represent the most direct legislation affecting collective bargaining. The Wagner Act gave unions the freedom to exist and identified employer unfair labor practices. Taft-Hartley balanced the power between unions and management by identifying union unfair labor practices.

3. **Identify the significance of Executive Orders 10988 and 11491, and the Civil Service Reform Act of 1978.** Executive Orders 10988 and 11491 paved the way for labor relations to exist in the federal sector. Additionally, Executive Order 11491 made federal labor relations similar to its private-sector counterpart. The Civil Service Reform Act of 1978 removed federal-sector labor relations from under the jurisdiction of the president and established a forum for its continued operation.

4. **Describe the union-organizing process.** The union-organizing process officially begins with the completion of an authorization. If the required percentage of potential union members show their intent to vote on a union by signing the authorization card, the NLRB will hold an election. If 50 percent plus one of those voting vote for the union, then the union is certified to be the bargaining unit.

5. **Describe the components of collective bargaining.** Collective bargaining typically refers to the negotiation, administration, and interpretation of a written agreement between two parties that covers a specific period of time.

6. **Identify the steps in the collective-bargaining process.** The collective-bargaining process is comprised of the following steps: preparation for negotiations, negotiations, and contract administration.

7. **Explain the various types of union security arrangements.** The various union security arrangements are the closed shop (made illegal by the Taft-Hartley Act); the union shop, which requires compulsory union membership; the agency shop, which requires compulsory union dues; and the open shop, which enforces workers' freedom of choice to select union membership or not.

8. **Describe the role of a grievance procedure in collective bargaining.** The role of the grievance procedure is to provide a formal mechanism in labor contracts for resolving issues over the interpretation and application of a contract.

9. **Identify the various impasse-resolution techniques.** The most popular impasse-resolution techniques include mediation (a neutral third-party informally attempts to get the parties to reach an agreement); fact-finding (a neutral third-party conducts a hearing to gather evidence from both sides); and interest arbitration (a panel of individuals hears testimony from both sides and renders a decision).

10. **Discuss how sunshine laws affect public-sector collective bargaining.** Sunshine laws require parties in the public sector to make their collective-bargaining negotiations open to the public.

DEMONSTRATING COMPREHENSION: *Questions for Review and Discussion*

1. What three pieces of legislation have been most important in defining the rights of management and unions?

2. What is the process for establishing a union as the legal collective-bargaining representative for employees?

3. Where are unionizing efforts focused today?

4. "All that is required for successful labor-management relations is common sense, sound business judgment, and good listening skills." Do you agree or disagree with this statement? Explain.

5. Given your career aspirations, might you join a union? Why or why not? Explain.

6. What is collective bargaining? How widely is it practiced?

7. Describe the collective-bargaining process.

8. What is the objective of collective bargaining?

9. Why do a union's initial demands tend to be long and extravagant?

10. "An employer might not want to stifle a union-organizing effort. In fact, an employer might want to encourage his employees to join a union." Do you agree or disagree with this statement? Explain your position.

CASE APPLICATION: *TEAM FUN!*

Kenny and Norton, owners of TEAM FUN!, a sporting goods manufacturer and retailer are kayaking in the LAGOON, their water gear area. Kenny splashes Norton, "Did you see the paper this morning?" Norton shakes his head no as Kenny continues, "I bet I know why Keith was talking about changing operations at his company and finding out how happy all his employees are. Those guys voted in a union. Honest. Front page of the business section." (Keith is one of their long time competitors.)

Norton frowns, "Why would they go union? He's a great guy. Tony found out that they pay better than we do. Say, do we need to worry about a union here?" (Tony is Director of Human Resources for TEAM FUN!)

Kenny reassures him, "No worries here. Besides, they have to let us know ahead of time if they are having a "certainization vote." I think he said 2 years, or maybe that's 2 months, before they organize one. We can go talk to all the employees if you want. Next month's picnic doesn't have a topic yet. We'll ask Tony as soon as he shows up. You'll never catch me in a union."

Norton: "We were in a union before the war. Remember that food processing plant in Texas where we shoveled frozen peas into boxcars? We paid dues, filed grease bandages, the whole bit. It was a closeted shop."

Kenny: "My fingers got frostbit there. See? I never paid dues." Norton holds up 3 fingers and Kenny says, "Oh, yeah. I thought I was bribing that guy not to tell when we came in late. I never had a closet for any of my stuff. That place wasn't anything like TEAM FUN! Ask Tony what he thinks about a union. Did you ever figure out why they called the complaint procedure a 'greased bandage?'"

Norton snorts, "I'll fire him if he thinks it's a good idea."

Kenny smiles, "We can just fire all of them if they think it's a good idea."

Questions

1. How accurate is Kenny's description of the union organizing process? Give details.
2. Explain to Norton the union activities he remembers from their Texas job.
3. Is TEAM FUN! likely to organize?
4. Should the organization resist or encourage such activities?

WORKING WITH A TEAM: *Handling a Grievance*

Break into teams of three. This role-play requires one person to play the role of the HR Director (Chris), another to play the role of the employee (Pat), and a third to play the role of the union steward (C.J.).

Each team member should read the following scenario and the excerpt from the union contract and then role-play a meeting in Chris's office. This role-play should take no more than 15 minutes.

Scenario: The head of security for your company has recently been focusing attention on the removal of illegal substances from the company's workplace. One morning last week, a guard suspected the possession of a controlled substance by an employee, Pat. The guard noticed Pat placing a bag in a personal locker, and subsequently searched the locker. The guard found a variety of pills, some of which he thought were nonprescription types. As Pat was leaving work for the day, the security guard stopped Pat with a request for Pat to empty the contents of the bag being carried. Pat was not told why the request was being made. Pat refused to honor the request, and stormed out of the door, leaving the company's premise. Pat was terminated the next morning by his boss for refusing to obey the legitimate order of a building security guard. Feeling as if they were unable to address the issue satisfactorily with Pat's supervisor, Pat and C.J. have set up this meeting with Chris.

Chris has just gone into a meeting with Pat and C.J. Chris wishes to enforce Pat's supervisor's decision to terminate Pat and justify the reason for it. C.J. and Pat, on the other hand, claim this action is a violation of the union contract.

Relevant Contract Language: The following is excerpted from the labor agreement: An employee who fails to maintain proper standards of conduct at all times, or who violates any of the following rules, shall be subject to disciplinary action.

Rule 4: Bringing illegal substances, firearms, or intoxicating liquors onto company premises, using or possessing these on company property, or reporting to work under the influence of a substance is strictly prohibited.

Rule 11: Refusal to follow supervisory orders, or acting in any way insubordinate to any company agent, is strictly prohibited.

Role for Chris: To handle this grievance, listen to the employee's complaint, investigate the facts as best you can, and make your decision and explain it clearly.

*E*NHANCING *Y*OUR *W*RITING *S*KILLS

1. In a two- to three-page report, discuss the pros, cons, and class perceptions of what it is/would be like to work in a unionized environment. Would you consider working in such an environment? Why or why not?

2. Visit the AFL-CIO's web site (www.aflcio.com). Research and summarize two current union issues the AFL-CIO is working on/supporting legislation for. End your report with your support for or against the union perspective.

3. Investigate how the Racketeering Influenced and Corrupt Organizations Act (RICO) has been used in the past five years to attack corrupt practices in labor unions. Cite specific examples found in your research.

www.wiley.com/college/decenzo

*E*NDNOTES

1. Adapted from K. Bradsher, "Behind the Labor Peace at Ford," *New York Times* (March 21, 1999), p. BU-2; Eric Torbenson, "Northwest Airlines Mediators Give Up," *Pioneer Planet* (February 11, 2001), p. 1; John Lippert, "Striking Similarities?" *Columbia Journalism Review* (January–February 2001), p. 10; and Deborah Solomon, and Yochi J. Dreazen, "Verizon Hit by Strike, But Talks progress—Phone Company Addresses Union Push to Organize Wireless Unit's Workers," *Wall Street Journal* (August 7, 2000), p. A-3.

2. Robert Kornfeld, "The Effects of Union Membership on Wages and Employee Benefits: The Case of Australia," *Industrial and Labor Relations Review* (October 1993), p. 114.

3. Marianne J. Koch and Greg Hundley, "The Effects of Unionism on Recruitment and Selection Methods," *Industrial Relations* (July 1997), p. 349.

4. See AFL-CIO, "Unions Raise Wages—Especially for Minorities and Women," www.aflcio.org/uniondifference/uniondiff4.htm, from U.S. Department of Labor, Employment and Earnings (January 2001).

5. Aaron Bernstein, "All's Not Fair in Labor Wars," *Business Week* (July 19, 1999), p. 43.

6. Readers should recognize that although the closed shop (compulsory union membership before one is hired) was declared illegal by the Taft-Hartley Act, a modified form still exists today. That quasi-closed shop arrangement is called the *hiring hall* and is found predominantly in the construction and printing industries. However, a hiring hall is not a form of union security because it must assist all members despite their union affiliation. Additionally, the hiring hall must establish procedures for referrals that are non-discriminatory.

7. Currently, 21 of 50 states are right-to-work states. These are Alabama, Arizona, Arkansas, Florida, Georgia, Idaho, Iowa, Kansas, Louisiana, Mississippi, Nebraska, Nevada, North Carolina, North Dakota, South Carolina, South Dakota, Tennessee, Texas, Utah, Virginia, and Wyoming. *Statistical Abstracts of the United States, 1999,* news release November 17, 2000, and www.aflcio.org/uniondifference/uniondiff7.htm.

8. There are, however, exceptions to this in the construction industry.

9. *Communication Workers of America v. Beck*, U.S. Supreme Court, 109LC (1988).

10. "The AFL-CIO's Dues Blues: Democracy Strikes Unions," *Fortune* (April 13, 1998), p. 36.

11. Ibid.

12. Aaron Bernstein and David Griesing, "Baseball's Strike Talk Turns Serious," *Business Week* (June 27, 1994), p. 34.

13. See, for instance, Michael Romano, "Hospital Accused of Iron-Fist Tactics," *Modern Hospital* (January 8, 2001), p. 16.

14. For a comprehensive review of labor laws, see Bruce Feldacker, *Labor Law Guide to Labor Law*, 4th ed. (Upper Saddle River, NJ: Prentice-Hall, 2000).

15. Bruce Feldacker, *Labor Law Guide to Labor Law*, 4th ed., p. 5.

16. The Railway Labor Act created the National Mediation Board, which works on matters of recognition, dispute resolution, and unfair labor practices in the railroad and airline industries only. The National Railroad Adjustment Board was also part of the Railway Labor Act, and this body arbitrated disputes between railroads and unions.

17. It is also important to note that the Wagner Act was also amended in 1974 with the Health Care Amendments. This amendment brought both nonprofit hospitals and health care organizations under the jurisdiction of the Wagner Act.

18. Michael J. Goldberg, "An Overview and Assessment of the Law Regulating Internal Union Affairs," *Journal of Labor Research* (Winter 2000), pp. 15–36.

19. L-M 2 reports are required of unions that have revenues of $200,000 or more and those in trusteeship. L-M 3 reports are a simplified annual report which may be filed by unions with total revenues of less than $200,000, and if the union is not in trusteeship. L-M 4 is an abbreviated form and may be used by unions with less than $10,000 in total annual revenues, and if the union is not in trusteeship. These reports are due within 90 days after the end of the union's fiscal year. See www.dol.gov/dol/esa/public/regs/compliance/olms/rrlo/repreq.htm.anfin.

20. It must be noted that when one discusses government labor relations, two categories emerge. One is the federal sector, the other the public sector. In a brief discussion of government labor relations, the focus is on the federal sector due to its federal legislation. However, one must realize that state

or municipal statutes do define practices for labor-management relationships for state, county, and municipal workers (typically police officers, fire fighters, and teachers). Because these laws differ in the many jurisdictions, it goes beyond the scope of this text to attempt to clarify each jurisdiction's laws.

21. Although government employees often face a no-strike clause, with the exception of the Air Traffic Controllers case, such restrictions are generally ineffective. Working to rules, "blue flues" and recorded sanitation, nursing, and teacher strikes across this country support the contention that a no-strike clause is weak.

22. United States Code Annotated, Title 18, Section 1961 (St. Paul, MN: West Publishing, 1984), p. 6.

23. Ibid., p. 228.

24. United States Code Annotated, Title 29, Section 186 (St. Paul, MN: West Publishing, 1978), p. 17.

25. See, for example, "The Liberation of the Teamsters," *National Review* (March 30, 1992), p. 35; and "Breaking the Teamsters," *Newsweek* (June 22, 1987), p. 43.

26. Only pure grievance awards can be solely determined by the FLRA. See Joseph R. Gordon and Joyce M. Najita, "Judicial Response to Public-Sector Arbitration," in Aaron et al., op. cit., p. 247.

27. Mark A. Spognardi and Ruth Hill Bro, "Organizing Through Cyberspace: Electronic Communications and the National Labor Relations Act," *Employee Relations Law Journal* (Spring 1998), pp. 141–151.

28. Jonathan A. Segal, "Expose the Union's Underbelly," *HRMagazine* (June 1999), p. 166.

29. Elections may not be the only means of unionizing. In cases where a company has refused to recognize a union because of a past unfair labor practice, the NLRB may certify a union without a vote.

30. Adapted from Stephen P. Robbins and David A. DeCenzo, *Supervision Today,* 3rd ed. (Upper Saddle River, NJ: Prentice-Hall, 2001), p. 494; Mary-Kathryn Zachary, "Labor Law for Supervisors: Union Campaigns Prove Sensitive for Supervisory Employees," *Supervision* (May 2000), pp. 23–26; Steven Greenhouse, "A Potent, Illegal Weapon Against Unions: Employers Know it Cost Them to Fire Organizers," *New York Times* (October 24, 2000), p. A-10; John E. Lyncheski and Leslie D. Heller, "Cyber Speech Cops," *HRMagazine* (January 2001), pp. 145–150; and Jeffrey A. Mello, "Redefining the Rights of Union Organizers and Responsibilities of Employers in Union Organizing Drives," *S.A.M. Advanced Management Journal* (Spring 1998), p. 4.

31. D. C. Bok and J. T. Dunlop, "Collective Bargaining in the United States: An Overview," in W. Clay Hammer and Frank L. Schmidt (eds.), *Contemporary Problems in Personnel* (Chicago: St. Clair Press, 1977), p. 383.

32. An international union, in this context, refers to a national union in the United States that has local unions in Canada.

33. If we take into account public-sector collective bargaining, then we have another exception—the public. The tax-paying voting public can influence elected officials to act in certain ways during negotiations.

34. Nicole Harris, "Flying into a Rage," *Business Week* (April 27, 1998), p. 119.

35. Mollie H. Bowers and David A. DeCenzo, *Essentials of Labor Relations* (Englewood Cliffs, NJ: Prentice-Hall, 1992), p. 101.

36. For a thorough explanation of the grievance procedure, see ibid., pp. 109–114.

37. See also, Mark I. Lurie, "The 8 Essential Steps in Grievance Processing," *Dispute Resolution Journal* (November 1999), pp. 61–65.

38. Adapted from Stephen P. Robbins and David A. DeCenzo, *Supervision Today,* 3rd ed. (Upper Saddle River, NJ: Prentice-Hall, 2001), p. 500.

39. Sue Shellenbarger, "Companies Are Finding Real Payoffs in Aiding Employee Satisfaction," *Wall Street Journal* (October 11, 2000), p. B-1.

40. To be accurate, a strike vote is generally held at the local union level in which the members authorize their union leadership to call the strike.

41. U.S. Department of Labor, *Statistical Abstracts of the United States, 1999* (Washington, D.C., GPO, 1999), p. 452.

42. See Michael A. Verespej, "Wounded and Weaponless," *Industry Week* (September 16, 1996), p. 46.

43. U.S. Department of Labor, *Statistical Abstracts of the United States, 1999* (Washington, DC., GPO, 1999), p. 452; and Fehmida Sleemi, "Work Stoppages in 1999," *Compensation and Working Conditions* (Fall 2000), p. 36.

44. "Business Brief—Kaiser Aluminum Corp.: United Steelworkers Finalize Labor Pact, Ending Lockout," *Wall Street Journal* (September 19, 2000), p. C-19.

45. Kevin Helliker, "Grocery Lockout: Food for Thought on Labor's Power—Union Mostly Prevails in Kansas After Replacement Workers Prove Hard to Attract," *Wall Street Journal* (June 30, 2000), p. A-2.

46. U.S. Bureau of the Census, *Statistical Abstracts of the United States, 1999*, p. 453.

47. "Why Labor Keeps Losing," *Fortune* (July 11, 1994), p. 178. It is also interesting to point out that President Clinton lifted the ban on hiring air traffic controllers who had been fired by President Reagan. Any air traffic controller fired by Reagan was not eligible to work again for the Federal Aviation Administration—the agency that hires air controllers. The removal of the ban came on August 12, 1993.

48. See Philip A. Miscimarra and Kenneth D. Schwartz, "Frozen in Time—The NLRB, Outsourcing, and Management Rights," *Journal of Labor Research* (Fall 1997), pp. 561–580. Outsourcing refers to a situation where work is taken away from unionized workers in a company and given to nonunionized employees in a separate location.

49. Department of Labor, U.S. Bureau of Labor Statistics, "Union Members Summary" (January 18, 2001), p. 1 [http://stats.bls.gov/news.release/union2.nr0.htm]; Yochi J. Dreazen, "Percentage of U.S. Workers in a Union Sank to Record Low of 13.5% Last Year," *Wall Street Journal* (January 19, 2001), A-2; and Yochi J. Dreazen, "Slower Growth Threatens Labor Unions—Leaders Fear Further Decline in Ranks as Economy Cools Off," *Wall Street Journal* (January 16, 2001), p. A-2.

50. "Multiple Indicators Show Labor Movement Organizing and Growing," *AFL-CIO* (January 25, 1999), p. 1 [http://aflcio.org/publ/press1999/pr0125.htm].

51. Carlos Tejada, "Graduate Students at Private Universities Have Right to Unionize, Agency Rules," *Wall Street Journal* (November 2, 2000), p. B-22; Vivienne Walt, "Labor's

Big Net," *U.S. News & World Report* (February 9, 1998), pp. 52–53; and Aaron Bernstein, "Sweeney's Blitz," *Business Week* (February 17, 1997), p. 56.

52. Timothy J. Loney, "TQM and Labor-Management Cooperation—A Noble Experiment for the Public Sector," *International Journal of Public Administration* (October 1996), p. 1845; and Bill Vlasic, "The Saginaw Solution," *Business Week* (July 15, 1996), pp. 78–80.

53. "Teamwork for Employees and Managers (TEAM) Act," *HR Legislative Fact Sheet* (June 1996), pp. 28–29; and Randall Hanson, Rebecca I. Porterfield, and Kathleen Ames, "Employee Empowerment at Risk: Effects of Recent NLRB Rulings," *Academy of Management Executive*, Vol. 9, No. 2 (1995), pp. 45–56.

54. For an interesting article on this topic, see Roy J. Adams, "Why Statutory Union Recognition Is Bad Labour Policy: The North American Experience," *Industrial Relations Journal* (June 1999), pp. 96–100.

55. "Team Act," *Journal for Quality and Participation* (January–February 1998), p. 7.

56. Legislation, called the "Teamwork for Employees and Managers (TEAM) Act," has been proposed in both the House of Representatives and the Senate. The Act, as proposed, was designed to "permit employers and employees to establish and maintain employee involvement programs—including various approaches to problem-solving, communication enhancement, productivity improvement programs." In May 1996, the Act was passed in the House and sent to the Senate for approval. By a vote of 53 to 46, the Senate approved the Act in principle but did not agree to some of its language. "Teamwork for Employees and Managers (TEAM) Act," *HR Legislative Fact Sheet* (June 1996), pp. 28–29.

57. See, for example, Leo Troy, "Why Labor Unions Are Declining," *Journal of Commerce* (August 1994), p. 6A; and S. Overman, "The Union Pitch Has Changed," *HRMagazine* (December 1991), pp. 44–46.

58. Bureau of Labor Statistics, "Union Affiliation of Employed Wage and Salary Workers by Occupation and Industry," *Union Member Survey* (January 18, 2001), Table 3.

59. Victor G. Devinatz, "Testing the Johnston 'Public Sector Union Strike' Hypotheses: A Qualitative Analysis," *Journal of Collective Negotiations in the Public Sector*, Vol. 26, No. 2 (1997), pp. 99–112.

60. Sunshine laws exist in eleven states: Alaska, California, Delaware, Florida, Idaho, Iowa, Minnesota, Texas, Ohio, Vermont, and Wisconsin. In addition, Indiana, Kansas, Maryland, Montana, and Tennessee have laws regarding the openness of the collective-bargaining process.

61. Wendy Zellner and Aaron Bernstein, "Up Against the Wal-Mart," *Business Week* (March 13, 2000), pp. 76–78.

62. U.S. Department of Labor, *Employment and Earnings* (January 2001), and AFL-CIO, http://www.aflcio.org/uniondifference/uniondiff5.htm.

63. Katherine Pfleger, "Unions Active in High-Tech Fields," *Editor and Publisher* (January 29, 2001), p. 1; and Aaron Bernstein and Rob Hof, "A Union for Amazon," *Business Week* (December 4, 2000), p. 86.

64. See, for example, Peter J. Dowling and Randall S. Schuler, *International Dimensions of Human Resource Management* (Boston: PWS-Kent Publishing, 1990), pp. 138–157.

65. David Woodruff, "The German Worker Is Making a Sacrifice," *Business Week* (July 28, 1997), pp. 46–47. See also Barrie Clement, "Nice Suit. Is That the Union Rep?" *Management Today* (March 1999), pp. 74–78.

66. See Joe Laws and Thomas Li-Ping Tang, "Japanese Transplants and Union Membership: The Case of Nissan Motor Manufacturing Corporation," *S.A.M Advanced Management Journal* (Spring 1999), pp. 16–25.

67. See, for example, Peter Dowling, Randall S. Schuler, and Denice E. Welch, *International Dimensions of Human Resource Management*, 2nd ed. (Belmont, CA: Wadsworth, 1994), pp. 201–203.

68. Brooks Tigner, "The Looming Crunch," in M. Mendenhall and G. Oddou (eds.), *Readings and Cases in International Human Resource Management* (Boston: PWS-Kent Publishing, 1991), pp. 412–417.

69. Based on R. Fisher and W. Ury, *Getting to Yes: Negotiating Agreement Without Giving In* (Boston: Houghton Mifflin, 1981); J. A. Wall Jr. and M. W. Blum, "Negotiations," *Journal of Management* (June 1991), pp. 295–96; M. H. Bazerman and M. A. Neale, *Negotiating Rationally* (New York: Free Press, 1992); David A. DeCenzo and Stephen P. Robbins, *Fundamentals of Management*, 3rd ed. (Upper Saddle River, NJ: Prentice-Hall, 2001), pp. 401–402.

70. "How to Negotiate with Really Tough Guys," *Fortune* (May 27, 1996), pp. 173–174.

GLOSSARY

Absolute Standards Measuring an employee's performance against some established standards.

Adjective Rating Scales A performance appraisal method that lists a number of traits and a range of performance for each.

Adverse (Disparate) Impact A consequence of an employment practice that results in a greater rejection rate for a minority group than it does for the majority group in the occupation.

Adverse (Disparate) Treatment An employment situation where protected group members receive different treatment than other employees in matters like performance evaluations, promotions, etc.

Affirmative Action A practice in organizations that goes beyond discontinuance of discriminatory practices, including actively seeking, hiring, and promoting minority group members and women.

Age Discrimination in Employment Act This act prohibits arbitrary age discrimination, particularly among those over age 40.

Agency Shop A type of union security arrangement whereby employees must pay union dues to the certified bargaining unit even if they choose not to join the union.

Albermarle Paper Company v. Moody Supreme Court case that clarified the requirements for using and validating tests in selection processes.

Americans with Disabilities Act of Extends EEO coverage to include most forms of disability, requires employers to make reasonable accommodations, and eliminates post-job-offer medical exams.

Application Form Company-specific employment forms used to generate specific information the company wants.

Assessment Centers A facility where performance simulation tests are administered. These are made up of a series of exercises and are used for selection, development, and performance appraisals.

Attribution Theory A theory of performance evaluation based on the perception of who is in control of an employee's performance.

Authorization Card A card signed by prospective union members indicating that they are interested in having a union election held at their work site.

Background Investigation The process of verifying information job candidates provide.

Behaviorally Anchored Rating Scales (BARS) A performance appraisal technique that generates critical incidents and develops behavioral dimensions of performance. The evaluator appraises behaviors rather than traits.

Blind-box Ad An advertisement in which there is no identification of the advertising organization.

Blue Cross A health insurer concerned with the hospital side of health insurance.

Blue Shield A health insurer concerned with the provider side of health insurance.

Bonafide Occupational Qualifications Job requirements that are "reasonably necessary to meet the normal operations of that business or enterprise."

Broad-banding Paying employees at preset levels based on the level of competencies they possess.

Bulletin Board A means a company uses to post information of interest to its employees.

Burnout Chronic and long-term stress.

Career The sequence of positions that a person has held over his or her life.

Carpal Tunnel Syndrome A repetitive motion disorder affecting the wrist.

Central Tendency The tendency of a rater to give average ratings.

Change Agent Individuals responsible for fostering the change effort, and assisting employees in adapting to the changes.

Checklist Appraisal A performance appraisal type in which a rater checks off those attributes of an employee that apply.

Civil Service Reform Act Replaced Executive Order as the basic law governing labor relations for federal employees.

Civil Rights Acts of 1991 Employment discrimination law that nullified selected Supreme Court decisions. Reinstated burden of proof by the employer, and allowed for punitive and compensatory damage through jury trials.

Civil Rights Act of 1866 Federal law that prohibited discrimination based on race.

Climate Survey Assessment of employees' perceptions and attitudes about their jobs and organization.

Collective Bargaining The negotiation, administration, and interpretation of a written agreement between two parties, at least one of which represents a group that is acting collectively, that covers a specific period of time.

Communication The transference of meaning and understanding.

Communications Programs HRM programs designed to provide information to employees.

Company Newsletter A means of providing information for employees in a specific recurring periodical.

Company-wide Meetings Frequently held meetings used to inform employees of various company issues.

Comparable Worth Equal pay for similar jobs, jobs similar in skills, responsibility, working conditions, and effort.

Compensation Administration The process of managing a company's compensation program.

Compensation Surveys Used to gather factual data on pay practices among firms and companies within specific communities.

Competency-based Compensation Programs Organizational pay system that rewards skills, knowledge, and behaviors.

Competitive Intelligence Seeking basic information about competitors

Complaint Procedure A formalized procedure in an organization through which an employee seeks resolution of a work problem.

Comprehensive Interviews A selection device in which indepth information about a candidate can be obtained.

Comprehensive Selection Applying all steps in the selection process before rendering a decision about a job candidate.

Concurrent Validity Validating tests by using current employees as the study group.

Conflict Resolution Attempts to get both parties to see the similarities and differences that exist between them, and look for ways to overcome the differences.

Consolidated Omnibus Budget Reconciliation Act Provides for the continuation of employee benefits for a period up to three years after an employee leaves a job.

Constraints on Recruiting Efforts Factors that can affect maximizing outcomes in recruiting.

Construct Validity The degree to which a particular trait is related to successful performance on the job e.g., IQ tests.

Content Validity The degree to which the content of the test, as a sample, represents all the situations that could have been included e.g., a typing test for a clerk typist .

Contingent Workers The part-time, temporary, and contract workers used by organizations to fill peak staffing needs, or perform work unable to be done by core employees.

Controlling A management function concerned with monitoring activities.

Core Competency Those organizational strengths that represent unique skills or resources.

Core employees An organization's full-time employee population.

Criterion-related Validity The degree to which a particular selection device accurately predicts the important elements of work behavior e.g., the relationship between a test score and job performance.

Critical Incident Appraisal A performance appraisal method that focuses on the key behaviors that make the difference between doing a job effectively or ineffectively.

Cut Score A point at which applicants scoring below that point are rejected.

Decline Period The final stage in one's career, usually marked by retirement.

Defined Benefit Plan A type of retirement program whereby a retiring employee receives a fixed amount of retirement income based on some average earnings over a period of time.

Delegation A management activity in which activities are assigned to individuals at lower levels in the organization.

Diary Method A job analysis method requiring job incumbents to record their daily activities.

Digital Media A form of communications that relies heavily on technology.

Discipline A condition in the organization when employees conduct themselves in accordance with the organization's rules and standards of acceptable behavior.

Dismissal A disciplinary action that results in the termination of an employee.

Documentation Used as a record of the performance appraisal process outcomes.

Domestic Partner Benefits Benefits offered to an employee's "live-in" partner.

Downsizing An activity in an organization aimed at creating greater efficiency by eliminating certain jobs.

Drug Testing The process of testing applicants/ employees to determine if they are using illicit drugs.

Drug-free Workplace Act Requires specific government-related groups to ensure that their workplace is drug free.

Dues Checkoff Employer withholding of union dues from union members' paychecks.

Dysfunctional Tension Tension that leads to negative stress.

Economic Strike An impasse that results from labor and management's inability to agree on the wages, hours, and terms and conditions of a "new" contract.

Employee Assistance Programs EAPS Specific programs designed to help employees with personal problems.

Employee Benefits Membership-based, nonfinancial rewards offered to attract and keep employees.

Employee Counseling A process whereby employees are guided in overcoming performance problems.

Employee Development Future-oriented training, focusing on the personal growth of the employee.

Employee Handbook A booklet describing the important aspects of employment an employee needs to know.

Employee Monitoring An activity whereby the company is able to keep informed of its employees' activities.

Employee Referrals A recommendation from a current employee regarding a job applicant.

Employee Relations Function Activities in HRM concerned with effective communications among organizational members.

Employee Retirement Income Security Act Law passed in 1974 designed to protect employee retirement benefits.

Employee Training Present-oriented training, focusing on individuals' current jobs.

Employment-at-Will Nineteenth-century common law that permitted employers to discipline or discharge employees at their discretion.

Employment Planning Process of determining an organization's human resource needs.

Empowering Affording employees more delegation, participative management, work teams, goal setting, and training.

Encounter Stage The socialization stage where individuals confront the possible dichotomy between their organizational expectations and reality.

Environmental Influences Those factors outside the organization that directly affect HRM operations.

Equal Employment Opportunity Commission The arm of the federal government empowered to handle discrimination in employment cases.

Equal Pay Act Passed in 1963, this act requires equal pay for equal work.

Essay Appraisal A performance appraisal method whereby an appraiser writes a narrative about the employee.

Establishment Period A career stage in which one begins to search for work. It includes getting one's first job.

Executive Search Private employment agency specializing in middle- and top-management placements.

Executive Order 11246 Executive order which prohibited discrimination on the basis of race, religion, color, or national origin by federal agencies as well as by contractors and subcontractors who worked under federal contracts.

Executive Order 11375 Executive order which added sex-based discrimination to Executive Order 11246.

Executive Order 11478 Superceded pars of Executive Order 11246 stating that employment practices in the federal government must be based on merit and must prohibit discrimination based on race, color, religion, sex, national origin, political affiliation, marital status, or physical disability.

Expatriates Individuals who work in a country in which they are not citizens of that country.

Exploration Period A career stage that usually ends in one's mid-twenties as one makes the transition from school to work.

External Career Involves the properties or qualities of an occupation.

Extrinsic Rewards Rewards one gets from the employer, usually money, a promotion, or benefits.

Fact-finder A neutral third-party individual who conducts a hearing to gather evidence and testimony from the parties regarding the differences between them.

Fair Credit Reporting Act Requires an employer to notify job candidates of its intent to check into their credit.

Fair Labor Standards Act Passed in , this act established laws outlining minimum wage, overtime pay, and maximum hour requirements for most U.S. workers.

Family and Medical Leave Act Federal legislation that provides employees up to twelve weeks of unpaid leave each year to care for family members, or for their own medical reasons.

Family-Friendly Benefits Flexible benefits that are supportive of caring for one's family.

Federal Mediation and Conciliation Service A government agency that assists labor and management in settling their disputes.

Flexible Benefits A benefits program in which employees are permitted to pick benefits that most meet their needs.

Forced-choice Appraisal A type of performance appraisal method in which the rater must choose between two specific statements about an employee's work behavior.

4/5ths Rule A rough indicator of discrimination, this rule requires that the number of minority members that a company hires must be at least 80 percent of the majority members in the population hired.

401(k)s Tax code section that permits employees to set aside a part of their salary for retirement on a pretax basis.

Functional Tension Positive tension that creates the energy for an individual to act.

Glass Ceiling The invisible barrier that blocks females and minorities from ascending into upper levels of an organization.

Global Village The production and marketing of goods and services worldwide.

Golden Parachute A protection plan for executives in the event that they are severed from the organization.

Grievance Procedures A complaint-resolving process contained in union contracts.

Griggs v. Duke Power Landmark Supreme Court decision stating that tests must fairly measure the knowledge or skills required for a job.

Group Interview Method Meeting with a number of employees to collectively determine what their jobs entail.

Halo Error The tendency to let our assessment of an individual on one trait influence our evaluation of that person on other specific traits.

Hawthorne Studies A series of studies that provided new insights into group behavior.

Health Maintenance Act Established the requirement that companies offering traditional health insurance to its employees must also offer alternative health-care options.

Health Maintenance Organization Provides comprehensive health services for a flat fee.

Holland Vocational Preferences An individual occupational personality as it relates to vocational themes.

Honesty Tests A specialized paper-and-pencil test designed to assess one's honesty.

Host-country national Hiring a citizen from the host country to perform certain jobs in the global village.

Hot-stove Rule Discipline should be immediate, provide ample warning, be consistent, and be impersonal.

Human Resource Management System A computerized system that assists in the processing of HRM information.

Imminent Danger A condition where an accident is about to occur.

Implied Employment Contract Any organizational guarantee or promise about job security.

Impression Management Influencing performance evaluations by portraying an image that is desired by the appraiser.

IMPROSHARE A special type of incentive plan using a specific mathematical formula for determining employee bonuses.

Incident Rate Number of injuries, illnesses, or lost workdays as it relates to a common base of full-time employees.

Individual Interview Method Meeting with an employee to determine what his or her job entails.

Individual Needs A basic want or desire.

Individual Ranking Ranking employees' performance from highest to lowest.

Initial Screening The first step in the selection process whereby inquiries about a job are screened.

Interactive Videos Videos that permit the user to make changes/selections.

Interest Arbitration An impasse resolution technique used to settle contract negotiation disputes.

Internal Search A promotion-from-within concept.

Intrinsic Rewards Rewards one receives from the job itself, such as pride in one's work, a feeling of accomplishment, or being part of a team.

Job Analysis Provides information about jobs currently being done and the knowledge, skills, and abilities that individuals need to perform the jobs adequately.

Job Description A written statement of what the job-holder does, how it is done, and why it is done.

Job Evaluation Specifies the relative value of each job in the organization.

Job Instruction Training A systematic approach to on-the-job training consisting of four basic steps.

Job Morphing Readjusting skills to match job requirements.

Job Rotation Moving employees horizontally or vertically to expand their skills, knowledge, or abilities.

Job Specifications Statements indicating the minimal acceptable qualifications incumbents must possess to successfully perform the essential elements of their jobs.

Karoshi A Japanese term meaning death from overworking.

Knowledge Workers Individuals whose jobs are designed around the acquisition and application of information.

Landrum-Griffin Act Also known as the Labor and Management Reporting and Disclosure Act, this legislation protected union members from possible wrongdoing on the part of their unions. Its thrust was to require all unions to disclose their financial statements.

Late-career Phase A career stage in which individuals are no longer learning about their jobs, nor is it expected that they should be trying to outdo levels of performance from previous years.

Layoff-survivor Sickness A set of attitudes, perceptions, and behaviors of employees who remain after involuntary employee reductions

Leading A management function concerned with directing the work of others.

Learning Organization An organization that values continued learning and believe a competitive advantage can be derived from it.

Leased Employees Individuals who are hired by one firm and sent to work in another for a specific duration of time.

Legislating Love Company guidelines on how personal relationships may exist at work.

Leniency Error A means by which performance appraisal can be distorted by evaluating employees against one's own value system.

Lockout A situation in labor—management negotiations whereby management prevents union members from returning to work.

Maintenance Function Activities in HRM concerned with maintaining employees' commitment and loyalty to the organization.

Maintenance of Membership If an individual chooses to join a union, that individual must remain in the union for the duration of the existing contract.

Management The process of efficiently getting activities completed with and through other people.

Management by Objectives (MBO) A performance appraisal method that includes mutual objective setting and evaluation based on the attainment of the specific objectives.

Management Thought Early theories of management that promoted today's HRM operations.

Marshall v. Barlow, Inc. Supreme Court case that stated an employer could refuse an OSHA inspection unless OSHA had a search warrant to enter the premises.

McDonnell-Douglas Corp. v. Green A four-part test used to determine if discrimination has occurred.

Medical/Physical Examination An examination indicating an applicant is physically fit for essential job performance.

Mentoring or Coaching Actively guiding another individual.

Merit Pay An increase in one's pay, usually given on an annual basis.

Metamorphosis Stage The socialization stage whereby the new employee must work out inconsistencies discovered during the encounter stage.

Mid-career Phase A career stage marked by a continuous improvement in performance, leveling off in performance, or the beginning of deterioration of performance.

Mission Statement The reason an organization is in business.

Motivation Function Activities in HRM concerned with helping employees exert high energy levels

Musculoskeletal Disorders (MSDs) Continuous motion disorders caused by repetitive stress injuries.

Myers-Briggs Type Indicator Uses four dimensions of personality to identify 16 personality types.

National Institute for Occupational Safety and Health (NIOSH) The government agency that researches and sets OSHA standards.

National Labor Relations Board Established to administer and interpret the Wagner Act, the NLRB has primary responsibility for conducting union representation elections.

Observation Method A job analysis technique in which data are gathered by watching employees work.

Occupational Safety and Health Act Set standards to ensure safe and healthful working conditions and provided stiff penalties for violators.

Office of Federal Contract Compliance Programs The government office that administers the provisions of Executive Order.

Open Shop Employees are free to choose whether or not to join the union, and those who do not are not required to pay union dues.

Ordering Method Ranking job worth from highest to lowest.

Organization Development The part of HRM that deals with facilitating systemwide change in the organization.

Organizing A management function that deals with what jobs are to be done, by whom, where decisions are to be made, and the grouping of employees.

Orientation The activities involved in introducing new employees to the organization and their work units.

Outsourcing Sending work "outside" the organization to be done by individuals not employed full time with the organization.

Paired Comparison Ranking individuals' performance by counting the number of times any one individual is the preferred member when compared with all other employees.

Pay-for-Performance Rewarding employees based on their performance.

Peer Evaluations A performance evaluation situation in which coworkers provide input into the employee's performance.

Pension Benefit Guaranty Corporation The organization that lays claim to corporate assets to pay or fund inadequate pension programs.

Performance-based Rewards Rewards exemplified by the use of commissions, piecework pay plans, incentive systems, group bonuses, or other forms of merit pay.

Performance Simulation Tests Work sampling and assessment centers focusing on actual job activities.

Perquisites Attractive benefits, over and above a regular salary, granted to executives "perks" .

Piecework Plans A compensation plan whereby employees are typically paid for the number of units they actually produce.

Planning A management function focusing on setting organizational goals and objectives.

Plant-wide Incentives An incentive system that rewards all members of the plant based on how well the entire group performed.

Plateauing A condition of stagnating in one's current job.

Point Method Breaking down jobs based on identifiable criteria and the degree to which these criteria exist on the job.

Polygraph Protection Act Prohibits the use of lie detectors in screening all job applicants. Often referred to as a "lie-detector" test.

Position Analysis Questionnaire A job analysis technique that rates jobs on elements in six activity categories.

Post-Training Performance Method Evaluating training programs based on how well employees can perform their jobs after they have received the training.

Pre–Post-Training Performance Method Evaluating training programs based the difference in performance before and after one receives training.

Pre–Post-Training Performance with Control Group Evaluating training by comparing pre- and post-training results with individuals who did not receive the training.

Prearrival Stage The socialization process stage that recognizes individuals arrive in an organization with a set of organizational values, attitudes, and expectations.

Predictive Validity Validating tests by using prospective applicants as the study group.

Preferred Provider Organizations Organization that requires using specific physicians and health-care facilities to contain the rising costs of health care.

Pregnancy Discrimination Act Law prohibiting discrimination based on pregnancy.

Privacy Act Requires federal government agencies to make available information in an individual's personnel file.

Programmed Instruction Material is learned in a highly organized, logical sequence, that requires the individual to respond.

Qualified Privilege The ability for organizations to speak candidly to one another about employees.

Railway Labor Act Provided the initial impetus to widespread collective bargaining.

Realistic Job Preview A selection device that allows job candidates to learn negative as well as positive information about the job and organization.

Recruiting The process of discovering potential job candidates.

Relative Standards Evaluating an employee's performance by comparing the employee with other employees.

Reliability A selection device's consistency of measurement.

Repetitive Stress Injuries Injuries sustained by continuous and repetitive movements of the hand.

Replacement Charts HRM organizational charts indicating positions that may become vacant in the near future and the individuals who may fill the vacancy.

Representation Certification The election process whereby union members vote in a union as their representative.

Representation Decertification The election pro-cess whereby union members vote out their union as their representative.

Reasonable Accommodations Providing the necessary technology to enable affected individuals to do his or her job.

Restricted Policy An HRM policy that results in the exclusion of a class of individuals.

Reverse Discrimination A claim made by white males that minority candidates are given preferential treatment in employment decisions.

Rightsizing Linking employee needs to organizational strategy.

Role Ambiguity When an employee is not sure what work to do.

Role Conflicts Expectations that are difficult to achieve.

Role Overload When an employee is expected to do more than time permits.

Scanlon Plan An organization-wide incentive program focusing on cooperation between management and employees through sharing problems, goals, and ideas.

Scientific Management A set of principles designed to enhance worker productivity.

Sexual Harassment Anything of a sexual nature where it results in a condition of employment, an employment consequence, or creates a hostile or offensive environment.

Shared Services Sharing HRM activities among geographically dispersed divisions.

Sick Building An unhealthy work environment.

Similarity Error Evaluating employees based on the way an evaluator perceives himself or herself.

Simulations Any artificial environment that attempts to closely mirror an actual condition.

Social Security Retirement, disability, and survivor benefits, paid by the government to aged, former members of the labor force, the disabled, or their survivors.

Socialization A process of adaption that takes place as individuals attempt to learn the values and norms of work roles.

Staffing Function Activities in HRM concerned with sourcing and hiring qualified employees.

Strengths Things that an organization does well.

Stress A dynamic condition in which an individual is confronted with an opportunity, constraint, or demand related to what he or she desires and for which the out-come is perceived to be both uncertain and important.

Stressors Something that causes stress in an individual.

Structured Questionnaire Method A specifically designed questionnaire on which employees rate tasks they perform on their jobs.

Suggestion Program A process whereby employees have the opportunity to tell management how they perceive the organization is doing.

Summary Plan Description An ERISA requirement of explaining to employees their pension program and rights.

Suspension A period of time off from work as a result of a disciplinary process.

SWOT Analysis A process for determining an organization's strengths, weaknesses, opportunities, and threats.

Taft-Hartley Act See Labor-Management Relations Act.

Team-based Compensation Compensation based on how well the team performed.

Team Building Activities associated with helping employees come together and work as a team.

Technical Conference Method A job analysis technique that involves extensive input from the employee's supervisor.

Telecommuting Employees who do their work at home on a computer that is then linked to their office.

360-Degree Appraisal Performance appraisal process in which supervisors, peers, employees, customers, and the like evaluate the individual.

Third-Party Intervention Using an outsider to assist employees in a group to change their attitudes, stereotypes or perceptions about one another.

Title VII The most prominent piece of legislation regarding HRM, it states that it is illegal to discriminate against individuals based on race, religion, color, sex, or national origin.

Total Quality Management A continuous process improvement.

Training and Development Function Activities in HRM concerned with assisting employees to develop up-to-date skills, knowledge, and abilities.

Type A Behavior Personality type characterized by chronic urgency and excessive competitive drive

Type B Behavior Personality type characterized by a lack of time urgency or impatience.

Union Organization of workers, acting collectively, seeking to protect and promote their mutual interests through collective bargaining.

Union Security Arrangements Labor contract provisions designed to attract and retain dues-paying union members.

Union Shop Employers can hire nonunion workers, but they must become dues-paying members within a prescribed period of time.

Validity The proven relationship of a selection device to some relevant criterion.

Validity Generalization Statistically corrected test that is valid across many job categories.

Vesting Rights The permanent right to pension benefits.

Virtual Reality A process whereby the work environment is simulated by sending messages to the brain.

Wage Structure A pay scale showing ranges of pay within each grade.

Wagner Act Also known as the National Labor Relations Act of , this act gave employees the legitimate right to form and join unions and to engage in collective bargaining.

Wards Cove packing Company v. Antonio A notable Supreme Court case that had the effect of potentially undermining two decades of gains made in equal employment opportunities.

Weakness Those resources that an organization lacks or does not do well.

Websumes Web pages that are used as resumes.

Weighted Application Form A special type of application form where relevant applicant information is used to determine the likelihood of job success.

Wellness Program Organizational programs designed to keep employees healthy.

Whistle-blowing A situation in which an employee notifies authorities of wrongdoing in an organization.

White-Water Metaphor Organizational change reflecting uncertain and dynamic environments.

Wildcat Strike An unauthorized and illegal strike that occurs during the terms of an existing contract.

Work-Force Diversity The varied personal characteristics that make the work force heterogeneous.

Work Process Engineering Radical, quantum change in an organization.

Work Sampling A selection device requiring the job applicant to actually perform a small segment of the job.

Worker Adjustment and Retraining Notification Act Federal law requiring employers to give sixty days' notice of pending plant closing or major layoff.

Written Verbal Warning The first formal step in the disciplinary process.

Written Warning First formal step of the disciplinary process.

PHOTO CREDITS

Chapter 1
Page 3: Courtesy Selective HR Solutions. Page 6: Pablo Bartholomew/Liaison Agency, Inc. Page 10: Courtesy Monster.com. Page 23: ©Jay Reed.

Chapter 2
Page 35: Zigy Kaluzny/Stone. Page 38: ©AP/Wide World Photos. Page 48: Courtesy Amy's Ice Creams, Inc. Page 53: ©Sergio Dorantes.

Chapter 3
Page 61: ©Todd Buchanan, Inc. Page 67: ©Scott Braman. Pages 74 & 83: ©AP/Wide World Photos.

Chapter 4
Page 93: Spencer Ainsley/The Image Works. Page 99: Alan Abramowitz/Stone. Page 105: Gary Parker/Liaison Agency, Inc. Page 114: ©Steve Boljonis.

Chapter 5
Page 125: Courtesy Team Petroleum. Page 127: Courtesy DeWalt Industrial Tools and Accessories. Page 136: Courtesy Sun Microsystems, Inc. Page 142: ©Larime Photographic, Inc.

Chapter 6
Page 149: ©AP/Wide World Photos. Page 154: Courtesy Recruiters OnLine Network, Inc., "Success by Association". Page 160: Terry Vine/Stone. Page 163: Courtesy interbiznet. Page 164: Michael Newman/PhotoEdit.

Chapter 7
Page 175: Michael Jang/Stone. Page 183: Mark Newman/PhotoEdit. Page 189: ©John Abbott Photography. Page 192: Courtesy Motherwear. Page 198: ©2000 Randy Glasbergen.

Chapter 8
Page 207: ©AP/Wide World Photos. Page 218: Chuck Keeler/Corbis Stock Market. Page 227: ©Pictor. Page 229: Terry Vine/Stone.

Chapter 9
Page 237: ©Marc Luinenburg. Page 241: ©Peter Gregoire Photography. Page 248: Rob McClaran/SABA. Page 257: ©Marc Royce.

Chapter 10
Page 267: Utsumi/Liaison Agency, Inc. Page 273: Barros & Barros/The Image Bank. Page 283: Bill Greenblatt/Liaison Agency, Inc. Page 290: Sergio Dorantes/Corbis Sygma.

Chapter 11

Page 299: Courtesy Coffey & Company. Page 305: Jim MacMillan/©Philadelphia Daily News/The Image Works. Page 315: Kim Kulish/SABA. Page 317: Jeff Christensen/Liaison Agency, Inc.

Chapter 12

Page 327: Reproduced with permission of WFD. Page 333: Matthew McVay/SABA. Page 342: ©Mark Katzman/Ferguson Katzman Photography. Page 346: Jason Grow/SABA.

Chapter 13

Page 357: Reuters/Jeff Mitchell/Archive Photos. Page 359: Reprinted with permission from US Dept. of Labor, OSHA. Page 365: Rachel Epstein/PhotoEdit. Page 374: Lara Jo Regan/SABA. Page 381: Michael L. Abramson/Woodfin Camp & Associates.

Chapter 14

Page 391: Courtesy Kingston Technology. Page 395: Paul Loven/The Image Bank. Page 402: Courtesy Townson University. Page 403: Dilbert reprinted by permission of United Feature Syndicate, Inc. Page 405: Courtesy Dana Corporation.

Chapter 15

Pages 413 & 417: ©AP/Wide World Photos. Page 429: Courtesy California Nurse's Association. Page 435: Chung Sung-Jun/Liaison Agency, Inc.

$\mathcal{I}$NDEX